Development of Economic Analysis

The Irwin Series in Economics

Consulting Editor   **Lloyd G. Reynolds**   *Yale University*

DEVELOPMENT OF ECONOMIC ANALYSIS

Ingrid Hahne Rima

Professor of Economics
Temple University

Third Edition   1978

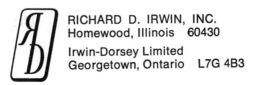

RICHARD D. IRWIN, INC.
Homewood, Illinois   60430
Irwin-Dorsey Limited
Georgetown, Ontario   L7G 4B3

ISBN 0-256-02030-2
Library of Congress Catalog Card No. 77–085802

Printed in the United States of America

1 2 3 4 5 6 7 8 9 0 A 5 4 3 2 1 0 9 8

To the Diamonds of Our Acres
In Memory of MAX HAHNE

Preface

To nonspecialists in the history of economics and, more particularly, to the lamentably large numbers whose formal study of economics excluded the history of the discipline as nonessential for the modern practitioner or student, it may come as something of a surprise that there is something "new" to be included in a book that deals chiefly with intellectual contributions long since chronicled.

One aspect of contemporary reflection on the present state of economics is a substantially revitalized interest in classical economics. This "return to the classics" has served, in particular, to heighten contemporary appreciation of the effectiveness with which writers of the past—the Physiocrats, Adam Smith, David Ricardo, Thomas Malthus, the Mills, and Alfred Marshall—addressed the problems of their day. While the concern of this book is with the concepts and analytical tools they developed, it is, nevertheless, clear that they never divorced analytical inquiry from matters of policy. Moreover, it is far from certain that present day economics is as capable of providing an understanding of contemporary problems (unemployment, inflation, discrimination, poverty) as the economists of yesteryear provided about the problems then confronting them.

There appears to be less certainty today than in the past several decades that scientific progress in economics occurs by means of the refutation of false hypotheses, and less conviction that there is little point to studying the (presumably) mistaken theories of the past. A renewed interest in the history of economics has accompanied the increasing perception, both in and out of the profession, that the economists' impressive accumulation of technical skills and analytical capabilities is of little use if it does not contribute more richly toward achieving better human arrangements. Thus, study of the history of economics may well be a humbling experience, particularly if it is true, as Paul Samuelson once observed, that "the economic scholar works for the only coin worth having—our own applause."

The applause in recent decades has been accorded chiefly to the refinements that have been added to the theory of the household and the firm, and to "The Grand Neo-classical Synthesis" forged as a result of casting J. M. Keynes's model into a general equilibrium framework. Both of the preceding editions of this book made a point of including these relatively recent contributions to the analytical tools and concepts of economic theory. It is gratifying that the reception accorded earlier efforts to bridge the gap between the history of economics and the present state of the discipline was generally favorable. It encourages me to think that now may be the right time to extend the earlier inquiry and address of some of the current controversies which are difficult to avoid, even in courses on the history of economics.

Several changes in format have been made to accommodate at least a brief inquiry into the current state of economics and the dissent it has provoked. One such change is the presentation of the subject matter in four parts, each preceded by a brief introduction, which serves as an overview to facilitate selective omission of certain chapters as dictated by time constraints and the personal academic interests of the professor. Several alternative outlines are suggested below.

Part I examines the preclassical period which preceded Adam Smith's *The Wealth of Nations* and the transition to classical economics. Part II explores "Classical Economics" with special emphasis on its major themes and points of view as well as on the specific contributions of Smith, Malthus, Ricardo, John Stuart Mill, and Nassau Senior. Emphasis on "themes" and "points of view" facilitates the treatment of Karl Marx's inquiry into the "laws of motion" of the capitalist system and provides a basis for examining "Marginalism" in Part III. The brief chapter which introduces Part III focuses on the early and isolated efforts of Gossen, Cournot, Dupuit, von Thünen, and Bernoulli. It is followed by an inquiry into the work of Jevons, Walras, and Menger—who comprise "the first generation" of marginalist thinkers. The work of "the second generation" (Edgeworth, Wicksteed, Wicksell, Wieser, Böhm-Bawerk, Fisher, and John Bates Clark) is treated in a separate chapter. The emergence of the "neoclassical" tradition as the result of Marshall's eclectic efforts is examined as the concluding chapter of Part III. Part IV, From Marshall to the Present, is comprised of seven chapters. These focus on contributions furthering the development of the neoclassical tradition and major expressions of dissent that are examined in the concluding chapter against the background of the tenets of mainstream thinking.

Since this book is intended for undergraduates who are studying economics at the intermediate level, Parts I, II, and III, in particular, are presented at a level which class testing assures to be suitable for readers who have not progressed beyond the Principles course. The glossary of terms and concepts introduced in the second edition is retained as an aid which more advanced students may also find useful. Parts I, II, and III provide an adequate background for most of Part IV, which examines contemporary theory. Some of the sections of Part IV may be too advanced for readers who have not studied intermediate micro- or macroeconomics. The Notes for Further Reading which have been appended to the chapters of this edition are primarily intended for more advanced readers.

The time constraint is an increasingly severe problem as semesters are shortened while reading lists are lengthened. My own experience is that in a typical 12- to 14-week semester, Parts I, II, and III which comprise the "traditional" course ending with Marshall and the neoclassical tradition, can be covered comfortably. If personal preference dictates lingering over particular favorites, the necessary "pruning" is accomplished most easily by omitting Chapter 10, Forerunners of Marginalism. If additional cuts are required, Chapter 7, Nassau Senior and John Stuart Mill, and Chapter 12, Second Generation Marginalists, seem least likely to be missed unless, of course, Senior or Mill happen to be "favorites."

For users who are attracted by the content of Part IV (and it is hoped there will be many), a suggested outline for a one semester course is to assign Chapter I on Origins of Analytical Economics and proceed to Part II which examines the classical tradition. By omitting Chapters 2, 3, 7, 10, and 12, it is possible to add selectively from Part IV. My own choice would be Chapters 14 and 17–20 inclusive. This arrangement offers an equivalent number of chapters, though they are somewhat longer, and also more technical.

Hopefully, there will also be a fortunate few who enjoy the unique luxury of two semesters to devote to the development of economic analysis.

My greatest intellectual debt in the preparation of this edition is to the architects of contemporary theory, some of whom I have been privileged to know personally. It is my hope they will not find my efforts to bring their ideas into the classroom unduly wanting. I am also appreciative of the encouragement provided by two anonymous reviewers of Part IV and of the suggestions they made. Finally, thanks are due to Benjamin Klotz for his helpful comments on some of the chapters in Part IV.

March 1978   *Ingrid Hahne Rima*

Contents

of Physiocratic Views: *Say and the Law of Markets. Adam Smith and the Productivity Concept.*

ductivity Theory of Distribution: *Clark's Generalization of Ricardo's Theory of Rent. Wicksell and the Adding-Up Problem. Clark's Ethical Interpretation of Marginal Productivity Theory. Limitations of the Marginal Productivity Theory of Distribution.* Fisher's Theory of Interest: *The Nature of Interest. Individual Equilibrium. Market Equilibrium. Real and Money Rates of Interest and the Price Level.* Wicksell's Theory of Capital and Interest: *Capital Accumulation and the Distributive Shares. The Wicksell Effect. The Indirect Mechanism of Price Change.*

Introduction: *Life and Times (1842–1924). Principles of Economics: Objectives. Methodology.* The Theory of Demand: *Utility and Demand. Demand Schedules and Curves. Consumer Surplus. Price Elasticity of Demand.* The Theory of Production: *The Laws of Return in the Short Run. The Laws of Return in the Long Run.* Costs of Production and Supply: *Real Costs and Money Costs. Diminishing Returns and Short-Run Cost Behavior. Long-Run Cost and Supply Curves.* The Theory of Price Determination: *Prices Which Deviate from Cost of Production. Long-Run Competitive Price Determination.* The Pricing of Productive Factors: *Distribution Theory in Relation to Value Theory. Marginal Productivity and Factor Demand. The Supply of Productive Factors. The Pricing of Productive Factors.* Macroeconomic Aspects of Marshall's Analysis: *Acceptance of Say's Law. The Theory of the General Price Level.*

An Overview of Modern Contributions

Introduction: *The Leading Participants.* Institutional Dissent: *The Veblenian Challenge. J. M. Clark's Rejection of Marginal Utility Theory.* Controversy about the Price Mechanism and Resource Allocation: *Sidgwick and Pigou on "Externalities." Pigou on Increasing and Decreasing Cost Industries. Clark's "Economics of Overhead Costs."* The Counterrevolution: Neoclassicism Defended: *Logical Positivism. Knight on the Methodology of Economics and Consumer Sovereignty. Knight's Response to Pigou.* Hicks on Demand Theory: *Indifference Curves and Optimum Allocation of Income. Derivation of a Demand Curve. Separation of Income and Substitution Effects.* The New Welfare Economics: *Logical Positivism and the New Welfare Economics. Optimum in the Consumer Sector. Optimum in the Producing Sector.*

Introduction: *The Contributors to Modern Price Theory.* Some Dark Spots in Neoclassical Value Theory: *Assumptions concerning the Firm's Demand*

Curve. Assumptions regarding the Laws of Return. The Monopoly Net Revenue Curve. Equilibrium of the Firm: *The Conditions of Stable Equilibrium. Equilibrium When Monopoly Price Discrimination Is Possible.* The Equilibrium of the Group: *Chamberlin's Concept of Small and Large Groups. Chamberlin's Equilibrium Analysis. Robinson's "Full Equilibrium." The von Stackelberg Approach.* Imperfect Competition and Factor Rewards: *Factor Rewards under Competition. Monopsony and Factor Exploitation.*

Economics: The Property Rights Approach to Pricing: *The Coase Theorem. The Chicago View of Public Utility Regulation.* The Chicago View of Developing Economies: *The Perspective. Trade versus Inflation as an Instrument of Development.*

The Participants and Issues of Current Controversy. The Galbraithian Challenge: *The "New Industrial State" and the "Technostructure."* The *Planning System.* The Challenge of Radical Economics: *The Radical Paradigm. Can Capitalism Survive?* The Challenge of Post-Keynesian Theory: *Weintraub's "Classical" Keynesianism. Instability, Uncertainty, and Finance. Growth and Dynamics.*

part one

PRECLASSICAL
ECONOMICS

AN OVERVIEW OF PRECLASSICAL ECONOMICS

WHILE MAN'S SPECULATION about his material environment can be traced
to ancient times, the development of analytical economics is of relatively
recent origin. Indeed, the emergence of economics as a separate field of
inquiry before the late 17th century was a distinct impossibility. Everything
militated against it: the nature and limited scope of economic activity, the
dominance of the state and church, the force of custom, and the religious
and philosophical beliefs which shaped prevailing attitudes toward human
activity for the acquisition of wealth. Economic activity for the satisfaction
of wants has of course taken place in every age of human history. And
since man is capable of intelligent inquiry, it is reasonable to infer that he
has always directed some thought to explaining the material aspects of his
life. Speculation on economic matters is therefore undoubtedly as old as
human society itself.

Analytical or theoretical economics, however, has much more recent
history. Not until the 18th century did the content of man's speculation
about economic phenomena begin to emerge as economic analysis rather
than as economic thought. Economics in its preanalytic stages did not exist
as a separate subject matter, nor were there analytical tools with which
thinkers probed into economic matters. Thus there are no economic tracts
or discourses we can study to learn about man's earliest speculations concerning his material environment. The economic ideas of the ancients are
largely unsystematic and must be extracted from the writings of priests,

1

lawgivers, and philosophers. While some of these ideas have survived into modern times, though usually in altered form, the content of ancient economic thought is little more than a series of unrelated observations and moral pronouncements on production, consumption, and exchange embedded in writings devoted primarily to religion, ethics, politics, or law.

Economic behavior increasingly became reflected in commercial activity from the 15th century onward. The revival of trade during the Italian Renaissance and the impulse it gave to finance nurtured an era of mercantilism, which sought to promote governmentally regulated national economies to increase state power at the expense of other states. Mercantilism shaped economic activity and thought in England, France, and northern Europe from the 16th well into the 18th century and beyond. Some of the theoretical ideas of economics can be traced to this early period, although mercantilistic thinkers were chiefly concerned with politics and practical rather than theoretical economic matters.

The period of the transition, which began about the middle of the 17th century and lasted roughly until Adam Smith's *The Wealth of Nations* was published in 1776, is usually regarded as the "dark age" which preceded the classical era. The general impression is that little of interest happened during this transition period with respect to economics. Viewed in this light, the ideas in Smith's great classic appear to have sprung, full-blown, from one mind. This conception of the intellectual climate of the transition period is, however, quite inaccurate, for it was, in fact, an era animated by many inquiring minds. While economics had not yet become established as a separate discipline, perhaps because there was so much theological and political controversy and such great interest in the natural sciences, the ground from which the classical tradition subsequently germinated was being prepared.

It was in France rather than England that a school of theoretical economics developed in the mid-18th century. The work of François Quesnay and his disciples who established the tradition of Physiocracy marks the beginning of economics as a discipline. Their efforts to identify general laws which govern the behavior of the social universe preceded those of Adam Smith. Because their perception of economic problems reflected the largely agrarian economy of prerevolutionary France, while Smith's thinking anticipated the changes which industrialization would bring, the work of the Physiocrats is, strictly speaking, preclassical, even though it represents the beginning of formal economics.

1

The Origins of Analytical Economics

EARLY BARRIERS TO ECONOMIC INQUIRY

EXAMINATION OF THE REASONS why inquiry into economic matters was such a minor aspect of intellectual speculation before the 18th century is a useful point of departure for an appreciation of the historical development of economic analysis. There is much to be learned about the positive aspects of analytical economics by inquiring into the impediments which confronted its early emergence as a discipline.

Dominance of the State

Ancient thinkers had only a limited interest in economic matters; thus their concern with politics and the role of the state is especially important. The greatest of the Greek thinkers believed that the purpose of man's existence is to live a good life and that this can be achieved only within the city-state (*polis*). To a Greek, the city-state was not merely a legal structure; it was a way of life. Every aspect of daily existence was intimately connected with it. The individual derived his importance from his relation to the state; he was viewed as a citizen who depends on the state and who can contribute to its welfare. But the state was omnipotent. Thus the attention of Greek thinkers was primarily absorbed by political theory, though the theory of the city-state embraced much more than politics in the narrow sense. It was at one and the same time ethics, sociology, and economics as well as political science.

The absorption of Greek thinkers with the origin and functioning of the ideal state and the subordination of the individual to the state necessarily limited the development of the kind of economic thought that emerged. Witness, for example, the contribution of the Greek historian Xenophon (441–*c.* 352 B.C.). His work *On the Means of Improving the Revenue of the State of Athens* begins with a description of the natural advantages of Athens as a commercial center attractive to foreigners. Foreigners were regarded as desirable because they were subject to the tax levied on aliens and were therefore a lucrative source of revenue. In similar vein, merchants and shipowners were regarded as superior citizens because they brought wealth to the city. Thus, Xenophon recommended various measures to the state to encourage merchant activity in Athens. He also urged enhanced production of silver and expressed the view that this metal would never lose its value.

These recommendations are noteworthy from our point of view because they reflect the preoccupation with the importance of the state that dominated the thought of the ancients. While emphasis on the state as an instrument to achieve socially optimal results is not, of course, incompatible with the emergence of what has come to be called social economics, it does preclude the emergence of economics as a body of theory which seeks to explain how socially optimal results can be achieved in the absence of a central authority directing the allocation of resources.

Philosophy

To Plato and Aristotle, man's happiness can be achieved only within the city-state. Thus the search for the good life was at one and the same time the search for the ideal state. But after the disintegration of the Greek city-states and the emergence of the empires of Alexander and later of Rome, the conception of man as inseparable from the self-sufficient city-state was supplanted by new schools of thought in which the search for the good life was no longer interwoven with the search for the good state. Thus began the divorce of politics from ethics and an appreciation of man as an individual being rather than a social being who is a dependent part of the whole.

Through Stoicism, the most influential of the post-Aristotelian schools, Greek philosophy was introduced into the western world. Though first conceived by Zeno (*c.* 335–263 B.C.), the philosophy of Stoicism received its most profound expression in the *Meditations* of the Roman emperor Marcus Aurelius (A.D. 121–80). According to the Stoics, the universe is systematic and rational, being governed by the all-pervading law of nature. The wise man lives according to nature; his reason guides his conduct so that his actions conform to the dictates of natural necessity. The greatest virtue is acquiescence to natural law through reason. "Be satisfied with your business and learn to love what you were bred to do, and as to the remainder of your life, be entirely resigned, and let the gods do their pleasure with your body and soul." This is the essence of the stoic philosophy. The belief that happiness is achieved by conforming to the inevitable law of nature suggests a kind of fatalism similar to that characteristic of Oriental philosophy, and is not conducive to improvements in the production or distribution of wealth.

Attitudes toward Want Satisfaction

Economics did not emerge as a separate field of inquiry until the satisfaction of man's material needs became a desirable goal of human activity. The thousands of years during which the pursuit of wealth was disdainfully regarded could scarcely have produced a systematic body of principles dedicated to explaining acquisition. Indeed, those ancient civilizations which had the least materialistic philosophies are, as might be expected, precisely those in which there existed the most notable paucity of economic ideas.

A negative attitude toward wealth among the ancient peoples is perhaps most clearly in evidence in the thinking of the Hindus and Chinese, although it is typical of Oriental thought in general. Oriental philosophy regards happiness as being achieved through a state of mind in which material wants become increasingly unimportant. It accepts poverty with fatalistic passivity and views wealth with relative indifference. The material renunciation of Oriental philosophy and its denial of the worth of man as an individual make it inconsistent with both economic progress and the development of economic thought.

The ancient Hebrews, while considerably less ascetic than the Chinese and Hindus, also believed that happiness could be achieved without wealth and that the pursuit of riches would lead to sin. The lives of these people were circumscribed by the rules of conduct set forth in the commands of Moses and the prophets. These minutely regulated every phase of human existence, guiding men in their relationships with one another as well as in their personal lives. The rules were detailed and complex, and understandably embraced also the economic aspects of life. For example, lending upon usury to fellow Hebrews was strictly forbidden with respect not only to money but also to goods. The term *usury* refers here not to an excessive interest rate, which is its present-day meaning, but to any interest charge. Since loans were made primarily for charitable reasons, the Old Testament proscription against the taking of usury introduced a moral standard into economic behavior. There are many other directives of an economic nature in the Old Testament, such as the rules concerning the restitution of property, the remission of debt, and the production and harvesting of agricultural output. Many of these rules commemorate events of religious significance such as the seventh day in the story of the creation. These are typical of the economic aspects of the Mosaic law and are of interest to us because they demonstrate that a separate science of wealth is incompatible with adherence to a religious and philosophical code which completely dictates economic behavior.

Even Greece, with its highly developed culture, did not produce a separate body of economic thought. This is not, however, because the Greeks were disdainful of material goods. On the contrary, Plato and Aristotle believed that a minimum amount of wealth is essential to the good life. According to Aristotle, the household (*oikos*) exists for the purpose of satisfying men's natural wants. Its activities properly include the production and storage of necessary and useful commodities and their acquisition by exchange for purposes of consumption. It is retail trade, which is exchange for the purpose of making money, that is unnatural, as are all chrematistic activities engaged in for the acquisition of wealth. The most unnatural chrematistic activity in which man can engage is usury. Money, said Aristotle, is intended to function as a medium of exchange and nothing else. It cannot beget money, and its use to make money is a perversion of its proper function.

Aristotle's discussion of the barrenness of money and his condemnation of usury are perhaps the best known and most influential of his economic ideas. Their importance in this discussion is to emphasize that he regarded only those activities that contribute to the attainment of the good life as natural and proper. Economic activities are natural and proper, but they are means to an end, not an end in themselves. The distinction between what is "proper" and "improper," "natural" and "unnatural" is not merely factual; it is moral. Within this framework, economic inquiry could only emerge as applied ethics.

The dominance of Scholasticism during the Middle Ages presented a similar barrier to economic inquiry. The revival of trade, industry, and town life during the 12th and 13th centuries was associated with numerous practices that were in conflict with Christian teaching. Thus, Saint Thomas Aquinas turned his attention in his *Summa Theologica* to such questions as: Is it lawful to sell a thing for more than it is worth? What are the obligations of buyers and sellers with regard to transactions? Is it a sin to take usury for money lent? In answering these and other questions that arose as a result of expanding commercial activities, Aquinas examined the civil law in the light of Christian teaching and the then recently rediscovered Aristotelian principles of logic. His studies had their basis in theology or, more precisely, Christian ethics. In contrast with modern economics, which seeks to explain economic phenomena, Aquinas and the Schoolmen sought to lay down a body of rules of conduct.

The profound impact of the Church and the Schoolman is particularly in evidence in their reinterpretation of Ptolemy's theory of celestial spheres to join it with Christian theology. Claudius Ptolemy (*c.* A.D. 140), the greatest of the Greek astronomers, developed a complex mathematical system to support his belief that the earth is a motionless body at the center of the universe which is surrounded by celestial spheres moving around it in their own epicycles. The planets Venus and Mercury were observed as always being close to the sun which, in terms of Ptolemy's theory of the universe, was interpreted as meaning that their epicycles were fixed in line with Earth and the sun.

The Scholastics melded Ptolemy's theory with Christian theology by adding their own interpretation concerning the celestial sphere beyond Saturn, the planet they thought furthest removed from Earth. Neptune and Uranus had not yet been identified and, according to their interpretation, God and the angels existed in "Heaven," the sphere beyond Saturn. This sphere was thought to be the universal energy source which propelled the other celestial spheres in their orbits around the Earth. The universe was thus conceived as a hierarchy leading up to God. God's creatures occupy the Earth, which is at the center between Heaven above and Hell below. The purpose of man's existence on earth is to prepare for an eventual union with God and the angels in the hereafter.

Condemnation of the pursuit of wealth followed readily from the Scholastics' conception of the universe and man's place in it. Avarice, a lust after earthly things, was viewed as one of the seven deadly sins. Only such economic activities as maintain individuals in the rank or order into which God has placed them were regarded as proper. The reader acquainted with Chaucer's *Canterbury Tales* will perhaps remember the words of the Parson who observes "God has ordained that some folk should be more high in estate and in degree, and some folk more low, and that everyone should be served in his estate and in his degree." By putting these words into the Parson's mouth, Chaucer reflects a synthesis of philosophy and theology—the essence of medieval thought. Within this framework society is seen as an integrated whole in which God, nature, and man each has its preordained place. The "good life" requires that each class, farmer, artisan, priest, and nobleman, perform its proper work according to the laws of God and nature. The ultimate test of the propriety of any exchange of goods or services is the preservation of the class structure. A seller's price is just when it is no more than what he needs to suitably support himself in his rank in life.[1] Thus, the concept of the just price is a

---

[1] W. J. Ashley, *An Introduction to English Economic History and Theory* (1893), *Part II,* chap. 6, p. 391 (New York: Augustus Kelley, 1969). But see also Raymond de Roover, "The Concept of the Just Price: Theory and Economic Policy," *Journal of Economic History,* 4 (December 1958), reprinted in Ingrid H. Rima, ed., *Readings in the History of Economic Theory* (New York: Holt, Rinehart and Winston, 1970). De Roover maintains that many medieval thinkers conceived of the just price as the competitive market price.

concept of applied Christian ethics whose dominance inhibited the emergence of economics as an autonomous discipline.

Writers who dealt with economic matters during and after the 18th century began from the premise that man's conduct is guided by self-interest. This self-interest manifests itself in the economic sphere in the desire for and pursuit of wealth. Modern writers typically abstract the moral aspects of acquisition; this contrasts with Adam Smith who, writing during the last quarter of the 18th century, stood in closer proximity to the Middle Ages and interpreted man's acquisitive instincts in such a way as to reconcile individual self-interest with the common good.

The Mode of Resource Allocation

Regardless of the simplicity or complexity of the arrangements and techniques used, the essence of economic activity is the use of human and material resources to satisfy wants. It is an inescapable fact that resources are scarce in comparison with the numerous alternative uses to which they can be put. The impossibility of satisfying all wants necessarily poses a twofold problem: first, which wants shall have priority; and secondly, how these wants will be satisfied. On an individual basis, these problems are relatively simple. The individual knows perfectly well what his preferences for goods, services, and leisure are and, if he is free to do so, will use his money income or labor to acquire them in an order which corresponds to his preference scale.

The adaptation of means to ends is considerably more complicated with reference to society as a whole. For while the problem of choice remains, there is no way in which the wants of its various individual members can be made commensurate. Nevertheless, every society must establish some priority among the material desires of its citizens, for scarcity of resources universally imposes the necessity of choice. The common characteristic of all societies before the 18th century is that decisions as to which wants would receive priority—and therefore what the allocation of resources would be—were dictated by central authority and reinforced by custom. How well a particular group or individual fared relative to others depended on his status in the social hierarchy, and this status reflected the importance attached to his function by society. Soldiers, scholars, priests, artisans, farmers, and tradesmen have performed their functions from time immemorial, but different societies have accorded them varying degrees of status.

In the feudal society of the Middle Ages, for example, the most exalted position was occupied by the lord of the manor who owned the land and everything on it. He was pledged to protect the lives of the serfs and freemen of his domain. The vacuum created by the fall of the western part of the old Roman empire was filled by the feudal lords who provided a substitute for the law and order of a central government. The serfs who were subject to them had the obligation to produce food and other products, and to serve in the lord's army. Everyone had a rigidly regulated place in society and a function to perform which custom perpetuated from generation to generation. Each manor constituted a self-sufficient economic, social, and political unit. Production, distribution, and consumption patterns were determined by the orders of the lord and the force of tradition.

In other early societies the source of authority and the criteria according to which wants were given priority differed. But there was an essential similarity: the prime mover of economic activity was compounded of custom and command, and was a reflection of the prevailing philosophical or theological standard for social and moral well-being. Economic decision-making was outside the scope of individual action; and individual acquisition, especially in the form of usury, was strongly censured. Within this framework, there was no soil for the development of economics as it is conceived of in the modern sense. Why resources were allocated as they were required no special explanation. It was a matter of law or tradition. While there was much for the thinker to speculate about, it was in the realm of ethics, theology, and politics, not economics. Not until the evolution of the market system of allocating resources did economics emerge as a separate field of inquiry.

The essence of the market system is freedom of the factors of production to seek out the most profitable opportunities of employment. Clearly, this mode of allocating resources could not assert itself until the propriety of individual gain became sanctioned by society. Nor could it assert itself until human and material resources came into existence as "agents of production." Land, labor, and capital have of course always existed in a physical sense. But they did not become agents of production until they, or their services, became available for sale. Before the 14th century, land was hardly ever sold, and there was certainly no such thing as a real estate market. Indeed, since land was the primary source of wealth and the base of the medieval social structure, every effort was made to insure that holdings would be preserved through such customs as primogeniture and entail, the inheritance of land by eldest sons and in perpetuity to their direct descendants. The Church was, of course, the largest single landholder. The entire structure of society was to experience profound changes before land was to become commercialized.

Similarly, there was no such thing as a labor market until the human being became emancipated from servitude, whether in the form of slavery, serfdom, or apprenticeship to a guildmaster. Not until he was free to sell his services in a competitive market would there be such a thing as labor in an economic sense. Nor did capital exist in the modern sense of the term. Though tools and equipment existed and funds were accumulated even in simple economies, there was no incentive to use them for pioneering new and more efficient techniques of production. In fact, during the Middle Ages the guilds strictly regulated the method and quantity of production.

STIMULI TO ECONOMIC INQUIRY

The dawning of the Renaissance unleashed the forces that were ultimately to provide the climate for the development of economics as a separate discipline. Historians are not in complete agreement as to the exact time span during which the many and complex forces that were to destroy feudal economic, political, social, and religious life were at work. Usually, the beginning of the Renaissance is placed at the time of the fall of Constantinople in 1453, though many of the events of the 11th and 12th centuries heralded the changes that reached fuller development in later centuries. Similarly, the end of the 17th century is generally thought of as marking the end of the Renaissance; though many medieval ideas and influences continued into the 18th century.

The precise dating of this momentous time in human history is, however, considerably less important than the recognition of the tremendous, though gradual, change that took place in every aspect of human life. From an economic and social point of view, it was a period during which commerce revived, new forms of wealth emerged, and a town life dominated by an entirely new social class came into existence. Politically it was a period which witnessed the growth of powerful national states; and intellectually it was a time of skepticism, increasing secularization, and a corresponding decline in the authority of the church in Rome. Each of these aspects of the Renaissance had an impact on economic activities and institutions. By creating the environment within which economic phenomena took place, each also served to stimulate economic inquiry.

The Decline of the Manorial System: The Rise of Trade and Capitalism

The most dramatic feature of the Renaissance was the decline of the manorial system, for it signaled the end of feudalism. More than any other economic phenomenon the disintegration of the manorial system heralded the Renaissance and the dawn of modern times. It should, of course, be recognized that the decline of feudalism was gradual and, if we view the experience of Europe as a whole, extended over several centuries.

The specific causes of the decline of the manor are exceedingly complex. A major force derived from the expansion of trade. There were two great commercial movements between the 11th and 16th centuries; one centered around the Mediterranean and Adriatic Seas, the other on the northern shores of Europe that were accessible via the North and Baltic Seas. In between lay the heartland of continental Europe, still overwhelmingly rural and slumbering in the unchanging institutions of feudalism. The catalysts for bringing commercial activity to the interior of the continent were the Crusades in southern Europe, which introduced new and exotic commodities from the East, and the regional specialization of production that developed in northern Europe because of the accident of natural resource distribution and the growth of population. For example, Flanders was so heavily populated by the 11th century that it began to concentrate on the production of cloth which it exported in order to get raw materials and food. Thus, wool from England and fish from Denmark and southern Sweden became the staples of interregional trade which centered in Flanders. Great international fairs developed in places located at road or river junctions. Champagne, a small principality near Paris where roads from Flanders, Italy, France, and Germany converged, became the most famous of several "commercial oases" to which merchants brought their wares.

The institutions which were to become an integral part of capitalism first began to flourish in conjunction with the commercial activities of medieval Europe. Italy, or more specifically Venice, is the birthplace of the financial institutions of capitalism. Besides her several important industries—among them the glass industry still flourishing and famous to this day—and her extensive commercial trade, Venice had financial institutions for dealing in bills of exchange, conducting credit transactions, and writing maritime insurance. The Florentines also excelled in banking; London's Lombard Street is a modern reminder of the place of the Lombards in the early history of banking. The Medici family also specialized in facilitating foreign exchange, i.e., exchanging the currencies of one locale into that of another. This activity was the natural outgrowth of the expansion of trade and the medieval fairs. Because these attracted merchants with different currencies from all over Europe, money changers provided facilities for conversion at some standard rate. Bills of exchange were used in long-distance trade because they reduced the need to ship gold and silver. Thus the banking activities of the merchant bankers of the late medieval period pioneered in the use of debt as a money substitute—a factor which became an essential feature of modern banking activity.

Another by-product of the expansion of trade was that it established an economic base for city life, which was virtually destroyed with the disintegration of the Roman Empire. Originally the feudal lords claimed jurisdiction over the towns adjacent to their lands; but the commercial activities of the towns were inconsistent with the restrictions inherent in feudal relationships. As a result, it was not uncommon for a town to purchase a charter granting political freedom from the feudal lords. The status of the townspeople was uniquely different from the servitude of most of the rural population, the majority of whom were not free men. The legal sanction to individual freedom provided by the town charters was an additional factor that contributed to the destruction of feudal institutions and their mode of economic behavior. The feudal lords were reduced to collecting revenues from the townspeople in exchange for political freedom, and the townsfolk directed their attentions to nurturing their economic gain through trade.

The merchant traders formed voluntary associations known as guilds, which banded together in caravans to better insure the safety of both merchandise and men as they pursued their trade over long distances. Various regional guilds joined to form national guilds and larger organizations of merchants in free German cities known as Hansas. The national guilds became typical in England, whereas Hansas developed and flourished even into modern times in areas like Germany which lacked strong central government. The Hanseatic League was the most powerful and famous of all. From the late Middle Ages until the political unification of Germany it served as a proxy for central governments while at the same time facilitating trade between the various regions of Europe.

During the latter part of the 13th century the center of northern European trade shifted from Champagne to Bruges, Antwerp, and Amsterdam. This change marked the transition from the traveling to the sedentary merchant as the chief participant in long-distance trade. It was accompanied by important developments in both business and market organization and in operating techniques. More specifically the bourse replaced the fair as a selling organization. The fairs of earlier eras had offered varying grades and types of merchandise sold by individual craftsmen. The bourses facilitated the sale and purchase of items which lent themselves to sufficient physical standardization that the actual goods did not need to be physically present. The institution of the bourse operated under conditions approximating those of pure competition, offering homogeneous commodities along with access to free markets. The latter was symbolized on the 16th century bourse building of Antwerp by the inscription "Open to the merchants of all nations." This further contributed to the vitality of economic activity.

The Putting Out System: Emergence of a Wage Class

Europe's population growth and natural resource endowments, coupled with improved techniques of production, facilitated both the expansion of production and the extension of markets. Growing markets made it possible for workmen to specialize in particular products and acquire skills as craftsmen. Specialization, and the division of labor which tends to accompany it, resulted in production for market rather than the more primitive form of production for self-consumption that was typical of the manor. Medieval handicraft industry is thus an intermediate step toward industrialization.

During the most advanced stage of the handicraft system, craftsmen contracted their outputs to merchants and thereby divorced themselves from the final consumer. At a still later stage, which developed as the market became further extended, merchants contracted for output directly with workers, who now worked for wages instead of functioning as independent craftsmen. The merchants frequently provided tools as well as raw materials and collected and sold the finished product. This system, which is known as the putting-out, or *domestic,* system, served as the intermediary step in the development of the factory system out of the more primitive handicraft system and marks the beginning of the first permanent wage-earning class.

Under the medieval craft system no wage class existed—apprentices typically became journeymen, who developed their skills and became masters themselves. Under the putting-out system, capital became a factor completely separate from labor, typically provided by rural folk working out of their own cottages. Thus, by the 14th century, the extension of the market was the primary force leading to the decline of the medieval handicraft system just as the expansion of trade was a primary force in destroying the manorial system two centuries earlier.

The Protestant Ethic

As the preceding discussion suggests, by the end of the 15th century only the last vestiges of a rural feudalistic economy remained. Many islands of capitalism flourishing in both northern and sourthern Europe were on the verge of expanding toward a position of dominance over European economic life as a whole. Only one essential prerequisite of capitalism was absent: an ethical standard that was compatible with accumulation. The prevailing ethical standard was negative toward activities undertaken for the pursuit of wealth. The teachings of Aquinas and Augustine were difficult to reconcile with the need to accumulate goods. If capitalistic production was to continue its growth, an entirely new ideology was required to give moral sanction to acquisitive behavior. The sanction came within the framework of a wholly new intellectual climate, which was to stimulate the birth not only of modern philosophy and the Protestant Reformation, but also of modern science.

Essentially, these developments have a common origin, which is the thesis that human reason, as distinct from divine revelation, is sufficient to discover truth. This thesis destroyed the nexus between faith and reason, and thus between theology and philosophy—a nexus forged by the Scholastics of the Middle Ages. To Aquinas, knowledge was the product not only of reason (philosophy) but also of revelation (theology). All branches of learning (logic, ethics, politics, and economics) were welded together into one great whole through theology. The union between philosophy and theology was, however, far from permanent and over a period of centuries, was challenged even from within the church itself.

The consequence of the eventual divorce between reason and faith was a secularism and a religious skepticism which was to characterize intellectual activity from the 15th through the 17th centuries. In essence, this intellectual revolution asserted the primacy of individual man as capable of reason and possessed of an individual will. These principles became fundamental to the spiritual revolution inherent in the Protestant Reformation.

Martin Luther's attack in the 16th century against the misuse of indulgences, the worship of images and relics, and other practices which he regarded as pagan is an expression of his emphasis on the individual and of the power of the human mind to discover truth. While Luther's interpretation of Christian teachings was not particularly sympathetic to industry and trade, the reform movements of John Calvin, John Knox, and the Puritans in the same century were much more so. Indeed, they adopted such strongly favorable attitudes toward acquisition by useful labor and the judicious and prudent use of wealth that their views have been described as the Protestant ethic, which launched and encouraged the development of capitalism in northern Europe. This thesis was advanced in the 19th century by Max Weber, the German sociologist and economist, in *The Protestant Ethic and the Spirit of Capitalism.*

Weber's hypothesis, of course, does not necessarily tell the whole story, for the fact that northern Europe and England were geographically well located for trade and had a climate and resources conducive to industry was undoubtedly also a factor in their industrial development. Nevertheless, Protestantism was congenial to the development of personal attributes which encouraged business activity. In this sense, the Reformation contributed toward capitalist development and economic thought. Protestantism considers acquisition a virtue rather than a sin, and instead of the merchant's being considered as un-Christian because of his activities for profit, he came to be regarded as a pillar of the church and the community. His pursuit of gain, unrelated to material needs and the virtue of frugality, became as integral a part of the Protestant ethic as the autonomy of the individual. Joined with the notion of the dignity and moral worth of work, Protestant emphasis on frugality served the capitalistic system well, for it stimulated thrift and capital accumulation.

New Political Concepts

Further stimulus to economic inquiry came from changing political developments and ideas. The Reformation was a major source of such political developments. Europe became torn by religious dissension as Protestants and Catholics fought for supremacy. The principal beneficiary of this struggle was absolute monarchy. As monarchy replaced feudal relationships, so taxation superseded personal service as a means of supporting the state. The emergence of national government and the necessarily associated need to find the best way to enhance its revenue marks the beginning of modern political economy. This was the era of mercantilism, during which economic decision-making was not yet liberated from the state and economics was still in its preanalytic phase. Subsequently, economics was divorced from politics and thus constituted, at last, a separate field of inquiry.

The divorce of economics from politics required the development of the concepts of the natural order and the natural law. These concepts became the vehicle for the political and economic liberalism of the Physiocrats and Adam Smith in the 18th century. Both derive from the Stoic philosophy, which eventually passed, through the writings of Cicero, into Roman legal conceptions. According to Roman jurists, natural law not only is universal and immutable, but is also the foundation of the state, since it existed before the founding of any state. Thus the state is "an assemblage of men associated in consent to law." This concept is different from the Greek view of the state as the outgrowth of natural necessity. Roman thinkers thus contributed two ideas which were to profoundly affect future political and economic thought: first, the idea of universal law; and secondly, the idea of the state being based on mutual consent. These two ideas provided the foundation for the conception of individual rights, without which modern capitalism would not have evolved. While Roman thinkers contributed little as far as the development of economic thought is concerned, it is Roman law, with its emphasis on private property and freedom of contact, which constitutes the basis for the legal doctrines and institutions of capitalism. These were given new expression during the 17th century and reflect one aspect of the new *Weltanschauung,* or conception of the world, which emerged during the Renaissance and Reformation.

The Renaissance and the Reformation gave birth to the idea of the "masterless man," the autonomous individual created in the image of God and therefore inherently good, but individually responsible for his own salvation. The idea of man as possessing an individual will and therefore power to think and do things gave the man of the Renaissance an estimate of his own worth and importance in the scheme of things that would have been inconceivable for the man of the Middle Ages. Thus, he challenged the uncompromising authority of the monarch who claimed to rule by divine right, for such authority was in conflict with the whole conception of an autonomous individual subject only to his own conscience and the dictates of "right reason." This 17th-century conception of natural law was propounded by the Dutch jurist Hugo Grotius.

Grotius' secularized version of natural law was especially significant in regard to defining the natural rights that reason demonstrates as belonging to individuals by virtue of their humanity. These are the inalienable rights which cannot be abrogated by law and which John Locke later formulated as the "right to life, liberty and property." The rising commercial classes were quick to embrace this philosophy, for it reflected their own growing aspirations. As a result of their enhanced economic status during the period of mercantilism, they eventually challenged privileges based on birth and social position. They believed in the rights of individuals to own property and the fruits of their own labor; to speak, to write, to assemble, and to worship as they chose; to have the right to fair trial and freedom from arbitrary imprisonment and cruel or unusual punishment. Thus the same burgher class which supported the absolutism of the Tudors in England during the 16th century led the Glorious Revolution which culminated in establishing the supremacy of Parliament in the 17th century. This protest against the unlimited power of the sovereign marked the first victory of liberalism over absolutism—a victory later echoed in the American Revolution for independence from Britain in 1776 and the French Revolution of 1789.

The growth of political freedom was paralleled by greater economic freedom, which gave rise to new economic problems and phenomena requiring explanation. As will become clear in Chapter 2, some headway was made during the period of mercantilism in the development of economic concepts and tools of analysis. But the subject of inquiry during this period was political economy rather than economic analysis. Purely economic analysis did not emerge until the Physiocrats concerned themselves with the economic conditions which prevailed in France during the 1750s. Their writings mark the emergence of economics as a separate subject matter with analytical tools and concepts appropriate to its purpose.

Modern Science

The new intellectualism brought with it a quest for new knowledge, new techniques for its acquisition, and new bases for its evaluation. In the process, the Ptolemaic conception of the universe in which the Earth is central in the universe gave way to a revolutionary new conception based on the studies of the Polish astronomer Nicolaus Copernicus (1473–1543). He noted that the actual movements of the planets Mercury and Venus did not coincide with the predictions of Ptolemy's system. The discrepancy which this inconsistency created led him to challenge the Ptolemaic theory. He hypothesized instead that the Earth rotates on an axis of its own and orbits the sun, as do the other planets. This alternative to the Ptolemaic system seemed to explain the relative positions of Venus and Mercury.

While Copernicus' theory that the spheres of the universe were sun centered was denounced by the Church as contrary to scripture, it nevertheless served to drive another wedge, besides Luther's earlier one, between faith and reason. Thus the Copernican revolution became important for the history of natural science and, eventually, for economics. Together with the later studies of Johannes Kepler (1571–1630) and Galileo Galilei (1564–1642), Copernicus precipitated an intellectual revolution that was to alter completely man's conception of the universe. Galileo, whose experiments with falling objects from Italy's tower of Pisa represented a breakthrough into the behavior of the physical universe, also looked through his telescope and, upon identifying the mountainous surface of the moon, surmised that "Heaven" was no more perfect than earth. He observed the satellites orbiting Jupiter and concluded that there are heavenly spheres that orbit neither the Sun nor the Earth. His studies brought him into conflict with the church which threatened him with excommunication until he retracted his heretical beliefs.

Not much later, in Germany, Kepler noted that the planets orbited earth in an elliptical rather than a circular motion. His observations, like those Galileo had made concerning falling bodies, proclaimed the existence of laws governing the behavior of the natural order. These special cases were ultimately encompassed in the mechanics of Isaac Newton (1642–1727) whose death came only four years after the birth, in 1723, of Adam Smith. Smith was later to describe the Newtonian system as "the greatest discovery ever made by man."[2] Newton saw the entire universe as governed by mechanical laws functioning with such precision that they can be formulated mathematically. He did not doubt that God had created a mechanically perfect universe. It is precisely because of this perfection that the universe is rational, predictable, and beneficent in its functioning for the benefit of all God's creatures without further intervention by Him.

Another aspect of the development of pure science which took place during the century of the Enlightenment deserves notice. Once it was recognized that the physical universe obeys certain laws that can be discovered by experimentation and observation, it was only a question of time before it was asked whether the same principles might not also be applied to the society to discover laws governing social phenomena. Just as Newton sought to discover the regularities governing the behavior of the physical universe and give them expression in a system of natural laws, the Physiocrats of France and the Scottish moral philosophers, among them David Hume, Francis Hutcheson, and his most eminent pupil, Adam Smith, sought to identify the natural laws ruling the behavior of society. Developments in the natural sciences, physics, and astronomy in particular, thus were greatly influential in determining the point of view and methodology which developed for the study of the behavior of the economic system.

How Does a Science Develop?

The historical relationship between economics and the natural sciences suggests that a brief inquiry into the process by which a science advances

---

[2] Adam Smith, "An Essay on the History of Astronomy," in *The Early Writing of Adam Smith* by Ralph Lindgren (New York: Augustus Kelly, 1967).

might be relevant. In this book we will examine the unfolding of economic theories and their related concepts from the period of mercantilism to the present. Each contribution, as will be seen, emerged during a particular period in history and was thus associated with the events and political problems of the period and the ideology and philosophy of the writers who developed them. Is this association a basis for explaining why particular theories emerged when they did? In the view of some historians of economic thought it is. The development of economic thought has been interpreted as an attempt to understand and rationalize the economic aspects of man's experience.[3] Other historians of economic thought have explained the development of economic doctrine in terms of the philosophical preconceptions of its authors.[4] At least one writer has advanced the hypothesis that particular theories were evolved by their authors in order to provide principles to support policies they regarded as politically and socially appropriate.[5]

A more recent interpretation of the history of economics views its development as an example of scientific advance in response to problems which the prevailing doctrine is unable to explain. Thomas Kuhn, a historian of science, advanced the hypothesis that the practitioners of a discipline (e.g., economists) are typically engaged in what he terms "normal science."[6] Together with their colleagues, they direct attention toward problems their scientific community identifies as "solvable" in terms of the principles of their discipline. These principles constitute the core of ideas or "paradigm" which the community of scholars accepts as a basis for the research that constitutes the day-to-day activity of "normal" science.

According to Kuhn, the study of paradigms . . . "prepares the student for membership in the particular scientific community with which he will later practice."[7] The problems which are selected and the rules for solving them are paradigm-directed. Such anomalies as occasionally appear are

---

[3] W. Stark, *The History of Economics in Its Relation to Social Development* (London: K. Paul, Trench, Truber and Co., Ltd., 1945), and Eric Roll, *A History of Economic Thought,* 3d ed. (New York: Prentice-Hall, Inc., 1956), are among those who interpret the development of economic thought primarily as an attempt to understand and rationalize experience.

[4] A classic example of a writer who has explained economic doctrine in terms of its philosophical foundations is James Bonar, *Philosophy and Political Economy,* 2d ed. (London: George Allen and Unwin, Ltd., 1909). Walter A. Weisskopf has given a psychological interpretation of the development of economic thought in *The Psychology of Economics* (Chicago: The University of Chicago Press, 1955).

[5] This relationship has led at least one writer to advance the hypothesis that particular theories evolved in order to lend support to policies and programs which seemed politically and socially appropriate at particular times in history. See Leo Rogin, *The Meaning and Validity of Economic Theory* (New York: Harper & Bros., 1956).

[6] Thomas Kuhn, *The Structure of Scientific Revolutions* (Princeton: Princeton University Press, 1970).

[7] Ibid, p. 176.

typically explained by qualifying or making relatively minor refinements in the principles which the scientific community accepts. But minor paradigmatic changes will not suffice when a science confronts a problem it cannot solve within the prevailing framework. It then experiences an intellectual crisis of the sort the Ptolemaic paradigm encountered when its inability to explain the behavior of Mercury and Venus became apparent. This crisis produced the Copernican revolution which was, in essence, a rejection of the Ptolemaic paradigm and its replacement by a new one which henceforth guided the researches of the scientific community.

The physical sciences have encountered intellectual crises since the challenges precipitated by the studies of Copernicus, Kepler, and Newton. Their paradigms have been replaced by alternatives which later practitioners in physics, astronomy, chemistry, and other natural sciences accepted as a superior framework for scientific inquiry. Have there been similar scientific revolutions in economics? We will have occasion, when we encounter major challenges to theory prevailing at particular times in history, to inquire whether they represent revolutions in the Kuhnian sense. This is, of course, a far less ambitious undertaking than to explain (or, at least, try to explain) why economic thought emerged as it did. To explain the structure of scientific revolutions in economics is considerably beyond the scope of this book. Our objective is more precisely to examine the development of the concepts and tools of analyses which have been evolved over time to explain economic phenomena.

Mainstream economics and economists are nowadays so often the subject of criticism (frequently from persons who are highly regarded members of the profession themselves) that some attention to the question of contemporary controversy also seems appropriate. Even though it will take us beyond the usual scope of a book in the development of economics, concern with intellectual crisis is very much the business of the historian of economics. Final judgment on the relevance for economics of Kuhn's hypothesis concerning the structure of scientific revolutions, which was advanced specifically with reference to the natural sciences rather than the social sciences, is still a long way off. But, because there is no question that the intellectual crises of today generate tomorrow's theories, the concluding chapter of this book will examine the more important challenges which are now being leveled against mainstream economic theory.

In between we will complete our brief inquiry into preclassical economics before proceeding to Part Two on classical economics, which begins with the economics of Adam Smith and concludes with Karl Marx's challenge to the classical paradigm. Part Three on marginalism examines an alternative challenge to the classical tradition which was associated chiefly with scholars working outside of England before it was incorporated into the great neoclassical synthesis fashioned by Alfred Marshall. Our concluding Part IV will examine the major developments which have taken place in economics during the present century and will conclude with a brief survey of modern iconoclasts and their contributions to current controversy.

NOTES FOR FURTHER READING

Historical events which contributed to the development of economic thought during the preclassical period are put into perspective by W. J. Ashley in *An Introduction to English Economic History and Theory,* vol. 1, part I (1888), chap. 3, Part II (1893), chapter VI (New York: Augustus Kelley, 1969). This background is further examined by Karl Polanyi, et al. in *Trade and Markets in Early Empires* (Glenco, Ill.: Free Press, 1957). Chapter 5 is especially recommended.

R. H. Tawney's *Religion and the Rise of Capitalism* (New York: Penguin Books, 1947) and Max Weber's *Protestant Ethic and the Spirit of Capitalism,* trans., Talcott Parsons (New York: Scribner, 1948) explore the relationship between religion and the rise of capitalism. Raymond De Roover, "The Concept of the Just Price: Theory and Economic Policy," *Journal of Economic History, 4* (December 1958), reprinted in Ingrid H. Rima, ed., *Readings in the History of Economic Theory* (New York: Holt, Rinehart and Winston, 1970) examines the influence of church doctrine on pricing during the Medieval period.

E. Ray Canterberry is particularly clear and interesting in his discussion of the relationship between the natural sciences and economics in *The Making of Economics* (Belmont: Wadsworth Publishing Company, 1976), especially chs. 1–5. Among the more sophisticated sources providing background for these chapters, see Thomas Kuhn, *The Structure of Scientific Revolutions* (Princeton: Princeton University Press, 1970), Henry Margenau, "What is a Theory" in S. R. Krupp, ed., *The Structure of Economic Science* (Englewood Cliffs, N.J.: Prentice-Hall, Inc., 1966), and Laurence Nabers "The Positive and Genetic Approaches" in the same volume.

GENERAL REFERENCES

History of Economic Analysis, the magnum opus of the late Professor Joseph A. Schumpeter is the most comprehensive and sophisticated treatise available. There are also numerous textbooks on the history of economic thought which can serve as useful collateral reading either because they include contributions of a less theoretical nature than those which are the focus of this book or because they provide interpretations and examine the impact of economic ideas in a way which is precluded by the scope of this inquiry. Two books on contemporary economic analysis are also included in the list which follows because of their historical orientation; each is marked with an asterisk.

Bell, John F. *A History of Economic Thought.* New York: Ronald Press Co., 1953.

*Blaug, Mark. *Economic Theory in Retrospect.* Homewood, Ill.: Richard D. Irwin, Inc., 1962, revised 1968.

Bonar, James. *Philosophy and Political Economy*. 2d ed. London: George Allen and Unwin, Ltd., 1909.

Canterberry, E. Ray, *The Making of Economics*. Belmont: Wadsworth Publishing Co., 1976.

Ekelund, Robert B. Jr. and Hébert, Robert F., *A History of Economic Theory and Method*. New York: McGraw-Hill Book Co., Inc. 1975.

*Fellner, William, *The Emergence and Content of Modern Economic Analysis*. New York: McGraw-Hill Book Co., Inc., 1960.

Ferguson, John M. *Landmarks of Economic Thought*. 2d ed. New York: Longmans, Green & Co., Inc., 1950.

Gide, Charles, and Rist, Charles. *A History of Economic Doctrine*. Trans. R. Richards. 7th ed. Boston: D. C. Heath & Co., 1948.

Gray, Alexander. *The Development of Economic Doctrine*. New York: Longmans, Green & Co., Inc., 1933.

Gruchy, Allan G. *Modern Economic Thought: The American Contribution*. New York: Prentice-Hall, Inc., 1947.

Haney, Lewis H. *History of Economic Thought*. 4th ed. New York: Macmillan Co., 1949.

Heibroner, Robert. *The Worldly Philosophers*. New York: Simon and Schuster, Inc., 1953.

Heimann, Eduard. *History of Economic Doctrine*. New York: Oxford University Press, 1964.

Homan, Paul T. *Contemporary Thought*. New York: Harper & Bros., 1928.

Hutchison, Terrence W. *A Review of Economic Doctrines, 1870-1929*. Oxford: Clarendon Press, 1953.

Landreth, Harry. *History of Economic Theory*. Boston: Houghton-Mifflin, 1976.

Lekachman, Robert. *A History of Economic Ideas*. New York: Harper & Bros., 1959.

Lekachman, Robert (ed.). *The Varieties of Economics*, 2 vols. Cleveland: The World Publishing Co., 1962.

Rogin, Leo. *The Meaning and Validity of Economic Theory*. New York: Harper & Bros., 1956.

Roll, Eric. *A History of Economic Though*. 3d ed. Englewood Cliffs, N.J.: Prentice-Hall, Inc., 1956.

Schumpeter, Joseph A. *History of Economic Analysis*. New York: Oxford University Press, 1954.

Seligman, Ben. *Main Currents in Modern Economics*. New York: Free Press of Glencoe, Inc., 1962.

Taylor, Overton H. *A History of Economic Thought*. New York: McGraw-Hill Book Co., Inc., 1960.

Whittaker, Edmund. *Schools and Streams of Economic Thought*. Chicago: Rand McNally & Co., 1960.

Zweig, Ferdynand. *Economic Ideas: A Study in Historical Perspective.* Englewood Cliffs, N.J.: Prentice-Hall, Inc., 1950.

There are also several collections of readings from original sources and essays on economic thought or about the works of specific contributors with which the reader will find it useful to be acquainted.

Abbot, Leonard D., ed. *Masterworks of Economics.* Garden City, N.Y.: Doubleday & Co., Inc., 1949.

Gheritity, James A., ed. *Economic Thought; A Historical Anthology.* New York: Random House, 1965.

Keynes, John Maynard. *Essays in Biography.* London: Macmillan & Co., 1933. Rev. ed. London: Rupert Hart-Davis, 1951.

Monroe, Arthur E., ed. *Early Economic Thought.* Cambridge: Harvard University Press, 1924.

Newman, Philip; Gayer, Arthur; and Spencer, Milton, eds. *Source Readings in Economic Thought.* New York: W. W. Norton & Co., Inc., 1954.

Patterson, S. Howard, ed. *Readings in the History of Economic Thought.* New York: McGraw-Hill Book Co., Inc., 1932.

Rima, I. H., ed. *Readings in the History of Economic Theory.* New York: Holt, Rinehart and Winston, 1970.

Schumpeter, Joseph A. *Ten Great Economists.* London: Oxford University Press, 1951.

Spengler, Joseph J., and Allen, W., eds. *Essays in Economic Thought: Aristotle to Marshall.* Chicago: Rand McNally & Co., 1960.

Spiegel, William H., ed. *The Development of Economic Thought.* New York: John Wiley & Sons, Inc., 1952.

Viner, Jacob. *The Long View and the Short.* Glencoe, Ill.: Free Press, 1958.

Wilson, George W., ed. *Classics of Economic Theory.* Bloomington, Ind.: Indiana University Press, 1964.

References which apply only to particular chapters and suggestions for further reading beyond what is noted under the General References given above will be appended to individual chapters. Most of these direct the reader to areas of controversy and interpretation, to background material and related disciplines, or to areas beyond the scope of this text.

2

Mercantilist Contributions to Economic Analysis

INTRODUCTION

The Period in History

THE ORIGIN of some theoretical concepts in economics can be traced to the period of mercantilism. Mercantilist thinkers, however, particularly in the early period, were practitioners dedicated to improving their own fortunes and those of their nation in the struggle against other states for supremacy. The ultimate test of the strong state was its ability to wage war, make conquests, and hold colonial areas. These national objectives presented problems different from those encountered during the Middle Ages. The lord of the manor recruited men and materials for warfare from his own domain. But the modern state depended on an army of mercenaries employed by the sovereign. The modern state needed money to acquire the sinews of war. The essence of mercantilism, therefore, was statecraft (*Staatsbildung*), and economic policy became a primary instrument to promote the simultaneous development and growth of the economy and the state.

The revival of trade during the Renaissance and the emergence of a money economy had already cemented the association between money and wealth. While the accumulation of precious metals was common in the ancient world and during the Middle Ages, England and the countries of Western Europe pursued the acquisition of gold as a matter of national policy well into the 18th century. Spain had an advantage over her rivals because of her colonizing ventures in the New World, for she alone had direct access to gold. The others, largely unsuccessful in their gold-seeking expeditions, had to devise other ways to increase their stocks of the precious metal. Thus, they directed their attention to policies designed to promote a favorable balance of payments, the presumption being that if they sold more to foreigners than they bought, the surplus would return to them in gold. They also regulated production, giving special attention to the growth and manufacture of exportable commodities and those which would promote domestic self-sufficiency, and encouraged the growth of population.

Regulations to accomplish these ends were especially stringent in France and reached their zenith under Jean Baptiste Colbert, who was minister of finance under Louis XIV from 1661 to 1683. During his administration, every aspect of production was brought under state control, including the relations between masters and workmen in the guilds, and methods and quality standards of manufacturers. Certain manufacturers, such as the famous Gobelin tapestry firm, were "royal manufacturers" owned and operated by the state. Dependence on foreign manufacturers was lessened by encouraging craftsmen to immigrate to France, and bounties were granted to encourage shippers and shipbuilders. Colbert's administration also witnessed the expansion of the French colonial empire and the growth of successful trading companies which conducted colonial trade as a monopoly of the crown. He was so thoroughgoing in introducing measures to stamp out remaining feudal elements and secure absolute power for the state that "Colbertism" is virtually synonymous with French mercantilism.

Sources of Early Mercantilist Thought

A tract entitled *A Brief Treatise on the Causes Which Can Make Gold and Silver Plentiful in Kingdoms Where There Are No Mines,* written by an Italian merchant, Antonio Serra, in 1613, is generally regarded as the earliest written exposition of mercantilistic thought. The last systematic presentation of mercantilistic doctrines was Sir James Steuart's *Inquiry into the Principles of Political Economy,* published in 1767. The ideas and policy recommendations to which the label mercantilistic has been given, may be extracted from the large volume of tracts, pamphlets, and articles which appeared between those dates. Examination of this literature, however, reveals such a diversity of ideas and recommendations that to describe them simply as mercantilistic tends to obscure and minimize their differences.

A considerable portion of the 17th century English writing came from the merchants, who naturally identified wealth with precious metals. While their funds were used to buy raw materials, tools, and labor, their businesses required the restoration of capital funds to monetary form through the sale of goods. Since they thought of domestic trade as merely circulating existing stocks of money, it was foreign trade they especially prized. Here, they looked to the state to facilitate their efforts by controlling the relationship of imports and exports, regulating interest rates and exchange rates, and chartering joint-stock trading companies with monopoly privileges such as the British East India Company and the Merchant Adventurers.

Since the accumulation of treasure was a primary aim of the sovereign, and its acquisition depended on the foreign trade balance, a unity of interest between the state and the merchants evolved. Insofar as a heterogeneous group of writers may be said to have a chief spokesman, Thomas Mun (1571–1641) is generally regarded as most representative of the English mercantile interests of his day.[1] That he was also the most influential appears evident from Adam Smith's famous critique of mercantilism in *The Wealth of Nations*. Smith discusses the nature and shortcomings of mercantilism almost exclusively in terms of Mun's *England's Treasure by Forraign Trade*, even though other writers had produced a voluminous number of papers, pamphlets, essays, and tracts and Sir James Steuart's *Inquiry into the Principles of Political Economy* had been published.

Mun was during his lifetime a successful merchant, a director of the East India Company, and a member of the Board of Trade. After the loss of a company vessel carrying a gold shipment, he wrote *A Discourse of Trade from England into the East Indies* (1621) to clear the East India Company of the bullionists' charge that its export of specie was contrary to the best interests of the country. The *Discourse* was so obviously a special interest plea that it is much less impressive than his later work *England's Treasure by Forraign Trade*, which was published posthumously.

Not all businessmen were, however, of one mind. Some were enthusiastic nationalists; others were provincial and favored a continuation of medieval localism; and still others thought in terms that transcended national boundaries. The arguments of such English exponents of mercantilism as Gerard De Malynes, Dudley Diggs, and Thomas Mun, while marking them as spokesmen for the business interests of their day, reflect wide differences in their ideas and policy recommendations. The flow of ideas from merchant authors, together with those of the philosophers, government officials, and scientists who also turned their attention to economic matters, resulted in a very heterogenous body of literature. It is no easy task, therefore, to set forth mercantilistic doctrines. We can examine the leading ideas on foreign trade, money and interest, and labor and production; and yet, our efforts will not yield a homogeneous body of thought.

---

[1] E. A. J. Johnson, *Predecessors of Adam Smith* (New York: Prentice-Hall, Inc., 1937), "Mun, the Strategist," p. 77. It is suggested that Mun's book was the model on which *The Wealth of Nations* unconsciously was patterned.

This is particularly the case when we deal with the more advanced mercantilist writers, such as Sir William Petty, David Hume, and Dudley North who are forerunners of economic liberalism, even though they dealt with mercantilistic problems. Although the end of the mercantilistic period is generally regarded as coinciding with the appearance of Adam Smith's *Wealth of Nations,* it must be borne in mind that, in England at least, many mercantilistic restrictions had already become obsolete by the middle of the 18th century, and those remaining were regarded with irritation rather than approval.

Compared with their English contemporaries, writers on economic matters in France, Germany, and Austria were considerably less numerous than in England. Nor were they predominantly merchants or members of the nobility. Most were civil servants who were even more exclusively concerned with applied economics than were their English counterparts, whose writings, though crude and unsystematic, laid the foundation for numerous concepts from which modern tools of analysis, especially in the area of international trade and monetary theory, were to develop.

ECONOMIC ANALYSIS

The Balance of Trade and the Acquisition of Wealth

The concept of the balance of trade is the most important tool of economic analysis developed by mercantilist writers. In modern terminology the term "balance of trade" includes only merchandise imports and exports, whereas the "balance of payments" includes, in addition, invisible exports and imports, long-term and short-term capital and gold. Merchandise and invisible exports, exports of monetary metals and transfers of claims on the domestic economy to the rest of the world are designated as plus items in the balance of payments. Commodity and invisible imports, imports of monetary metals and acquisitions of claims *vis a vis* the rest of the world set up an outward flow of foreign exchange to other countries and are negative items in the balance of payments.

If a country has a surplus of commodity and invisible imports, this will be balanced by an outward movement of specie, new foreign debts, or diminished foreign assets. Conversely, an excess of merchandise and invisible exports will be offset by an inflow of gold or the acquisition of claims on the rest of the world. It is in this sense that the balance of payments, which is nothing more than an accounting statement of a country's foreign transactions, must always be in balance. That bullionist, mercantilist, and cameralist writers did not understand this principle is evident in their argument that a nation should strive for a favorable balance of trade as a matter of national policy. By this, they meant an excess of merchandise and invisible exports relative to imports which would be offset either by a flow of gold or by foreign credits. Since their primary concern was the acquisition of treasure, they advocated policies that would insure gold imports to compensate for a surplus in the balance of trade.

What was the rationale for the pursuit of this objective? This is a question which became a matter of almost endless controversy. The least sympathetic interpretation was Adam Smith's. In the *Wealth of Nations* he viewed the mercantilist position as being nothing more than the translation of private merchants' interest in acquiring gold into a national policy of protectionism by a gullible Parliament. A more charitable interpretation, also associated with Smith, is that the mercantilists identified specie with wealth. There were several among the later mercantilists who understood that money is not capital; but most of the early mercantilist writers were persuaded that the wealth of the nation consists of its stock of precious metals rather than goods for consumption or further production. Many were so wedded to this notion that they failed to perceive the advantages inherent in geographical specialization of production. Relatively few mercantilists showed any awareness that wealth consists of goods for consumption or further production. Since the supply of gold is relatively fixed, they believed that the wealth of one nation could only be augmented at the expense of other nations. This conception of wealth provided the mercantilist rationale for theoretical analysis as well as policy prescriptions.

Although all writers, regardless of national origin, were essentially in agreement concerning the goal of building a strong state through the accumulation of treasure, some presented cruder theoretical analyses and narrower policy recommendations than others. For example, the English bullionists urged complete prohibition of the export of bullion and the establishment of the Office of Royal Exchanger to regulate foreign exchange transactions. These proposals grew in vehemence after the loss of an East India Company vessel carrying a large shipment of gold. The most heated protest against the privilege to ship gold came from Gerard DeMalynes who urged the state to control the exchange dealings of private financiers, whose transactions he believed not only caused bullion to flow out but also raised interest rates by decreasing the amount of bullion in the realm.[2]

DeMalynes' arguments reflect a strong medievalist view of moral justice. While he recognized that bills of exchange facilitated foreign trade, he argued that only transactions taking place at exchange rates that are *par pro pari* (that is, at rates reflecting the bullion content of the currencies involved) are consistent with the requirements of moral justice. A divergence of exchange rates from parity was viewed as the result of corrupting

---

[2] Gerard DeMalynes, *A Treatise on the Canker of England's Commonwealth* (London, 1601); *The Maintenance of Free Trade* (London, 1622); *The Center of the Circle of Commerce* (London, 1623).

activities by dealers in exchange which imposed an injustice on one of the parties and also caused bullion movements to take place. DeMalynes thought that bullion would either flow into a country or be drained away, depending on the direction of the movement of exchange rates above or below par. Only at stable exchange rates would no bullion movement take place. His proposed remedy was that the Royal Exchanger should handle all foreign exchange transactions, and that such transactions, in being made only at the *par pro pari,* would preserve the treasures in the kingdom.[3] The modern counterpart of DeMalynes' *par pro pari* is the mint par of exchange, which is today, of course, divorced from moral connotations.

Some mercantilists took exception to the proposal that all bullion exports should be prohibited, maintaining that the outward flow of specie would actually contribute to the goal of achieving a favorable overall export balance. No one presented this view with greater vigor and clarity than Thomas Mun. His central argument in *England's Treasure by Forraign Trade* was that the export of specie results in purchases of goods which, when reexported at advantageous prices, bring back more specie than had originally been exported. The defense of the special cause of the East India Company is abandoned in this work, and the argument is presented from the viewpoint of the statesman or greatly enlightened businessman who was conscious primarily of the interests of the nation.

Mun begins by distinguishing between natural and artificial riches as a basis for national opulence. A notion of capital which is generally identified with stock or financial capital, though it is sometimes confused with both money and wealth, is subsequently introduced. Drawing an analogy between the kingdom and a private estate which can be impoverished by careless spending or enriched by an orderly conversion of goods into money and money into goods. Mun designates as "stock" that portion of natural or artificial wealth which is used to yield a surplus. He argues that the wisest way to employ stock is in foreign trade, for this will increase wealth and treasure if care is taken to achieve a favorable balance. In Mun's own words:

> The ordinary means, therefore, to increase our wealth and treasure is by Forraign Trade wherein we must ever observe this rule; to sell more to strangers yearly than we consume of theirs in value. For suppose that when this Kingdom is plentifully served with Cloth, Lead, Tin, Iron, Fish and other native commodities, we doe yearly export the over-surplus to forraign Countreys to the value of twenty two hundred thousand pounds, by which means we are enabled beyond the Seas to buy and bring in

---

[3] Another supporter of policies to restrict bullion exports was Edward Misselden, with whom DeMalynes engaged in arguments regarding trade and exchange regulations. However, in defending his views in *The Center of the Circle of Commerce,* DeMalynes reversed his position and argued favorably for the export of bullion to purchase goods abroad. See Johnson, *Predecessors,* chap. 4, "Misselden, the Critic."

forraign wares for our use and Consumptions, to the value of twenty hundred thousand pounds; By this order duly kept in our trading, we may rest assured that the Kingdom shall be enriched yearly two hundred thousand pounds, which must be brought to us in so much Treasure, because that part of stock which is not returned to us in wares must necessarily be brought home in treasure. . . .[4]

It is thus that Mun adopts Misselden's notion of the balance of trade and emphasizes that it is the relationship between *aggregate* imports and exports that is crucial, not the relationship between specific imports and exports. Mun is also well aware of the significance of invisible items of trade as a source of additional foreign credits, for he says: "The value of our exportations may be much advanced when we perform it ourselves in our own Ships, for then we get not only the price of our wares as they are worth here, but also the Merchants gains, the charges of ensurance and freight to carry them beyond the seas. . . ."[5] In order to cultivate a favorable balance, he urges that the country should strive for self-sufficiency to diminish its imports and practice frugality to have more available for export. The consumption of luxuries is to be discouraged, but "if in our rayment we will be prodigal, yet let this be done with our own materials and manufactures, as Cloth, Lace Imbroideries, Cutwork and the like, where the excess of the rich may be the employment of the poor, whose labours notwithstanding of this kind, would be more profitable for the Commonwealth, if they were done to the use of strangers."[6]

The advantages from trade can be maximized only if judgment is used in pricing. Commodities should be sold at high prices only "so far forth as the high price cause not a less vent in the quantity." Where there is competition from other suppliers or substitutes are readily available, "we must strive to sell as cheap as possible we can, rather than lose the utterance of such wares." These observations concerning the relationship between price and the quantity of a commodity which can be sold reveal Mun's understanding of what in modern terminology is called demand elasticity. Similar awareness of the relationship between price and demand is also evident in his recommendations regarding export and import duties. High export duties, he reasoned, may be harmful, for by "indearing them [English exports] to the strangers use, it hinder[s] their vent." Import duties, on the other hand, should be high enough to discourage consumption of foreign goods in England and low on goods intended for reexport.

The most controversial matter pursued by Mun concerned the export of specie as a means to increase England's treasure. It was this issue that

---

[4] Thomas Mun, *England's Treasure by Forraign Trade* (London; 1664), in John R. McCulloch, ed., *Early English Tracts on Commerce* (Norwich: Jarrold and Sons, Ltd., 1952), pp. 125–26.

[5] Ibid., p. 129.

[6] Ibid.

brought him into conflict with the bullionists who advocated complete prohibition of gold exports. The essence of his argument was that when gold is used in trade to acquire goods which are subsequently reexported at advantageous prices, even more gold will be returned to England than was originally sent out. To keep gold in the kingdom does not multiply wealth; on the contrary, it will raise prices and diminish exports. Money must be used as capital in order that more wealth will ultimately emerge. Outward movements of gold to acquire goods for reexport are analogous to the seedtime and the harvest, says Mun, for "if we only behold the actions of the husbandman in the seed-time when he casteth away much good corn into the ground, we will rather accompt him a mad man than a husbandman: but when we consider his labours in the harvest which is the end of his endeavours, we find the worth and plentiful increase of his actions."[7]

Monetary Analysis

Most mercantilists were aware of the direct relationship between the quantity of money and the level of prices, maintaining that "plenty of money in a Kingdom doth make the native commodities dearer." The earliest theoretical analysis of the relationship between the quantity of money and inflationary price increases was made by the 16th century French political philosopher Jean Bodin. He attributed the marked price rise experienced by western Europe in his time primarily to the inflow of monetary metals from South America, thus emphasizing what is today treated as M (monetary means of payment) in our modern equations of exchange. He also observed that monopolies, through their policies of restricting output, and large demands by consumers for luxury commodities contributed to price increases. Thus, he was not unaware of the significance of what is today designated as T and V in the transactions version of the equation of exchange (see below).

In the now familiar form introduced by Irving Fisher in the 1920s, the equation of exchange states:

$$MV = PT$$

In this equation, M designates the monetary means of payment available for conducting transactions in the economy, V designates the average number of times the units of payment change hands in a given period of time, P stands for the average level of prices, and T for the quantity of goods and services available to be purchased. The equation, as it stands, is nothing more than the truism that the monetary value of the goods and services paid for is equal to the monetary value of the goods and services

---

[7] Ibid., p. 141.

sold. It becomes analytically useful only within the framework of a hypothesis as to how the elements in the equation behave. Fisher, making certain assumptions with respect to T and V, maintained that there is a direct casual relationship between the quantity of money and the general price level. He argued that, other things being equal, the general price level will vary directly with the quantity of money. This is a conclusion with which mercantilists were in accord, though they lacked the analytical framework that was later developed.

Since few mercantilists favored inflation, their recommendations for a continuous accumulation of monetary metals via a favorable balance of trade appear contradictory. But this seeming contradiction of objectives is reconciled if changes in M affect T rather than P. They reasoned that increases in the amount of money "quicken trade" instead of producing an inflation of prices and thereby rescued their advocacy of a favorable balance of trade, with its associated inflow of specie, from a seeming contradiction of objectives.

This line of reasoning reflects an awareness that a growing volume of money and credit is essential to continued expansion of the physical volume of trade. Since the embryonic state of the credit system at that time precluded a well functioning system of note issue (demand deposit creation being a still later phase of banking development), mercantilist emphasis on the desirability of accumulating greater quantities of gold in order to expand the money supply is more comprehensible than it would be if the credit system had been better developed. They reasoned that an inflow of hard money would keep interest rates low, while the downward pressure on prices which would result from an inadequate supply of money would serve to dampen further expansion of economic activity.

While the relationship between the quantity of money, prices, and interest rates was not clearly understood until much later, when a distinction was made between the money rate and the real rate of interest, the mercantilists seemed to sense the necessity of avoiding downward pressure on prices if commercial activity is to be expanded. Though they thought of these relationships in purely monetary terms, real factors, which they did not understand, are involved. An economic analysis is being conducted in real terms when it views money as facilitating exchanges by serving as a unit of account without affecting relative commodity or factor prices or the level of economic activity in any way. A monetary analysis, on the other hand, regards money as capable of exerting an effect on the magnitudes of the economy.

Mercantilists overlooked the interaction between real and monetary factors when they failed to see that falling prices raise the real rate of interest, which impedes economic expansion. It is the value of a loan in terms of the goods and services it represents, rather than money rates as such, which affects the worthwhileness of borrowing. If the price level is falling, the principal value of a loan in real terms is necessarily rising, since the borrower contracts to repay a given number of dollars which will purchase more goods and services at low prices than at higher prices. What the mercantilists failed to understand was that the reason an increased quantity of money is associated with a lower rate of interest is not simply due to the greater supply of funds thus available for borrowing, but because this is generally associated with an increase in real income. This is a relationship which the mercantilist monetary theory of interest overlooked. It was not until the writings of David Hume, Anne Robert Jacques Turgot, and Richard Cantillon that real as opposed to monetary theories of interest began to evolve.

Mercantilist Views on Production and Related Matters

Preoccupation with the aggrandizement of the state and the acquisition of treasure set the stage for a number of corollary doctrines and policies designed to foster the achievement of these goals. The theory of production is of major importance in this connection, for the creation of the largest possible export surplus necessarily required maximum utilization of the factors of production. To some writers, natural resources were the basis for wealth, while others regarded labor as a more important factor than natural resources. Lewes Roberts, for example, viewed the earth as "the fountaine and mother of all riches," while Petty said that "labor is the father and active principle of wealth as land is the mother." The policy counterpart of both viewpoints is to be found in measures to increase natural resources and the productivity of labor by discouraging idleness and introducing specialization. Even before Smith's celebrated description of the advantages of division of labor in the manufacture of pins, Petty observed that "cloth must be cheaper when one cards, another spins, another weaves, another draws, another dresses, another presses and packs, than when all the operations above were clumsily performed by the same hand."

Mercantilistic writers distinguished between productive and unproductive labor in terms of its contribution to national opulence. Manufacturers and farmers were regarded as productive, though the warmest praise was, understandably, reserved for the merchants. Retailers, clergymen, doctors, lawyers, and entertainers were generally regarded as unproductive; and it was urged that the government hold the number of unproductive people to a minimum in order to direct their labor to some more useful occupation. Mercantilistic ideas on production are part of their legacy from the Scholastics of the medieval period, who viewed God's bounty as the origin of wealth and production as the exploitation of this bounty by labor. Thus, Thomas Hobbes wrote that "plenty God usually either giveth freely, or for labor selleth to mankind."[8] Emphasis on the appropriation of natural or divine bounty by the efforts of man's labor is to be found throughout British economic literature in the period before Adam Smith wrote. Virtually without exception, it was urged that government must increase both the quantity and the utilization of "natural" wealth and labor. Thus, Mun advocated the growing of hemp, flax, cordage, and tobacco on wastelands,[9] and the exploitation of fisheries in the North Sea, which are "our own natural wealth and would cost nothing but labor."[10] Similarly, Roger Coke proposed that idle workers be employed to reclaim wastelands.[11] Willful idleness was not to be tolerated, and there is an abundance of literature setting forth proposals to make England's population as productive as possible. This is the responsibility of government, for if people are idle, "that is for want of being rightly governed."[12]

Still another aspect of mercantilistic emphasis on the importance of labor in production is the encouragement of population growth, not for the sake of mere numbers but to increase the size of the working force. Attention was frequently called to Holland, a very prosperous country which, though it had few resources, was enriched through the industry of its people; and Spain, which was impoverished through its sparse population, though it was rich in colonial mines. Proposals to increase population by encouraging early marriage and immigration are so common to most of the English writers of this period that they cannot be typically associated with the name of anyone specifically. It was generally accepted that a large population, by keeping wages close to subsistence levels, would not only reduce the cost of producing goods but would also discourage the idleness that might become associated with higher wage levels.

One of the most interesting bits of mercantilistic reasoning incorporating views on both labor and balance of payments is the argument which appeared in successive issues of the *British Merchant* regarding foreign-paid incomes.[13] Briefly, the line of reasoning pursued was that when goods were exported, foreigners would pay the wages of the workmen employed in making them, whereas imports would involve like payments to foreigners. The obvious duty of government would therefore be to minimize foreign imports in order to achieve a favorable balance of foreign-paid income. The most desirable import is bullion, not only because it is wealth

---

[8] Thomas Hobbes, *Leviathan* (London, 1691), p. 127.

[9] *England's Treasure by Forraign Trade,* in McCulloch, *Early English Tracts,* p. 127.

[10] Ibid., p. 130.

[11] Roger Coke, *A Discourse of Trade* (London, 1670), pp. 16–17.

[12] Attributed to Malachy Postlethwayt in E. A. Johnson, *Predecessors,* p. 287.

[13] See Johnson, *Predecessors,* Chapter 15, for a complete description of these views.

but also because it has little labor incorporated in it as compared with the manufactured commodities which England concentrated on exporting.

THE TRANSITION TO CLASSICISM

The Environment and Leading Contributors

A reaction to mercantilistic views began in the second half of the 17th century which caused economic thought to enter a transitional phase. During this phase the businessman was displaced as the chief inquirer into economic questions, and the attitude and methodological approach which later characterized the writings of the classical era slowly began to appear. The newly emerging attitude was one of increasing liberality; people began to believe that greater freedom from governmental restrictions would be advantageous to themselves as well as to the economy. This attitude reflected the gradually evolving idea that the economic system is a self-generating autonomous organism which does not require management from above, but functions best when allowed to regulate itself. A hedonistic philosophy of material gain and enjoyment, as opposed to the medieval view of the virtue of self-denial, was also gaining acceptance. According to this philosophy, prodigality is not immoral but is the life of trade. Economic progress thrives under the stimulus of self-interest and higher levels of personal consumption. Later 17th and early 18th century writers gave ideological expression to these beliefs in the doctrine of laissez-faire and sought to discover the laws which govern the functioning of self-regulating economic systems.

These liberal trends in economic thinking were particularly evident in England, whose growing middle class included many who were engaged in trade and industry. France and Holland also had some early proponents of liberalism, but Italy and Germany as yet shared little disposition to displace mercantilistic ideas. Thus, English writers in the main gave currency to more liberal ideas and prepared the ground for the development of economic theory. Before 1660, economic theory was virtually nonexistent; after 1776, with the publication of Adam Smith's *Wealth of Nations,* economics was firmly launched as a discipline.

At the beginning of the transition period, the individuals best suited by experience and interest to write on economic matters were businessmen like Josiah Child (1630–99) and Nicholas Barbon (1637–98). Child was a merchant who sold supplies to the English navy and eventually became the largest single stockholder in the East India Company.[14] His most famous work is a pamphlet, *Brief Observations,* published in 1668, in which he undertook to prove that England could equal the prosperity of the

---

[14] A most interesting account of the lives and works of some leading writers of this transitional period in the history of economic doctrine is given in William Letwin, *The Origins of Scientific Economics* (London: Methuen and Co., Inc., 1963).

Dutch if she would follow policies which he believed to be the source of Holland's great wealth. He believed a low rate of interest to be the most important of these and strongly advocated that the legal rate of interest be reduced.

Nicholas Barbon was also a businessman, though he earned an M.D. degree from the University of Utrecht in 1661. His earliest business interest was in building, and he had become prosperous as a result of the destruction of most of the city of London by the Great Fire. He was also astute enough to develop the first workable plan for writing fire insurance and ventured into mortgage banking. He wrote many pamphlets on fire insurance, building, and banking, but his leading work is *Discourse on Trade* (1690).

Though the social benefits of commerce were more appreciated at the time Child and Barbon wrote than previously, merchants were still not highly esteemed. On the contrary, their recommendations were so generally suspect that merchant-authors often preferred to write anonymously or preceded their writings with prefaces which denied that their policy recommendations would benefit them privately.[15] These denials notwithstanding, the fact is that private interests were seldom really subordinated to the public good, and public suspicion of merchant-supported proposals was more frequently justified than not. Their recommendations that the legal rate of interest and the bullion content of silver coins be reduced (the latter was done in 1696) provided reason for suspicion. Though the prosperity of the Dutch was generally thought to be associated with their relatively low interest rate, the fact that low interest rates would also benefit borrowers, such as Child and Barbon were, raised doubts about the honesty of their denials. Nor was the argument that devaluation would make the country richer as convincing as it might have been if it were not apparent that it would also benefit those who had hoarded bullion or old coins whose silver content had not been reduced by clipping. As a banker Barbon had this opportunity, although he pointed out that banks would also profit if coins were fewer and heavier, for "nothing can be of greater advantage to banks than scarcity of money when men will be glad to take a bank note for want of it."[16]

The recommendations which men like Barbon and Child made were virtually unsupported by any kind of economic analysis. Typically, they argued for their proposals on the ground that they had worked well previously or because current policies produced unsatisfactory results. An-

---

[15] Josiah Child's *Discourse about Trade* (1690), an anonymous republication of his earlier *Brief Observations,* is typical of efforts to conceal authorship. The Preface was written by the publisher, who assured the reader that the writer was not a trader and that the manuscript came to him very accidentally.

[16] Nicholas Barbon, *A Discourse concerning Coining the New Money Lighter, in Answer to Mr. Locke's Considerations about Raising the Value of Money* (London: 1696).

other technique of argumentation was to refute the objections others made against the policies they recommended. But there was no attempt to derive the general principles on which the policies recommended must necessarily rest if they were to work as was claimed. It is plain, therefore, that what was most urgently needed in order that economics make headway as a science was a deductive system which derives its conclusions from a set of premises. The only critique that can then be made is that the premises are false or inappropriate, or that the reasoning is imperfect. Failing this, the conclusions are valid, irrespective of the personal interests of the author, for the conclusions are inherent in the premises. In short, economics required the methodology which René Descartes had already introduced in his *Discourse on Method* in the mid-17th century to lay a foundation for natural science.

The method followed by Sir Dudley North (1641–91) in his pamphlet, *Discourse upon Trade,* is essentially Cartesian, though it was constructed by a man with relatively no formal education. Though he came from a family which was fairly accomplished academically, North had so little inclination for classical study that he was sent to writing school, where he became skilled in penmanship, arithmetic, and weights and measures. He then was apprenticed to a merchant with the Levant Company. Many of the next 20 years were spent abroad, principally in Turkey, where he accumulated enough from his various trading activities to return to England and a life of ease in his early 40s. He had also acquired such vast technical information about every aspect of trade that in 1683 he was appointed Commissioner of Customs and later elected to Parliament.[17] During this period North became increasingly aware that private and public interests frequently diverge and that it is necessary to separate the two when inquiring into economic matters. The method by which he thought this could be accomplished is described by his brother Roger North in the preface to *Discourse upon Trade* (1692). Here, the extent to which private interests might interfere with objective thinking in economic matters is candidly recognized, and it is asserted that objective thinking in economic matters requires that conclusions be "built on clear and evident truths." It is, in short, necessary to lay down premises that are incontrovertible and to reason from these premises to the conclusions they imply. Thus the earliest beginning of deductive analysis in economics is Sir Dudley North's pamphlet, *Discourse upon Trade.* Unfortunately, this pamphlet made little impression and was soon forgotten. As was subsequently often the case in the history of economic thought, its rediscovery came too late to be of more than historical interest.

The writings of Sir William Petty and John Locke mark a turning point in the development of economics because neither was associated in even

---

[17] Roger North, *Lives,* 3 vols. (London: George Bell & Sons, 1826), vol. 2, pp. 132 ff., 153–54, 180–82.

the remotest way with the business world. Sir William Petty (1623–87) served for a time in the Royal Navy before studying medicine in the Netherlands.[18] He subsequently served as physician general to the army in Ireland during the Civil War. Afterwards, he was commissioned to survey the lands which were to be distributed among Oliver Cromwell's soldiers. The experience familiarized him with land rents and taxes, and encouraged him to pioneer an empirical approach to economic inquiry. His *Political Arithmetick* (1690) presented an impressive array of numbers concerning land, cattle, houses, shipping, gold, merchandise, people, etc.; but these were illustrative rather than actual data, so that Petty's technique was essentially that of deductive logic, in which premises and conclusions were given expression in hypothetical numerical terms. Though he liked to think of himself as an empiricist, his work is much more in the nature of a contribution to economic theory. This is particularly true of his *Treatise of Taxes and Contributions,* which predated his work on political arithmetic.

The philosopher John Locke (1632–1704) was another contributor to the literature of the transition period. He received a thoroughly classical education at Christ Church, Oxford, where he also took a medical degree.[19] Like Petty, Locke practiced his profession only on a limited scale. He became personal physician to Lord Ashley, who was chancellor of the Exchequer, and soon also became his personal secretary and assistant. In this way he was brought into contact with matters of trade, such as the proposal concerning the reduction of the interest rate. He drafted a reply to Child's *Brief Observations* in which he examined, from the standpoint of natural law, the effect which a reduction in the rate of interest would have. He also became so well versed in colonial problems that he was appointed in 1673 as Secretary to the Council for Trade and Plantations. He returned to private life two years later and turned his attention to such works as the *Treatise of Civil Government* and the *Essay Concerning Human Understanding,* which established him as one of the great philosophers of his day. But he also continued to interest himself in economic questions. Monetary problems, in particular, claimed his attention and led to his book *Some Considerations of the Consequences of Lowering of Interest and Raising the Value of Money.* This work examined the nature and determination of interest, rent, and the value of land, from the standpoint of natural law. He asserted that the inexorability of natural laws makes any statute which is contrary to the laws of nature inappropriate. Adherence to this principle led him to the conclusion that natural law, not man-made law, should determine interest rates and the value of coins.

Locke's approach to examining economic questions had profound impli-

---

[18] Details of Petty's life are readily available in Emil Strauss, *Sir William Petty* (London: Bodley Head, 1954).

[19] Maurice Cranston, *John Locke* (New York: Macmillan Co., 1957).

cations for the development of economics. It suggested that society is governed by a body of laws precisely as is the natural universe. Locke's work, therefore, helped establish the pattern of later economic analysis. Whereas 17th century writers typically addressed themselves directly to practical questions and policy proposals, the method of approach subsequently became to discover the principles concerning particular phenomena such as value, price, interest, etc., in order to examine the relevance of these principles to particular problems.

David Hume (1711–76) is also among the transitional thinkers whose economic writings helped to break the influence of mercantilistic principles. Though he was primarily a philosopher, his *Political Discourses* (1752) include numerous essays which contain some significant contributions to theoretical economics, the most significant of which are "Of Money," "Of Interest," "Of Commerce," and "Of the Balance of Trade."[20]

The significance of the contribution made by the Irish-born English financier Richard Cantillon (1680–1734) to economic theory is debatable; if it is judged in terms of the merit of its content, it is probably not overgenerous to regard him as the cofounder, along with Adam Smith, of the classical school. But if we judge instead on the basis of the impact he had in his own time, his role in the history of economic analysis is considerably less significant. His *Essay on the Nature of Commerce in General* was not published until 20 years after his death and then forgotten until it was rediscovered and rescued from virtual oblivion by William Jevons in 1881.[21] The most significant impact of the essay was on the Physiocrats, particularly as regards their emphasis on land as the source of wealth. Victor Riquetti, Marquis de Mirabeau, had a copy, and several of the ideas developed in his *L'Ami de Homme* (1760) paralleled those introduced by Cantillon in his essay.

The subject matter of economic inquiry was also undergoing a change. Although the Industrial Revolution was not yet under way, commercial capitalism was already evolving into industrial capitalism. Compared with its status in the previous century, manufacturing, as contrasted with agriculture, had grown greatly in importance. New products and modes of production, new forms of enterprise and credit facilities had been developed. These changes were accompanied by the pauperization of numerous farmers, the decay of many agricultural areas, the impoverishment of many handcraftsmen, and considerable technological unemployment. During the heyday of commercial capitalism the central problem was trade and the

---

[20] The economic writings of Hume are available in Eugene Rotwein, *The Economic Writings of David Hume* (Edinburgh: Nelson, 1955).

[21] This essay was originally written in English and translated into French by Cantillon to make it available to a friend. It was reprinted in facsimile (1892) by G. H. Ellis for Harvard University and subsequently translated by Henry Higgs (Macmillan, 1931).

growth of merchant capital through profitable exchange. With the growth of industry, production rather than exchange became the central problem.

Not every writer of this period found himself in conflict with every aspect of mercantilistic thinking or policy. On the contrary, all were mercantilists to some degree, though certain aspects of their thinking were closer to the ideas of Adam Smith and the Physiocrats, who wrote during the 18th century, than to those of their predecessors. Classification of writers such as Petty, North, Locke, Hume, and Cantillon is therefore somewhat arbitrary. They may be treated either as later or liberal mercantilists, or as forerunners of economic liberalism. While sufficient reason can be advanced for either treatment, the important thing to recognize is the transitional nature of their thought.

CHANGING CONCEPTS DURING THE TRANSITION PERIOD

The Nature of Wealth

The mercantilist concept that gold and silver are the wealth of a nation and that every effort should be made to preserve and augment the supply of precious metals was rapidly becoming outmoded during the transition period. Even some of the merchants were becoming free of the bullion illusion. Nicholas Barbon was among the first to recognize that while gold and silver have characteristics which make them particularly satisfactory for coining, there is no greater advantage to be derived from accumulating them than any other commodity. "If there could be account taken of the balance of trade, I can't see where the advantage of it could be. For the reason that's given for it—that the overplus is paid in bullion and the nation grows so much richer . . . is altogether a mistake. For gold and silver are but commodities, and one sort of commodity is as good as another so be it of the same value."[22]

Dudley North attacked another aspect of the mercantilist view of trade when he disassociated riches from gold and silver. Mercantilists viewed trade as being essentially warfare; one nation gained what the other lost. North asserted, on the contrary, that trade is mutually advantageous, for no one will accept a smaller value in exchange than he gives up. Moreover, he asserted, it is not trade which enriches men the most, but production, particularly of manufactured goods; "he who is most diligent, and raiseth most Fruits or maketh most of Manufactory, will abound most in what others make or raise; and consequently be free from Want and enjoy most Conveniences, which is truly to be Rich, altho there were no such things as Gold, Silver or the like amongst them."[23]

---

[22] Barbon, *A Discourse,* p. 40.

[23] Dudley North, "A Discourse Concerning the Abatement of Interest," in McCulloch, *Early English Tracts,* p. 516.

David Hume also disputed the mercantilist identification of wealth with money and trade. His essay "Of Money" asserted that money merely represents "the real strength of the community" which is "men and commodities."[24] Though he recognized that an increase in its quantity will raise prices and serve as a temporary stimulus to trade, he mentioned that the happiness of people is not affected by the quantity of money.

Hume also examined the old mercantilist dogma that the prosperity of other countries will undermine domestic employment and industry. His essay "Of the Jealousy of Trade" maintained that international specialization is the basis of prosperity and remarked that "as a British subject, I pray for the flourishing commerce of Germany, Spain, Italy and even France itself."[25] His unique attitude eventually bore fruit in the commercial treaty concluded with France in 1786.

The Quantity Theory

Although the notion that the level of economic activity is related to the supply of money was already common in mercantilist days, John Locke gave the principle, now known as the quantity theory of money, a more refined statement than had been given previously. In particular, he pointed out "the necessity of some proportion of money to trade," though he recognized that it is hard to determine what that proportion should be. The quantity of money needed to carry on trade is hard to determine because it depends also on "the quickness of its circulation[;] . . . to make some probable guess we are to consider how much money it is necessary to suppose must rest constantly in each man's hands as requisite to the carrying on of trade." This recognition of the importance of the velocity of circulation was the most sophisticated treatment of quantity theory which had yet been offered. Later writers formulated these ideas on the velocity of circulation and the volume of trade with greater precision, but Locke deserves credit for a greatly improved statement of the quantity theory of money. Unfortunately, however, he was led via his quantity theory of money to advocate the desirability of an export surplus. He thought this would be to England's advantage because it would cause specie to flow in and thereby would enable her to sell at high prices and buy cheaply in other countries which would have low prices because they would have less bullion.

David Hume saw the fallacy of Locke's thinking and recognized the relationship between the quantity of money, the price level, and international flows of specie. Whereas mercantilists believed that a nation can

---

[24] David Hume, "Of Money," *Essays* (London: Longmans, Green & Co., 1912), vol. 1, p. 319.

[25] David Hume, "Of the Balance of Trade," *Essays* (1912).

continuously accumulate gold if it has a favorable balance, Hume pointed out that it is not possible for gold to flow continuously in one direction. A nation which has a favorable balance, and therefore acquires gold, will also experience a rise in its domestic price level. This will cause it to lose its export trade and stimulate imports for domestic use. Specie will therefore always adjust itself to the actual needs of trade. Thus "a government has great reason to preserve with care its people and its manufactures. Its moneys it may safely trust to the course of human affairs."[26] Hume also examined the transformation which takes place as a primitive barter economy develops into a money economy. He noted that exchange economies experience increasing specialization and growth. The power of the state is also enhanced in a money economy, for the sovereign may then "draw money by his taxes from every part of the state, and what he receives goes farther in every purchase and payment."

Cantillon recognized that Locke's inquiry into the effect of an increase in the quantity of money on the general price level did not consider the mechanism through which this occurs. Starting with the assumption that new mines are discovered, he traced the spread of inflation through the economic system as a result of the additional purchasing power received by those engaged in mining. These people are able to outbid others whose incomes are fixed with the result that the additional money will cause generally higher prices as it is absorbed into the economy. It will also alter the *structure* of prices, in a way which reflects the source of the new injection of money and the relative demands for goods by those who receive it.

The concept of the differential impact of new money on the structure of prices has become known as the Cantillon effect. Cantillon used it to compare the effect of an increase in specie which originates from an export surplus with that which results from new mines or an expansion of paper currency. An increase in specie which originates from an export surplus is more likely to stimulate trade than new money originating from an expansion of paper currency or the discovery of new mines. New gold production is more like to increase prices without accompanying increases in output. Rising prices in any country will, quite naturally, cause people to expand their purchases from countries in which prices have not yet risen. The home market will therefore become depressed, and gold will leave the country to pay for foreign imports until eventually prices will again be low enough to induce domestic buyers to buy at home rather than abroad. He concluded, therefore, that no country permanently benefits from the discovery of precious metals.

Cantillon also noted that inflationary price increases can result from an increase in the supply of paper money as well as from more metallic

---

[26] Ibid., p. 346.

money. He thought that price increases resulting from increased paper money are likely to prove disastrous because paper, lacking an intrinsic value, is likely to be refused acceptance. This is precisely what happened in France following John Law's famous experiment with a paper currency in 1716. Cantillon refused to endorse that proposal when it was presented to him, predicting that it would have unfortunate results.

The Propriety of Interest and Determination of Its Rate

The problem of interest, especially as regards the establishment of a legal rate, generated a large volume of literature throughout the period. The earliest of these contributions, like Josiah Child's, contained virtually no theory. Child was quite simply in favor of reducing the legal rate of interest in order to duplicate the advantages enjoyed by Dutch traders. He asserted it would make the country richer but offered no explanation why he thought it would have this effect.

Petty's views on interest were also relatively unsophisticated but do offer a theoretical explanation which relates the interest rate to the rent which land can earn. He thought that if a lender can demand repayment of a loan at any time, he is not entitled to interest. But if money is lent for a fixed period of time, the lender is entitled to "a compensation for this inconvenience which he admits against himself." Then, anticipating the Physiocratic analysis of a century later, he maintained that if the security of a loan is undoubted, the rate of interest is equivalent to the "Rent of so much Land as the money lent will buy."[27] He also suggested that if the security of a loan is in doubt, "a kind of ensurance must be interwoven with the simple natural interest."[28] These observations led him to conclude that it is useless to try to fix interest rates by law.

Nicholas Barbon, who was also opposed to fixing interest rates by law, had a more sophisticated view of the relationship between interest and rent. Land is "natural stock" and earns rent. Capital is "wrought stock"; its return is therefore like the return to land. "Interest is commonly-reckoned for money, because the money borrowed at interest is to be repaid in money. But this is a mistake, for the interest is paid for stock; the money borrowed is laid out to buy goods or pay for them before bought. No man takes up money at interest to lay it by him and lose the interest of it."[29]

The "wrought stock" to which Barbon referred consists of processed goods which merchants sell as distinct from the unprocessed goods farmers sell exactly as nature produces them. Farmers hire land and pay rent to

---

[27] Charles H. Hull, *Economic Writings of Sir William Petty* (1899), vol. 1 (New York: reprinted by A. M. Kelley, 1963–4), p. 48.

[28] Ibid.

[29] Barbon, *A Discourse,* p. 31.

acquire "natural stock"; merchants acquire processed goods, or "wrought stock," intended for sale. Dudley North had much the same idea when he talked of the "stock lord" who receives a return called interest for permitting others to use the property he has accumulated in the form of money.

Perhaps if Barbon's and North's inquiries had not been associated so specifically with the activities of the merchant, they would have formulated more clearly the principle of interest as the net yield of capital. But they did not conceive of stock as a separate factor of production which is entitled to a functional reward. Later, in the 19th century, "wrought stock" was plainly identified as a separate factor of production, distinct from labor and land, and entitled to a return equivalent to its net yield. But this is a much more advanced notion than either Barbon or North had of stock and its return.

Just as the 17th century concept of stock related generally to money rather than real capital goods, so interest was explained as a monetary rather than a real phenomenon. Thus, Locke wrote: "That which most sensibly raises the rate of interest of money is when money is little in proportion to the trade of the country."[30] North similarly applied price analysis to the explanation of interest rates. "That as more Buyers than Sellers raiseth the price of a Commodity, so more Borrowers than Lenders, will raise Interest."[31] David Hume also argued that the rate of interest depends on the demand and supply of borrowers and lenders. If there is "a great demand for borrowing but little riches to supply that demand," the rate of interest will be high. Viewing profits as interdependent with interest, he asserts that it is not the quantity of gold and silver that causes the interest rate to be high, but the volume of industry and commerce. The commercial classes, especially, contribute to a reduction of the interest rate, for their frugality and rivalry for gain reduces not only profit but interest.

Rent and the Value of Land

Though the problem of interest was frequently approached from the standpoint of the rent of land, the problem of rent was also dealt with in connection with the value of land itself. How much, asked Petty, would rent-yielding land be worth? He was apparently unaware that the value of land is related to the rate of interest. Thus, instead of capitalizing the return in terms of the rate of interest, he suggested that the purchase price that will be paid for land depends on the number of years a prospective purchaser and his immediate descendants are likely to enjoy the yield. In

[30] From Locke's early manuscript on interest in William Letwin, *The Origins of Scientific Economics,* app. 5, p. 278.

[31] North, "A Discourse concerning the Abatement of Interest," in McCulloch, *Early English Tracts* (London: Methuen and Co., Ltd., 1963), p. 522.

the *Treatise of Taxes,* he estimates that three generations of males may be expected to live concurrently for 21 years, and that the value of land is therefore equal to that number times its annual rent.

John Locke, however, was aware of the relationship between the price of land and the interest rate. He reasoned that the value of land depends on the income that can be derived from it, and that the value of land and its income bear the same relationship to each other as the principal of a loan bears to the interest it earns. The value of land (and other assets) is established by capitalizing its rental income in terms of the interest rate. Thus, given a certain rental income, the value of land will be raised if the interest rate in terms of which it is capitalized is lowered.

The Value of Commodities

The problem of the value of commodities was also beginning to be of concern to the thinkers of the transition period, although it was not yet a distinct topic of inquiry for most. Petty's value theory must, for example, be extracted from his inquiry into the "mysterious nature" of rent. Rent, he maintained, is the agricultural surplus which remains after the seed and the farmer's subsistence are deducted from the proceeds of his harvest. This view of rent as a differential surplus, which is price-determined rather than price-determining, anticipates by some 150 years the theory of rent which, during the classical era, was to become associated with David Ricardo. Petty thought that the value of an agricultural worker's product in excess of his own subsistence may be considered as rent. Since the value of a laborer was regarded as the cost of producing his subsistence, the monetary value of his product would be equal to the amount of gold that could be produced in the same labor time as the worker's food. Thus, if equivalent amounts of labor time are involved in producing different commodities, they would tend to have equal values in exchange for one another. Labor time, therefore, became the common denominator of all values for Petty. He thus foreshadowed the labor theory of value which subsequently was associated with Adam Smith, David Ricardo, and Karl Marx.

Although Petty considered labor more important than land in creating value, he also struggled with the problem of attributing some part of value to land. He maintained that all things should be measured by "two natural denominations, which is Land and Labor," and regarded the establishment of a natural par between these two elements as a major problem of political economy. This would imply that rent is price-determining and that land and labor are joint determinants of value. Petty struggled with this difficulty time and again, but he was unable to resolve it.

Cantillon arrived at essentially the same explanation of value as Petty. He attributed value to the amount of labor and land required in production; the cost of labor and materials drawn from land were seen as determining the "intrinsic value" of commodities. The latter would, he thought, never vary. But the market price will fluctuate above or below the intrinsic value, depending on the state of demand and supply. By demonstrating how increasing or decreasing demand will raise or lower the price of a commodity and thereby encourage or discourage production, Cantillon advanced an explanation of the nature and functioning of the price system as the automatic mechanism through which an otherwise unregulated economy regulates itself. This view of the self-regulatory nature of a price-directed economy was later to become the core of the classical and neoclassical systems of economics. Thus, Cantillon may be considered as an early classicist or, at least, as a forerunner of classical economic thinking.

CONCLUDING REMARKS

During the era of mercantilism, economic behavior began to manifest itself through commercial rather than exclusively household and other non-commercial activities. Accordingly, mercantilist thinkers emphasized the importance of commerce and industry, and the role of the state in promoting economic development and national wealth. They looked to the state to pursue policies that encouraged the growth of the labor force by natural increase and immigration, and fostered its employment in productive activities.

The possibility of increasing productivity by specialization was appreciated, but the role of innovation in increasing the productivity of labor was still too infrequently observed to receive much attention. The importance of increasing efficiency in the use of land and other natural resources in order to reduce the cost of wage goods was also given considerable attention. All these measures were thought of as contributing to the maintenance of a favorable balance of trade which served to increase the supply of money and precious metals. Money was thus thought of as playing an active role in economic development because it supposedly kept interest rates low and prevented unfavorable price movements.

The economic analysis which emerged in connection with these recommendations was crude and unsystematic by modern standards. The early mercantilists, especially, were practitioners rather than theorists, and their interest was in economic policy rather than in analysis. Much of their analysis was implicit in their discussions on policy, and even when given explicit formulation, it lacked the rigor that was to become associated with the inquiries of writers of the transition period. The distinction between money and wealth, and the explanation of the international specie flow mechanism especially, are principles which rank with those discovered by preclassical writers. Indeed, some of the inquiries into the determination of the interest rate which were made by later mercantilists during the transition are more advanced than many which followed. It was however necessary for mercantilistic ideas of long standing to be sloughed away before the newer, more liberal ideas could take hold. It was necessary for a new conception of the economic order to be established, namely, the conception that the economic order is essentially a self-regulating organism. Medieval attitudes toward the propriety of acquisition and consumption also needed to be replaced by a hedonistic psychology which regarded material self-interest as being not only proper but essential to prosperity. All these changes in attitudes and values were taking place during the transition period. Without them, Adam Smith's work could not have commanded the reception it got. From this point of view, the philosophic and attitudinal changes of the period are even more significant than are the actual theoretical developments, though the latter are by no means insignificant. The distinction between money and wealth and the explanation of the international specie flow mechanism especially are principles which rank with those discovered by classical writers; and some of the inquiries into the determination of the interest rate which were made during the transition are more advanced than many which followed.

GLOSSARY OF TERMS AND CONCEPTS

Economic literature is full of expressions and terms that serve almost as a shorthand to identify various economic relationships and phenomena. These are frequently of historical origin and have survived, though sometimes in altered form, beyond their initial context. Because at least some of the continuity between contemporary theory and older theoretical doctrines is reflected in concepts of this sort, it appears useful to identify these briefly at the end of the chapter in which they are first introduced to build a familiarity which will facilitate understanding of later theoretical developments.

Balance of payments.   Summary of the monetary value of a country's transactions with the rest of the world, including merchandise and invisible exports and imports, capital movements and gold.

Cantillon effect.   The effect of an injection of money on the *structure* of prices (as opposed to the level of prices) dependng on its source and its impact on recipients.

Equation of exchange. $MV = PT$ expresses the identity between aggregate demand (MV) and aggregate supply (PT) in monetary terms.

Quantity theory of money.   A hypothesis which relates changes in P, the general price level to changes in M, the quantity of money, assuming that V, velocity, and T, transactions are given magnitudes in the short run.

Real analysis v. monetary analysis.   A real analysis is one in which money has no influence on relative factor and commodity prices or the level of economic activity. A monetary analysis is one in which money is not viewed as passive but exercises an independent influence (through mechanisms that differ from writer to writer) over the economic magnitudes.

Reverse specie flow mechanism. David Hume's principle concerning the return flow of specie which results when a country experiences a reduction in exports in consequence of a price level which is high relative to that of other countries.

NOTES FOR FURTHER READING

Eli Hecksher's classic article, "Mercantilism," in *Encyclopedia of The Social Sciences* is reprinted in H. W. Spiegel, ed., *Development of Economic Thought* (New York, John Wiley and Sons, 1952). Thomas Mun's, "England's Treasure by Forraign Trade," is in John R. McCulloch (ed.), *Early English Tracts on Commerce.* (Norwich: Jarrold and Sons, Ltd., 1952).

John Maynard Keynes, in his "Notes on Mercantilism" at the conclusion of *The General Theory of Employment, Interest and Money* (1936) credited the mercantilists with anticipating some of his own thinking. He reasoned that their recognition of the stimulating effect of low interest rates on the level of investment indicates their awareness that there is a tendency for the propensity to save to be high relative to the inducement to invest and that this factor underlies underemployment equilibriums. Since modern techniques of monetary management and public investment to stimulate employment were not then at hand, Keynes regarded the mercantilist policy of encouraging inflation through a favorable trade balance as a perfectly rational way of expanding the money supply, thereby lowering interest rates and stimulating investment and employment.

A similar hypothesis is advanced by W. D. Grampp in his provocative article, "Liberal Elements in English Mercantilism," *Quarterly Journal of Economics, 46* (November 1952). Grampp takes the position that the main objective of mercantilist policy was to achieve full employment rather than a favorable balance of trade per se.

It is not difficult to perceive a Keynesian flavor in mercantilist warnings against holding money idle and in their references to the employment-creating effects of a favorable trade balance. The analogy must, however, not be carried too far; Keynes' analysis was intended to explain the experience of modern industrial economies. The type of unemployment experienced by predominantly agrarian economies, such as England was before the Industrial Revolution, is very different from the involuntary type associated with insufficient aggregate demand and underinvestment as it manifests itself in advanced economies. Keynes' extension of his hypothesis to analyze mercantilist thought is questionable because it is predicated on an institutional framework which is entirely foreign to its historical period.

J. D. Gould rationalizes mercantilist trade policy in terms of the unique nature of their East Indian trade in "The Trade Crisis of the Early 1920's and

English Economic Thought," *Journal of Economic History, 15* (no. 2, 1955), 121–32. This selection is reprinted in Ingrid H. Rima, ed., *Readings in the History of Economic Theory* (New York: Holt, Rinehart and Winston, 1970). Further insight into mercantilist contributions to the analysis of international trade is provided by Jacob Viner in *Studies in the Theory of International Trade, Chaps.* 1–2 (New York: Harper & Bros., 1937) and "Power vs. Plenty as Objectives of Foreign Policy in the Seventeenth and Eighteenth Cenuries," *World Politics,* 1948, reprinted in Jacob Viner, *The Long View and The Short* (1958).

Contributions associated with the period as a whole are examined by E. A. Johnson, *Predecessors of Adam Smith* (New York: Prentice-Hall, Inc., 1937), and by William Letwin in *The Origins of Scientific Economics* (London: Methuen & Co., Ltd., 1963).

The philosophical foundations of the transition to classical thinking are examined with particular insight by Alfred F. Chalk in "Natural Law and the Rise of Economic Individualism in England," *Journal of Political Economy, 59* (August 1951), 332–47. This selection is reprinted in Ingrid H. Rima, ed., *Readings in The History of Economic Theory,* (New York: Holt Rinehart and Winston, 1970). The discussion by H. M. Robertson in *Aspects of the Rise of Economic Individualism.* (Cambridge: Eng., The University Press, 1933) is also valuable.

Douglas Vickers provides a comprehensive study of early contributions to monetary theory in *Studies in the Theory of Money, 1690–1776* (Philadelphia: Chilton Co., 1959), and Keith J. Horsefield reviews the monetary experiences of the period in *British Monetary Experiments, 1650–1760* (Cambridge: Harvard University Press, 1960). Part 2 is especially useful.

Value theory did not figure prominently in mercantilist writings, but there is value theory before Smith which is admirably detailed in an early article by H. R. Sewall, "The Theory of Value before Adam Smith," *Publications of the American Economic Association,* series III, vol. *2,* no. 3 (1901).

3

Physiocracy: The Beginning of Macroeconomic Analysis

INTRODUCTION

Origins and Philosophy of Physiocracy

THE REACTION AGAINST the doctrines and restrictive practices of mercantilism was, if anything, more violent in France than in England. France had prospered little from the industry-stimulating measures introduced by Jean Baptiste Colbert, since the French economy, unlike the English, was basically agrarian. Added to this, the wealth of France was drained by unsuccessful colonial wars and extravagant expenditures at court, both of which required high taxes to support them. The difficulty of assessing personal income and the exemption of the clergy and nobility from taxation caused the burden to fall almost exclusively on the commoner landowner and the peasant. This situation impoverished the rural classes to such an extent that demands for reform became increasingly insistent until, at last, they culminated in the French Revolution. But before this great explosion, the Physiocrats presented an eloquent plea for "revolution from above."

Some of the observations and recommendations which were made by the Physiocrats were anticipated in the writings of Pierre Boisguilbert (1646–1707) and Sébastien de Vauban (1633–1707). Both writers reacted against adverse conditions which prevailed in France late in the reign of Louis XIV. Understandably they put their greatest emphasis on tax reforms and the abolition of export duties on grain. Boisguilbert, foreshadowing the Physiocrats, regarded land as the primary source of wealth and criticized mercantilist emphasis on precious metals. He viewed wealth as consisting of the supply of necessary and convenient things required by man to satisfy his diverse wants. The primary requisite for the creation of wealth, he maintained, is the elimination of man-made obstructions to natural harmony, such as tax abuses, customs duties, monopolistic guild practices, court extravagances, and large public debts. Vauban made tax reform his particular concern and proposed that a single poll tax replace all other direct taxes.

Unfortunately, the reforms proposed by Boisguilbert and Vauban brought them dishonor rather than praise. The absolute monarchy of the *ancien régime* tolerated little criticism. Their writings were suppressed; but their ideas nevertheless survived, and many were incorporated in reform efforts which came later with the Physiocrats. Pleas for reform and even programs for reform, such as the *Project for the Royal Tithe* which Vauban offered in 1707, failed to catalyze change. What was needed, in addition, was a philosophy and a systematic analysis to provide a rationale for reform by explaining the source of the ills which plagued the French economy. The Physiocrats, or "economists," as they preferred to call themselves, were to supply these needs.

An abundance of materials had been stored up by the middle of the 18th century out of which a new discipline, to be known as economics, would soon emerge. Though Greek philosophy was its ultimate source, its beginnings were more precisely to be found in the emergence of modern science during the post-Renaissance period. The investigations and researches which culminated in the Newtonian system indirectly stimulated the rise of social science. The recognition that physical events obey certain laws made it reasonable to inquire whether there also are laws governing human events, and whether ways of improving the social environment might be prescribed on the basis of these principles. The Physiocrats scrutinized social processes with a view to discovering causation and a principle of regularity, just as Sir Isaac Newton (1642–1727) and other physical scientists had done before them with respect to natural phenomena, and as John Locke had attempted to do with the social phenomena he examined.

The Physiocratic system is primarily associated with François Quesnay, physician to Madame de Pompadour and later Louis XV, who, partly as a result of his early experiences with farming and partly as a result of his belief in the primacy of nature, interested himself in the plight of the French peasantry and its relationship to the ills of France. Quesnay directed his inquiries toward explaining the nature and creation of wealth, and the relationship which the mode of its circulation bears to the well-being of the economy. The inference was plain that something definite might be done to prevent the progressive diminution of the country's wealth which had been taking place during the long and ill-fated reign of the Bourbon kings. The idea of reform was, of course, not new. What made the Physiocratic program unique was, first, that it was articulated with a theoretical system which purported to explain the creation, circulation, and reproduction of the nation's wealth; and secondly, that it was predicated on the continuance of monarchy and the existing class structure.

The term *physiocracy* came from the French word *Physiocrate,* first used by Dupont de Nemours in 1776 after Quesnay's death. It means "the rule of nature." Quesnay accepted the idea that a divine providence has ordained the existence of a universal and inherently perfect natural order. Conformity to the laws of the natural order will insure maximum happiness, whereas infringement of the fixed laws of nature will call forth correspondingly disastrous consequences. Man, as a rational creature created by a benevolent providence, will tend to conform in all his activities to a design above himself. This philosophy suggests that it is both unnecessary and undesirable for governments to regulate. Legislation which conforms to nature is superfluous, and that which is in conflict with nature is certain to be defeated because, in the long run, the law of nature is supreme. This rationale is the basis for the famous maxim, *Laissez faire, laissez passer* ("Let it be, let it go"), which was to figure so importantly in the subsequent development of economic theory. With it, the Physiocrats unavoidably invited comparison between France as it was under the absolute rule of a divine right monarchy and the France that might have been under a system of perfect liberty.

So great was the discrepancy between the *ancien régime* and the ideal that it would appear Physiocratic philosophy and doctrines heralded the French Revolution. It was not, however, their intent to alter the social status quo. On the contrary, the Physiocrats were enthusiastic supporters of monarchy and nobility. They interpreted the rule of nature as the absence of unnecessary legislation but not lawlessness. The function of the sovereign is to give expression to the divine wisdom that already rules the universe, and in so doing, he should be an absolute despot.

Contrary to the popular notion that the task of governing is extremely complicated, the Physiocrats maintained that in practice, there would be relatively little for kings to do, for every reasonable person would obey the rule of nature if only he were acquainted with it.[1] Every enlightened individual would recognize that the king is merely the instrument through which the laws of nature are carried out. The Physiocrats thus held the principle of political liberty in contempt because elected representatives cannot always link personal and group interests for the entire nation. Only the hereditary monarch, permanent and without self-interest, can harmonize the interest of all. It should be obvious, therefore, that the Physiocrats were not proponents of democratic self-government. Nor were they

---

[1] An oft repeated anecdote associated with this contention concerns the visit of the Physiocrat Mercier de la Rivière to Catherine the Great of Russia to advise her concerning reforms in government. He is purported to have told her that the wisest policy she could follow was simply to let things alone to take their own course, for nature would rule, to which advice she responded by wishing him a prompt goodbye.

pleading for benevolent despotism. They wanted merely an enlightened despot, who, recognizing that the only road to happiness is to acquiesce to the rule of nature, would bring about revolution from above.

ECONOMIC ANALYSIS

Methodology

The work of Quesnay and his disciples marks the beginning of economics as a discipline. Using the process of abstraction, they were the first to seek out the existence of general laws according to which economic phenomena behave. By closing the gap between free will and natural law that had so long divided theology and science, they laid the groundwork for the systematic study of social phenomena on an empirical level.

Philosophers such as Descartes, Hobbes, and Hume had already abandoned acceptance of supersensual sources of knowledge, holding instead that knowledge is achieved postnatally and that the facts thus perceived constitute the whole of human wisdom. The Physiocrats dealt with facts, the facts of a society sick with abuses and already on the verge of revolution; and from these observations they constructed their theory of an ideally functioning economy which would tend automatically to achieve optimum results but for the disturbances injected by human beings uneducated in the ways of the natural order.

While the predetermined providentialism which made their economic laws inexorable in their operation is quite different from the "necessity" attaching to generalizations known to us today as economic laws, they nevertheless laid additional groundwork for Adam Smith and all those after him who used the deductive method. They also constitute the first group of thinkers whose ideas were, in general, so acceptable to all that most individual identities, with the exception of Quesnay, are lost in that of the group as a whole, so that they are the first economic thinkers to constitute a school of thought.

Concepts

We are indebted to the Physiocrats for an analysis of production and wealth which, although imperfect, is greatly in advance of mercantilist views. In mercantilist thinking, it will be remembered, wealth consisted of treasure, and it was believed that only trade could make a nation prosperous. The Physiocrats maintained that wealth consists of goods which are produced with the aid of nature in industries such as farming, fishing, and mining. This line of thought is in advance of the mercantilist idea, even though the restriction of wealth to the output of the primary industries is unduly narrow.

Their belief that only land is the source of wealth led them to think that only labor engaged in primary occupations, farming in particular, is productive. They conceived of the economy as being comprised of three classes: the proprietor class, the cultivator class, and the sterile class. The nature of each of these classes and its role in the economy are to be understood and appraised in relation to what the Physiocrats called the *produit net,* or net product. A class is productive only if it is capable of producing a net product, that is, an output of greater value than its own subsistence requirements. The cultivator class, whose numbers are primarily tenant farmers renting land from the proprietors, are uniquely able to do this. They and others who work with the land, such as miners, fishermen, and the like, were thought to be the only ones capable of producing a net product because they alone have the advantage of the assistance of nature. Nature, as it were, labors alongside those engaged in primary pursuits. Its bounty manifests itself in a net product which is a true surplus in excess of the subsistence requirements of the labor involved.

The sterile class, on the other hand, which includes all those not belonging to the other two classes, produces no such surplus. Finished products produced by artisans, for example, have a value in excess of the raw materials they embody, which is equivalent only to the labor expended in the transformation process. There is therefore no surplus associated with their efforts, and this is the reason why they are termed sterile or unproductive. While only the cultivators and others engaged in primary occupations are members of the productive class, it must be emphasized that it is the land rather than their labor which is the source of the surplus.

The status of the proprietors in Quesnay's social classification is a matter about which there is no agreement. Quesnay himself was not entirely consistent in his earlier and later writings. In his earlier expositions, he regards the proprietors as being sterile because they are not directly engaged in raw material production. This suggests that he thought of their rental incomes as being unearned. Later, he took the position that landowners are at least partly productive because they maintained the permanent improvements made on land and also performed the necessary functions of government. Mercier de la Rivière and Abbé Baudeau, two of Quesnay's more ardent followers, both took the position that the landlords are productive because they, or their forebears, bore the original cost of clearing and draining the land, and that these efforts gave them a claim to its fruits which took precedence over those of the present cultivators. In any event, the Physiocrats reasoned that in order to preserve the flow of the net product to the landlord, the cultivators, like the artisans, are entitled only to subsistence.[2]

---

[2] The classification of artisans, domestic servants, merchants, financiers, and anyone else who is not a cultivator as "sterile" is an unfortunate and inconsistent choice of terms, for it does not distinguish between those who are, within the framework of Physiocratic thinking, capable of producing their own subsistence and those who are not. Quesnay himself was not completely consistent, for in an unpublished article,

The Physiocrats regarded the activity of artisans as considerably more acceptable than that of those engaged in trade and finance, for those so engaged do add value to the raw materials they fabricate. Artisans have legitimate values to exchange against agricultural commodities. The incomes they receive are therefore earned and tend to equal the values they create. Their presence in the economy is also necessary for maintaining a *bon prix* (good price) for farm commodities Manufacturing industry, however, is desirable only if it does not diminish the agricultural market or inhibit the growth of agricultural capital.

Since the primary industries, agriculture in particular, are the source of the net product upon which the prosperity of the nation rests, agriculture would be specially encouraged in an ideally functioning economy. This would require that the number of persons engaged in trade and finance be kept to an absolute minimum. The Physiocrats viewed the activities of tradespeople and financiers with disdain because they were thought to be incapable of producing any new values whatever. They merely engaged in exchanging values created by others. Some middlemen were of course regarded as necessary to the functioning of the economy; but, maintained Quesnay, retailers are present in far greater numbers than is required for the distribution of goods. Moreover, the large merchant capitalists are engaged in *trafic* (trade) which is frequently speculative and directed toward a favorable balance of trade, thereby helping artificially to channel resources into industry, to the consequent detriment of agriculture. The incomes merchants receive are parasite incomes which can only represent a deduction from the net product. Since merchants themselves produce no values, and the farmers and artisans receive no more than their subsistence, it is certain that such tradespersons are supported out of the net product. This injury to the economy is compounded by the waste of much of their income on luxury commodities which are subsidized by the state or imported from abroad.

The "Tableau Economique"

The Physiocrats regarded their description of the creation and circulation of wealth among the three classes to be their primary contribution to the science of economics. Inspired by William Harvey's discovery of the circulation of blood in the human body, Quesnay constructed a table which, by means of zigzag lines crossing over from one column to another, as in Figure 3–1, is intended to demonstrate the interdependence of economic classes which nourish and sustain one another by means of their expenditures.

"Hommes," he said that domestic servants may be indirectly productive if they free some of the energies of the agricultural classes. See Henry Higgs, *The Physiocrats* (New York: Macmillan Co., 1897), p. 127.

FIGURE 3–1
The "Tableau Economique"

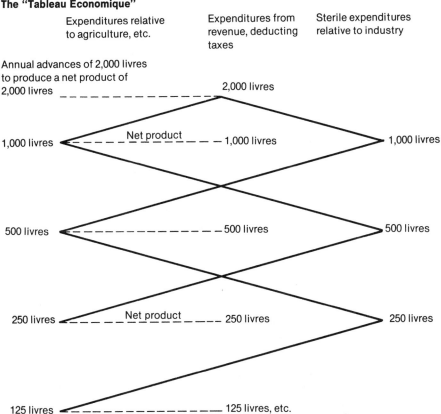

Source: From a presentation by Marquis de Mirabeau in *Elements de la Philosophie Rurale.*

The *Tableau Economique* is the first attempt to demonstrate the nature and achievement of equilibrium from a macroeconomic point of view. It depicts an economy which is assumed to be closed and stationary; that is, foreign trade is absent, and savings are equal to the replacement needs of capital. It is also assumed that there is private property in land, the owners receiving rent from the cultivators who supply their own capital and employ whatever wage labor they require. The analysis is limited to the agricultural sector of the economy; and the net product, which is the focal point of the analysis, is explicitly the output of the agricultural sector. No attention is directed to the sterile sector of the economy nor to individual enterprises or financial organizations, and all exchanges are interclass exchanges rather than interindividual exchanges. In short, the *Tableau* is designed to explain the manner in which the net product is created and circulated among the three classes of society and ultimately reproduced the following year.

Quesnay's table consists of three columns which are headed "Expenditures Relative to Agriculture," "Expenditures from Revenue," and "Sterile Expenditures Relative to Industry." That the circulation of both goods and money is involved is not entirely clear from the *Tableau,* though it is implicit in the analysis. It is, however, stated by Nicolas Baudeau, Quesnay's disciple, and implied in Quesnay's discussions that at the end of the harvest the farmers have the money stock of the nation as well as the economy's entire net product. The size of the net product reflects the capital investment (*advances annuelles*) made in agriculture during the year. Such investments are assumed by Quesnay to produce a net product of 100 percent over and above the expenses of production, which are taken to include the farmer's profit. Thus, if 2,000 livres are invested, there will be a net product of 2,000 livres available to be paid to the landlords as rent. Payment of these rents, shown by dotted horizontal lines moving from the first column to the second, initiates the circular flow of money and goods during the ensuing year.[3] Landlords' expenditures out of the incomes they receive are assumed to be directed in equal proportions toward the purchase of agricultural products and products produced by the artisans and other members of the so-called sterile class. Lines moving outward from the center column to the left and to the right illustrate the expenditure streams by which purchasing power is circulated from the proprietor class to the other two classes of society in return for the products they produce. By expending its revenue of 2,000 livres equally upon agricultural and nonagricultural products, the proprietor class has caused both the productive and the sterile classes to receive 1,000 livres, out of which they purchase their subsistence needs, raw materials, capital requirements, services of various kinds, etc.

Since the result of expenditures made on primary products, as represented by the flow of purchasing power to the column on the left, is quite different from that associated with the expenditures on manufactured products or services, these two expenditure streams must be examined separately. All expenditures directed toward production on the land, whether in agriculture, mining, fishing, or forestry, will yield a net product which Quesnay assumes throughout to be 100 percent. Thus a net product of 1,000 livres is again created and is paid as rent to the landlords, as shown by dotted horizontal lines moving from the first column to the second. This is the amount over and above the farmer's expenditures, including replacement of his capital and his profit. Actually, the income of the farmer in Quesnay's *Tableau* is really equivalent to a wage of manage-

---

[3] The livre is a former French money of account originally equal to a pound of silver. It was gradually reduced in value and replaced by the franc.

ment and interest on capital rather than profit. Profit, in its modern conception, is thought of as a reward for the entrepreneurial function of risk bearing. The concept of the entrepreneur and the concept of profit as a distinct income share rewarding his function was introduced later by Jean Baptiste Say in the early 19th century.

Assuming once more that landlord revenues, which now amount to 1,000 livres, are equally divided between purchases from the productive class and the sterile class, 500 livres will again be spent on products of the land. This investment will again yield a net product of 100 percent, or an additional 500 livres, which will flow to the landlords as rent. Each subsequent expenditure for the products of the productive sector will reproduce itself in the same way. It would, however, complicate the table unnecessarily to follow the expenditure of successive rental payments. The *Tableau* shown in Figure 3–1, therefore, traces only the circulation of the first 2,000 livres.

Unlike expenditures made on primary products, landlord purchases from the sterile class are incapable of facilitating the creation of a net product. Returning to the assumption that landlords expend their revenue of 2,000 livres equally on the products from the other two classes, the sterile class is now also in receipt of 1,000 livres. This amount is shown on the right side of the table and represents all expenditures in the economy except those associated with the extractive industries. It includes such items as interest payments, transportation costs, purchases of foreign goods and services, payments to domestics, and lodgings, as well as payments for manufactured goods. Again assuming an equal division of expenditures, one half, or 500 livres, is spent on the products of the extractive industries, and the other on the products and services of the other members of the sterile class. Thus, one half of their revenues, as indicated by the diagonal lines moving to the left-hand side of the table, are used "productively" and will result in a net product, and the other half is consumed "unproductively" and is therefore not conveyed to the left side of the table. All expenditures made by the landlords and artisans on products produced by the extractive industries facilitate new investment in these fields and thus assist in the creation of a net product. Conversely, if the consumption of goods and services provided by the sterile classes increases, it will be at the expense of agricultural products which will contribute to a decline in annual advances and annual reproduction. Excessive expenditure by the sterile classes themselves or by others on their products, was seen as inimical to the well-being of the entire economy because it destroyed the pattern of expenditures which the Physiocrats regarded as essential to the prosperity of the nation.

They were concerned also about the rate of savings and, unlike most thinkers who were to follow them, did not consider savings in the economy to be desirable, regardless of their source or the use to which they are put.

They saw money as more than the "wheel of circulation" Smith thought it to be. They were concerned with hoards and the impact which these would have on the *bon prix* of agricultural products and, therefore, the net product. The manner of living pursued by the landlords, especially the king as the largest landholder, and members of the sterile class therefore determines not only the kind of economic activity conducted in the nation but also the level of national wealth. The moral of this observation is obvious and is the basis for most of the reform measures proposed by the Physiocrats.

The Physiocrats, their followers, and admirers considered that this demonstration of the circular flow of money and goods had great significance. Typical of the esteem in which it was held was the observation of Mirabeau that there have been three great inventions since the world began. The first is writing, the second is money, and the third is the economic table.[4]

PROPOSALS FOR REFORM

Tax Reform

The real meaning of the *Tableau* emerges when its pure theory is articulated with Physiocratic proposals for reform.[5] The essence of the theory which the *Tableau* intends to support and demonstrate is that only nature can produce a net product and that an ideal economy would maintain only those activities and practices which would not encroach upon its creation. France, under Louis XIV, XV, and XVI, was far from this ideal. It suffered a variety of tax abuses, trade impediments on a national as well as an international level, an unnecessarily large merchant class, an unsound agricultural organization, monopolized industrial enterprises, and an ever expanding public debt associated with unsuccessful colonial wars and lavish court expenditures.

Proposals for tax reform had long been a central issue in France. In a predominantly agricultural country, it is obvious that the bulk of governmental revenues had to be derived from the land, especially in view of the difficulty of taxing less tangible forms of wealth. Tradition, however, exempted the clerical and lay nobility from the *taille,* as the land tax was known, thus shifting the bulk of the taxes to the third estate. The burden imposed thereby on the poor, miserable peasant became intolerable; but what is more, the revenues collected fell so short of the needs of government that large-scale public loans from professional speculators and fi-

---

[4] Higgs, *The Physiocrats,* p. 57.

[5] An interesting interpretation of Physiocracy is given by Norman J. Ware, "The Physiocrats: A Study in Economic Rationalization," *American Economic Review,* vol. 21, no. 4 (December, 1931).

nanciers were necessary. Many of these individuals further enriched themselves through the privilege of tax farming (paying a fixed sum for taxes collected and pocketing the difference) as well as farming out trading rights in certain commodities. Much of the fortune they accumulated tended to be drained into speculation at home or abroad, or hoarded. In either case the Physiocrats believed these practices lessened the demand for agricultural commodities and contributed to the impoverishment of agriculture. These moneyed interests, however, became so essential to the sovereign that it was virtually impossible for such men as Richelieu, Colbert, and Turgot to introduce economy measures in the court.

The Physiocrats proposed not only that hereditary land tax exemptions be eliminated, but also that the entire complex conglomeration of taxes currently levied be replaced by one single tax, the *impôt unique,* to which all landholders would be subject according to their respective shares of the net product. Needless to say, this proposal met violent opposition not only because of the financial burden it would have imposed on those previously free from taxes, but also because it would have deprived them of a cherished symbol of class status.

The logic of the Physiocratic proposal was quite clear and simple. Only land was capable of yielding a net product, or surplus, in excess of the subsistence requirements of those who labored on it. The supply price of laborers' services tended to be no more than the value they added to the product; and consequently, they were regarded as being incapable of bearing taxes. Any taxes levied on them, reasoned the Physiocrats, came to rest ultimately on the only possible source of payment, namely, the net product. We encounter here, in embryonic form, our modern theory of tax shifting, according to which taxes can under certain circumstances be shifted forward to the purchasers of the product by being added to the price they pay, or shifted backward to the factors of production if it is possible to reduce the payments made to them.

The Physiocrats thought of tax shifting not in this, the modern sense, but rather associated it with the reduction of the net product that would take place if taxes were imposed on the members of the cultivator or sterile classes. They reasoned that if taxes were levied on the farm laborers, it would necessarily reduce their ability to finance the next crop, thereby reducing the net product that would become available after the next harvest. In this way, the proprietor class would come to bear the burden of the tax. In like manner, if the tax were imposed on the sterile class, it would reduce their purchases from the cultivators, which would diminish the net product. Thus the Physiocrats reasoned that it would be sounder and more economical to levy a tax on the net product in the first instance. It was suggested that this *impôt unique* would not need to absorb more than one third of the net product. They expected that if expenditures were curbed and the productivity of agriculture was increased, a levy of this size would be adequate to meet the revenue needs of the state.

The Reorganization of Agriculture

The improvement of agricultural productivity was regarded as fundamental to the successful functioning or the single-tax system, and this the Physiocrats proposed to accomplish by reorganizing agriculture on a more capitalistic basis. French agriculture was typically conducted on a small scale, each individual tenant farmer cultivating a small acreage with a minimum investment. Only by the introduction of *grande culture* in the place of the present *petite culture* could agricultural productivity be enhanced, and thereby the net product be substantially increased. From the standpoint of the social and economic structure, this would of course mean that the relatively large number of small peasant farmers would be superseded by relatively few capitalistic farmers, who would be able to introduce the more progressive methods of production that are practical only when conducted on a larger scale. From the standpoint of its impact on productivity, the Physiocratic proposal for agricultural reorganization undoubtedly makes sound sense, but it should also be obvious that a measure which promised to convert a major portion of the land-hungry peasantry into wage labor was not likely to gain popular support.

Trade

It has already been noted that the Physiocrats regarded the activities of traders as unproductive, because they thought trade merely involved the exchange of equal values. Such activities were therefore thought incapable of producing new wealth whether the exchange took place on a domestic level or internationally.

The difference between Physiocratic reasoning about trade and that of the mercantilists should be immediately obvious. The latter held that trade is the only way to increase the wealth of a nation and that every effort should be made to secure a favorable balance. Under Colbert, trade in France was strictly regulated with precisely this end in view. Clearly, the Physiocrats were to find themselves in opposition to both the mercantilist and Colbertist points of view, for both were directed toward achieving a favorable balance of trade. In terms of Physiocratic thinking, the latter was not merely incapable of creating any new wealth; it actually tended to diminish wealth by reducing the demand for agricultural products.

How, then, can we explain the Physiocratic support of free trade? Is it not inconsistent with their position that commerce is unproductive? Present-day supporters of free trade, after all, do so on the ground that it will enhance the wealth of the participating countries, not by increasing their gold holdings but by securing them a greater quantity and better quality of goods and services than they could enjoy on the basis of their domestic production alone. But this is not the line of reasoning pursued by the

Physiocrats, although theirs is the first free-trade position of note, and they are generally regarded as the first supporters of free trade. This support, it should be noted, focused chiefly on freedom to export grain, which was restricted while the import of manufactured goods was encouraged. They viewed restrictive measures that deprived farmers of foreign markets as incompatible with maintaining the *bon prix* of agricultural products which they thought essential to the growth of the *produit net.*

CRITICISMS OF PHYSIOCRATIC VIEWS

Say and the Law of Markets

Physiocratic denial that money is always promptly restored to the income stream called forth the criticism of Jean Baptiste Say (1767–1832). Say had considerable business experience before he was appointed to a chair of political economy at the Conservatoire des Arts et Metiers and later the College de France. Like the Physiocrats, Say recognized that interruptions to the circular flow are injurious to the economy, but he denied that prosperity required a pattern of consumption in which a large fraction of total expenditures is for raw produce. In the first edition of his *Traité* (1803), Say presented the thesis, later known as the law of markets, that production and not consumption underlies prosperity. He reasoned that production automatically generates the purchasing power required for consumption. The surplus of each producer exchanges against that of others, with money serving as a medium of exchange, and the aggregate value of the goods demanded to be bought is exactly equivalent to the value of those given in exchange for them.[6] It is possible for too much of one product to be produced, on occasion, to clear the market at a satisfactory price; but it is impossible to produce too much of all products, since the aggregate demand for products is identical with the aggregate supply which has been produced.

Say used his law of markets to criticize those who, like the Physiocrats, argued that "parsimony" results in underconsumption and overproduction, and that unproductive consumption is better than frugality. He argued, on the contrary, that consumption is an effect of production and that it is necessary to curb unnecessary unproductive consumption because saving is necessary to facilitate capital formation. The sixth edition of his *Traité* specifically emphasized the importance of frugality to the progress of opulence.[7] While this view coincided substantially with that of Adam Smith, whose work Say undertook to interpret for French readers, the entire question of the relationship between saving, investment, and prosperity was shortly to become a very controversial issue.

---

[6] Jean Baptiste Say, *Traité,* 1st ed. (Paris: 1803), pp. 175–77.

[7] Say, *Traité,* 6th ed. (Paris: 1827), pp. 112–22.

Adam Smith and the Productivity Concept

Though Smith had great admiration for many aspects of Physiocratic thinking, he correctly considered their concept of wealth as originating only in the agricultural sector to be unduly restrictive. He thought they erred in representing artisans, maufacturers, and merchants as altogether unproductive.

> We should not call a marriage barren or unproductive, though it has produced only a son and a daughter to replace the father and the mother, and though it does not increase the number of human species, but only continued it as it was before. . . . A marriage which affords three children is certainly more productive than a marriage which affords only two, so the labour of farmers and country labourers is certainly more productive than that of merchants, artificers and manufacturers. The superior produce of one class, however, does not render the other barren or unproductive.[8]

These criticisms, while interesting and constructive, indicate that Smith himself made an untenable distinction between productive and unproductive labor. Actually, the idea that only agricultural labor is productive is somewhat difficult to comprehend, even within the confines of Physiocratic thinking, since the Physiocrats maintain that it is really nature that is the source of the net product rather than labor. For how can they justify the receipt of the net product by landowners if they themselves are not productive? Are they not mere parasites enjoying fruits they did not bring forth? The high respect in which the landowners were held certainly gives no evidence of this point of view. To the Physiocrats the existence of private property was a part of the natural order, and landed proprietors existed by the will of God. In short, the right of private property is regarded as a divine institution from which the prior claim to the net product by the landlords is derived. This line of reasoning seems metaphysical to the modern reader. But a classic work suggests it be recognized that the Physiocrats knew no organization of society other than a feudalistic one and inferred that this may have persuaded them of the necessity of landed property in much the same way that Aristotle defended slavery.[9]

CONCLUDING REMARKS

The Physiocrats concerned themselves with both the level of economic activity and the allocation of resources. The crucial factor, in their view, insofar as the level of economic activity is concerned, is that the continuity

---

[8] Adam Smith, *An Inquiry into the Nature and Causes of the Wealth of Nations,* Ernest Rhys edition (London: Everyman's Library, 1910), vol. 2, pp. 168–69.

[9] Charles Gide and Charles Rist, *A History of Economic Doctrines,* 7th. ed., trans. by R. Richards (Boston: D. C. Heath and Co., 1948), p. 41.

of the circular flow be maintained by means of an appropriate pattern of consumption. It is not consumption as such which is required, they thought, but the kind of consumption that will cause a sufficient portion of national income to be spent on a raw produce.

Money was regarded as being essentially a medium of exchange which facilitated the transfer of goods and services among the three classes. Thus the *Tableau* emphasized the real as opposed to the pecuniary nature of exchange and the importance of expenditures in maintaining the circular flow. Their emphasis on the interdependence of production and consumption was probably the inspiration of Say's law, though Say emphasized the primacy of production as opposed to consumption, thereby disputing not only the importance of agricultural as opposed to other kinds of production but also the importance of avoiding hoarding.

We are also indebted to the Physiocrats for their demonstration of the appearance of a surplus, a phenomenon which was subsequently to occupy the attentions of Adam Smith, David Ricardo, and Karl Marx. Clearly, in the history of production, man must pass beyond the stage of bare subsistence before a surplus of any kind is a possibility. Since the earliest and simplest civilizations are fundamentally agrarian, the first appearance of a surplus is likely to be in the agricultural sector. Such an economy is not likely to be an exchange economy, but rather one in which the use values created are directly appropriated.

Although the exchanges described in the *Tableau* are expressed in terms of money, it is the circulation of the use values in which the Physiocrats are interested. Thus the problem of determining exchange value, which was to loom so importantly in the later development of economic thought, was virtually ignored by the Physiocrats. Furthermore, there was no appreciation of the subjective elements that affected the determination of value and price. The prices for which goods sold in the market were implicitly cost-of-production prices which are a summation of the subsistence costs of those who participate in making goods available for sale. Turgot, whose thinking along these lines was considerably more advanced than that of his contemporaries, appreciated that there were many factors an individual would take into consideration in valuing a good. But it remained for Etienne de Condillac to present a more thoroughgoing consideration of value. He wrote: "Value is not an attribute of matter, but represents our sense of its usefulness, and this utility is relative to our need. It grows or diminishes according as our need expands or contracts."[10] Furthermore, he realized that scarcity, which makes want satisfaction more difficult, and abundance, which makes it less difficult, cause exchange values to be greater or less, depending upon the quantities available relative to the demand for them. Thus, he established not merely the psychological basis of value, but

---

[10] Etienne de Condillac, *Le Commerce et le gouvernement* (Paris: 1776), p. 15.

also anticipated what in the later French, English, and Austrian analysis became known as final or marginal utility, that is, the additional satisfaction associated with the last unit of a good acquired. But it was to take approximately a hundred years before a similar approach found its way into English political economy.[11]

Physiocratic doctrines did not attract many followers in England. Most were more impressed with Smith's view that the manufacturing sector rather than agriculture has the greatest potential for further advance. It is, no doubt, Smith's correct surmisal of much that was about to occur in England's economic environment that causes us to regard *The Wealth of Nations,* rather than the writings of the Physiocrats, as the starting point of modern economic theory. Further, it is because changes took place in the direction he anticipated that there are aspects of Smith's writings that are relevant today.

Although Smith greatly admired aspects of Physiocracy, there were several fundamentals of Physiocratic thinking he categorically rejected, among them their views on parsimony. Smith's view, and that of Say, that "saving is spending" came to predominate in England. Indeed, Say's law had such a formidable influence that it virtually eliminated the question of the level of economic activity from theoretical speculation and focused attention chiefly on the question of resource allocation and pricing. Not until the 1930s was there again substantial interest in the level of economic activity and inquiry into the impact of hoarding. It is interesting to note in this connection that, as crude as the Physiocratic concept of hoarding was, it is surprisingly suggestive of Keynes' treatment, in which hoarding is related to a reduction in effective demand.

Although we can accept neither the Physiocrats' notion that the gross product of an economy consists only of agricultural goods nor their concept of productive labor, this does not alter the originality or usefulness of their demonstration of the production and circulation of output and income for the economy as a whole. They demonstrated conclusively that the economic process consists of a flow of goods and a flow of money income. Our modern concepts of gross national product and gross national income are based on the recognition of the fact that the total income earned in a given period of time is exactly equivalent to the value of the total product produced. Similarly, our concept of net national product is arrived at by making appropriate deductions from the gross national product. Only depreciation is deducted in the modern scheme of national income and product accounting, whereas Quesnay, deducting also the subsistence requirement (i.e., wages) of the cultivators, conceived of the net product as representing only the surplus available to the landlord as rent. The Physiocrats, however, no less than present-day national product estimators, had a

---

[11] William Jevons' *The Theory of Political Economy,* was first published in 1871.

concept designed to arrive at the net results of the economy's performance for a given period of time. It is perhaps unnecessary to add that they did not make quantitative estimates of the sort that are today compiled by the United States Department of Commerce.

GLOSSARY OF TERMS AND CONCEPTS

Circular flow. The circulation of goods and money incomes throughout the economic system which results from economic interdependency.

Law of markets (Say's law or Say's equality). Aggregate demand is necessarily sufficient to clear the markets of the economy of the aggregate supply of all good because the production process simultaneously creates goods and generates purchasing power. Equality between aggregate demand and supply requires that there be no interruption to the circular flow.

Single tax. A single levy on the economic surplus yielded by land. Such a tax was originally recommended by the Physiocrats. Their recommendation was later revived in the 19th century by the American social reformer Henry George on the premise that its collection will not reduce production and that the amount collected will be adequate for revenue needs.

Product net (net product). The surplus produced by workers employed in the primary industries in excess of their own subsistence requirements.

Tableau Economique. The economic table that depicts the circulation of the net product among the three classes of society and the return of the net product to the farmer and to support future investment in agriculture.

Unproductive labor. Workers who are sterile in the sense that the values they create do not yield a surplus, but are sufficient only to provide their subsistence. The labor of artisans is unproductive in this sense.

NOTES FOR FURTHER READING

Henry Higgs *The Physiocrats* (New York: Macmillan Co., 1897) remains the classic reference. Charles Gide and Charles Rist add further background and insight in *A History of Economic Doctrines,* trans. by R. Richards, 7th ed. (Boston: D. C. Heath & Co., 1948), chap. 1.

The unique role of Quesnay in the history of Physiocracy is examined by T. P. Neill in "The Physiocrats' Concept of Economics," *Quarterly Journal of Economics,* vol. 63 (November 1949). Warren Samuels analyzes Physiocratic policy and institutions in "The Physiocratic Theory of Property and State," *Quarterly Journal of Economics,* vol. 75 (February 1961), and "The Physiocratic Theory of Economic Policy," *Quarterly Journal of Economics,* vol. 76

(February 1962). J. J. Spengler suggests that the Physiocrats' theory of consumption may have contributed to the formulation of Say's Law in "The Physiocrats and Say's Law of Markets," *Journal of Political Economy,* vol. 53 (September–December 1945), reprinted in Joseph J. Spengler and W. Allen, eds., *Essays in Economic Thought: Aristotle to Marshall* (Chicago: Rand McNally & Co., 1960).

Arthur Bloomfield explores Physiocratic views on foreign trade and notes the limited extent of their contribution in "Foreign Trade Doctrines of the Physiocrats," *American Economic Review,* vol. 28, no. 4 (December 1938). Ronald Meek, *Economics of Physiocracy, Essays and Translations* (Cambridge, Mass.: Harvard University Press, 1962) includes a selection of Quesnay's writings and essays on various aspects of physiocracy.

part two

CLASSICAL ECONOMICS

AN OVERVIEW OF CLASSICAL ECONOMICS

THE YEAR 1776 marks a fateful year for economics. The influence of Physiocracy was virtually ended when Anne-Robert Turgot was deposed as the French finance minister; the publication of Adam Smith's *Wealth of Nations* in the same year introduced a set of principles that became the cornerstone of what was to become the classical tradition. The efforts of Petty, Steuart, North, Cantillon, Hume, and the Physiocrats were only stepping stones to the preparation of the work which, in scope and content, became the point of departure for all who followed, whether in the classical tradition or in opposition to it.

Appreciation of classical economics is facilitated by a preview of its several major themes and special points of view. Beginning with Adam Smith (1723–1790), the classicists' central theme of inquiry, as it had been for the Physiocrats, is economic growth. The growth phenomenon was further explored by Thomas Malthus (1766–1834), David Ricardo (1772–1823), and John Stuart Mill (1806–1873). These followers of Smith articulated their concern with economic growth to such related questions as the behavior of population, the tendency toward diminishing returns, the principles of international trade, and the ultimate movement toward a stationary state.

In *The Wealth of Nations* Smith also laid the foundation for the second major theme of classical economists, namely their concern with the problem of exchange value and the role of the price mechanism in allocating labor and other resources among the sectors of the economy. His exposition of value in use and value in exchange posed the problem of the relationship between utility and cost of production in determining value. The so-called paradox of value, which his followers interpreted as signifying that utility is relatively unimportant in explaining why commodities have value in exchange, is among the results of his inquiry. After Adam Smith, Thomas Malthus, David Ricardo, John Stuart Mill and others who followed in their tradition, offered value theories that emphasized the governing role of costs of production as opposed to utility.

In the hands of Karl Marx, who follows in the classical tradition in the sense that he too sought to explain the long-run tendencies of the capitalistic system, cost of production was narrowly construed to mean socially necessary labor cost. When applied to explaining the market value of labor power and the wages of labor, Marx's interpretation of the Smithian cost-of-production theory of value became articulated with his theory of exploitation and thus the tendency of the capitalistic system toward ultimate destruction.

The problem of distribution, i.e., the sharing of the nation's product among the three great social classes in the form of wages, profit, and rent, is the third major theme of the classical writers. Smith is the first to integrate the problem into his analysis, but it is Ricardo and John Stuart Mill who gave special focus to the question of income shares. The policy orientation of the classical school whose members, from Smith to John Stuart Mill, were political economists rather than pure theorists, is particularly apparent in association with such questions as the Corn Law and the Poor Law that relate to the distribution of income.

Nassau William Senior (1790–1864), was the only leading figure among members of the classical school who maintained that the concern of economics as a science is exclusively to deduce general laws about the behavior of the economic system and that the formulation of policy is outside its proper domain. The influence of his view is evident in the publication of books concerned with principles of economics rather than principles of political economy as the period associated with the establishment of the classical tradition came to an end.

4

Adam Smith: From Moral Philosophy to Political Economy

INTRODUCTION

Life and Times (1723–1790)

The Wealth of Nations (1776) is the second book in the trilogy planned, but never completed, by the Scottish moral philosopher Adam Smith. Smith dealt at length with the ethical values of life in *The Theory of Moral Sentiments* (1759) before turning his attention to subjects which today constitute the major concern of economic inquiry. He viewed *The Wealth of Nations* as a capstone to his work as a philosopher. He lectured at the University of Glasgow on the whole field of moral philosophy after the manner of his teacher Francis Hutchieson, who classified his subject into four branches: natural theology, ethics, jurisprudence, and political economy.

Like most great works, *The Wealth of Nations* is the product of the man and the times. With respect to the times, it may be observed that during the last quarter of the 18th century the English business scene was already dominated by the capitalist enterpriser who hired wage labor and frequently did business using the corporate form of organization. Agriculture was still the most important industry, and the rural classes were still well off; but the technical strides being made, particularly in the textile and metalworking industries, were soon to call forth the Industrial Revolution. England had passed through its most extreme period of protectionism, and its foreign trade was making great forward progress as the huge trading companies of bygone decades gradually lost their privileges. Nevertheless,

69

the restraints were still numerous and onerous, especially with the colonies, and the psychological moment to dissent had now come. *The Wealth of Nations* is, first and foremost, an attack against the principles and practices of mercantilism.

The Wealth of Nations is not, as is sometimes erroneously contended, a plea for extending industrialization and advancing the interest of business-men. On the contrary, Smith directs some of his most pungent criticisms against manufacturers and traders, reserving his sympathies for the work-ingman and his warmest plaudits for agriculture. It must also be re-membered that the Industrial Revolution was still in its most embryonic stages. True, the spinning jenny and the water frame had already been invented to transform the textile industry, and James Watt had patented his steam engine in 1769; but their widespread practical application was still in the future. The wool and linen industries, which were among the largest, were still organized in domestic units rather than in factories. In short, the England of Smith's day was primarily commercial and agricultural rather than industrial.[1] But it was not to take many more decades before the Industrial Revolution was to emerge.[2]

It was also a time of changing social and political relationships. Ideas of political liberalism had come to the forefront in England even before the French Revolution sounded the call of freedom elsewhere in Europe. Within this framework, economic theory also was acquiring new concepts and broadening its scope. Cantillon's *Essai sur la Nature du Commerce en Géneral* (1755) and Sir James Steuart's *Inquiry into the Principles of Political Economy* (2 vols., 1767) represented a serious effort in the direc-tion of systematic study of the operation of the economy. Petty had suc-cessfully stated the problem of value, which was to become the focal point of classical theory. There were also advances in understanding the nature of money, the determination of interest, and the importance and advan-tages of free trade. But despite the brilliance of some of these pioneering efforts, economic investigation was still far from systematic. It is the great achievement of Smith and those who followed him in the classical tradition that they brought order into a field of inquiry that was still largely hap-hazard and unsystematic.

---

[1] Some notion of Smith's perception of the declining relative importance of agri-culture may be gleaned from his estimate in *The Wealth of Nations* that the annual value of agricultural output amounted to 60 million pounds whereas the *Lectures* (about 1763) inferred that "the whole annual produce of lands must be about 72 millions." See Adam Smith, *Lectures on Justice, Police, Revenue and Arms,* (1763) ed. E. Cannan, first published, 1896 (New York, 1964), p. 224, and Adam Smith, *An Inquiry into the Nature and Causes of the Wealth of Nations* vol II, p. 775. This and following references to this work are to the edition of Ernest Rhys (London: Everyman's Library, 1910).

[2] Among the several themes of Samuel Hollander's *The Economics of Adam Smith* (Toronto: University of Toronto Press, 1973) is that Smith did not fail to anticipate the Industrial Revolution as has sometimes been charged.

What was there about Smith that made his efforts more fruitful than those of his several able contemporaries whose intellectual curiosity led them to explore along many of the same paths as he? It has often been suggested that there was nothing really unusual about Adam Smith, the boy or the man. He himself is said to have remarked: "I am a beau in nothing but my books." He lived a rather uneventful life with his widowed mother, devoting himself largely to academic pursuits, although he also served as Commissioner of Customs in Edinburgh from 1778 until his death in 1790. Except for his sojourn in France as tutor to the young Duke of Buccleuch, which position brought him a lifetime pension, he traveled little. Even so, his natural talents, coupled with his educational experiences at Glasgow College and later at Balliol College, Oxford; his contacts with such associates as Francis Hutcheson, who was his teacher at Glasgow, David Hume, his friend of a lifetime, the Physiocrats whom he met during his travels in France, as well as the opportunity for firsthand observation in the expanding commercial metropolis of Glasgow enabled him to produce the great creative work which is *The Wealth of Nations.*

THE WEALTH OF NATIONS

Philosophical and Psychological Background

The concern of moral philosophy, said Smith, is human happiness and well-being. Of this, the ancient moral philosophers were well aware, for they sought to examine "the happiness and perfection of a man, considered not only as an individual but as a member of a family, of a state, and of a great society of mankind. . . ."[3] This view was sharply different from that which had flourished during the Middle Ages, when it was believed that happiness is inconsistent with virtue and that the only true virtue is self-denial. Although the material progress of the modern world rendered the medieval view of morality increasingly indefensible, it nevertheless persisted into the 18th century. It was much in evidence, for example, in an essay entitled *The Fable of the Bees, or Private Vices and Publick Benefits,* written by Dr. Bernard de Mandeville. Mandeville's thesis was that man's vices, specifically the quest of luxuries and material gain, generate wealth. His implication was that if the virtue of self-denial were practiced, material progress would come to a standstill.[4]

The *Fable* attracted wide attention; most of Mandeville's contemporaries considered it worthy of a reply. Smith regarded his system of moral philosophy as "wholly pernicious," for it "seems to take away altogether

---

[3] Adam Smith, *An Inquiry into the Nature and Causes of the Wealth of Nations,* vol. 2, p. 255.

[4] From the Preface, *The Wealth of Nations.*

the distinction between vice and virtue."[5] Smith himself saw the desire for worldly gain in an entirely different light. He viewed the pursuit of riches as merely one aspect of every individual's desire to better himself. This desire, says Smith, is with us from the womb to the grave and operates in every sphere of our lives. "It is not from the benevolence of the butcher, the brewer, or the baker that we expect our dinner, but from their regard to their own interest. We address ourselves not to their humanity, but to their self love, and we talk to them not of our necessity, but of their advantages."[6] Self-interest is thus seen as manifesting itself in every aspect of man's behavior and activity. In the economic sphere, it prompts the division of labor and the accumulation of capital, thus enhancing productivity. In the field of justice, it operated, Smith believed, to promote a high degree of efficiency in the English courts which tried to hear as many cases as possible because they functioned on the basis of the fees they collected from parties who came before them.[7]

It was precisely the absence of the principle of self-interest that Smith found so deplorable with regard to English universities. His years at Oxford convinced him of the adverse effect on the quality of instruction where professors are paid without due regard for their efforts. By contrast, the teachers of ancient Greece, who were compensated on the basis of the number of students they attracted, were much more efficient, in Smith's opinion, then the majority of those he encountered at Oxford. Self-interest, then, is the motive which naturally drives men, and impediments to its operation generally have an adverse effect. Moreover, this is precisely the motive which *ought* to prevail, for, says Smith, "I have never known much good done by those who affected to trade for the public good."[8]

To some Smithian scholars, the emphasis on self-love and self-interest which we encounter in *The Wealth of Nations* appears to be somewhat at odds with the principle of sympathy advanced in his *Theory of Moral Sentiments*. That volume begins with the observation: "How selfish soever man may be supposed, there are evidently some principles in his nature which interest him in the fortune of others and render their happiness necessary to him though he derives nothing from it except the pleasure of seeing it." It is, says Smith, imagination which prompts even the mean individual to sacrifice his own interests at times to the greater interests of others, for only his own imagination enables him to have a conception of anyone else's sensations. Individual morality is thus seen as being shaped through introspective psychology. "If, upon placing ourselves in his situa-

---

[5] Adam Smith, *The Theory of Moral Sentiments*, p. 451. This and subsequent references to this work are to the edition published by George Bell & Sons, Ltd., 1911.

[6] Smith, *The Wealth of Nations*, vol. 1, p. 13.

[7] Ibid., vol. 2, p. 208.

[8] Smith, *The Wealth of Nations*, vol. 1, p. 400.

tion, we thoroughly enter into all the passions and motives which influence it, we approve of it, by sympathy with the approbation of this supposed equitable judge. If otherwise, we enter into his disapprobation and condemn it."[9]

Our own experience thus underlies the growth of moral sentiments. If man grew up in isolation without communication, it would be impossible for him to conceive of any of these sentiments, but "bring him into society and he is immediately provided with the mirror that he wanted before."[10] We see the world through our own senses; and because we desire, above all, the sympathy and approbation of our fellowmen, it is necessary for each of us to regard his happiness not in that degree in which it appears to himself but in that degree in which it appears to mankind in general. Thus the desire of the individual for the approval of society, as well as the censure of his own conscience, tends to keep him doing right. The individual and society move naturally toward the same end, and mankind will prosper in proportion as the individual is permitted freedom to choose his own way. Conscience and sympathy will always deter undesirable conduct in the economic sphere as well as in every other. Thus, belief in the morality of sympathy and the influence of social experience leads Smith ultimately to faith in the role of liberty in the functioning of the natural order.

The theory of the social origin of moral judgments and standards is fundamental to the doctrine of the harmony of individual and national interests which pervades *The Wealth of Nations*. All of the economic interests the individual pursues are largely acquired in the course of his social experience. The individual, as a product of the society in which he lives, is of necessity concerned with social approbation. It appears reasonable, therefore, to interpret the doctrine of sympathy as developed in *The Theory of Moral Sentiments* as the conceptual antecedent of the doctrine of the natural order set forth in *The Wealth of Nations*.[11]

The philosophy on which Smith's economic principles are based is nowhere specifically mentioned in *The Wealth of Nations*. Yet, it pervades his entire work to an even greater extent than the philosophy of naturalism colored the writings of the Physiocrats. Above all, Smith was dedicated to "the simple system of natural liberty." Standing at the center of his system is the individual who follows his own interests while promoting the welfare

---

[9] Smith, *The Theory of Moral Sentiments,* p. 162.

[10] Ibid.

[11] See Glenn R. Morrow, "Moralist and Philosopher" in J. M. Clark et al., eds., *Adam Smith, 1776–1920* (Chicago: University of Chicago Press, 1928), for an interesting essay on the relationship between *The Theory of Moral Sentiments* and *The Wealth of Nations*. Jacob Viner has explored the same issue, taking the point of view that there are divergences between *The Theory of Moral Sentiments* and *The Wealth of Nations* which are impossible to reconcile. His essay, "Adam Smith and Laissez-Faire," is included in the same volume.

of society as a whole, for such is the nature of the natural order. The Physiocrats also equated the existence of the natural order with the ideal society, but with a difference. For the Physiocrats, the natural order was to be discovered through the intellect and brought to fruition through enlightened despotism. For Smith, the existence of the natural order is a fact. It exists in spite of human interferences.

A variety of beneficent economic institutions are spontaneously generated within the framework of the natural order. Among them are the division of labor, the development of money, the growth of savings and the investment of capital, the development of foreign trade, and the adjustment of supply and demand to each other. These and other institutions of the spontaneous order spring into existence as a result of man's self-interested behavior and operate for the benefit of society as a whole.

Smith's psychology must likewise be culled out of his writings, as it is not specifically set forth anywhere. He does, however, appear to follow David Hartley, John Locke, and his good friend David Hume in regarding sensation as the source of ideas and knowledge.

Plan and Scope

The Wealth of Nations is divided into an introduction, which sets forth the plan of the author, five books, and an appendix. The first book is "Of the Causes of Improvement in the Productive Powers of Labour, and of the Order According to Which Its Produce Is Naturally Distributed among the Different Ranks of the People." Book II is "Of the Nature, Accumulation and Employment of Stock," and Book III is "Of the Different Progress of Opulence in Different Nations." These three books are primarily a presentation of economic principles. Book IV, "Of Systems of Political Economy," and Book V, "Of the Revenue of the Sovereign or Commonwealth," take Smith into the area of political economy.

Even today *The Wealth of Nations* is an interesting book to read. Its author knew how to intersperse facts with illustrations and persuasive reasoning. The result is neither repetitious or complicated in its logic, but rather, remarkably straightforward and simple, with a genuine feeling for his fellow man unmistakably in evidence.

Smith is the first of the great eclectics who wove into a harmonious whole the more important ideas of predecessors and contemporaries alike. The influence of Hutcheson and Hume is particularly in evidence; he also owed much to Turgot and the Physiocrats, especially Quesnay and such liberal mercantilists as North, Petty, Child, and Tucker. Other important ideas germinated from his disagreement with Mandeville. It is worth noting that *The Wealth of Nations* contains remarkably few references to the writings of other authors and that Smith was perhaps less scholarly in this regard than he might have been. He knew precisely, however, what to extract from other works and how to use it to make his final product in every way unique and peculiarly his own, though many individual ideas and even illustrations are not original with him.

THE THEORY OF PRODUCTION

The Nature and Sources of Wealth

"The annual labour of every nation is the fund which originally supplies it with all the necessities and conveniences of life which it annually consumes, and which consists always either in the immediate produce of the labourer, or in what is purchased with that produce from other nations."[12]

This is the statement with which Adam Smith begins his inquiry into the nature and causes of the wealth of nations. It alerts us to the central theme of *The Wealth of Nations,* which is the growth of national wealth. His chief focus thus parallels that of the Physiocrats, whose concern was the increase of the nation's net product. The primary difference between Smith's conception of the nature and source of wealth and that of the Physiocrats is thus immediately brought into focus. Not nature but human effort makes commodities available.

It is also evident that Smith considered a nation to be well off in accordance with its supply of "necessaries and conveniences" in relation to the number of its inhabitants. Goods, not gold, thus constituted the wealth of a nation. This becomes abundantly clear in Book IV, which deals at length with mercantilism. A stinging criticism is delivered here against policies which artificially allocate labor and capital into foreign trade rather than agriculture, mining, or manufacturing and thereby adversely affect the growth of per capita income.

Though it served to distinguish his position from that of the Physiocrats, his initial emphasis on labor also laid the groundwork for future misunderstanding. He was subsequently interpreted as taking the position that labor and labor alone is the source of weath, though he nowhere excluded stock and land as productive factors. The term *factors of production* is not to be found in Smith's work; but, as will be seen later, his treatment of income shares as functional rewards suggested that he thought of labor, stock, and land as separate factors of production which are entitled to receive their separate shares of the annual product in the form of wages, profit, and rent. His emphasis on labor was not intended to deny the importance of either capital stock or land but rather to call attention to labor, as opposed to the forces of nature, as the prime mover of production. Without the cooperative efforts of labor, neither land nor capital would be able to bring forth anything.

---

[12] Smith, *The Wealth of Nations,* vol. 1, p. 1.

The Division of Labor

Having emphasized the importance of labor in production, Smith proceeds in Book I to inquire how the productive powers of labor may be enhanced. Drawing on the trade of the pinmaker for illustrative purposes, Smith tells us that labor is most effective in production when division of labor is practiced.[13] He calculates that division of labor makes it possible for ten workers to produce 48,000 pins per day, so that each worker produces the equivalent of 4,800. Without division of labor, a worker might not even make one pin in a day, and certainly not 20. He was greatly impressed with this enhancement of the productivity of labor, and his description has become a classic, though he was certainly not the first to describe either the process or its effects. It should also be noted that while his illustration of division of labor is drawn from a relatively small-scale operation, Smith was well aware that there were already some large-scale operations in Great Britain, chief among them the iron works at Carron in Scotland.[14]

He observes that division of labor enhances the dexterity of each worker, saves time by making it unnecessary to shift from one type of work to another, and also stimulates the invention of laborsaving devices. The result is a great increase in the quantity of work that a given number of people can perform. It is to the division of labor that Smith attributes the relatively high standards of living that prevailed during his day for even the lowest ranks of people and concludes "that the accomodation of an European prince does not always so much exceed that of an industrious and frugal peasant as the accomodation of the latter exceeds that of many an African King. . . ."[15]

Division of labor comes into existence spontaneously without the necessity of human wisdom, planning, or intervention; it is the consequence of the "propensity to truck, barter, and exchange one thing for another."[16] This inclination to trade is found only in man and is but one expression of his self-interested behavior. Only by exchanging his surplus with others can he acquire all the goods he has need of; and in order to serve his own interests, he appeals to the self-interest of his fellowmen. "As it is by treaty, by barter and by purchase that we obtain from one another the

---

[13] Ibid., vol. 1, p. 7. While Smith regards the division of labor to be the fundamental basis for progress, an alternative interpretation has been offered in regard to the point of view encountered in Book 5 which suggests that its effect on labor may be stultifying. For an interesting discussion on this point see N. Rosenberg, "Adam Smith on Division of Labor: Two Views or One?" *Economica vol. 32*, May 1965. Reprinted in Ingrid H. Rima, ed., *Readings in the History of Economic Theory* (New York: Holt, Rinehart and Winston, 1970).

[14] *Wealth of Nations,* vol. 1, p. 76.

[15] Ibid., p. 11.

[16] Ibid., p. 12.

greater part of those mutual good offices which we stand in need of, so it is the same trucking disposition which originally gives occasion to the division of labour."[17]

Manufacturing generally lends itself better to division of labor than agriculture, and although the richest countries generally excel their neighbors in agriculture as well as manufacturing, their superiority is usually greater in manufacturing.[18] Everywhere, the practicality of engaging in division of labor is limited by the size of the market to be served.[19] Thus Smith anticipates later discussions concerning the limits of what is today known as increasing returns to scale. He also observes that regions of relatively sparse population afford little opportunity to carry on division of labor, whereas well populated areas and those made easily accessible by good water and land transportation will be more likely to enjoy its advantages.

Productive and Unproductive Labor

Both the mercantilists and the Physiocrats employed the notion of productive and unproductive labor. For the former, the criterion of productivity was the degree to which the effort contributed to securing a favorable balance of trade, while the latter believed that only workers engaged in agriculture and the extractive industries were productive, in that they were assisted by nature, which alone is capable of creating a surplus. Unfortunately, Smith also thought in terms of productive and unproductive labor, and created considerable confusion with his distinction not only as regards the discussion itself, but also as regards its compatibility with other parts of his theory.

In the third chapter of Book II, he observes that some labor realizes itself in a vendible commodity and is thus to be considered as productive, while certain other labor is unproductive in that it does not "fix or realize itself in any particular subject . . . which endures after that labour is past and for which an equal quantity of labour could afterwards be purchased." The labor of domestic servants, entertainers, professional men, government servants, and others among "the most respectable orders in the society" fall into this class.

The foregoing distinction between productive and unproductive labor is also coupled with two other grounds on which the one type of labor is distinguished from the other. The first is the relationship of labor to the creation of value. Thus, he observes that productive labor "adds to the value of the subject on which it is bestowed." The effort of labor engaged

---

[17] Ibid., p. 13.

[18] Smith, *The Wealth of Nations,* vol. 1, p. 6.

[19] Ibid., p. 15.

in manufacturing is in this class, while that of menial servants is not. Elsewhere, he observes that productive labor creates a surplus which goes to the owner of stock.

> Thus, the labourer of a manufacturer adds, generally, to the value of the materials which he works upon, that of his own maintenance and of his master's profit. . . . Though the manufacturer has his wages advanced to him by his master, he, in reality, costs him no expense, the value of those wages being generally restored, together with a profit, in the improved value of the subject upon which his labourer is bestowed.[20]

The notion of labor as the creator of a surplus is pursued in a somewhat different vein in Book IV, in which Smith writes of the Physiocratic system. Here he makes the observation that the labor of artisans and traders is not as productive as that of farmers because agricultural workers produce not only their own subsistence and profit on the stock of their employer, but also rent for the landlord. Like the Physiocrats Smith was persuaded that in agriculture nature labors alongside man and produces a surplus. His predilection for agriculture is equally apparent in Book II, which is devoted to the accumulation and employment of capital, and in which he insists that capital employed in agriculture is the most productive. "The capital employed in agriculture, therefore, not only puts into motion a greater quantity of productive labour which it employs, it adds a much greater value to the annual produce of the land and labour of the country, to the real wealth and revenue of its inhabitants."[21] It was on these grounds that Smith believed that a nation should give preference to agriculture and pursue other economic activities only as its increasing capital accumulation permits. He regarded manufacturing as the second most productive activity, followed by domestic trade. To him, foreign trade was the least advantageous field of investment, returning lower profits and being more difficult of supervision than capital invested at home.

Smith's distinction between productive and unproductive labor is untenable and created confusion in at least three areas of economic thinking. First, his exclusion of services as part of the national product and the designation of the work of those who render them as unproductive labor was later recognized as incorrect. Secondly, his identification of revenues in excess of wages in manufacturing enterprises as a "surplus" blurred the difference between profit and interest. This was unfortunate because profit and interest are functional returns rewarding two distinct activities, namely, the entrepreneurial function of risk bearing and management, and the lender's function of making available funds. The third area of confusion concerns the productive powers of land and its relationship to the appearance of rent. Like the Physiocrats, Smith entertained the idea that there is

---

[20] Ibid., p. 295.
[21] Smith, *The Wealth of Nations,* vol. 2, p. 325.

something unique about the productive powers of land which created an erroneous idea of the nature of rent and the circumstances under which it arises. Smith, however, unlike the Physiocrats, recognized that profit is a separate form of surplus, i.e., as distinct from rent. Thus profit and rent were both viewed by Smith as a source of saving and investment, whereas the Physiocrats regarded profit as a deduction from rent.

The most meaningful interpretation of Smith's distinction between productive and unproductive labor is in connection with saving and capital accumulation. It is clear from his third chapter in Book II, "On the Accumulation of Capital or of Productive and Unproductive Labor," that he is concerned with the effect of using savings to satisfy the desire for luxuries by those who are prodigal instead of channeling them into uses that will enhance the supply of fixed or circulating capital. He is, in effect, arguing that savings should be used in such a way that they will create a flow of income and new equipment, and that failure to use savings in this manner is an impediment to economic growth. This line of reasoning is somewhat obscured by his observation that "what is annually saved is as regularly consumed as what is annually spent, and in nearly the same time too; but it is consumed by a different set of people."[22] This seems to imply that it matters little whether income is used for consumption or saving because savings flow back into the income stream via investment. Hoarding is implicitly regarded as an exceptional occurrence in this context. While Smith seemed to be aware that people sometimes have a demand for money as a store of value, he believed that money is primarily desired as a medium of exchange. In effect, therefore, he eliminated the store-of-value function of money and did not seriously entertain the idea that hoarding could diminish the flow of income payments in the economy. On the contrary, he pictured the frugal man as contributing to the public welfare because his savings are used to set productive labor into motion and to add to the stock of fixed capital. This view of the relationship of savings and investment anticipates the dictum which subsequently became important in economic analysis as Say's law.

THE THEORY OF VALUE AND EXCHANGE

The Origin and Use of Money

Having considered production and the manner in which division of labor enhances man's ability to create goods. The theme of production and economic growth is thus set aside to explore a host of other matters which tend, particularly for the uninitiated reader, to diffuse Smith's central concern with the problem of economic growth. The growth problem is not

---

[22] Smith, *The Wealth of Nations,* p. 302.

specifically addressed until it is examined from an historical point of view in Book III, as a prelude to issues related to mercantilism, which are examined in Book IV. The concerns of the first two books, however, lay the microeconomic foundation for those that follow and, for the alert reader, ought not to obscure Smith's central theme of economic growth.

The use of money, like the division of labor, is viewed by Smith as a spontaneous development resulting from man's self-interested behavior. The use of money eliminates the inconvenience of barter situations. Thus, Smith tells us that "in order to avoid the inconvenience of such situations, every prudent man in every period of society, after the first establishment of the division of labour must naturally have endeavoured to manage his affairs in such a manner as to have at all times by him, besides the peculiar product of his own industry, a certain quantity of some one commodity or other such as he imagined few people would be likely to refuse in exchange for the produce of their own industry."[23] Many different commodities, he observes, have served this purpose, but the precious metals seem particularly well suited to it. These observations are, of course, commonplace today, and every discussion since has been couched in almost identical terms.

Use Value and Exchange Value

Having examined the origin of money, Smith proceeds next to his consideration of value. In the closing paragraph of Chapter 4, Book I he notes that commodities may have use value or exchange value and that:

> Things which have the greatest value in use have frequently little or no value in exchange; and on the contrary, those which have the greatest value in exchange have frequently little or no value in use. Nothing is more useful than water; but it will scarce purchase anything, scarce anything can be had in exchange for it. A diamond, on the contrary, has scarce any value in use; but a very great quantity of other goods may frequently be had in exchange for it.[24]

Today's student of economics will probably have little difficulty in discerning several errors in the sentences just quoted. First, a commodity cannot possibly command other commodities in exchange unless it has value in use; only the ability to yield satisfaction to a user would make a commodity worth acquiring by giving up other goods or money. Smith's failure to recognize this rather obvious relationship was most significant for the future development of value theory, for it led to the attempt to explain exchange value without reference to utility. Some hundred years were to

---

[23] Ibid., p. 20.

[24] Smith, *The Wealth of Nations,* p. 25.

elapse before English political economy specifically took utility into consideration in explaining value.[25]

A further error of Smith's famous opening statement on value is his failure to recognize the significance of the relative scarcity of the commodity at the margin. It is clearly misleading to compare a single diamond to the total supply of water. If he had compared the utility of a single diamond with the utility of a single unit of water, he could not have been misled. The fact that some goods are free illustrates beyond doubt that the utility afforded by a commodity may be quite unrelated to its exchange value. But it was not until it was recognized that it is the ratio of exchange between individual units that should be compared that the paradox of the diamond and the water was resolved. Such a comparison makes it perfectly plain that water commands little or nothing in exchange while a diamond commands a great deal because the supply of diamonds is so much smaller in relation to the intensity of the desire for them than is the case with water. It is surprising that Smith was unaware of this relationship, for it had been clearly pointed out by John Locke[26] and others.[27] Finally, Smith applied a personal moral standard in deciding that a diamond has no use value. The fact that one does not approve of the consumption of a particular commodity, or that its use may be harmful or even illegal, does not deprive the commodity of its utility. The mere fact that a commodity can command a price is sufficient evidence of its utility.

Labor and Value

Having thus failed to consider utility, Smith turned his attention next in chapters 5 through 7 of Book I to the role of labor as a determinant of value. It is no simple matter to describe or comprehend his account of the relationship between labor and value, for it is at many points contradictory and confused. He begins by telling us that "The value of any commodity, therefore, to the person who possesses it, and who means not to use or consume it himself, but to exchange it for other commodities is equal to the quantity of labour which it entitles him to purchase or command. Labour, therefore, is the real measure of the exchangeable value of all commodities."[28] Elsewhere, he says, "its value to those who possess it, and who want to exchange it for some new production is precisely equal to the quantity of labour which it can entitle them to purchase or command."[29]

---

25 See Chapter 11 below.

26 See his early manuscript on interest in Letwin, *The Origins of Scientific Economics,* appendix 5, p. 291.

27 See H. R. Sewall, "The Theory of Value before Adam Smith," *Publications of the American Economic Association,* Series III, 2, no. 3, 1901, pp. 66–124.

28 Smith, *The Wealth of Nations,* vol. 1, p. 26.

29 Ibid.

These statements express what may be referred to as the labor command theory of value, according to which a commodity has a value equivalent to the labor it can command in exchange for itself either directly or indirectly in the form of some other commodity. When used in this sense, labor serves as a measure of value.

Other statements, however, just as clearly put forth the idea that labor is the cause or determinant of value. Thus, says Smith, "the real price of everything, what everything really costs to the man who wants to acquire it, is the toil and trouble of acquiring it."[30] But he also says:

> In that early and rude state of society which precedes both the accumulation of stock and the appropriation of land, the proportion between the quantities of labour necessary for acquiring different objects seems to be the only circumstance which can afford any rule for exchanging them for another. . . . It is natural that what is usually the produce of two days' or two hours' labour, should be worth double of what is usually the produce of one day's or one hour's labour.[31]

These statements put forth a labor cost theory in which labor is the cause or determinant of value rather than simply the measure of value.

Several questions concerning these relationships may now be asked: First, if labor is the measure of value, why are values commonly expressed in money prices? Secondly, can labor not be both the cause and the measure of value—that is, can we not assign a value to a commodity in accordance with the amount of labor it contains and measure its worth in terms of some other commodity or group of commodities containing the same amount of labor? If this is possible, there is no incompatibility between the labor command theory and the labor cost theory. Finally, is it not possible that Smith intended the labor theory of value to apply only in "that early and rude state of society" and considered that the cause of value after the appropriation of land and the accumulation of stock might not be labor alone? The latter two questions are especially pertinent in trying to understand Smith's theory of value.

In regard to the first question, Smith says that once barter ceases, it becomes "natural" to exchange commodities for money rather than other commodities. Gold and silver are the most satisfactory monetary media, but they vary in value, like all other commodities, depending on the quantity of labor required to mine them. Corn (grain) also can be used to measure value, but it too will vary in value, depending on the quantity of labor required for its production.[32] He concludes, therefore, that labor is the only universal as well as the only accurate measure of value, or the only standard by which we can compare the values of different commodi-

---

[30] Ibid.

[31] Ibid., p. 41.

[32] Smith, *The Wealth of Nations*, vol. 1, p. 31.

ties at different times and places, in spite of the fact that values are commonly expressed in terms of money.[33]

The problem of explaining the determination of exchange value is analytically distinct from the problem of measuring value, though Smith himself saw no difficulty in conceiving of labor both as a cause and as a measure of value. He reasoned that commodities will have greater or less exchange value depending on the quantity and quality of the labor they contain. It does not matter, then, whether we speak of the value of the commodity or the value of the labor in it. Thus, Smith tells us in the beginning of the sixth chapter of his Book I that in "the early and rude state of society" which antedates private property in land and the accumulation of capital, a commodity has value in accordance with the amount of labor congealed in it, and commodities containing equal amounts of labor will be exchanged equally for one another. Under these circumstances, there is no difficulty concerning the use of labor both as a cause and as a measure of value because factors other than labor do not exist, and all transactions involve equivalents of labor. The labor cost of a commodity is exactly equal to its labor command.

The only problem that Smith conceived to exist in this state had to do with the fact that equivalents of labor time are not automatically equivalents of labor content, since some labor is more difficult, unpleasant, or dangerous, or requires more training, dexterity, or ingenuity. But this does not introduce a major difficulty, for such differences in the quality of labor will be reflected in different rewards. "In the advanced state of society, allowances of this kind, for superior hardship and superior skill, are commonly made in the wages of labourer; and something of the same kind must probably have taken place in its earliest and rudest period."[34] He took it for granted that the market process of wage-rate determination will automatically result in a wage commensurate with the labor performed by each worker and that wage differentials will be reflected in commodity values. The subject of wage differentials is thus introduced into the discussion of the value problem. The subject is not pursued further until a later chapter, but it is already apparent that Smith believed the market sets commodity prices in accordance with the worth of the labor embodied in the commodities. Thus, he concluded that commodities would be exchanged for one another in accordance with their content of labor, the latter being the product of time, hardship, and ingenuity. "If among a nation of hunters, for example, it usually costs twice the labour to kill a beaver which it does to kill a deer, one beaver should naturally exchange for or be worth two deer."[35]

---

[33] Ibid., p. 32.

[34] Ibid., p. 42.

[35] Smith, *The Wealth of Nations,* vol. 1, p. 41.

No problems of interpretation are involved with respect to Smith's discussion of the precapitalist era which antedates land ownership and capital accumulation. The only factor of production is labor, and commodities are exchanged for one another in accordance with the labor they contain. Labor is thus both the cause and the measure of value. Moreover, in this state of things the whole product belongs to labor. There is neither landlord nor capitalist with whom it must be shared. Not until land becomes privately owned and the accumulation of capital has taken place does a share of the product go to the owner of stock and the landlord. In this state of things, the whole produce of labour does not always belong to the labourer. He must, in some cases, share it with the owner of the stock which employs him.[36] ". . . As soon as the land of any country has all become private property the landlords, like all other men, love to reap where they never sowed, and demand a rent even for its natural produce."[37]

These statements have great significance for Smith's labor theory of value. For if the worker must share the product with the owner of the stock and the landlord, it must be concluded either that labor does not create the whole product in an advanced society and that the shares going to the landlord and the capitalist are just rewards that they have earned, or that the laborer is being deprived of a part of the product that is rightfully his. The first interpretation is tantamount to recanting the labor theory of value, at least as it applies to the advanced state; and the second interpretation introduces a theory of labor exploitation. Which interpretation approximates most closely Smith's position? Our examination of the nature of profit and rent and their relationship to natural and market price will help us to decide.

Profit, Rent, and Natural and Market Price

Smith tells us that as soon as stock becomes accumulated, the value of a product resolves itself into two parts: wages and profits. The profits of the stock are not to be conceived of as payment for a special kind of labor, namely, the labor of inspection or direction, because they bear no relationship to the disutility of the labor. "They are regulated altogether by the value of the stock employed and are greater or smaller in proportion to the extent of this stock. . . . In the price of commodities, therefore, the profits of stock constitute a component altogether different from the wages of labor and are regulated by quite different principles."[38]

Not only are profits distinct from wages as regards their origin, but what is more, there is no indication that Smith considered the receipt of profits as being anything but justified. He tells us that the owner of stock would

---

[36] Ibid., p. 43.

[37] Ibid., p. 44.

[38] Ibid., p. 43.

have no interest in employing his stock if his revenues did not leave something over and above the cost of materials and wages to reward him for the hazards he assumes.

Profits are not the only additional income share that will be encountered in an advanced society. Rent, too, will make its appearance as soon as the land of a country has become privately owned.

> The wood of the forest, the grass of the field and all the natural fruits of the earth, which when land was in common, cost the labourer only the trouble of gathering them, come, even to him to have an additional price fixed upon them. . . . This portion, or what comes to the same thing, the price of this portion, constitutes the rent of land, and in the price of the greater part of commodities makes a third component part.[39]

Smith's attitude toward the receipt of rent by the landlords is less than warm, for he tells us that landlords love to reap where they have never sowed.[40] But they are no different from other men in this respect, and Smith regards the receipt of rent as being quite as "natural" as the receipt of profits.

There exists in every society or neighborhood an average or ordinary rate of wages, profits, and rents which is "natural" with respect to the time and place it prevails. Thus, when a commodity sells for a price which is just high enough to compensate the worker, the landlord, and the owner of stock at the natural rate, the commodity is being sold at its "natural price." It is then being sold for precisely what it is worth.[41] This is not to say that a commodity will always sell for its natural price. From time to time, changes in the relationship between the demand for it and the supply of it will cause the market price to rise above or fall below the natural level. But such a deviation tends to be corrected, for the supply will naturally tend to suit itself to the effective demand, thus causing the market price to rise or fall, as the case may be, until it again equals the natural price. "The natural price, therefore, is, as it were, the central price to which the prices of all commodities are continually gravitating. Different accidents may sometimes keep them suspended a good deal above it, and sometimes force them down even somewhat below it. But whatever may be the obstacles which hinder them from settling in this centre of repose and continuance, they are constantly tending towards it."[42] Thus, the long-run natural price is seen by Smith as a long-run equilibrium price which tends always to be reestablished as a result of short-run adjustments of demand and supply.

Smith did not think of demand and supply in the schedule sense in which we think of them in modern analysis, but rather as the willingness of

---

[39] Ibid., p. 49.

[40] Ibid.

[41] Ibid., p. 51.

[42] Ibid., p. 44.

market participants to buy or sell at a particular price rather than at various possible prices. Nevertheless, it is useful for us to think of the restoration of the market price to the level of the natural price as a result of short-run shifts of the supply schedule. Thus, when Smith refers to the supply of a commodity as too small to satisfy the "effectual demand," so that the market price rises above the natural price, he is really thinking in terms of an upward shift in the supply curve. Conversely, when the supply is too large for the effectual demand, market price will sink below natural price because, in modern terminology, the supply curve will shift downward. Only when the quantity brought to market is just sufficient to supply effectual demand and no more will market price be equal to natural price. It is clear, therefore, that Smith conceived of the interaction of demand and supply as determining prices in the short run under competitive conditions.

The long-run, or the natural, price was, however, thought to be independent of demand forces. Smith believed it is determined solely by the costs incurred on the supply side of the market. These costs were implicitly assumed to be constant, that is, not affected by the rate of output. More than a century later, Alfred Marshall in the 19th century was to demonstrate that in a constant-cost industry, demand exerts no influence on price but merely determines the level of output.[43] But this is a special case, and Smith erred in neglecting the role of demand in the determination of the long-run equilibrium price. A similar neglect of demand was to become typical until the advent of the marginal revolution toward the end of the 19th century.

Smith's awareness of the role of competition in the pricing process becomes clear in his seventh chapter. Here, he notes not only the significance of a large number of sellers, but also the effect of market knowledge and resource mobility in limiting the ability of market participants to influence price. Indeed, the only prerequisite of pure competition which he did not note is product homogeneity. His treatment of monopoly, however, is very cursory. He makes reference to articles that are in fixed supply because they are not reproducible and to the possibility of monopoly prices on account of "secrets of manufacture." He thinks of monopoly price as being "upon every occasion the highest which can be squeezed out of buyers," indicating that he has some appreciation of the role of demand as setting the upper limit to monopoly price.

What is the significance of Smith's explanation of natural price for the labor theory of value? Smith nowhere denies the right of the owner of stock to receive profit or of the landlord to receive rent. On the contrary, he regards the existence of these shares as being "natural" once "that early and rude state of society" (before the advent of privately owned land and accumulated stock) is past. What this implies from the standpoint of the

---

[43] See Chapter 13 below.

value problem is that the cost of production tends to be the long-run determinant of value. Smith does not, of course, say this. Nowhere is the validity of the labor theory of value specifically limited to a primitive society. The dilemma thus becomes obvious. Does labor create all value, so that the deduction of a share for the landlord and the owner of stock represents exploitation of what rightfully belongs to the worker? It never occurred to Smith to reason along these lines, for his was a beneficent society in which there is no dichotomy of class interests. But the door to a theory of class conflict was opened to those who, like Karl Marx, would later argue that the deduction of rent and profit from the total revenue of the sale of a commodity necessarily meant a discrepancy between its labor cost and its labor command.

THE THEORY OF DISTRIBUTION

Classical Distribution Theory

When Smith addressed himself to the matter of distribution, he perceived the problem requiring explanation to be the division of the nation's product among the laboring class, the capitalist class, and the landlord class. All who followed him in what became the classical tradition explained wages, profits, and rents as the incomes of "the three great social classes."

This approach is very different from that of modern economists who conceive of labor, capital, and enterprise as factors of production receiving functional returns for their productive contribution to the economy's product. The interdependence between the problems of value and distribution which modern writers perceive is not a matter emphasized by Smith.[44] Indeed, his original lectures at Glasgow dealt only with production. The inclusion of four chapters on distribution in Book I of *The Wealth of Nations* conceivably reflects the influence of the Physiocrats or, as suggested by Edwin Cannan, Cantillon's *Essay on the Nature of Commerce in General*. Moreover, his explanation of the distributive shares as component parts of natural price which tend toward competitive rates under his "obvious and simple system of liberty" is not of major significance as far as the central theme of *The Wealth of Nations* is concerned. But as England became more industrialized and the great conflict between the landed interests and the rising manufacturing class and between the latter and the

---

[44] Samuel Hollander's book *The Economics of Adam Smith* (1973), which reinterprets Smith's work from the perspective of the modern neoclassical view, argues that while the formal analysis of general equilibrium is given relatively little attention in *The Wealth of Nations,* Smith's perception of the interdependence between the problems of value and distribution are evident in the applied chapters which deal with restraints on imports and colonial trade.

growing class of wage earners became intensified, his discussion of the distributive shares assumed great social significance.

Wages

Smith's discussion of wages suggests virtually every conceivable theory of wage rate determination. He begins by referring once again to the early and rude society which precedes the accumulation of capital and the private ownership of land, and tells us that under those conditions the produce of labor constitutes the natural recompense or wages of labor.[45] In this state, it is unnecessary to share the product with either the owner of stock or the landlord, and labor's share would have increased with all the improvements in its productive powers resulting from the division of labor if this state had continued. This utopian state being no longer in existence, Smith proceeds to discuss the various factors that are operative in the determination of wage rates.

The first explanation offered is the bargaining theory. He maintains that "what are the common wages of labour depends everywhere upon the contract usually made between these two parties, whose interests are by no means the same. . . . It is not, however, difficult to foresee which of these two parties must, upon all ordinary occasions have the advantage in the dispute, and force the other into a compliance with their terms.[46]

Although employers generally have the advantage in the wage bargain, even the poorest grade of laborer must receive at least enough to maintain himself and his family. Subsistence, Smith believed, sets the minimum below which wages cannot fall in the long run. Wages may of course rise considerably above this rate if the demand for workmen is great in precisely the same way a commodity price may rise above its natural level.

The demand for labor, says Smith, is governed by the size of the wage fund which employers have available to give employment. Stock comes to be accumulated "in the hands of particular persons" who constitute a class distinct from the worker. The independent workman, who used stock he owned himself and who received both profits and wages, became atypical. Instead, says Smith, "in every part of Europe, twenty workmen serve under a master for one that is independent; and the wages of labor are everywhere understood to be, what they usually are, when the laborer is one person and the owner of the stock which employs him another."[47] The owner of stock has accumulated it out of revenues in excess of his own living requirements and the capital requirements of business. "The demand for those who live by wages, therefore, necessarily increases with the in-

---

[45] Smith, *The Wealth of Nations,* vol. 1 p. 57.

[46] Ibid., pp. 58–59.

[47] Ibid., p. 66.

crease of the revenue and stock of every country, and cannot possibly increase without it. The increase of revenue and stock is the increase of national wealth. The demand for those who live by wages, therefore, naturally increases with the increase of national wealth, and cannot possibly increase without it."[48]

Thus, Smith relates increasing wages to increasing national wealth. He continues with a discussion of the level of wages in different parts of the world, noting that wages are especially high in North America because of its small population and the rapidity of increase in its national wealth. China, on the other hand, has a very low level of wages because it has long been stationary. Wage rates in Great Britain are not so high as in North America, but they are above subsistence for even the poorest grade of labor. This is evident, says Smith, from the fact that summer wages are always higher than winter wages, although living costs are greater in the wintertime.[49]

In his observation on wage rates in different parts of the world, Smith also notes the relationship between the rewards of labor and the growth of population. He notes that "every species of animals naturally multiply in proportion to the means of their subsistence and no species can ever multiply beyond it."[50] Thus, when wages are high, as they are in North America, the rate of population growth tends to be high, whereas low wage rates are associated with a stationary population. This relationship was later to become the subject of a detailed inquiry by Thomas Malthus. Smith, however, did not entertain the attitude of general pessimism that is encountered in Malthus' essay with respect to the growth of population, for while the latter was concerned in the main with the dire consequences of population pressure and the available means of subsistence, Smith noted that high wage rates also increase the "industry of the common people" and thus contribute to the rising standard of living associated with greater division of labor.

Smith believed that the long-run trend of wages would be upward and considered that this was not merely a symptom of an advancing economy but also a cause of progress. For though rising wages are dependent upon increases in stock, they also enhance the productive powers of labor and thereby facilitate the accumulation of capital. Even though population tends to expand to the very limits of subsistence, Smith evidently believed that the incentive to save rather than to be prodigal is so strong that additions to the wage fund coupled with the productivity increases associated with capital accumulation would tend to make the living standard of wageworkers rise. Thus the specter of a stationary state, in which the great

---

[48] Ibid., p. 61.

[49] Ibid., pp. 62–65.

[50] Ibid., p. 71.

mass of people live in misery, did not loom upon Smith's horizon. Not until the day of Malthus and Ricardo was the optimism of Smith to be replaced by an attitude of such general pessimism that economics became known as the "dismal science."

Profits on Stock and Interest

The profits of stock, says Smith, are closely related to the wages of labor, falling when wages rise and increasing when wages decline. Their average level depends on the accumulation of stock. The nature, accumulation, and employment of stock are not discussed until Book II, in which it is explained that not until an individual has accumulated financial reserves (stock) in excess of his own subsistence requirements will he try to use these reserves in a manner which will earn additional income. "His whole stock, therefore, is distinguished into two parts. That part which, he expects, is to afford him revenue is called his capital. The other is that which supplies his immediate consumption. . . ."[51]

Fixed capital consists of machinery, tools, buildings, and improvements on land which "yield a revenue or profit without changing hands," whereas circulating capital creates a revenue only by "circulating or changing masters." It consists of money, the stock of provisions, raw materials, and partly manufactured and completed goods not yet disposed of to their proper consumers. All useful machines and instruments are originally derived from and must be supported by circulating capital in order to afford a revenue.

> All capital is the result of savings.
> Capitals are increased by parsimony, and diminished by prodigality and misconduct. Whatever a person saves from his revenue he adds to his capital, and either employs it himself in maintaining an additional number of productive hands, or enables some other person to do so, by lending it to him for an interest, that is, for a share of the profits.[52]

Thus, it is evident that Smith thought of increases in stock as the source of additions to the wage fund. The size of this fund determines the demand for labor; and depending upon the size of the laboring population, it determines whether the average level of wages will rise or fall. Increases in stock are generally associated with falling profits as well as rising wage rates, for mutual competition in the same trade will reduce the rate of return.[53]

The level of profits, says Smith, is so fluctuating that it cannot be ascertained precisely. The most reliable gauge of the level of profits is the level

---

[51] Ibid., p. 243.

[52] Ibid., p. 301.

[53] Ibid., p. 78.

of interest. "It may be laid down as a maxim that whenever a great deal can be made by the use of money, a great deal will commonly be given for the use of it; and that whenever little can be made by it, less will commonly be given for it. . . . The progress of interest, therefore may lead us to form some notion of the progress of profit."[54]

Smith expressed his opposition to the prohibition of interest, maintaining that such prohibition increases rather than diminishes the evil of usury, for nobody will lend without such a consideration for the use of his money as is suitable not only to the use that may be made of it but to the difficulty and danger of evading the law.[55] It is clear, therefore, that the term "interest" is used by Smith, and indeed by others before him, as a payment made for the use of borrowed funds. He tells us that there is a minimum rate of interest which must compensate for the risk of lending, and the lowest rate of profit must be enough to compensate the investor after he has made interest payments to the lender. Interest is thus regarded by Smith as part of gross profit, and "net profit" is a rate of return on capital whose level can be inferred from the market rate of interest. The entire income of a businessman who provided all or most of his capital, as was not uncommon when businesses were predominantly organized as proprietorships or partnerships, was simply regarded as profit. Today, of course, the return on equity capital would be labeled as interest rather than profit. But early thinkers on the subject, not only Smith but Malthus and Ricardo as well, made no functional distinction between interest and profit. They thought of the profit of the businessman as being essentially a yield on his capital investment. That the businessman performs other functions, such as risk bearing, management, and innovation, and is not necessarily a provider of funds, was still unrecognized or given only passing notice. Their primitive theory of profit was therefore essentially a yield-on-capital explanation of interest.

With regard to the rate of profit, Smith believed that the average would be in the neighborhood of approximately double the rate of interest on well-secured loans.[56] Reasoning that there is competition for the employment of capital, which is largely mobile enough to flow from one part of the economy to another in response to profit opportunities, Smith concluded that the same *rate* of return would tend to prevail in all industries, though the actual *amount* would vary, he believed, with the amount of capital invested. The rate of profit would tend to decline with the progress of accumulation relative to the supply of labor. While the explanation of the decline in the rate of profit was not associated by Smith with the tendency toward diminishing returns as additional quantities of labor and capital are

---

[54] Ibid., p. 79.

[55] Ibid., pp. 85–86.

[56] Ibid., p. 87.

applied to a fixed supply of land, as was later emphasized by Ricardo, his discussion of the trend of income shares in areas abundantly populated and capital-rich, as compared with newer and still underdeveloped economies, anticipates the Ricardian analysis of the effect of progress on income distribution.

Rent

Although some consideration has already been given to rent as a component part of natural price, along with profit and wages, Smith devotes his lengthy closing chapter of Book I to this matter. Here, he virtually abandons his earlier view of rent and makes it a differential return.

> Rent, it is to be observed, therefore, enters into the composition of the price of commodities in a different way from wages and profits. High or low wages and profits are the causes of high or low prices; high or low rent is the effect of it. It is because high or low wages and profits must be paid in order to bring a particular commodity to market, that its price is high or low; but it is because its price is high or low, a great deal more, or very little more, or no more, than what is sufficient to pay those wages and profits, that it affords a high rent, or a low rent, or no rent at all.[57]

Land which is used to produce food is the only land which "always and necessarily affords some rent to the landlord."[58] How much this rent will be depends on the fertility and location of the land. The greater the demand for the product, the higher the price which the landlord, as a monopolist, will be able to demand for his product above the minimum necessary to pay wages and profit. This is the essence of the differential surplus theory presented later by Ricardo, and it is perhaps superior to it in some respect because it discusses different conditions under which rent will emerge.

Smith concludes his lengthy chapter on rent with some observations about the long-run trend of the various income shares and the role which their recipients play with respect to the society as a whole. It is his expectation that every improvement in the economy as a whole will raise the real rent of land either directly or indirectly. This is not because of the efforts of the landlords, a class of men whom Smith considered to be naturally indolent, but rather because of the reduction in labor requirements resulting from improvements. It was not Smith's intention, however, to single out the landed gentry as the object of his attack. Opposition to the landed interests did not become an issue until industrialization had become sufficiently advanced to make cheap labor, and therefore cheap food, a primary requisite. But a basis for the destruction of the harmony of social interests

---

[57] Smith, *The Wealth of Nations,* vol. 1, p. 132.

[58] Ibid., p. 147.

had clearly been laid, though the eventual conflict was, for the time being, obscured by Smith's philosophy of a beneficent natural order. If anything, Smith's criticism was reserved for traders and manufacturers. They are "an order of men whose interest is never exactly the same with that of the public, who have generally an interest to deceive and even to oppress the public and who accordingly have upon many occasions, both deceived and oppressed it."

THE ARGUMENT FOR ECONOMIC LIBERTY

Economic Progress among Different European Nations

Book III, "Of the Different Progress of Opulence in Different Nations," provides a historical perspective for the devastating attack on infringements against economic liberty which Smith delivers in Book IV. In it, he reviews the development of European industry and agriculture from the time of the decline of the Roman Empire. He notes that in many nations the progress of opulence has been impeded by the pursuit of policies that conflict with what he regards as the natural course of things. If the natural course of development is allowed to assert itself, the capital of every nation will be directed first to agriculture, then to manufacturing and domestic trade, and last of all to foreign commerce.[59] This is the order of capital development which he believed to be most profitable and most conducive to welfare.

Having completed this comparatively brief historical survey, Smith proceeds with his examination of different systems of political economy. This is done in Book IV, which is devoted to the commercial and agricultural systems.

The Attack on Mercantilism

The task of exposing the fallacies of the commercial system is begun by examining the policy of seeking a favorable balance of trade to augment the nation's gold supply and wealth. Smith argued that the idea that a nation is rich if it has a great deal of gold, just as a man who has gold is wealthy, is erroneously to identify money with wealth. While the inflow of gold is undoubtedly in the interest of the merchants, for a country that has no mines of its own to gain gold by pursuing a favorable balance of trade is as unnecessary as it is foolish. It is unnecessary because a country can always acquire all the gold it has need of in the same way it acquires any other commodity it does not produce at home, namely, by trade, which will automatically respond to the effective demand for a commodity. "We trust

---

[59] Smith, *The Wealth of Nations,* vol. 1, p. 340.

with perfect security that the freedom of trade, without any attention of government, will always supply us with the wine which we have occasion for; and we may trust with equal security that it will always supply us with all the gold and silver which we can afford to purchase or to employ, either in circulating our commodities, or in other uses."[60] The special characteristics of gold and silver are, in fact, such that they are more easily transported than most commodities. But if for any reason it is impossible to satisfy the effective demand for the precious metals, this shortage will cause less inconvenience than would be encountered in regard to virtually any other commodity because a well regulated paper money could supply the need for a medium of exchange, "not only without any inconveniency, but, in some cases, with some advantages."[61] Nor is it necessary to accumulate treasure in order to carry on foreign wars, for "fleets and armies are maintained, not with gold and silver, but with consumable goods."[62]

Foreign trade is desirable, in Smith's view, when it appears spontaneously in the natural course of a country's economic development. But the acquisition of gold and silver is an insignificant benefit to be derived from it. The primary gain from trade is that it provides a market for a country's surplus products and, by extending the market, facilitates further division of labor.[63] The great gain derived from the discovery of America was not the additional good it brought to Europe, but the advantage to all trading countries of acquiring commodities cheaper than they could be produced at home. "Whether the advantages which one country has over another be natural or acquired is in this respect of no consequence. As long as the one country has those advantages, and the other wants them, it will always be more advantageous for the latter rather to buy of the former than to make."[64] Thus, there is a natural distribution of products among the different countries of the world which will come into existence automatically if only restrictive measures do not prevent their development. Later on, David Ricardo and John Stuart Mill were to elaborate the basis for territorial specialization in their theory of comparative cost and to point out the advantages accruing to the consumer if there is free trade. Smith was more concerned with the disadvantages of mercantilist restrictions on traders and producers; but unlike the arguments of the early antimercan-

---

[60] Ibid., p. 381.

[61] Ibid., p. 383.

[62] Ibid., p. 386.

[63] Although Smith's main argument in favor of trade is that it provides a "vent for surplus" in that it utilizes the output of factors that would otherwise be unemployed, Ricardo subsequently noted that Smith's treatment of trade would have been more consistent with the main theme of *The Wealth of Nations* if he had emphasized the advantage of foreign trade as facilitating a more efficient utilization of resources. See David Ricardo, "Principles of Political Economy" in *The Works and Correspondence of David Ricardo,* Piero Sraffa, ed. (Cambridge: 1951), pp. 294–95.

[64] Smith, *Wealth of Nations,* vol. 1, p. 403.

tilists, his were the first such arguments to be made by a personally disinterested individual. The Physiocrats were, of course, also free traders, but their hostility to restrictive measures was an aspect of their program for agricultural reform, and there was no attempt to demonstrate the positive advantages of international trade. Smith, however, undertook to demonstrate that protection is not only useless but may actually be disadvantageous to the economy because it will tend to bring about a different allocation of capital than would occur under conditions of free trade. "No regulation of commerce can increase the quantity of industry in any society beyond what its capital can maintain. It can only divert a part of it into a direction into which it might not otherwise have gone; and it is by no means certain that this artificial direction is likely to be more advantageous to the society than that into which it would have gone of its own accord."[65] There are, in general, only two circumstances in which it is desirable to lay some burden on foreign industry for the encouragement of the domestic; the first is when the industry is necessary to the defense of the country, and the second is when a tax levied on a foreign commodity would merely equal the tax imposed on the domestic commodity. The later policy "would leave the competition between foreign and domestic industry, after the tax as nearly as possible upon the same footing as before it."

The Agricultural System

Having devoted eight chapters to an analysis and criticism of mercantilism, Smith turns his attention, in the concluding chapter of Book IV, to Physiocracy. During his travels to France, he had personal contact with the authors of that system. While he regarded their argument that agriculture is the sole source of revenue and wealth, and that artificers, manufacturers, and merchants are unproductive, as being incorrect, he nevertheless had warm praise for them.

> Though in representing the labor which is employed upon land as the only productive labour, the notions which it inculates are perhaps too narrow and confined; yet in representing the wealth of nations as consisting, not in the unconsumable riches of money, but in the consumable goods annually reproduced by the labour of the society, and in representing perfect liberty as the only effective expedient for rendering this annual reproduction the greatest possible, its doctrine seems to be in every respect as just as it is generous and liberal.[66]

He commended them not only for understanding the true nature of the wealth of nations, but also for realizing the essential role of economic freedom in promoting its growth.

---

[65] Ibid., p. 398.

[66] Smith, *The Wealth of Nations*, vol. 2, p. 172.

CONCLUDING REMARKS

Although *The Wealth of Nations* was, in the main, an attack on the English commercial system, it was also intended as a policy guide—a key to the wealth of nations. Smith believed that the natural trend of economic development is upward and that this trend is most likely to manifest itself within the framework of an "obvious and simple system of liberty." Interpreted in modern terminology, this is a system which embodies the characteristics of perfect competition.

His principal concern was to maintain the system of natural liberty that would facilitate the accumulation and direction of capital into those avenues that his theory of different employments of capital emphasizes as being most desirable from the standpoint of maximizing welfare. The premature diversion of resources away from the agricultural sector was his great concern. Capital employed in agriculture is most productive, in Smith's view, for it yields not only wages and profit but also a surplus which is paid as rent to the landlord. Manufacturing ranks second in the hierarchy of productive employments, followed by domestic trade and finally foreign trade. The implication is that if businessmen are free to seek out the best opportunities for maximizing gains, the most productive employments will be sought out first. It is also implied that the activities in which the state engages will be minimal because the labor of the sovereign and other governmental servants is "unproductive." The incomes they receive are transfers and do not correspond to value added.

Despite his emphasis on the desirability of economic freedom, Smith's concern with identifying legitimate areas of intervention by government should not be overlooked. He did not, for example, favor wholesale removal of protective trade duties, for this would precipitate dislocation and unemployment in the domestic economy. "The public tranquility" would, he believed, require control over the corn trade, and he considered duties whose intent is to retaliate against those imposed on domestic products by foreign countries as justified.

While Smith's treatise expressed a harmony of social interests, it also showed how and why social conflict might arise. His labor theory of value and his theory of surplus laid the foundation for a definite dichotomy of class interests. He expressed his faith in the operation of the "invisible hand" in securing the interests of all members of society, but also had second thoughts about the role which different classes played with respect to the society as a whole. Of landowners, he entertained a low opinion indeed; they are frequently not only incapable of understanding the significance of any proposed change in policy but are actually ignorant of their own interests. The recipients of profit are, by training and inclination, best able to understand proposed changes in policy, but they are a class of men who are "interested to deceive and even oppress the public." Thus, elements of disharmony were present in Smith's analysis, but social conditions were not yet ready for them to ripen into actual conflict.

Conflict did not emerge until the mechanization of industry became widespread. Until that time, increases in capital were primarily associated with increases in the wages fund, just as Smith contended, and, therefore, with the improvement in the welfare of the mass of workers. But the subsequent appearance of capital in the form of machinery was to make questionable Smith's doctrine that the accumulation and employment of capital would automatically coincide with the advancing material progress of all classes of society. That the large mass of people would always benefit from the policy of laissez-faire, which Smith applauded so warmly, was also to be challenged.

But these challenges do not diminish in the least the brilliance of Smith's insight into the optimizing results of perfect competition. If there is perfect competition, there is no area of conflict between private and social interests. Each individual, independently seeking to maximize what he considers to be his own selfish interest, will nevertheless contribute to the social welfare. This thesis, in addition to counteracting the then prevailing view that every action for private gain is necessarily antisocial, also laid the groundwork for future propositions concerning the optimal characteristics of perfect competition. Precisely why these results would obtain under perfect competition was not clearly understood. But with Smith's analysis of the operation of the invisible hand, a major step was taken in the direction of understanding the significance of perfect competition in optimizing the results of economic activity. Reliance on perfect competition to achieve optimum results was subsequently built into classical as well as neoclassical analysis, though a thorough examination of the requirements of the economic optimum and their relation to perfect competition was delayed until the 1930's, when they were explored by writers on socialism in connection with economic planning to achieve maximum welfare.[67]

GLOSSARY OF TERMS AND CONCEPTS

Circulating capital. That portion of the economy's stock of capital which the production process converts into finished goods in a year or less such as raw materials and the "wage goods" which comprise the worker's subsistence. Fixed capital, i.e., tools, machinery, equipment depreciate over a much longer period.

Division of labor. Concentration of labor effort on particular tasks in order to improve skill, save time, and promote better use of capital.

Exchange value. The ability of a good to command another good in ex-

---

[67] See Chapter 14, pp. 333, 336 n.

change for itself. This is predicated on its having value in use (though Smith did not recognize this relationship).

Invisible hand.   The harmonizing of individual profit-maximizing actions with the social good through the operation of competitive market forces.

Labor theory of value.   The hypothesis that the rate at which a commodity will exchange for another is equal to the value of the labor effort congealed in it. A less rigorous version is that exchange value tends to be proportional to the value of the labor effort a commodity contains.

Price.   Exchange value expressed in terms of a common denominator: money.

Use value.   The ability of a good to yield satisfaction.

Wages fund.   Food and other items comprising the subsistence requirements of labor, or their monetary equivalent. In classical theory the wages fund constitutes the bulk of the economy's supply of capital. The size of this fund, relative to the size of the working population, determines the average wage rate.

NOTES FOR FURTHER READING

General

The bicentenary of *The Wealth of Nations* has been commemorated with the Glasgow edition of *The Works and Correspondence of Adam Smith* in six volumes with two associated volumes: *The Life of Adam Smith* by I. S. Ross and *Essays on Adam Smith,* A. S. Skinner and Thomas Wilson eds. (London: Clarendon Press, 1975). In *Essays on Adam Smith* those essays in Part II which include selections by a distinguished group of historians of economic thought are of particular interest. The selections are preceded by a useful analytical table in which the editors provide a brief summary of each.

The *Proceedings of the Second Annual Convention of the Eastern Economics Association* (1976) also commemorates the bicentenary and includes a large number of relevant articles. Samuel Hollander, *The Economics of Adam Smith* (Toronto: University of Toronto Press, 1973) undertakes a comprehensive reexamination of *The Wealth of Nations,* including several new themes, chief among which is Smith's perception of the general equilibrium tendencies of a competitive economy.

An earlier collection of interpretations of Smith's economic contributions, which marked the sesquicentennial of *The Wealth of Nations* is J. M. Clark, ed., *Adam Smith 1776–1926* (Chicago: The University of Chicago Press, 1928).

On Smith's Value Theory

The literature is so vast that it is impossible to suggest more than some of the more relevant selections, each of which includes a bibliography. With this in mind, see M. A. Stephenson, "The Paradox of Value: A Suggested Reinterpretation," *History of Political Economy,* vol. 4 (Spring 1974); H. M. Robertson and W. L. Taylor, "Adam Smith's Approach to the Theory of Value," *Economic Journal,* vol. 67 (June 1957); Paul H. Douglas, "Smith's Theory of Value and Distribution," in J. M. Clark, et al., *Adam Smith 1776–1926* (Chicago: University of Chicago Press, 1928). This classic article is still worth reading. For a more recent and contrary interpretation which argues that Smith's theory did not neglect utility, see Samuel Hollander, "The Role of Utility and Demand in The Wealth of Nations," *Essays on Adam Smith,* A. S. Skinner and T. Wilson, eds. (London: Clarendon Press, 1975).

On Labor

Alternative interpretations of Smith's theory of division of labor are presented by E. G. West, "Adam Smith's Two Views on Division of Labor," *Economica,* vol. 31 (February 1964) and Nathan Rosenberg, "Adam Smith on Division of Labor, Two Views Or One?" *Economica,* vol. 32 (May 1965). The latter is reprinted in *Readings in The History of Economic Theory,* Ingrid H. Rima, ed. (New York: Rinehart, Holt and Winston, 1970). V. W. Bladen examines the notion of productive and nonproductive labor in "Adam Smith on Productive and Non-Productive Labor," *Canadian Journal of Economics and Political Science,* vol. 26 (1960).

On Money

Douglas Vickers examines Smith's contribution to monetary theory in "Adam Smith and the Status of the Theory of Money," *Essays on Adam Smith,* A. S. Skinner and T. Wilson, eds. (London: Clarendon Press, 1975).

On Profits

The role of profit in classical economics is explored by Ronald Meek in "Adam Smith and the Classical Concept of Profit," *Scottish Journal of Political Economy,* vol. 1 (June 1954), and in "Physiocracy and Classicism in Britain," *Economic Journal,* vol. 61 (March 1951), reprinted in Ingrid Rima ed., *Readings in the History of Economic Theory* (New York, Rinehart, Holt and Winston, 1970). Nathan Rosenberg writes on "Adam Smith on Profits— Paradox Lost and Regained" in *Essays on Adam Smith,* A. S. Skinner and T. Wilson, eds. (London: Clarendon Press, 1975).

On Growth

J. J. Spengler, "Adam Smith's Theory of Growth," *Southern Economic Journal,* vol. 25 (April 1959) is particularly recommended and is usefully supplemented by W. O. Theatt "A Diagrammatic Presentation of Adam Smith's Growth Model," *Social Research,* vol. 24 (July 1957). The relationship between growth and class conflict is examined by Ingrid Rima in "Conflict and Economic Growth: Some Thoughts Suggested by "The Wealth of Nations,"

Proceedings of the Eastern Economics Association (1976). Among the more recent inquiries into Smith's growth theory are Adolph Lowe, "Adam Smith's System of Equilibrium Growth," and W. A. Ellis, "Adam Smith's Theory of Economic Growth" in *Essays on Adam Smith,* A. S. Skinner and T. Wilson, eds. (London: Clarendon Press, 1975).

On International Trade

Arthur Bloomfield reexamines Smith's "vent for surplus" view of international trade in "Adam Smith and the Theory of International Trade," *Essays on Adam Smith,* A. S. Skinner and T. Wilson, eds. (London: Clarendon Press, 1975).

On Early Writings and Social Philosophy

The work of J. R. Lindgren is particularly useful. See his *The Early Writings of Adam Smith* (New York: Augustus Kelley, 1966) and *The Social Philosophy of Adam Smith* (The Hague: Nijhoff, 1973).

5

Thomas Malthus: The Political Economy of Population Behavior

INTRODUCTION

Life and Times (1766–1834)

AN ANONYMOUS ESSAY which was to become one of the most discussed works of modern times was published in 1798. It bore the title *An Essay on the Principle of Population, as It Affects the Future Improvement of Society with Remarks on the Speculations of Mr. Godwin, M. Condorcet and Other Writers*. It had been written by Thomas Malthus, an ordained minister of the Church of England. Relatively few copies of the original edition circulated, for its subject matter was both unpopular and controversial. But the *Essay* soon became the center of heated discussion, and six editions appeared during the author's lifetime. The original is substantially different from subsequent ones, in length and content, for the author added numerous qualifications and evidence to document his thesis.

Malthus was born in 1766 to a distinguished family. His father, Daniel, a lawyer by profession, was a friend of such men as Rousseau and Hume. He sent his son to be educated in Cambridge; upon graduation, Malthus entered the ministry of the Church of England, and was in charge of a parish at the time his famous essay was written. It was subsequently revised after extensive travel in Germany, France, and the Scandinavian countries. Shortly afterward, in 1805, he was appointed professor of history and political economy at the East India College, where he remained for the rest of his life. During these years he enjoyed a close friendship with David Ricardo and helped found the Political Economy Club in 1821 and the Statistical Society of London in 1834.

The span of Malthus' lifetime coincided with years that were revolutionary in the industrial as well as in the political world. The Industrial Revolution, still in its embryonic stage when Adam Smith wrote, brought with it not only improved methods of production and transportation, new forms of business organization, and better banking and credit facilities, but also the factory system with its many attendant evils. The ever growing urban population, whose employment opportunities were reduced by technological progress, presented a troublesome problem. These difficulties were compounded by recurrent economic crises which gave rise to periodic commodity gluts. The problem of overproduction therefore became an issue, as did the whole question of the "effect of machinery." The possibility that French revolutionary ideas might spread into England as a result of difficulties of the working class was the great fear that haunted the wealthy. The practical aim of English politics became to forestall a similar uprising by improving the conditions of the urban working class enough to safeguard the existing social structure. William Pitt's bill of 1798, calling for the extension of relief to large families, is typical of the sort of "safety valve" measures proposed.

The economic burdens of the urban poor became especially acute when the Napoleonic wars ended in 1815. While England was relatively prosperous during this lengthy and expensive struggle, its termination was accompanied by a state of general depression. The problem of widespread unemployment was complicated by continued high food prices, whose relationship to the Corn Laws became a major issue to which Malthus and his contemporary, David Ricardo, were to address themselves. The Corn Laws, which had been in existence since mercantilist times, were intended to stabilize the price of grain through a system of import duties and bounties which became effective in accordance with the domestic supply. In years of good harvest the market price of grain fell, and the duty became effective, whereas in years of poor harvest the market price of grain rose, and the duty was decreased. Under this system, English imports were virtually duty-free from 1795 to 1812 because the continued growth of population caused grain prices to remain high in spite of increased acreage and better cultivation methods.[1] Thus the Corn Laws themselves had little to do with keeping the price of grain high during the Napoleonic wars. Landlords, however, became especially concerned about their continuation when the return of peacetime conditions and the prospect of large imports threatened to lower crop prices. Manufacturers and merchants, on the

---

[1] Edwin Cannan, *A History of the Theories of Production and Distribution in English Political Economy* (London: Staples Press, 1953), pp. 148–52.

other hand, were quick to realize the advantages which free trade would yield them because of the relationship between wage rates and low food prices.

The Philosophical Aspects of Post-Smithian Economics: Utilitarianism

Post-Smithian economics, of which Malthus was a leading figure, was predominantly pessimistic in its outlook. It addressed itself chiefly to the problem of explaining the distribution of income among the three social classes. In this approach, it reflected problems which were too pressing and widespread to be obscured by belief in a natural order in which harmony is always assured. Thus the thinkers who followed Smith described an economic system whose laws of operation they conceived to be dictated by a supreme but by no means beneficent natural order. Instead of the "invisible hand" operating to promote the good of all, though this is no part of man's intention, emphasis was now placed on the necessity of man's adaptation to the exigencies of nature in order to avoid the unpleasant consequences of his own shortcomings.

Post-Smithian economics also reflects the effect of Utilitarian ethics on the thinking of the political economists of the day. Utilitarianism sought, on the one hand, to introduce a principle, analogous to Sir Isaac Newton's in the natural sciences, on which a science of moral and social life could be founded and, on the other, to provide a basis for a reform movement known as philosophical radicalism. This movement was associated primarily with Jeremy Bentham and James Mill, although the ideas on which it is based are drawn principally from David Hume and the French philosopher Claude Adrien Helvétius.[2] Like Hume, Bentham believed that human behavior is the product of sense experience rather than reason. By identifying the pleasant sensations which individuals can be observed to experience with moral goodness, and painful sensations with evil, Bentham made Hume's hedonism the foundation for a system of social ethics. The practical application of this ethical system required a "felicific calculus," or quantitative measurement of the pleasures and pains associated with various actions or modes of behavior. Bentham's view was that pleasures and pains differ quantitatively, depending upon their intensity, duration, certainty or uncertainty, propinquity or remoteness, fecundity, and extent, but they do not differ qualitatively. In his system, therefore, there are no pleasures which are superior or inferior and, consequently, none which rank higher or lower from a moral standpoint. Only the individual can judge which actions or experiences give him quantitatively more pleasure and which are, in this sense, better.

---

[2] Elie Halévy, *The Growth of Philosophical Radicalism* (New York: Augustus Kelley, 1949), chap. 1.

Bentham thought it possible to sum up pleasures and set them against pains, conceived of as negative pleasures. "The balance, if it be on the side of pleasure, will give the good tendency of the act upon the whole, with respect to the interests of that individual person; if in the side of pain, the bad tendency of it upon the whole."[3] By assuming that all individuals count equally and that a given action is associated with identical experiences of pleasure or pain for everyone, he extended the felicific calculus to society as a whole. He concluded that conduct should be judged morally according to its effects on the balance of human happiness. But this conclusion necessarily raises the question as to whether the egoisms which motivate human conduct are harmonious with each other, as Smith maintained, or are in conflict with each other. The French philosopher Helvétius took the position that individuals do not spontaneously identify their interests with the general interest. It was his influence which led Bentham to the idea that education and legislation will contribute to the greatest happiness of the greatest number. Education will contribute to the more perfect attainment of the goal of maximum utility by impressing on people more appropriate "associations"; while reform, particularly of the legal system, will penalize unacceptable behavior and provide an incentive for behavior which will promote the social welfare.

Malthus' Political Philosophy

Although Malthus did not write a treatise on political philosophy, his views on the pressing issues of his day indicate that he was largely guided by Utilitarian principles. He considered that the goal of politics is the greatest happiness of the greatest number and that the rule for achieving that end is observation, based on experience, of what actually secures the desired end within the particular institutions and interest of England as a nation. But he differed in several ways from other Utilitarians of his day; specifically, he tended to be conservative, perhaps even reactionary, where others were philosophical radicals. Thus, he defended the traditional English class structure, which most others criticized. Furthermore, he shared neither their anticlerical views nor their optimism for greatly improving the lot of the large mass of humanity.

While Malthus' work does not have a predominantly religious quality, though he was a clergyman in good standing, his Utilitarianism has its foundation in his theological views. It is the intention of the Creator to procure what is good for His creatures, and it is this apparent purpose which mankind must fulfill. It is man's reason which must select among the various human impulses in order to carry out the design of the Creator.

---

[3] W. Stark, ed., *Jeremy Bentham's Economic Writings* (London: George Allen and Unwin, Ltd., 1954), vol. 3, pp. 436–37.

This design is to be discovered by applying the principle of utility to our actions. It is by examining the consequences of our impulses and subjecting them to the test of utility that we shall gradually acquire the habit of gratifying them only when they will add to the sum of human happiness and thus promote the intention of the Creator. This is the only test by which we can know, independently of the revealed will of God, whether an impulse should be acted upon.

Theological postulates behoove us to discipline our impulses to promote not only our own happiness but that of the great majority of our fellowmen as well. The happiness of the whole is the natural outgrowth of the happiness of individuals. It is not institutions and laws, as Godwin maintained, but ourselves who bear the responsibility for human unhappiness. Human happiness is, Malthus argued, most likely to be attained within existing institutions, specifically the existing form of English constitutional government. His counsel was thus for the preservation of the existing legal, social, and economic status quo. Regardless of the issue, whether the Poor Laws, the Corn Laws, or the problem of maintaining effective demand, he was consistently in favor of preserving the then existing class structure and relying on the principle of utility to improve human society.

THE ESSAY ON POPULATION

Philosophical Background

Malthus' original interest in the population problem was incidental to the much broader question of the reforms proposed by the philosophical radicalists. The spark that kindled the *Essay* was struck as a result of discussions between himself and his father, Daniel Malthus, concerning the arguments of William Godwin, whose new book *The Enquirer* had recently been published. Godwin's earlier *Political Justice* had already proposed a "simple form of society, without government," in which the perfectibility of man will ultimately be realized. This volume, which has been called the first textbook of philosophical radicalism, held that the institutions of the present society, especially as they affect the distribution of wealth, militate against the achievement of perfection and happiness. Reason, argued Godwin, dictates that an equal division of wealth will provide for simple wants and leave ample leisure time for an intellectual and moral improvement which will ultimately establish perfection and happiness on earth.

The French philosopher Marquis de Condorcet had much the same vision, though he relied more on science than morals to produce the ideal society. Like Godwin, he believed in the perfectibility of man, but he emphasized the progress inherent in the cumulative character of knowledge in the arts and sciences, which would produce advances to offset the growth of population. The prospect of overpopulation was viewed as existing only in a future too distant for present contemplation. It was this utopian dream of a golden age of equality and happiness which Malthus' *Essay* was to shatter, for he foresaw the specter of excessive population as a permanent impediment to the improvement of society.

The Postulates

Malthus argued that he required only two postulates to prove the unattainability of the millennium Godwin and Condorcet foresaw: the first, "that food is necessary to the existence of man"; the second, that "the passion between the sexes is necessary, and will remain nearly in its present state."[4] The first postulate is axiomatic; and the second, Malthus argued, Godwin had failed to disprove. He maintained that the instinct for marriage is permanent, though there are admittedly individual exceptions, and that the operation of the principle of population would make it impossible to attain the millennium. The potential increase of population, when unchecked, is in a geometrical ratio, whereas subsistence can increase only in an arithmetical ratio.

> A slight acquaintance with numbers will shew the immensity of the first power in comparison with the second.
> By that law of nature which makes food necessary to the life of man, the effects of these two unequal powers must be kept equal.[5]

This implies that there must exist a strong and constantly operating check on population because of the difficulty of obtaining subsistence. This difficulty must necessarily be severely felt by a large proportion of mankind.

Mathus supports his contention that the growth power of population is geometrical only by the experience of the United States, in which population doubled itself in 25 years. This growth potential was then compared with the potential increase of the annual food supply. Our knowledge of the qualities of land, reasons Malthus, indicates that under the most ideal conditions imaginable the increase which can be achieved in 25 years might equal the present produce.

> Let us then take this for our rule, though certainly far beyond the truth; and allow that, by great exertion, the whole produce of the Island might be increased every twenty-five years, by a quantity of subsistence equal to what it at present produces. The most enthusiastic speculator, cannot suppose a greater increase than this. In a few centuries it would make every acre of land in the Island a garden. Yet this ratio of increase is evidently arithmetical.[6]

---

[4] Thomas Malthus, *First Essay on Population* (*1798*), Reprints of Economic Classics (New York: Augustus Kelley, 1965), p. 11.

[5] Ibid., p. 14.

[6] Ibid., p. 22.

It is obvious therefore that the growth powers of population greatly exceed those of the food supply.

Diminishing Returns

Although Malthus did not explicitly set forth the tendency of diminishing returns on land, it is implicitly assumed in his ratios. For while man's subsistence consists of lower forms of animal and vegetable life which, unchecked, also tend to increase in a geometrical ratio, so that it might be presumed that the human population and its food supply would be equally capable of growth, this is the case only when the supply of land is large enough to accommodate the expansion. Because the earth's surface is limited, increasing the food supply necessarily means the application of added productive effort at the margin, where the returns are proportionately less, unless the existing land supply can be made more productive via technological improvements. The problem begins to show itself as soon as a given quantity of land has been brought under cultivation and the animal and human population have consumed all available food, for then only more effective use of the given supply of land can increase its food-producing potential. This, in Malthus' view, is assuredly more difficult than the increase of living beings by their own act, for he has in mind such increases in the food supply as are made possible by the same methods and techniques as made available the old supplies.

The disparity between the growth rate of population and food supply is readily apparent if it is accepted that to raise additional food, in the absence of changes in productive methods, requires more labor per unit of output. Bringing new population into the world is independent of such requirements. This does not imply, as is sometimes suggested, that Malthus believed a geometrical increase is characteristic of man alone, while plants and animals increase arithmetically. All things living can increase geometrically when furnished with the proper amount of nourishment. The power of increase of the lower plants and animals is perhaps even greater than that of man, but their actual increase is quite slow for want of the land supply from which all subsistence, human and otherwise, must be derived. If good land could be gotten in abundance, the increase of food from it would be in a geometrical ratio even greater than that of man. But because good lands are limited in supply and ultimately all under cultivation, increasing the food supply eventually becomes a laborious process which yields increases only at a diminishing rate. Thus, even if one could create an ideal social system, such as Godwin envisioned, in which checks on population would be eliminated or greatly reduced, it would not be long before the pressure of checks would reassert itself, not from any fault of man but because the earth's productiveness does not expand with population.

That there is a tendency toward diminishing returns had, of course, already been noted. Turgot in particular had stated the matter quite lucidly.[7] James Anderson, a Scot, who was a prolific writer on economic subjects besides being a farmer, discussed diminishing returns in relation to rent.[8] But the 19th-century English economists appear to have been influenced less by the work of their predecessors than the actual experience of England during the Napoleonic wars. For not only did agricultural prices increase significantly, but large tracts of previously untilled lands were brought under cultivation. It was also recognized that the high price of raw produce, which enables land to yield a high rent, is due to diminishing returns. It would probably have been surprising if the relationship between increasing population and recourse to poor soils had not stimulated inquiry. The observations of Edward West are particularly pertinent in this connection, for it is he, rather than Malthus or Ricardo, who gave the law of diminishing returns precise formulation, although the latter are more responsible for its prominent place in English political economy.

Checks on Population Growth

From the contradiction between the geometrical ratio of population growth and the arithmetic ratio of the growth of the food supply, Malthus concluded that population increase must necessarily be checked in some manner. In his first edition of the *Essay,* he surmised that such checks would be resolvable into either misery or vice, and that Godwin's hypothesis regarding the ultimate perfectibility of man was therefore rendered untenable. Godwin and Condorcet were wrong, he argued, in attributing all inequality to human institutions. Rather, it is human nature, with its tendency to marry and multiply, which is the most serious obstacle to improvement. No other conclusion is possible if we begin, as Malthus did, by assuming that the desire for food and the desire for marriage are equally urgent and that there is a strong tendency toward diminishing returns from land.

The principle of population thus presented was received as a major contribution to political economy, though it also provoked great protest.[9] Even Godwin acknowledged its value while pointing out that among the more enlightened classes it was not uncommon to postpone marriage to avoid the burden of too great a family, and that this prudence was precisely the ideal behavior he foresaw as being attainable for the entire population.

---

[7] Anne Robert Jacques Turgot, *Observations sur le Memoire de M. de Saint-Peravy* (Paris, 1768).

[8] James Anderson, *An Inquiry into the Nature of the Corn Laws with a View to the New Corn Bill Proposed for Scotland* (London: 1777).

[9] Kenneth Smith, *The Malthusian Controversy* (London: Routledge and Kegan Paul, 1951), Book 2, "The Development of Controversy."

History has since indicated that this mode of behavior is not beyond man and demonstrated that if Godwin overrated the role of reason, Malthus equally overrated the role of passion.

Malthus eventually saw that he had perhaps placed undue emphasis on vice and misery as checks, and made revisions over the next five years before republication of his *Essay*. In the new edition, he took the position that while man cannot remove the necessity of checks, because there is always a tendency of population to outrun subsistence, he can, with his own self-control, alter their mode of operation. For in addition to the positive checks of misery and vice, there is the preventative check of moral restraint. Moral restraint is interpreted to mean the postponement of marriage until such time as a family can adequately be supported, and the practice of continence outside of marriage. He observed that vice and misery were the primary checks in ancient and primitive societies, whereas moral restraint predominates in modern civilizations. Prudential restraint became the only morally acceptable check to Malthus. Educate the individual, he urged, to postpone marriage until he is capable of supporting a family and to avoid irregular gratification.

This can best be accomplished, Malthus believed, within the framework of a social system which will encourage people to practice moral restraint. The system which promises the most desirable results in this regard is the existing one of private property, including its characteristics of economic inequality and social class structure, provided it also assures opportunity to those who are ambitious and prudent to rise by their own efforts. The Poor Laws encourage indolence and raise the level only of the weakest members of society, and this is at the expense of the others. If people knew they could not count on parish relief, the ordinary motives of self-interest would force them to help themselves. It was on these grounds that Malthus became an enthusiastic supporter of popular education which would teach enlightened self-interest; at the same time, he opposed the continuation of poor relief.

The Tendency toward Subsistence Wages

One of the main implications deriving from the Malthusian theory of population is that the level of real wages will tend toward subsistence unless the rate of population growth is sufficiently checked by moral restraint. Malthus and his contemporaries thought of the wage rate as depending on the ratio between the labor force and the size of the wage fund.

Since it was generally assumed that the wage fund represents a constant proportion of the capital stock, it follows that the continued growth of population, and thus the labor force, will depress the wage rate to the lowest level compatible with subsistence. This tendency could of course be offset if capital stock, and therefore the wage fund, increases more rapidly than the population. Thus, Malthus associated rising wage rates with a high ratio of capital to labor, whereas falling wage rates were associated with a low ratio of capital to labor. This is a conclusion with which modern economists are in accord, but for a different reason. Modern analysis maintains that a high ratio of capital to labor affects labor's marginal productivity and consequently its claim to income.

The Tendency for Rents to Rise

Just as the growth of population tended to be associated with a downward pressure on wage rates if there was a wage fund of a given size, so it was also associated with a tendency for rents to rise. Malthus' *The Nature and Causes of Rent* addressed itself primarily to the question of whether rent is, as implied by Smith and even the Physiocrats, a monopoly income.[10] The inquiry was also associated with the Corn Law controversy. Malthus observed at the outset of his inquiry that this subject "has perhaps a particular claim to our attention at the present moment on account of the discussions which are going on respecting the Corn Laws, and the effects of rent on the price of raw produce and the progress of agricultural improvement." His pamphlet antedated the appearance of Ricardo's *Essay on the Influence of a Low Price of Corn on the Profits of Stock.*

Malthus advanced three reasons for the appearance of rent. He argued, first, that land produces more than enough to maintain its cultivators.[11] This fact alone makes rent "a bountiful gift from providence" rather than the result of monopolistic scarcity. Secondly, he argued, the necessaries of life are uniquely capable of "creating their own demand or of raising up the number of demanders in proportion to the quantity of necessaries produced."[12] It is because population increases with the food supply that its price rises above its cost of production and creates a surplus. Must we not therefore grant, Malthus asks, that its appearance is a clear indication of a most inestimable quality in the soil, which God has bestowed on man—the quality of being able to maintain more persons than are necessary to work it?"[13] Here Malthus clearly regards the appearance of rent as being inherent in the progress of society according to the dictates of natural law. The third cause of rent is that the most fertile land is comparatively scarce, and, except in a new country, there is not enough to supply all our wants.

---

[10] This was also the position of David Buchanan, whose argument that rent is the result of a monopoly of land appears to have had a good deal to do with Malthus' inquiry.

[11] Thomas Malthus, *Principles of Political Economy, 2d ed.* (1836), Reprints of Economic Classics (New York: Augustus Kelley, 1964), p. 140.

[12] Ibid.

[13] Ibid., p. 147.

When it becomes necessary, because of population growth and diminishing returns, to resort to inferior lands, the products produced thereon will have to be high enough in price to pay their costs of production, and superior lands will then receive rent.

The comparative scarcity of fertile land was viewed in a very different light by Malthus than by his contemporary, David Ricardo. To Malthus, it seemed obvious that not all land can be equally fertile or equally well situated. The superiority of the best land is thus regarded as "a bountiful gift from providence." This view is expressed in his *Principles of Political Economy* in which he concludes his chapter "Of the Rent of Land" with the statement that "in every point of view, then, in which the subject can be considered, that quality of land which, by the laws of our being, must terminate in rent, appears to be a boon most important to the happiness of mankind; and I am persuaded that its value can only be underrated by those who still labour under some mistake, as to its nature, and its effects on society."[14] Ricardo, on the other hand, was persuaded that rent was due to the niggardliness of nature, which not only caused rents to rise but caused them to absorb a progressively larger proportion of the national product in an insulated economy. It was on these grounds that he advocated the repeal of the Corn Laws in opposition to Malthus.

THE PROGRESS OF POPULATION AND WEALTH

The Effectual Demand for Labor

In the *Essay,* Malthus was especially concerned with examining the laws which regulate population growth. In the *Principles,* this inquiry was extended to examine the factors which determine increases in subsistence and therefore make the growth of population possible. Subsistence consists of the supplies of food and other necessaries which the worker and his family require. The ultimate limit on the growth of subsistence derives from the supply of land, its fertility, and the state of progress of the arts which govern production. The size of the population is ultimately limited by subsistence; however, Malthus thought that in many countries the number of inhabitants was actually *fewer* than could be supported in relative comfort. This led him to inquire what sort of obstacle or impediment existed to prevent the population from increasing to a size compatible with the physical possibility of providing subsistence. He concluded that the chief impediment to increasing the number and well-being of the population is the failure of what he termed "effectual demand" for labor.[15]

While the thesis that the growth of population depends on the effectual

---

[14] Ibid., p. 217.
[15] Ibid., pp. 231–40.

demand for labor is implicit in the *Essay,* it is overshadowed by his concern with the relationship between population and the food supply and the checks of vice, misery, and moral restraint. Later, however, he became increasingly concerned with examining the factors which determine what he called the effectual demand for labor and its relationship to the growth of population.[16]

The effectual demand for labor is reflected in the extent of its employment. Employment regulates the wages of labor, and the latter determine the power of the laborer to acquire food and necessaries for the support of himself and his family. Employment therefore also regulates the size of the family the worker is able to support. The demand for labor is, in turn, "proportioned to the rate of increase in the quantity and value of those funds, whether arising from capital or revenue, which are actually employed in the maintenance of labor.[17] Accumulation is therefore essential to the progress of population and wealth, for it makes it possible to augment the wage fund out of which labor is supported. Effectual demand for labor requires that there be additions to the wage fund. But there must also be a demand for commodities. Without a demand for commodities, the demand for labor will diminish. If income receivers are too thrifty, there is likely to be a depression of wealth and population which is caused by the presence of gluts.[18]

Commodity and Capital Gluts

During the first decade and a half of her war with France, Great Britain enjoyed an era of almost continuous prosperity. The post-Napoleonic war years, however, were interrupted by periods of severe industrial stagnation. Domestic depression was aggravated by failure of revival in foreign trade and by a poor harvest, which raised the price of bread. Moreover, the new Corn Law of 1815 effectively excluded foreign grain. This chain of events led Malthus to maintain that Great Britain was experiencing the effects of an insufficient demand for capital as the result of a decline in the demand for consumer goods.[19] He thought that the English social structure, and consequently the distribution of income, encouraged such a large volume of saving that it produced a glut of commodities as well as capital. Another important reason, he believed, for the fall in the demand for goods and the

---

[16] This aspect of Malthus's work is discussed in an interesting essay by Joseph J. Spengler, "Malthus' Total Population Theory: A Restatement and Reappraisal," *Canadian Journal of Economics and Political Science,* vol. 11 (February–May 1945).

[17] Malthus, *Principles of Political Economy,* p. 234.

[18] Ibid., pp. 314–30.

[19] Ibid., pp. 413–37.

resulting redundancy of capital was the decrease in governmental military expenditures in the transition from war to peace. The cessation of these expenditures, coupled with the expanded productive capacity made possible by earlier rapid accumulation, resulted in a volume of production which was too great for the revenue that was available to purchase it.

Malthus was by no means the only or perhaps even the first student of economic crisis. Karl Marx, in fact, maintained that the Swiss historian and economist Jean Charles Sismondi was responsible for ideas generally attributed to Malthus. While Sismondi's first theoretical work *De la richesse commerciale* (1803) was strongly in the tradition of Adam Smith, his later *Nouveaux Principes de l'Economie politique* (1819), written against the background of the crises of the early 19th century, questioned the self-equilibrating character of the capitalistic system. It laid particular emphasis upon the ever increasing productive powers of the modern capitalistic system and reasoned that the worker, having only the purchasing power of subsistence wages, is unable to purchase all the products the system is capable of producing. Periodic excess and unemployment are the inevitable outcome, which, with the progress of further technological advances, will necessarily become worse because competition among capitalists to employ capital profitably will intensify overproduction. Thus Sismondi emphasized the atomistic competitive character of production which, in conjunction with the inadequacy of consumer purchasing power, manifests itself in the most striking feature of economic crises: overproduction.

Contemporaries such as Jean Baptiste Say, James Mill, and David Ricardo regarded depressions as inevitable concomitants of economic progress. But they emphatically denied that there could be either a general overproduction of goods or an overaccumulation of capital in the long run. This conclusion derived from their acceptance of Say's law, which maintained that aggregate effective demand is necessarily the equivalent of aggregate supply.[20] Since goods are intended to be exchanged for other goods, every act of production simultaneously creates a market for the whole product produced by making available the monetary means of purchasing it. Specific commodities may at times be produced in greater quantities than the demand for them warrants, but a state of general overproduction, or glut, is impossible. Even such maladjustments, however, will tend to correct themselves. If the supply of a given commodity is excessive, the losses incurred in its production will soon diminish its supply; while, conversely, if the supply falls short of current demand, the resulting high profits will expand output so that individual demands and supplies tend to be balanced. In a barter economy an excess supply of all goods relative to

---

[20] Jacob Hollander has maintained that the generalization known as Say's law was, in fact, conceived by James Mill before it was developed by Say. See Hollander's *Introduction to Ricardo's Notes on Malthus* (Baltimore: Johns Hopkins Press, 1928). In any event, Mill evidently taught the principle to Ricardo.

the aggregate demand for them is a logical impossibility. Aggregate demand and aggregate supply are "necessarily" equal.[21]

Ricardo drew still another conclusion, namely, that an overaccumulation of capital is also an impossibility. Capital, he argued, will never be accumulated in a greater quantity than can be productively employed. Its accumulation depends on the long-run trend of profits, and this is contingent on the productivity of labor and the margin of cultivation. If accumulation proceeds at a greater rate than can assure profitablility, the motive for continued accumulation will disappear. Low rates of profit would make "unproductive consumption," by which Ricardo and Malthus meant expenditures not aimed at further production, more attractive. In short, Ricardo took it for granted that low rates of profit would alter the proportions of spending and savings so that less capital would accumulate.

Malthus, on the other hand, maintained that capital accumulation is not automatically limited by a decline in the rate of profits. He observed that "while it is quite certain that an adequate passion for consumption may fully keep up the proper proportion between supply and demand, whatever may be the powers of production, it appears to be quite as certain that an inordinate passion for accumulation must inevitably lead to a supply of commodities beyond what the structure and habits of such a society will permit to be consumed."[22] While he fully agreed that some degree of frugality is necessary and desirable, he held that saving pushed to excess will destroy the motive for production by reducing what he termed the "effective demand" for commodities.

Although Malthus did not specifically define the term *effective demand,* he apparently meant the ability and willingness of the community to buy a commodity at a price equivalent to its labor command value, that is, at a price which will enable the producer to cover his costs plus profit at the prevailing rate. He regarded the market price of the commodity, which results from the interaction of supply and demand, as much more important than the natural price. For while he agreed with Ricardo that rising food costs would gradually eliminate profits through their impact on wages, since wages and profits vary inversely, he maintained that a theory which

---

[21] It has become conventional to refer to the "necessary" equality between aggregate demand and aggregate supply in real terms as Say's equality. Say's equality assumes that money serves only as a medium of exchange and not as a store of value. If money also serves as a store of value, an excess supply of all commodities necessarily means that there is an excess demand for money. Aggregate demand will equal aggregate supply in money terms only if the demand for cash balances is zero. This version of Say's law, which is known as Say's identity boils down to making a money economy function like a barter economy. This distinction between that version of Say's Law which has come to be called Say's equality and the version known as Say's identity should alert us that the meaning of Say's law is not as simple as it first appears to be. But its interpretation did not become a major issue until it was raised by J. M. Keynes. See chapter 17 below.

[22] Malthus, *Principles of Political Economy,* p. 325.

explains short-run variations in profits is necessary to explain the phenomenon of gluts. He maintained that when profits rise, "there will be a tendency to spend a smaller proportion of the gains and to save a greater." This increase in savings results in the employment of more "productive" laborers and thus in a greater quantity of goods available for purchase. But because the number of persons remains the same in the short run, and because it takes time to learn new habits of consumption, the effective demand for consumer goods is not large enough to offset the reduction which results from the savings of capitalists and other wealthy persons. The result is that goods can be sold only at prices lower than the costs of production, so that ultimately the reduction of profits destroys the capacity to save.

Malthus believed that James Mill and David Ricardo committed a serious error in maintaining that accumulation of capital would assure a demand for goods. Their argument, he said, proceeded on the premise of a handicraft economy in which money serves merely to implement the exchange of commodities for one another; whereas, in fact, in a society which is composed of a class of proprietors and a class of laborers, exchange also involves the exchange of capital in the form of the wage fund and labor. Malthus maintained that in dealing with the problem of gluts, Mill, as well as Ricardo, in effect assumed away the capitalistic labor market by conceiving that exchange consisted in the main of the exchange of commodities, which had value in accordance with the labor they embodied. He, on the other hand, equated value with labor command. Thus, within the framework of Malthus' definition of values, Say's law could not hold because the aggregate demand for goods consists of subsistence wages (labor commanded), while aggregate supply consists of this quantity plus profit. The inadequacy of effective demand and gluts is therefore the logical counterpart to his theory of value.

Unproductive Consumption

Malthus reasoned that in a society comprised of proprietors and laborers, the origin and use of most income-shares militate against an adequate level of effective demand for commodities. Specifically, wages impinge upon profits, and capitalists are more interested in accumulation than in making large expenditures on consumer goods. Their savings increase productive capacity and therefore aggravate the problem of maintaining effective demand. It is for this reason that Malthus looked to the expenditures of the rentier class and other unproductive consumers to maintain the level of effective demand. Since rent is a differential surplus, its expenditure adds to effective demand without adding to costs of production, whereas other forms of income are costs of production as well as sources of purchasing power.

There are other classes of unproductive consumers—menial servants, statesmen, physicians, judges, lawyers, clergymen, etc. The expenditures of these persons also add to the effective demand for goods and thus offset the deficiency of consumer demand which arises out of the savings process. Malthus maintained that it is absolutely essential for an economy with great powers of production to have a body of unproductive consumers. Unproductive consumption is the safety valve which he viewed as diminishing the undesirable effects of too rapid accumulation. Without it, the economy will experience periods of commodity glut and capital redundancy.

Progress and the Structure of the Economy

The effective demand for labor, and therefore the growth potential of population, is also affected by the structure of the economy. Malthus thought that the effective demand for labor is best maintained in an economy in which the balance between the industrial and agricultural sectors is such that the country is always independent of foreign sources of food. Unlike Ricardo, he was in favor of restricting free trade in corn on the ground that it would contribute to maintaining the effective demand for labor. His argument is presented in his *The Grounds of an Opinion on the Policy of Restricting the Importation of Foreign Corn* (1815). In it, he argues that it is desirable for England to encourage domestic production of grain on a scale that would make her independent of foreign supplies, even though it would tend to raise English crop prices. This position is, he tells us, mainly the result of French legislation restricting the export of corn. Since England was greatly dependent on exports from France to supplement her home supply, he argued that a system of free trade would render domestic supplies inadequate in years of scarcity abroad. In view of England's special circumstances, therefore, he argued in favor of protection.

His second reason for advocating a restricted corn trade for England was his observation that increased industrialization tends to be accompanied by more frequent and more severe business fluctuations, which particularly burden the lower classes, and that it is therefore desirable in England, which is "the most manufacturing [country] of any ever recorded in history," "that its agriculture should keep pace with its manufactures, even at the expense of retarding in some degree the growth of manufactures."[23] He thus concluded that in England, agricultural protection was in the interest of general abundance and advantageous to the working class by protecting it against adverse price movements originating abroad as well as minimizing the evil effects which would be associated with rapid industrialization.

He observed that while predominantly agricultural economies also tend

---

[23] Malthus, *Observations on the Effects of the Corn Laws* (1814).

to be poorer than those which are more industrialized, the "premature check" to the progress of the population is due to the remains of the feudal system. While he asserted the primary importance of agriculture in promoting the progress of population and wealth, subsequent editions of his *Principles* became increasingly cognizant that industrialization also contributed to maintaining and enhancing the effective demand for labor.

CONCLUDING REMARKS

The impact of an individual's work may manifest itself in a variety of ways. First, and perhaps foremost, it may influence subsequent work in terms of method or content in its own discipline. It may also become incorporated in some way into policy measures and so guide the solution of practical problems. Finally, it may inspire new work in other fields of knowledge. Malthus' efforts have the distinction of having borne fruit in all these directions.

There is, first of all, his contribution to the development of pure economic theory. In Malthus' day the principles which subsequently became known as the laws of classical economics were only beginning to be forged and he contributed greatly to their development, in terms of both content and methodology. At a time when the emphasis of inquiry was at least as much on practical policy as on the discovery of principles Malthus used the deductive method to establish formal principles. Both the principle of population and the principle of effective demand are propositions he established by means of deductive logic.

In establishing these principles, Malthus pioneered in applying the methods of deductive logic to the complex world of daily events. These events crystallized themselves to Malthus chiefly in the form of worker misery. The poverty suffered by the laboring classes before the Napoleonic wars was afterward compounded by unemployment. Malthus directed his attention to both aspects of the poverty problem. His approach was that of the moral scientist schooled in the *a priori* method of the Cambridge tradition. To this, he added a wealth of historical and contemporary factual information which guided him in the proper selection and formulation of the premises from which he ultimately arrived, by means of deductive logic, at his conclusions. His principle of population was offered to explain the determination of the supply of labor and was the basis for the conclusion that the only way of improving the standard of living of the laboring classes was the control of numbers. His principle of effective demand maintained that the aggregate demand for labor is derived from the aggregate demand for commodities and determines the ability of population to grow. Malthus maintained, on the basis of this principle, that excessive savings are associated with gluts of commodities and capital, and therefore with an inadequate demand for labor.

The importance of Malthus' principle of effective demand has come to be appreciated only in this century. Not until the worldwide depression of the 1930s was the principle of effective demand to be reiterated and extended by John Maynard Keynes. In the long interim the conclusions derived from Say's law were presented with such effectiveness that it was accepted that any economy whose operation is guided by a freely operating price system will tend, automatically, to fully employ its resources. Thus, Malthus' name is even now remembered only by relatively few for his principle of effective demand though it has been immortalized by his principle of population behavior.

In the western world the triumphs of technology and the practice of contraception have intervened to counteract the dire implications of Malthus' theory of population growth. But given the premises from which Malthus started, no other conclusion is possible than the one at which he arrived. This is all too evident in areas of the world like Asia, in which the premises on which Malthus rested his conclusions are empirically verifiable.

Though the *Essay* prompted angry protests when it first appeared, its eventual impact on the English Parliament is apparent in the passage of a new Poor Law in 1834 which, in comparison with the earlier legislation, greatly limited aid to the poor, particularly of illegitimate birth. Malthus' principle of population was also significant in causing the first census to be taken in 1801. It also inspired innumerable empirical and theoretical works on demography, besides serving as an inspiration to Charles Darwin in the development of his theory of evolution.[24]

GLOSSARY OF TERMS AND CONCEPTS

Atomistic production.   Production which is uncoordinated with demand and which tends to result in commodity gluts.

Commodity gluts.   An insufficiency of aggregate effective demand which results in unsold goods.

Diminishing returns.   In a given state of the arts, the productive capacity of land increases at a decreasing rate beyond a certain point. Malthus inferred from this principle that the food supply could only be increased at an arithmetical rate.

Hedonism.   The explanation of human behavior in terms of the objective of maximizing pleasure and minimizing pain. In economics, the counterparts of pleasure and pain are monetary gains and losses.

Principle of population.   The hypothesis that, in the absence of restraints, population will tend to increase at a geometrical rate as long as there is a food supply.

Say's identity.   Equality between aggregate demand and supply *in money terms.* It is predicated on the assumption that the demand for cash

---

[24] *Life and Letters of Charles Darwin,* New York: D. Appleton, 1897, vol. 1, p. 83.

balances is zero. *Say's equality* assumes that money serves only as a medium of exchange and not as a store of value.

Utilitarianism.   A system of ethics, principally associated with Bentham and other philosophic radicals which maintained that the ideal of "the greatest good for the greatest number" could be achieved by educative and punitive measures to promote the kinds of individual choices which would maximize human happiness.

NOTES FOR FURTHER READING

Thomas Malthus' "First Essay on Population" (1798) is to be found in Reprints of Economic Classics (New York: Augustus Kelley, 1965). His *Principles of Political Economy,* 2d ed., 1836, is also among Reprints of Economic Classics (New York: Augustus Kelley, 1964).

For general assessments of Malthus' work, see James Bonar's classic *Malthus and His Work* (London: George Allen and Unwin Ltd., 1924) and the more recent assessment of Lionel Robbins, "Malthus as an Economist" *Economic Journal,* vol. 77 (June 1967). On Malthus' relation to Utilitarianism, see Elie Halévy, *The Growth of Philosophical Radicalism* (New York: Augustus Kelley, 1949).

J. J. Spengler examines the relationship between Malthus' theory of population and his theory of aggregate demand with great insight in "Malthus' Total Population Theory: A Restatement and Reappraisal," *Canadian Journal of Economics and Political Science,* vol. 11 (February–May 1945), reprinted in Spengler and Allen, eds., *Essays in Economic Thought: Aristotle to Marshall* (Chicago: Rand McNally & Co., 1960). The relationship between Malthus' wage theory and his argument for retaining the Corn Laws is explored and evaluated by William D. Grampp in "Malthus Money, Wages and Welfare," *American Economic Review,* vol. 46, no. 25 (December 1956), reprinted in Ingrid H. Rima, ed., *Readings in The History of Economic Theory* (New York: Holt, Rinehart and Winston, 1970). An alternative interpretation of Malthus' position is given by J. J. Spengler in "Malthus the Malthusian vs. Malthus the Economist," *Southern Economic Journal,* vol. 24 (July 1957).

6

David Ricardo: Economic Analysis of the Distributive Shares

INTRODUCTION

Life and Times (1772–1823)

THE CLASSICAL TRADITION achieved the apex of its development with the work of David Ricardo. It is remarkable that a person of his background should have made such a distinguished contribution to economics, since he was destined, as a youth, to a business rather than an academic career. His father, a native of Holland, of the Jewish faith, settled in England and eventually became a member of the Stock Exchange. Young David was already in his father's employ at the age of 14, and it was fully expected that this would be his lifework. Indeed, he amassed a fortune in the exchange at such an early age that he had ample time to devote himself to such studies as took his fancy. This was accomplished largely on his own resources, for his marriage to a Quaker and subsequent conversion to Christianity estranged him from his father.

His first acquaintance with the subject to which he was to contribute so importantly was through Smith's *Wealth of Nations,* which came into his hands in 1799.[1] A decade was to elapse, however, before anything bearing Ricardo's name was to appear in print. The subject matter of his contributions clearly reflected the transformation England had undergone in the 40-

---

[1] John R. McCulloch, ed, *The Works of David Ricardo* (London, 1886), pp. xvi-xxxiii, "Life and Writings of Mr. Ricardo."

odd years that had elapsed since the appearance of Smith's great work. Population, in spite of emigration, had increased substantially. Though England was still able to feed herself and even exported some grain as late as 1812 and 1813, the price of bread became a major issue. Nor was industrialization to relieve the problem, for manufacturing processes were also dependent on products of the soil. Moreover, the introduction of machinery created new problems quite unlike those which confront a predominantly agricultural nation.

Ricardo's initial writing was stimulated by the currency question. The English monetary system had, like the rest of the economy, undergone substantial change. In Smith's day, money consisted largely of coin and paper notes, redeemable in gold, issued by the Bank of England and relatively few rural banks. The subsequent growth in the number of rural banks, largely unregulated with respect to their issue of paper currency, led the Bank of England to assume central bank functions. When, however, that bank was forced, toward the end of the Napoleonic wars, to suspend the redemption of its notes in gold, the value of English currency was no longer related to the value of gold. For Ricardo, the rise in the market price of bullion and the fall of the exchange rate which took place was the stimulus to a careful inquiry. His analysis of these phenomena, intended for his own edification, was shown to the editor of the *Morning Chronicle,* who persuaded him to allow its publication in letter form. The response to his observations was sufficiently great to induce him to enlarge upon his subject in a tract entitled *The High Price of Bullion: A Proof of the Depreciation of Bank Notes.* With its publication, Ricardo became an active participant in the famous bullion controversy, one of the major issues of the day.[2] The issue was the cause of the great depreciation of paper money and the associated rise in prices, an upheaval of such proportions that an investigation was undertaken by the Bullion Committee. Ricardo found the cause of these phenomena in the overissue of paper money.

In 1815, Ricardo published his *Essay on the Influence of a Low Price of Corn on the Profits of Stock,* in which he advanced a strong argument for free trade in grain, in opposition to Malthus. In the following year, he made another contribution to the literature on money and banking with his *Proposals for an Economical and Secure Currency with Observations on the Profits of the Bank of England.* The latter essay concerned itself with the value of money; and in it, Ricardo took the position that it is unnecessary for a currency to have intrinsic worth. Rather, what is essential is that the supply of a paper currency be sufficiently limited to maintain its value on a par with the value of gold. He offered a plan for maintaining the value of paper currency on a par with gold without making it convertible into

---

[2] See below, pp. 141–43.

coin in order to save the expense associated with metallic currency. This plan, which was subsequently adopted by the Bank of England, proposed that bank notes be made convertible into bars of gold bullion of a standard weight and purity instead of making them into gold coin. Although the plan was effective in checking the overissue of notes, it was later decided to continue a mixed currency, even though it was more expensive to maintain than one which consisted exclusively of paper, because the pound notes which replaced sovereigns became subject to forgery.[3]

By the time Ricardo published his *Principles of Political Economy and Taxation* in 1817, he had already earned a considerable reputation as a writer on current issues. This interest was ultimately to carry him into the House of Commons. He took his seat in 1819 as a member for Portarlington and exercised considerable influence. His contributions to the literature on current affairs continued. In 1820, he contributed an article to the Supplement of the *Encyclopaedia Britannica* on the "Funding System" and, in 1822, his tract on *Protection to Agriculture,* which, even if he had never written anything else would, in the opinion of his biographer, "have placed him in the first rank of political economists."[4]

Although his style of writing was extremely abstract, there was nothing unrealistic about the issues to which Ricardo addressed himself. Indeed, the problems were many and pressing, and hinged closely on the fact that the country was becoming ever more populous while restrictions on the importation of grain continued. England had long since experienced diminishing returns on land, and yet the landed interests exerted pressure for an increase in protection at a time when its abolition appeared to be called for. It was largely because of the pressure of diminishing returns that Ricardo found himself unable to share Smith's optimism regarding the future well-being of the large mass of the population. Without free importation of corn, he argued, food could not be cheap. Wages, therefore, would necessarily rise, and this would tend to lower profits and impede further accumulation. His analysis was thus oriented to the question of economic progress; but unlike Smith, he regarded progress as being closely associated with the trend of the distributive shares. This was an intensely practical issue which necessarily led Ricardo into the policy question of the Corn Laws. It is important to recognize that Ricardo's analysis, particularly as it relates to the trend of the distributive shares, is presented within the context of an "insulated" economy, that is, an economy which does not import agricultural products. As such, it is specifically oriented to the issue of the Corn Laws and the consequences inherent in their continuance.

---

[3] McCulloch, *Works,* pp. xxii–xxiii.

[4] Ibid., p. xxix.

PRINCIPLES OF POLITICAL ECONOMY AND TAXATION

Introduction

The major part of Ricardo's *Principles* was written in a single year and incorporated many of the ideas which had already been presented in his tracts and pamphlets. It appears to have been undertaken at least partly at the urging of James Mill.[5] The issues to which he addressed himself were pressing, and he could not allow himself a long period for revision and reflection, as did Smith. Partly on this account, and perhaps because of his own lack of academic training, his book suffers from a poor arrangement of subject matter and is generally less than polished. His style is abstract in the extreme and seldom relieved by digressions into history or philosophy of the sort we find in Smith's work. His rigorously deductive method was to set the pattern for much of the subsequent work in the field of political economy. This is not to say that political economy became divorced from philosophy and psychology, but rather that many of the observations which were previously made concerning human behavior and social institutions could now be accepted as postulates on which subsequent analysis could be based. The high degree of abstraction we encounter in Ricardo's work should not, however, blind us to the fact that he was an intensely practical man with wide experience and knowledge of his contemporary world.

THE THEORY OF EXCHANGE VALUE

The Measurement of Exchange Value

Smith, it will be recalled, regarded labor as the only unvarying measure of value. Ricardo disagreed and maintained that the value of labor is no less variable than that of gold or silver or corn. Its value is determined in precisely the same manner as the exchangeable value of any other commodity. There is no commodity which is truly an invariable measure of value. "Of such a measure it is impossible to be possessed, because there is no commodity which is not itself exposed to the same variations as the things the value of which is to be ascertained; that is, there is none which is not subject to require more or less labour for its production."[6] Ricardo, however, recognized that his analysis of price could be greatly facilitated by identifying an invariable measure of value. If this could be accomplished it would make it possible to separate the problem of changes in

---

[5] John Stuart Mill, *Autobiography* (London: 1873), p. 27.

[6] David Ricardo, *Principles of Political Economy and Taxation,* in *The Works and Correspondence of David Ricardo,* 10 vols., Piero Sraffa and Maurice Dobb, eds. (Cambridge, England: The University Press, 1951–55), vol. 1, p. 43–44. Subsequent references are to this edition of Ricardo's work unless otherwise noted.

price due to changes in the value of money from those that reflect changes in exchange value.

In order to accomplish this separation analytically, Ricardo suggests that the production of gold might be viewed as taking place with the aid of a combination of fixed and circulating capital which approximates the average quantity employed in most industries. If this assumption is granted, we may regard money made of gold as an invariable standard of value. It can then be concluded that changes in commodity prices are the result of changes in their exchange values rather than changes in the value of the standard in terms of which prices are being measured. Ricardo's analysis of exchange value, therefore, is premised on the assumption that the value of the monetary unit of account, in terms of which values are expressed, does not change.

Ricardo's assumption of the constancy of the general price level conceives of money as a passive unit of account which facilitates convenient and efficient exchanges, but in no way alters the final relationships which result. While increases or decreases in the money flow will tend to raise or lower all prices and temporarily alter exchange ratios because some money prices move more rapidly than others, these are short-run disturbances. The explanation of value in exchange relationships quite properly assumes such variations to be absent. Thus, when Ricardo refers to price, it is synonymous with exchange value; and unless he specifically refers to "market price," he means "natural price," or the price in terms of embodied labor.

The Source of Exchange Value

Ricardo began his analysis of exchange value by recalling Smith's distinction between value in use and value in exchange. He asserts that for a commodity to have value in exchange, it is essential that it have utility, although utility is not a measure of that value. Having utility, commodities derive their exchangeable value from their scarcity and from the quantity of labor required to obtain them.[7]

Some commodities derive value from their scarcity alone. Such objects as rare pictures, books, coins, and other art objects which no amount of labor can reproduce are in this class. The implication is that when supply cannot be adjusted, demand will rule in the determination of exchange value. The great bulk of commodities are, however, reproducible and therefore derive their value not from scarcity but from the labor requirements of production.

Commodities have past labor as well as present labor embodied in them. Though Smith talked of that early and rude state of society which preceded

---

[7] Ibid., p. 12.

the accumulation of capital, there was never a period in history, Ricardo observed, when capital was nonexistent. "Without some weapon neither the beaver nor the deer could be destroyed; and therefore their value would be regulated not solely by the time and labour necessary for their destruction, but also by the time and labour necessary for providing the hunter's capital, the weapon by the aid of which their destruction was effected."[8] Thus, Ricardo appears to identify capital with labor.

He was of course conceiving of real capital rather than money capital and included within this category, as did Smith, not only such instruments of production as buildings, machines, tools, and equipment but also circulating capital, which is comprised primarily of the wage fund out of which productive workers are supported. The primary role of capital, with Ricardo as with Smith, therefore, is the employment of labor through advances from the wage fund. Consumer goods purchased by workers are part of the real investment of the economy. Their sale merely reimburses the wage advances previously made plus profits. Exchange value, therefore, is proportional to the direct labor involved in production, and that which is "bestowed on the implements, tools, and buildings with which their labor is assisted."[9]

Though Ricardo accepted the principle that the ratio of exchange between goods will reflect their cost of production, including not only the current rate of wages but also the current rate of profits, he has often been regarded as an exponent of the labor theory of value.[10] Actually, he was not particularly concerned with explaining the ratio of exchange between commodities. His primary interest was in explaining *alterations* in exchange values because such variations affect the distributive shares going to laborers, capitalists, and landlords.[11] Ricardo resasoned that *changes* in the rate at which two commodities are exchanged for one another derive from changes in their relative content of past and present labor. This implies that exchange values are not affected by wage rate differences between workers, or by changes in the level of wages and profits, or by the inclusion of rent in the price of a product. Let us proceed with each of these in turn, bearing in mind that Ricardo's theory of value is a labor theory only in a very special sense.

---

[8] Ibid., p. 23.

[9] Ibid., p. 24.

[10] Consult Oswald St. Clair, *A Key to Ricardo* (New York: Kelley and Millman, Inc., 1957), pp. 26–27 and Mark Blaug, *Ricardian Economics* (New Haven: Yale University Press, 1958), pp. 33–37 for a discussion of this issue.

[11] See John M. Cassels, "A Reinterpretation of Ricardo on Value," *Quarterly Journal of Economics,* vol. 49 (May 1935), pp. 518–32, reprinted in I. H. Rima, ed., *Readings in the History of Economic Theory* (New York: Holt, Rinehart and Winston, 1970). See also "Introduction to Ricardo's Works," written by Sraffa, in *Works,* vol. 1, secs. IV–V.

The Influence of Wage and Profit Levels on Exchange Values

Labor is not homogeneous, and different commodities are certain to be produced with different kinds and qualities of labor as well as different quantities. Qualitative differences between labor of the same duration will be reflected, Ricardo maintained, in the wage rates prevailing in the market. But, he argued, these differences will not affect exchange values. If the labor embodied in one commodity is superior in some way, and therefore more highly paid than that embodied in some other commodity, the effect is precisely the same as if a greater quantity of labor had been used.

Nor did Ricardo think that variations in the level of wages would have any influence on exchange values. A change in the wage level will only affect the level of profits. This results because Ricardo, like Smith before him, conceived of wages and profits as varying inversely with each other. Thus the exchange value of two goods remains the same if their labor content does not change. Only the ratio between wages and profits is changed by an alteration in the level of wages and profit.

While there necessarily will be wage rate differences among different kinds of labor, Ricardo believed that capital is sufficiently mobile and the opportunities for its employment are sufficiently competitive to insure a uniform rate of profit throughout the economy in the long run. The prices of all commodities would thus comprise the same percentage of profit on all the capital invested in their production, so that variations in the level of profits are not a source of variations in exchange value. While this principle is later qualified to take cognizance of different proportions of fixed and circulating capital and capitals of unequal durability, it enabled Ricardo to conclude, after also eliminating rent as a determinant of exchange values, that variations in the relative values of commodities are derived from variations in the quantities of labor required to produce them.

The Influence of Land Rent on Exchange Values

Ricardo's initial examination of the phenomenon of rent in the *Principles* is occasioned by the necessity of inquiring whether "the appropriation of land, and the consequent creation of rent, will cause any variation in the relative value of commodities, independently of the quantity of labour necessary to production."[12] He defines rent as the compensation which is paid to the owner of land for the original and indestructible powers of the soil. Such rent is distinct from the return resulting from capital improvements on land or the presence of valuable commodities such as coal, stone,

---

[12] Ricardo, *Principles of Political Economy and Taxation*, vol. 1, p. 67.

or timber. The latter give rise to profits rather than rent, and these are regulated by different factors than those which regulate rents.[13]

When a country is first settled and there is rich and fertile land available in abundance relative to the size of the population to be supported, there will be no rent on any part of the land. Land is, in effect, a free good under such circumstances. It is not until the growth of population and the progress of society require land of a second degree of fertility to be brought under cultivation that rent will emerge on land of the first quality. This rent will depend on the difference in the productive powers of the two pieces of land. With each subsequent need to bring less productive land under cultivation, rent will appear on land which previously yielded none and will increase on those lands which already yield rent.

This principle can be demonstrated by envisioning the application of a given quantity of labor and capital to lands which, because of their fertility and/or situation may be regarded as the best grade. The output which is produced will have an exchange value which reflects the labor and capital embodied in it. The whole price will therefore be absorbed by wages and profit, and the land itself will command no return. If, in consequence of a growing population, it becomes necessary to employ land which is inferior to that first employed, and an equal amount of labor and capital is applied in cultivating it, a smaller output will now be obtained. It costs more to produce the same product on second-grade land. The value in exchange of units of a product so produced is regulated by the same principle which ruled with respect to the output produced on the best grade of land, namely, the labor and capital embodied in its creation. However, there cannot be two rates of exchange for different units of the same product when they are sold in the same purely competitive market. Thus the exchange value of the entire output is regulated by the least favorable production requirements. The exchange value or price of units of a commodity produced under more favorable circumstances is precisely the same as that of units of the same commodity produced under less favorable circumstances. To whom does the difference go, and why? Since only one rate of wages and one rate of profit can prevail, it goes to the owner of superior land in the form of rent. Ricardo therefore concluded that rent is not a cause of the exchangeable value of a product, but the result of it.

Precisely the same result would obtain if additional labor and capital are employed on land already under cultivation instead of bringing in new

---

[13] Ricardo, however, was not always consistent in his use of the term *rent*. For example, he says that the payments to the owner's of mines for permission to work them are for the minerals removed and not for the original and indestructible powers of the soil. He also suggests, in a note at the end of his chapter on poor rates, that a portion of the capital used by landlords may be "amalgamated with the land, and [so] tends to increase its productive powers, [that] the remuneration paid to the landlord for its use is strictly of the nature of rent, and is subject to all the laws of rent."

land. This is the alternative which will be chosen if it will produce a greater product than can be gotten from the cultivation of additional land.

> In such case, capital will be preferably employed on the old land, and will equally create a rent; for rent is always the difference between the produce obtained by the employment of two equal quantities of capital and labour. . . . In this case, as well as in the other, the capital last employed pays no rent.[14]

The payment of rent does not cause an increase in the exchangeable value of raw produce. Exchange value is regulated by the quantity of labor bestowed in production on that land which pays no rent. Thus, says Ricardo, "corn is not high because a rent is paid, but a rent is paid because corn is high, and it has been justly observed that no reduction would take place in the price of corn, although landlords should forego the whole of their rent."[15]

The Ricardian theory of rent lends itself readily to modern terminology and apparatus, for it is in essence a marginal productivity theory.[16] Assume a situation in which a product, say wheat, is produced on four grades of land of equal area. Production proceeds with the application of successive equal doses of labor and capital to these fixed quantities of land. The total and marginal outputs yielded are summarized in Table 6–1. The left-hand portion of the table which relates to total output reflects the tendency toward diminishing returns as additional equal doses of labor and capital are applied to lands A through D, each being progressively less productive than the preceding one. The right-hand portion of the table relates to the additional or *marginal* output associated with the application of additional doses of labor and capital to each grade of land. Strictly speaking, marginal analysis should involve very small increments, whereas the numbers used

TABLE 6–1
Diminishing Returns on Land

Inputs of Labor and Capital	Total Output of Wheat				Marginal Output of Wheat			
	A	*B*	*C*	*D*	*A*	*B*	*C*	*D*
0	0	0	0	0	—	—	—	—
1	400	300	200	100	400	300	200	100
2	600	475	300	—	200	175	100	—
3	750	575	—	—	150	100	—	—
4	850	—	—	—	100	—	—	—

[14] Ricardo, *Principles of Political Economy and Taxation,* vol. 1, pp. 71–72.

[15] Ibid., p. 74–75.

[16] J. B. Clark and Philip H. Wicksteed first appreciated this aspect of Ricardo's theory of rent. See J. B. Clark, "Distribution by a Law of Rent," *Publications of the American Economic Association, Series* 3, IV (1903), pp. 15–65 and P. H. Wicksteed, *Co-ordination of the Laws of Distribution* (1894) (London: London School Reprint No. 12, 1932).

here are quite large, but they suffice to illustrate the relationship between the total and the marginal product.

Table 6–1 enables us to visualize the number of doses of labor and capital which can economically be applied to each grade of land. Assume that each dose of labor and capital costs $100 to employ and that the price of wheat on the market is $1. It is obvious that the output potential of land grade A warrants the application of four doses of labor and capital, whereas land D warrants the application of only one. This is the case because the marginal cost of these inputs is exactly equal to the marginal value product, which is the marginal physical product multiplied by the market price. The market price is equal to the marginal cost of production and, under competitive conditions, is the same to all sellers. On Grade D land the cost of labor and capital absorbs the entire product, whereas lands C, B, and A yield a surplus of $100, $275, and $450, respectively. These amounts go to the landlord as rent; and grade D land, the marginal land, is no-rent land. This is the extensive margin of cultivation, yielding an output whose value is just equal to the labor and capital cost of producing it.

The same principle is applicable to intramarginal land; thus, it pays to cultivate grades A, B, and C intensively until the value of the marginal product produced is just equal to the marginal cost of producing it. Cultivation will therefore continue until the returns at the intensive margin of cultivation are equal to those at the extensive margin. The variable factor, that is, the labor and capital component, receives the value of the marginal product as its return, while the fixed factor, land in this instance, receives the difference between the total revenue and the portion going to labor and capital. This difference is the surplus Ricardo called rent. It is not part of the cost of production in that its elimination (for example, by a tax levied on it) would not affect the size of the product which a given quantity of labor and capital could produce. Only the costs of labor and capital must be met to assure that the output will be forthcoming. Thus, the price must be high enough to cover the labor and capital cost of using marginal land, or its output will not be forthcoming. But a product price equal to the marginal cost of producing on marginal land leaves a surplus on better than marginal land. It is in this sense that rent is determined by price and will increase with every rise in the labor and capital cost of producing output as the extensive margin of cultivation is extended.

Ricardo's Qualification of the Labor Theory of Value

While Ricardo was at great pains to demonstrate that changes in the rate at which two commodities are exchanged for one another derive from changes in their relative content of past and present labor, and are not affected by the rate of wages or profit, his examination of the effect of *different capital structures* actually introduced a modification to this principle. He observed that when the ratio of fixed to circulating capital is increased, or capital of greater durability is employed, it has the effect of increasing the length of time which must elapse before the final products can come to market. Capitalists must therefore be compensated for the greater time lapse by greater profits. It follows that goods produced with equal amounts of fixed capital or capital of greater durability cannot sell at the same price as those produced with more circulating capital or less durable capital, even if the same quantity of direct labor is involved. Thus the effect of different capital structures is to qualify the principle that relative values are proportional to the relative quantities of labor used in production.

The significance of this qualification has been a source of controversy and discussion from the outset. Ricardo himself seemed unclear on the matter. On the one hand, he minimized the importance of the modification and maintained that commodities are valuable in proportion to the quantity of labor bestowed on them.[17] On the other, he seemed to sense that the qualification he proposed brought to the forefront the role of capital in the production process and involved the cost of the capital component. The classic case in which he and his contemporaries came to grips with this problem was their effort to explain why wine has a greater value than grape juice, though no additional labor has been applied.[18] Ricardo eventually concluded that there must be some element other than accumulated labor in capital and that this other element is *waiting*. Thus, he appeared to be on the very brink not only of adopting a more sophisticated concept of capital, but also of giving up the proposition that exchange values are in proportion to the relative quantities of labor.

To appreciate why Ricardo, in fact, did neither of these things, we need only remind ourselves that with respect to the value problem, he was concerned with explaining *changes* in exchange values rather than the ratio of exchange between goods at any moment of time. Furthermore, he was concerned with the value problem only insofar as it affected the determination of the distributive shares. Different capital-labor ratios necessarily mean that a change in the level of money wage rates, and therefore the rate of profit, must have an impact on the price *structure*. Ricardo realized that if the level of wages is rising, it will cause the prices of goods produced with a smaller capital-labor ratio to rise relative to those produced with a greater capital-labor ratio and relative to gold which, it will be recalled, serves Ricardo as an invariable measure of value by virtue of his assumption that it is produced with an average capital-labor ratio.

The price of agricultural products, which are produced by methods that

---

[17] "Letters to J. B. Say," in the *Works* . . . *of David Ricardo,* vol. 9, p. 169.
[18] "Letter to McCulloch," Ibid., p. 330.

are more labor intensive than either gold or manufactural goods, will rise when wages rise. On the other hand, the prices of manufactured goods will fall, for they are produced under capital- rather than labor-intensive conditions. This effect, which subsequently came to be called the Ricardo effect, later became the basis for the inference that a rise in real wages will lengthen the average period of production in the economy because it leads to a substitution of machinery for labor.[19] Since Ricardo assumed that wage goods consist of agricultural products, while manufactured products are the luxuries consumed by capitalists and landlords, he was also able to conclude that though the long-run trend of the economy's total product is up, the share going to labor in real terms will not increase.

DISTRIBUTION

Rent as a Distributive Share

Ricardo's theoretical analysis was directed primarily to the examination of the problem of distribution. His attention was focused on explaining the determination of rent, wages, and profit, and their probable future trend. "To determine the laws which regulate this distribution is the principal problem in Political Economy; much as the science has been improved by the writings of Turgot, Steuart, Smith, Say, Sismondi, and others, they afford very little satisfactory information respecting the natural course of rent, profit and wages."[20]

While his primary emphasis is on rent, it is the trend of the rate of profit which is most significant for economic progress. For high rents do not cause but rather accompany low profits. The latter, in turn, are the result of the high cost of labor, which depends on the cost of producing food at the margin of cultivation. The productivity of labor in the production of non-wage goods is relatively unimportant, in Ricardo's view, to the progress of profit and wealth. The doctrine of land rent is therefore the heart of his whole distribution theory; the explanation of the trend of wages and profits is articulated with the progress of rent.

It has already been seen that Ricardo identified rent as a differential which appears on superior land. Its appearance hinges, first, upon the law of population growth and, second, on the inability of additional applications of labor and capital to presently employed lands to yield anything but decreasing returns. Neither of these principles is, of course, original with Ricardo, but it remained for him to deduce a new theory of rent from them. Although he made some reference to the possibility of improvements

---

[19] See F. A. Hayek, "The Ricardo Effect," *Economica*, vol. 9, 1942, reprinted in F. A. Hayek, *Individualism and the Economic Order* (Chicago: University of Chicago Press, 1948).

[20] David Ricardo, *Principles of Political Economy and Taxation*, vol. 1, Preface.

in agriculture, he nevertheless believed them to be greatly inferior to those attainable in the manufacturing industries and thus concluded that the progressive decline in the fertility of land would necessarily be associated with rising food prices and therefore rising rents. The portion of the annual revenue which goes to the landlord will increase in the normal course of economic development because the exchange value of products produced on the land will increase relative to manufacturing commodities.

The tendency for rent to increase is crucial to the future of both wages and profits, and thus to the generally pessimistic conclusions which are associated with Ricardo's analysis. It is also fundamental to the dichotomy of class interests which emerges so clearly in his thinking and which forms the theoretical basis for his position on the Corn Laws and other questions of policy. For while rent seemed a perfectly legitimate form of income to Malthus, who shared the Physiocratic view that it is a bounty of nature, Ricardo viewed it instead as the outcome of the niggardliness of nature. He regards the absence of rent in a new country in which land is still abundant as proof that this contention is valid. Rent emerges as soon as the pressure of population necessitates resort to inferior lands because there is then an increase in the quantity of labor required to produce raw produce on such lands. The interests of landlords are thus antagonistic to those of every other class in society. For while other classes have an interest in the improvement of production techniques in agriculture and free importation of raw produce, the interests of the landed proprietor are best served by a rapid growth of population and a continuation of the Corn Laws.

The hypothesis that land rent is a differential surplus rather than income produced by labor effort had decidedly antisocial implications, not so much to Ricardo as to some of his contemporaries. James Mill, for example, argued in favor of the confiscation of rent. Ricardo admits the possibility of doing this by means of taxation, for a tax on rent would affect rent only; it would fall wholly on landlords and could not be shifted to any class of consumers.[21] Nevertheless, he appears reluctant thus to burden the owners of property.

Wages

Ricardo's explanation of rents is central to his theory of distribution, for it determines the proportions of the income shares received by labor and capital. The wages of labor may be considered first. What effect is the operation of law of population and the tendency toward diminishing returns, from which Ricardo deduced his law of rent, likely to have on the income that goes to labor? The prospects are far from optimistic. The total amount which is available to be paid out to all who live by wages is the

---

[21] Ibid., p. 235.

equivalent of the wage fund, which is that portion of the supply of real capital consisting of consumer goods customarily bought with wages. At any moment of time, therefore, the wage per worker is determined by the size of the wage fund and the number of workers to be paid. The total amount available in the wage fund cannot be increased except as a result of savings by the capitalist class, and it was implicitly assumed that in the short run, at least, there were unlikely to be any substantial additions. The average real wage per worker in the short run, therefore, is nothing more than the ratio of the wage fund to the labor supply.

It is likely that in the long run, there will be new capital formation and thus additions to the wage fund. But there will also be a continuous growth in population and consequently a persistent tendency for the real-wage income to approximate the subsistence level of the worker and his family. This is the essence of Ricardo's statement that "the natural price of labour is that price which will enable the labourers one with another to subsist and perpetuate their race without increase or diminution."[22] In the short run, the real wage can of course rise above this level, but such a rise would encourage larger families, both by encouraging earlier marriages and more births and by enabling more children to survive to maturity. Conversely, if the level of real wages should fall temporarily below the minimum support level, the resulting decline in the birth rate and higher mortality rate would limit population growth and the labor supply, and therefore facilitate the return of the wage rate to its natural level.

The natural level of wages is the rate which reflects and equals the cost of the subsistence requirements of the worker and his family. It is because real wages are constantly tending toward their natural level that even with increases in the supply of capital and the wage fund, and improvements in the state of the arts, Ricardo foresaw little, if any, long-run improvement in the workers' economic status. Agricultural production lends itself less to scientific improvement than does manufacturing, and advances in the latter do little to make the resort to inferior lands unnecessary. Simultaneously, continuous population growth tends to offset whatever real gains are made.

Money wages will of course tend to rise, for the increasing labor cost of producing raw produce at the margin of cultivation will raise the money price of provisions and therefore the nominal wage the worker must receive in order to support himself and his family. It is even conceivable that a decrease in real wages will be obscured by an increase in money wages—that the worker may be less well-off in terms of goods even though his money wages are rising. The only hope for permanent improvement in the workers' lot is therefore to be found in the restriction of numbers. This is precisely in accord with Malthus' observation, but Ricardo had less faith than Malthus in the check of moral restraint on population growth.

---

[22] Ibid., p. 93.

Profits

It has already been noted that Ricardo believed the rate of profit from different employments of capital would always tend toward equality. But what of the trend of this uniform rate? Ricardo, like Smith, believed that profits and wages always vary inversely with one another. He had already reasoned that the money wage-rate would necessarily rise because of the increasing labor cost of producing food at the margin of cultivation. The future trend of profits therefore is necessarily downward. Profit, it will be recalled, was conceived by Ricardo, as well as by Smith and Malthus, as consisting of the entire net income received by businessmen who own, manage, and generally provide the capital funds for their enterprises. Part of this net income, namely, the return on capital provided by the businessman himself, would be called interest today. Ricardo, however, was less concerned with presenting a functional explanation of profit than with explaining its future trend in relation to economic progress.

The rate of profit depends on the rate of wages; the worker must at least get his subsistence, and the remainder goes to the capitalists in the form of profit. As long as the rate of profit is high enough to enable capitalists to save and invest, the supply of capital, and therefore the wage fund, will increase. This facilitates the support of an increased labor supply. But with the continued growth of population, which necessitates resort to inferior soils, the growth rate of national income will tend to be reduced as the labor cost of producing food and other raw produce increases. The share going to land rent increases, as does the nominal wage rate. Although this serves to reduce profit levels, the worker is no better off in terms of what his money wages will purchase.

Ultimately, profits will fall so low as to discourage all further growth of capital and, consequently, population. This cessation of growth ushers in the "stationary state," in which neither capital nor population experiences further growth. In this state the level of wages is barely adequate to support the population at subsistence levels, while rents absorb the bulk of the national income, and profits are at a minimum. Whether this minimum is equivalent to a zero profit, Ricardo did not say. He did not address himself to the question as to whether some minimum rate of profit is necessary not merely to continued growth, but simply to stimulate the capitalist into continuing to perform his function within the framework of the stationary state. Ricardo's failure in this regard is an aspect of his neglect of the functional nature of profit. We have no answer from him, therefore, as to whether the profit residuum will eventually disappear altogether, or whether its presence in some minimal amount is essential to the continued existence of the system.

The chief adversaries in the Ricardian system are the capitalists and the wage earners, for while the normal trend of rent is upward, high or low rents do not cause either low profits or high wages. High rents are the result of an inexorable law of production according to which the yields of progressively poorer land cause the total output to increase at a diminishing rate. But the division of the remainder between profits and wages is the result of the distribution process. Increases in either share can only be at the expense of the other; and since rising food costs necessitate a progressive increase in money wages, profits are ever pressed downward. But the gain of the worker is in money terms only; real wages tend to remain at subsistence levels as growing population pressure forces the cultivation of progressively poorer land.

The Effect of Machinery

In his last revision of the *Principles,* Ricardo introduced a chapter "On Machinery," which examined the effect on the distributive shares of converting circulating capital into fixed capital. This examination was introduced because he felt it necessary to alter his conclusion concerning the effect which the introduction of machinery would have on the various income shares. He had originally concluded that apart from the inconvenience attendant on shifting labor from one employment to another, the introduction of machinery was beneficial to all classes. Landlords, capitalists, and laborers would, under long-run competitive conditions, all enjoy the advantage of buying commodities produced with the aid of machinery at a lower price. His reexamination of the effect of lengthening of the period of production, however, caused him to alter his view. When a rise in real wages favors capital-intensive rather than labor-intensive production, the effect "is often injurious to the interest of the class of labourers."

To illustrate the basis for the change in his conclusion, he hypothesizes a situation in which a capitalist employs a capital of £20,000 in carrying on a business in which he is jointly a farmer and a manufacturer. Ricardo supposes that £7,000 of the total capital is allocated to fixed capital such as buildings and implements, while the remaining £13,000 is used as circulating capital in the support of labor. The capital is assumed to yield a profit of 10 percent, or £2,000, so that annual gross revenue amounts to £15,000. Thus the capitalist has £2,000 annually for his own consumption and £13,000 for the maintenance of labor in the subsequent year.

If, in the following year, the capitalist employs half his men in producing food and necessaries as usual, and half in producing a machine, he will as usual pay out £13,000 as wages. The composition of his product, however, will be altered, for he will now obtain a machine worth £7,500 and food and necessaries worth £7,500. After deducting £2,000 for his own expenses from the revenue gotten from the sale of the food and necessaries, he will have a circulating capital of only £5,500. Since the wage fund previously amounted to £13,000, the equivalent of £7,500 worth of labor will become redundant as a result of the change in the proportions between fixed and circulating capital. Thus, Ricardo concluded that the introduction of machinery could be harmful to the working class when its introduction is associated with a reduction in the size of the wage fund. This conclusion is subsequently modified by the observation that these undesirable effects need not materialize if machinery is financed out of savings rather than by converting circulating capital into fixed capital.

Ricardo's focus on the problem inherent in the substitution of capital for labor in the short run moves away from the two-factor assumption which characterized his previous analysis. By restricting himself to the substitution of capital for labor along given production functions, his analysis neglects the long-run factors which might mitigate these short-run effects. The analysis does not, for example, consider the effect of unemployment on wage rates, which, if perfect competition is assumed, must be flexible in a downward direction and therefore lead directly or indirectly to the reabsorption of labor. Secondly, while Ricardo realizes that mechanization will increase productive efficiency in the sense of reducing the labor requirements for production, it also means that under competition the total output of goods will increase, and the prices of these goods will fall. Even though money wages decline in consequence of unemployment in a particular case, the real wages of those who are employed may be no lower, and those of workers elsewhere in the economy will certainly be higher. Thus the real value of the wage fund may be maintained even without additional saving because of the effect of machinery on the production of a larger output. In any event, it is clear that the machinery question should not be examined exclusively, as Ricardo did, from the standpoint of its effect on the income shares, but must be integrated into the examination of commodity and factor values. Failing to do this, the whole discussion leaves the impression of being an afterthought which is superimposed on the original analysis. It does, however, reflect the growing concern with the problem of technological unemployment.

Concluding Remarks on the Wage-Fund Doctrine

The preceding discussion of the determination of wages and profits and the way in which they are likely to be affected by the conversion of circulating into fixed capital indicates that the wage-fund theory performed a dual role in that it was used, at one and the same time, as a theory of wages and as a theory of capital. As a theory of capital, it conceived of the capitalists of the economy as setting aside a predetermined portion of their revenue for making advances to labor during the course of the production process. Labor therefore subsists on that part of the economy's real capital which consists of the wage goods it consumes. The sale of labor's output merely replenishes the capital stock which was advanced to the laborers, plus the capitalists' profit. As a theory of wages, it conceived of the average wage rate as being determined by the ratio of the wage fund and the population.

The weakness of applying the wage-fund doctrine to any but a strictly agricultural economy is that production is a continuous process. Output does not typically become periodically available for sale, as is implicitly assumed in the wage-fund model, but flows continuously into inventories at more or less the same rate as inventories are depleted by consumption. The net effect, therefore, is that capital, interpreted as a supply of wage goods, is maintained intact.

Another difficulty of the wage-fund doctrine is that it provides no basis for explaining the proportions in which a business will employ labor and capital. These proportions depend both on the relative marginal cost of using labor and capital and on the value of their marginal products. Without the concepts of marginal cost, productivity, and factor substitution it cannot be explained why the proportions between circulating capital and fixed capital are what they are to begin with, or why the proportions change.

Nevertheless, the wage-fund doctrine enabled the classicists to reach substantially correct conclusions with respect to the possibility of raising the average wage for a given labor force with a given level of technology. They concluded that the average wage rate can rise *only* if the capital stock rises. Today, we recognize that increasing wage rates do indeed require an increase in capital; however, we explain rising wages not in terms of an increasing wage fund but in terms of the increase in the marginal productivity of labor when it is combined with more capital. But whereas marginal productivity theory provides a basis for understanding the proportions in which the factors will be used in production, the wage-fund doctrine does not.

It should, however, be recognized that the wage-fund doctrine was fruitful in another direction, namely, in providing a foundation for the theory of capital. The idea that the wage fund is the source of capitalist advances to the worker ultimately led to the idea that capital bridges the time gap between production and consumption, and that there is a necessary cost inherent in shifting resources from producing goods for immediate consumption as opposed to producing goods whose final products become available only after a lapse of time.

INTERNATIONAL TRADE AND FINANCE

Income Shares and the Corn Laws

Ricardo's interest in and contribution to international trade theory is closely related to his analysis of value and distribution. Specifically, great care was lavished on explaining the inverse relationship between wages and profits, and thus the impossibility of increasing profits except by means of a reduction in wages. Any measure that operates to reduce wages, maintained Ricardo, will simultaneously operate to increase profits.

The extension of foreign trade is precisely such a measure. He is therefore critical of the Corn Laws and, in opposition to his contemporary Malthus, advocates the reduction of protection, especially on agricultural commodities, which are the "wage goods" consumed by the working class. The importation of these commodities rather than those consumed by the rich helps to check the rise in the cost of food and thus in wages and prevents a decline in the rate of profit which is harmful to continued growth. "Foreign trade, then, though highly beneficial to a country . . . has no tendency to raise the profits of stock, unless the commodities imported be of that description on which the wages of labour are expended."[23] It is thus through the effect of free trade in agricultural products on wage rates and profits that Ricardo articulates his views on the Corn Laws with his analysis of value and distribution. The ever present tendency toward diminishing returns from land, which puts constant upward pressure on the labor cost of producing food at the margin of cultivation, is seen as raising money wages and consequently the rent of land. Rising money wages, however, do not make the worker better off, for his corn wage remains at subsistence and at the same time depresses the rate of profit, thereby harming not only the capitalist but also impeding the accumulation of capital upon which the advancement of society depends. It was on these grounds that Ricardo urged that a transition toward freer trade be gradually effected. Only by importing a cheaper food supply could England hope to minimize the dire consequences of diminishing returns. A continuance of protection would simply reinforce the inexorable tendency for money wages and rents to rise and for profits to fall.

Protection for manufactured commodities was considered less of an issue, not only in principle but also as concerns policy. This is because Ricardo regards the rise of manufactured commodity prices above their natural levels as temporary gains that will be eliminated by the inflow of capital into those undertakings, with a consequent reduction of profits. Only the protection of agricultural commodities can exert a permanent influence on profits, and this in a downward direction, because it affects the real cost of labor's subsistence.

Actually, Ricardo did not contemplate so rash a program as complete elimination of agricultural protection. Rather, he argued that duties on raw produce should be made high enough to offset the relatively greater tax burden of the landowning class.[24]

---

[23] Ibid., p. 133.

[24] *Hansard's Parliamentary Debates,* Speeches of May 8, 1820; April 3, 1822; April 29, 1822 (N.S., vols. 6–7).

Comparative Cost

The advantages of free trade had already been taken note of by Adam Smith, who observed that under free-trade conditions a nation will specialize in producing the goods for which it is best suited. While this observation is correct enough as far as it goes, it does not embrace all aspects of geographical specialization. What, for example, if a nation is naturally superior in the production of several commodities, or perhaps even in all commodities? Or conversely, what if a nation does not enjoy any natural superiority? What then determines the area of specialization and which goods will tend to be exported or imported under conditions of free trade? Ricardo's doctrine of comparative advantage was formulated with a view to providing guidance on such questions and is a distinct improvement over 18th-century antimercantilist writings. The latter arguments for free trade generally expressed the advantage to a country of importing those commodities that could either not be produced at home at all or could only be produced at an absolutely greater cost than they could be produced abroad. Adam Smith, at least, did not elaborate the case for free trade any further than this. Ricardo, however, emphasized comparative rather than absolute differences in cost as the basis for specialization and exchange.

His now classic illustration hypothesizes a situation in which the labor of 120 men in England could produce a quantity of wine which could be produced in Portugal by the labor of 80 men, while a quantity of cloth could be produced in England with the labor of 100 men and in Portugal with the labor of 90 men. Portugal thus produces both wine and cloth at a lower labor cost than does England, but she produces wine at a comparatively cheaper cost than she does cloth. Similarly, England produces cloth at a comparatively lower labor cost than wine. Thus, under free-trade conditions, England will specialize in producing cloth and will import wine. That is, the wine-to-cloth ratio in England is 6/5 whereas it is 8/9 in Portugal. England can therefore gain more wine by importing it from Portugal in exchange for cloth than she can by producing wine herself. Precisely the same thing is true in Portugal with respect to cloth. It requires relatively less labor to produce wine in Portugal than to produce cloth.

Ricardo did not indicate how the ratio at which wine and cloth would be exchanged for each other would be determined, but he assumed that the commodities would be exchanged for one another at a ratio of one unit of cloth to one unit of wine. This is close to being midway between their comparative cost ratios, and the gains of trade are almost equally divided at this ratio.[25] This gain manifests itself in the saving of labor made possible by importation. England is saving the equivalent of 20 labor-hours

---

[25] The ratio exactly midway between the comparative cost ratio is one cloth to 47/48 wine.

by importing wine, for it would have cost her 120 labor-hours to acquire wine by producing it at home. Similarly, Portugal, in exchanging one unit of wine for one unit of cloth, will save herself 10 labor-hours by importing cloth instead of relying on domestic production. Both countries will therefore gain from specialization and exchange because England can obtain more wine per labor-hour by importing it than by producing it herself; conversely, Portugal can obtain more cloth per labor-hour by importing it than by producing it herself. The movement of commodities will therefore be advantageous to both countries.

Precisely how the gains from trade will be divided between the participants is not made clear by Ricardo, but the implicit assumption that one unit of wine will be exchanged for one unit of cloth suggests that the terms of trade must lie between 6/5 and 8/9, which is approximately a ratio of one to one. It is not clear how he arrived at this ratio. James Mill and J. R. McCulloch, however, also stated that the benefits from trade would generally tend to be equally divided.[26] Subsequently, it was pointed out that the terms of trade are determined by reciprocal demand, that is, by the relative strength of the demand by the two countries for each other's products. Robert Torrens appears to have been the earliest exponent of this idea, but it was John Stuart Mill who developed this notion in a manner which gained it general acceptance among economists. Discussion of the concept of reciprocal demand will therefore be postponed to the chapter on Mill which follows.

The Ricardian illustration of comparative cost involves a number of implicit assumptions. These assumptions are that trade takes place in two commodities only, and only between two countries; that labor costs are constant and reflect the real or psychic costs of production to labor; that competition is free and there is adequate time for long-run adjustment. It then follows that the supply prices of the two commodities tend to be proportional to the labor costs of production. Credit for formulating the doctrine of comparative cost is sometimes claimed for Torrens, and he was indeed the first to use the term "comparative cost."[27] But it appears that the doctrine was not integrated with other aspects of Torrens' thinking and that major credit for the doctrine and its general acceptance is due to Ricardo.

The International Financial Mechanism

David Hume had already put forward the hypothesis that under a metallic currency system the amount of metal in each geographical area is self-regulating. Ricardo elaborated on this idea, maintaining that the distribution of precious metals among trading countries will be such that

---

[26] John R. McCulloch, *Principles of Political Economy*, 4th ed. (1849), p. 147.

[27] Lionel Robbins, *Robert Torrens and the Evolution of Classical Economics* (New York: St. Martin's Press, 1958), pp. 21–24.

transactions among them will tend to constitute a barter relationship. That is, the balance of payments will have a tendency to be in equilibrium without the necessity of using gold or silver to settle differences.[28] Should this distribution not exist, forces will come into play which will tend to restore equilibrium and bring about a distribution of precious metals which is compatible with it. The operation of these forces involves the international application of the quantity theory of money. Thus, if there is disequilibrium in the balance of payments between two countries, the one with the favorable balance will experience an increase in its exchange rate, while the one with the unfavorable balance will experience a decrease in its exchange rate.

Ricardo maintained that the invariable cause of an unfavorable balance of trade, and therefore of international gold flows, is the relative "redundancy" of currency.[29] The issue of redundancy was central to the bullionist controversy in which Ricardo was an active participant. The events leading up to this controversy may be reviewed briefly.[30] Largely because of the demands for advances made on it by the government starting with the outbreak of the war with France in 1793, the Bank of England found it necessary to suspend specie payments of its notes beginning early in 1797. This suspension initially induced an inward flow of bullion, which eased the strain on the bank and produced a general resurgence of confidence. Subsequently, however, toward the end of 1799, and more particularly from 1809 to the end of the war, the sterling exchange rate fell, and bullion was quoted at a substantial premium over paper. This would of course not have occurred over such a prolonged period of time on a fully convertible international gold or bimetallic standard. Before the suspension of specie payments, England was by law on a bimetallic standard, though the undervaluation of silver at the mint kept her in fact on a gold standard. Gold coin, however, could not legally be melted down, nor could gold bullion be exported.[31] Metallic money was supplemented by Bank of England notes, which circulated largely in the London area, bills of exchange drawn on local banks, and, to a limited extent, bank deposits subject to check.

On a metallic standard, convertibility into either gold or silver of all

---

[28] Ricardo, *Principles of Political Economy and Taxation,* vol. 1, p. 137.

[29] Ibid., vol. 6, pp. 25–26.

[30] N. S. Silberling, "Financial and Monetary Policy of Great Britain during the Napoleonic Wars," *Quarterly Journal of Economics,* vol. 38 (February–May 1924).

[31] There were no dealings in gold coin at a premium over paper, for this would lead to suspicion of intent to violate the law against melting down coins. Full-weight coins, however, tended to pass out of circulation, disappearing into hoards either for export on government account or for illegal export. Ricardo observed that repeal of the law against melting and export would cause gold coin to have the same premium as bullion over paper money. Conversely, if the law against melting and export were strictly enforced, exportable bullion would command a premium over both gold coin and paper money. (See Jacob Viner, *Studies in the Theory of International Trade* [New York: Harper & Bros., 1937], p. 137.)

claims circulating as part of the monetary stock would have prevented more than temporary divergence from par. The situation was such, however, that the sterling exchange was at a marked and prolonged discount, while bullion commanded a premium over paper. At the same time, English prices rose substantially relative to those prevailing abroad. The cause of these relationships constituted the central theoretical issue of the bullion controversy. The issue was whether or not the paper pound was depreciated.

The bullionists, with whom Ricardo aligned himself, took the position that sterling was depreciated. The most impressive rebuttal to his views was made by a Mr. Bonsanquet, a merchant who presented his opinions in his *Practical Observations*. Ricardo subsequently published his *Reply to Mr. Bonsanquet's Practical Observations on the Report of the Bullion Committee,* which is generally regarded as one of the most brilliant essays ever written on a controversial issue in the field of economics. This essay set forth the view that the premium of bullion over paper currency, the relative rise in English prices over those abroad, and the fall of the sterling exchange below par are prima facie evidence of depreciation. He attributed this depreciation to the fact that the quantity of currency was greater than that which it would have been possible to maintain if the principle of convertibility had been adhered to.

The Report of the Bullion Committee called attention to the continued high premium on gold and low foreign exchanges as evidence of the existence of excess currency, and advocated resumption of cash payments at the old par to be undertaken within two years. Ricardo found himself in complete accord with this proposal. He urged that the Bank of England gradually diminish the volume of notes in circulation until the price of gold and silver returned to their Mint par. Unless this was done, he maintained, the foreign exchange would be unfavorable to England, and gold would continue to be exported, while domestic prices would continue high and currency values continue depreciated.

> If the Bank directors had kept the amount of their notes within reasonable bounds; if they had acted up to the principle which they have avowed to have been that which regulated their issues when they were obliged to pay their notes in specie, namely, to limit their notes to that amount which should prevent the excess of the market above the Mint price of gold, we should not have been now exposed to all the evils of a depreciated, and perpetually varying currency.[32]

Thus, Ricardo concluded that if the price of bullion rises above its Mint price by more than the cost of shipping it abroad, this is conclusive proof

---

[32] D. Ricardo, "The High Price of Bullion" in J. R. McCulloch, ed., *The Works of David Ricardo,* p. 287.

of overissue, or redundancy.[33] Such redundancy, as has already been noted above, was regarded by Ricardo as the "invariable" cause of disequilibrium in the balance of trade. He recognized, however, that redundancy can also be produced by "a diminution of goods or by an actual increased quantity of money (or, which is the same thing, by an increased economy in the use of it) in one country; or by an increased quantity of goods or by a diminished amount of money in another."[34] In other words, redundancy can be caused either by forces operating on the supply of goods or by the supply of money.

CONCLUDING REMARKS

Ricardo's primary theoretical concern was the division of the nation's product among the three main social classes in the form of wages, profit, and rent. In his view, the probable long-run tendency of these shares is governed by the cost of producing labor's subsistence. Since he implicitly assumed a given level of agricultural technology as well as a constantly growing population, the tendency toward diminishing returns forced a resort to progressively inferior lands and, consequently, rising food costs. Thus, he regarded freedom to import food products from countries which have a comparative advantage in terms of labor cost as the most effective way of alleviating the upward pressure on food costs which underlies the determination of the income shares in the long run.

It is because Ricardo's main concern was the problem of distribution that he addressed himself primarily to explaining changes in exchange values over a period of time. The price of a good would, he thought, reflect its cost of production, including not only the current rate of wages but also the current rate of profits. Ricardo's value theory can therefore be interpreted as a labor theory only in a very special sense. And even this adherence to the labor theory is limited by his recognition that the relative values of commodities are not governed exclusively by the quantities of labor embodied in them, but depend also on the proportions between fixed and circulating capital and on the durability of capital, because these affect the length of time which elapses before commodities can come to market.

While Ricardo conceived of different capital structures as influencing the time flow of labor-created values to market, as will be seen in the next chapter, Nassau Senior had a far better understanding of the nature of

---

[33] In order to prevent disturbances to the balance of payments arising from excess issue, the bullionists recommended that the note issue be made convertible. The adherents of the currency school, however, contended that convertibility alone is an inadequate safeguard and that what is required is the regulation of note issue in such manner as to correspond to the fluctuations that would have taken place if the currency were purely metallic.

[34] Letter to Malthus, *Works and Correspondence of David Ricardo,* Sraffa and Dobb, eds., vol. 6, pp. 25–26.

capital and its role in the production process, and a broader concept of the cost of production emerged from his analysis. It will also be seen that while John Stuart Mill's restatement of the theory of value was intended to be essentially Ricardian in nature, what he actually produced is quite un-Ricardian. The labor theory of value did not, therefore, survive among those whom we may collectively refer to as the orthodox economists. Rather, it was perpetuated, though with a difference, among the economic heretics, chief among them Karl Marx.

The cost of capital is not the only cost element Ricardo neglected to treat; rent is another such element. Rent in the Ricardian sense applies only to land as a whole because there is no necessary supply price which must be met in order to call forth the supply of land in the aggregate. But once it is recognized that there are competing uses for land and that land can be shifted from one alternative use to another, it follows that it will tend to be used in that alternative in which it is most productive and that it will command a scarcity payment in that alternative, which is just as much a cost factor, and hence a price determinant, as the necessary costs of labor and capital. This type of payment is now known, quite appropriately, as the "transfer price" of the agent. From the point of view of the individual firm hiring a factor, transfer prices are part of the production cost, even though they are a surplus from the point of view of the entire industry or the economy as a whole in the sense that their elimination would not affect the supply of that factor. Only if the services of a factor, say land, are limited to a single alternative is the entire reward considered to be rent from both an individual and a social point of view because its transfer price is then equal to zero. When such rewards accrue to factors other than land, they are known as quasi rents. Such rents are unlikely, however, to exist in the long run because no factor is completely nonreproducible or incapable of alternative uses.

Modern economists have little inclination for a special theory to explain the rent of land. They recognize, in the first place, that land, far from being a free gift of nature, requires the outlay of developmental and maintenance costs, and that there are few, if any, resources available for use without such costs. In this sense, land is not very different from capital goods or even reproducible human labor, even though its supply is less elastic than that of other factors. Furthermore, it is unrealistic to think of land as being used only to produce a particular agricultural product. This is the sense in which Ricardo thought of it. He conceived of land beyond the extensive margin of agricultural use as being left in idleness, whereas a given area of land is likely to have several alternative uses to which it can be put. It will command a scarcity payment in any of these alternatives and will actually be employed in that alternative in which it is most productive. The transfer price associated with this employment is necessarily a cost to the hiring firm and will therefore be price-determining rather than price-determined.

While the explanation of value generally accepted in Ricardo's day was a cost-of-production theory, there were some who argued that utility must not be neglected. Samuel Bailey, in particular, pointed out that the relative nature of value implies that utility is a cause of value and not just a prerequisite, as Ricardo maintained.[35] It is plain from his observation that Ricardo's dictum that reproducible commodities derive their value from the quantity of labor required to make them, rather than scarcity, is untenable. Reproducible goods may be less scarce relative to the demand for them than those which exist permanently in fixed supply, but they are scarce nonetheless. Thus, demand and utility, as well as cost of production and supply, determine exchange values, whether the commodities being exchanged are reproducible or not.

Those who criticized Ricardo for neglecting the demand side of the price problem were, however, unable to show how demand affects price. Jean Baptiste Say, for example, while he emphasized that exchange value is dependent on utility, failed to recognize the relationship between utility and supply. Consequently, he was unable to explain why water, for all its utility, does not command a price. Nassau Senior, although he too emphasized utility as a cause of value, also failed to perceive this relationship. The net result was that criticisms of Ricardo's theory of value on the ground of its failure to recognize the role of utility more specifically came to naught until the marginal revolution of the 1870s.

With respect to its long-term significance, Ricardo's demonstration of the construction and use of rigorous deductive analysis is no doubt a primary contribution. It was he who perfected the technique of abstraction; and this, rather than his substantive conclusions, is the basis for his long-term influence on economic analysis. His doctrine of comparative cost remains, of course, as a substantive contribution to modern principles. The differential theory of rent is significant primarily as a forerunner of the marginal productivity theory of distribution rather than as the basis for explaining distributive shares among the different classes of society. The problem of distribution is handled very differently by neoclassical economists; and even though Alfred Marshall was to revitalize Ricardo's cost-of-production theory of value, he did so with major additions and alterations as will be seen in Chapter 13.

GLOSSARY OF TERMS AND CONCEPTS

Economic (Ricardian) rent. A differential surplus appearing on better than marginal land because of its greater fertility or better location than "no-rent land," which only produces enough to pay for the

---

[35] Samuel Bailey, *A Critical Dissertation on the Nature of Measures and Causes of Values; Chiefly in Reference to the Writings of Mr. Ricardo and His Followers* (London, 1825).

labor and capital employed on it. Rent in this sense is not a cost of production and therefore not price determining.

Principle of comparative advantage.   Under conditions of free trade a region will tend to specialize in the production of those goods in which it has the greatest comparative advantage, in terms of cost, or the least comparative disadvantage.

Ricardo effect.   The lengthening of the average period of production which results when a rise in real wages favors capital-intensive as opposed to labor-intensive production.

Stationary state.   The ultimate state, according to classical theorists, toward which the economy is evolving. It is characterized by a stable population (i.e., the birth rate equals the death rate), a constant stock of capital (i.e., new investment merely replaces depreciated capital), and a constant income per capita.

NOTES FOR FURTHER READING

Ricardo's complete works have been edited by Piero Sraffa and M. H. Dobb in *The Works and Correspondence of David Ricardo,* 10 vols. (Cambridge, Eng.: The University Press, 1951–55.) Mark Blaug's *Ricardian Economics* (New Haven: Yale University Press, 1958) is the most recent comprehensive interpretation of Ricardo's works written after Sraffa's discovery and publication of important additional materials contained in Ricardo's extensive correspondence, especially with James Mill. Some of the differences between Blaug's interpretation and J. J. Hollander's early work, *David Ricardo* (Baltimore: The Johns Hopkins Press, 1910) are traceable to the Sraffa edition of Ricardo's works.

The influence of James Mill on Ricardo has always been a matter of speculation and is among the questions treated by Hollander and Blaug. The general view, which reflects Sraffa's interpretation of the Ricardo-Mill correspondence, is that Mill contributed little more than friendly, though persistent, encouragement. An alternative interpretation is offered in Ingrid H. Rima, "James Mill and Classical Economics: A Reappraisal," *Eastern Economics Journal,* vol. 2, no. 2 (April 1975), and by William O. Theat "James Mill and the Early Development of Comparative Advantage," *History of Political Economy,* vol. 8, no. 2 (Summer 1976). In "James Mill and Ricardian Economics," soon to be published, T. W. Hutchison concurs with those assessments of James Mill's positive influence on Ricardo.

Ricardo's labor theory of value has long been a matter of particular interest. In addition to the interpretation of Blaug and Hollander see especially George Stigler, "Ricardo and the 93% Labor Theory of Value," *American Economic Review,* vol. 48, no. 3 (June 1958) and the reinterpretation by John M. Cassels, "A Reinterpretation of Ricardo on Value," *Quarterly Journal of Economics,* vol. 49 (May 1935), reprinted in Ingrid H. Rima, ed., *Readings in the History of Economic Theory* (New York: Holt, Rinehart and Winston, 1970). This last article relates Ricardo's value theory to his theory of distribution. R. L.

Meek examines the close of Ricardo's system in "Decline of Ricardian Economics in England," *Economica,* vol. 17, no. 65 (February 1950). Ricardo's relationship to Adam Smith is examined with great insight and with particular reference to the theory of value and Ricardo's case against the Corn Laws, by Maurice Dobb, "Ricardo and Adam Smith" in *Essays on Adam Smith,* A. S. Skinner and Thomas Wilson, eds. (London: Clarendon Press, 1975).

7

Nassau Senior and John Stuart Mill: Classicism Comes of Age

INTRODUCTION

WHILE THE CONTRIBUTIONS of Nassau Senior (1790–1864) and John Stuart Mill (1806–73) to economic theory have not secured them a leading place in its history, it would be a serious omission to neglect their work. Mill was undoubtedly a thinker of greater stature and influence than Senior, though Senior's contributions have generally been less appreciated than they deserve.[1]

As the son of James Mill, John Stuart Mill was reared in an intellectual environment consciously designed by his father to train him to carry on the tradition of both Bentham and Ricardo. Mill's *Autobiography* (1861) relates his first introduction to the study of economics at the age of 13 under his father's careful supervision via Ricardo's *Principles of Political Economy and Taxation*. This was followed by an equally intensive study of Adam Smith. Mill subsequently spent a year in France, partly at the home of Jean Baptiste Say, and upon his return to England was assigned the task of preparing marginal notes for his father's *Elements of Political Economy* (1821). He was only 19 when he began contributing articles on economics to the *Westminster Review*. In addition, he had also studied Utilitarian philosophy and became a member of the circle of philosophic radicals. He was not yet 20 when he edited the five volumes of Bentham's *Rationale of Evidence*.

---

[1] See R. A. Seligman, "Some Neglected British Economists," *Economic Journal*, vol. 8 (1903), pp. 335–63; pp. 511–35; reprinted in his *Essays in Economics* (New York: Macmillan, 1925).

Not long afterward, however, Mill experienced a severe mental crisis which he described in his *Autobiography* as a "conviction of sin," the sin being his acceptance of Utilitarianism. Actually, he never rejected Utilitarianism in its entirety, though he became sharply critical of certain features of Bentham's system. Specifically, he rejected the view that human behavior was entirely governed by self-interest, as Bentham implied, and even ventured to suggest that the reason why Bentham attached little importance to sympathy and benevolence as influencing conduct was because he himself was devoid of these characteristics.[2] He also maintained that there are qualitative differences among pleasures and that the estimation of pleasure does not depend on quantity alone. But these criticisms seem to constitute, in the final analysis, a revision or qualification of Benthamism rather than a rejection, for Mill was a hedonist who thought that the morality of behavior is to be judged in terms of its effects on happiness.

Mill attempted to fill the void created by his dissatisfaction with Utilitarianism by reaching out for new ideas to the writings of the English Romanticists, such as Samuel Taylor Coleridge and Thomas Carlyle, and the philosopher Auguste Comte. He was also greatly interested in the views of the utopian socialists. The ideas he derived from these sources created an intellectual dilemma for Mill, for he tried to reconcile them with the earlier and deeply ingrained influences of Benthamism and Ricardianism. Consequently, Mill's standard approach to almost every subject was to begin with a preliminary statement of received doctrine which he subsequently proceeded to qualify and revise until much of the original principle was swept away. While these qualifications stemmed largely from his deep sense of humanitarianism and social purpose, they nevertheless created conflicts which he was unable to resolve. He was, for example, a great champion of individual liberty; the eloquence of his defense of freedom on the basis of its own moral worth made his essay *On Liberty* (1859) a classic in the English language. He was also a great social reformer. But his political theory provided no criterion for judging the circumstances in which a society is justified in placing a limitation on personal freedom. Rather, the case which he made for social legislation is derived from his humanitarian ideals.[3]

His treatment of economics presents a similar problem of consistency. He started with Ricardian principles, but was so much impressed with Comte's objective of creating a complete science of society that he came to view political economy as a study of people, institutions, and customs and not just as the formulation of laws governing production, exchange, and distribution. Thus the aim of his *Principles of Political Economy* was to

---

[2] "Bentham," reprinted in John Stuart Mill, *Dissertations and Discussions,* 3d ed., (1875), vol. 1, p. 353.

[3] George Sabine, *A History of Political Theory,* rev. ed. (New York: Henry Holt & Co., Inc., 1950), pp. 705–15.

provide not only an exposition of Ricardian theory but, more important, to examine the social and political milieu within which Ricardian generalizations work themselves out. Since Mill conceived of these environmental factors as exerting their main influence on the distribution of wealth, the logic of his distinction between pure economics and applied economics was to provide a foundation for a broad program of reform designed to alter the institutions which affect this distribution. This approach enabled Mill to be sympathetic with the dreams of the utopian socialists to establish cooperative communities while he was also the last great exponent of classicism.

Compared with Mill, the details of Nassau Senior's life present a rather colorless picture. He was the son of a vicar, was educated at Oxford, and was admitted to the bar in 1819. He became a member of the Political Economy Club in 1823 and in 1825 became first Drummond Professor of Political Economy at Oxford. He held the post for five years and was appointed for a second time in 1847. During the interim, he was professor of political economy at King's College in London, though he resigned under pressure when he advocated the confiscation of some of the revenues of the Established Church of Ireland for the benefit of Roman Catholics. He also was a member of the commission for administering the Poor Laws and wrote a large number of pamphlets and letters on the Poor Laws and the Factory Acts. The first edition of his *Outline of the Science of Political Economy* was published in 1836 and incorporated his Oxford lectures on that subject.

Though Senior had a wide range of opportunity to concern himself with policy questions in economics, he was particularly concerned to keep this aspect of his inquiries strictly separated from those of a theoretical nature. He believed that this separation was essential to the development of economics as a science, for as long as the science of political economy is associated with controversial issues of public policy, it cannot develop a body of universal truths. Thus, his own discussions of social problems were always undertaken as a moralist or statesman and not as an economist. His efforts to present economics as a body of generalizations deduced from a small number of postulates give him the distinction of being, methodologically speaking, the first of the pure theorists in England.

SENIOR'S CONTRIBUTION TO ECONOMICS

The Four Postulates

While the technique of establishing economic laws by the process of deduction was already well established when Senior published his *Outline of the Science of Political Economy* (1836), he was the first to give explicit statement to the postulates or axioms on which economic theory is constructed.[4] His list is extremely circumscribed in that it includes only four postulates from which economic reasoning is properly to proceed. It is preceded by a definition of wealth as all goods and services which possess utility and are scarce.

The first of Senior's propositions is: "That every person is desirous to obtain, with as little sacrifice as possible, as much as is possible of the articles of wealth." This proposition was, of course, an integral part of economics long before Senior's explicit formulation. The only difference derives from his definition of wealth as including services as well as material goods. While this conception of wealth obscures the difference between the stock of tangible goods and the flow of money income, it has the advantage of facilitating inquiry into the pricing of services as well as goods. It also facilitates more specific attention to the role of demand in the pricing process than was given by Ricardo. Senior was extremely critical of Ricardo's failure to deal more specifically with utility and demand in the pricing process and considered his premise on the nature of human choice as a basis for constructing a theory of value which would take cognizance of utility.

Senior's three remaining propositions are significant for the theory of production and distribution as well as value. His second proposition is as follows: "That the Population of the World, or, in other words the number of persons inhabiting it, is limited only by moral or physical evil, or by a fear of a deficiency of those articles of wealth which the habits of the individuals of each class of its inhabitants lead them to require." Though this proposition is reminiscent of Malthus, Senior did not accept the popular doctrine that population tended to expand more rapidly than the food-producing potential of land. He maintained instead that with the advance of civilization, there is a natural tendency for subsistence to increase in a greater ratio than population. The basis for the difference between his position and Malthus's on this matter is his third proposition, which is stated as follows: "That the powers of labour, and of the other instruments of production which produce wealth, may be indefinitely increased by using their products as the means of further production." This proposition, as will be seen, is also the basis of Senior's theory of capital and interest, which was to broaden significantly the theory of the cost of production by adding abstinence as a separate factor of production. It is fundamental to Senior's conception of increasing returns in manufacturing as the result of the application of additional labor. In contrast, the application of additional labor in agriculture results in diminishing returns. Thus the fourth proposition is: "That agricultural skill remaining the same, additional labor employed on the land within a given district produces in general a

---

[4] Nassau Senior, *Outline of the Science of Political Economy,* 6th ed. (London: George Allen & Unwin, Ltd., 1872), p. 22.

less proportionate return, in other words, that though, with every increase of the labor bestowed, the aggregate return is increased, the increase of the return is not in proportion to the increase of the labor."

Though these four propositions had already been stated by Senior in his lectures, they assumed a new importance in his *Outline of the Science of Political Economy,* published in 1836, apparently because Senior became impressed with the desirability of separating economic science from questions of policy. Although Senior had earlier conceived of economists as dealing with the "art" as well as the science of wealth, he now conceived of it as "the science which treats the nature, the production and the distribution of Wealth."[5] The significance of this definition is that it limited economics exclusively to pure theory in order to make it an exact science based on the four postulates and the definition of wealth noted above. Within this conception of the scope of economics, all questions of policy are part of the science of legislation and are not the concern of the economist.

Capital and Its Return

There are two aspects to Senior's contribution to the theory of capital and its return: first, his explanation of the relationship between capital and what he termed abstinence; second, his explanation of the productivity of waiting. While he is better known for his concept of abstinence than for his explanation of the gain to be derived from roundabout production, the latter concept, although it is not fully developed, is a new idea in English thinking, whereas the desirability of waiting is not. The desirability of waiting was, after all, inherent in Smith's concept of parsimony and in Ricardo's explanation of why the values of commodities produced with more fixed capital or more durable capital deviated from their labor quantity.

What Ricardo did not see is that the use of capital, besides entailing a longer waiting period until the final product matures, is also more productive and that the return on capital is related to the productivity of waiting as well as to the real cost or disutility of waiting. He thus failed to recognize the substance of Senior's third postulate, namely: "That the powers of Labour and other instruments which produce wealth may be indefinitely increased by using their products as means of further production." While it is, of course, not true that the use of intermediate products can indefinitely increase the productivity of labor and natural agents, this proposition gives expression to the idea of roundabout production. The productivity of waiting derives from the greater productivity of the roundabout method and thus provides a basis for explaining the demand for capital.

---

[5] Ibid., p. 1.

The supply of capital depends on abstinence; abstinence expresses "the conduct of a person who either abstains from the unproductive use of what he can command, or designedly prefers the production of remote to that of immediate results." While the second part of this definition implies that abstinence is waiting in the Ricardian sense, the first part implies that revenues are permanently being withdrawn from consumption in order to create intermediate products. It is on this basis that Senior regards abstinence itself rather than the capital goods it creates as a separate factor of production. "By the word abstinence, we wish to express that agent, distinct from labour and the agency of nature, the concurrence of which is necessary to the existence of capital, and which stands in the same relation to profit as labour does to wages."[6] The significance of this statement is that it specifically makes capital a distinct factor of production, the cost of which must be included along with wages as part of the total cost of production. It thus completes the destruction of the view that labor cost is the only cost. Actually, Ricardo himself initiated this destruction when he observed that the values of commodities which are produced with more fixed capital must deviate from their labor value because the producer must be compensated in consequence of the greater lapse of time before his product can come to market.

A weakness of Senior's abstinence theory is the implication that saving is always associated with disutility. Savings by persons in higher income groups may involve little, if any, sacrifice; nor are business savings amenable to explanation in terms of personal sacrifice. Thus the abstinence theory does not provide a satisfactory explanation of the scarcity of capital. Neither does it provide a satisfactory explanation of the interest rate. It is merely a theory of the supply of savings which must be coordinated with a theory of the demand for investment funds. While Senior's conception of the productivity of capital pointed in this direction, the interaction of demand and supply forces was not examined until Alfred Marshall integrated the waiting theory of interest with the productivity theory.

Value and Distribution

Senior's theory of abstinence is significant for his theory of value because it results in a broadening of the concept of cost to include the cost of capital as well as the cost of labor. Moreover, Senior conceived of costs not merely in a money sense but in a real sense, i.e., as payments for the sacrifices incurred in producing goods. Although this conception of cost could have been fruitful in explaining the distributive shares, Senior unfortunately adhered to the wage-fund doctrine and confined himself to an examination of the relative proportions of rent, profit, and wages.

---

[6] Ibid., pp. 58–59.

Senior's inquiry into the value problem also reflects an attempt to introduce utility as a value determinant by insisting that value depends not only on the difficulty of acquiring goods as reflected in their labor and abstinence costs, but also on utility. While he recognized that the utility of additional units of one and the same good diminishes as additional units are acquired, he did not understand the relationship between scarcity and the utility of the marginal unit. Thus the relationship between utility and demand was not explored in a way which sheds much light on price determination. His discussion of monopoly prices is, for example, designed to illustrate that prices will equal costs of production only under competition. But he does not show that utility limits in any way the extent of the deviation.

His analysis of monopoly price does, however, lead in another direction. Because monopoly returns are essentially a surplus, Senior included them in his concept of rent. He also suggested that when a worker receives an "extraordinary" remuneration because of extraordinary natural talents, the surplus may be termed rent. He thus anticipated the generalization of the Ricardian theory of rent which was to be fully developed subsequently by Alfred Marshall in his analysis of quasi rent.

In summary, then, Senior had a number of potentially fruitful ideas. But his most substantive contribution is in the area of capital theory. His analysis in this area led not only to the broadening of the concept of cost of production but also to an abstinence theory of interest.

MILL'S PRINCIPLES OF POLITICAL ECONOMY

The Laws of Production and Distribution

Mill's *Principles of Political Economy* enjoyed a position of unchallenged leadership from the time of its publication in 1848 until the publication of Marshall's treatise in 1890. Mill's object was to modernize *The Wealth of Nations* in the light of "the more extended knowledge and improved ideas of the present age," and to examine economic principles with respect to "their application to social philosophy."[7] The latter objective sets the tone of the book. Mill is less concerned with theoretical analysis for its own sake than with the application of the doctrines of Malthus and Ricardo, in which he had been steeped since childhood, to the solution of the problems of the age. Thus, he is led at the very outset of his work to distinguish between the laws of production and those of distribution. The laws governing the production of wealth are physical truths, whereas "those of Distribution are partly of human institution. . . . But though governments of nations have the power of deciding what institutions shall exist,

---

[7] John Stuart Mill, *Preface, Principles of Political Economy*, W. J. Ashley, ed. (London: Longmans, Green & Co., Inc., 1923).

they cannot arbitrarily determine how those institutions shall work. The conditions on which the power they possess over the distribution of wealth . . . are as much a subject for scientific inquiry as any of the physical laws of nature."[8]

His distinction between the laws of production and the laws of distribution became the vehicle by which Mill reconciled his concern for reform with Malthusian and Ricardian economic principles. The distinction later became unacceptable to neoclassical writers because it implies that the income shares of the factors are independent of the process of production and the determination of exchange values. However, from the standpoint of Mill's reform objectives, the distinction enabled him to tackle questions of social justice on a different basis than questions of productive efficiency.

Production

Book 1 of Mill's *Principles* treats the various aspects of production and begins with the identification of labor and natural agents as the two requisites of production. He perpetuates the distinction between productive and unproductive labor, and defines labor as productive if it results in the creation of wealth.[9] The latter is conceived as the stock of the products of past labor. While nonproductive labor may be as useful or more useful than productive labor, "it does not render the community, and the world at large, richer in material products but poorer by all that is consumed by the labourers while so employed."[10] Similarly, consumption is productive or unproductive if it contributes directly or indirectly to the maintenance of productive labor.

The significance of Mill's distinction between productive and unproductive labor and consumption is that it leads directly to his theory of capital. While labor and natural agents are the primary requisites of production, all but the most primitive operations also require an accumulated stock of the products of past labor. Labor is maintained out of the wage fund, whose size depends on the decision of capitalists to expend their earnings on advances to productive labor rather than in unproductive consumption. Thus, Mill, like Ricardo, maintained that the demand for labor is enhanced by the capitalists' abstinence, for wages represent the advances which capitalists make to workers. From this it follows that "industry is limited by capital," which implies that employment can only be increased by new capital.

This leads Mill to his second fundamental proposition with respect to capital, namely that "capital is the result of saving." It is at this point that

---

[8] Ibid.

[9] Ibid., p. 45.

[10] Ibid., p. 49.

the Smith-Say principle that "saving is spending" is invoked. According to this principle which has come to be known as Say's identity, purchasing power is not destroyed or lost; income not used for consumption expenditures will be used for investment. The essence of this generalization is that it denies the likelihood that money will be hoarded; that is, that it may be desired not only as a medium of exchange, but also as an asset. The role of money as an asset and its significance for the economic process became a major issue of the Keynesian revolution and continues to be a matter of concern to contemporary theorists.

Since the wage fund is part of circulating capital, the Ricardian question of the effect on employment of increasing the ratio of fixed to circulating capital is examined, though, unlike Ricardo, Mill focuses his attention on fixed capital devoted to land. His conclusion, too, is different from Ricardo's, for he concludes that improvements in production are seldom injurious, even temporarily, to the working class in the aggregate.[11] The basis for this conclusion is not, however, the compensation principle, which Mill regards as fallacious, on the ground that a demand for commodities is not a demand for labor.[12] According to his reasoning, employment has been maintained in industries like cotton manufactures and printing not because of machine-engendered cost reductions which facilitate the absorption of displaced labor, but by the accumulation of additional savings which have made possible increases in circulating capital in addition to the increase in fixed capital. He also maintains, however, that if the "sinking or fixing of capital in machinery or useful works were ever to proceed at such a pace as to impair materially the funds for the maintenance of labour, it would be incumbent on legislators to take measures for moderating its rapidity. . . ."[13]

The causes and advantages of large-scale production in achieving increasing returns to scale are also examined by Mill with considerable insight. The test, says Mill, of the relative productive efficiency of large-scale versus small-scale establishments in the same business is the ability to sell more cheaply.[14] However, large-scale production is necessarily accompanied by the existence of large capital in few hands. The result may then be higher than lower prices, for "where competitors are so few, they always end up by agreeing not to compete."[15] Mill therefore suggests that when a firm produces its output under conditions of natural monopoly, it is best to treat it as a public utility.

Though Mill appreciates the possibilities and significance of increasing returns to scale in manufacturing, he is nevertheless a true Ricardian in

---

[11] Ibid., p. 97.

[12] Ibid., pp. 79–90.

[13] Ibid., p. 99.

[14] Ibid., p. 143.

[15] Ibid.

pronouncing the law of diminishing returns to labor in agriculture as "the most significant proposition in political economy. Were the law different, nearly all the phenomena of the production and distribution of wealth would be other than they are."[16] This law operates because a given quantity of land is cultivated in a "given state of agricultural skill and knowledge." Though he agreed with Henry Carey, Ricardo's American critic, that the order of cultivation does not always proceed from the best lands to the poorest, but may proceed from the poorest to the best, he maintained that diminishing returns will ultimately assert itself because land is fixed in quantity. Its impact may be temporarily controlled or offset as man gains control over nature. But, the limited supply of land, along with the deficiency of capital, presents fundamental impediments to continued increases in production without proportionately greater increases in cost of production. Thus, his statement of the principle of diminishing returns emphasizes that, given the state of the arts in agriculture, returns will eventually diminish regardless of the order in which lands are cultivated. Economic progress is therefore dependent on maintaining a rate of technical improvement in agriculture to offset the tendency toward diminishing returns.

Distribution

While the modern reader would expect the subject of exchange value to be treated immediately after production, Mill's examination of the distributive shares precedes his discussion of exchange value. Since he regards these shares as the result of human institutions, he apparently considers their determination as unrelated to the price-making forces that operate in commodity markets. His opening chapter, "On Property," examines the origin of private property and proceeds to an extremely sympathetic discussion of socialism and communism. He observes that if

> the choice were to be made between Communism with all its choices, and the present [1852] state of society with all its suffering and injustices; if the institution of private property necessarily carried with it as a consequence, that the produce of labour should be apportioned as we now see it, almost in an inverse ratio to the labour . . . if this or Communism were the alternative, all the difficulties, great or small of Communism would be but as dust in the balance.[17]

Mill is not, however, prepared to take an unequivocal stand in favor of communism, feeling that we must first consider "the regime of individual property, not as it is, but as it might be made."[18] His zeal as a reformer of the present system is nowhere in greater evidence than in this statement.

---

16 Ibid., p. 177.

17 Ibid., p. 208.

18 Ibid., p. 208.

Mill takes the position that the basic tenet of the institution of property is the right of each person to the "exclusive disposal of what he or she may have produced by their own exertions. . . ."[19] Thus, each is entitled to the product of his labor and his abstinence.[20] When the institution of private property prevails, the division of the produce among the various claimants is determined primarily by competition, though it may be modified by custom. Wages are regulated primarily by competition, that is, by the supply and demand for labor.

Though Mill was subsequently to recant the doctrine of the wages fund, he maintained in his *Principles,* as did Ricardo before him, that there is a fund of predetermined size which is destined to maintain labor in production which sets a limit, or ceiling, on the size of the annual wage flow. He therefore reasoned that the average wage depends on the number of participants in the market and that there is nothing which can be done, either by government or by labor unions, to raise the wages of labor as a whole. The wages of any particular group may of course be raised, but only at the expense of other groups.

The fallacy of this explanation of the average wage rate, as Mill himself was later to recognize, is that the wage flow may be altered by employers and other nonwage groups. If these groups reduce their own consumption expenditure and divert it to giving more employment, neither the wage fund nor the flow of wages is predetermined. It was this line of reasoning which led Mill in 1869 to recant the wage-fund doctrine in an article in the *Fortnightly Review,* and to take the position that it was not inherently impossible for wages to rise to a point at which they absorb not only the funds initially intended for the maintenance of labor, but also funds intended by the capitalist for other businesses and personal expenses.[21] He therefore concluded that even under competition, there are numerous possible wage rates at which the supply of labor can be absorbed. Since the employer generally has greater bargaining power than the individual employee, however, the wage bargain will usually be to the employer's advantage. Labor unions can therefore, within limits, raise the wage rate by reducing the disparity between the relative strength of the parties to the wage bargain. Thus the practical significance to Mill of recognizing the fallacy of the wage-fund doctrine was that it provided him with a theoretical basis for supporting labor combinations.

Mill's discussion of wages is followed by his inquiry into profits, which

---

[19] Ibid., p. 218.

[20] While Mill admits that those who have inherited the savings of others have an advantage, which he believes should be curtailed as much as is consistent with justice to those who left their savings to their descendants, he also points out that laborers share in this advantage (ibid., p. 219).

[21] John Stuart Mill, *Some Unsettled Questions on Political Economy* (London: London School of Economics, 1924), p. 108.

are "according to Mr. Senior's well chosen expression, the remuneration of abstinence."[22] The reward for abstinence is more specifically identified as net profit and interest, for gross profit includes also a return for the risks and superintendence of the "undertaker."[23] Thus, Mill, unlike Senior, specifically recognizes that interest and profit are returns which are associated with the performance of different functions. His explanation of the level of the interest rate leaves much to be desired, however, for it proceeds only in terms of abstinence and the supply price of savings. The demand for savings based on the productive services of capital is not part of Mill's thinking. This is evident in his observation that capital, strictly speaking, has no productive power, but only sets productive labor into motion. Thus, while he adopts Senior's concept of abstinence, he apparently does not appreciate the significance of Senior's third postulate in connection with explaining the rate of interest.

Gross profit will, Mill observes, tend to be equalized under competitive conditions because of the transfer of capital from one employment to another. Extraordinary rates of profit can long prevail only under conditions of monopoly. The rate of profit, says Mill, depends, first, upon the size of the product and, secondly, on the proportion of that produce which is obtained by workers in the form of wages. Thus, he arrives at the Ricardian conclusion that the rate of profits depends on wages or, more specifically, on the cost of labor. This, he insists, and accurately, is an important alteration to Ricardo's wording, for it recognizes that there is a difference between wages and the cost of labor. The cost of labor may be at its highest when wages are at their lowest. Labor may be cheap but inefficient, so that the cost of using it is high. Conversely, though wages may be high, labor may be cheap to use if it is efficient, especially if the cost of the commodities it consumes is cheap, as it is in the United States. In this case, high wages and high profits can coexist.

While Mill's observations that it is not wages per se but the cost of using labor that is important, what is missing in his discussion is the role of capital in improving the efficiency of labor. This lack undoubtedly derives from his conception of capital as consisting primarily of an inventory of wage goods out of which advances are made to workers during the course of the production process. While he subsequently gave up the notion that there is a fixed fund out of which these advances are made, the conclusion that profits and wages vary inversely is conceptually derived from the wage-fund model which was at one and the same time a theory of wages and a theory of capital.

Though Mill emphasized the importance of capital accumulation, he

---

[22] Mill, *Principles of Political Economy,* p. 405.

[23] Mill remarks in a footnote that it is regrettable that the French term *entrepreneur* was not familiar in England.

believed that the rate of profit tended to a minimum level at which there would be zero net savings. The limited supply of land limits the capacity to increase agricultural output, so that wages and rents increasingly encroach upon profits, which, in turn, limit capital formation and population growth. These tendencies become pronounced in the absence of continued improvements in mankind's control over nature and lead eventually to the stationary state. Mill, however, viewed the stationary state as the millennium; unlike Smith and Malthus, he did not conceive of the progressive state, in which life is a continual struggle toward progress as ideal. The best state for human nature, Mill believed, is one

> in which while no one is poor, no one desires to be richer nor has any reason to fear being thrust back by the efforts of others to push themselves forward. . . . There would be as much scope as even [in the stationary state] for all kinds of mental culture, and moral and social progress; as much room for improving the Art of Living, and much more likelihood of its being improved, when minds ceased to be engrossed by the art of getting on.[24]

Exchange Value

Mill's discussion of exchange value, as already observed, is peculiarly placed, for the matter of factor-price determination had already been dealt with in Book 2 before the problem of exchange value is finally examined in Book 3. Mill begins by classifying goods into three categories: (1) commodities which are absolutely limited in supply, (2) commodities whose supply can be indefinitely increased at a constant cost, and (3) commodities whose supply can be indefinitely increased but not without an increase in cost.

The significance of this classification is that it leads to an explanation of price which recognizes the relative influence of demand and supply forces in determining price under different circumstances. Thus, in the case of perfectly inelastic supply, demand is relatively more important; while in the case of perfectly elastic supply, supply and the cost of production are relatively more important. Since the supply of commodities in the third class can be augmented only under conditions of increasing cost, their value is governed by the cost of producing them under the least favorable circumstances. While he does not draw demand and supply curves, his discussion leaves no doubt that he conceives of demand and supply in the schedule sense, that is, as a function of price. Hence, he recognizes that the equilibrium price is the price which equates demand and supply. This is a novel conception in English economics and one on which Alfred Marshall was to build in an important way, though Mill, ironically enough, re-

---

[24] Ibid., pp. 748–49, 751.

marked: "Happily, there is nothing in the laws of value which remains for the present [1848] or any future writer to clear up; the theory of the subject is complete."[25]

Though Mill was aware of the law of demand and supply, he nevertheless followed Ricardo in conceiving of short-run prices as being governed by demand and supply, and long-run prices as being determined by costs. Indeed, he categorically states that value depends almost entirely on the quantity of labor required to produce goods, though he includes in the cost of production the cost of conveyance to market. Neither variations in wages nor variations in profits have any effect on value. Nor does rent enter into the cost of production unless the factor in question has a scarcity value, because of the possibility of alternative employment. The latter qualification to Ricardo's rent doctrine is of course important, for land is seldom without alternative uses, though Mill did not develop the significance of this point.

The labor theory of value is, however, qualified by Mill under conditions of joint supply, for when a given production process yields two or more products in fixed proportions, it is impossible to allocate costs on any but an arbitrary basis. The greater the demand for a joint product, the larger the proportion of the total cost which will be covered by the price of the product. Demand and supply conditions for each of the products will establish the price at which the market will be cleared of both, and the sum of the prices established will equal their joint costs of production. This analysis is one of Mill's original contributions to economic theory.[26]

Comparative Cost and Reciprocal Demand

Mill's exposition of the principle of comparative advantage proceeded in terms of the comparative effectiveness of labor rather than the comparative cost of labor. Ricardo, it will be recalled, took as given the output of each commodity in two countries and assumed their respective labor costs to be different. Mill, however, assumed a given input of labor in each of the two countries, so that the comparative efficiency of labor in production is reflected in differing outputs. The product in which a country has the greatest comparative advantage, or the least comparative disadvantage, can then be determined in terms of the comparative efficiency of labor in producing the outputs in question. The barter terms of trade, that is, the rate at which the product of one country will be exchanged for that of a second country, depends on the state of reciprocal demand, and it is the latter principle which explains how the gains from trade will be divided.

---

[25] Ibid., p. 436.

[26] G. J. Stigler, "Originality in Scientific Progress," *Economica,* vol. 22 (November 1955), pp. 296–99.

Ricardo, it will be recalled, simply assumed that the gains from trade will be equally divided.

The nature of the principle of reciprocal demand and the way in which it supplements the principle of comparative cost may be explained in terms of a simple example which is summarized in Table 7–1. Assume two countries, X and Y, which have different capabilities in terms of the labor cost of producing commodities A and B. Assume that in country X, 10 labor-hours, costing $2.00 per hour, can produce 100 units of commodity A at an average cost of 20 cents per unit, or 400 units of commodity B at an average cost per unit of 5 cents. In the absence of trade, both goods would be produced, and their domestic exchange ratio based on labor cost would be $A = 4B$. Assume also that in country Y, 10 labor-hours can produce 80 units of A at an average cost of 25 cents, or 40 units of B at an average cost of 50 cents. If both goods are produced, the domestic exchange ratio between A and B in country Y will be $A = B/2$.

If there is freedom to trade commodities A and B internationally, each country will specialize in producing that commodity which it can produce most efficiently. In the example given, country X can produce both commodities at an absolutely lower real-labor cost, but it enjoys a comparative advantage in the production of B. Country Y is at a disadvantage in the production of both commodities, but it has the smallest disadvantage in the production of A. Thus, there is a basis for specialization and trade.

Each country will be willing to trade its specialty for that of another country at any ratio of exchange which improves on that which would obtain if both goods were produced domestically. Thus, country X will trade B for A at any ratio which is better than $A = 4B$; for example, $A = 3B, A = 2B, A = B/2$. The fact that country Y can produce the commodities at a ratio of $A = B/2$, however, sets a limit to the exchange ratio, for if it is necessary to export more than one unit of A to acquire one-half unit of B by trade, Y will be as well off to produce B domestically. Similarly, country Y will be willing to trade at any ratio which is better than $A = B/2$. But again, the limit to the barter terms of trade is imposed by the ratio of the domestic costs of A and B in the exporting country. Thus the barter terms of trade in this example must necessarily be between $A = 4B$ and $A = B/2$.

The actual barter terms of trade depend, according to Mill's doctrine of

TABLE 7–1
The Labor Costs of Two Commodities in Two Countries

		Country X		Country Y	
Input of Labor	*Total Labor Cost*	*Output*	*Average Cost per Unit*	*Output*	*Average Cost per Unit*
10 hours to A	$20	100	$0.20	80	$0.25
10 hours to B	20	400	0.05	40	0.50

reciprocal demand, on the relative strength of the demands which the two countries have for each other's products. In Mill's own words: "It may be considered therefore, as established, that when two countries trade together in two commodities, the exchange value of these commodities relatively to each other will adjust itself to the inclinations and circumstances of the consumers on both sides, in such manner that the quantities required by each country, of the articles which it imports from its neighbor, shall be exactly sufficient to pay for one another."[27] It does not follow, however, that the gains from trade will be equally divided. If, for example, country X has a relatively greater demand for commodity A than country Y has for commodity B, the actual rate of barter exchange would favor country Y. That is, Y would be acquiring commodity B by exchanging it for A at a relatively greater saving in terms of labor than that which is enjoyed by country X in importing A from country Y. This idea is expanded by recognizing that the benefit of cost-reducing improvements in the production of a good which is exported may be enjoyed entirely by the importing country if its demand for the product increases proportionately with the reduction in price. Mill thus demonstrates his appreciation of what is today called the price elasticity of demand. Mill also recognized that the benefits from trade are reduced by increases in transportation costs and that transportation costs may make it uneconomical to trade certain goods regardless of their production costs.

SOME CONCLUDING COMMENTS ON MILL AND THE CLASSICAL SYSTEM

Mill and Ricardianism

Though John Stuart Mill examined a number of theoretical issues with genuine originality, the essentials of his theoretical inquiries, particularly as they relate to the determination of factor prices and their long-run trends, represent a refinement of Ricardo's principles. The critical element is the labor cost of producing wage goods which are, in the main, the products of agriculture. While technical progress operates to reduce these costs, Mill believed the law of diminishing returns to scale is the most important principle of political economy because of the limited supply of land. His conclusion with respect to the long-run trend of the income shares is therefore necessarily Ricardian, though his conception of the opportunity for social and moral progress in the stationary state injects an optimistic tone which is conspicuously absent in Ricardo's analysis.

Mill's treatment of value includes a correct statement of the law of demand and supply, and the idea of price as representing the equilibration

---

[27] Ibid., p. 587.

of demand and supply conceived of in a schedule sense. However, like Ricardo, he apparently thought of supply and demand as determining short-run prices, while costs determine long-run prices. Alfred Marshall was later to maintain that the same principle rules in both cases, though demand is relatively less important in the long run because of the elasticity of supply. Thus the role of demand never achieves the importance of Mill's analysis that it does in the analysis of subsequent writers on the value problem such as William Stanley Jevons and Alfred Marshall. The notable exception is in his analysis of the barter terms of trade, which he explains with the aid of a distinctly new concept; reciprocal demand. The role of demand is also recognized in his explanation of the prices of commodities produced under conditions of true joint supply. Neither of these problems had been dealt with by Ricardo, and Mill's treatment is both original and correct. Indeed, Mill's theoretical analysis seems at its best when he ventures into areas which Ricardo had not previously dealt. Elsewhere, Ricardian principles seemed to impose a constraint that stifled originality, though Mill's interest in reform proposals rather than pure theory is undoubtedly another reason why so much of his theoretical analysis emerged as a restatement, though a very refined one, of Ricardo's doctrines.

Economic reform is Mill's essential objective. While he believed that individual and social interests are generally compatible with each other within the framework of a competitive economy, there are numerous exceptions to the laissez-faire principles he recommended. These include taxation of the unearned increment on land, control of the rate at which technological changes are introduced, and social control of natural monopolies. He also emphasized the necessity of worker education, particularly with respect to the importance of controlling their numbers, and favorably regarded labor combinations as contributing to the improvement of the position of the working class.

These reforms, clearly premised on the principle of the greatest good for the greatest number, were conceived of as necessary improvements in the system of individual property which functions within the framework of man-made, and therefore alterable, institutions. Thus, his distinction between the laws of production and exchange and the laws of distribution enabled Mill to go beyond pure theory while at the same time adhering to the "immortal principles" of Ricardo. From the standpoint of doctrine, therefore, the work of Ricardo virtually completed the architecture of classical political economy, though Mill gave the doctrine its most refined statement. This system remained substantially intact, commanding respect and attention throughout most of the 19th century, though it encountered criticisms and reactions on several fronts. Except for the efforts of Karl Marx to construct an alternative system on classical foundations, however, no new system of economic analysis was to emerge until that of the marginal utility economists in the latter part of the 19th century.

GLOSSARY OF TERMS AND CONCEPTS

Abstinence. Postponement of consumption in order to facilitate the production of "intermediate" (i.e., capital) goods. In Senior's view this act is rewarded by profit.

Barter terms of trade. The ratio (in physical terms) at which two goods exchange in international exchange.

Joint supply. A production process which yields two or more products. If these are produced in fixed supply, production costs must be arbitrarily allocated and cost of production is not the determinant of price.

Reciprocal demand. The relative urgency of demand which trading partners have for one another's goods. This concept was introduced by J. S. Mill to explain how the benefits from trade would be shared. Unlike Ricardo, Mill did not assume they would be shared equally.

NOTES FOR FURTHER READING

Senior's contribution is carefully examined in Marion Bowley, *Nassau Senior and Classical Political Economy* (New York: Augustus Kelley, 1949). Senior's *Outline of the Science of Political Economy,* 6th ed., is available as a reprint (New York: Augustus Kelley, 1951).

Mill's *Principles of Political Economy* is included as vols. 2 and 3 in *Collected Works of John Stuart Mill* (1965) with an introduction by V. W. Bladen and much of Mill's correspondence on topics related to the work. There is no better introduction to Mill's life than his own *Autobiography* (London: Oxford University Press, 1924). His modern biographer is M. St. J. Packe, whose *Life of John Stuart Mill* (New York: Macmillan, 1954) examines his political and philosophical ideas in addition to those on economics. On Mill's philosophical background there is no better analysis than Jacob Viner's "Bentham and J. S. Mill: the Utilitarian Background," *American Economic Review,* vol. 39, no. 2 (March 1949), reprinted in Viner's *The Long View and The Short* (Chicago: Free Press, 1958).

Since Mill's most highly regarded contribution to economics is in the field of international trade, the review by F. Y. Edgeworth, "The Theory of International Values" *Economic Journal,* 1894, reprinted in *Papers Relating to Political Economy,* vol. 2 (New York: Macmillan, 1925) pp. 20–25 is particularly valuable. This area of Mill's work is also summarized by Jacob Viner in *Studies in the Theory of International Trade* (New York: Harper and Bros., 1937). Mill's "terms of trade arguments" are more recently reviewed by Harry Johnson in, "Optimum Tariffs and Retaliation," *Review of Economic Studies,* vol. 21, no. 2 (1953–1954), pp. 142–53.

On the controversial issue of Mill's adherence to the wage-fund doctrine see A. C. Pigou, "Mill and Wage Fund," *The Economic Journal,* vol. 57, 1949, reprinted in Ingrid H. Rima, ed., *Readings in the History of Economic Theory*

(New York: Holt, Rinehart and Winston, 1970); see also William Breit, "The Wage Fund Controversy: A Diagrammatic Exposition," and his longer "The Wage Fund Controversy Revisited," *The Canadian Journal of Economics,* vol. 53, no. 4 (November 1967) also reprinted in Ingrid H. Rima, ed., *Readings in the History of Economic Theory* (New York: Holt, Rinehart and Winston, 1970). Scott Gordon adds further interpretation in "The Wage-Fund Controversy: The Second Round," *History of Political Economy,* vol. 5 (Spring 1973), pp. 14–35.

After Mill's recantation of the wage-fund doctrine, J. E. Cairnes made an attempt to rehabilitate it in *Some Leading Principles of Political Economy Newly Expounded* (London: 1874). There was considerable correspondence between Mill and Cairnes on many topics including the wage fund. Some of this is presented in G. O'Brien, "J. S. Mill and J. E. Cairnes" *Economica,* (November 1943).

In light of the usual assessment of Mill as lacking in originality, George Stigler's "The Nature and Role of Originality in Scientific Progress," *Economica,* vol. 22 (November 1955), pp. 296–99 is particularly relevant. The present relevance of Mill's social philosophy is examined with great insight by Pedro Schwartz, *The New Political Economy of John Stuart Mill* (Durham, N.C.; The Duke University Press, 1973).

Senior and Mill were by no means the only able economists during the period. Robert Torrens is remembered for his "terms of trade" argument in favor of tariffs. His views are examined in a full-length study by Lionel Robbins in *Robert Torrens and the Evolution of Classical Economics* (New York: St. Martins Press, Inc., 1958) which also examines his participation in the currency controversy. The work of John Elliot Cairnes, who attempted to revive the wage fund doctrine and to argue for classical principles in *Some Leading Principles of Political Economy Newly Expounded* (1874), is also noteworthy.

8

Classical Theory in Review

Scope and Method

IN THE FIRST HALF of the 18th century, France and not England had a school of theoretical economists; the Physiocrats conceived of political economy as the science which sought the laws governing the distribution of wealth. Adam Smith, on the other hand, made virtually no attempt to distinguish between economics as a science and economics as a branch of politics. It was Smith's French disciple, Jean Baptiste Say, who concentrated on the use of the deductive method to derive the laws which govern the production, distribution, and consumption of wealth. His method, as well as his logical arrangement of the subject matter of economics, has become classical. It was probably introduced into England through James Mill, who studied the work of the Physiocrats and was also well acquainted with Say.[1] Mill taught the deductive method to David Ricardo, whose work became the prototype for a school of thinkers who sought to discover universal laws of production, exchange, and distribution by reasoning from premises which were accepted a priori, or which had been previously arrived at by deduction.

This tradition continued with the contributions of Nassau Senior, John Stuart Mill, John Elliott Cairnes, and J. R. McCulloch. All of these thinkers elaborated and refined in some way the economic principles and methodological tools introduced by the Physiocrats, Smith, and Say, while at the same time avoiding their use to forge a rival system of thought. The

---

[1] Elie Halévy, *The Growth of Philosophical Radicalism* (New York: Augustus Kelley, 1949), pp. 266–82.

use of the term *classical* in connection with their work is therefore intended to convey the virtually universal acceptance of their methodology and economic principles up to about 1870, and to distinguish their work from that of the various dissenting schools which made their appearance coincidentally or shortly afterward, not only in England but to a greater extent on the Continent.

While the product of their efforts was more rigorous than *The Wealth of Nations,* it also had less popular appeal. Nevertheless, the classicists believed that their laws were a scientifically arrived at and universally applicable body of principles which depicted the operation of the economic system regardless of time, place, or existing institutions. Institutions were regarded as being largely an expression of simple and universal laws of human behavior and therefore irrelevant to the functioning of specific societies. This is consistent with the associationist and hedonistic psychology on which Jeremy Bentham constructed Utilitarianism, even though the laws of classical economics do not themselves rest on utilitarian foundations.

The conception of economics as a science which seeks to discover the laws governing the production, exchange, and distribution of wealth, restricted the scope of inquiry more narrowly than that of Adam Smith in *The Wealth of Nations.* Smith was concerned with policy quite as much as he was with analysis. But later members of the classical school generally took the position that for economics to be a science, it must restrict itself to analyzing the functioning of the economy and not intrude into the realm of policy making, where value judgments necessarily come into play and inject a bias.

Economists have attempted ever since, at least in principle, to preserve the distinction between pure economics and applied economics. The former seeks only to establish laws, while the latter is normative and seeks to alter the results which emanate from economic laws. Thus the classicists conceived of production and exchange as being governed by immutable laws whose operation they sought to discover. Distribution, on the other hand, has some laws which are not of man's creation which political economy seeks to discover, but it is primarily the result of human institutions. The classicists, therefore, conceived of the laws of distribution as being alterable by human intervention and for this reason different from the laws of production and exchange. This distinction became particularly important in the writings of later classicists such as John Stuart Mill.

The Laws of Classical Economics

The generalizations or "laws" deduced by classical economists all relate in some way to their central theme of economic growth and the tendency toward an ultimate stationary state. Philosophically speaking, most post-

Smithian economists were of Utilitarian persuasion. But their economic analysis was more specifically predicated on the Smithian conception of the psychology of individual behavior which emphasizes the natural inclination of people to maximize their personal gains, including those which come to them in monetary form, if they are free to do so. This does not imply that people's only interests are pecuniary, but rather that pecuniary interests have been singled out for special consideration. Thus the classicists envisaged businessmen as seeking to decrease costs to maximize profits and minimize losses, while workers seek to increase wages and work fewer hours, and landlords and moneylenders seek to maximize rent and interest. This view of human behavior owes nothing to Utilitarianism, though it is compatible with it. Smith conceived of individuals as acting in precisely the same way, though he derived his conception of human behavior from the philosophy of the natural order rather than hedonistic psychology.

Bearing in mind the philosophical and psychological foundations of classical economics and the limitations of lists, the laws of classical economics may be conveniently collected in summary form as follows: (1) the law of value, (2) the quantity theory of money, (3) the law of comparative advantage, (4) the law of diminishing returns, (5) the law of population, (6) the law of wages, (7) the law of capital accumulation, (8) the law of rent and (9) the law of markets. These laws were regarded as irrevocable but, in the hands of later classical writers, were not viewed as preordained for the benefit of mankind. They were thought to operate in the same impersonal way as physical laws and, unlike the laws of Physiocrats and Smith, are neither good nor bad, moral nor immoral, in and of themselves. Naturally, not all who are collectively referred to as classical economists dealt exhaustively with each of these laws or accepted all of them without modification.

The independence of classical economics from Utilitarianism is particularly evident in their emphasis on cost of production in the determination of value in exchange. Even though Smith and his followers explained the oscillations of market price around natural price in terms of demand and supply, they had little understanding of the relationship between utility and demand. Otherwise Bentham's felicific calculus might have added a new dimension to post-Smithian economics by leading to a greater appreciation of utility, if not to a utility theory of value. This, in turn, could have led to an understanding of the conditions of maximum consumer satisfaction and optimum resource allocation. Bentham did, after all, perceive the principle of diminishing marginal utility, which was later to figure so importantly in the thinking of the marginal utility theorists, when he observed that while happiness is associated with the possession of wealth, each addition to an individual's wealth will not produce a corresponding increase in his happiness. On the contrary, "the quantity of happiness produced by a particle of wealth, each particle being of the same magnitude, will be less and less at every particle. The second will produce less than the first, the third less than the second and so on."[2] This observation, however, did not lead him to a utility theory of value. The fact that his felicific calculus was nothing more than a table or list of the various sources of human pleasure is probably a major reason why it did not serve as a fruitful beginning for a utility-oriented theory of value. The development of this sort of theory took place only after it was perceived that a mathematical calculus, which proceeds in terms of balancing infinitely small increments of utility and disutility, is needed to define the conditions under which consumer satisfactions are maximized.

Conceivably, the orientation of economic analysis to explaining the behavior of businessmen rather than consumers is another reason why the role of utility was so generally underemphasized by the classicists. While it was shown that the competitive market will lead to an optimum allocation of resources among different industries, the effectiveness of this process was interpreted in the light of monetary gains for the businessman, rather than the maximization of consumers' satisfaction. Thus the classicists chose to develop Smith's labor cost theory of value instead of developing a value theory premised on a theory of consumer behavior. Only Say and Senior gave utility a significant role by maintaining that prices are proportional to utilities, but their failure to recognize that it is the utility of the marginal unit that is important prevented them from developing a utility-oriented theory of value. Not until the advent of the marginal utility school in the 1870s was the economic problem to be conceived of primarily in terms of the relationship between maximum consumer satisfaction and the allocation of resources among alternative uses. Thus, Utilitarianism did not influence the classical theory of value because it did not lead to an examination of the relationship between utility and demand.

The classical explanation of exchange value is, in essence, a cost of production theory. It was recognized, after Smith, that commodities must have utility in order to have value in exchange, but difficulty of attainment was conceived to be the essential determinant of value. Commodities have values which are commensurate with their labor and capital costs and command prices which tend, over time, to reflect production costs including the current rate of wages and profits if competition is free.

What is the classical view of the relationship between individual commodity prices and the general price level? The answer to this question requires that we recall their explanation of the general price level and the role of money. The mature classical formulation of the quantity theory recognized what has already been identified as the Cantillon effect. Mill was aware that an increase in the quantity of money would alter relative prices if the proportions in which different commodities are demanded

---

[2] W. Stark, ed., *Jeremy Bentham's Economic Writings* (London: George Allen and Unwin Ltd., 1954), vol. 3, p. 441.

became altered as a result of the increase. But if the extra cash is distributed "neutrally," a change in the quantity of money will only alter the general price level. Even the mature classicists, like Mill, reasoned that this is usually the case. Thus their approach was to analytically dichotomize the pricing process in that they examined the determination of individual commodity prices as though the process was quite unrelated to the determinants of the general price level.

The classicists conceived of international trade as being governed by the same laws which govern individual exchange. Like individual exchange, international exchange yields a gain to both participants. If there is freedom to buy in the cheapest market, the tendency will be to buy from abroad those commodities which would impose the greatest costs if produced domestically. The value of a commodity imported from abroad depends on the cost of producing the commodity exported in exchange for it. This is the essence of Ricardo's famous law of comparative cost, which was further elaborated by John Stuart Mill.

The law of diminishing returns holds an especially prominent place in classical thinking. It expresses the relationship between a constant factor, land, and a variable factor, labor, in the production process and leads to the conclusion that there is a limit to the practicality of using additional doses of labor with a given quantity of natural resources. The law of diminishing returns, together with the law of population, according to which population will tend to increase directly with and to the limits of subsistence, led to the classical theory of economic development, which conceived of the tendency toward the stationary state as the irrevocable final stage. It also provided the basis for the pessimistic bent of English economics after Smith. Concern with the pressure which a growing population would put on the food supply led even such an ardent champion of freedom as John Stuart Mill to consider the desirability of restricting liberty in order to reduce the birth rate.

The law of wages conceived of the wage rate as being dependent on the relationship between the number of workers seeking employment and the size of the wage fund available. The wage fund consisted of previously produced wage goods, principally food products, which are advanced to workers during the production process, and was therefore identified with the real capital fund of society. The concept of the wage fund thus provided the basis for the development of an abstinence theory in which interest is conceived as a reward to those who made present goods available. It also leads to the classical notion that the rate of capital accumulation depends on the willingness of capitalists to curtail unproductive consumption in favor of the productive employment of labor. The only practical mode of raising the level of wages was therefore thought to be encouraging the accumulation of capital or discouraging population growth, or both.

The law of rent emerges because the tendency toward diminishing returns forces a resort to the inferior margin of cultivation, and competition causes price to equal the cost of producing a product on the least productive land in cultivation. A differential surplus, namely, rent, will therefore make its appearance on superior grades of land. This principle is primarily associated with Thomas Malthus and David Ricardo, and was later elaborated by Nassau Senior and John Stuart Mill.

Finally, the classical economists, with the notable exception of Malthus, accepted the proposition known as Say's law of markets, that there cannot be a general glut or overproduction of all goods. According to this proposition, which was introduced into English political economy by James Mill, specific individual goods may be produced in excess of the demand for them, with the consequence that other specific goods are produced in smaller quantity than dictated by demand. But such an occurrence with respect to all goods was regarded as an impossibility because every act of production creates not only goods but also the purchasing power with which to take them off the market. Although it was recognized that income is saved as well as spent, it was further reasoned that savings cannot create a deficiency of aggregate effective demand because the capital which results from savings is also consumed as wage advances are made during the course of the production process. It was on these grounds that the classical economists extended the identity known as Say's law to arrive at the conclusion that a glut of capital is impossible.

Say's work has not been examined separately because only his concept of the law of markets was incorporated into the principles of classical economics. It is worth noting, however, that Say developed other concepts which were subsequently adopted. Specifically, Say, unlike the classicists, accorded a unique role to the entrepreneur who organizes and manages production. He also recognized that factor values, and therefore distribution shares, reflect factor contributions to production. This treatment of the relationship between production and distribution was considerably in advance of the thinking of the English classicists, who treated distribution simply as the sharing of income among the social classes instead of as functional rewards. He also recognized the role of utility as a determinant of value, although he did not have a concept of the margin. But he was in many ways in advance of English writers, and it is unfortunate that the barrier of language prevented Say's work from being more widely studied than was apparently the case.

Classicism as a Theory of Economic Development

In formulating and elaborating the laws noted above, the classical economists believed that they had succeeded in providing a realistic and universal, though abstract, description of the production of goods, the establishment of domestic and international prices, and the distribution of the income of the economy among the three social classes. But they were even more concerned with the long-run trend of wages, profits, and rent. Indeed, the central problem of classical economics after Smith was that of long-run economic development rather than the problem of value and price. The latter was subsequently to become the focal point of neoclassical theory.

Economic development was envisaged in the classical model as the result of population growth and capital accumulation. Population was seen as growing in response to the availability of subsistence, as evidenced by the market rate of wages. The higher the market rate of wages in relation to labor's requirements, the greater the stimulus to population growth. The market rate, in turn, was thought to depend on the initial size of the labor force and the willingness of capitalists to provide the wage fund out of which subsistence is advanced. Growth also required a net accumulation of capital. Smith's dictum that "parsimony and not industry is the immediate cause of the increase of capital" is fundamental to what was to become the classical conception of the growth process.

The classicists conceived of growth in much the same way as we do today, i.e., in terms of an increase in per capita income. It is perhaps intuitively obvious that the growth phenomenon is a dynamic process in which one or more magnitudes that relate to the determination of income in the present "carry over" and determine the income level achieved in the succeeding period. In the classical model, growth was contingent on a sufficiently large product to leave a residual for profit after the wage requirements of the laboring population and the rental payments of the landlord class had been met. This provided the basis for "parsimony" and the accumulation of the capital stock. In Smith's model the capital stock is the preceding harvest of corn. That is, the capital in Smith's model is circulating capital in the form of the wages fund. This is the fund which supports the laborers who are part of the process through which one year's harvest is transformed into the next.

The mature classical approach to the growth process, which is best exemplified by Ricardo, differs relatively little from Smith's. Because of its special orientation to the issue of the Corn Laws, it was imperative for him to distinguish the agricultural sector from the rest of the economy. Nevertheless, his model is like Smith's for two reasons. First, the agricultural sector is taken as a mechanism for converting corn which appears first in the form of the wages fund into corn which appears in the form of a finished good. Second, the fixed capital of Ricardo's model is stored-up labor; fixed capital is therefore, in effect, reduced to circulating capital. These features are responsible for the character of classical growth models. The model is essentially static because there is no real linkage from one period to the next. The essence of the process is the conversion of "corn" into "corn"; each period is thus self-contained.[3]

---

[3] A more technical discussion is presented in J. R. Hicks, *Capital and Growth* (London: Oxford University Press, 1965), chap. 4.

Continued growth was impossible in the classical model. Eventually, the tendency toward diminishing returns would raise the cost of maintaining the laborer and his family to a level which leaves too small a margin of profit after wages and rents to stimulate further accumulation. The stationary state, in which both population growth and net capital accumulation cease, will then come into existence.

Classicism and Liberalism

The inherent disparity of interests among the receivers of rent, profit, and interest was an important conclusion of post-Smithian thinkers. This dichotomy made the proper role of government an issue. Laissez-faire had been the policy counterpart of Physiocratic as well as Smithian thinking, in which individual conscience was regarded as the instrument through which the ideal of individual freedom under law was to be realized. But once the thesis of the natural harmony of interests fell into discard, another basis for policy recommendations was required. Classical political economists were primarily concerned with the discovery of laws, but insofar as they concerned themselves with matters of policy, Bentham's Utilitarianism provided them with the foundation they needed. They accepted Bentham's principle that the greatest good for the greatest number should be the governing consideration and, for the most part, believed that this objective is served by a laissez-faire policy coupled with education and appropriate legislative reforms to reconcile divergent class interests. It is interesting to note in this connection, however, that Bentham himself originally believed that the reforms he sought would be accomplished more quickly under a system of enlightened despotism than by political liberalism. But he later abandoned this view, largely under the influence of James Mill, in favor of a program of reform which called for broader representation in Parliament and universal male suffrage.

Appraisal of Classicism

Classical economic theory attempted to provide, first of all, a simplified model of the operation of the actual economic system. It attempted secondly, to offer a hypothesis concerning its probable future long-run development. Finally, its philosophical and psychological foundations were thought to offer a basis for a policy of economic and political laissez-faire. How well were these objectives satisfied?

The conception of the operation of the economic system which is fundamental to the classical analysis is that its functioning is comparable to a self-correcting physical mechanism which is capable of automatic adjustment to external forces disturbing its equilibrium. This assumption proved to be most valid while the economy was in its preindustrial stage of development. Later, as industrialization altered the system, the assumption of automatic adjustment became less valid and rendered analyses conducted on that assumption less tenable. Malthus' theory of gluts is in the nature of an internal attack on the classical system in this regard. The impact of this theory was, however, greatly softened by the prominence which Say's law of markets assumed in Ricardo's thinking. Ricardo's views on this matter were so persuasive that subsequent analyses of the nature and cause of economic crisis came largely from heretics such as Jean Charles Sismondi and Karl Marx.

The classical system was conspicuously successful for a long time in providing a basis for political theory. Philosophically, the roots of its political system stem from John Locke's conception of the natural order in which labor was conceived as a source of property and consequently as the foundation for all claims to wealth. Intervention of any sort was regarded as violating the property relations of the natural order. Thus, political laissez-fair became the logical counterpart of an economic theory predicated on labor. Not everyone agreed, however, that the property relations which came into existence in the course of time coincided with the requirements of the natural order.

Bentham's system of Utilitarianism, which is a later expression of the philosophy of natural law than Locke's, can be used to lend support to a radical movement as well as a conservative one.[4] The principle of utility provides an unequivocal basis for laissez-faire only if egotistic behavior can be relied on to produce socially altruistic behavior, as would be the case if the same basic desires can be attributed to all men, so that they engage in essentially the same behavior to maximize pleasure and avoid pain. But this presupposes not only that every individual is in fact the best judge of his own interests and that the pleasures and pains of different persons are homogeneous and comparable, but also that individuals commonly and regularly make rational calculations with respect to the pleasures and pains associated with the various modes of behavior open to them. If these conditions are not realized, it is a simple matter to make out a case for state intervention. If, for example, competition cannot be relied upon to assure everyone his just share of society's product, or if general overproduction is possible, or if the urge for procreation is so powerful that population tends to multiply without reference to the supply and fertility of land, there is a basis for arguing that the state should properly intervene to improve and correct these conditions.

Bentham himself prescribed that governmental intervention in economic matters be limited, but the limits he suggested were not so narrow as to support the doctrine that there exists natural harmony of interests in a

---

[4] Halévy, *Philosophical Radicalism,* part III, chap. 1.

society unregulated by government.[5] While the classical economists who followed him advocated laissez-faire as a general rule, they also recognized that legislation is sometimes required to identify naturally divergent interests and recommended numerous exceptions to laissez-faire on the basis of the principle of utility. The schism between liberalism and intervention is particularly apparent in the writings of John Stuart Mill, but the frequently encountered notion that the classicists regarded the functions of government as being wholly negative is quite erroneous in spite of its persistence.[6] It was, however, the case the classicists made for laissez-faire which, more than its technical analysis, gave it continued authority.

Classical analysis was not conspicuously successful as a theory of economic development. Its shortcomings as regards its visions of the stationary state are evident. The pessimistic results associated with the tendency to diminishing returns and population growth failed to materialize as technological developments, emigration, and birth control alleviated population pressures. These were factors which Malthus, Ricardo, and John Stuart Mill did not foresee. They were essentially unhistorical in their outlook and took it for granted that the behavior they observed among their contemporaries was inherent in human nature and that their conclusions concerning them were valid for all eternity. This is the essence of the criticisms which the German historical school directed against classicism.

The historical school took the position that the laws of the classical school were neither absolute nor perpetually valid either in terms of economic theory or as a basis for policy. They argued that economic laws, if they can be discovered at all, must necessarily be relative to time and place. Because economic laws operate within the framework of constantly changing environments, they argued that it is necessary to replace the classical method of deduction by induction in order to discover the nature of these environments. Induction would, they felt, also shed new light on the motives of human conduct, which, in their view, the classicists interpreted all too simply as being only the product of self-interest. The study of political economy should proceed by collecting a mass of historical data from which generalizations will eventually be drawn. Precisely what the nature of these generalizations will be cannot be determined in advance, for the necessary data must first be assembled.

German scholars such as Wilhelm Roscher of the older historical school, Karl Knies and Gustav Schmoller, who carried on his tradition of *historismus,* took the position that the historical method is the only way of studying political economy and that nothing of importance can be learned by using the deductive method. They embarked on an ambitious program of

---

[5] Jacob Viner, "Bentham and J. S. Mill: The Utilitarian Background." *American Economic Review,* vol. 39, no. 2 (March 1949); reprinted in Viner's, *The Long View and the Short* (Glencoe, Ill.: Free Press, 1958).

[6] This question is examined at length by Lionel Robbins, *The Theory of Economic Policy in Classical Political Economy* (New York: Macmillan Co., 1952).

study which resulted in the accumulation of a remarkable volume of historical detail. But their contribution is primarily of a descriptive character. Their charge that theoretical economics neglects relevant facts undoubtedly made deductive economists more selective regarding their premises and more cautious in putting forward their generalizations. But the historical school contributed little to the body of economic analysis. Eventually, the disagreement over methodology (*Methodenstreit*), which reached England but found few enthusiastic adherents, resolved itself as participants to the dispute recognized that both deduction and induction have their place in economic analysis and mutually fructify one another.

The criticism of the socialists against classicism was much more formidable than that of the historicists. Revolutionary in character, the socialist movement was inspired in part by the exploitation and genuine misery which the Industrial Revolution imposed on the working class. But it had still another root, and this one was philosophical. It has already been suggested that the doctrine of the natural order and the natural law governing it could as readily be used to support radical political views as conservative ones. Indeed, the emergence of capitalism, sweeping away as it did feudal institutions and the vested interests of the medieval era, was itself revolutionary. Since capitalism in turn gave rise to new vested interests and abuses, the same liberal philosophy which sired capitalism could now be called upon to sanction further reform. The English socialists for example, started with the Ricardian theory of value but also gave a revolutionary twist to Bentham's Utilitarianism. Their interpretation of the principle of the greatest good for the greatest number did not lend sanctity to the existing social order but required instead a more egalitarian system of income distribution in which each would receive the whole product of his labor.

These early English socialists, as well as their French counterparts, were part of Marx's inspiration. Philosophically, however, Marxian socialism was grounded on the Hegelian dialectic rather than philosophical radicalism. As an economist in the classical tradition, Marx was to forge a system which rivaled the classical one. His analysis of the origin, functioning, and inevitable destruction of the capitalistic system is not only the most complete and best articulated rival to the classical analysis but also the one having the greatest impact on future generations. As such, the work of Marx is deserving of a separate chapter, which follows.

GLOSSARY OF TERMS CONCEPTS

Classicism. The school of English political economy which elaborated and refined the methodology and economic principles of Smith, Say, Malthus, and Ricardo relating to production, distribution, value, and economic development. This tradition continued with the contributions of Senior, John Stuart Mill, and Cairnes.

Dichotomization of the pricing process. The examination of individual commodity prices as though the process were unrelated to the determination of the general price level.

Economic liberalism. The economic policy of allowing the market process to reconcile divergent individual interests on the assumption that all people have the same basic desires and are equally capable of asserting themselves in the economic decision-making process.

Methodenstreit. The methodological dispute (chiefly between the Austrian and the German historical school) concerning the appropriateness of deduction as opposed to the historical method in economics.

NOTES FOR FURTHER READING

Understanding the philosophical aspects of the mature classical tradition requires an appreciation of its Utilitarian background. This is lucidly presented by Jacob Viner in "Bentham and J. S. Mill: The Utilitarian Background," *The American Economic Review,* vol. 66 (June 1956), and by T. W. Hutchison in "Bentham as an Economist," *Economic Review,* vol. 66 (June 1956). The nature of Utilitarianism and its impact on the thinking of Bentham and Mill is also treated by Etienne Halévy in *The Growth of Philosophical Radicalism* (New York: Augustus Kelley, 1949).

An important and relatively new book by Robert V. Eagley, *The Structure of Classical Economic Theory* (New York: Oxford University Press, 1974) investigates the analytical structure of classical economic theory and finds it grounded in the concept of capital. A central theme of Eagley's analysis is that the transition from mercantilist thinking to classical theory involved a shift from a theory within which "money matters" to a theory in which "capital matters."

The classical theory of economic growth commands particular interest, and there are many articles and books, recent and not so recent, which treat this topic. William Baumol's chapter 2 in *Economic Dynamics,* 3d ed. (New York: The Macmillan Co., 1970) is especially recommended. Two articles which offer particular insight are Adolph Lowe's "The Classical Theory of Economic Growth," *Social Research* (Summer 1951). Reprinted in Ingrid H. Rima, ed., *Readings in the History of Economic Theory.* New York: Holt, Rinehart and Winston, 1970; and Hla Myint, "The Classical View of the Economic Problem," *Economica,* N.S., vol. 13 (May 1946); republished in Joseph Spengler and William R. Allen, eds. *Essays in Economic Thought* (Chicago: Rand McNally, 1960) pp. 442–53. Hla Myint's *Theories of Welfare Economics,* Chap. 5 (Cambridge: Harvard University Press), 1948 is also recommended.

The political aspects of classical economics are examined by Lionel Robbins in *The Theory of Economic Policy in Classical Economy* (New York: Macmillan Co., 1952).

Karl Marx: An Inquiry into the "Law of Motion" of the Capitalist System

INTRODUCTION

Life and Times (1818–1883)

THE NAME OF KARL MARX is not only most intimately associated with the socialist movement, but his ideas have also had a more influential impact than those of any other socialist advocate. It is to him that we may attribute the rise of "scientific" socialism—that distinctively Marxian fusion of philosophy, socialism, and economics put forward as a "revelation" of the ultimate collapse of capitalism and the inevitable triumph of socialism.

Marx was born in the German Rhineland, the son of a moderately well-to-do Jewish lawyer who became a convert to Lutheranism and raised his children in that faith. At 17, Marx entered the University of Bonn to study law but transferred after a year to the more stimulating atmosphere of the University of Berlin, where his interests became directed primarily to philosophy and history. His religious views now abandoned, he became an avowed atheist and materialist. Intellectually, he was, like many others of his generation, profoundly affected by the ideas of the philosopher Georg Hegel (1770–1831) whose views of the individual, the state, and the mode of historical change were in sharp contrast with the tenets of rationalism which characterized the Age of Enlightenment. Initially, Hegelian ideas led Marx in the direction of what became known as the "higher criticism." This sought to examine religious views within the framework of the historical method and was at least partly an outgrowth of the strict control of the Prussian authorities over political inquiry and action. As a result of these curbs, intellectual activity, particularly of a critical nature, became directed toward religious issues.

Intellectually trained but unable to secure a university post, largely because of his unpopular religious views, Marx turned his attention to journalism. He became the editor of the *Rheinische Zeitung* in Cologne, a moderately liberal paper sponsored by business interests. In this post Marx became interested in social and economic questions. The suspension of the newspaper a year later caused him and his wife to take up residence in Paris, which he felt to be a base of operations more congenial to his liberal views. Here he made contact with a gamut of revolutionary socialist and communist ideas. This was the period during which Marx became a serious student of history, politics, and economics. Pierre Proudhon appears to have initially suggested the possibility of interpreting economic phenomena in Hegelian terms. This idea was eventually to become the foundation stone for the whole Marxian system, though Proudhon was later denounced by Marx as an incompetent exponent of the dialectic.

His period in Paris also brought Marx into close personal contact with Friedrich Engels, with whom he had an intellectual and personal association that spanned a lifetime. Engels' family was in the textile business in Barmen (Germany), and he later became the prosperous part-owner of a cotton business in England. His intimate knowledge of economic and social conditions in that country, the basis for his work on *The Condition of the Working Class in England* (1844), was invaluable to Marx. It was also through Engels that he made contact with the English socialists of the day.

Marx's sojourn in Paris was brief, lasting a little more than a year. At the request of the Prussian government, he was expelled from France and moved to Belgium. By this time, his intellectual system had already taken shape, and he turned his attention for the first time to political activity. He helped found a German Workers' Union which joined with other such groups into an international Communist League. Marx and Engels together drafted a statement of principles they called the *Communist Manifesto* (1848), which became the best known of all Marxist writings. A powerful and brilliant document which is now available in virtually all languages, the *Manifesto* was intended to present a theoretical basis for communism, a critique of utopian socialist movements, and a program of socialist aims and methods for achieving them.

The year 1848 brought many revolutionary uprisings in Europe. The outbreak which took place in France forced the abdication of Louis Philippe and the proclamation of the new Second French Republic. Though there were efforts to direct the new government in accordance with socialist principles, the coup of 1852 established Louis Napoleon as Emperor Napoleon III. In all likelihood, Marx's *Manifesto* had little to do with the revolution. Nevertheless, he was deported from Belgium for revolutionary activity, and he returned first to Paris and then briefly to Germany. London became his ultimate refuge, and it was there that he lived the remainder of his life, supported largely by gifts and loans from friends, relatives, and sympathizers (Engels in particular), and stipends from intermittent journalistic activity. The most noteworthy of the latter was his work as foreign correspondent for the *New York Tribune,* an association which lasted from 1851 to the 1860s. This was also the period during which he utilized the facilities of the British Museum to gather material for the first volume of *Das Kapital,* which appeared in print in 1867. The remaining two volumes were put together by Engels from partial drafts and notes. This was the trilogy that Marx intended to represent the reconstruction of the science of political economy.

THE BACKGROUND FOR MARXIAN ECONOMIC THEORY

Socialist Thought

Fundamentally, Marxian theory is a theory of capitalist economic development rather than a theory of socialism. Indeed, Marx had remarkably little to say about socialism, the system he expected ultimately to succeed capitalism. Marxian analysis, however, derives partly from the social reform movements of the Enlightenment. The earlier roots of socialism are of course to be found in the ideals of Christian brotherhood; but another and perhaps more important source is the emergence during the Enlightenment of the idea that human society can be rationally reconstructed to promote the best interests of its members.

There were two broad views as to how this reconstruction might take place. The first, continuing the tradition of classical liberalism, maintained that society's best interests are served by assuring freedom to its individual members, who, in seeking their own best interests, would automatically also assure the ideal functioning of the whole. Philosophical radicalism was this sort of reform movement. It stressed the preservation of private property rights and individual enterprise within the framework of minimal government functions.

The socialist-anarchist movement was similar to philosophical radicalism in its aims but fundamentally different in the modus operandi it visualized to achieve them. It was socialistic in its view that the only rational society is one which substitutes collective for private ownership of the means of production as a foundation for an egalitarian distribution of income. It was anarchistic in its conception of government as the outgrowth of the inequities and abuses of a society in which the property rights of the wealthy required the coercive influence of the state in order to survive.

Like classical liberalism, the socialist-anarchist movement was initially an idealistic one and attracted intellectual rather than working class support. It had its primary early development in the France of the early 19th century, which had not yet experienced an industrial revolution and its associated labor discontent. The Revolution had destroyed the political power of the absolute monarchy of the *ancien regime,* but it brought the bourgeoisie to such a high level of economic and political power that it generated a milieu which nurtured heterodox ideas. Comte Henri de Saint-Simon (1760–1825) called for the reorganization of society on the model of the factory. The new industrial state should, he urged, supplant the church as the supreme authority if mankind is to achieve harmony. He envisioned a society in which all will benefit from the spirit of cooperation that characterizes factory life besides enjoying the advantages of an industrial system built on the basis of capital and science.[1] Saint-Simon favored drastic reforms in the ownership of land but did not advocate the abolition of private property. On the contrary, he maintained that capital as well as labor is legitimately entitled to some form of remuneration.

Charles Fourier (1772–1837), another Frenchman who developed a theory of socialism almost contemporaneously with Saint-Simon, maintained that he had discovered a principle of mutual attraction, akin to Newton's physical principles, which underlies social relations. He argued that the industrial world ought to be organized on the principle of mutual attraction and proposed the group as the basic social unit composed of at least seven persons of similar tastes who pursue a common art, science or industry. Five or more groups would constitute a series, and a union of series would comprise a phalanx. Each phalanx, consisting of approximately 1,600 persons would, in his scheme, occupy about 500 acres of land and its members would live together in a great Phalanstory, or Palace. Since the organization of the Phalanx is essentially like that of a joint-stock corporation, Fourier does not propose the abolition of private property. Profits would not however be distributed solely among those who own stock: five twelfths would go to labor, four twelfths to capital, and three twelfths to talent. Thus, the wage system would be abolished in Fourier's scheme because labor would be rewarded by a share in profits.

Not all of the early French socialists shared the view of Saint-Simon and Fourier that it is not necessary to abolish private property in order to achieve major reforms. Proudhon's contrary view is typical. "Property," he said, "is theft"; when there is private property, the state becomes the agency required to perpetuate it. He reasoned that after private property has been abolished and men have renounced their acquisitive ambitions in

---

[1] Cited by E. Gide and C. Rist, *A History of Economic Doctrine* 2d English ed. (London: George G. Harrap and Co., 1948), p. 214.

favor of cooperation for the common good, government will be abolished because it has no further function to perform.

While Saint-Simon and Fourier approached reform on an intellectual level, Robert Owen (1771–1858) attempted to put some principles of a socialist society into practice. He bought an impoverished textile village at New Lanark, Scotland, where approximately 2,500 persons participated in the model community he sought to establish. He also purchased a tract of land in the state of Indiana in the United States and established a settlement which become known as New Harmony. The success of these communities was, however, short lived. But the experiment is an interesting chapter in the history of what Karl Marx dubbed "Utopian" socialism.

Marx acquired many ideas from the early socialists and incorporated them into his system. He was in substantial agreement with them about the aims of socialism and shared many of their visions of the future society. But he felt they were unrealistic in believing that a major transformation of existing society could be brought about simply by an appeal to reason. The prosperous upper classes, in particular, could never be led by reason alone to accept the reforms proposed by the socialists. Even the workers were not yet ready, in his view, for a radically different society. It was not until the effects of the Industrial Revolution became more widespread that socialism became a mass movement of the working class. It is perhaps worth noting, in this regard, that the German Workers' Union which Marx helped found while he was in Belgium had no workers in it, but existed primarily to study socialist thought. Marx maintained that workers would not be ready for socialism until the evils of the present system greatly worsened their positions. It became his aim to demonstrate how deterioration of the working class would inevitably come about and necessarily call forth socialism. This is the difference between Marx's "scientific" socialism and the earlier (in his view) "utopian" movements. He sought to demonstrate that the advent of socialism will be the inevitable result of an evolutionary process which could be hastened by proper strategy and tactics, and that the approach of the utopians would in fact serve to hinder rather than serve that ultimate aim. Precisely why socialism was inevitable according to Marxian thinking turns upon the use he made of Hegel's philosophy of history.

Hegel's Philosophy of History

The development of the Marxist system appears to have begun with its general philosophy. Marx was still a student at the University of Berlin when he came under the influence of Hegel's philosophy of history. This was the first systematic exposition against the philosophy of natural rights. The revolt against reason which began with Rousseau and culminated in Hume's *Treatise of Human Nature* virtually destroyed all claims to validity of the doctrine of natural law and, along with it, its applications to religion, ethics, law, and politics. Specifically, Hume maintained that the concept of reason as used in the system of natural law is ambiguous and cannot, therefore, be a source of knowledge. Immanual Kant sought to rescue the problem of knowledge from this abyss by effecting a synthesis between rationalism and empiricism. Knowledge, he maintained, is acquired in three ways: via the senses, via the intellect, and via moral will. The knowledge gotten through the senses and the intellect cannot be of the world as it really is, but only as it appears to be, because our minds impose upon these things a quality which has no existence in the things themselves. Thus, it is only through moral will that we can have contact with the real world. Morality belongs to the noumenal world, that is, to the world of reality, whereas science belongs to the phenomenal world, that is, the world as it appears to be. The realms of science and morality are therefore regarded by Kant as autonomous and separate.

But Kant's "solution" to the problem posed by Hume made the schism between science and religion more acute by placing one in the realm of fact and the other in the realm of value. Hegel, however, maintained that there is a necessary and logical relationship between them which is demonstrable via the dialectic, the only instrument of analysis through which truth can be discovered.[2]

The dialectic is the self-propulsion of ideas through the process of synthesis. Its origin is to be found in ancient Greek philosophy, in which it referred to the method by which two persons engaged in argument or debate modify, and eventually correct, one another's views until they arrive at a third view which incorporates elements of both. Thus, there is a thesis which is confronted with a conflicting antithesis. The controversy between them leads to corrective argument and modification until a synthesis emerges in which thesis and antithesis are reconciled. This is the method which was used by Plato in his *Dialogues* and which was later an important intellectual tool of the Scholastics.

Hegel's adaptation of the dialectic was little concerned with the opposing ideas of individual human beings. He conceived of the dialectic as the process by which change takes place in the universe. There is, he thought, an inherent pattern according to which this development takes place about which we can learn from the study of history. Under his influence, European scholars came to believe that a knowledge of the past is necessary in order to foresee and influence the future. Conservative and radical thinkers alike embraced anew the study of history; and there followed an age, particularly in Germany but also elsewhere in Europe, in

---

[2] Excellent treatments of Hegelian philosophy are available in George Sabine, *A History of Political Theory*, rev. ed. (New York: Henry Holt Co., Inc., 1950), and H. B. Acton, *The Illusion of the Epoch*, part 1 (Boston: Beacon Press, 1957).

which the historical method became regarded as the only truly scientific one and was applied to virtually all fields of inquiry.

Hegel himself undertook to utilize the dialectic to predict the next stage of German history. The next and inevitable step, he maintained, would be the amalgamation of the several German states under a single monarchy. The new German state would thus be the apex of history. Hegel's political philosophy not only rejected individualism on the ground that it failed to recognize the intimate relationship between the individual and society, but also endowed the state with a spirit all its own. This is the conception of the state which characterized German political theory even into the 20th century.

Ricardian Economics

Ricardian economics or, more specifically, Ricardo's labor theory of value, was the third source of inspiration for Marx's analysis of the functioning of the capitalistic system. Ricardo, it will be recalled, wrote as follows: "Possessing utility [which he discarded both as a cause and as a measure of value] commodities derive their exchangeable value from two sources: from their scarcity and from the quantity of labour required to obtain them."[3] Scarcity was regarded as being of primary significance when a commodity, like a rare work of art, is not reproducible. Most commodities, however, being the product of labor, can be supplied "almost without any assignable limit, if we are disposed to bestow the labour necessary to obtain them."[4] He then proceeded to reason that rent, as a differential surplus, is not a determinant of exchange value, and that since neither variations in wages or nor variations in profits could affect value in exchange, commodities would be exchanged in proportion to the labor used in their production.

Marx's serious study of economics dates from his early Paris days, and he was greatly impressed with the treatment that Smith, and more particularly Ricardo, gave to labor as the cause of value. The latter were, however, favorably disposed toward competitive capitalism and laissez-faire policy, whereas Marx was hostile to that system in every form on the ground that the laboring class is exploited by capitalist employers. He regarded their labor theory of value, however, as providing an essential foundation for his hypothesis concerning labor exploitation and the eventual destruction of the capitalist system. Indeed, Marx considered himself to be, intellectually speaking, a lineal descendant of the great classical tradition.

---

[3] David Ricardo, "Principles of Political Economy and Taxation" in *The Works and Correspondence of David Ricardo,* Piero Sraffa and Maurice Dobbs, eds. (Cambridge, Eng.: The University Press, 10 vols., 1951–55), vol. 1, p. 11.

[4] Ibid., p. 12.

THE ORIGIN, NATURE, AND FUNCTIONING OF CAPITALISM

The Economic Interpretation of History

Marx's objective was "to lay bare the economic law of motion of modern society."[5] The prime mover of social change was, he maintained, to be found in changes in the mode of production. This premise was a firm part of his convictions considerably before he published Volume I of *Capital*. In the preface to *A Contribution to the Critique of Political Economy*, he wrote as follows:

> The mode of production in material life determines the general character of the social, political and spiritual processes of life. It is not the consciousness of men that determines their existence, but on the contrary, their social existence determines their consciousness. At a certain stage of their development, the material forces of production in society come in conflict with the existing relations of production, or—what is but a legal expression for the same thing, with the property relations within which they had been at work before. From forms of development of the forces of production these relations turn into their fetters. Then comes the period of social revolution. With the change of the economic foundation the entire immense superstructure is more or less rapidly transformed.[6]

The impetus to social change is thus to be found in the "mode of production." The mode of production prevailing in a particular period is associated with a given set of social relationships which reflect the ownership and use of the material means of production which have developed in the process of social production. As the mode of production becomes altered, as it will in the course of time, new social relationships, more appropriate to the altered production relationship, will be required. It is the contradiction that develops between the altered mode of production and existing social relationships that generates change. This is the Hegelian aspect of Marx's thinking. But unlike Hegel, Marx considered that conflicts are not in the realm of ideas, but in the material world with its existing social system. The mind of man, far from originating the conflicting thesis and antithesis which Hegel stressed, merely perceives the material world around him. This is the essence of Marx's materialism as opposed to Hegel's idealism. The conflicts to be resolved are between social classes—the ruling class of the epoch versus the exploited class. Thus, Marx began the *Communist Manifesto* with the observation that "the history of all hitherto existing society is the history of class struggles."

The economic source of class conflict was also of particular interest to

---

[5] Karl Marx, *Capital,* trans. from the 3d German ed. (1883) by Samuel More and Edward Aveling, and edited by Friedrich Engels (Moscow: Foreign Languages Publishing House, 1959), preface to 1st ed., vol. 1, p. 10.

[6] Karl Marx, *A Contribution to the Critique of Political Economy,* trans. by N. I. Stone (Chicago: Charles H. Kerr & Co., 1904), p. 11.

the classicists. This is precisely what Ricardo meant by "the distribution of the produce of the earth." In his view, the basic antagonism between social classes was that which existed between the landlords and the industrial capitalists. It was for this reason that the doctrine of rent loomed so large in the Ricardian analysis. Marx, however, regarded the emphasis on land and rent to be inappropriate in a bourgeois economy, for the latter is a society in which the antagonistic classes are the bourgeoisie and the proletariat. It is the relationship between them which determines the nature of the mode of production and hence of the whole society.

In analyzing the relationship between these two classes, Marx relies heavily on the deductive methodology which is so strongly associated with Ricardo and his followers. The manner of Marx's application is of course different, in that it is oriented toward demonstrating the transitory nature of capitalism. To do this, Marx finds it necessary to isolate the capital-labor relationship from all other social relationships in order to examine its basic character. Reduced to its simplest form, this relationship is one of exchange. The commodity which is being bought and sold Marx identifies as "labor power." This commodity, the only one labor has available for sale, is merely one commodity among many, and the exchange relationship that results from its sale is one among many. Thus, Part 1 of the first volume of *Capital* is entitled "Commodities" and is an analysis of the general phenomenon of exchange. It begins with simple commodity production such as takes place when each individual owns his own means of production and satisfies those wants he cannot fulfill directly by exchanging his surplus with others. Such is not the case under capitalism; here, the ownership of all the means of production is vested in one class, the bourgeoisie, while the work is performed by the members of the proletariat. The means of production and labor power are thus given commodity form, and exchange relationships are involved in their purchase and sale. This is the mode of production that is typical of capitalism.

That the concept of the mode of production does not refer to the technical aspects of production alone should now be obvious. It includes not only the technology surrounding the physical means of production, but also the social relationships deriving from the whole complex of the socioeconomic, political, and cultural institutions which pertain to a given stage of development. This superstructure is a major aspect of the mode of production and therefore plays a role in the historical process. Thus, what is so often referred to as the "economic interpretation of history" is at least as much in the realm of sociology as of economics.

Use Value and Exchange Value

The manner in which the conflict between the mode of production and the superstructure of social organization will make itself felt and the reason the capitalistic system will eventually become untenable are questions which Marx's economic analysis is intended to answer. His analysis is focused on the value problem. Marx begins by noting that every commodity has a use value and an exchange value. Though he uses these terms in their usual sense, he regards the analysis of use value as lying outside the sphere of political economy because it involves a relation between a consumer and an object of consumption. Political economy, in Marx's view, properly involves only social relations. The study of use values does not come within the province of the political economist because they involve a relationship between a person and an object. But exchange values between goods, though they seemingly do not involve social relationships, are of particular concern to the political economist because every exchange of commodities is also an exchange of labor. Marx thus conceives of the value problem as having a qualitative aspect as well as a quantitative one. It has been suggested that the great originality of Marx's value theory lies in its attempt to deal simultaneously with both.[7]

Marx's insistence that an object can have exchange value only if it represents embodied labor led him to distinguish between value and price. An object like uncultivated land may command a price but is devoid of exchange value because there is no labor congealed in it.[8] While he thought that all value derived from labor, Marx, like Smith and Ricardo before him, was aware that labor is not homogeneous but is sometimes more proficient because of natural ability or superior training. When a more effective worker is employed in a given line of production side by side with one who is less productive, their comparative efficiency is measurable in physical terms. Once the ratio of their output has been established, the two kinds of labor can be reduced to a common denominator, namely, "human labor pure and simple." "Skilled labor counts only as simple labor intensified, or rather, as multiplied simple labor, a given quantity of skilled labor being considered equal to a greater quantity of simple labor."[9] The labor congealed in a commodity is thus measurable in time units which express the proportion of the community's labor force a commodity absorbs. From this, Marx deduces that there is a correspondence between the labor-time ratios involved in the production of two commodities and their exchange ratios.

There is an obvious qualification to this principle: The fact that more labor time is lavished on a commodity does not necessarily give it greater value. Unnecessary or inefficient expenditures of labor time do not enhance value. Only "socially necessary" labor time contributes to value. "The labor time socially necessary is that required to produce an article under the normal conditions of production, and with the average degree of

[7] See Paul M. Sweezy, *The Theory of Capitalist Development* (New York: Oxford University Press, 1942).

[8] Marx, *Capital,* vol. 1, p. 102.

[9] Ibid., p. 44.

skill and intensity prevalent at this time."[10] Thus, commodities are exchanged for one another at a rate which is determined by the quantity of socially necessary labor each embodies. When this ratio of exchange prevails in the market between any pair of commodities, the producers of neither commodity will have an incentive to shift from the production of one to the production of the other, and the price of each will be proportional to the labor time required to produce it. In other words, if the forces of supply and demand have free play, an equilibrium price which is proportional to labor time will be established. Competitive market forces, then, are the mechanism through which deviations between market prices and real (labor) values are eliminated. Thus the supply and demand explanation of price determination is really an essential part of the labor theory, though Marx did not always express this point clearly.

Marx did not completely overlook the role of demand in determining exchange values, though it is frequently maintained that he did. He specifically emphasized that use value is a prerequisite for exchange value and that therefore the social need for a commodity is the determining factor of the amount of social labor which is to be allocated to a particular type of production. Thus, if too much of a commodity has been produced, or if more labor has been expended than is socially necessary, it will be reflected in a reduced exchange value. Nevertheless, it is true that he did not approach the value problem from the standpoint of consumer choice, any more than did Smith or Ricardo. It has been suggested that to have done so would have been inconsistent with his objective of investigating the causes of social change, for consumer wants, except insofar as they originate in physical requirements, are a reflection of the mode of production and are therefore passive as regards the process of change.[11]

Surplus Value

There is a significant difference between a system of simple commodity production and that which prevails in a capitalistic system. Under simple commodity production, each producer owns his own means of production and sells the product he produces. He exchanges his commodities for money and then reconverts money into commodities. Symbolically, the process is described as $C—M—C$ by Marx. Under capitalism, the means of production are owned by one group of individuals, the capitalists, but actively used in production by another group, the workers. The capitalist, who produces nothing, starts the process with money. He purchases commodities in the form of means of production and labor and, after the completion of the production process, converts the commodities once again

---

[10] Ibid., p. 39.

[11] Sweezy, *Capitalist Development,* p. 51.

into money. Thus the process is *M—C—M'*. *M'* must necessarily be greater than *M* in order to make the process worthwhile. The difference between *M* and *M'* is the surplus value, the income of the capitalist and the aim of the production process.

Surplus value has its origin in the difference between the value of the commodities workers are able to produce in a given period and the value of the labor power they sell to the capitalists for use in the production process. Its nature will be most clearly understood if it is recognized that the worker, because of his inability to accumulate capital goods, is unable to utilize his own labor power and therefore has no choice but to sell it to an employer. This commodity, his labor power, is bought and paid for at its going competitive price, which is the market wage-rate. The products produced by the employment of this labor power are also sold at their going competitive prices. Surplus value, therefore, does not originate either from selling commodities above their real value or buying labor power at less than its real value. The worker receives the full value of his labor power. Thus, Marx avoided the moralistic interpretation which the Ricardian socialists gave the labor theory of value when they maintained that labor is robbed of its own fruits.

It may of course happen that wages and/or commodity prices temporarily deviate from their norms and thereby enhance or diminish profits. But surplus value is a permanent and normal phenomenon of capitalist production. It is neither the product of dishonesty nor monopsonistic power on the part of the capitalist, but merely part of the normal operation of the capitalistic system. The operation of this system, because of capitalist ownership of the means of production, requires the worker to sell his labor power. This is a commodity whose value is determined in precisely the same way as any other, namely, by its socially necessary labor cost.

> The value of labor power is determined, as in the case of every other commodity, by the labor time necessary for the production and consequently, also the reproduction of this special article. . . . Therefore, the labor time requisite for the production of labor power reduces itself to that necessary for the production of those means of subsistence, in other words, the value of labor power is the value of the means of subsistence necessary for the maintenance of the laborer.[12]

In this manner, Marx establishes that the exchange value of labor power is determined by the labor cost of producing the goods that the physical requirements of life demand and the degree of civilization in the country generally regard as essential. Subsistence, in other words, need not be interpreted as the bare minimum for survival, but only as a more or less definite quantity of physical goods which represent the congelation of a given amount of labor power. The worker receives money wages corre-

---

[12] Marx, *Capital*, vol. 1, p. 171.

sponding to the value of his labor power. In short, his labor power is sold for precisely what it is worth. The product the worker produces is in turn also sold for precisely what it is worth, as determined by the labor power absorbed in its production. Thus the laws that regulate the exchange of commodities have in no way been violated; and yet, in the process, surplus value is somehow created.

Surplus value, Marx maintains, arises because the capitalist in buying labor power and paying its equivalent exchange value actually receives its use value for an entire working day. Thus, if the average working day is, let us say, twelve hours, and the worker can produce the equivalent of his own subsistence in six hours, then six hours remain during which the worker continues to create new exchange values. The working day is, therefore, divisible into two parts, necessary labor and surplus labor. The output resulting from necessary labor accrues to the worker in the form of wages; but the product of surplus labor goes, in the form of surplus value, to the capitalist. Under the assumptions made above, the rate of surplus value will be 100 percent. The surplus value realized by the capitalist is indicative of the degree of exploitation.

The rate at which surplus value can be created depends on three factors: the length of the working day, the productivity of labor, and the quantity of commodities comprising the worker's real wage. Individually, or in combination, these factors can be altered by the capitalist to increase surplus value. It is obvious from this that Marx associated the creation of surplus value strictly with labor. That part of the machinery and tools actually used up and the materials utilized in the production process are incapable of creating a surplus, but only transfer an equal value to the final good. These Marx calls "constant capital," represented by the letter c. Only variable capital, v, which represents payments to labor and tends to be equal to labor's subsistence, creates a surplus, s, for v is transformed into labor power. Every commodity produced, therefore, has a total value comprised as follows: $c' + v + s$, where c' represents the used-up portion of constant capital. The rate of surplus value (s'), which measures the extent of exploitation derives directly from this formulation and is written by Marx as $s' = s/v$. Because labor tends to move from low-wage areas to high-wage areas and producers utilize productive techniques as efficient as those used by their competitors, Marx maintains that the rate of surplus value will tend to be the same for all firms within an industry and also among all the industries in the economy.

The Equalization of Rates of Profit

In Volume I of *Capital,* Marx maintains that the rate of surplus value is equalized. In Volume III of *Capital,* however, it is argued that surplus values are reshuffled among the different industries in such a way that rates of profit rather than rates of surplus value are equalized. In other words, it is the ratio

$$\frac{s}{c + v}$$

rather than s/v which tends to equality under competitive conditions.

It is more realistic to maintain that rates of profit rather than rates of surplus value tend to be equalized because businessmen are not interested in profit per unit of labor cost, but in profit per unit of total invested capital. Only if the rate at which capital depreciates annually and the turnover rate of inventory were the same in every industry, which it clearly is not, would it be immaterial to conceive of rates of surplus value rather than rates of profit as being equalized. This does, however, appear to vitiate the labor theory of value, for it leads to the conclusion that a commodity will sell not at its labor value, but at its cost of production. Marx's critics have maintained that the problem of transforming values into prices necessarily undermines the entire labor theory of value.[13] Marx himself recognized the problem it posed, for he said: "It would seem therefore, that here the theory of value is incompatible with the actual process, incompatible with the real phenomena of production, and that for this reason any attempt to understand these phenomena should be given up."[14] He did, however, offer a "solution" to the problem. The essence of this solution is that the market transforms values into prices that individually will differ from labor-determined values of commodities. Some capitalists will sell above value and enjoy more surplus value, and others will sell below value and enjoy less surplus value. Capitalists will share in the aggregate of surplus value not in accordance with their variable capital component, but in accordance with their total capital.

Marx himself explained the transformation of values into prices by means of a numerical example, reproduced in Table 9–1. He assumed five industries with different organic compositions of capital, with each enjoying the same rate of surplus value, namely, 100 percent. That is, the rate of surplus value is equal throughout the economy to the variable capital component. The capital for each industry is equivalent to 100 and is regarded as a part of one single capital of 500. In the process of production a portion of the constant capital will be "used up" and thus become congealed in the commodity. These figures, indicated in column 4, are arbitrarily selected. The value of the commodities produced by each industry on the basis of socially necessary labor time may now be computed as $c' + v + s$, indicated in column 6. The total value of each of the outputs equals the cost price plus the surplus.

---

[13] See, in particular, Eugen Böhm-Bawerk, *Karl Marx and the Close of His System* (New York: Augustus Kelley, 1949).

[14] Marx, *Capital,* vol. 2, p. 151.

TABLE 9–1
The Transformation of Values into Prices

Capital Composition by Industry	Surplus Value	Rate of Surplus Value (s/v)	Used Up (c)	Cost Price	Value of Commodities (c' + v + s)	Rate of Profit ($\frac{s}{c+v}$)
1. 80c + 20v	20	100%	50	70	90	20%
2. 70c + 30v	30	100	51	81	111	30
3. 60c + 40v	40	100	51	91	131	40
4. 85c + 15v	15	100	40	55	70	15
5. 95c + 5v	5	100	10	15	20	5
390c + 110v	110					

If each industry's commodities were sold at their values, each industry would experience a different rate of profit, as indicated in the last column of Table 9–1. This is, however, incompatible with the operation of competitive forces. These forces, Marx maintains, will tend to redistribute the total amount (110) of surplus value in such a fashion that each producer will receive a share of the aggregate surplus value that will yield him a rate of profit equivalent to that of his competitors. As shown in Table 9–2, each will receive a rate of profit equal to the average, which is 22 percent. This equalization is brought about by interindustry capital movements. If the rate of profit is above average, as is the case in industries, 1, 2, and 3, in Table 9–1, capital will tend to be attracted from industries 4 and 5, where the rate of profit is lower than average, until the average rate of profit is the same for all, as in Table 9–2.

The implications of the equalization of the rate of profit are twofold. It implies, first of all, that products will be sold not at their value, but at what Marx calls their "price of production." This is determined by $c' + v + p$. Individual commodity prices will therefore deviate from value. As is shown in Table 9–2, which demonstrates the effects of equal rates of profit of 22 percent on each individual capital of 100, individual prices now will deviate from values by the amounts shown in the last column. It will be noted, however, that these deviations of prices from values cancel one another out. These deviations had their origin in the manner in which

TABLE 9–2
Deviation of Prices from Values Based on 22 Percent Profit

Capital Composition by Industry	Cost Price of Commodities	Value of Commodities	Price of Commodities	Rate of Profit	Deviation of Price from Value
1. 80c + 20v	70	90	92	22	+ 2
2. 70c + 30v	81	111	103	22	− 8
3. 60c − 40v	91	131	113	22	− 18
4. 85c + 15v	55	70	77	22	+ 7
5. 95c + 5v	15	20	37	22	+ 17

profits were distributed throughout the system. Since total profits are equal to total surplus value, and the latter amount is unchanged, the total of the prices of production is the equivalent of the sum of the values. This is the manner in which Marx "rescues" the labor theory of value from the abyss into which it appears to fall as a result of the problem of transforming values into prices.

Capital Accumulation and the Tendency toward a Falling Rate of Profit

It has already been noted that the rate of profit, which is the ratio of surplus value to total capital,

$$\frac{s}{c + v}$$

is more significant to the capitalist than the rate of surplus value and is the real inducement to investment. The rate of profit depends not only on the rate of surplus value, but also on the organic composition of capital, i.e., the relationship between constant and variable capital. The tendency for the rate of profit to become equal throughout the economy implies not only that commodity prices will deviate from their values in the manner discussed above, but also that individual capitalists, in order to increase their shares of the aggregate surplus value, will make additions to constant capital which will enhance the productivity of labor.

The original source of capital funds is something Marx explains with his economic interpretation of hitory. Primitive accumulation, which occurred in England during the late 15th and early 16th centuries, created, for the first time, the "free" proletarian (in the sense of his being emancipated from the soil and therefore free to sell his labor) and the money-owning capitalist. Describing the demise of the feudal system and the related destruction of the agricultural economy, Marx observes:

> The spoilation of the church's property, the fraudulent alienation of the state domains, the robbery of the common lands, the usurpation of feudal and clan property, and its transformation into modern private property under circumstances of reckless terrorism, were just so many idyllic methods of primitive accumulation. They conquered the field for capitalistic agriculture, made the soil part and parcel of capital, and created for the town industries the necessary supply of a "free" and outlawed proletariat.[15]

After the era of primitive accumulation is over, further accumulation takes place from additions derived from surplus value. The accumulation of capital is accompanied by an increased mechanization in the production process. A given amount of labor, now combined with a greater supply of

---

[15] Ibid., vol. 1, p. 732.

more efficient equipment, will be able to process a greater volume of raw materials into finished goods. Though labor productivity is enhanced, the organic composition of capital is altered. More and more constant capital relative to total capital is now acquired by the capitalist. Since only variable capital yields a surplus, the ratio

$$\frac{s}{c+v}$$

will fall. From this, Marx deduced his "law of the falling tendency of the rate of profit." The latter naturally tends to dampen the enthusiasm for new investment and encourages the capitalist to seek ways of counteracting it.

Since the rate of profit is a function of both the rate of surplus value and the organic composition of capital, it follows that any factor which tends to raise the rate of surplus value or reduce the constant capital component of total capital will tend to keep the rate of profit from falling. Marx notes six such counteracting factors, the most obvious one of which is the lengthening of the working day, which operates to increase the amount of surplus labor. The speedup has essentially the same effect. The increase in surplus value tends to keep the rate of profit from falling. The technique of cutting wages is not one which Marx seriously entertains, for he assumes that wages, like prices, are determined in a purely competitive market.

Marx, however, saw a tendency for wages to be depressed downward as a result of the growing constant capital component rather than aggressive employer wage policy. This growth creates a situation of technological unemployment which Marx regards as the primary factor operating to keep wages at subsistence levels. He regarded as a "libel on the human race" the population theory by which Malthus and Ricardo explained the tendency of the market wage to equal the natural wage. He emphasized instead the development of a surplus population. The workers who are set free by machine power constitute an industrial reserve army which depresses the rate of wages and thereby tends to raise the level of surplus value. Technological changes are regarded by Marx not as the fortuitous occurrences that the classicists regarded them to be, but as conscientiously sought-after laborsaving devices necessary to the continued existence of capitalist production. The existence of a reserve army is necessary for the maintenance of surplus value. Thus, Marx observed in the *Communist Manifesto:* "The bourgeoisie cannot exist without constantly revolutionizing the instruments of production, and thereby, the relations of production, and with them the whole relations of society." It is in this manner that Marx lays bare an area of inherent conflict within the framework of capitalism, from which he deduces one of the laws of motion of the capitalistic system.

The human aspect of these observations is "the increasing misery of the proletariat." On the one hand, the degree of worker exploitation is enhanced through the speedup and the lengthening of the working day; and on the other, the value of the worker's labor power is depressed through the reduced labor requirements of producing labor's subsistence.[16] It is another of capitalism's internal contradictions that the increasing productivity of labor is associated with increasing exploitation and diminished ability to consume goods.

Capitalist Crisis

The classical economists, as has already been noted, largely assumed away the problem of economic crisis by their acceptance of Say's law.

Marx rejected Say's law because he regarded it as applicable only to a barter economy. In a capitalistic economy, commodities are exchanged first for money and then for one another. In the process, qualitatively different use values represent quantitatively equal exchange values. The exchange value of commodities is transformed into money form and then back again to commodity form. The transformation of commodities into money and back into commodities is not necessarily synchronized with regard to time and place. It is for this reason, Marx maintains, that endogenously created crises are inherent in capitalism. "If the interval in time between two complementary phases of the complete metamorphosis of a commodity becomes too great, if the split between the sale and the purchase becomes too pronounced, the intimate connection between them, their oneness, asserts itself by producing a crisis."[17] Thus, Marx regarded crisis as being indicative of and taking the form of a state of general overproduction. Crisis is the process by which equilibrium between the production and circulation of goods is forcibly restored. The actual cause of periods of general overproduction is among the problems to which Marx returned again and again in his various works. Nowhere, however, does he present a systematic and thorough treatment of the subject. He seems more concerned to show, contrary to the fundamental theorem of Say's law, that partial gluts are always possible in a capitalistic system and that, instead of being corrected, they tend to culminate in general overproduction.

Marx offered several hypotheses concerning the manner in which a crisis, which will manifest itself in the form of overproduction, may be precipitated. Marxist interpreters and revisionists, however, have considerably more to say on the specific causes of crisis than Marx himself, though in some instances arguments which are in reality the product of a follower have been erroneously attributed to him.[18] His followers extended and

---

[16] A different interpretation is presented by Thomas Sowell, "Marx's Increasing Misery Doctrine," *American Economic Review,* vol. 50, no. 1 (March 1960); reprinted in Ingrid H. Rima, ed., *Readings in the History of Economic Theory* (New York: Holt, Rinehart and Winston, 1970).

[17] Marx, *Capital,* vol. 1, pp. 113–14.

[18] Sweezy maintains that ideas put forward by Michael Tugan-Baranowsky have been erroneously attributed to Marx. See Sweezy, *Capitalist Development,* pp. 159–60.

embellished hypotheses that may be found in his original works, but which are incompletely developed.[19]

Among the hypotheses suggested by Marx on the matter of crisis is the view that this phenomenon is associated with the declining rate of profit. One interpretation stresses the fact that the growth of accumulation stimulates the demand for labor power, thus raising the level of wages and diminishing profits. Diminished profits, in turn, discourage further accumulation and precipitate a crisis, the immediate cause of which, in more modern terminology, is underinvestment. In other words, an interruption to the circular flow takes place as a result of a decline in the rate of profit below normal. This hypothesis finds its modern counterpart in the Keynesian hypothesis of the declining marginal efficiency of capital, although the Marxian formulation is far less well developed, especially as regards its failure to take into account the significance of the interest rate, the money market, institutional credit arrangements, and the role of expectations. Some writers, such as Maurice H. Dobb, have concluded that Marx regarded the tendency of the rate of profit to fall as the primary explanation of crisis.[20]

Another hypothesis regarding economic crisis which may be derived from Marx's fragmentary observations is that crisis is traceable to the atomistic character of capitalist production. The essence of this view is that crises originate because individual businessmen have, at best, only partial knowledge of the market they are serving and tend to produce either too much or too little. These errors call forth adjustments, but only small errors can be corrected without general disturbance. Michael Tugan-Baranowsky, especially, is associated with this view.

A third hypothesis regarding crisis, and the most clearly stated by Marx himself, stresses the role of underconsumption. The capitalist, he maintains, creates surplus value in the process of production in the form of commodities. But in order that he may "realize" his surplus value, he must sell his product. The consumption of the great mass of the people, however, is restricted by low wage rates and unemployment with the result that the capitalist has to sell his product at prices below the cost of production. Labor is not less exploited, but the capitalist benefits little from this exploitation. Consumption is further restricted by the tendency to accumulate and expand capital in order to introduce laborsaving technological improvements. These are undertaken in order to improve the level of profits, but the reduction in variable capital relative to constant capital defeats this goal through its impact on the labor component, which is the source of

---

[19] The subsequent discussion is greatly indebted to the analysis presented by Sweezy, ibid., part 3.

[20] See Maurice H. Dobb, *Political Economy and Capitalism* (New York: International Publishers, 1944), especially chap. 4.

surplus value. The quest for profit is thus the reason for its falling rate. Although this tendency is counteracted from time to time (the problem of timing was not specifically dealt with), it is nevertheless an inexorable tendency which will grow more pronounced as the counteracting forces become attenuated. Thus, crises will become increasingly severe, "putting the existence of the entire bourgeois society on trial each time more threateningly."

Monopoly Capitalism

Marx's entire economic analysis is intended to demonstrate the impossibility of an indefinite expansion of the capitalistic system and the consequent inevitability of a revolutionary period during which the proletariat will overthrow the existing structure of production and its associated social relations and establish in its place a socialistic organization of production. The prelude, in Marx's thinking, to the ultimate overthrow of capitalist production is the change in the organic composition of capital. The proportion between constant and variable capital will grow and the fixed component of constant capital, that is, the proportion in buildings, machinery, and equipment as opposed to raw materials will increase. As a result, there is an increase in the optimum size of the production unit. This implies not only concentration of capital, but what Marx called centralization of capital. "This process differs from the former in this, that it only presupposes a change in the distribution of capital already to hand and functioning; its field of action is therefore not limited by the absolute growth of social wealth, by the absolute limits of accumulation. Capital grows in one place to a huge mass in a single hand because it has in another place been lost by many. This is centralisation proper, as distinct from accumulation and concentration."[21]

The causes of the centralization of capital are only briefly sketched by Marx. The major factor is, of course, the economies inherent in large-scale production. As the optimum-size production unit grows larger, "the larger capitals beat the smaller."[22] In other words, interfirm competition for profits is, in itself, a force of centralization. In addition, the credit system, which Marx conceives of as including not only banks but all financial institutions, facilitates the development of the large corporation, which alters the production structure from one in which there is competition among a large number of producers to competition among a few. In the process of this phase of capitalist development, there is a divorce between the ownership of capital and the entrepreneurial function.[23] The owner of capital becomes a shareholder, and the actual function of the entrepreneur

---

[21] Marx, *Capital,* vol. 1, pp. 625–26.

[22] Ibid., p. 626.

[23] This aspect of Marx's work was greatly extended by Rudolph Hilferding in *Das Finanzkapital* (Berlin: Dietz, 1955), first published 1923.

is assumed by professional managers. The ultimate stage in the development of the capitalistic system gets under way when corporations unify in the form of cartels, trusts, and mergers in order to control production and prices. At the same time, there is also the tendency, because of the close relations between the banks and industry, for capital to be concentrated in the stage of "monopoly capitalism," in which social production is under the virtual control of a single bank or a small group of banks.

During this phase of capitalist development the contradictions of capitalism become even more acute. Monopoly tends to increase the rate of accumulation out of surplus value, since centralization of capital, in decreasing the number of competitors, tends to increase the portion accruing to each one. Monopolists, however, tend to invest in the remaining competitive areas of the economy rather than in their own industry in which the marginal rate of profit is low, though the average rate may still be high. This tends to strengthen the tendency in those sectors toward a declining rate of profit. Also, to the extent that additional monopoly profits are a deduction from labor's share, the tendency toward underconsumption is further strengthened. The declining rate of profit further encourages the adoption of laborsaving technology, with a resultant expansion in the size of the industrial reserve army. Monopoly, therefore, intensifies the contradictions inherent in capitalism and strengthens the forces leading to social revolution. "Centralization of the means of production and socialisation of labor at last reach a point where they become incompatible with their capitalist integument. The integument is burst asunder. The knell of capitalist private property sounds. The expropriators are expropriated."[24] Thus the internal contradictions created by capitalist production ultimately make its continuation untenable. Conditions are then ripe for the proletariat to seize the instruments of production and establish socialism, which is the first stage of full communism. This, in Marx's view, could not come about without violent revolution. The question as to precisely what the pattern and tactics of revolution should be or the nature of the proletariat state, while interesting, is not only outside the scope of economic analysis, but is also a matter to which Marx himself gave little expression.

CONCLUDING REMARKS

While Marx's technical apparatus was built on Ricardian foundations, the political implications he derived from the Hegelian interpretation he gave to the labor theory of value made his analysis unacceptable in orthodox circles, whose inquiries were directed by the classical paradigm. Then, too, Marx adhered to the tradition of the labor theory of value at a time when Austrian thinkers were stressing the importance of utility and the subjective cost elements inherent in interest and profit. His theory therefore

---

[24] Marx, *Capital,* vol. 1, p. 763.

met with an attitude of almost complete rejection except among those who sympathized politically. His analysis of capitalism was indicative of an intellectual crisis, but his rejection of the classical paradigm failed to generate a scientific revolution in economics. However, Marx's observations about the functioning of capitalism were taken more seriously when such problems as monopoly, mass unemployment, excess production, recurrent crises and other phenomena which he had described, became so prevalent that they could no longer be glossed over.

Marx's theory of socially necessary labor as the determinant of value has been widely criticized. But the ultimate use to which he put his theory of value—namely, as the basis for a model in which economic breakdown is ascribed to internal insufficiencies—was a pathbreaking conception. Marx's precapitalist model of simple commodity production envisages an economy in which there is no technical progress and no change in the capital-labor ratio. Thus, there is no net accumulation of capital. But his model of a capitalist economy is one in which there is capital accumulation and, consequently, a continuous reduction in the labor requirements of production. This is associated with a declining rate of profit which affects not only the process and composition of capital accumulation but the entire structure of the system. He envisaged constant capital as increasing more rapidly than the output of consumer goods, so that the economic structure will become increasingly disbalanced.

This principle is very suggestive of the later Keynesian conception, in which a declining marginal efficiency of capital causes a lack of effective demand. But Marx went even further, for his model implies that stable economic growth requires a proportionate expansion of both the consumer and the capital goods industries. Thus the law of capitalist motion which Marx discovered is also surprisingly anticipatory of the principle recently established by modern growth theorists that a growing equilibrium requires that the rate of increase in capacity must equal the rate of increase in income and that both must be expanding at a compound interest rate in order to avoid deflationary tendencies.[25] The change that is required to update Marx's model is, of course, partly substantive, especially insofar as it hinges on the labor theory of value; but once the philosophical and sociological overtones are removed, it is largely terminological. The long underestimated richness of his legacy can best be appreciated if we abstract the Hegelian elements and the sociology of revolution which obscure the contribution of Marx as economist.

GLOSSARY OF TERMS AND CONCEPTS

Capitalistic "law of motion."   A Marxist expression referring to the dynamic tendencies of the capitalistic system which drive it inevitably

---

[25] See Chapter 17 below.

toward a zero rate of return and toward economic crises that threaten the continued existence of the entire bourgeois society.

Constant capital (*c*). That portion of total capital which is unable to create surplus value. Specifically it consists of machinery, tools, equipment, and materials which are used in production but only transfer an equal value to the final good.

Dialectic. A process through which the phenomenon of change has been explained. Conflict between a thesis (in the real world or in the world of ideas) and an antithesis results in a synthesis which provides the basis for subsequent conflicts and further change.

Economic interpretation of history. The hypothesis (principally associated with Marx) that the history of mankind is basically the product of economic forces which determine the character of the other aspects of human experience.

Industrial reserve army. A Marxian term referring to labor which becomes unemployed as variable capital is converted into constant capital.

Mode of production. A distinctively Marxian term referring to the social relationships inherent in ownership and use of the material means of production.

Monopoly capitalism. The last phase through which the capitalistic system will pass according to Marxian theory. It is characterized by an increase in the optimum size of the production unit, the concentration of capital in hands of a few large financial institutions, and a separation between the ownership of capital and the function of entrepreneurship.

Proletariat. A class which is "property-less" in the sense that it owns only its labor power .

Surplus value. A distinctively Marxian term referring to the difference between the value of the commodities workers produce in a given period, and the value of the labor power they sell to the capitalists hiring them. The surplus value realized by the capitalist is indicative of the degree of labor exploitation. The rate of surplus value is the ratio s/v.

Transformation problem. Critics of the Marxian theory of value have argued that the proposition, found in Volume III of *Capital,* that rates of profit, $s/(c + v)$, are equalized as opposed to the equalization of rates of surplus value, $s/v,$ as is argued in Volume I, undermines the labor theory of value. Marx's own "solution" to the transformation problem was that individual commodity prices might well deviate from their labor costs of production and that capitalists would not share equally in surplus value. But these deviations would cancel one another out, so that commodity prices would, on the average, reflect their labor content.

Variable capital (*v*).   That portion of total capital which is used in the support of labor. It tends to be equal to labor's subsistence and creates a surplus, *s,* because *v* is transformed into labor power.

NOTES FOR FURTHER READING

The antiMarxist position of the Austrians has already been noted. Their criticisms are expounded with particular vigor by Eugen Böhm–Bawerk in *Karl Marx and the Close of His System,* which is available as a reprint. (New York: Augustus Kelley, 1949).

Paul M. Sweezey provides an excellent, now classic, summary of Marxian theory in *The Theory of Capitalist Development* (New York: Oxford University Press, 1942). A more recent and very readable review is Ernest Mandel's *An Introduction to Marxist Economic Theory* (New York: Pathfinder Press, 1970), His *Marixst Economic Theory,* 2 vols., trans. by Brian Pierce (New York: Monthly Review Press, 1968), poses a severe challenge to Marxian analysis. See also his briefer work (also trans. by Brian Pierce), *The Formation of the Economic Thought of Karl Marx* (New York: Monthly Review Press, 1971).

The matter of Marx's "transformation problem" has long been a matter of controversy. See J. Winternitz, "Values and Prices: A Solution of the So-Called Transformation Problem," *Economic Journal,* vol. 58 (June 1948). See also A. Mays, "A Note on Winternitz's Solution," *Economic Journal,* vol. 58 (December 1948), and Ronald Meek, "Some Notes on the Transformation Problem," *Economic Journal,* vol. 66 (March 1956). The debate was subsequently reopened by Paul Samuelson in "Understanding the Marxian Notion of Exploitation: A Summary of the So-Called Transformation Problem between Marxian Values and Competitive Prices, *Journal of Economic Literature,* vol. 9 (June 1971). Joan Robinson and Martin Bronfenbrenner offer their comments on the issues raised in the December 1973 issue. William Baumol and Michio Moreshima entered the debate in the March 1974 issue, which also contains Samuelson's "final word."

Among modern interpretations of Marx, none is more provocative than Joan Robinson's "Marx and Keynes," *Economica Critica* (1948), reprinted in *Collected Economic Papers* (Oxford: Basil Blackwell, 1951) and her *Essay on Marxian Economics* (London: Macmillan and Company, Ltd., 1966), in which she maintains that Marx's argument concerning the destruction of capitalism does not depend on the labor theory of value.

A very different but none the less interesting reinterpretation of Marx is Thomas Sowell's "Marx's Increasing Misery Doctrine", *American Economic Review,* vol. 50, no. 1, March 1960, reprinted in Ingrid H. Rima, ed., *"Readings in the History of Economic Theory* (New York: Holt, Rinehart and Winston, 1970).

part three

MARGINALISM

AN OVERVIEW OF MARGINALISM

THE TWO DECADES following the appearance of John Stuart Mill's work were comparatively sterile as far as the development of economic analysis is concerned. Not until the 1870s was economic analysis revolutionized by the introduction of a new point of view and a powerful new tool. The new point of view concerned the role of utility in the determination of value; the new tool was the concept of the additional or marginal increment.

Discovery of the concept of the margin and the development of precision in its use provided the economist with an analytical tool which has become indispensable. Its initial application was to the kind of analysis which is termed "microeconomic" in the sense that it examines particular segments of the economy, such as the household, firm, or industry, with a view of explaining commodity and factor prices and the allocation of resources among alternative uses. This type of economic analysis predominated from the 1870s into the 1930s and continues to be a major facet of modern economic analysis.

A number of early and isolated efforts to develop and use the concept of the margin in connection with problems of value, production, and distribution were made, notably by Wilhelm Gossen, Augustin Cournot, Jules Dupuit, Johann Heinrich von Thünen and Daniel Bernoulli. Their embryonic efforts, however, did not bear fruit. The marginal concepts they identified had to be developed anew before they became incorporated into the body of economic analysis in the 1870s.

The first generation of marginalists, William Jevons in England, Leon Walras in Switzerland, and Carl Menger in Austria, appeared virtually simultaneously in the 1870s in their independent efforts to reconstruct the theory of value. The common thread in their work is their emphasis on marginal utility rather than cost of production as the determinant of value in exchange.

Little work was done with respect to reformulating the theory of distribution. Indeed, there was no separate and distinct theory of distribution in the 1870s in the sense of a body of principles which explained the division of the economy's product among those who perform different functions in the production process or supply different factors. The problem of distribution was still being approached in the classical manner which viewed rent, wages, and profits as the income shares of the three main social classes, rather than as functional returns to productive factors which are, at one and the same time, costs of production and factor incomes. What was needed, therefore, to bridge this hiatus was the formulation of a theory of distribution which was integrated with the theory of value. This was undertaken by "second generation" marginalists.

With the exception of Francis Edgeworth, Philip Wicksteed, and Alfred Marshall, the second generation marginalists were non-English. Chief among them were the Austrians, Friedrich von Wieser and Eugen Böhm-Bawerk, who followed in the tradition established by Carl Menger as did the Swedish economist Knut Wicksell. John Bates Clark and Irving Fisher were the chief American contributors. Except for Marshall, these individuals made their most substantive contributions in the area of distribution theory and the related fields of production theory and the theory of capital and interest. Only Marshall and Wicksell attempted comprehensive treatises concerning the whole subject matter of economics in the manner of Smith, Ricardo, and Mill, and only Marshall was sufficiently inspirational and persuasive to stimulate what may be termed a "school."

These thinkers addressed themselves to three major questions. The first is the theory of production, the second is the explanation of factor rewards according to their productive contributions at the margin, and the third is the special problem of capital and interest. The result of their efforts was a substantial reconstruction of the whole theory of distribution by means of the application of the marginal principle to explain factor rewards, including that earned in the form of interest and profit.

The approach of the marginalists to the problem of explaining the distributive shares reflects, at least in a general way, the economic and social changes that accompanied the evolution of industrial capitalism. There was little evidence that the dismal Malthusian and Ricardian prophecies were being fulfilled. In general, the real wages of labor were rising, and rates of profit did not exhibit significant downward pressure; nor was rent increasing relative to other income shares. On the contrary, emigration, falling birth rates, and freer trade were reducing population pressures; and technological improvements such as Malthus and Ricardo had never envisioned were improving production potentials in both industry and agriculture. The vision of the "stationary state" therefore receded and the analyses of Alfred Marshall and the neo-classicists who followed in the tradition he founded focused on the problems of allocating resources among alternative uses and pricing commodities and factor services. Under Marshall's influence the doctrine of economic harmony, as being inherent in the functioning of a system guided by self-interest, gained new adherents. Thus, there was a revival of the optimism that had characterized the thinking of the late 18th century, but which was unable to survive the stern realities of the first part of the 19th.

This spirit of optimism again found expression in the doctrine of laissez-faire, though few economists sought to present a philosophical basis for their views. Indeed, the scope of economics was becoming more narrow and specialized. Theoretical economists after John Stuart Mill were much more concerned with the formulation of economic laws than with policy prescriptions. They sometimes began with assumptions about the institutional setting and human behavior which did not always coincide with observable reality. Though their abstractions were intended to facilitate the establishment of propositions which represented only a first approximation to the truth, and which therefore required amendment and qualification, there was sometimes a tendency to overlook the tentative nature of their conclusions. The ideal was sometimes equated with reality; and as a result, the body of economics which developed after Mill occasionally appears to have an apologetic bias in favor of the system of private capitalism.

10

Forerunners of Marginalism

WHILE THE "MARGINAL REVOLUTION" dates from the 1870s there were several thinkers who had a remarkably clear understanding of the concept of the margin and who used it to seek answers to specific questions before marginal analysis came into general vogue. The efforts of Jeremy Bentham to give expression to the concept of marginal utility in the 1840s has already been noted. Jules Dupuit (1804–66) of France used the concept of marginal utility even earlier, while Wilhelm Gossen of Germany (1810–54) gave a remarkably polished statement not only of the principle of diminishing marginal utility, but also of the principle of individual consumer equilibrium, in 1854. Earlier still, Daniel Bernoulli (1700–1782) of Switzerland used the concept of marginal increments of income, while Augustin Cournot (1801–77) of France and Johann Heinrich von Thünen of Germany (1780–1850) are remembered for their respective discoveries and applications of the concepts of marginal revenue and marginal productivity.

All these early and isolated efforts to develop and use the concept of the margin took place, so to speak, before their time. They were scarcely known and little appreciated. Bentham's felific calculus, it will be recalled, had no effect on the development of value theory in England. The efforts which will be examined here shared a similar fate; they were overlooked in their own time and had to be "rediscovered" after the so-called "marginal revolution" was on its way. They are therefore examined here as a background to the marginal approach which came into general vogue around the 1870s, even though, chronologically speaking, many of the contributions described here antedated John Stuart Mill's *Principles of Political Economy* of 1848.

THE UTILITY CONCEPT BEFORE THE MARGINAL REVOLUTION

The Classical and Early Continental Conception

The concern of classical economists with the problem of exchange value and their failure to perceive any relationship between value in use and value in exchange caused them to give little emphasis to the role of utility and demand in the determination of prices. They conceived of utility as a general characteristic of a commodity rather than as a relationship between a consumer and a unit of a commodity. This was true even of Senior, who was more aware of the subjective aspects of value than most other English thinkers. Thus the "paradox of value" posed by Smith's example of the diamond and the water went unresolved for lack of the concept of the marginal increment.

Continental rather than English thinkers were the first to use the concept of the marginal increment. Daniel Bernoulli was one of its earliest anticipators. His special contribution was his understanding of the significance of the margin as it relates to increments of income. His hypothesis, presented in the 1730s, was that the importance of an additional dollar to an individual is inversely proportional to the number of dollars already in his possession. From this relationship, he deduced that in a situation of uncertainty with respect to future receipts, an individual will not be guided exclusively by the mathematical probability of gain or loss, but will also be influenced by the significance of given gains or losses in terms of his means.[1] He did not, however, explore the concept of the margin as it relates to utility, consumer behavior, or the determination of exchange value.

The concept of marginal utility expresses the subjective value or want-satisfying power of an additional unit of a given good to a particular user. The importance an individual attaches to an additional unit of a particular good depends in part on its relative scarcity. The larger the supply of a given commodity, the smaller will be its relative significance at the margin. Thus the reason why water usually commands no price is because its supply is so large relative to the demand for it that the utility of the marginal unit is zero. Joseph A. Schumpeter noted that there were a number of 18th-century Italian and French thinkers who understood this paradox of value and that its existence did not, as Smith thought, bar the way

---

[1] Some of the more sophisticated aspects of economic behavior under conditions of uncertainty have only recently been explored. See, for example, John von Neumann and Oskar Morgenstern, *The Theory of Games and Economic Behavior* (Princeton, N.J.: Princeton University Press, 1944).

to a theory of exchange value based upon value in use.[2] While these thinkers realized that utility is more than the condition or prerequisite of value David Ricardo thought it to be, none of them understood the significance of scarcity. They thus continued to be confounded by the paradox of value. Although they appreciated the importance of utility, they lacked the concept of the margin. A marginal utility theory of value was therefore unable to germinate from their efforts.

It is interesting to speculate why Continental thinkers were appreciative of the role of utility in the determination of value so much earlier than their English counterparts. One suggested hypothesis is that Protestant theology, with its greater emphasis on the virtue of work, was more compatible with a labor-oriented theory of value than the more subjective doctrine of Catholicism.[3] Dominance in England of Protestant theology may conceivably be a reason for the general lack of interest of the classical economists in consumer wants, while thinkers in Catholic countries like France and Italy placed greater emphasis on utility.

Gossen's Conception of Utility

The German writer Wilhelm Gossen introduced the concept of marginal utility in *Development of the Laws of Human Commerce and of the Consequent Rules of Human Action* (1854). Using the term *Werth* to express utility, Gossen noted that there is no such thing as absolute utility, but rather that *Werth* is a relationship between an object and a person. He observed that as an individual acquires additional units of the same kind of good, each successive act of consumption yields continuously diminishing pleasure up to the point of satiety. This principle later became known as the law of satiable wants, or Gossen's first law.

If we are willing to assume that pleasure or utility can be measured in cardinal numbers, the relationship between increases in consumption and the behavior of total and marginal utility inherent in Gossen's first law may be demonstrated graphically by means of a hypothetical curve of total utility. This is done in the upper portion of Figure 10–1, in which the maximum utility derived from the consumption of a given commodity is reached when quantity OX is consumed per unit of time. The relationship between total utility and marginal utility may be easily perceived from this graph. If an individual is assumed to be taking quantity X_0 per unit of time

---

[2] Schumpeter in his *History of Economic Analysis,* specifically mentions the Neapolitan Abbé Ferdinando Galiani (1728–87) and the French Abbé Etienne de Condillac (1714–80) in this connection. J. B. Say, the early 19th-century French thinker who is best known for popularizing *The Wealth of Nations,* also appreciated the significance of utility as a value determinant, though he lacked the concept of the margin.

[3] See R. S. Howey, *The Rise of the Marginal Utility School, 1870–1889* (Lawrence: University of Kansas Press, 1960), p. 2.

FIGURE 10–1

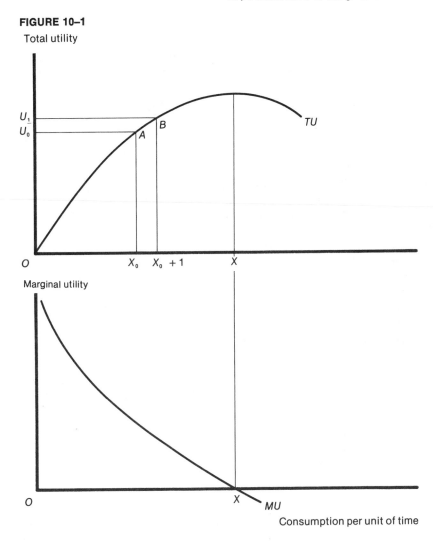

Total utility

U_1

U_0

A

B

TU

O

X_0 $X_0 + 1$ *X*

Marginal utility

O

X

MU

Consumption per unit of time

and he increases his consumption to $X_0 + 1$, his total utility increases from U_0 to U_1. The marginal utility of the unit $(U_0 + 1) - X_0$ is therefore $U_1 - U_0$ and is approximately equal to the average slope of the total utility curve between points *A* and *B*. If the change in quantity and the utility associated with it are both infinitely small, marginal utility at any given level of consumption is equal to the slope of the total utility curve at that point. Symbolically, the slope of the curve is equal to

$$\frac{dTU}{dX}$$

It is evident from the total utility curve that marginal utility decreases as consumption per unit of time increases between O and X. Thus the slope of the total utility curve becomes progressively less until it is zero when quantity OX is consumed, and it is negative beyond that point.

In the lower section of Figure 10–1 a marginal utility curve is abstracted from the total utility curve shown above. The marginal utility of each unit of consumption is plotted on the ordinate axis. Since the slope of the total utility curve is decreasing as consumption level OX is approached and reaches zero at that level, the marginal utility curve slopes downward and passes through the horizontal axis when OX units are consumed. The curve MU represents the marginal utility for all levels of consumption per unit of time including those which yield diminishing total satisfaction. This function is significant because it subsequently became the basis for drawing consumer demand curves.

In addition to the law of satiable wants, Gossen is also given credit for formulating a law which expresses the optimum allocation of income among alternative uses. Since separate units of the same good yield different degrees of satisfaction, each individual will, in general, derive utility only from a limited number of such units. Continued consumption beyond this point does not, therefore, continue to add to total satisfaction. From this Gossen inferred that each person should distribute his available money income among the various goods he consumes in such a manner that the last unit of money spent on each commodity yields an equal degree of satisfaction. His statement of the equimarginal principle as it applies to consumption has become known as Gossen's second law.

While Gossen must be credited with the statement of the basic principles on which the marginal utility theory of value is grounded, the fact is that he did not utilize them in connection with the problem of value and price, and his work attracted virtually no attention until it was rediscovered by William Jevons of England in the 1870s. But this rediscovery came too late to make it a significant force in the development of marginal utility doctrine, though Jevons admitted that "Gossen has completely anticipated me as regards the general principles and method of the theory of Economics."[4]

Dupuit's Conception of Utility

Those who inquired into the monopoly problem, especially as it is associated with large fixed and low variable costs, and therefore increasing returns to scale, are also among the pioneers of the marginal utility analysis. These cost conditions are typical of railroads and other public utilities. Those who dealt with the pricing problems of these industries, therefore, also contributed to the rise of the marginal utility analysis.

---

[4] William Jevons, *The Theory of Political Economy,* Preface to 2d ed. (1879).

The contribution of Jules Dupuit, a French railway engineer, is particularly noteworthy in this connection. The essence of his thinking is contained in an article published in 1844, "On the Measurement of the Utility of Public Works."[5] In this article, he maintained that exchange value cannot be used, as Say suggested it might, as a measure of utility. The utility of everything which is consumed, observed Dupuit, varies according to the person consuming it. This may be illustrated by noting the reaction of consumers to a tax which the government imposes on some commodity. For example, a tax of five sous per bottle of wine will cause its price to rise by that amount but adds nothing to the utility of the product. Thus, if a bottle of wine is bought for 15 sous instead of 10, it is because the buyer finds at least an equivalent utility in it. Were he willing to pay more than 15 sous, but only had to pay that price, the difference would be what Dupuit called *utilité relative,* consumer surplus. He subsequently used this concept as a basis for a theorem on taxation and for a theory of pricing in which he showed that an enterprise which charges a single price to all its customers and sustains a loss might become profitable if it adopted a policy of price discrimination. Such a policy would charge different groups of buyers different prices, depending on the strength of their demands.

Dupuit provided a graphic explanation of his concept of consumer surplus and its relation to price. To do this, he drew a downward sloping demand curve premised on the principle that the quantity of a commodity purchased tends to increase as the price falls. He conceived the curve to become increasingly elastic as the price falls, as does DD in Figure 10–2 because each price reduction brings the commodity into a price range which a larger number of consumers can afford.[6] Given a demand schedule for a commodity such as DD, which Dupuit also took to be a total utility curve, the quantity which would be taken at a price of OP would be OM.[7] If a tax is imposed which raises the price to OP_1, the quantity demanded will be OM_1. As shown in Figure 10–2 the tax yield will be accompanied by a loss of utility which is proportional to the square of the tax. From this Dupuit concluded that the yield of a tax is no measure of the loss its collection imposes on society.

The foregoing conclusion led Dupuit to inquire into the tolls which should be charged for publicly used goods such as canals, bridges, and roads. He reasoned that different objectives require that different tolls be

---

[5] *Annales des Ponts et Chaussées* (1844). This article was not available in English until it appeared in *International Economic Papers,* No. 2 (London and New York: Macmillan & Co., 1952), pp. 83–110.

[6] Dupuit showed price on the horizontal and quantity on the vertical axis. These have been reversed to conform to standard practice in economics today.

[7] Jevons was acquainted with Dupuit's work and recognized its merit as a beginning of the utility approach. Leon Walras, Jevons' codiscoverer of the marginal utility concept in the 1870s, was, however, quite critical of Dupuit's failure to distinguish between the utility curve and the demand curve.

FIGURE 10–2

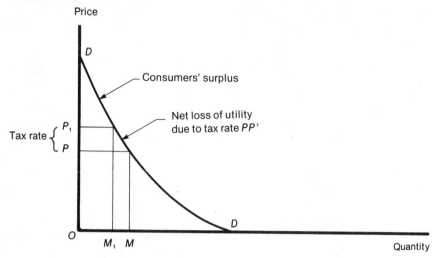

charged. If, for example, the objective is to set a toll sufficient to raise a sum of money to cover the cost of capital expended in making a bridge available, then, given a demand curve for its services of $y = f(x)$, Dupuit reasoned that the appropriate toll can be established by solving the equation $A = xy$ where A is the required amount of money. If, on the other hand, the objective is to raise the maximum revenue possible, given the demand for the service, it is necessary to set a toll at which the marginal revenue will be zero. This requires solution of the equation[8]

$$\frac{dyx}{dx} = 0.$$

Figure 10–3 helps us to appreciate the difference which results when the first equation rather than the second is used as a basis for establishing a toll rate. If the value of x derived from the first equation is equivalent to Op the total revenue yielded by that rate will be $Ornp$. Granting Dupuit's interpretation of a demand curve as a utility curve, the utility of the bridge to those who use it is the area under the curve denoted by the triangle pnP, while the utility which will be lost by the public when this rate, as opposed to a zero rate, is charged is the triangle nrN. A maximum revenue of $ORTM$ can be achieved by charging the higher toll OM as in Part B of Figure 10–3. The utility of the bridge to those who would use it at that rate is equivalent only to the triangle PMT while the loss of utility is represented by the triangle NTR. From this Dupuit concluded that, ideally, the tolls imposed

---

[8] "On the Measurement of the Utility of Public Works," in *International Economic Papers*, pp. 107–8.

FIGURE 10–3

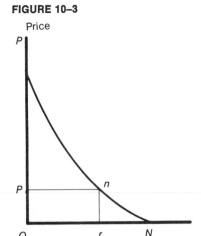

Part A

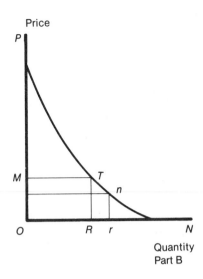

Part B

for the services of publicly used goods like bridges, canals, and roads should be set at the lowest rate consistent with providing a revenue which will cover costs. He also reasoned that if consumers can be grouped according to the utility each category of user derives from the same service it is possible to increase the revenue collected and diminish the loss of utility to consumers by choosing an appropriate combination of tolls.

COST AND REVENUE CONCEPTS BEFORE THE MARGINAL REVOLUTION

The Classical Conception

Just as the classical school made no use of the marginal concept with respect to utility, so it also had no need for it with respect to the cost of production. The classicists generally assumed that production costs are constant, i.e., that additional units of output are produced at the same average cost as preceding units. There was therefore no necessity to deal with a divergence between average and marginal cost.

Marginal cost is the change in total cost associated with an additional unit of output. It is calculated by dividing the increase in total cost associated with the production of added output by the change in output. This measure of cost becomes important whenever it is not realistic to assume that production is associated with a given level of unit costs regardless of the volume which is produced. As a rule, changes in the level of a firm's output will be associated with changes in the average total cost and, therefore, with the marginal cost of output. But this principle was not understood by the classical economists any more than they recognized that the principle of diminishing returns from successive inputs of labor and capital is applicable to all forms of production, and not just to agriculture. While their recognition of the operation of the latter principle in agriculture marked the beginning of marginal analysis in productivity theory, classical analysis did not explore the behavior of cost as output changes. They could not, therefore, discover the concept of marginal cost. But if, instead of examining merely the change in output associated with the application of successive doses of labor or capital to a given quantity of land, which is what Ricardo did in explaining the emergence of rent, they had also examined the effect of output changes in terms of additions to cost, they would have discovered the concept of marginal cost.

Nor did the classical economists have an appreciation of the concept of marginal revenue. Marginal revenue identifies the change in total revenue which is associated with the sale of an additional unit of output. Since the classical analysis of price assumed a purely competitive market, the individual firm is implicitly assumed to be able to sell additional units of output without having to reduce its selling price. Expressed in modern terminology, the classicists thought of a firm as being confronted with an infinitely elastic demand curve. Under these conditions, the marginal revenue which can be gotten from the sale of output is necessarily equal to its average revenue. Thus the emergence of the concept of marginal revenue was delayed until attention was directed to the problem of determining price in a market which is not purely competitive.

Cournot and Marginal Revenue

The first to appreciate the nature and significance of additional increments of revenue with respect to the behavior of the individual firm was Augustin Cournot, who developed the concept in connection with his analysis of monopoly profit maximization.[9] He recognized that increments of revenue are related to increments of demand, and his mathematical training enabled him to perceive the demand for a commodity as a function of its price. Accordingly, he wrote the demand function as $q = f(p)$. Although he made no effort to relate demand to utility, he apparently realized, taking the demand for a commodity as a whole, that more would be bought only at a lower price, so that the demand function for an industry would be negatively sloped, i.e.,

$$\frac{dq}{dp} < 0.$$

---

[9] Augustin Cournot, *Researches into the Mathematical Principles of the Theory of Wealth* (1838), translated by Nathaniel Bacon (New York: Macmillan Co., 1897).

In the case of pure monopoly, which Cournot thought of as the polar opposite of "illimited competition" (our pure competition), the firm is the entire industry, so that the monopolist is confronted with the same demand curve as the industry.

While price is a parameter to a pure competitor who maximizes profits by adjusting output, a monopolist can maximize profits with respect to variations in either price or output. Given the demand curve, he can select the output he wishes to sell and let consumers determine the price, or he can set the price and let consumers determine the quantity they will take. His demand curve $q = f(p)$, therefore, has a unique inverse, $p = f(q)$. Thus, if a monopolist's selling price is p and his demand curve is $p = f(q)$, his total revenue may be written as $R = p(q)$. It may also be expressed functionally as $R = R(q)$. His total cost may also be expressed as a function of output. Thus, $C = C(q)$. The difference between total revenue and total cost is profit. This difference is maximized when the additional revenue associated with an extra increment of output is equal to the additional cost of that increment. It follows that a monopolist will maximize profit when he sets a price which equates the first derivative of total revenue with the first derivative of total cost or, what amounts to the same thing, when marginal revenue equals marginal cost.[10]

Although Cournot did not identify the first derivative of total revenue as marginal revenue, his proof that profits are maximized when $MR = MC$ is a fundamental which is now contained in every textbook on economic principles. It was, however, neglected after Cournot initially introduced it in his *Researches* in 1838. This is due partly to Alfred Marshall's subsequent analysis of monopoly profit maximization in terms of the monopolist's total net revenue rather than in marginal terms. Marshall's procedure, coupled with the fact that neoclassical price analysis, until the 1930s, was typically conducted under the assumption that the structure of the market is purely competitive, accounts for the neglect, subsequent to Cournot, of the concept of marginal revenue.

Although Cournot recognized that a monopolist can set the price for his product in such a way as to maximize his total revenue by offering to sell that volume of output at which marginal revenue will equal marginal cost, he apparently failed to appreciate the additional opportunities for adding to total profits that are inherent in discriminatory pricing. This is the policy of offering a product or service to different groups of demanders at different prices, rather than at the same price, depending upon the strength of their demands. Total profits will then be maximized when the marginal revenue in each separate market is equated to marginal cost. The success of this

---

[10] $P = R(q)$, where P is profit,

$$\frac{dP}{dq} = R'(q) - C'(q) = 0$$

$$R'(q) = C'(q)$$

type of policy depends on the ability of the monopolist to segregate his buyers according to the urgency (elasticity) of their demands and his ability to keep those who are able to buy from him at low prices from reselling to those to whom the product is made available only at higher prices. There was already a lively appreciation of this aspect of the theory of price discrimination by Dupuit and others in the applied fields, transportation in particular.

Cournot on Duopoly

Cournot sketched out the kinds of market conditions which lie between pure monopoly and what he termed "illimited competition" (our pure competition). His most famous case was that of duopoly—two competing monopolists whom he assumed to be selling a costless homogeneous commodity (water from a mineral spring). Assuming, to begin with, that one seller is in possession of the entire market, he proceeded to examine what will happen if a second seller enters to compete with the first. Cournot's explanation of the nature of the ultimate equilibrium position derived from the assumption he made about the behavior of the two rivals.

Cournot assumed that neither seller has the power to name a price. But each has the power to adjust the quantity he offers for sale and, as a result, influences buyers bidding for his product. Thus a rival who enters the market to compete with a former monopolist is conceived to offer that quantity which will maximize his total revenue, on the assumption that the former monopolist will not alter the quantity he offers for sale. But, says Cournot, this assumption on the part of the newcomer will prove to be invalid, for his sales cut into the former monopolist's market and force him to make adjustments in price and output. These adjustments are similarly assumed by Cournot to be made on the invalid premise that the rival seller will not alter his output. Each seller in his turn will always have to adjust to the new situation created by the change his rival makes in the quantity offered for sale. This will necessitate corresponding adjustments by his rival until a stable equilibrium is reached. He reasoned that in an equilibrium situation the amount offered in any market which is not purely competitive can be determined according to the formula

$$\frac{n}{(n+1)}$$

times the competitive output. Thus, the amount offered in a duopoly equilibrium is equal to two thirds the competitive output, with half the amount being offered by each of the sellers.[11] The equilibrium price will be below

---

[11] Cournot's formula, $\frac{n}{(n+1)}$ times the competitive output is applicable to any number of sellers. Competitive output is approached as the number of sellers (n)

the monopoly price and above the competitive price, and any departure from this level will cause its reestablishment as a result of "a series of reactions, constantly declining in amplitude."

The Cournot solution of the duopoly problem is only one among several that are possible, for there are numerous behavior assumptions which might be made. Cournot assumed that a duopolist maximizes his profit on the basis of a conjectural variation of zero with respect to the rival's output. His solution was subsequently criticized by Joseph Bertrand, who offered an alternative solution based on the assumption that each seller tries to maximize his profit, on the assumption that his rival will not alter his price.

Actually, neither Cournot's solution nor Bertrand's is based on realistic assumptions, for duopolists, as well as oligopolists, are likely to realize that their decisions with respect to both price and output are interdependent. Various behavior patterns may result from this interdependence. For example, the monopolists may agree to cooperate and both set a monopoly price, or they may engage in a price war designed to drive the competitor out of business. This is why it has often been said that the problem posed by Cournot is indeterminate. That is, there is no general solution possible without introducing further assumptions about the behavior of the two competitors.

PRODUCTIVITY AND DISTRIBUTION THEORY BEFORE THE MARGINAL REVOLUTION

The Classical Theory

It has already been noted that the observation of the tendency toward diminishing returns on land marked the beginning of marginal productivity theory, but failed to develop the concept of marginal cost. Ricardo, as well as Malthus, understood that if additional doses of labor and capital are applied to a given land area, output will increase at a decreasing rate beyond a certain point. These observations were made in connection with the emergence of rent and the apparent tendency of this share of income to increase. The unique social and political implications of the rent problem undoubtedly helped to obscure the fact that the principle of diminishing returns, or productivity, is equally applicable to labor and capital. Thus the classicists simply treated the problem of distribution as the sharing of the social income among the three main economic classes of society. No attempt was made to explain income shares from a functional point of view, that is, as a problem of valuing the services of factors in the production process under conditions of competition or monopoly.

---

increases; whereas when the number of sellers decreases, the monopolistic situation is approached. Monopoly output is half the competitive output.

Von Thünen and the Marginal Product

A brilliant pioneer effort was made by a little known German thinker, Johann Heinrich von Thünen, to explain factor rewards in terms of the contributions that marginal increments make to the total product. This explanation was developed in conjunction with his effort to explain the location of different kinds of agricultural production in relation to the market. His analysis, as set forth in his leading work, *Der Isolierte Staat* (The Isolated State) in 1826, supposes a city surrounded by uniformly fertile agricultural land which is isolated by an impenetrable wilderness from the rest of the world. The problem which von Thünen postulates is that of explaining to what use the land will be put as the distance from the city increases. He reasoned that the further lands are removed from the city, the less intensive production will become. The more distant areas will concentrate on products that are relatively nonperishable and yet valuable enough to bear the cost of transportation to market. He depicted the location of the different types of production which will develop with varying degrees of proximity to a city by a series of concentric circles. The lands represented by the first circle, immediately surrounding the city, are devoted to garden and dairy products which are highly perishable and/or difficult to transport. The lands represented by the next circle are devoted to forests which provide fuel and building materials. Beyond that, one encounters various kinds of extensive farming and, in areas still farther away from the city, stock raising.

The principle involved in this example is that production must be guided by the additional or marginal cost incurred by moving away from the market. Von Thünen concluded that the added application of a factor should stop when the additional cost exactly equals the value of the added product and that the return to a factor is determined by the productivity of the last unit employed. Thus, he anticipated the marginal productivity theory of factor rewards, though he never used the term, in the process of developing his location theory. His contributions were, however, largely unnoticed; and it was not until the 1890s, as will be seen in Chapter 13, that the marginal productivity principle was rediscovered and the theory of distribution revolutionized.

CONCLUDING REMARKS

Two observations appear to be in order with respect to early efforts to develop the marginal concept as an analytical tool. The first is that while the concept of the margin is obviously applicable to any magnitude of economic significance, such as utility, cost, revenue, and productivity, not one of the individuals who pioneered in its use perceived the possibility of its general application. Bernoulli understood the concept of the margin and applied it to increments of income. Gossen and Dupuit appreciated the concept of marginal utility and its relationship to consumer behavior. Cournot developed the concept of marginal revenue and its relationship to marginal cost in a profit-maximizing situation. Von Thünen understood the relationship between additional applications of a factor of production and its marginal output, and used these concepts as a basis for developing a theory of location and an explanation of factor rewards. All, however, understood the concept of the margin and its significance only in relation to a particular problem. They therefore failed to develop the marginal concept as a general analytical tool.

A second and perhaps related observation is that their embryonic efforts failed to bear fruit; indeed, as is so often the case, essential truths had to be rediscovered or developed anew by others before they could become incorporated into the body of economic analysis. Thus the reconstruction of the theory of value and distribution was delayed until the 1870s, when the marginal concept was reintroduced through the virtually simultaneous and independent efforts of William Jevons in England, Leon Walrás in Switzerland, and Carl Menger in Austria. The contributions of this trio will be examined in the next chapter.

GLOSSARY OF TERMS AND CONCEPTS

Bernoulli's Law. In a case of uncertainty about future receipts, behavior is guided not only by the mathematical probability of gain or loss, but also by the significance of gains and losses in relation to the individual's financial capability.

Cardinal utility. Measurement of satisfaction in terms of cardinal numbers e.g., 1, 2, 3 . . .

Consumer surplus. If a consumer would have been willing to pay more for a particular good than the price he actually paid, he may be said to be enjoying a consumer surplus.

Diminishing marginal utility. The satisfaction an individual derives from additional quantities of a particular good diminishes as more units are consumed in a given finite period of time.

Gossen's Law. From the principle of diminishing utility, Gossen inferred that if an individual distributes his income among the various goods he consumes in such a way that the last unit of each good he consumes will satisfy him equally, he will have maximized his satisfaction; i.e., a reallocation of expenditures cannot increase his satisfaction.

Marginal analysis. An analysis which focuses on infinitely small increments of such economic magnitudes as utility, cost, output, revenue, etc.

Ordinal utility. The ranking of preferences. The statement that A is preferred to B means that a particular individual prefers A to B. It does not imply that the extent of the preference is measurable.

Von Thünen's Law.   The principle that each factor will tend to receive a return equivalent to the value added by the last unit employed.

NOTES FOR FURTHER READING

Augustin Cournot's *Researches into the Mathematical Principles of the Theory of Wealth,* trans. by Nathaniel Bacon (New York: Macmillan Co., 1897) is also published as a Kelley reprint (1960). Generous excerpts of this work have been compiled into a small paperback, *Classics in Economics,* Lloyd Reynolds and William Fellner, eds. (Homewood, Ill.: R. D. Irwin, Inc., 1963) Fritz Machlup provides a particularly readable review of the Cournot-Bertrand-Edgeworth solutions to the problem of duopoly in *The Economics of Sellers' Competition* (Baltimore: The Johns Hopkins University Press, 1952).

Jules Dupuit's "On the Measurement of the Utility of Public Works" in *Annales des Ponts et Chaussées* (1844) is published in *International Economic Papers* (London and New York: Macmillan Co., 1952). His contributions are assessed by George Stigler in "The Development of Utility Theory," *Journal of Political Economy,* vol. 58 (August and October 1950), reprinted in *Essays in the History of Economics* (Chicago: University of Chicago Press, 1965). R. B. Eklund, Jr. examines Dupuit in relation to marginal cost pricing in "Jules Dupuit and the Early Theory of Marginal Cost Pricing," *Journal of Political Economy,* vol. 76 (May–June 1968). Dupuit's role in the development of public finance theory in France is explored by Eklund jointly with R. F. Hébert in "Public Economics at the École des Ponts et Chaussées 1830–1850," *Journal of Public Economics,* vol. 2 (July 1973). Arthur H. Leigh, "Von Thünen's Theory of Distribution and the Advent of Marginal Analysis," *Journal of Political Economy,* vol. 54 (December 1946) is reprinted in J. J. Spengler and W. Allen, eds., *Essays in Economic Thought: Aristotle to Marshall* (Chicago: Rand McNally & Co., 1960). Vol. I of Thünen's *Isolated State* is available in translation by Carla Wartenberg and edited by Peter Hall (Oxford: Pergamon Press, 1966).

11

First Generation Marginalists and the Austrian School

THE FIRST AREA of economic theory to be revolutionized through the rediscovery of the marginal principle was the theory of value. Three brilliant men, William Stanley Jevons (1835–82), Carl Menger (1840–1925), and Leon Walras (1834–1910) working in England, Austria, and Switzerland, independently formulated a theory of exchange value based on the principle of diminishing utility. Jevons' work *The Theory of Political Economy* (1871) was preceded by *Notice of a General Mathematical Theory of Political Economy*. Menger's *Grundsätze der Volkswirtschaftslehre* was also published in 1871, and Walras' *Elements d'economie politique Pure ou theorie de la richesse sociale* appeared 1874–77.

The principle which unites the efforts of Jevons, Walras, and Menger is their emphasis on the role of marginal utility as opposed to cost of production as the determinant of exchange value. They established the nexus between value in use and value in exchange which Smith's "paradox of value" obscured and which Ricardo and Marx failed to recognize. Their analyses thus mark a clear departure from the cost of production and labor theories of value of the classical paradigm and Marxian theory.

Jevons was only 24 years old and a graduate student at the University of London when he adopted the concept of marginal utility into his thinking. His private correspondence indicates that he arrived at the marginal utility principle as early as 1860, which is an earlier date than the initial efforts of either Menger or Leon Walras. Although his theory of production and distribution is essentially classical, his subjective theory of value and its exposition in mathematical terms set it apart from the classical tradition.

But the classical school of thought was so dominant in England that Jevons attracted few followers to build on the ideas he introduced.

Leon Walras was the most mathematically inclined of the first generation of marginal utility economists and lavished his greatest concern on the formulation of his general equilibrium equations. This is his great contribution to economic theory; in the opinion of Schumpeter, it has earned him the distinction of being rated as the greatest of the pure theorists. He built on the work of Quesnay, Condillac, Say, Cournot, and his father Augustin Walras, who was professor of philosophy and an economist in is own right. From his father he drew the notion of the general interdependence of all social phenomena; from Quesnay, the idea of the general equilibrium of the economic system; and from Say, the notion that value derives from utility and scarcity rather than cost of production. He hoped to produce separate volumes on price theory, applied theory, and social economy; but unfortunately his work in the latter two fields did not develop into treatises.

Walras invited a young Italian nobleman, Vilfredo Pareto, who left his country because of political disturbances, to succeed him at Lausanne. Pareto adopted Walras's concept of the general equilibrium of the static state and developed a technique, already introduced by Francis Edgeworth and known as an indifference curve, as an analytical tool for the purpose of defining the nature of the economic optimum. Since the indifference curve technique has come into general use only since the 1930s, particularly in connection with the theory of rational consumer behavior and welfare theory, Pareto's contribution will be examined in a later chapter along with recent developments in microeconomic theory.

The Austrian Carl Menger is the first generation marginalist whose work had the greatest immediate impact. A whole group of able economists, who collectively became known as the Austrians, followed in his footsteps. Friedrich von Wieser (1851–1926) and Eugen Böhm-Bawerk (1851–1914) directed their considerable talents toward advancing the cause of theoretical analysis as opposed to the historical method and extended Menger's opportunity cost principle to the problem of valuing goods of a higher order (productive resources). In addition, both forged ahead in new directions, Wieser in the area of utility theory and Böhm-Bawerk in the area of capital theory. Their joint efforts were persuasive in diminishing the intellectual influence of Karl Marx as well as that of the German historical school.

Their preference for a literary approach to economics sets the work of the Austrians apart from that of Jevons, who utilized caculus to express his notion of the final degree of utility (which is equivalent to marginal utility), and Walras who invented general equilibrium equations. But in spite of this methodological difference, their emphasis on individual utility maximization as the key to the problem of valuation provides a rationale for grouping the work of Jevons, Walras, and Menger together in a single chapter.

THE ECONOMICS OF WILLIAM STANLEY JEVONS (1835–1882)

The Subjective Aspects of Exchange Value

Jevons maintained that investigation of the "nature and conditions of utility . . . doubtless furnishes the true key to the problem of Economics.[1]

Since "the whole theory of Economics depends upon a correct theory of consumption,"[2] "we must necessarily examine the character of the wants and desires of men."[3] The influence of Bentham's felicific calculus is apparent in Jevons' definition of a commodity as "any object or, it may be, any action or service which can afford pleasure or ward off pain," while utility is "the abstract quality whereby an object serves our purposes, and becomes entitled to rank as a commodity." Its negative counterpart is disutility. In the process of gaining utility, an individual necessarily makes sacrifices, or incurs disutility. In the language of Jevons: "To satisfy our wants to the utmost with the least effort, to procure the greatest amount of what is desirable at the expense of the least that is undesirable, in other words, to maximize pleasure, is the problem of Economics."[4]

Neither utility nor disutility are inherent in a commodity but are "a circumstance arising out of their relationship to man's requirements." Thus Jevons conceives of the marginal utility of a commodity as a diminishing function of the quantity in a consumer's possession, for example, $U_a = f(A)$, $U_b = f(B)$ etc. The magnitude of utility can not be measured, but Jevons was optimistic that it might become so at some future time, for the numerical data of economics are both abundant and precise.[5] His subsequent discussions and that of his contemporaries, however, imply that utility can be measured in cardinal terms and that utility functions are additive.[6] He thus represented the total utility of an individual as $f(A) + f(B) + f(C) +$ . . . .

[1] William Jevons, *The Theory of Political Economy,* 5th ed. (New York: Kelly and Millman, 1957), p. 46.

[2] Ibid., p. 47.

[3] Ibid., p. 46.

[4] Ibid., p. 37.

[5] Jevons, *Theory,* pp. 9–12. The technique of indifference curves which Francis Edgeworth and Vilfredo Pareto developed independently was not developed until the 1880s. It assumes only that utilities can be ranked ordinally.

[6] Jevons' single variable utility functions ignore the possibility that the utilities of some commodities, at least, are interrelated rather than independent of the quantities and prices of other goods, changes in income (and therefore the marginal utility of money), and other peoples' utility functions. Commodities may be complementary to one another or rivals of one another. In the case of complementarity, the more of a given good acquired by a consumer, the higher his marginal utility curve for a complementary good becomes. Or, if commodities are rivals (substitutes), the more a consumer acquires of one of them, the lower is the marginal utility of the second (rival) good. The assumption of universal independence of utility functions also has the implication that there are no "inferior" goods, that is, goods of a kind of which

While Jevons had considerable insight into the subjective side of the value problem, he lavished less attention on it than did the Austrians and proceeded early in his analysis to move on to the matter of exchange value. His approach is in terms of two individuals each with a stock of goods (corn and beef). Having recognized that the marginal or "final degree" of utility acquired by an individual decreases with each increase in total supply, he explains that exchange will take place until both individuals maximize their positions by bartering units from their given stock in exchange for the commodity they do not have, until exchange is no longer profitable. His concern is to deduce the limits of exchange and define the nature of the equilibrium position. This condition is achieved when the ratio of exchange of any two commodities is the reciprocal of the ratio of the final degrees of utility of the quantities of the commodity available for consumption after the exchange is completed.[7]

Following Jevons' notations, let a denote a quantity of corn held by one person, while b denotes a quantity of beef held by a second. Each exchanges successive small increments of the commodity he has for successive small increments of the commodity he does not have. If x of corn is traded for y of beef and the market is purely competitive, there will only be one ratio of exchange, that is

$$\frac{dy}{dx} = \frac{y}{x}$$

After exchange has taken place, one person will have $(a - x)$ of corn and y of beef, and the second will have x of corn and $(b - y)$ of beef. If now $\phi_1(a - x)$ and $\psi_1(y)$ are the marginal utilities of beef and corn to the first person, while $\phi_2(x)$ and $\psi_2(b - y)$ are the marginal utilities of corn and beef to the second person, the conditions of maximum satisfaction for each of the two parties in a barter exchange is expressed by the following equation:

$$\frac{\phi_1(a - x)}{\psi_1(y)} = \frac{y}{x} = \frac{\phi_2 x}{\psi_2(b - y)}$$

This equation expresses the principle that neither party to an exchange of two goods will be satisfied unless the ratio of the marginal utilities between them is inversely proportional to their ratio of exchange.[8]

While Jevons' example was intended to demonstrate the limits of barter

---

fewer are purchased as income increases. Yet, there are many goods, particularly if commodity classifications are narrowly defined, which are inferior for certain income ranges. There is also the possibility that the utility of a commodity to a given individual is affected by the quantities consumed by other people. None of these issues were, however, addressed at this stage of the development of marginal utility theory.

[7] Ibid., p. 95.

[8] Ibid., p. 100.

exchange, the equimarginal principle easily explains also how a consumer will allocate his income to maximize his total satisfaction. Given his income, the rational consumer will allocate it among two or more goods in such a way that the marginal utility of the last cent spent on good A is equal to that of the last cent spent on good B. If this were not the case, the consumer could add to his total satisfaction by buying more of the commodity that offers greater marginal utility per additional expenditure because the loss of utility associated with giving up a unit of the second good would be less than the gain gotten from buying more of the first. This principle is of course applicable for any number of goods the consumer might buy.

Rational allocation of money income does not imply that a consumer will spend *the same dollar amount* on every commodity. Rather, it means that *differences in expenditures must be balanced by differences in utility,* so that if the expenditure on good A is twice as high as on good B, the marginal utility associated with good A will be twice as high as that associated with good B. In other words, the marginal utility of the expenditure on any good is found by dividing the price of the good into its marginal utility. The marginal utilities of the goods themselves would be equated only in the event that their prices are the same. Thus, it may be concluded that a consumer who makes a rational allocation of expenditures on any pair of goods acquires them in proportions which will make

$$\frac{\text{Marginal utility of good A}}{\text{Price of good A}} = \frac{\text{Marginal utility of good B}}{\text{Price of good B}}$$

which is the same as making

$$\frac{\text{Marginal utility of good A}}{\text{Marginal utility of good B}} = \frac{\text{Price of good A}}{\text{Price of good B}}$$

This is a conclusion which is not dependent on the cardinal measurement of utility. That is, even if utility cannot be measured directly in terms of real numbers, the expression of quantities in terms of a ratio has the effect of eliminating the unit of measurement. Thus the principle laid down by the marginal utility theorists concerning the maximization of satisfaction is not contradicted by later work in demand theory which introduced a system of ordinal ranking of consumer preferences instead of assuming that utility is cardinally measurable, as it is implicitly assumed to be in the older analysis.

The Concept of the Trading Body

While Jevons' equation

$$\frac{\phi_1(a - x)}{\psi_1(y)} = \frac{y}{x} = \frac{\phi_2 x}{\psi_2(b - y)}$$

was designed to illustrate equilibrium in the case of an isolated exchange taking place at fixed prices, he attempted to make a transition from the subjective valuations of two trading individuals to multiple exchange and the formation of market price. To do this, he employed the concepts of the trading body and the law of indifference. The trading body is comprised of the aggregate of buyers and sellers of a commodity in a purely competitive market, and the law of indifference implies that only one price can prevail for a given commodity in a competitive market. These concepts were used by Jevons to extend the conclusion arrived at with respect to the nature of the equilibrium achieved by two traders to the case of a large number of traders engaged in multiple exchange.

Jevons' logic was supplemented by a graph which is reproduced, with minor changes, in the accompanying Figure 11–1. Trading body (A) with its stock of beef (a) is presumed to exchange increments from its stock with trading body (B) which has a stock of corn (b). Quantities of corn and beef are measured along the horizontal axis and the marginal utilities associated with increases and decreases in the quantities held by each trading body are assumed to be expressed as functions (increasing or decreasing) of the change in the quantities held and are represented by the two curves *MU* corn and *MU* beef. Thus an increase in the quantity of corn held by A, as represented by the line segment $a'a$ implies a decrease in his stock of beef and loss of the utility represented by area $afka'$. The marginal utility associated with increased quantities of corn is represented by $aeca'$ which implies a *net* gain from trade of *feck*.

Trading party B acquires a comparable gain equivalent to area *hdig* when it decreases the stock or corn in order to acquire additional beef. Both parties will continue their trading activities until equilibrium is reached at *m*, which represents the optimum division of both stocks between the trading bodies in the sense that further trade would reduce the net gain of each of the parties.

Jevons' approach involves some rather obvious difficulties, even apart

FIGURE 11–1

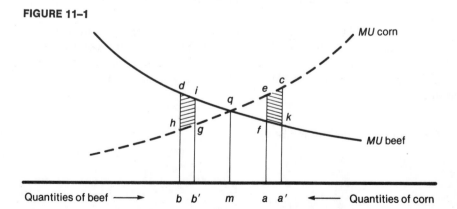

from the fact that it is possible that the relative utilities of the two commodities to either or both traders may be such as to preclude all exchange. The latter limitation is recognized in his discussion of the Failure of the Equations of Exchange.[9] He is also aware that utility functions may not be continuous, although his analysis proceeds on the premise that marginal utilities vary continuously with variations in the quantities held. He maintains, however, that while the single individual may not vary the quantity he buys with every small variation in price, this will not be true of a large number of individuals. The concept of the trading body, whose composition may range from the single individual to the sum total of a country's inhabitants, poses other difficulties. It implicitly assumes that the utilities of different individuals are additive, which Jevons himself recognized is not possible.[10] Moreover, the equilibrium rate of exchange is *assumed* as given at the outset, and is thus not explained, so that the analysis begs the question of price determination. What Jevons' analysis really amounts to, therefore, is a definition of consumer equilibrium with given supplies. Only within the framework of given commodity stocks do utility functions determine exchange ratios or relative prices.

Jevons himself seemed to sense these limitations. While he stated categorically "that value depends solely on the final degree of utility," he amended this principle by asserting: "Cost of production determines supply; supply determines the final degree of utility."[11] Thus, it would seem that while Jevons emphasized the role of utility in determining exchange value, he was groping toward an analysis of price which would also take the role of supply into account. The marginal utility explanation of market price is valid only when supplies are given. It is capable only of demonstrating that each consumer with given tastes and income maximizes his utility position relative to given prices so as to obtain the same marginal utility per dollar expended on every product he buys. It omits the whole problem of variations over time in supply and cost of production, and their effect on exchange value. Just as each consumer maximizes utility, so each producer maximizes his profit position within the framework of factor prices by employing factors in proportions that will yield an equal marginal value product per dollar of factor outlays. This is the sort of analysis which was suggested by Fleeming Jenkin and actually undertaken by Alfred Marshall, who solved the problem of the determination of particular prices without resorting to the fiction of the trading body by explaining that the price of a commodity is determined by the interaction of the schedule of demand for it and its schedule of supply.[12]

---

[9] Jevons, *Theory,* pp. 118–27.

[10] Ibid., p. 21.

[11] Ibid.

[12] Fleeming Jenkin, *The Graphic Representation of the Laws of Supply and Demand and Other Essays on Political Economy 1868–84* (London: London School of Economics and Political Science, 1870, reprinted 1931).

Jevons' extension of his theory of utility to explain the relationship between the supply of labor effort and the disutility of work is a particularly perceptive aspect of his work. He conceived of labor as the "painful exertion of mind or body undergone partly or wholly with a view to future income." The worker is envisioned as "trading" the disutility of work against the utility of the real wages his labor can command. Work, in Jevons' view, entails disutility as well as utility. Initially the disutility inherent in effort offsets whatever pleasure work yields. Later, there is some range of production over which the utility of work outweighs the disutility. Beyond some point the utility from work is exceeded by disutility, so that the net "pain" of labor is first a decreasing function of the rate of production and then an increasing function.

Assuming that a worker is paid by the piece, and that the utility of additional increments of real income is subject to the principle of diminishing marginal utility, his rate of production determines his real wage. The worker's rate of production (i.e. the time he will allocate to work) is determined by precisely the same principle as governs trade in commodities. Individuals offer additional increments of commodities from their stocks as long as the net utility they gain is positive. Analogously, they engage in work as long as the net reward (in terms of the utility of real wages) exceeds the net "pain" from labor. The logic of Jevons' analysis is thus essentially the same as that which underlies a labor supply curve which is represented as sloping upward until at some point it bends backward to represent the greater gains from leisure in comparison with the gains from work.

THE ECONOMICS OF LEON WALRAS

The Subjective Aspects of Value

Unlike Jevons, who insisted that inquiry into the subjective value of goods is the necessary foundation for the theory of exchange value, Walras introduced his analysis of marginal utility (*rareté*) after his inquiry into the theory of exchange value. But like Jevons, he was fully aware that utility is subjective and that it has no direct or measurable relationship to time or space. However, he proceeded boldly and suggested:

> We need only assume that such a direct and measurable relationship does exist, and we shall find ourselves in a position to give an exact mathematical account of the respective influences on prices of extensive utility, intensive utility and the initial stock possessed. . . . I shall, therefore, assume the existence of a standard measure of intensity of wants or intensive utility, which is applicable not only to similar units of the same kind of wealth, but also to different units of wealth.[13]

---

[13] Leon Walras, *Elements of Pure Economics,* William Jaffe, trans. (London: George Allen and Unwin, Ltd., 1954), p. 11.

This is the basis on which Walras proceeded to the solution of the two-commodity exchange problem and the derivation of individual demand curves.

The Derivation of Individual Demand Curves

Walras' primary objective was to demonstrate the establishment of *general equilibrium,* that is, to show that the prices of *m* commodities and *n* factors (land, labor, and capital) are mutually determined. The first portion of his analysis, however, is devoted to the solution of individual demand curves. Whereas Augustin Cournot had neglected the relationship between utility and demand and Jevons had interpreted demand curves as representing individual utility curves, Walras was fully aware of the relationship between utility and demand. (However, his discussion of marginal utility or *rareté,* follows his analysis of demand curves and equilibrium market conditions.) Thus, he introduces the theorem of maximum utility which, in substance, holds that an individual maximizes satisfaction by equating the ratios of marginal utility and price for all commodities.

If there are *m* commodities and one is selected as a *numeraire* (common denomination) in terms of which all other prices are expressed, so that $P_1 = 1$, the individual will maximize his satisfaction when

$$MU_1 = \frac{MU_2}{P_2} = \frac{MU_3}{P_3} = \ldots \frac{MU_n}{P_n}$$

That a price reduction will increase the quantity demanded, while a price increase will decrease the quantity demanded, follows directly from this rule. Postulating a market in which there are definite quantities of only two good, and in which the price of one good is expressed in terms of units of the other, Walras showed how to establish a consumer demand curve for either good. He followed the standard mathematical procedure of placing the independent variable, the price, on the abscissa and the quantities demanded on the ordinate as the dependent variable. The derivation of a consumer's demand curve for a commodity, say A, begins with his initial equilibrium position. The coordinate of the initial price, Pa_1, and the quantity, Qa_1, taken at that price constitute one point on the demand curve shown in Figure 11–2, which follows the economist's practice of placing price on the ordinate axis.[14] The problem is how to establish other price-quantity relationships with respect to commodity A. If the price of A is assumed to increase to Pa_2, a consumer who buys the same quantity at the higher price as he did initially would be left with less income to spend on commodity B. It would also mean that the marginal utility per dollar

---

[14] The procedure of placing price on the ordinate axis and quantity on the abscissa was introduced by Alfred Marshall.

FIGURE 11–2

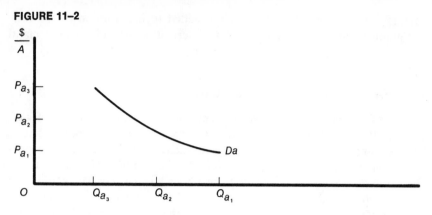

expended on A would have decreased, whereas the marginal utility of a dollar's worth of the now smaller quantity of B at an unchanged price would have increased. That is:

$$\frac{MU_{Qa2}}{Pa_2} < \frac{MU_{Qb1}}{Pb_1}.$$

The purchase of the same quantity of good A, after the price has risen to Pa_2, will not maximize the consumer's satisfaction. He can improve his position by transferring a part of his expenditures to commodity B as long as the marginal utility of a dollar's worth of A is less than a dollar's worth of B. This transfer will continue until he has again equalized the marginal utility of his expenditure on both commodities—in other words, when

$$\frac{MU_{Qa2}}{Pa_2} = \frac{MU_{Qb2}}{Pb_1}$$

The relationship between the quantity Qa_2 and the price Pa_2 yields a second point on the consumer's demand curve for A. This procedure may then be repeated until a whole series of price-quantity relationshps for commodity A is obtained. These price-quantity combinations constitute a demand schedule and may be presented graphically as in Figure 11–2. It should not be inferred, however, that Walras conceived of an individual's demand for a given commodity as a function of its price alone. Cournot, and later, Alfred Marshall, defined the demand curve as $D = f(p)$, a form which continues to be used in present-day partial equilibrium analysis. Walras' demand function is the relationship between the quantity of a commodity and all prices.[15] Only money income and tastes are assumed constant, whereas the Marshallian demand curve assumes also that all prices other than that of the commodity in question are held constant.

---

[15] See his general equilibrium analysis below.

GENERAL EQUILIBRIUM ANALYSIS

The rationale for a general equilibrium approach to the problem of price determination had been clearly perceived by Cournot who wrote that "for a complete and rigorous solution of the problems relative to some parts of the economic system, it is indispensable to take the entire system into consideration."[16] It was, however, Leon Walras who constructed a mathematical system to demonstrate general equilibrium. His analysis, instead of embracing only two commodities and seeking to establish the equilibrium rate of exchange between them, is broadened to include simultaneous equilibria in all commodity and factor markets. Like a partial analysis, a general equilibrium analysis is constructed on the basis of certain assumptions. In Walras' system, these "givens" are (1) the quantities of m finished goods to be consumed in a given period of time; (2) the supplies of n factors of production which may be offered for hire in the factor market or employed directly by their owners; (3) the technical coefficients of production, that is, specific combinations of land, labor, and capital which are required by technical considerations to produce finished goods; and (4) the marginal utility, or *rareté,* functions of individuals for goods and self-employed factor services. These are the data of Walras' system.

The system seeks to determine four sets of unknowns: the quantities of n productive services offered for sale, the quantities of m finished goods demanded, the prices of n productive services, and the prices of m finished goods. In practice, of course, quantities and prices are determined in the marketplace through the interaction of demand and supply forces. But Walras demonstrated that, given the necessary data, it is possible to achieve a solution mathematically. If one of the commodities whose prices we seek to establish is chosen as a common denominator in terms of which all prices are expressed, so that $Pa = 1$, there is one less price to be established, so that there are $2m + 2n - 1$ unknowns to be determined. Therefore, $2m + 2n - 1$ independent equations must be written. Thus the solution of Walras' general equilibrium equations is precisely like the solution of a system of simultaneous equations.

The achievement of general equilibrium in all markets is premised on the achievement of simultaneous individual equilibria. Assuming that the quantities of productive resources available to be supplied by each household is known once commodity and factor prices are established, two conditions must be satisfied before each individual consumer of finished goods or supplier of resources can be in a state of general equilibrium. Both of these conditions can be expressed in terms of equations. The first is

[16] Augustin Cournot, Nathaniel Bacon, trans. *Researches into the Mathematical Principles of the Theory of Wealth* (1838), (New York: Macmillan Co., 1897), p. 127.

that the marginal utilities of the finished goods bought and the productive services of self-owned factors retained by individuals for their own use must be proportional to their prices. If this condition is not satisfied, maximum satisfaction from expenditures is not achieved.

The second condition derives from the fact that every individual is subject to a budget constraint imposed by the requirement that individual expenditures must equal individual receipts. Individual budget equations, together with marginal utility equations, determine the quantity of each good bought or factor retained by the household for its own use. These consumer equations express the optimum allocation of income for each individual among alternative goods and services when their prices and the marginal utilities consumers derive from them are given. By contrast, Jevons' equation of the ratio of exchange expressed the conditions of maximum satisfaction for two parties to a barter exchange.

Consumer utility and budget equations provide part of the information needed to define the conditions of general equilibrium for the economy as a whole. Individual demands for each good, expressed as a function of all commodity and factor prices, are aggregated into a group of market demand equations. There are m such equations, each of which is a summation of individual consumer demand equations for each good. Unlike a particular equilibrium analysis in which the demand for each good is expressed as a function of its price alone, each of the m equations of demand in the Walrasian general equilibrium analysis is expressed as a function of all commodity and factor prices. Similarly, individual supply equations for productive resources, expressed as a function of individual commodity and factor prices, are aggregated to provide a group of equations of factor supplies. There are n such equations.

The technical coefficients of production (which are one part of the data of Walras' system) and the demands for finished goods establish the quantity of each resource required to produce each good. Since Walras assumed full employment, it is axiomatic that the sum of these requirements is equal to the total supply of each resource. This, too, may be expressed in terms of a group of equations which are n in number. A final group of equations expresses equality between the prices of consumer goods and their average costs of production. Since one of these goods is the *numéraire* or common denominator, there are $m - 1$ such equations. Summing up, then, there are $2m + 2n - 1$ independent equations to solve for the same number of unknowns, so that the system is determinate.

The preceding verbal description of the Walrasian system may be supplemented by a symbolic presentation. Let the quantity of finished goods to be consumed be designated as

$$a, b, \ldots m$$

Let the supply of factors used to produce these goods be designated as

$$s_{f1}, s_{f2}, \ldots s_{fn}$$

Let the technical coefficients, i.e., the quantities of the various factors f_1, $f_2, \ldots f_n$ that enter into the production of finished goods $a, b, \ldots m$ be designated as

$$a_{f1}, a_{f2}, \ldots a_{fn}$$
$$b_{f1}, b_{f2}, \ldots b_{fn}$$
$$\ldots \ldots \ldots \ldots$$
$$m_{f1}, m_{f2}, \ldots m_{fn}$$

Let the quantities of finished goods demanded be designated as

$$d_a, d_b, \ldots d_m$$

and let the demands for the services of owner-employed factors be designated as

$$d_{f1}, d_{f2}, \ldots d_{fn}$$

The marginal utility, or *rareté*, functions of each of the m consumer goods and n productive services retained by owners are

$$u_a = \phi_a(d_a)$$
$$u_b = \phi_b(d_b)$$
$$\ldots \ldots \ldots \ldots \ldots$$
$$u_m = \phi_m(d_m)$$
$$u_{f1} = \phi_{f1}(s_{f1} - d_{f1})$$
$$u_{f2} = \phi_{f2}(s_{f2} - d_{f2})$$
$$\ldots \ldots \ldots \ldots \ldots$$
$$u_{fn} = \phi_{fn}(s_{fn} - d_{fn})$$

No equation is required for good a, which is the *numéraire* or common denominator in terms of which values are expressed. The total number of equations is $n + m - 1$, which is sufficient to determine n unknown factor supply functions, as follows:

$$s_{f1} = f_1(p_{f1}, p_{f2}, \ldots p_{fn}, p_b, p_c, \ldots p_m)$$
$$s_{f2} = f_2(p_{f1}, p_{f2}, \ldots p_{fn}, p_b, p_c, \ldots p_m)$$
$$\ldots \ldots \ldots \ldots \ldots \ldots \ldots \ldots \ldots$$
$$s_{fn} = f_n(p_{f1}, p_{f2}, \ldots p_{fn}, p_b, p_c, \ldots p_m)$$

and $m - 1$ unknown demand functions, as follows:

$$d_b = f_b(p_{f1}, p_{f2}, \ldots p_{fn}, p_b, p_c, \ldots p_m)$$
$$d_c = f_c(p_{f1}, p_{f2}, \ldots p_{fn}, p_b, p_c, \ldots p_m)$$
$$\ldots \ldots \ldots \ldots \ldots \ldots \ldots \ldots \ldots$$
$$d_m = f_m(p_{f1}, p_{f2} \ldots p_{fn}, p_b, p_c, \ldots p_m)$$

The summation of individual demand and supply functions results in two of the four sets of equations Walras required to define the conditions of general equilibrium for the economy as a whole. There are n equations of supply for productive services, as follows:

$$S_{f1} = \Sigma s_{f1} = F_{f1}(p_{f1}, p_{f2}, \ldots p_{fn}, p_b, p_c, \ldots p_m)$$
$$S_{f2} = \Sigma s_f = \ldots\ldots\ldots\ldots\ldots\ldots\ldots\ldots\ldots\ldots$$
$$\ldots\ldots\ldots\ldots\ldots\ldots\ldots\ldots\ldots\ldots\ldots\ldots\ldots\ldots$$
$$S_{fn} = \Sigma s_{fn} = \ldots\ldots\ldots\ldots\ldots\ldots\ldots\ldots\ldots\ldots$$

There are also $m - 1$ equations of demand for finished goods, as follows:

$$D_b = \Sigma d_b = F_b(p_{f1}, p_{f2}, \ldots p_{fn}, p_b, p_c, \ldots p_m)$$
$$D_c = \Sigma d_c = \ldots\ldots\ldots\ldots\ldots\ldots\ldots\ldots\ldots\ldots$$
$$\ldots\ldots\ldots\ldots\ldots\ldots\ldots\ldots\ldots\ldots\ldots\ldots\ldots\ldots$$
$$D_m = \Sigma d_m = \ldots\ldots\ldots\ldots\ldots\ldots\ldots\ldots\ldots\ldots$$

The third group of n equations expresses equality between the quantity of productive services employed to produce each good, given the technical coefficients of production, and the quantity offered:

$$a_{f1}D_a + b_{f1}D_b + \ldots m_{f1}D_m = S_{f1}$$
$$a_{f2}D_a + b_{f2}D_b + \ldots m_{f2}D_m = S_{f2}$$
$$\ldots\ldots\ldots\ldots\ldots\ldots\ldots\ldots\ldots\ldots\ldots\ldots$$
$$a_{fn}D_a + b_{fn}D_b + \ldots m_{fn}D_m = S_{fn}$$

Finally, the fourth group of equations expresses equality between the prices of m consumer goods and their average costs of production. Thus, there are m equations, as follows:

$$a_{f1}p_{f1} + a_{f2}p_{f2} + \ldots a_{fn}p_{fn} = 1$$
$$b_{f1}p_{f1} + b_{f2}p_{f2} + \ldots b_{fn}p_{fn} = p_b$$
$$\ldots\ldots\ldots\ldots\ldots\ldots\ldots\ldots\ldots\ldots\ldots\ldots$$
$$m_{f1}p_{f1} + m_{f2}p_{f2} + \ldots m_{fn}p_{fn} = p_m$$

Summing up, there are $2m + 2n - 1$ independent equations to solve for the same number of unknowns. The determinateness of the system is assured by the equality of the number of independent equations with the number of unknowns. This demonstration has become the inspiration for all subsequent work on general equilibrium.

It is not difficult to appreciate some of the problems inherent in the general equilibrium approach. To establish and solve such a system of equations is certainly to perform Herculean labor. Furthermore, equality between the number of equations and the number of unknowns will not necessarily mean that there will be a single positive solution. Sets of simultaneous equations may have multiple solutions or may be satisfied by zero or negative prices, which imply that the good is either a free good or a nuisance good. Negative prices for goods are more easily accommodated in the equations than negative factor prices, for the latter imply that factors are paying firms to employ them. Yet, it is obvious that if factor supplies and technical coefficients of production are fixed, as Walras assumed them to be, it may not always be possible to satisfy the market-clearing equations at positive factor prices.

Walras took his analysis a step beyond demonstrating the determinacy of a general market equilibrium. He tried to show that the problem for which he gave a theoretical explanation is, in practice, solved in the market by the mechanism of free competition through a process of recontracting. People are presumed to come to the market with certain stocks of commodities and certain dispositions to trade, from which a set of prices will emerge. If demand and supply are equal at these prices, there is an immediate equilibrium. If, on the other hand, demand and supply are not equal, people will recontact until none of the parties see any advantage in further recontracting. The price ultimately established by this process is the equilibrium price.

The two cardinal points in Walras' description of exchange equilibrium are (1) that the amounts demanded and supplied by particular individuals depend on the system of market prices and (2) that there must be an equilibrium between demand and supply in particular markets. What Walras does not make clear in his analysis of exchange equilibrium is whether exchanges do or do not take place at the prices originally proposed if these prices are not equilibrium prices. If there is no actual exchange (or "false trading") until the equilibrium prices are reached by bidding, Walras' explanation of the way in which a position of stable equilibrium is reached seems unrealistic. But if there is false trading so that exchanges do take place at prices which are not equilibrium prices, the final equilibrium prices are bound to be affected by them. That is, the final position of equilibrium is not independent of the path followed to reach the equilibrium position.

THE ECONOMICS OF THE AUSTRIAN SCHOOL

Menger on the Subjective Aspects of Value

Menger gives even more detailed attention than Jevons to the subjective aspects of value. In his inquiry into what he terms *Güterqualität* (prerequisites for status as goods), he notes that there must be a human want for an object and that it must have characteristics which will satisfy this want.[17] Further, consumers must be aware of its want-satisfying power and have the object at their disposal. *Güterqualität* is thus seen as deriving from human wants. Because objects having *Güterqualität* are generally in smaller supply than the needs (*Bedarf*) for them, people will economize in their use. The individual will therefore classify his wants in accordance

---

[17] Carl Menger, *Grundsätze der Volkswirtschaftslehre,* vol. I, Reprint No. 17 (London: London School of Economics, 1870), p. 3.

TABLE 11–1

I	II	III	IV	V	VI	VII	VIII	IX	X
10	9	8	7	6	5	4	3	2	1
9	8	7	6	5	4	3	2	1	0
8	7	6	5	4	3	2	1	0	
7	6	5	4	3	2	1	0		
6	5	4	3	2	1	0			
5	4	3	2	1	0				
4	3	2	1	0					
3	2	1	0						
2	1	0							
1	0								
0									

with their importance. Menger illustrates this hypothesis with an arithmetical example which presents a hierarchy of wants from the point of view of an individual consumer designated by Roman numerals from I to X as in Table 11–1. Arabic numbers listed in each column represent the satisfaction associated with a unit increase in the stock of goods acquired to satisfy that want. Declining numerical values were selected to represent the diminishing want-satisfying power of additional units of the same good. No additions are made to any stock when the utility of the marginal increment becomes zero.

THE THEORY OF IMPUTATION

Menger's Theory of Negative Imputation

Menger was the first economist to consider the problem of the valuation of the factors of production on the basis of their contributions to the value of their products. He conceived of factors of production as *goods of a higher order* whose value is determined by imputation from the anticipated value of the goods of a lower order in whose production they serve. Menger thought that the correct procedure for establishing this value was to withdraw one unit of a good of a higher order from production and observe the effect on total output. The loss in the total product is the marginal product of the variable factor in question, and the utility of the product which is forgone establishes the value of the unit of the good of a higher order in the production process. This value may also be conceived of as the alternative or opportunity cost of using the factor in the production of some other good. This alternative cost is equal to the difference in utility which results from the withdrawal of a unit of the resource in question.

Within the framework of Menger's reasoning, it is immaterial whether the factors are used in fixed proportions or variable proportions. In the case of fixed proportions the withdrawal of a unit of one resource necessitates the employment of some portion of cooperating resources elsewhere. The total loss of product minus the product produced by the complementary factors in their new employment establishes the loss of utility, and thus the value, of the variable factor.

In the more usual case of variable factor proportions, Menger implies that the withdrawal of one unit of a factor necessitates a rearrangement of complementary factors. The loss of utility associated with the reduction of the product determines the value of the withdrawn factor unit. What is not made clear in Menger's analysis is the effect which the tendency toward diminishing returns exerts on output when the input of one variable resource is altered. Nor does he examine the problem as to whether his method of valuing the factors will result in payments which will exactly exhaust the total product. This is a question which was to be a major issue of the marginal productivity theory of distribution. A theory of capital is also absent from Menger's theory of distribution. That is, he does not distinguish between capital goods themselves and the services they render. Menger's explanation of the value of productive factors, as far as it went, however, was significantly better than any previously offered hypothesis.

Von Wieser's Theory of Positive Imputation

Friedrich von Wieser extended Menger's theory of imputation by emphasizing that the process identifies the *economic* contribution rather than the physical contribution of a factor. He also maintained that Menger's procedure of valuing the factors by negative imputation was inaccurate. The withdrawal of a unit of any one agent reduces the productivity of remaining agents. The reduction in the total product is not due just to the withdrawal of an individual unit of the factor in question. Hence, he proposed the alternative method of positive imputation, which measures the product gained by adding a unit of the factor in question.

Wieser assumed that factors are combined in fixed proportions in each industry, though these proportions vary from one industry to another. By assuming that the values of the factors are simply reflections of the marginal utility of consumer goods, and therefore equal to the value of the product, he was able to demonstrate that factor payments just exhaust the final product. However, this procedure does not prove that a factor's reward is determined by the value of its marginal product, because the separate productivity of a factor cannot be imputed at all when factors are combined in fixed proportions. A factor's marginal product can be isolated *only* if proportions are variable and substitution is possible. Otherwise, the concept of marginal product is without meaning.

A further limitation of the Austrian theory of imputation is its interpretation of the marginal value product of a factor as a reflection of consumer satisfaction in an aggregate sense. The concept of social marginal utility implies that individual utilities are additive. Moreover, the Austrian formulation implies that factor values (i.e. the values of goods of a higher order) are determined by commodity values which are themselves determined by social marginal utility. Actually, the relationship between commodity and factor values is a reciprocal one because consumer incomes, which are derived from the sale of productive services, underlie the demands for commodities.

BÖHM-BAWERK'S AGIO THEORY OF INTEREST

The Value of Present versus Future Goods

Eugen Böhm-Bawerk's special contribution was the extension of theory of imputation to provide an explanation for the income share received by the capitalists of society. Schumpeter's well known description of Böhm-Bawerk as "the bourgois Karl Marx" stems from the political and sociological implication that the receipt of interest and profit by capitalists is justified in a capitalistic system.

Böhm-Bawerk's agio theory is the earliest of the nonmonetary theories of interest to emerge during the first decade of the 20th century as a special aspect of distribution theory. Interest theory during this period sought, in the main, to explain the real rate of remuneration of capital relative to the prices of other factors of production. It was not concerned with the relationship between changes in the interest rate and the general price level or changes in the level of aggregate income, output, and employment.

Böhm-Bawerk's point of departure was Menger's marginal utility theory of value, to which he added his own solution, different from von Wieser's, of the imputation problem. His theory of capital and interest was developed within this typically Austrian conception of the problem of valuation. It was presented in a three-volume *magnum opus* entitled *Capital and Interest,* whose first volume, *History and Criticism of Interest Theories* (1884) set the groundwork for the two subsequent volumes. This volume presents a detailed review and criticism of all the theories on the subject of interest which had been previously formulated. It thus provides the background for Böhm-Bawerk's definitive statement of his own views on capital and interest in his *Positive Theory of Capital* (1889), the second of his three volumes.

The key to the problem of capital as a means of production and as a source of a net return is, in Böhm-Bawerk's view, an understanding of the nature of the production process in which the original factors, labor and resources, transform matter into want-satisfying goods. These may be consumer goods or "produced means of production." When production proceeds with the aid of produced means of production, the same input of original factors results in a larger total product than when direct methods of production are employed. This observation, which was not completely original with Böhm-Bawerk, but which had never been given detailed formulation before, became one of the pillars of his theory of capital and interest. He reasoned that the net return to capital must result from the effect which the greater productivity of the roundabout method has on the formation of value and also must be related to the postponement of consumption inherent in roundabout production. This is the reason why he sees the problem of capital and interest as part of the broader problem of value. Goods have value only because they have utility; the want-satisfying power of a particular unit of a given good depends not only on the total quantity which is available, but also on the dimension of time in which it is available.

Capital goods are, in Böhm-Bawerk's view, not original and independent factors of production, but intermediate products which yield final goods after a period of waiting. The more capitalistic, or roundabout, a process of production is, the longer will be the interval of waiting time which will elapse before the final goods emerge from the production process. Any good which is available in the present has a greater value than an equal quantity of the same kind available at some time in the future. Present goods, therefore, command an agio, or premium, over future goods.

The Three Reasons for Interest

Böhm-Bawerk advanced three separate reasons for the higher value placed on present goods. The first two are of a psychological nature and are relevant to the demand for consumer loans, namely, the hope which most people entertain of being better able to provide for future wants and the all too human tendency to underestimate future wants. These factors reinforce one another and enhance the value of present goods. The third reason for the greater value of present goods is technical rather than psychological and relates to the demand for producer loans. Presently available goods are "technically superior" instruments for the satisfaction of human wants and therefore yield a higher utility than future goods.

Böhm-Bawerk illustrates this principle with an example intended to demonstrate that the want-satisfying power of any presently available productive resource, say 30 days of labor, is greater than that of 30 days of labor used in the same production process which will become available in a year's time.[18] By the same reasoning, 30 days of labor which became available last month are technically superior to the same quantity which became available only this month. Precisely the same principle applies to the utilities which are produced by capital goods. Unless there is a change

---

[18] Eugen Böhm-Bawerk, *Capital and Interest,* vol. 2: *Positive Theory of Capital,* trans. G. D. Huncke (South Holland, Ill.: Liberaterian Press, 1959), pp. 273–89.

in the state of the arts which will enhance the productivity of still-to-be-produced capital goods, those capital goods which are already on hand are "technically superior" to those which are not yet available because the time interval which must elapse before they generate finished goods is shorter than that which would necessarily elapse if these intermediate products were not yet available. Thus, presently available intermediate goods have a greater value productivity and are therefore technically superior with respect to want satisfaction than those not yet available. Hence, their use in time-consuming roundabout methods of production will yield a product which contains a surplus value.

The concept of the period of production is an integral part of the Austrian theory of capital. If only the third reason for interest were operative, the greater productivity of the roundabout method would result in an infinitely long period of production. The operation of the first and second reasons, however, which cause the value of future goods to be discounted in the present, implies that the period of production cannot be infinitely long. It is therefore the interaction between the first two and the third of Böhm-Bawerk's "three grounds" which will determine the optimum length of the production period in terms of its yield of present value. Thus the agio in the exchange of present for future goods derives, on the one hand, from the fact that future values are discounted in the present for psychological reasons and, on the other, from the fact that the roundabout method of production yields a greater value product. It is precisely because the three grounds for the value agio of present over future goods are not equally operative for all individuals that there is a market for exchanging present against future goods. The preference at the margin for present versus future goods is objectively expressed in the rate of interest. This rate is the price phenomenon which reflects the difference in value between present and future commodities.

The Forms of Interest

Böhm-Bawerk considers the simplest manifestation of interest to be that which arises in connection with consumer loans. A borrower must pay interest to the lender who makes the funds available in order to acquire present goods. Profit to entrepreneurs is, however, the principal form in which interest manifests itself. The latter buy remote goods, such as raw materials, tools, machines, and the use of land and labor, and transform them into finished products ready for consumption. According to Böhm-Bawerk they receive a gain which is proportioned to the amount of capital invested in their business. This gain, which has variously been called "profit," "surplus value," and "natural interest on capital," is in addition to the compensation received for managerial services. It arises, according to Böhm-Bawerk, from the fact that the goods of remote rank which the businessman transforms are, economically speaking, future commodities.

Higher order goods are incapable of satisfying wants in their present form and need to be transformed into consumption goods in order to do so. They are, in effect, therefore, future commodities which have a lower present value than they will have when the transformation process is complete. The increase in value is, according to Böhm-Bawerk, the profit of capital.[19] Profit is therefore a price agio which appears in exchange transactions between capitalists, on the one hand, and workers and landlords who own the original means of production, on the other. Differently expressed, profit is a discount from the money value of the future marginal product of the original means of production. It follows that even in a socialist society the value of a worker is the equivalent only of the discounted value of his product rather than the whole product, and the same is true of land. That is, both rent and wages are the monetary expression of the marginal products of a given quantity of labor and land discounted to the present. This would, in Böhm-Bawerk's view, be equally true in a socialist society, for labor and land can in any case receive only the present or discounted value of their future product.[20]

CONCLUDING REMARKS

The threads of the preceding examination may now be drawn together to see what positive contribution to economic analysis was made by the marginal utility theorists and how they differed from their classical predecessors. The most significant contribution is their use of the marginal utility apparatus to deduce the exchange ratios that will be established between commodities in competitive markets. In so doing, they established the nexus between value in use and value in exchange which Smith, Ricardo, and Marx failed to recognize. Their analysis thus marks a clear departure from labor and cost of production theories of value. While they did not emphasize the weaknesses of the labor theory of value as a basis for advancing their views on marginal utility, they pointed out that a labor theory of value is deficient in several respects. They noted first that a large expenditure for labor will not necessarily result in a high commodity value, because future demands may be inaccurately forecast. They also noted that a labor theory of value lacked generality, for it does not explain the value of land or objects like works of art that exist in permanently fixed supply.

---

[19] Ibid., pp. 299–302.

[20] The American theorist Frank Taussig combined the marginal productivity theory of factor rewards with Böhm-Bawerk's theory of time preference to develop the hypothesis that competitive wages tend to be equal to the discounted value of labor's marginal product because wages represent an advance made by employers against the finished product. See *Wages and Capital* (New York: Appleton & Co., 1898).

While the role of marginal utility appears somewhat less obvious in Walras' analysis than in that of Menger and Jevons, because it is overshadowed by the theory of general equilibrium, Walras nevertheless regarded the notion of marginal utility as fundamental, for it constituted the basis for his demand functions and thus the whole production process.

The preoccupation of the marginal utility economists with the theory of exchange made it appear that the theory of maximizing behavior was a special case rather than a tool of general application. The subsequent development of marginal economics, however, consisted primarily of the extension of the marginal principle to the theory of production and distribution. The concept of the margin has significance not only in relation to consumer goods but also in relation to producer goods. Menger called them "goods of a higher order," which differ from consumer goods only in terms of their nearness to the final user. Their value is therefore dependent on the marginal utility of the goods in whose production they assist. Though Menger himself was too preoccupied with the problem of subjective value to make the transition to the problem of factor valuation, and therefore income distribution, his ranking of goods into various "orders" became the basis for later important analysis which demonstrated how the productive contribution of separate factors to the utility of the total product could be isolated. This is the route by which later Austrians were to discover the principle of imputation.

It is something of an enigma that the marginal productivity theory was not clearly developed alongside the theory of subjective value. It seems that once the revolutionary concept of explaining the value of consumer goods in terms of marginal utility theory was developed, the next logical step would have been to explain how the values of the productive services themselves are determined. Yet, it was approximately 20 years later that the marginal productivity theory finally made its appearance. As in the case of marginal utility, it also appeared more or less simultaneously in several countries. These developments will be treated in the following chapter which examines the contributions of the "Second Generation" Marginalists.

GLOSSARY OF TERMS AND CONCEPTS

Agio.   The premium commanded by present goods over future goods.

Inferior goods.   Goods of a kind purchased less as income increases.

Imputation.   The process of valuing factors of production (goods of a higher order" in Austrian terminology) on the basis of their contributions to the value of production

Numéraire.   A commodity arbitrarily chosen to serve as a common denominator of unchanging value, i.e., as "constant value money," in terms of which all other prices are expressed. Thus all prices vary relative to P_a where $P_a = 1$.

Opportunity cost. The price a factor of production can command in its best paying alternative use.

Recontracting. Walras' notion of hypothetical resales of commodities as a process for establishing a true equilibrium.

Walras' Law of general equilibrium. Demonstration of simultaneous individual equilibriums in all commodity and factor markets. A mathematical solution can be found if it is possible to write as many equations on the basis of known data as there are unknown prices to be established.

NOTES FOR FURTHER READING

Among the several available sources that examine the work of the marginal utility school as a whole, those which are particularly recommended are R. S. Howey, *The Rise of the Marginal Utility School, 1870–1889* (Lawrence: University of Kansas Press, 1960) and T. W. Hutchison, *A Review of Economic Doctrines, 1870–1929* (Oxford: Clarendon Press, 1953), particularly chaps. 1, 2, 6, 9, and 13.

On the development of marginal utility theory see Emil Kauder's "The Retarded Acceptance of the Marginal Utility Theory," *Quarterly Journal of Economics,* vol. 67 (November 1953), reprinted in Ingrid H. Rima, ed., *Readings in the History of Economic Theory* (New York: Holt, Rinehart and Winston, 1970); and George Stigler, "The Development of Utility Theory," *Journal of Political Economy,* vol. 58 (August and October, 1950). This selection is reprinted in Joseph Spengler and W. Allen, eds., *Essays in Economic Thought: Aristotle to Marshall* (Chicago: Rand McNally & Co., 1960).

On Jevons' work, J. M. Keynes' "William Stanley Jevons," in *Journal of the Royal Statistical Society,* vol. 49 (1936) is especially recommended, as is Lionel Robbins' "The Place of Jevons in the History of Economic Thought," *The Manchester School,* vol. 7 (1935). Keynes' article is reprinted in his *Essays in Biography* (London: Macmillan and Co., Ltd., 1933). R. D. Collison Block contributed an important interpretation of Jevons' work in "Jevons, Marginalism and Manchester," in *The Manchester School,* vol. 40 (March 1972), which commemorates the 100th anniversary of the publication of Jevons' *Theory of Political Economy.* Marian Bowley contributed "The Predecessors of Jevons: The Revolution That Wasn't" to the same volume. George Stigler analyzes Jevons' contribution in *Production and Distribution Theories* (New York: McGraw-Hill, 1941.) Reference should also be made to the rest of Jevons' work; see, in particular, Jevons' own *Investigations in Currency and Finance,* H. S. Foxwell, ed. (London: Macmillan and Co., Ltd., 1909) and Harriet A. Jevons, ed. *Letters and Journal* (London: Macmillan and Co., Ltd., 1886), which includes his correspondence with Walras and others and his chronicle detailing his Australian and American visits and his growing interest in economics and the social sciences.

Leon Walras' *Elements* (1874) has been translated by William Jaffé (Homewood, Ill.: R. D. Irwin, Inc., 1954). Jaffé has also edited *Correspondence of Leon Walras and Related Papers,* 3 vols. (Amsterdam: North-Holland Publishing Co., 1975) and contributed an article, "Leon Walras" to *International Encyclopedia of the Social Sciences* (New York: The Macmillan Co., 1968), vol. 16, pp. 447–52. A succinct summary of the general equilibrium system has been contributed by Milton Friedman in "Leon Walras and His Economic System," *The American Economics Review* (December 1955), reprinted in Ingrid H. Rima, ed., *Readings in the History of Economic Theory* (New York: Holt, Rinehart and Winston, 1970). J. R. Hicks presents a nontechnical exposition in "Leon Walras," *Econometrica,* vol. 2 (October 1934).

George Stigler examines the work of Carl Menger in "The Economics of Carl Menger," *Journal of Political Economy,* vol. 45 (April 1973), which is reprinted in Joseph J. Spengler and W. Allen, *Essays in Economic Thought: Aristotle to Marshall* (Chicago: Rand McNally & Co., 1960). Frank Knight provides a highly favorable review and assessment of Menger's work in his introduction to James Dingwalls and Bert Hoselitz trans. and ed. of Menger's *Principles of Economics* (Chicago: Free Press, 1950).

Böhm-Bawerk's *History and Critique of Interest Theories* (1884) is translated by G. D. Hunke and H. F. Sennholz (South Holland, Ill.: Liberation Press, 1959). Frederick Wieser's *Natural Value* (1893) has been translated by R. Mulloch (New York: Stechert, 1930).

12

Second Generation
Marginalists

CONTINENTAL and American contributions to economics appeared with increasing frequency and commanded a wider audience after 1870 than was the case in the preceding century. The leading role of the Austrian school has already been noted. They gave inspiration to many others including Knut Wicksell (1851–1926) of Sweden whose principal works are *Value, Capital and Rent* (1893); *Interest and Prices* (1898; trans. in 1936); and *Lectures on Political Economy,* two volumes, published in 1901 and 1906 and translated into English in 1934–35. These identify him as a thoroughgoing marginalist who integrated the utility theory of value with the marginal productivity theory of distribution. His special contribution to the theory of distribution, for which he shares the honor of discovery with Philip Wicksteed of England (1884–1927), is the theorem concerning the exhaustion of the product.

Böhm-Bawerk's work in the theory of capital and interest was a source of particular stimulus to Wicksell. But he had neither the intellect nor the temperament of a follower. The originality of his thought is nowhere more in evidence than in the area of monetary theory. His work was begun during his graduate school days and came to full fruition during the period between 1900 and 1916, while he held the chair of political economy at Lund University in Sweden.

John Bates Clark (1847–1938) is the most distinguished American marginalist who contributed to the development of distribution theory during the period under consideration. He brought to economics a lifelong interest in philosophy and ethics acquired in his undergraduate days at Brown University and Amherst College. This philosophic bent led him to the view that the economic aspects of life cannot be divorced from questions of morality. From 1895 well into the 1920s, he was a professor of economics at Columbia University, publishing articles and three books: *The Philosophy of Wealth* (1885), *The Distribution of Wealth* (1899), and *Essentials of Economic Theory* (1907). His reputation rests chiefly on *The Distribution of Wealth,* in which he presented the hypothesis that the functional distribution of income will be determined in the long run under static and perfectly competitive conditions according to the principle of factor productivity at the margin.

Most of Clark's work aligns him with the orthodox tradition of English economists and makes him an intellectual cousin of his English contemporary, Alfred Marshall. There is little, especially as regards his mature work, to mark his contribution as distinctively American. The early Clark, as reflected in his first work, *The Philosophy of Wealth,* gave promise of a departure from English tradition in its criticism of the assumptions on which classical economics rested. In it, Clark undertook to question the premise that man's economic behavior is motivated by material self-interest and urged the necessity of a more valid psychological basis for economic inquiry. He also questioned the inherent desirability of competition as the regulator of economic life and introduced into economics the Spencerian conception that society is an organic whole. While many of these ideas were novel when Clark introduced them into economics, the body of economic analysis which he ultimately perfected and which is given expression in *The Distribution of Wealth* places him, in terms of viewpoint, among the ranks of the orthodox thinkers who believed that competitive forces could be relied upon to work economic justice and social harmony. Thus, while Clark gave promise of leading the revolt against the body of orthodox economics, it was in fact his student, Thorstein Veblen, who became the most prominent critic of received doctrine.

Irving Fisher (1867–1947) was another noted American theorist, who was a statistician and mathematician as well as an economist. All of his work aimed at advancing economic theory in relation to mathematics and statistics. This objective was already evident in his first work, *Mathematical Investigations in the Theory of Value and Prices* (1892), which first appeared as his Ph.D. thesis. He is perhaps best known for *The Purchasing Power of Money* (1911), in which he attempted to measure the elements in the equation of exchange in order to test the relationship between changes in the quantity of money and changes in the general price level.

From the standpoint of the development of distribution theory, Fisher's special contribution is in the theory of the interest rate. His ideas are given their most fully developed exposition in *The Theory of Interest* (1930), a revision of his earlier volume, *The Rate of Interest* (1907). The central idea of this book, which is dedicated to both Eugen Böhm-Bawerk and his forerunner, John Rae, is that interest is not a separate form of income but is an element common to all income shares which accrue over a period of time.

THE THEORY OF PRODUCTION

Edgeworth on the Laws of Return in the Short Run

The chief problem of the second generation of marginalists was to relate the income shares of land, labor, and capital to their productive contributions at the margin. The theory of distribution is therefore necessarily related to the theory of production which concerns the relationship between factor inputs and product outputs.

Although the concept of a production function is implicit in von Thünen's analysis and in the classical theory of diminishing returns, Leon Walras was the first to express these relationships in the form of a mathematical function. His initial assumption with respect to the production function was that the coefficients of production are fixed, so that there is only one possible combination of inputs which will yield any product. The significance of this assumption from the standpoint of the theory of distribution is that it makes it impossible to isolate the productive contribution of any individual factor. It is interesting to note that Walras never arrived at a theory which related the distributive shares to the marginal productivities of their factors, even though he eventually introduced the concept of variable proportions into his theory of production.

It is only in the very short run that the extreme situation in which factor substitution is a complete impossibility that it is likely to be encountered. It is more than likely that at least one of the inputs will be variable. Ricardo's theory of rent was premised on a production function of this sort. The presence of a fixed factor (land) was recognized as imposing a constraint on the production process which causes the returns to the variable factor (labor) to increase at a decreasing rate beyond a certain number of inputs. The operation of this law accounted for the emergence of rent as a differential surplus on better than marginal land.

This analysis had its shortcomings both as a theory of production and as a theory of distribution. Not only did it fail to distinguish between diminishing average and marginal product, but it also implied that the law of diminishing returns applied only to land and agricultural output. Classical theorists therefore failed to recognize that it is possible to generalize Ricardo's theory of rent. That is, the return to any factor may be conceived either as a differential product or as the equivalent of its marginal product, depending upon whether the factor is a fixed constant or a variable in the production function.

While the classical theorists stated the law of diminishing returns, Francis Edgeworth is credited with making a clear-cut distinction between proportional and incremental changes in the output which can be gotten from a variable factor. He also made it plain that when for any reason it is not possible to vary all factor inputs, diminishing returns are due to the change in the ratio in which the factors are used. In order to demonstrate the distinction between diminishing average and marginal returns, he assumed that successive small doses of labor and capital are applied to a given plot of land and that the total output, marginal output, and average output behave as recorded in Table 12–1.[1] This table provides a clear demonstration that there is a difference between diminishing marginal returns and diminishing average returns, though the two were usually confused.[2]

The behavior of marginal product and average product when the land-to-labor ratio is varied may also be shown graphically. Figure 12–1 plots the labor-to-land ratios from Table 12–1 on the horizontal axis, and the average and marginal product associated with varying the labor-to-land ratio on the vertical axis. It is evident that as long as additional increments of a variable factor can cause total output to increase at an increasing rate, both marginal and average output will increase, and the marginal physical product of the variable factor will be greater than its average product. The marginal product curve will then be above the average product curve.

When additional units of the variable factor can no longer raise the total product at an increasing rate, as in the case in Edgeworth's example after the application of the 15th dose of labor and equipment, the marginal product will diminish, and the marginal product curve will slope downward. When additional inputs of the variable factor can no longer raise the average product beyond the maximum already reached, the average

TABLE 12–1
Returns from Varying Amounts of Labor and Equipment
Applied (in small doses) to a Given Plot of Land

Day's Labor of Man with Team and Tools	Total Crop in Bushels	Increments Due to Successive Doses	Bushels per Day's Labor
—	—	—	—
13	220	—	16.92
14	244	24	17.43
15	270	26	18.00
16	294	24	18.38
17	317	23	18.65
18	339	22	18.83
19	360	21	18.95
20	380	20	19.00
21	396	16	18.86

---

[1] Francis Edgeworth, *Collected Papers Relating to Political Economy,* vol. 1 (London: Macmillan & Co., 1925), p. 68.

[2] Even Alfred Marshall was among those who confused the two concepts. See Chap. 13, pp. 283–85.

product of the variable factor will equal the marginal product. Beyond that point, additional applications of the variable factor will cause the average product to diminish. This takes place, in Edgeworth's example, with the application of the 21st dose of labor and equipment to a given plot of land. The marginal physical prodct is then smaller than the average product.

While Table 12–1 and Figure 12–1 do not show it, additional applications of the variable factor to a given amount of a fixed factor will, at some point, be associated with an absolute decrease in total product. The average product of the variable factor will then decrease, and the marginal product will be negative.

Edgeworth's distinction between diminishing average productivity and diminishing marginal productivity is fundamental to understanding the behavior of production costs in the short run. It is also fundamental to an understanding of entrepreneurial demands for factors of production. Just as a consumer maximizes his gains by allocating his income among alternative uses until the ratios of the marginal utilities of the goods he consumes are equal to the ratios of their prices, so a producer maximizes his gains from his factor inputs when he equates the ratios of the marginal revenue products of the factors he hires to the ratios of their prices.

Euler's Theorem: Wicksteed on Returns to Scale

Philip Wicksteed appears to have been the first to appreciate the fact that when it is not possible to vary all factor inputs, the laws of return are different from those which govern when all inputs are variable.[3] The out-

FIGURE 12–1
Average and Marginal Product of a Variable Factor

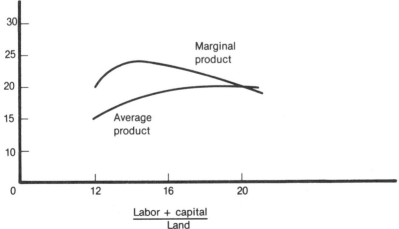

---

[3] Philip Wicksteed, *The Commonsense of Political Economy*, Lionel Robbins, ed. (London: George Routledge & Sons, Ltd., 1935), p. 529.

put possibilities when all factors are variable are now commonly described by the term *returns to scale*. There are three possibilities: constant returns, increasing returns, and decreasing returns.

If an increase in all factor inputs increases output proportionately, the returns to scale are constant. The production function in this case also satisfies the requirement the 18th-century mathematician Leonhard Euler laid down in his theorem concerning linear homogeneity. A function is linearly homogeneous if the multiplication of every variable it contains by a given real number increases the value of the total function by the same multiple. Applying this principle to the relationship between factor inputs and the resulting product, a production function is homogeneously linear if a given increase in all factor inputs increases the total product in precisely the same proportion. If, however, a proportionate increase in all factor inputs increases output more than proportionately, the returns to scale are increasing. Conversely, if a proportionate increase in all factor inputs increases output less than proportionately, the returns to scale are decreasing.

Wicksteed was especially concerned with the relevance of returns to scale to the problem of "coordinating" the laws of distribution.[4] He conceived the latter problem to involve the demonstration that each of the distributive shares is governed by the principle of marginal productivity, and that the total product available for distribution is the exact sum of the shares which that principle assigns to each of the several factors. He understands that it is possible to pay each factor the equivalent of its marginal product and exactly exhaust the total product only if returns are constant. In this case the marginal product of the factors is independent of the absolute amount of the factors employed, and a proportionate change in the quantity of all factors does not affect their marginal product. The increase in total product resulting from additional quantities of all factors is precisely equal to the sum of the marginal products of each of the separate factors. The problem Wicksteed posed concerning the exhaustion of the total product thus revealed what neoclassical thinkers perceive to be an essential link between the theory of production and the theory of distribution.

THE MARGINAL PRODUCTIVITY THEORY OF DISTRIBUTION

Clark's Generalization of Ricardo's Theory of Rent

The marginal productivity theory is an alternative hypothesis to the Austrian theory of imputation for explaining the functional distribution of income. The individual most closely associated with this theory is John

---

[4] Philip Wicksteed, *An Essay on the Co-ordination of the Laws of Distribution* (London: Macmillan & Co., 1894).

Bates Clark, who gave this hypothesis its fullest exposition in *The Distribution of Wealth* (1899). He had already formulated, independently of Jevons, Menger, and Walras, the hypothesis that the value of a commodity expresses the utility of the marginal unit to society as a whole. Examination of the problem of distribution was therefore the logical sequel to his inquiry into the problem of value.

The starting point of the marginal productivity theory of distribution is the demand for and the supply of the factors to individual hiring firms. Firms are assumed to have production functions in which factor proportions are variable and in which the contribution of the variable factor to the total product increases at a decreasing rate beyond a certain point. The result is that added inputs then cause the marginal physical product curve to be downward sloping. Given a competitive market price for its product, the marginal physical product curve of a variable factor can be translated into a marginal revenue product curve by multiplication, i.e., $MPP(P) = MRP$. This curve is also the firm's demand curve for the factor in question because it indicates the revenue an additional unit of that factor will add.

Firms are also assumed to be confronted with factor supply curves which are perfectly elastic at the ruling market price. In other words, the factor market is assumed to be purely competitive. If, in addition, each firm is assumed to hire its factors in profit-maximizing proportions, each variable factor will be employed until the marginal revenue product it produces is equal to its price of hire. Since all factor inputs are variable in the long run, all factors will be employed in proportions which will make the ratio of their marginal revenue products equal to the ratio of their prices. The marginal productivity theory is, therefore, from the point of view of an individual firm, a theory of employment.

The market demand curve for a homogeneous factor represents the summation of the demand curves of individual firms with the necessary adjustment in the market price of the commodity being sold. The commodity price is, of course, no longer a parameter when the analysis is extended from the individual firm to the industry as a whole. Since the market price of a competitively produced product will fall as output is increased, the industry demand curve for a factor will fall more rapidly than the marginal revenue product curve of a factor to a firm. Given the supply of the factor which is available for employment, the productivity theory therefore establishes the market price per unit which will tend to prevail for a homogeneous factor in a static state. According to Clark's conception, a static state would exist "if labor and capital were to remain fixed in quantity, if improvements in the mode of production were to stop, if the consolidation of capital were to cease and if the wants of consumers were never to vary."[5]

---

[5] John Bates Clark, *The Distribution of Wealth* (London and New York: Macmillan & Co., 1899), Preface.

Both Clark and Wicksteed recognized that the marginal productivity theory of distribution is a generalization of Ricardo's theory of rent.[6] Ricardo's theory viewed rent as the differential surplus which appears on land as a result of the difference between the value of the total product and the value of the marginal product of labor and capital in their intramarginal applications. There is no rent at the margin of cultivation because the marginal product of capital and labor is exhausted by wages and interest. In his case, land is assumed to be the fixed factor to which variable labor-capital inputs are applied. The surplus he called rent arises because the payment to the variable factor is determined by the productivity of labor and capital at the margin.

Wicksteed and Clark showed that if the input of labor (including that congealed as capital) is assumed to be fixed and land is the variable factor, rent is the marginal product of land, while wages constitute the residual surplus. Figure 12–2 represents the gist of their reasoning graphically. The right-hand portion of the diagram shows the classical case in which a fixed quantity of land is combined with increasing quantities of a given grade of labor. The curve *DC* represents the diminishing marginal product of labor. Since all units of labor are assumed to be homogeneous, and therefore perfect substitutes, the marginal productivity curve of labor establishes *BC* as the demand price per unit. Thus the rectangle labeled "Wages" represents labor's share of the total product on the basis of its productive contribution when the total product is *ABCD*. The area under the marginal productivity curve is, therefore, the return to land as the fixed factor. Rent is thus a differential surplus which remains after the payment of wages at a rate established by the marginal productivity of labor.

The left-hand portion of the diagram utilizes the same vertical axis to

FIGURE 12–2

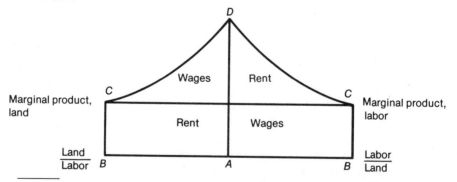

[6] Wicksteed's generalization of Ricardo's theorem appears in *An Essay on the Co-ordination of the Laws of Distribution.* Clark's first exposition is in "Possibility of a Scientific Law of Wages," in *Publications of the American Economic Association,* vol. 4, no. 1 (1889); also "Distribution as Determined by the Law of Rent," *Quarterly Journal of Economics,* vol. 5 (Oct. 1890-July 1891), pp. 289–318.

facilitate comparison; labor is assumed to be the fixed factor and land is the variable factor. It has also been assumed that the same total product, *ABCD,* is produced by varying land as by varying labor, and that the productivity curve is now that of land. In this case, rent is determined by the marginal productivity of land, while wages are a residual surplus. From this, Wicksteed and Clark deduced that all factors will be rewarded according to their marginal productivities, and that the total product will be exhausted when each factor is paid the equivalent of its marginal product. Proof of this proposition was, however, not provided by either Clark or Wicksteed, but by A. W. Flux in his review of Wicksteed's book.[7] Flux recognized that the distribution of factor rewards whose sum will equal the sum of the marginal products of the factors is consistent with production functions which are linearly homogeneous.

Wicksell and the Adding-Up Problem

Some of the most penetrating observations on the "adding-up problem," as the question of whether the total product is exactly exhausted by factor rewards equal to their marginal products has become known, were made by the Swedish economist Knut Wicksell. He recognized that the sum of the marginal products will equal the total product if the production function is homogeneous and linear, or if the presence of pure competition causes firms to achieve optimum size in the long run.[8] The entry and exodus of firms in response to short-run profits or losses will result in a tendency for firms to operate at an output level which is consistent with the lowest point of their long-run average-cost curve. When output is at this level, it will coincide with that point on the production function which is linear and homogeneous. Thus, even if the production function as a whole is not linearly homogeneous, Euler's theorem applies at the long-run, least cost point, for at this point returns are constant.

If either increasing or decreasing returns to scale prevail, the payment of the factors in accordance with the value of their marginal products cannot exactly exhaust the value of the total product. In the case of increasing returns, the marginal return to outlay is greater than the average return; while in the case of decreasing returns, it is smaller. Thus, in the case of increasing returns, the value of the total product is too small to reward all factors according to the value of their marginal products; and in the case of decreasing returns, a surplus will remain after the factors have received rewards equal to the value of their marginal products.

Wicksell maintained that neither increasing or decreasing returns to

---

[7] In *Economic Journal,* vol. 4 (June 1894), p. 305.

[8] Knut Wicksell, *Lectures on Political Economy* (New York: Macmillan Co., 1934), vol. 1, pp. 126–31.

scale are likely to prevail in the long run under competition because of the tendency for firms to achieve optimum size and, therefore, to operate under conditions of long-run constant cost. Instead of conceiving of increasing returns, decreasing returns, and constant returns as being mutually exclusive situations, Wicksell regarded these conditions as governing different phases of a firm's long-run cost curve. Increasing returns are likely to prevail in the initial phases of a firm's expansion and decreasing returns will assert themselves beyond some point. The transitional phase, in which these forces are balanced, is the stage of constant returns and costs, which is the optimum long-run condition for a firm under pure competition. The output at which long-run marginal cost equals long-run marginal revenue is also the one at which total cost equals total revenue. Therefore, the payment of the factors according to the value of their marginal product would exactly exhaust the value of the total product.

Clark's Ethical Interpretation of Marginal Productivity Theory

The "natural laws" of income distribution which Clark sought to formulate in *The Distribution of Wealth* are those which would operate in a static state from which all changes have been abstracted. These laws, if they were able to work without friction, "would give to every agent of production the amount of wealth that agent creates."[9] Thus, Clark's conception of the problem of functional distribution was, at the very outset, placed squarely in the realm of ethics. The position taken was that if everyone receives precisely the value of what he or the resources he owns creates, there is no basis for grievance. If, on the other hand, a factor does not receive its full product, there is "institutional robbery" and therefore a potentially disruptive condition in the society. Hence, in Clark's view, an understanding of the laws of distribution is basic to providing insight into the "right of society to exist in its present form, and the probability that it will continue so to exist. . . ."[10]

While Clark's earlier work, *The Philosophy of Wealth,* questioned the efficiency and justice of competition in the economic sphere, a fundamental change of attitude is evident in *The Distribution of Wealth* with respect to the role of competitive forces as a beneficial influence. In the earlier volume, he conceived of competition as being self-destructive and the immorality of the marketplace as being incompatible with economic justice and social harmony. In the later volume, competition is viewed in a different light, namely, as the force which "insures to the public the utmost that the existing power of man can give in the way of efficient service."[11]

---

[9] Clark, *The Distribution of Wealth,* Preface, p. v.

[10] Ibid., p. 3.

[11] Ibid., p. 77.

The logic by which Clark came ultimately to have faith in competition as a perfect regulatory mechanism is not difficult to perceive. Competition forces product prices to equal costs of production. Pure profits are therefore absent because all the changes associated with entrepreneurial risk are absent and the entrepreneurial function is reduced to that of a special kind of labor. Incomes which accrue in excess of contractual costs and imputed wages and interest to the owner exist only because they are imperfectly eliminated by competitive forces, or because new frictions develop. These frictions are the source of what Frank Knight, writing during the 1920s, called "uncertainty."[12] In Knight's view, it is the entrepreneur's uncertainty about the demand for his product, and therefore the price at which he can sell it, that causes him to hire productive factors, not on the basis of the actual value of their marginal products, but on the basis of expected value. Profits or losses thus materialize if actual product values diverge from those which are anticipated.

Competition also forces all factor rewards to be equal to the value of the factor's marginal product. The fact that entrepreneurial demands for factors are based on their marginal revenue product rather than their marginal value product creates no difficulty within Clark's framework of perfect competition, for in this case the two are equal. Thus, Clark argued that in the static state, competition among workers would keep the wage rate from rising above the point at which the value of the marginal product of labor equals its marginal revenue product, while competition among employers would prevent it from being less. Competition among the suppliers of capital funds and those who demand them would likewise assure that the interest rate is neither more nor less than that at which the value of the marginal product of capital is equal to its marginal revenue product.

A further reason for Clark's laudatory attitude toward competition stems from the relationship he perceived to exist between the natural laws of distribution and the natural laws of value. Although Clark does not systematically develop a theory of value, he accepts as correct the Ricardo-Mill view that the natural price of a commodity is its cost price.[13] But whereas the classicists conceived of prices as being determined by cost of production in the long run, Clark conceived of price as being an indication of the social cost of commodities. Money costs, therefore, reflect the pain and sacrifice incurred by factors in production. These costs are measured subjectively by individuals, as are the utilities of goods. The market, however, transforms individual costs into social costs and individual utilities into social utilities. The "universal law" of economics is that costs and benefits are everywhere equalized. The social organism as a

---

[12] Frank Knight, *Risk, Uncertainty and Profit* (Boston and New York: Houghton Mifflin Co., 1921).

[13] Clark, *The Distribution of Wealth*, p. 230.

whole is visualized as capable of rationally weighing the social marginal utility of goods against the social marginal cost of acquiring them and maximizing the social welfare by balancing them one against the other. Thus the static state constitutes the ideal for Clark in much the same way that the natural order was ideal for the thinkers of the 18th century. The major impediment, in his view, to the attainment of this millennium is the growth of monopoly power and the consequent necessity for government regulation to hold its spread in check.

Limitations of the Marginal Productivity Theory of Distribution

The marginal productivity theory of income distribution maintained that in the long run under perfect competition, all factors of production, including entrepreneurs, tend to receive a real rate of return equal to the "social value" of their marginal physical product. Since the profits of entrepreneurs tend to be no higher than normal, i.e., they tend to equal the marginal productivity of that kind of labor, the total product of society is exactly exhausted by the payments made to the factors.

This theory is premised on the behavior of an individual firm under perfect competition with respect to the purchase of a single variable factor when all other factor inputs and their prices and the state of the arts are fixed. In this case a firm is always confronted with a given sales price for its output, so that its total revenue is a function of its output. Its marginal revenue, therefore, expresses the share of the sales proceeds of a firm which will be available to pay any given factor of production.

The marginal productivity theory was not, however, intended simply as a theory of the behavior of the individual firm with respect to the employment of a homogeneous factor at the going market price. It was also intended as a theory of per unit price determination. There are limitations inherent in its use for this purpose. Specifically, the marginal productivity theory neglects completely the influence of factor supplies in determining factor prices. The marginal productivity of a factor explains the demand for a factor, but a complete theory of factor price determination must also consider the economic and social factors which determine factor supplies. This is precisely why Alfred Marshall, the foremost English contributor of the period, shied away from a marginal productivity theory of distribution in favor of a theory which recognized the interaction of demand and supply forces.

A much more formidable difficulty is encountered in making the transition from the demand for a variable factor by a firm to the demand by an industry, and from there to the demand by the economy. The marginal revenue product of a factor to a given firm is calculated on the basis of an assumed product price. This price is itself premised on a given product demand curve, which is drawn up on the assumption that consumer preferences, the prices of other goods, and the level of income are given. The latter assumption poses a special difficulty for the theory of income determination because every change in the marginal revenue product of a factor, and therefore in its compensation, must necessarily affect the product demand curves of the firms in the economy. This must, in turn, affect the marginal revenue product on which the demand for the factor depends. Nevertheless, marginal productivity theory implicitly ignores the interdependence of factor demand curves and product demand curves. This is the reason why John Maynard Keynes, writing during the 1930s, objected to wage cuts as a suitable method for dealing with the problem of mass unemployment. A wage cut will cause an individual firm to employ additional workers until the marginal revenue product of labor equals the new wage rate because the demand for its product is not likely to be affected. But if wage rates everywhere are reduced, product demand curves, and therefore the demand for labor itself, are altered, so that the derivation of industry and market demand curves for a factor cannot be accomplished by the simple process of summing up individual firms' factor demand curves. Marginal productivity theory has a microeconomic bias which limits the validity of the conclusions it can yield when its application is extended. What the marginal productivity principle provides is not an explanation of factor prices but rather a basis for understanding an employer's demand for a particular factor of production at a given market price.

The normative implications inherent in the marginal productivity theory have been another source of criticism. The theory implies that if a factor is compensated according to the value of its marginal product, it is receiving a just payment. Yet, when a firm hires a factor in a market which is not purely competitive or sells its product in a market which is not purely competitive, the value of its marginal product (i.e., the marginal physical product multiplied by the sale price of the good) is not equal to its marginal revenue product (i.e., the marginal physical product multiplied by the marginal revenue the sale of a product yields). It follows that the absence of pure competition, either in the product market or in the factor market, is associated with "exploitation" in the sense that the marginal increment of the factor cannot then receive a compensation which is equivalent to the value of its marginal product.[14]

FISHER'S THEORY OF INTEREST

The Nature of Interest

The issue as to whether the "third reason" which Böhm-Bawerk advanced as a basis for a positive rate of interest is really independent of the

---

[14] See Chapter 15 below.

other two has given rise to a considerable body of literature.[15] Böhm-Bawerk himself regarded the technical superiority of presently available goods as a separate reason, though others, Irving Fisher in particular, have argued that a positive rate of interest could not arise from this reason alone. Fisher's argument was that the greater productivity of roundabout methods of production explains only the willingness of borrowers to pay a premium. But the necessity of paying a premium derives from the first two reasons, which explain why people discount the future.

The distinctive features of Fisher's theory of interest derive from his conception of interest as "an index of the community's preference for a dollar of present over a dollar of future income." This notion was first advanced in *The Rate of Interest* (1907) which, when revised in 1930 as *The Theory of Interest* was received as "the peak achievement, so far as perfection within its own frame is concerned, of the literature of interest."[16] Fisher suggested that the nature of interest and its determination can best be understood if interest is conceived in relation to income rather than capital because "capital wealth is merely the means to the end called income, while capital value is merely the capitalization of expected income."[17] He therefore objected to that part of Böhm-Bawerk's explanation of interest which relates to the technical superiority of present goods. He objected to the concept of the production period and also to the thesis that the longer the period of production, the larger the final product will be. But he considered Böhm-Bawerk's fatal error to be the notion that the greater productivity of lengthier processes over shorter ones, which makes present goods technically superior to future goods, is an independent cause of interest.[18]

Fisher did not deny the technical superiority of present goods in Böhm-Bawerk's sense of the term, but maintained that this is not an independent cause of interest but one which operates through its effect on wants and the provision for them in the present and in the future. The fact that capital is productive will not, in and of itself, cause people to prefer income today in preference to income tomorrow. But the productivity of capital will affect the relative abundance of present and future goods, and therefore the willingness of people to pay a premium for income available today instead

---

[15] See, in particular, Eugen Böhm-Bawerk, *Positive Theory of Capital* (1889; William Smart, tr. London: G. E. Stechert & Co., 1923), pp. 260–75; Irving Fisher, *The Theory of Interest* (New York: Macmillan Co., 1930), pp. 476–85; Guy Arvidsson, "On the Reasons for a Rate of Interest," A. Williams, trans., *International Economic Papers*, no. 6 (New York: Macmillan Co., 1956), pp. 23–33, from *Ekonomisk Tidskrift*, March 1953.

[16] Joseph A. Schumpeter, *Ten Great Economists* (London: Oxford University Press, 1965), p. 230.

[17] Fisher, *The Theory of Interest*, p. 61.

[18] Irving Fisher, *The Rate of Interest* (New York: The Macmillan Co., 1907), p. 55.

of in the future. Thus, Fisher sees the interest rate as being determined by the actions of people to alter the time flow of their income receipts.

Individual Equilibrium

The alteration of the time flow of the income stream is made possible by the existence of a loan market and a market in which capital assets can be purchased and sold. Thus Fisher sees the interest rate as being determined in part by a subjective element analogous to Böhm-Bawerk's first and second grounds, which he calls "human impatience." This factor interacts with an objective factor, which Fisher calls the "principle of investment opportunity." It is the interaction of these two factors which determines the rate of interest to which each individual adjusts himself, and therefore the time flow of his income according to his degree of impatience and his opportunity for investment.

Fisher's demonstration of the way in which these factors interact begins on an individual level with an examination of adjustments to an already established rate of interest and proceeds to an explanation of market equilibrium. For an individual, the adjustment is a matter of altering the time shape of his income stream to bring his marginal preference rate into harmony with an already established interest rate. If his preference rate is above the market rate, he will "sell some of his surplus future income in return for an addition to his meager present income, i.e., he will borrow. . . . On the other hand, the man, whose temperament or whose income stream or both give him a preference rate below the market rate, will buy future income with some of his abundant present income, i.e., he will lend."[19]

One's income stream can also be modified by selecting among investment opportunities which offer alternative ways of utilizing resources such as capital, land, labor, or money to produce an income stream.[20] The relative attractiveness of alternative investment opportunities depends on the rate of interest which prevails. Fisher calls the hypothetical rate of interest which will equalize the present worth of two investment options the "rate of return over cost." Individuals select those investment opportunities which maximize the present worth of their income stream by equating the expected marginal rate of return over cost with the rate of interest. Changing expectations, which reflect individual estimates of the technical possibilities of alternative investments, cause shifts among alternative investment opportunities.

Fisher supplemented his description of the way an individual adjusts his rates of time preference, or impatience, and his opportunities for invest-

---

[19] Fisher, *The Theory of Interest,* p. 104.

[20] Ibid., p. 151.

FIGURE 12–3

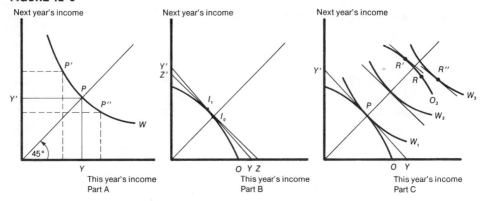

| This year's income
Part A | This year's income
Part B | This year's income
Part C |

ment to the real rate of interest confronting him with graphic demonstrations. As in Figure 12–3, Fisher measures absolute amounts of this year's income along the horizontal axis and equivalent amounts of next year's income on the vertical axis.[21] Part A of Figure 12–3 shows that, in the absence of a market in which an individual can lend, borrow, and invest, the modification of the time incidence of his income stream is impossible. Thus the income position of an individual who has a certain real income at present and an expected claim to an equivalent amount of future income can be denoted by some point, P, along the vector which represents a constant income stream. Additional points along this vector represent larger or smaller combinations of present and future income. But if there is no market in which he can trade some of this year's income for some of next year's, or vice versa, his income combination will always lie along this line, no matter what his preferences about the time incidence of his income may be.

There are any number of possible combinations of real present and future income with which the individual might be equally well satisfied. He may, for example, be willing to sacrifice, either by lending or investing, two units of this year's income for three units of next year's. This willingness is represented by point P' in Part A of Figure 12–3. Or he may be willing to sacrifice one unit of next year's income in exchange for an addition of two units to this year's income, as represented by point P''. The connection of a series of these points results in a curve like W, which Fisher calls a "willingness line." There will be a whole family of willingness lines for each individual in which more preferred combinations of this year's and next year's income will be to the right of W and less preferred combinations to the left. Fisher drew his willingness lines, which might also be called

---

[21] A lucid graphic description of Fisher's interest theory is included in J. W. Conard, *An Introduction to the Theory of Interest* (Berkeley: University of California Press, 1959), chap. 4.

"indifference curves," convex to the origin, on the assumption that present income is preferred to future income.

Whether an individual will alter the time flow of his income depends on his degree of impatience, his investment opportunities, and the interest rate to which he must adjust himself. Fisher's graphic demonstration of an individual's possibility for altering the time flow of his income stream utilized what he called an "investment opportunity curve." Such a curve is an "envelope," like the one marked "O" in Part B of Figure 12–3, of the most profitable investments among which an individual can choose. Each such curve is concave to the origin because of the principle of diminishing returns from investment. Given the rate of interest, it will be profitable for an individual to invest in real capital goods along his opportunity curve until the rate of return over cost is equal to the rate of interest. Assuming an interest rate of $Y'Y$, this equality exists when the opportunity curve is tangent at I_1 to the interest line. If, however, the opportunity curve is tangent to an interest line like $Z'Z$ at I_0, which coincides with the constant income line, there will be no inducement to invest because the expected rate of return over cost is zero.

But the investment opportunity curve only illustrates the range of possibilities which are open to an individual to alter the time flow of his income by investing. His inclination to avail himself of these opportunities is shown by the slope of his willingness line at its point of tangency with the interest rate line. A willingness line such as W_3 in Part C of Figure 12–3, which has a slope greater than unity, indicates a positive time preference; i.e., the individual will borrow. If the point of tangency intersects the vector representing the constant income stream, as is the case when an individual willingness curve is such as W_2, the individual's time preference at interest rate $Y'Y$ is neutral. Such an individual will neither borrow nor lend nor invest at that rate.

Individuals whose willingness lines are such as W_1, which has an absolute slope less than one at its intersection with the line representing a constant income stream, have a negative time preference at interest rate $Y'Y$. If such individuals are also confronted with an investment opportunity curve like O, they will optimize the stream of present and future income by (1) investing an amount of present income which will yield an expected rate of return equal to the rate of interest and (2) lending an amount of present income to acquire a claim on additional future income. These reduce this year's income until its present value is equal to the interest rate. Thus the individual will have maximized his position with respect to borrowing, lending, saving, and investing to alter the time flow of his income. This is represented graphically by tangency between his willingness curve and his investment opportunity curve to each other and the interest line at point P, as is the case for willingness curve W_1 and opportunity curve O in Part C of Figure 12–3.

The double adjustment pictured with the help of the investment opportunity line and willingness line W_1 is only one among many. Another individual might begin with an income combination of R. Given the interest line, he will first move along the investment opportunity line to point R', where the opportunity line is tangent to the interest line. He will then move along the interest line to R'', where the interest line is tangent to a willingness line. That is, given the rate of interest, the individual will shift in such manner that the marginal rate of return over cost and the marginal rate of time preference will both be equal to the market rate of interest. The sequence of this adjustment is that the point of tangency on the investment opportunity line is always found first. This is because "there is only one opportunity line and only one point on it at which the slope corresponds to the rate of interest, while there are an infinite number of W lines with a point on each having that slope or direction."[22]

Market Equilibrium

In a purely competitive market in which income streams can be freely modified by lending, borrowing, and investing, expected rates of return over cost and rates of impatience for present over future income for all individuals will become equal to each other and the rate of interest at the margin. From the standpoint of the market as a whole, the exploitation of alternative investment opportunities is the objective factor which interacts with the impatience principle to establish the rate of interest. "The more we invest and postpone our gratification, the lower the investment opportunity rate becomes, but the greater the impatience rate; the more we spend and hasten our gratification, the lower the impatience rate becomes but the higher the opportunity rate."[23] Individuals' adjustments to differentials in these rates will ultimately push all impatience rates and all opportunity rates to equality. When this equality obtains, the real rate of interest is in equilibrium and exactly reflects the premium people are willing to pay for present as opposed to future income.

Whether this rate will be positive "depends entirely on the conformation of the O curve and the W curves of each person in the loan market."[24] If the slope of both the willingness and the opportunity curves is greater than unity at their point of tangency with each other, the real rate of interest will be positive. By the same logic, Fisher concluded that the real rate could be zero only if the slope of both the willingness curve and the investment opportunity curve were unity at their point of tangency because the degree of time preference is then neutral and the net productivity of capital zero.

---

[22] Fisher, *The Theory of Interest,* p. 272.

[23] Ibid., p. 177.

[24] Ibid., p. 283.

Real and Money Rates of Interest and the Price Level

Fisher also investigated the relationship between the real and the money rates of interest. The relationship between these two rates depends, he thought, on the behavior of the general price level, whose determination he fully investigated in *The Purchasing Power of Money* (1911).

His explanation of changes in the general price level sought to relate the price level (P) with the quantity of money in circulation (M), its velocity of circulation (V), and the volume of trade (T). The statistical measurement of these components led him to introduce checking deposits (M') and their velocity (V'), so that his equation of exchange reads $MV + M'V' = PT$. His statistical studies concluded that in virtually all cases of subtantial price change, the active variable in the equation of exchange was M, the quantity of money in circulation. One basis for this conclusion is that P is "normally the one absolutely passive element in the equation of exchange."[25] In addition, V and V', which reflect the spending habits of the community, are short-run constants. Moreover, autonomous variations in M' cannot take place because there is a stable relationship between primary money, bank reserves, and the volume of checking deposits. Thus, Fisher concluded that changes in the quantity of money are the source of changes in the general price level.

What bearing does a change in the general price level have on money rates of interest? Fisher's inquiry into the interaction of the impatience principle and the investment opportunity principle explained only the phenomenon of the real rate of interest. If, however, the price level is changing, this will be reflected in the behavior of the money rate. More specifically, the money rate of interest on a risk-free loan will be equal, says Fisher, to the real rate as determined by the opportunity to invest, plus or minus the change in the general price level.[26]

WICKSELL'S THEORY OF CAPITAL AND INTEREST

Capital Accumulation and the Distributive Shares

Wicksell's concern with the theory of capital and interest is the outgrowth of his examination of Böhm-Bawerk's works. His critical examination and restatement of the latter's theory is a contribution in and of itself, particularly as it relates to his introduction of the concept of the capital structure. The capital structure reflects the "height" and the "width" of the land and labor inputs invested in real capital goods. The width of the

---

[25] Irving Fisher, *The Purchasing Power of Money,* 2d ed. (New York: The Macmillan Company, 1922), p. 172.

[26] Fisher, *The Theory of Interest,* chap. 19.

capital structure is the number of input units invested, while its height reflects the length of time over which such inputs must remain invested before the maturation of their services in production. The economic value of this structure can be determined by multiplying the input units by the relevant rate of wages and rent, and then applying the rate of interest, properly compounded, over the average length of the investment period. Or, expressed in terms of Böhm-Bawerk's agio principle, the value of a capital structure is equal to the discounted value of the products which the invested inputs yield until they mature.

The usefulness of Wicksell's concept of the capital structure is that it provided new insight into the effect of capital accumulation and invention on national income and the relationship between the distributive shares. He reasoned that, given a constant supply of labor and land, net investment initially expands the capital structure by extending its width. Subsequent expansion extends its height; i.e., in more modern terminology, it is "capital deepening" as opposed to "capital widening." Expansion of the capital structure always increases the national income by the marginal product of new investment. But it will affect the share going to capitalists differently from that going to workers and landowners. Capital widening, i.e., net investment which proportionately increases capitals regardless of their maturity, decreases the marginal productivity of capital so that the interest rate tends to fall while wages and rents tend to rise. This was essentially the conclusion of the classical economists, too. Eventually, however, accumulation increases the height or intensity of capital as well as the width because the profitability of investments of longer maturity becomes relatively greater as wages and rents rise. This effect, Wicksell maintained, serves to retard their further increase and slows down the reduction of the relative share going to capital. It cannot, however, stop the increase in the share going to land and labor or prevent the decline in the relative share going to capital.

Wicksell also examined the effect of technological change on the distributive shares. He reasoned that even in the absence of net investment, technological improvements always increase national income if there is perfect competition because they increase the average and marginal productivity of all factors, although not all are affected equally. Even though labor may experience hardship because of displacement by capital and a consequent fall in wages, it will find employment elsewhere. Thus, Wicksell concluded that invention does not in and of itself seriously reduce labor's share of the national income because of its productivity-enhancing nature.

Invention injures labor only if it serves to make long-term capital absolutely more profitable than before. Net investment will then result in the relative deepening of capital. When this occurs, a smaller quantity of capital will be used in current production, so that its marginal productivity rises both relatively and absolutely. If the supply of land and labor is constant, this has the effect of reversing the downward trend of the interest rate and the increase in rent and wages which normally results when there is net capital accumulation. Wicksell thus concluded that "the capitalist saver is fundamentally the friend of labor though the technical inventor is not infrequently its enemy."[27]

The Wicksell Effect

Wicksell's analysis of the effect of net accumulation led him to the conclusion that in addition to technical invention, there is still another factor which tends to halt the downward trend of the interest rate. The classicists, it will be recalled, anticipated that the trend toward a zero rate of interest would accompany the tendency toward a stationary state. Wicksell argued that a zero rate of interest would not come about in an economy in which there is capital formation. Part of the increase in real capital is continually absorbed, Wicksell argued, by rising rents and wages so that the quantity of capital never gets large enough to reduce its marginal productivity to zero. This principle is generally referred to as the Wicksell effect.

Wicksell utilized the principle of the partial absorption of the product of capital by labor and land in the form of rising wages and rents as the basis for his argument that the marginal productivity principle applies in a different way to real capital than it does to labor and land. According to the marginal productivity principle, or von Thünen's law, as Wicksell called it, every factor will tend to receive the equivalent of its marginal social product.

The social marginal productivity rate of real capital is determined by dividing the increment of output by the increase in real capital. According to von Thünen's law, the rate of interest should tend to be equal to the social marginal productivity rate of real capital. But this is not the case, according to Wicksell, because part of the social marginal productivity of capital is absorbed by rising wages and rents. The quantity of capital actually created is smaller than it would have been if part of net saving had not been absorbed in this manner. The rate of interest therefore tends to be equal not to the marginal social product of capital, but to the somewhat smaller marginal product of the real capital actually created. Thus, Wicksell concluded, von Thünen's law cannot apply to real capital for the economy as a whole, but can only apply on a microeconomic level.

The reason why the application of von Thünen's law is qualified only in the case of capital and not in the case of labor and land is not hard to find. It is the result of the valuation process. Wicksell conceives of the value of

---

[27] Knut Wicksell, *Lectures on Political Economy,* 2 vols., 1901 and 1906; trans. 1934–35 (New York: Macmillan Co., 1934), vol. 1, p. 164.

the capital stock as being determined by its physical size multiplied by the rate of wages and rent relevant to the labor and land inputs which comprise it, discounted to the present. Thus, when the stock of capital increases, given a constant supply of labor and land, it alters the rate of wages and rent and thus its own value.

The Indirect Mechanism of Price Change

Wicksell's greatest contribution was his pioneering effort to integrate monetary analysis with real analysis. Monetary analysis, in Wicksell's day, was largely concerned with the behavior of the general price level and proceeded on the implicit assumption that changes in the value of money are unrelated to real phenomena such as the level of output and employment. Changes in the price level and the value of money were thought to reflect only changes in the quantity of money and its velocity. The level of output, on the other hand, was thought to depend on the supply of resources and the state of the arts that determined the efficiency of their use at full employment. The acceptance of Say's law made it axiomatic that the resources of the economy would always tend to be fully employed.

It was Wicksell's contention that monetary phenomena and real phenomena are interrelated in that changes in the general price level take place not directly, as implied by the quantity theories of money, but indirectly as a result of changes in the interest rate. He took the position that any theory of money worthy of the name must show the interrelationship between changes in the quantity of money, the interest rate, and the price level.[28] To demonstrate these interrelationships, he conceived of a natural rate of interest and a market rate of interest. The natural rate of interest is the rate at which the demand for loan capital, which reflects the demand for capital for investment purposes, is equal to the supply of savings. It is also the rate which corresponds to the yield on newly created capital. The market rate of interest is the money rate charged by banks. Unlike the natural rate, its level can be objectively determined. Whether it coincides with the natural rate or diverges from it can, Wicksell believed, be inferred from the behavior of price.

If, for example, there is an increase in the demand schedule for funds, reflecting perhaps innovation and an improvement in the marginal productivity of capital, it will cause the natural rate of interest to rise. There is, however, no reason for the market rate of interest to rise as long as banks have excess reserves. The rise in the natural or real rate above the money rate "will provide a stimulus to trade and production and alter the relation between supply and demand for goods and productive services."[29] That is, the total demand for goods increases as a result of an increase in invest-

---

[28] Ibid., vol. 2 (1935), p. 160.

[29] Knut Wicksell, *Interest and Prices* (1899) trans. Richard F. Kahn (London, 1936; reprinted New York: A. M. Kelly, 1965), p. 89.

ment demand. The expansion of bank credit is the source of this increased demand. It enables the businessman receiving these credits to bid factors away from the consumer goods industries. The rise in factor prices increases factor income at a time when fewer consumer goods are available because factors have been diverted to the capital goods industries. Rising consumer goods prices deprive the consumer of increased real consumption out of higher incomes; they create a situation of "forced saving," which may moderate the price rise.

The expansion made possible by the divergence of the natural rate and the money rate of interest, however, is cumulative and self-perpetuating in a pure credit system. The rise in prices will continue indefinitely unless a shortage of reserves forces the bank rate up to the market rate. This will eventually happen under gold standard conditions because the loss of specie by external drain as well as internal drain into currency circulation will ultimately bring about a shortage of reserves. Such shortages will cause banks to raise the market rate. Their action will bring the expansion to a halt.[30] Needless to say, such an expansion could never have gotten started within the framework of a banking system requiring 100 percent reserves.

Wicksell's analysis also demonstrated how a reduction of the natural rate below the market rate would produce a cumulative contraction. The demand for investment funds is diminished in this situation. Falling factor prices and incomes are accompanied by reduced employment and production. The contraction is cumulative because the deficiency of demand associated with falling factor incomes offsets the stimulus arising from falling money costs. Demand will remain insufficient until either investment demand or consumption increases, and this cannot take place so long as the banks absorb funds. This requires either that the market rate of interest is reduced to the natural rate or that the natural rate rises until it is above the market rate. The implication of Wicksell's analysis is, therefore, that if the monetary authority will act to prevent divergences between the natural rate of interest and the market rate, it can prevent cumulative expansion and contraction and achieve a stable price level. The existence of a stable price level is indicative of and consistent with a monetary equilibrium in which money is "neutral."

Wicksell's conception of a divergence between the market rate and the natural rate of interest may be thought of in terms of savings and investment magnitudes as they exist *ex ante* and as they are realized *ex post*. *Ex ante* phenomena are those which refer to planned magnitudes of income, saving, investment, and consumption. *Ex post* phenomena refer to realized magnitudes, as opposed to those which are merely planned or expected. A natural rate of interest above the market rate implies an excess of planned investment over planned savings out of expected incomes. As was subsequently shown by writers of the modern Swedish school, an *ex ante* excess

---

[30] Wicksell, *Lectures,* vol. 2, pp. 200–201.

of planned investment creates an expansionary process.[31] Conversely, if *ex ante* investment is smaller than savings, a cumulative contraction will be initiated. In either case the process of expansion or contraction is accompanied by changes in the level of realized income. The volume of savings that are actually realized at the new income level will be such that they are equal to realized investment. Savings and investment are always equal *ex post,* though they may well diverge *ex ante.* Such an *ex ante* divergence appears to be what Wicksell had in mind when he conceived of inequality between the natural rate and the market rate, and the process of cumulative expansion or contraction which he envisioned as resulting.

One difficulty in Wicksell's analysis derives from the implicit assumption that the economy is fully employed when the expansion initiated by the divergence of the natural rate from the market rate begins. If there are unemployed resources, the expansion of the capital goods sector will not bid up factor prices. Nor will it necessitate the cutback in consumer goods output which leads to forced saving when the increased factor incomes are expended for diminishing supplies of consumer goods. Thus the usefulness of this portion of the analysis is limited to those periods during which an economy has reached full-employment levels. Until this point is reached, or bottlenecks develop in key sectors, inflationary pressures will not manifest themselves.

In spite of this shortcoming, Wicksell's analysis is a major innovation in several respects. First, it is intended to demonstrate that the price level changes not directly, as is implied by the quantity theory of money, but indirectly as a result of changes in the rate of interest. Secondly, by relating changes in investment to changes in the interest rate, and therefore factor and commodity prices, it provides an explanation of the process of income determination. It is to be noted, however, that it presents an income theory which emphasizes only changes in investment demand. The level of consumption expenditures is ignored. Wicksell's emphasis on fluctuations in the marginal productivity of capital, coupled with the lagging response of the market rate of interest, was itself only a theory of cumulative expansion and contraction, but it became a foundation for subsequent monetary theories of the business cycle.[32]

CONCLUDING COMMENTS

The marginal productivity theory of distribution, which is associated most particularly with John Bates Clark, is an hypothesis which relates the

---

[31] See, in particular, Gunnar Myrdal, *Monetary Equilibrium* (London: W. Hodge and Co., 1939); and Eric Lindahl, *Studies in the Theory of Money and Capital* (New York: Farrar and Rinehart, 1939).

[32] A variety of monetary theories of the cycle developed in the period after 1900. See T. W. Hutchison, *A Review of Economic Doctrines, 1870–1929* (Oxford: Clarendon Press, 1953), pp. 390–97.

price per unit of a homogeneous factor of production to the value of the product it produces in its marginal application. This theory is premised on the assumption that factor proportions are variable and that the return to the variable factor will increase at a decreasing rate beyond a certain point. Is is, therefore, a generalization of Ricardo's theory of rent, in that any factor, not just land, may be the fixed factor whose return appears as a differential surplus which remains after the variable factor is paid at a rate which is established by its marginal productivity.

In Clark's interpretation, the payment of factor rewards which are determined according to the marginal productivity principle is consistent with the natural law of income distribution. In his view, every agent is justly compensated when it receives the equivalent of its own product; and the payment of each factor according to the value of its marginal product will, in the competitive long-run static state, exactly exhaust the total product. This is an hypothesis which Alfred Marshall specifically rejected, for reasons that will be elaborated in the chapter that follows.

Marshall's work, which reaffirmed the classical principles of Ricardo and Mill while integrating them with the principle of marginal utility, became the core of the neoclassical tradition. Its influence was so great that it eclipsed the Austrian school as well as the tradition Walras founded at Laussane. General equilibrium analysis is enjoying a substantial revival at the present time, and there are many economists even today, among them Gottfried Haberler, Fritz Machlup, and the late Oskar Morgenstern, whose work reflects their Austrian forbears. But, after the publication of Marshall's *Principles of Economics* in 1890, it dominated the intellectual scene among economists, just as Mill's work had dominated after 1848.

GLOSSARY OF TERMS AND CONCEPTS

The "adding-up" problem. The question as to whether the total product is equal to the sum of the marginal products.

Deepening of capital. The process in which the structure of capital is altered in such manner that investment in capital of longer maturity is increased.

Euler's Theorem. A mathematical theorem concerning the properties of linearly homogeneous equations. An equation is linearly homogeneous if a change in any of the variables on one side of the equation proportionately changes the other side. Applied to a production function this means that a given increase in all factor outputs will increase the total product in precisely the same proportion.

Ex ante magnitudes. Planned or expected magnitudes (e.g., ex ante income or savings) as opposed to *ex post* magnitudes which are actually realized (e.g., actual income or savings).

Fisher's concept of capital. Any asset which yields a stream of income over time. Thus, assets which yield rent (i.e., land) as opposed to interest are merely different forms of capital. Contemporary theorists (e.g., Gary Becker and T. W. Schultz) have extended Fisher's concept to also include "human" capital.

Fisher's equation of exchange. $PT = MV + M'V'$ where P is the general price level, T the volume of trade, M the quantity of money, V its velocity of circulation, M' the amount of bank credit and V' its velocity.

Generalization of Ricardian rent.   The principle that the returns of any factor which exists in fixed supply (not just labor) may be viewed as "rent."

Imputation.   The process of valuing factors of production (goods of a "higher order" in Austrian terminology) on the basis of their contributions to the value of production.

Indirect mechanism of price change.   Wicksell's hypothesis that the general price level does not change directly as implied by the quantity theories of money, but indirectly as a result of changes brought about by divergences between the natural and money rates of interest.

Marginal productivity theory of distribution.   The theory that in the long run, under competition, all factors would tend to receive a real rate of return equal to the value of their marginal physical products.

Opportunity cost.   The price a factor of production can command in its best paying alternative use.

Production function.   A mathematical expression concerning the relationship between the ouput, O, of good a and the factors required to produce it. For example $O_a = f(x,y,z)$.

Returns to scale.   An expression describing the behavior of the production function in the long run when all inputs are variable. If an increase in inputs, say, x,y,z increases the output of a proportionately, the returns to scale are said to be *constant*. This means the production function has the property of linear homogeneity. If returns increase proportionately more than inputs, returns to scale are *increasing*. Conversely, if output increases proportionately less, returns are *decreasing*.

NOTES FOR FURTHER READING

The Clarkian approach to distribution theory is available in abbreviated form in his "Distribution," *Encyclopedia of the Social Sciences,* vol. 5 (1931); reprinted in *Readings in the Theory of Income Distribution* (Philadelphia: Blakiston Co., 1949). His preface to *The Distribution of Wealth* (London and New York: Macmillan & Co., 1899) also provides insight into his philosophy and analysis.

The scholarly examination in George Stigler's *Production and Distribution*

Theories (New York: Macmillan Co., 1941) is required reading for anyone seeking knowledge beyond the elementary level of the Marginalists. Chapters 1–7 and 12 are particularly relevant. See also his "Production and Distribution in the Short Run," *Journal of Political Economy,* vol. 47 (June 1939); reprinted in American Economics Association, *Readings in the Theory of Income Distribution* (Homewood, IL: Richard D. Irwin, Inc., 1949).

T. W. Hutchison's *A Review of Economic Doctrines, 1870–1929,* particularly Chaps. 5, 10, and 15 (Oxford: Clarendon Press, 1953), is also recommended.

Wicksell's work is interpreted by Carl G. Uhr in *The Economic Doctrines of Knut Wicksell* (Berkeley: University of California Press, 1960). Some highlights are emphasized in Uhr's "Knut Wicksell: A Centennial Evaluation," *American Economic Review,* vol. 41, no. 4 (December 1951); reprinted in Joseph J. Spengler and W. Allen, eds., *Essays in Economic Thought: Aristotle to Marshall* (Chicago: Rand McNally & Co., 1960).

Joan Robinson's classic article "Euler's Theorem and the Problem of Distribution," reprinted in *Collected Economic Papers,* vol. 1 (London: Basil Blackwell & Mott Ltd., 1951) analyzes the economic meaning of product exhaustion.

Paul Douglas' *Theory of Wages* (New York: Macmillan Co., 1934), chaps. 1 and 2, reviews the history of marginal productivity theory with respect to labor. Clark's generalization of Ricardo's theory of rent is conveniently available in Philip Newman et al., eds., *Source Readings in the History of Economic Thought* (New York: W. W. Norton and Co., 1954).

The most accessible and readable presentation of Irving Fisher's theory of interest and his controversy with Böhm-Bawerk is still J. W. Conard's *An Introduction to the Theory of Interest* (Berkeley: University of California Press, 1959), chap. 4.

13

Alfred Marshall and the Neoclassical Tradition

INTRODUCTION

Life and Times (1842–1924)

UNTIL HE CAME under the influence of Darwinian ideas, Alfred Marshall planned to make the ministry his lifetime work. But he became a mathematician who developed an interest in economics after reading John Stuart Mill's work on political economy. Like Mill, he was a reformer at heart and devoted himself with an almost religious zeal to the problems of human improvement. These he approached with a Utilitarian spirit inherited from Mill and an analytical approach firmly anchored in Ricardianism.

Marshall came into economics at a time when the influence of the classical tradition was on the wane. The twist which Marx gave to Ricardian doctrines, coupled with the attack of the German historical school and the reaction of the marginal utility school, contributed to its deterioration. While Marshall believed in the essential validity of Ricardo's principles, he maintained that utility must be accorded a greater role in the determination of value and that the evolutionary approach derived from Darwin's thesis could be utilized to revitalize Ricardian economics. He thus founded a new tradition known as neoclassicism and became the fountainhead from which much of modern economic thought and analysis springs. Even those who later reacted against the tradition he founded employed concepts and analytical tools which are Marshallian in origin.

His greatest theoretical work, and the source of most of this chapter, is his *Principles of Economics,* published in 1890. The success of this treatise was so great that for many decades afterward it almost totally eclipsed works of lesser stature. The study of economics became perforce, in the United States as well as in England, the study of Marshall's *Principles*. It is generally agreed that it is unfortunate that he devoted so much time to its original formulation that publication was delayed until 1890, and that he labored over seven revisions, none of them substantive, instead of turning his attention to other work. His other publications are *Industry and Trade* (1919), which is a historical study of the development of industry and has little analysis; *Money, Credit and Commerce* (1923); and a brief book which he coauthored before the *Principles* with his wife, Mary Paley Marshall, in addition to numerous occasional papers and lectures.[1]

PRINCIPLES OF ECONOMICS

Objectives

Marshall begins the *Principles of Economics* with the observation that "political economy or economics is the study of mankind in the ordinary business of life; it examines that part of individual and social action which is most closely connected with the attainment and with the use of the material requisites of well-being."[2] Unlike Nassau Senior, therefore, he intends to study economics as a science of human behavior rather than as a science of wealth.

He is concerned, above all, that his analysis be scientific, that is, that it shall bring to light such regularities or patterns of orderliness as are inherent in economic phenomena. Once discovered, these regularities can be given expression in the form of generalizations or laws describing the behavior of the economic forces which have been examined. The primary aim of the *Principles* is, therefore, to study the economic aspects of human behavior in order to derive the laws governing the functioning of the economic system.

Though the primary aim of the *Principles* is the analysis of the functioning of the economic system, Marshall believed that the system he was analyzing reflected the progress of western civilization, not only in terms of material achievement but also in the improvement of human character. In his eyes the present system is the product of a gradual but progressive extension of individual independence, freedom, and competitiveness. Though fully aware that competition can have negative results both from a social and from an individual standpoint, he regarded the rivalry of men against

---

[1] Consult Arthur C. Pigou, ed., *Memorials of Alfred Marshall* (London: Macmillan & Co., 1925), pp. 500–508 for a list of Marshall's writings.

[2] Alfred Marshall, *Principles of Economics,* 8th ed. (London: Macmillan & Co., 1920), p. 1. (This work is hereafter cited in the footnotes as *Principles.*)

one another as the source not only of economic gain but, equally important, the source of a wholesome effect on individual character and behavior. He believed that as individuals gain in freedom, they also become more rational in their goals and decision-making, more sportsmanlike and socially conscious of their behavior, so that in seeking their own success, they also promote the common good. The study of economics can contribute to this progress because the laws it discovers reveal more than knowledge for its own sake; they also contribute to the solution of social problems.[3] Humanitarian motives thus pervade all Marshall's enquiries. He is interested not only in that which is, but equally in that which ought to be. His pure analysis of the economy's functioning is therefore frequently interspersed with what Schumpeter has called Marshall's "Victorian moralizing."

Methodology

Marshall recognizes that the complexity of the economic system he is studying is so great and the motives of human behavior so diverse that it is necessary to devise techniques for their systematic study. This requires that the number of variables be reduced to manageable proportions and that some method be devised to subject their behavior to measurement. Accordingly, Marshall introduces the method of abstraction to single out one variable or sector of the economy at a time, on the assumption that its behavior is incapable of exerting any appreciable influence on the rest of the economy. This does not necessarily imply that the rest of the economy remains unchanged, but rather that if the small sector being analyzed is subjected to an external change, it adjusts itself without producing more than a negligible effect on the rest of the economy. This is Marshall's principle of the negligibility of indirect effects. By invoking this principle, all of the effects and countereffects which take place in the real world between a sector and the rest of the economy are impounded by the assumption *ceterus paribus,* other things remaining equal.

The regularities Marshall is seeking can be discovered only if the forces which underlie them can be subjected to measurement. Since these forces are themselves the product of human behavior, which is governed by a wide variety of motives, the economist must abstract those human motives which lend themselves to objective measurement. Not all motives are measurable; hence, they defy scientific investigation. But, Marshall observed, fortunately for the problem at hand, so much of man's life is oriented to the pursuit of economic gain that economic motives, at least, become measurable in terms of a single common denominator: money. He notes that this common denominator is probably unreliable when applied to

---

[3] Ibid., p. 42, margin.

single individuals for whom the marginal utility of money is different, but its application to the large group or social organism is valid because it involves a sufficiently large number of individuals to average out differences in income. For the group as a whole, therefore, Marshall conceives of economic motives as being measurable in terms of money.[4] This is not to say that economic motives are unique, but rather that those motives which underlie action in the marketplace give rise to results that are measurable in terms of market prices. Thus the primary area of inquiry with respect to the discovery of the regularities in economic activity Marshall was seeking became the study of prices—commodity as well as factor.

Marshall's famous Book 5 of the *Principles* has become the classic example of the use of the technique of abstraction to investigate the interaction of demand and supply forces to explain the emergence of an equilibrium price. Here, he treats the individual industry that is so small relative to the rest of the economy that he can draw up industry demand and supply curves which are completely independent of one another. That is, it is assumed that indirect effects are so negligible that changes in the quantity of output produced by the industry do not have a sufficient impact on the incomes earned in that industry to shift even the demand curve for its product, much less the aggregate demand for output as a whole.

The assumption of an industry which is a miniscule part of the whole implies that the market is perfect; the industry supply curve is comprised of the outputs of a large number of small firms. These outputs are perfectly homogeneous from the point of view of the buyers, so that the industry faces a definite market demand curve which, when set against the supply curve, will result in a single market price for all buyers. This schematic is, of course, most satisfactory when we are satisfied with approximations, when it is not necessary to take specifically into consideration the effect which a change in the conditions of production surrounding one commodity will have on national income, and via national income on the demand for some other commodity.

The use of the term *competition* in connection with Marshall's *Principles* can be confusing to modern students of economics who are already conversant with the more precise terms of *pure competition* and *perfect competition*. He himself thought that the term *competition* is not well suited to describe the special characteristics of industrial life in the modern age.[5] He suggested "Freedom of Industry and Enterprise" or, more briefly, "Economic Freedom," because these terms are without moral implication. It would be convenient if Marshall had committed himself to the precise assumptions on which he constructed his analytical model of the industry. Such assumptions are, however, nowhere precisely set forth; on

---

[4] Ibid., p. 19.

[5] Ibid., p. 9.

the contrary, he avoided them in the belief that each real problem investigated would require modifications in the model. Marshall's followers, rather than Marshall himself, have supplied us with such rigorous concepts as pure and perfect competition.

The concept of pure competition, as it is used in modern economics, involves rather precise requirements with respect to both the demand side and the supply side of the market. It requires, on the demand side, that the commodity is one which absorbs only a small portion of the consumer's income and on which the total expenditures constitute only a small part of the nation's income. It requires, on the supply side, a sufficiently large number of small selling units offering a homogeneous product, so that only one selling price can emerge as a result of the interaction of demand and supply forces. The concept of perfect competition is even more rigorous, requiring, in addition, perfect knowledge on the part of market participants and perfect mobility of buyers and resources. It represents an ideal set of circumstances which, if they existed, would facilitate the perfect functioning of the economy. The precise results which would obtain under these conditions were subsequently to be detailed by the modern welfare school.[6]

Marshall's concept of economic freedom was considerably less refined than these more modern concepts. But he conceived himself as describing the functioning of an economy within the framework of enough of the elements of what is conceived as pure competition to make the typical firm an insignificant part of the whole industry. Each individual firm produces such a small portion of the total market output that output variations cannot affect either the total supply of the product or the price which emerges.

The passage of time poses a major difficulty in the explanation of prices because the strength and the relative importance of the forces operating both on the side of demand and on the side of supply may change. Marshall has too keen an appreciation of the impact of change to ignore these possibilities. Reasoning from unchanging static assumptions would result in an analysis incompatible with change. On the other hand, he is committed to uncovering regularities, that is, to explain the "normal" behavior of prices. The method he chooses is therefore a compromise which does not eliminate change but reduces it to manageable proportions by introducing the assumptions of the "stationary state." In the stationary state, consumer tastes and production techniques remain unchanged. Population and capital are allowed to increase slowly and at the same rate. Business enterprises grow and decline, but always there will be certain firms which may be regarded as being representative of the others in an industry. Change is therefore not entirely absent, but has been abstracted from sufficiently to show how prices would be adjusted in the long run if the conditions under

---

[6] See Chapter 14.

which they are determined are sufficiently stable to allow these forces the opportunity to work themselves out.

There are times when Marshall seems to imply that the long-run results he describes actually occur in the real world.[7] But except for occasional lapses, he reminds his reader that his concept of the stationary state is an analytical construct designed to cope with the many variables operating in the real world. For while Marshall aimed at realism, his method was to start with simplifying assumptions. He singled out variables and impounded them; that is, he treated them as data in order to arrive at conclusions that represented tendencies or, at least, first approximations.

He recognized that these generalizations must necessarily be modified as the passage of time alters the institutional framework of behavior, and therefore behavior itself. Marshall's sense of history kept him from inferring that the generalizations economists arrive at are universal and permanent. "That part of economic doctrine which alone can claim universality has no dogmas. It is not a body of concrete truth, but an engine for the discovery of concrete truth."[8] Thus, when he spoke of long-run normal laws, paralleling the classical conception of long-run natural laws, he was conceiving of abstract analytical propositions which are indicative of tendencies in the economic system rather than concrete truths which express actualities. He never lost sight of the complexity and changeability of the universe within which economic forces operate and of the consequent difficulty of arriving at valid generalizations. His reluctance to claim universality for economic propositions is evident in his paper "The Old Generation of Economists and the New," in which he maintains that qualitative analysis, by which he meant deductive analyses, "will not show the resultant drift of forces. . . . The achievement of quantitative analysis stands over for the 20th century."[9]

These observations appear to suggest that in Marshall's view, pure theory has been carried as far as it fruitfully can be for the present, besides being unable to yield universal or permanent laws. In fact, he frequently depreciated even the present significance of pure analysis; for example, he hesitated to publish his diagrammatic analyses, fearing that "if separated from all concrete study of actual conditions they might seem to claim a more direct bearing on real problems than they in fact had."[10] He regarded theory as essential, but he warned against regarding it as economics "proper." What is today conceived of as economic principles Marshall regarded as "a very small part of economics proper." Much of modern

---

[7] See Claude W. Guillebaud, "Davenport on Marshall," *Economic Journal,* vol. 47 (March 1937), p. 35.

[8] Pigou, *Memorials,* p. 159.

[9] Ibid., p. 30.

[10] Ibid., p. 21.

microeconomic analysis, however, has developed out of Marshall's theory of value and distribution.

THE THEORY OF DEMAND

Utility and Demand

While Marshall's theory of value is fully developed in Book 5, which treats the "General Relations of Demand, Supply and Value," the analysis presented there is predicated on the two books which precede it. Book 3, "On Wants and Their Satisfaction," begins with the observation that insufficient attention has been paid to demand and consumption until just recently. He was alluding here, in particular, to Jevons, who "did excellent service by calling attention to it [the demand side of the theory of value] and developing it."[11]

But while Marshall regarded consumer wants and their satisfaction as an important part of the theory of value and was himself an important contributor to the development of demand theory, he believed that to accord the dominant role to marginal utility in the explanation of value was to commit a serious error. Ricardo, he agreed, tended to slight the role of demand; but he did not, as Jevons maintained, think of value as being governed by cost of production without reference to demand. Thus, while the theory of utility and demand supplemented and rounded out the classical analysis, the Ricardian emphasis on cost of production remained, for Marshall, the fundamental basis for explaining long-run normal values. His analysis was therefore designed to demonstrate the *interaction* of demand and supply forces. As a result of this approach, he has frequently been thought of as a synthesizer of the Ricardian cost-oriented type of analysis with the newer approach of the marginal utility theorists. Marshall himself was, however, irritated at being cast in the role of an eclectic, though his failure to publish earlier his own work on utility and demand makes such an interpretation understandable, even though incorrect.[12]

Demand Schedules and Curves

Marshall proceeds with his analysis of demand by translating the law of diminishing utility into terms of price. He reasons that the larger the quantity of a commodity a person has, the smaller (other things being equal) will be the price he will pay for a little more of it. Impounded in the phrase "other things being equal" is the assumption that the amount of

---

[11] *Principles,* Appendix I.

[12] See, for example, Joseph A. Schumpeter's discussion of Marshall's originality in *History of Economic Analysis* (London: Oxford University Press, 1954), pp. 835–40.

money the individual has available and its purchasing power remain constant. By assuming a constant marginal utility of money, and thereby ruling out any income effects resulting from price changes, the marginal utility curve for a commodity is converted into a demand schedule and then into a demand curve.

The demand of any individual for certain commodities may be discontinuous, that is, it will not always vary continuously for every small change in price. The aggregate demand of many persons on a market, however, will vary and the quantity which will be taken per unit of time gives the demand curve a characteristic downward slope to the right.[13] It is also the basis for the generalization known as the law of demand: "The amount demanded increases with a fall in price and diminishes with a rise in price."[14] Thus, there will be a movement along a *given* demand curve as a result of a change in the price of the commodity itself if none of the other factors which can influence the demand for it—for example, tastes, or the prices of other goods—have changed.

Only if the factors which have been held constant in defining a given demand situation become altered does the position, and perhaps shape of the demand curve itself, change. In a schedule sense, this means that buyers will be willing to buy either more or less of the commodity per unit of time at every possible price. This will shift the entire demand schedule from its original position, either upward to the right or downward to the left.

Consumer Surplus

The concept of consumer surplus is a distinctively Marshallian idea which was destined to figure importantly in what later became known as welfare economics. Marshall himself used the concept in more than one sense. He first defined it as the monetary value of the utility a consumer gains when the price at which he can purchase a good is lower than the price he would pay rather than go without it. He then proceeds to add individual surpluses together in order to arrive at the consumer surplus as the area under a market demand curve, given the price of a commodity. Figure 13–1 shows the area $DA'p_1$ as the consumer surplus when the market price is p_1 and the area $DB'p_0$ as the surplus when the price is p_0.

If a demand curve is asymptotic to the price axis, so that it is not tangent at D, as in Figure 13–1, the consumer surplus cannot be calculated as the area under the demand curve because the integral under the curve is infinite. Marshall was of course aware of this difficulty and avoided it by

---

[13] Marshall introduced the now standard practice of putting price on the ordinate axis.

[14] *Principles,* p. 99.

FIGURE 13–1

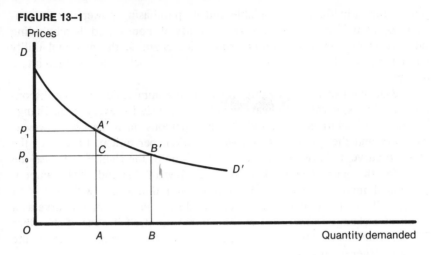

concentrating on the *change* in consumer surplus when price changes from one level to another. This change is represented by the triangle *A'CB'* in Figure 13–1. This is the sense in which Marshall used the concept of consumer surplus in his tax subsidy analysis. This application of the consumer surplus concept will be examined later in connection with the price and output results of increasing- and decreasing-cost industries.

The main criticisms of Marshall's attempt to measure consumer surplus are that it treats individual utilities as being additive, and that it assumes that the marginal utility of money remains constant as the price of a good changes. The latter assumption rules out changes in real income resulting from price changes, as well as substitution effects between the good in question and other goods consumers might buy. This assumption is obviously valid only if the good is a very unimportant item in all budgets; otherwise, changes in its price will have income as well as substitution effects. Many modern economists have therefore avoided both the concept of marginal utility and that of consumer surplus by utilizing the indifference curve technique of Francis Edgeworth and Vilfredo Pareto.[15]

Price Elasticity of Demand

While the law of demand expresses the inverse relationship between the demand for a commodity and its price, it does not indicate how sensitive the demand for a commodity is to a change in price. The concept of the *price elasticity* of demand is needed to supply this sort of information. The simplest way to determine whether the demand for a particular commodity

---

[15] See Chapter 14.

is elastic or not is to observe the behavior of total expenditures when the price of the good in question is changed. If total expenditures are greater at a lower price than at a higher price, the demand is elastic. Conversely, if total expenditure is smaller at a lower price, the demand for the good is inelastic. The limitation of this method is that it cannot indicate the degree of demand elasticity or inelasticity.

Demand elasticity can also be measured by the slope of the demand curve, that is, by relating the change in price to the change in quantity as the initial price is assumed to change. For example, if a 10-cent price reduction results in a 500-pound increase in the quantity demanded, the slope of that portion of the demand curve is

$$\frac{-10}{500} \text{ or } \frac{-1}{50}.$$

If the unit in terms of which prices are measured is changed from cents to dollars, however, the slope of the same segment of the demand curve is

$$\frac{\frac{-1}{10}}{500} \text{ or } \frac{-1}{5,000}.$$

A change in the measurement unit thus produces a very great decrease in the slope of the demand curve; yet there has been no change in the demand curve itself. A similar alteration of slope would result from altering the unit in terms of which quantities are measured—for example, a shift from pounds to bushels.

It is because the measurement of elasticity by the slope of the curve is unreliable that Marshall defined elasticity as the percentage change in quantity demanded divided by the percentage change in the price when both changes are infinitely small.[16] In symbols, then:

$$E_d = \frac{\frac{dQ}{Q}}{\frac{dP}{P}} = \frac{dQ \cdot P}{dP \cdot Q}$$

Because the resulting number (coefficient) is derived by dividing one percentage by another, it is independent of the units in terms of which prices and quantities are measured. The coefficient denoting elasticity will always be negative, since price change and quantity change take place in opposite directions and therefore have different signs. In speaking of demand elasticity, however, it is customary to ignore signs and refer to the numerical values of elasticity magnitudes simply as equal to one, greater than one,

---

[16] *Principles,* mathematical appendix, note III.

or smaller than one. When elasticity equals one, it is referred to as unitary elasticity. When elasticity is greater than one, demand is said to be elastic; and when it is less than one, it is said to be inelastic.

The Marshallian formula is now a standard analytical tool for calculating the degree of sensitivity of the demand for a commodity to a change in its price. It lends itself to measuring elasticity either at any point on a given demand curve or between two points on a demand curve. The latter measurement involves the computation of what is known as arc elasticity. The application of the formula to computing elasticity between two points on a demand curve will result in two different elasticity coefficients, however, depending on the direction in which the change is measured.[17] The further

	Price	*Quantity*
A	$2.00	100,000
B	1.00	200,000

Using the formula to measure elasticity from point *A* to *B*, the demand is elastic:

$$E_d = \frac{\dfrac{100,000}{100,000}}{-\dfrac{1}{2}} = \frac{1}{-\dfrac{1}{2}} = -2$$

But measuring from *B* to *A*, it is inelastic:

$$E_d = \frac{\dfrac{-100,000}{200,000}}{\dfrac{1}{1}} = \frac{-\dfrac{1}{2}}{\dfrac{1}{1}} = -\frac{1}{2}$$

apart these points are, the greater will be the discrepancy between the resulting elasticity coefficients.[18] Greater precision can therefore be achieved if price-quantity data are sufficiently continuous to result in any two points *A* and *B* which are very close together on the curve. This is prescisely why Marshall's elasticity formula is intended to measure very small changes in price and quantity.

THE THEORY OF PRODUCTION

The theory of production is the foundation for the analysis of costs and the supplies of goods. It is also fundamental to explaining the pricing of the factors, their allocation among alternative uses in the economy, and the

---

[17] This can be easily verified by measuring elasticity from point *A* to *B* and then from *B* to *A* using the data in the accompanying table:

[18] This discrepancy may be reduced by modifying the formula for calculating elasticity as follows: Calculate the change in price from the lower of the two prices and the change in quantity from the smaller of the two quantities. This results in an average of the two results obtained in the original formula. For the problem given in note 17, elasticity would be −1.

distribution of the economy's product among the various claimants. Thus, Marshall's discussion of the agents of production and the laws of return under which they operate is placed in Book 4 before the analysis of price determination, which is the burden of Book 5, and the analysis of income distribution is in Book 6.

The laws of return are significant in the short run and in the long run, but not in the market period, which, since the time of Marshall, is conceived to be a situation in which the available output has already been produced and is on hand. Physical supply in this period cannot be increased, and it can be decreased only by sale or destruction. During the short run, however, the supply of a product may be varied by altering some, though not all, of the factor inputs required to produce output. The long run is a period during which the supply of a product can be varied by altering all of the factor inputs. Only those changes in output associated with economic growth or decline are absent.

The Laws of Return in the Short Run

Since a production unit is always confronted with one or more fixed factors and a given state of technology in the short run, its production function is governed by the law of diminishing returns. Marshall, like his classical predecessors, examined this tendency with respect to agricultural production and concluded that when land is a fixed constant in the production function, "the application of increased capital and labor to land will add a less than proportionate amount to the produce raised, unless there be meanwhile an increase in the skill of the individual cultivator."[19] This "final statement" of the law of diminishing returns thus emphasizes that *average* output begins to decline after a certain quantity of the variable factor (labor) has been employed in conjunction with a given quantity of the fixed factor (land). He also states the principle in its marginal sense; "a continued increase in the application of capital and labor to land must ultimately result in a diminution . . . of the extra produce which can be obtained by a given extra amount of capital and labor."[20] The distinction between these two concepts, however, is not so clear in Marshall's analysis as in Edgeworth's.[21]

Marshall's treatment of diminishing returns has been termed disappointing because he restricted its operation to agriculture. But he undoubtedly knew that any variable factor of production will yield diminishing marginal returns if it is combined in production with a given quantity of a fixed

---

[19] *Principles,* p. 153.

[20] Ibid.

[21] Edgeworth is generally given credit for the earliest clear distinction between proportionate and diminishing marginal returns. See Chap. 12, p. 248.

factor.[22] This is implied by his principle of substitution, according to which the desire to maximize profits causes the businessman to substitute less expensive for more expensive factors. It is precisely because one factor is not a perfect substitute for another that diminishing returns occur. If the ratio of a variable factor, A, to a fixed factor, B, is progressively increased, A becomes a less effective substitute for B, and returns to the variable factor increase at a decreasing rate. According to the principle of substitution, a firm will alter the proportions in which it uses its variable inputs in order to achieve the least cost combination. It will experiment with different combinations of its variable factors until it achieves the greatest revenue product for a given expenditure. Given the cost of its variable factors, it will maximize its product (minimize its cost) by distributing its factor expenditures in such a way that the marginal revenue product of a dollar's worth of one factor is exactly equal to the marginal revenue product of a dollar's worth of each of its other variable factors. Thus, if P_a and P_b are the prices of factors A and B, the total product will be maximized with a given expenditure when

$$\frac{MPP_a}{P_a} = \frac{MPP_b}{P_b}$$

A firm's demand curve for a factor is therefore related to its marginal productivity in much the same way as a consumer demand curve is related to marginal utility. The best combination of variable resources depends on the respective marginal physical products of these resources, the cost at which they can be employed and the price at which the product they produce can be sold.

To minimize the cost of a given amount of product or, conversely, to maximize the product which can be gotten from a given expenditure requires that variable factors be combined so that the ratio of the marginal revenue product for each factor to price is equal. This principle is analogous to that previously examined with respect to the maximization of consumer satisfaction. The consumer maximizes his satisfaction by distributing his income among different goods so as to equate the marginal utility of each dollar's worth of goods purchased. A firm achieves its objective of maximizing its product (minimizing its cost) by distributing its expenditures so as to equate the marginal revenue product of each dollar's worth of variable resources it purchases.

Because the marginal productivity of a factor underlies the demand for it, it will also affect, in an important way, the price the factor will be able to command in the market. *The marginal productivity principle therefore serves to integrate Marshall's theory of value with his theory of income*

---

[22] George Stigler, *Production and Distribution Theories* (New York: Macmillan Co., 1941), pp. 66–67.

distribution. It enters into the theory of value through its effect on the cost and supply of commodity outputs, and it enters into the theory of distribution through its effect on factor demands.

The Laws of Return in the Long Run

Marshall's concern with the laws of return in the long run was to establish a basis for depicting the long-run supply curve of an industry. He identified three possible output behavior patterns which might result when an industry expands in the long run. In the case of constant return, output will increase proportionately with an increase in factor input; in the case of increasing return, the increase in output will be proportionally greater than the increase in factor input; in the case of diminishing return, it will be proportionately smaller. Increasing and diminishing returns were conceived of as forces which "press constantly against one another";[23] ". . . the part which nature plays in production shows a tendency to diminishing return, the part which man plays shows a tendency to increasing return."[24] When the two forces are balanced, there is a tendency toward constant returns.[25]

Marshall distinguished between external and internal economies which facilitate the production of a proportionately larger output with a given increase in expenditures. External economies are those which result from the general progress of the industrial environment and enable the firms of an expanding industry to experience decreasing costs. The development of better transportation and marketing facilities, and improvements in resource-furnishing industries, are possible sources of such economies which Marshall specifically mentions.[26] Internal economies are those which accrue to a firm as it enlarges its size to achieve greater advantages of large-scale production and organization.[27] Marshall observed that "an increase of labor and capital leads generally to improved organization, which increases the efficiency of the work of labor and capital."

It is not clear from the preceding statements that Marshall conceived of the laws of return in the long run as relating strictly to the results associated with changes in *all* factor inputs, i.e., to changes in scale. Only in the case of increasing returns resulting from internal economies is it clear that a change in the scale of production is involved. Increasing returns resulting from external economies, that is, "the general progress of the industrial environment," may or may not involve a change in scale. But, diminishing

---

23 *Principles,* p. 319.

24 Ibid., p. 318.

25 Ibid., p. 310.

26 Ibid., p. 317.

27 Ibid., p. 318.

returns is a short-run phenomenon which occurs because a change in scale is not possible. In the short run, as has already been noted, the impossibility of varying all factor inputs results in a production function which is governed by the law of diminishing returns beyond some point. It is therefore not possible for the tendency toward diminishing returns and increasing returns to "press against one another" in the manner conceived by Marshall, as these tendencies are operative in different time periods.[28]

Marshall's distinction between internal and external economies as the source of increasing returns in the long run has important implications with respect to competitive tendencies in the economy. He was aware that a condition of increasing returns is incompatible with competition. "Insofar as the economies of production on a large scale are 'internal,' i.e., belonging to the internal organization of individual firms, the weaker firms must speedily be driven out of existence by the stronger." He did not think it possible, however, for such economies to continue indefinitely. "The continued existence of weaker firms is an evidence that a strong firm cannot indefinitely increase its output, partly because of the difficulty of extending its market and partly because the strength of a firm is not permanent."[29] The reason, he suggested, is that the growth of individual enterprises would be limited by the probably inferior business talents of the descendants of present business leaders.[30] He also envisaged increased difficulties of marketing as limiting the possibilities for securing advantages of large-scale production.[31] Increasing long-run returns were therefore attributed by Marshall to the presence of external rather than internal economies. The basis for subsequent disagreement with this conclusion is discussed in Chapter 15.

COSTS OF PRODUCTION AND SUPPLY

Real Costs and Money Costs

Examination of Marshall's inquiry into production costs is a logical extension of the preceding inquiry into his theory of production. Except in the short run, when the supply of a good has already been produced, costs of production underlie the supply schedules of firms and industries. While these costs are necessarily monetary, Marshall is also concerned with the real costs imposed by the disutilities of labor and the "abstinences or rather the waitings required for saving the capital" required to produce capital goods.[32] All factors of production except land, which is a free gift of

---

[28] See Stigler, *Production and Distribution,* p. 68.

[29] *Principles,* pp. 808–9 n.

[30] Ibid., p. 316.

[31] Ibid., pp. 286–87.

[32] Ibid., p. 339.

nature requiring neither abstinence nor labor effort, impose a real cost when they are used in production. The money costs of production are, then, in Marshall's view, the prices which must be paid "in order to call forth an adequate supply of the efforts and waitings that are required for making it; or, in other words, they are its [a commodity's] supply price."[33]

Marshall's emphasis on the subjective or psychological aspects of cost reflects a continuation of the Utilitarian philosophy of the classicists. Insofar as the classicists explained money costs, they referred them back to the discomforts of labor and saving. Marshall followed this tradition, adding also the effort and waiting of the labor of enterprise.[34] Some "normal" rate of profit is therefore included by Marshall as part of the cost of producing a commodity.

The money costs of production consist of prime costs and supplementary costs. Prime costs, or operating expenses, vary directly with output, whereas supplementary costs are standing charges which do not vary with output. Marshall's classification corresponds to the current distinction between variable and fixed costs. In the short run, the inputs represented by supplementary costs are fixed. Only variable inputs, and therefore prime costs, are subject to change. In the long run, all inputs, and therefore all costs, are variable.

Diminishing Returns and Short-Run Cost Behavior

Although Marshall's discussion of diminishing returns implies that it is a land law, he is aware that the employment of increasing quantities of any variable input used in conjunction with a fixed factor will yield diminishing returns and that this will be reflected in the behavior of the average and marginal costs of production. Average prime costs reach their minimum when marginal physical product is at a maximum and rise as marginal physical product diminishes. Marginal costs, which fall and rise more sharply than average prime costs, also reach their minimum when marginal physical product is at its maximum and then rise as marginal physical product diminishes. Since marginal cost represents the additional cost a firm incurs in supplying one additional unit of output, the marginal cost at each level of output is the firm's supply price of that output, except for those outputs for which marginal cost is less than average prime cost. Production of the profit-maximizing (loss-minimizing) output (i.e., $MC = MR$) will therefore cause the firm to be producing on the rising portion of its marginal cost curve. Its short-run supply curve will therefore be rising.

While Marshall did not make cost calculations of the sort which have now become standard in most texts on economic principles or draw the cost curves these calculations describe, such calculations are implicit in his

---

[33] Ibid.
[34] Ibid., p. 362.

distinction between prime and supplementary costs. They are also useful in understanding why Marshall drew upward-sloping industry supply curves for the short run. Since the industry supply curve is a summation of individual firms' supply curves, it must be positively inclined in the short run. This is not necessarily the case in the long run. But in the short run the presence of fixed factors in the firm's production function confronts it with rising marginal costs in consequence of the tendency toward diminishing marginal returns to the variable factors. Individual firms and the industry as a whole will therefore offer larger quantities only at higher prices. The typical upward slope of the supply schedule of a purely competitive industry in the short run reflects this relationship.

Long-Run Cost and Supply Curves

There is no reason to assume that the cost curves of individual firms are the same in the short run, even though all firms are assumed to purchase factors in a purely competitive market. Some firms may enjoy lower costs because of superior capital equipment, more favorable location, or better management. These advantages will yield what Marshall terms "quasi rents" in the short run. These incomes accrue in the short run from using factors that are fixed in supply and are akin to the economic rent of land.

In the long run, quasi rents tend to be eliminated, either through an increase in the supply of a reproducible factor or, in the case of one which is not reproducible, through a price rise which results from competitive bidding for its use. In the long run under competition, therefore, each firm will tend to produce along identical cost curves which include the quasi rents of the short run. These costs may be explicit or imputed, depending on whether the firm hires the factor in the market or owns it.

Marshall himself did not examine the long-run cost curves of the individual firm, but dealt only with the long-run supply curve of the entire industry.[35] He conceived of the shape of the industry supply curve in the long run as depending on whether it is one of constant returns (constant cost), decreasing returns (increasing cost), or increasing returns (decreasing cost). The predominant tendency in each industry will manifest itself in the experience of what Marshall terms the "representative firm." This is a firm which "has had a fairly long life, and fair success, which is managed with normal ability and which has normal access to the economies, external

---

[35] This problem was later dealt with by Jacob Viner in his article, "Cost Curves and Supply Curves," *Zeitschrift fur Nationalökonomie*, vol. 3 (1931), pp. 23–46; reprinted in Kenneth E. Boulding and George Stigler, eds., *Readings in Price Theory*, vol. 6 (Homewood, Ill.: Richard D. Irwin, Inc., 1952), and in R. V. Clemence, ed., *Readings in Economic Analysis* (Reading, Mass.: Addison-Wesley Publishing Co., Inc., 1950), vol. 2.

and internal, which belong to that aggregate volume of production; account being taken of the class of goods produced, the conditions of marketing them and the economic environment."[36] This firm is not an actual firm, but rather an analytical tool which Marshall conceived of for the purpose of identifying cost of production, and therefore the supply schedule of a commodity, in the long run. "[The] normal supply price of any amount of that commodity may be taken to be its normal expenses of production (including gross earnings of management) by that firm."[37] Thus, Marshall examines the long-run supply curve of the industry with reference to the costs of the representative firm.

The concept of the representative firm is presented within the framework of a biological analogy. The life cycles of business firms are compared to those of trees in a forest, which first grow to maturity and then decay. During its growth phase, a firm will enjoy internal economies of scale; in its declining phase, these economies will be offset by diseconomies which limit its growth potential and its ability to experience decreasing costs as a result of internal economies. A firm therefore cannot, in Marshall's view, expand its size to an extent which will enable it to dominate an industry. Competition remains pure, and an increase in the output of the industry in the long run results from an increase in the number of firms rather than an increase in the size of firms.

Given pure competition, the long-run supply curve of an industry may be constant, upward sloping, or downward sloping as the industry expands in size to accommodate an increase in demand. The case of constant cost implies that the internal and external economies of production are canceled out by internal and external diseconomies. Increasing quantities of the product can therefore be supplied at a constant long-run average cost.

The long-run supply curve may also be upward sloping. This will be the case, for example, if the expansion of the industry raises the average cost curve of each firm, because the increasing scarcity of a nonreproducible factor increases the cost of using it. The quasi rents which accrued as a producer's surplus in the short run are capitalized in the long run and become embodied in long-run cost curves and supply curves when the supply of factors which gave rise to them is less than infinitely elastic. Increasing quantities of the product can then be supplied only at increasing long-run average costs, and the industry supply curve will be upward sloping.

Marshall believed that the long-run supply curve could also be downward sloping in a competitive industry. This kind of supply curve would obtain, he believed, when the availability of external economies to the firms enables them to experience falling average costs as the industry expands in

---

[36] *Principles*, p. 317.

[37] Ibid., p. 343.

size. Since external economies reflect input or output advantages which accrue to the firms in the industry, but which cannot be charged for by any factor, they have the effect of reducing costs rather than creating rents. Therefore, increasing quantities of the product can be supplied at decreasing long-run costs.

Decreasing costs deriving from external economies must not be confused with decreasing costs associated with internal economies. Internal economies are under the control of the firm and can be achieved by enlarging its scale of plant. External economies are those which accrue to firms in an industry from its general expansion. But these forces are outside the control of the firm, which is merely the beneficiary of gains or improvements in which all firms share, but for which no factor of production can charge a price. The chapter which follows will discuss the difficulty of identifying the source of such external economies and the reasons for which later economists questioned and eventually rejected Marshall's explanation of decreasing long-run cost.

THE THEORY OF PRICE DETERMINATION

Prices Which Deviate from Cost of Production

In Marshall's view, price is governed neither by cost of production alone nor by marginal utility alone, but by the interaction of these forces as they express themselves in the demand for and the supply of a good. Normally, the price of a commodity will, Marshall believed, tend to be equal to its long-run cost of production. That is, the longer the relevant period of time, the more accurately is it possible to adjust supply to changes in demand when there is freedom of enterprise. It follows that there are three cases in which the price of a product will reflect the state of the demand for it rather than its cost of production. One of these, namely, the case of competitive price determination in the market period, requires little elaboration. When the supply of a commodity has already been produced, the force of demand will necessarily be relatively more important than supply in determining price, so that there is no necessary tendency for price to approximate the cost of production. Marshall's explanation of the reason why long-run price bears no necessary relationship to price in the case of true joint supply or in the case of monopoly, however, warrants separate examination.

Marshall reformulated Mill's principle that the joint prices of products produced in fixed proportions cannot be governed by the cost of producing them because these individual costs cannot be determined. That is, if two or more products are produced in fixed proportions, the marginal cost of one product no longer exists. We can speak only of the marginal cost of a combined unit of production, i.e., the marginal cost of a bushel of wheat and so many pounds of straw, but we cannot separate the cost of the wheat from the cost of the straw. Thus, Marshall concluded that the price of a particular joint product will be governed, even in the long run, by the relative intensity of the market demand for it rather than its cost of production. Further, whenever a change in the demand for one joint product induces a change in the joint supply, their prices will vary inversely with each other. Marshall showed that if, for example, there is an increase in the demand for wool, the supply of both wool and mutton will increase as the high price of wool stimulates the production of sheep. The increased cost of output is as attributable to the extra output of mutton as it is to the extra output of wool, but since there is no change in the demand for mutton, its price must fall. Uniform prices for two jointly produced products would result only in these accidental cases in which the demand schedules for both of the jointly produced products are exactly alike. Only the case of joint cost with variable proportions presents no unusual value problem because it is possible to assign a separate supply price to each of the products.[38]

Marshall likewise noted that in a monopoly situation the cost of production is no guide to the price which will be charged. "The prima facie interest of the owner of a monopoly is clearly to adjust the supply to the demand not in such a way that the price at which he can sell his commodity shall just cover its expenses of production, but in such a way as to afford him the greatest possible total net revenue."[39] The price a monopolist will charge, given the demand schedule for his product, may be determined, Marshall tells us, by calculating the monopoly revenue associated with the production and sale of various quantities of output. In order to calculate what portion of the total revenue will be the monopoly net revenue at every level of output, it is necessary to draw up a supply schedule which represents the normal expenses of production of each of the several amounts supplied, including the interest on all capital and managerial salaries. For small outputs, the supply price, or average cost, will be high, so that the supply curve will be above the demand curve; for larger outputs, average cost of production will diminish, and the supply curve will therefore lie below the demand curve before it ultimately rises again. If the supply price of each quantity of output is subtracted from the corresponding demand price, the differential which remains is the monopoly net revenue. The object of a monopolist is to select that volume of output which, given the demand for the product, will make the aggregate net revenue the greatest.

Marshall's method of finding the price-quantity combination at which monopoly net revenue is at a maximum will produce the same results as

---

[38] Ibid., p. 388.

[39] Ibid., pp. 477–88.

FIGURE 13–2

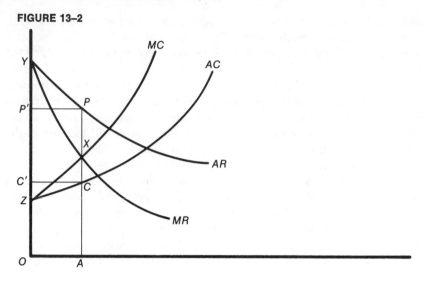

Cournot's method of equating the first derivative of total cost with the first derivative of total revenue.[40] Net revenue is at a maximum when marginal revenue and marginal cost are equal. That is, we can measure monopoly profit as the difference between average cost and average revenue multiplied by output. Or alternatively, we can measure monopoly profit as the difference between the area lying under the marginal revenue curve (aggregate revenue) and the area lying under the marginal cost curve (aggregate cost). Thus, in Figure 13–2, monopoly profit is equal to the area YXZ and to the area $P'PCC'$ when output OA is produced at an average cost of AC.

Long-Run Competitive Price Determination

In the absence of monopoly and production under joint supply, the long-run or normal price of a commodity, as Marshall calls it, will be equal to the cost of production, including the normal earnings of management, of the representative firm. This is the competitive equilibrium toward which the industries in the economy are always moving. His emphasis on the predominant influence of cost of production in the determination of value in the long run led him to conclude "that the foundations of the theory as they were left by Ricardo remain intact; that much has been added to them, and that very much has been built upon them, but that little has been taken from them."[41] This is as much of a concession as he was willing to

40 This was demonstrated by Joan Robinson, *Economics of Imperfect Competition* (London: Macmillan and Co., Ltd., 1933), p. 56.

41 Ibid., p. 503.

make to the marginal utility theory of value. He accorded utility a role, but by no means the dominant one, in the determination of competitive price. The longer the period of time under consideration, the greater the influence of cost of production on price. In the long run, when all the forces of adjustment have had time to work themselves out, price will be equal to the cost of producing the supply needed to satisfy the demand for the product.

The long-run cost tendencies which prevail, coupled with the demand for an industry's product, determine whether the long-run price will be higher, lower, or the same as an industry expands or contracts in response to changes in demand. A change in demand will cause output to expand or contract in the long run in a constant cost industry, but the long-run equilibrium price will be neither higher nor lower than that which prevailed in the short run.

If, on the other hand, the firms in an industry experience diseconomies as they expand their factor inputs, the industry's long-run supply curve will slope upward, and it will produce a larger output at a higher cost than previously if increases in demand cause it to expand. Conversely, if external economies cause resource prices, and therefore the cost curves of an industry, to decrease as its scale is increased, an increase in demand will enable the industry to produce a larger output than before at a lower price. Marshall regarded these cases as constituting a possible basis for interfering with the free operation of the price mechanism through a system of taxes and subsidies.

Marshall's analysis of the effect of imposing a tax or granting a subsidy in different industries clearly demonstrates that he did not share the position of the classical and utility schools that welfare is always maximized under free competition. When production takes place under long-run increasing cost or long-run decreasing cost, there will be a loss in economic welfare under laissez-faire conditions. These cases lend themselves best, Marshall believed, to the partial type of analysis in which it is possible to concentrate on net changes in economic welfare as a result of given changes in particular sectors of the economy, the rest of the system being assumed constant. Marshall measures these changes in terms of the effect which altered opportunities to buy or sell a particular commodity have on the surpluses consumers are able to reap. The change in consumer surplus is measured in terms of a sum of money which will offset the gain or loss resulting from price changes brought about by the imposition of a tax or the granting of a subsidy in industries operating with different laws of return.

The effects a tax or subsidy will have are most easily demonstrated in a constant cost industry. Assume the imposition of a tax raises the long-run supply curve from SS' to ss' as in Figure 13–3. The demand curve DD will then cut the new supply curve at W and output will be contracted from OB to OA. Consumer surplus will be reduced from DYS before the tax to DWs after the tax. The loss in consumer surplus due to the tax is therefore

FIGURE 13–3

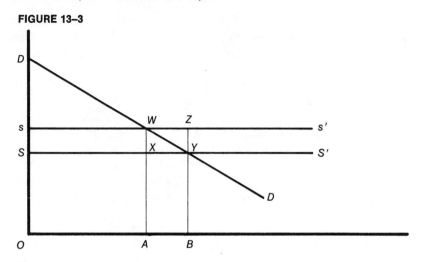

sWYS, while tax receipts are *sWXS.* Thus the loss of consumer surplus is greater than the tax receipts by the amount *WXY.* This triangle on the graph represents the net loss to the community.

The effect of a subsidy given to the same commodity can be demonstrated by similar logic. Assume *ss′* is the original supply curve and *SS′* is the new supply curve that results when a subsidy of *sZYS* facilitates an expansion of output from *OA* to *OB.* In this case the gain in consumer surplus is smaller than the subsidy spent to acquire it, and the triangle *WYZ* represents the net loss to the community. Marshall concludes, therefore, that the imposition of a tax or the granting of a subsidy to a constant-cost industry can make no positive contribution to the economic well-being of consumers.

It may be desirable, however, to tax an industry which operates under diminishing returns and subsidize one which operates under increasing returns. A tax will be beneficial in an industry subject to sharply diminishing returns because in this case a small reduction in output is associated with a substantial reduction in cost, so that the receipts from the tax will be greater than the loss in consumer surplus. Conversely, a subsidy will increase welfare in an industry operating under increasing returns if a small increase in output is associated with a considerable reduction in cost, for here the gain in consumer surplus will be greater than the amount spent on the subsidy. Thus, Marshall concludes that it might be "for the advantage of the community that the government should levy taxes on commodities which obey the laws of diminishing returns, and devote part of the proceeds to bounties on commodities which obey the law of increasing returns."[42] He warns, however, that his analysis does not, in and of itself, "afford a valid ground for government interference."

---

[42] Ibid., p. 475.

THE PRICING OF PRODUCTIVE FACTORS

Distribution Theory in Relation to Value Theory

Marshall's theory of distribution, as already observed, is an application of his theory of value to the pricing of the factors of production. Factor prices are envisaged as being determined through the interaction of demand and supply forces precisely as are commodity prices. The prices that rule in the factor markets are, at one and the same time, costs of production to the businessmen who give them employment and incomes to the factors. Since, under free competition, long-run commodity prices are equal to production costs, they are also equal, in the aggregate, to long-run factor incomes. Thus, Marshall established an interdependence or complementarity between value theory and distribution theory that was absent in the thinking of his classical predecessors. He also included organization, or enterprise, in his classification of the factors of production, along with land, labor, and capital. The incomes of these factors, which in the aggregate constitute the national dividend, are rent, wages, interest, and profit. Each of these shares, with the exception of the profit residuum, is a market-determined price which needs to be explained in terms of the demand and supply conditions which are operative in the long run as well as in shorter periods.

Marginal Productivity and Factor Demand

Marshall emphasized that the demand for a factor of production by a firm or industry is a derived demand which depends on the value of its services in the production of output. Since the employment of increasing quantities of a variable resource which is combined with one or more fixed resources will result in diminishing marginal returns to that resource beyond some point, it follows that the marginal revenue which the sale of its output yields will also diminish beyond some point. A firm's demand curve for a variable resource will therefore be downward sloping.

The market-demand curve for a factor is also downward sloping. All firms using a given variable factor will experience diminishing returns beyond some point as they employ greater quantities of it. But in addition, the increased product of a variable factor employed by all the firms in an industry is likely to depress the sale price of the product, and hence the marginal revenue product of the variable factor. A market-demand curve for a factor cannot, therefore, be drawn on the basis of an assumed product price as is done for a single firm.

While the marginal revenue product of a factor governs the demand for it, it does not, in Marshall's view, explain the price it will command any more than utility governs the price of a commodity. An explanation of the distributive shares therefore requires an examination of the factors influencing the supply of various productive agents, for the interaction of demand and supply forces governs factor prices as well as commodity prices. "The nominal value of everything, whether it be a particular kind of labor or capital or anything else, rests, like the keystone of an arch, balanced in equilibrium between the contending pressures of its two opposing sides; the forces of demand press on the one side, and those of supply on the other."[43]

The Supply of Productive Factors

Time is relevant to the examination of the supply of productive factors, just as it is with respect to the supply of commodities. Marshall maintained that while the short-run supply of the factors is for all practical purposes fixed, the long-run supply of reproducible factors exhibits the reflex influence of remuneration.[44] Thus the supply of labor in the aggregate and of each grade, including that of enterprise and organization, is conceived of as a positive function of the wage rate, and the supply of savings and capital is seen as being responsive to the interest rate.

Turning specifically to the supply of labor, Marshall recognizes that there are complex sociological influences at work which he examines with great insight. But he maintains that the supply of various kinds of labor responds to economic factors in the long run e.g., unusually high wages in the short run in specific occupations increase the supply of that type of labor in the long run. His emphasis on the functional relationship between the remuneration of labor and its supply is somewhat reminiscent of Malthus' position. Unlike Malthus, however, he conceived of the growth of the labor supply as including not merely the increase in numbers, but also the additional quantity of labor associated with the increased efficiency that accompanies a rising standard of life.

Marshall's explanation of the motives for saving and the supply of capital also emphasizes the reflex influence of remuneration on supply. Thus, he states that "a rise in the rate of interest offered for capital . . . tends to increase the volume of savings. . . . It is a nearly universal rule that a rise in the rate increases the desire to save; and it often increases the power to save."[45] Although it is recognized that the motives for saving are very complex and that the rate of interest frequently has little effect on individual savings, the long-run supply of savings in the aggregate is seen as being responsive to a rise in the demand price for it. Only land and other gifts of nature are unique in that their supply in a settled country is fixed even in the long run, so that earnings have no influence on their supply.

---

43 Ibid., p. 526.

44 Ibid., bk. 6, chap. 2.

45 Ibid., p. 236.

The Pricing of Productive Factors

Because the rewards of reproducible factors are similar to that of land when their supplies are relatively fixed, as they are in the short run, it is convenient to examine land rent first and then proceed to the incomes of the other factors. Because the supply of land is fixed in a settled country, Marshall envisages the various parcels that make up the total supply as being transferred from one use to another as the demands, supplies, and prices of various crops alter the opportunity for gain. The active factor determining the uses to which land will be put is the relative demand for the various crops it can produce. "Each crop strives against others for the possession of the land; and if any one crop shows signs of being more remunerative than before relatively to others, the cultivators will devote more of their land and resources to it."[46] Thus the rent secured from any one use must equal that possible from any other use in an equilibrium situation. Therefore, from the point of view of the individual landowner, land is not notably different from capital, for free capital can be invested either in land or in industrial equipment. In either case, the income is a rate of return on an investment whose value is established by capitalizing the income it yields.

Where land is leased to a tenant, the payment he must make for its use is obviously related to the return the owner could earn by cultivating it himself. The rent he pays is therefore one of the costs which must be covered by the market price of his product. This conclusion is at odds with the Ricardian view that rent is price-determined rather than price-determining. The notion that rent is not a cost of production is valid only within the framework of the implicit Ricardian hypothesis that land is used only to produce the raw products of labor's subsistence and that it has no alternative use. Since the long-run price of any agricultural commodity must cover the cost of the marginal application of the labor and capital required to produce it, all units of land on which labor and capital are not marginal yield a surplus which is rent in the Ricardian sense. Conceived of in this way, Marshall agreed, rent is not a cost of production and exerts no influence on price. When rent is looked at from a private point of view, however, it is not a surplus but a competitive price which must be paid in order to bid land away from an alternative use.

The difference between Ricardo's treatment of rent and Marshall's stems largely from the problems with which they dealt. Ricardo, it will be recalled, was primarily concerned with explaining the incomes of various social classes, particularly as they were affected by the Corn Laws. He conceived of rent as making its appearance when population growth required less fertile or less well-situated land to be taken out of idleness and

---

[46] Ibid., p. 435.

used in the production of raw produce. His concern was not with the rent paid by particular agricultural products for particular fields, but with the rent paid by raw produce as a whole for agricultural land as a whole. Competing uses of land for different kinds of raw products, or for nonagricultural uses, were not considered because his concern was chiefly to determine the laws which regulate the distribution of the produce of the earth among the three social classes under the names of rent, profit, and wages.

Marshall, however, was concerned primarily with the problem of exchange value as it applies to commodities and factors of production. Since the problem of exchange value always relates to particular commodities, Marshall recognized that part of the expense of producing a commodity is the competitive price it is necessary to pay for land in order to take it away from other uses. In this case, rent is a necessary payment; in the other, it is not. Thus, it is the difference in the hypotheses from which they started which is at the root of the issue as to whether rent is a cause or an effect of price. Marshall's own conclusion was that "it is wisest not to say that 'Rent does not enter into the cost of production because that will confuse many many people.' But it is wicked to say that 'Rent *does* enter into the cost of production,' because that is sure to be applied in such a way as to lead to the denial of subtle truths. . . ."[47]

In the short run, the rewards of labor and capital are governed by essentially the same principles as the rent of land. Since their supply is relatively fixed, the demand for them is the primary factor governing their remuneration. Their marginal productivity rules the demand for them, and the application of each factor up to its profitable margin of use causes the marginal increment of each factor to earn a reward equivalent to its addition to the value of the total product. Competition among homogeneous units of the same factor will operate to secure the same reward for each increment of a factor as the marginal one, since all units are inerchangeable. Short-run factor rewards are therefore adjusted by the current market situation without reference to the cost of producing the factor. They may thus exceed the cost of bringing the factors to market, so that a surplus in the form of quasi rent is contained in their prices.

The tendency of short-run factor rewards to equal the contribution of the factor at its margin of employment is not, however, in Marshall's view, a theory of distribution. It merely serves to "throw into a clear light the action of one of the causes" which govern factor rewards. This cause operates on the demand side. But supply forces must also be taken into account. Thus, *Marshall's theory of distribution is not a marginal productivity theory of distribution,* but one which holds that we must look to the margin to discover the forces which govern the determination of factor rewards. Supply forces as well as those of demand are operative.

---

[47] Pigou, *Memorials,* p. 436 (from letter to Francis Edgeworth).

Unlike land, labor and capital are reproducible. While the reflex action will be slow, their supply will tend to increase with their remuneration. With respect to labor, the marginal productivity of each grade will govern the demand for it, so that wages will tend to equal the marginal revenue product of labor. At the same time, however, wages also bear an indirect and complex relationship to the cost of rearing and training labor, and therefore to its supply. Thus, Marshall, unlike the classicists, does not see the real wage of labor as a constant determined in the long run by the cost of producing raw produce at the margin. Resorting once more to static assumptions, he concludes that if the economic conditions of a country remain stable for a sufficiently long period of time, the adjustment of the supply of labor to the demand for it will cause human beings to earn an amount which corresponds fairly well to their cost of rearing and training.[48] It follows that there is a separate rate of wages for each grade of labor which depends in the long run on the amount of that grade demanded and supplied.

Demand and supply forces are similarly at work in the determination of the income of capital. Such capital may be free capital which is available for new investment, or capital which has already been invested in concrete appliances. The present rate of interest reflects the temporary equilibration of the current demand for and supply of funds. Because the supply of capital is relatively fixed its short run earnings are not necessarily equal to the present rate of interest. Its earnings reflect the market values of its products and are comparable to the earning of land. Such earnings are properly conceived as quasi rents rather than interest, though they can be expressed as a percent by capitalizing them at the current rate of interest.

The long-run earnings of capital reflect the influence of altered supplies of industrial equipment over time. Types of capital yielding high returns will tend to be augmented in the long run, while those which yield relatively lower earnings will be decreased in supply. As a result, all types of capital will tend to yield a normal rate of return in the long run which corresponds to the additional amount of value product created by the capital applied at the margin.

Marshall's theory of profits involves much the same reasoning as his inquiry into wages and interest. Each industry will tend to evolve the type of organization which provides the greatest opportunity for profit at the margin of advantage. That portion of profit which represents the "wages of management" is governed by the same principle as governs the determination of wages. These are the normal profits which are part of the normal costs of production and which therefore enter into the long-run supply prices of goods. Pure profits exist under competitive conditions only as a

---

48 *Principles,* p. 577.

short-run phenomenon. Like other quasi rents, they tend to be eliminated, so that, in the long run, there remains only the normal rate of profit which is required to attract the appropriate type of entrepreneurial ability into each industry. Thus, we see that Marshall's theory of distribution is an integral part of "a continuous thread running through and connecting the applications of the general theory of the equilibrium of demand and supply to different periods of time. . . ."

MACROECONOMIC ASPECTS OF MARSHALL'S ANALYSIS

Acceptance of Say's Law

Since Marshall's analysis is almost wholly microeconomic in character and is little concerned with the behavior of the economy as a whole, it seems appropriate to reflect briefly on the reasons for his apparent lack of interest in what is today called macroeconomic analysis. Macroeconomic analysis, it will be recalled, began with the Physiocrats. The *Tableau Economique* was concerned not only with the allocation of resources, but also with the size of the net product. While the Physiocratic theory of the unique productivity of land and the prime importance of consumption in maintaining the circular flow was subsequently found unacceptable, it is nevertheless to the Physiocrats that we are indebted for a fundamental concept of macroeconomic analysis. This is the concept that production creates incomes which constitute the source from which the circular flow is maintained. Say's law is derived from this basic relationship, though it was directed against those aspects of the Physiocratic analysis which Say regarded as untenable.

The conclusions which Ricardo and Mill drew from Say's law effectively limited further macroeconomic analysis on the part of their classical contemporaries and followers because they used it as the basis for their conclusion that overproduction for the economy as a whole is an impossibility and that there cannot be an overaccumulation of capital.

Marshall, like his classical forebears, was much more interested in the "normal" equilibrium tendencies of the economy than in its tendency to generate crises and cycles. He paid but limited attention to the problem of oscillations in trade in his treatise on economic principles. Say's law with respect to the impossibility of overproduction for the economy as a whole was implicitly accepted. He also concluded that the labor resources of the economy would tend to be fully employed and receive a real wage equivalent to the value of its marginal product. Full employment is assured because the tendency for money wages to fall where there are unemployed workers is associated with corresponding reductions in *real* wages. Since the latter govern the profitability of hiring, wage rate reductions were regarded as a reliable mechanism for assuring full employment. Thus, the relationship envisioned by neoclassical thinkers between the behavior of money wages and real wages is closely related to their conception of the behavior of the general price level, which is examined next.

The Theory of the General Price Level

The best known hypothesis about the behavior of the general price level is Irving Fisher's transactions version of the quantity theory of money, which emphasized changes in M, the quantity of money, as the causal factor in bringing about changes in the general price level.[49] Marshall's formulation, unlike Fisher's, emphasized changes in the use of money. The public holds some portion of the annual money value of goods and services in its cash balances at any moment of time.

Marshall thought the essential reason why people demand cash or, in modern terminology, have a preference for liquidity is to bridge the time gap between the receipt of money income and its disbursement. If the demand for money for transactions purposes is such that the money stock turns over, say, at a rate of four times a year, the equivalent of one fourth of the annual money value of output will be in cash balances at any moment of time. Thus the demand for cash, which Marshall represented by the letter k, is equivalent to $\frac{1}{V}$. which is the reciprocal of V, the velocity of circulation. By substituting k for velocity in the equation $MV = PT$ and rearranging, Marshall's equation of exchange reads $M = PTk$, where M is the quantity of money at any instant of time and $PT \cdot k$ is the average level of prices, given the volume of trade and the demand for cash to satisfy transaction needs.

Marshall's introduction of cash balances into the equation of exchange has the advantage of facilitating examination of changes in the price level initiated by changes in the liquidity preferences of the public as well as changes which are initiated by alterations in the quantity of money itself. Marshall's introduction of the k factor, however, did not lead to any different conclusions than those associated with Fisher's quantity theory. This is because k in the Marshallian formulation, like V in the Fisher formulation, is a stable factor. The demand for money for transactions purposes is a function of the level of income and institutional factors such as the frequency of the pay period. It is therefore not subject to autonomous variations which will affect the general price level independently of the quantity of money.

While Marshall recognized the possibility that people might have a demand for money as an asset, he viewed holding cash as somewhat irrational. He reasoned that people finding themselves with excess cash balances, because of wage and price reductions associated with unemployment

---

[49] Irving Fisher, *The Purchasing Power of Money* (New York: The Macmillan Co., 1911, revised 1922). See above pp. 301–2 for a discussion of Fisher's quantity theory.

somewhere in the economy, would simply increase their expenditures on other goods (perhaps indirectly through investments in capital goods). This mechanism would maintain the general price level in the face of money-wage rate-reductions and was, therefore, seen as facilitating the real wage reductions essential to promoting re-employment of labor if there were layoffs anywhere in the economy. Thus, for Marshall, the problem of levels of resource use was considerably less challenging than the need to explain individual commodity and factor prices. It was consequently left to the proponents of underconsumption doctrine such as John A. Hobson and Thorstein Veblen and the proponents of the disproportionate investment doctrine, such as Michael Tugan-Baranowsky, Arthur Spietoff, and Joseph A. Schumpeter, to challenge Say's law and give the problem of crisis its place in the economic theory of the period between 1870 and 1914.

Marshall also left to others the examination of the relationship between changes in the general price level and the demand for money as an asset. His approach was to dichotomize the pricing process; that is, the forces operating in the money market were seen as operating separately from those operating in the commodity markets, as though there were no relationship between them. This is, of course, the case if there is no demand for money as an asset. In effect, this assumption has it that a money economy functions like a barter economy. The demand for cash balances is then zero, and the money market is always in a state of equilibrium. This implies that the money received from the sale of commodities is always used to purchase other comodities, which is to say, the requirements for Say's identity are fulfilled in Marshall's analysis as they were in the classical analysis which preceded his.

While Marshall regarded the holding of cash in excess of transactions needs as irrational, his introduction of the concept of a demand for cash balances was subsequently to become an important part of the thinking of John Maynard Keynes who emphasized the speculative motive for holding cash.[50] He viewed the demand for cash as a function of interest rates (bond prices) and, by showing the relationship between interest rates and the investment demand schedule, integrated monetary theory with the theory of income and output. But until this was done, monetary theory dwelt largely in a compartment separate from the theory of income, output, and employment, and its content was virtually limited to the quantity theory of money.

CONCLUDING REMARKS

While Marshall intended to complete and generalize Mill's exposition of Ricardo's theory of value and distribution with the aid of mathematical techniques, he actually produced, as our presentation has shown, a more

---

[50] See Chapter 17.

complete transformation than he himself originally anticipated. The main features of this transformation consist of (1) the explicit introduction of demand equations in the explanation of commodity values; (2) recognition that the technical coefficients of production are not fixed but vary with the costs of factor substitution at the margin, and that this will affect the marginal cost of producing a commodity in the short run; (3) inquiry into the laws of return which govern cost of production in the long run; (4) recognition that the real wage of labor is not a constant which depends on the cost of producing raw produce at the margin, and that there is a separate wage rate for each grade of labor which depends in the long run on the amount of that grade demanded and the amount supplied; (5) recognition that the return to capital is distinct from that of organization; and (6) recognition that factor prices and commodity prices are interrelated, and that the theories of value and distribution are therefore different aspects of a single problem.

While Marshall chose to conduct his analysis with the aid of the partial equilibrium technique, he also developed concepts which led outside its confines. The concept of demand elasticity, particularly in such modern developments as cross elasticity and income elasticity, the principle of substitution and consumer surplus all lead toward the exploration of interrelationships. So do his concepts of joint demand, joint supply, composite demand, and composite supply. His treatment of these cases in his Note 21 leads him to the formulation of equations of the Walrasian type and the conclusion that "however complex the problem may become, we can see that it is theoretically determinate, because the number of unknowns is always exactly equal to the number of equations which we obtain." Marshall himself saw the general equilibrium analysis of the Walrasian type as the logical complement of his partial analysis. But even within the framework of his partial analysis, the principle of substitution at the margin—involving as it does the balancing of small increments of payments and satisfaction, costs and receipts, effort and income, by conusumers, producers, and factors—provides the connecting link among all sectors of the economy. Thus the principle of interdependence and mutual determination pervades every aspect of Marshall's analysis, even though the technique of abstraction is employed to reduce the number of variables to manageable proportions.

Marshall also went beyond Ricardo and Mill in emphasizing the efforts and sacrifices which constitute the real costs of production and the satisfactions of consumption. Ricardo and Mill consistently thought of costs in objective rather than in subjective terms. But Marshall emphasized the psychological factors which underlie behavior in the marketplace and considered them measurable in terms of money. Though the first edition of the *Principles* equated optimizing behavior with the hedonistic pleasure-maximizing, pain-minimizing choices of Utilitarian ethics, subsequent editions sought to avoid the terminology of Benthamism, if not the spirit.

While Marshall examined the nature and sources of monopoly power, most of his analysis was conducted within the framework of the assumption that there is "freedom of industry and enterprise"—not perfect competition but pure competition of the atomistic variety in which there are a sufficiently large number of small economic units to prevent any one of them from exerting a dominant force in the market. He believed in the power of competitive forces to overcome the forces leading to monopoly. He also valued competition as a stimulus to individual initiative and achievement, and believed it would lead to social progress more surely than any form of socialism. He was not, however, opposed to reform measures so long as they did not tend to stultify individual opportunities for growth.

The main departure which modern theory has made from the *Principles* has been in the realm of macroeconomics. Whereas Marshall regarded money as a passive factor with respect to the level of economic activity and accepted the conclusions inherent in Say's law, modern macroeconomic theorists explain the determination of output on non-Sayian assumptions. Their concern is, therefore, to explain the level of resource use rather than the allocation of resources. Even though many Marshallian concepts and tools are indispensable to their analysis, much of the inspiration for modern macroeconomic analysis derives from contributions to the theory of economic crisis and business fluctuation which were made by persons not associated with the neoclassical tradition. Neoclassical theorists literally assumed away the whole problem of explaining economic fluctuations as a result of their acceptance of Say's law; and in the preoccupation with real phenomena, they also failed to appreciate the role of monetary phenomena in the determination of real magnitudes. It is not until the "Keynesian revolution" that the role of money and interest rates with respect to the level of employment and income began to be understood. But once this understanding was gained, its practical significance became so great that microeconomic analysis was almost shunted aside as macroeconomic analysis came to dominate contemporary economic theory. The earliest criticisms leveled against the neoclassical tradition, however, were directed at its microeconomic aspects. The notion of consumer sovereignty and the reliability of the price mechanism with respect to maximizing welfare were primary issues in the revolt against neoclassicism which began to gather momentum during the nineteen twenties. The chapter which follows examines this aspect of the challenge against neoclassicism, and the reaffirmation of the tradition which the criticism provoked.

GLOSSARY OF TERMS AND CONCEPTS

Cambridge Equation. $M = PTk$ where M is the quantity of money and $PT \cdot k$ is the average level of prices given the volume of trade and the transactions for cash. The latter is written as $1/V$, which is reciprocal of V, the velocity of circulation in the Fisherine equation $PT = MV$.

Ceterus Paribus. A Latin phrase meaning "other things remaining equal." In microeconomic analysis, it is customary to assume that tastes, incomes, the price level, and the level of technology remain unchanged.

Demand (supply) schedule. A list of the quantities of a given good which buyers (sellers) would be willing to purchase (offer) at a corresponding schedule of prices.

External economies. Economies associated by Marshall with "the general progress of the industrial environment." Because they are equally available to all firms, they do not tend to reduce competition. (Both Marshall's conception of external economies and his estimate of their impact on competition were later challenged.)

Internal Economies. Economies which are achieved by *individual firms* as they expand their scale of production and organization. Because they are not equally available, their effect is to reduce competition.

Joint supply. An output situation in which two or more products are simultaneously produced (e.g., cotton seed and fiber) so that individual costs are not separable. Individual costs can be identified only if proportions are variable.

Law of demand and supply. The price of a commodity varies directly with the quantity demanded and inversely with the quantity supplied.

Neoclassical economics. The integration, principally associated with Marshall, of the utility theory of values with the cost of production theory of the classicists. Its main concern is to explain commodity and factor prices and the allocation of resources with the aid of marginal analysis.

Partial equilibrium analysis. An analysis which focuses on the determination of individual commodity or factor prices, unlike a general equilibrium analysis in which all prices are determined simultaneously.

Perfect competition. A market characterized by perfect information on the part of participants and perfect resource mobility, in addition to the requirements associated with pure competition.

Price elasticity of demand. The percentage change in the quantity of a good demanded divided by the percentage change in price when both changes are infinitely small.

Pure competition. A market characterized by a large number of suppliers of a homogeneous commodity on which a large number of buyers spend only a small part of their income with the result that only one selling price emerges from the interaction of supply and demand forces.

Quasi rents. Returns to factors which are temporarily in excess of the value of their marginal products.

Representative firm. A hypothetical firm which has "average" access to resources, information, and markets, and is in this sense typical of the experience of the industry as a whole.

NOTES FOR FURTHER READING

The "Editorial Introduction" of the 9th edition of Marshall's *Principles of Economics,* vol. 2 by Claude W. Gilleband (London: Macmillan and Co., 1961) provides particularly useful insight into Marshall's work. An excellent summary and analysis is also available in T. W. Hutchison's, *A Review of Economic Doctrines, 1870–1919,* ch. 4 (Oxford: Clarendon Press, 1953). Book V of Marshall's *Principles of Economics,* 8th ed. (London: Macmillan and Co., 1920) is also recommended.

J. M. Keynes, who is among Marshall's many students, provides a knowledgeable portrait of the man and his ideas in "Alfred Marshall, 1842–1924," *Economic Journal,* vol. 34 (September 1924), pp. 311–72. His chapter on Marshall in *Essays in Biography,* rev. ed. (London: Rupert Hart-Davis, 1951), chap. 14, is also recommended as a biographical account, as is Arthur C. Pigou, ed., *Memorials of Alfred Marshall* (London: Macmillan & Co., 1925) in which Keynes's memorial article is reprinted. A less than admiring appraisal of Marshall's work is offered by J. A. Schumpeter in "Alfred Marshall's Principles: A Semi-Centennial Appraisal," *American Economic Review,* vol. 31 (June 1941); reprinted in Schumpeter's *Ten Great Economists* (New York: Oxford University Press, 1951).

The technical aspects of Marshall's *Principles* are analyzed by G. F. Shove in "The Place of Marshall's 'Principles' in the Development of Economic Thought," *Economic Journal,* vol. 52 (December 1942). This selection is reprinted in Joseph J. Spengler and William Allen, eds., *Essays in Economic Thought: Aristotle to Marshall.* (Chicago: Rand McNally & Co., 1960). See also George Stigler's *Production and Distribution Theories* (New York: Macmillan Co., 1941), Chap. 4; and Jacob Viner, "Cost Curves and Supply Curves," *Zeitschrift für Nationalökonomie,* vol. 3 (1931). This selection is reprinted in R. V. Clemence, ed., *Readings in Economic Analysis,* vol. 2 (Reading, Mass.: Addison-Wesley Publishing Co., Inc. 1950), and in George Stigler and Kenneth Boulding, eds., *Readings in Price Theory,* vol. 5 (Homewood, Ill.: Richard D. Irwin, Inc., 1952). Viner's article develops the notion of the firm's "envelope" or planning curve on the basis of Marshall's long-run analyses.

Many modern writers have investigated special aspects and particular topics relating to Marshall's work. See, for example, Milton Friedman's "The Marshallian Demand Curve," *Journal of Political Economy* vol. 57 (December 1949) on which Martin J. Bailey comments in "The Marshallian Demand Curve," *Journal of Political Economy,* vol. 62 (June 1954). George Stigler analyzes the possibility of a positively sloped demand curve in "Note on the History of the Giffen Paradox," *Journal of Political Economy,* vol. 55 (April 1947). The matter of the Giffin paradox is examined again in a recent article by William P. Gramm "Giffen's Paradox and the Marshallian Demand Curve," *The Manchester School,* vol. 38 (March 1970). Marshall's interest in business cycles is examined by J. N. Wolfe, "Marshall and the Trade Cycle," *Oxford Economic Papers* (February 1956); reprinted in Ingrid H.

Rima, ed., *Readings in the History of Economic Theory* (New York: Holt, Rinehart and Winston, 1970).

The historical and sociological aspects of Marshall's work are examined by Talcott Parsons in two classic articles, "Wants and Activities in Marshall," *Quarterly Journal of Economics,* vol. 46 (November 1931), and "Economics and Sociology: Marshall in Relation to the Thought of His Time," *Quarterly Journal of Economics,* vol. 46 (February 1932). See also Marshall's own view of the changing nature of economic inquiry in "The Old Generation of Economists and the New," *Quarterly Journal of Economics,* vol. 11 (January 1897).

part four

FROM MARSHALL TO THE PRESENT

AN OVERVIEW OF MODERN CONTRIBUTIONS

THE ANALYTICAL TRADITION of neoclassicism after Alfred Marshall's *Principles* and the laissez-faire policy conclusions which most interpreters inferred from it, dominated economic thought for at least the first three decades of the 20th century. But its dominance did not go unchallenged. Scholars who associated themselves with a movement known as Institutionalism became the chief American economists to lead the dissent. Other challenges came from younger members of the German historical school who carried on *historismus*. The tradition of the historical method, which had already clashed with orthodox economics during the *Methodenstreit* of the late 19th century, was imported to America under the influence of large numbers of young scholars who studied at German universities.

This disassociation from the orthodox tradition was joined, though for different reasons, by Arthur Cecil Pigou (1877–1959), who was among Marshall's most brilliant students and his successor at Cambridge. Much of his work places him firmly in the mainstream of neoclassicism. But his inquiry into the conditions required for maximizing welfare asserts his dissent from tradition. His argument concerning the need for special concern about social costs and benefits generated a heated controversy with Frank H. Knight (1885–1972) of the University of Chicago. Knight's views about private property rights, which prevailed over Pigou's contrary emphasis, reflects a reaffirmation of traditional thinking during the 1920s.

Another thread of the counterrevolution in support of orthodoxy during the 1930s came from Professor John R. Hicks (1904–   ). Unlike Pigou, Hicks' objective was to identify the conditions under which the divergent interests of consumers seeking to maximize their satisfaction can be reconciled with those of profit-maximizing producers by the operation of the competitive price mechanism. His work is a major contribution toward the reaffirmation of the neoclassical tradition in response to the issues of dissent that were being raised by the Institutionalists and Pigou. These matters are examined in Chapter 14.

The theory of commodity and factor price determination is an aspect of neoclassical economics that was substantially extended and refined during the 1930s. Chapter 15 discusses the contributions of Joan Robinson of Cambridge (England) and Edward Chamberlin of Harvard University who examined the optimizing problem from the standpoint of the individual firm with special reference to markets that are neither purely competitive nor purely monopolistic. Although their analyses differed in important ways from Marshall's theory of price determination, their price theories are essentially Marshallian. Their emphasis on the imperfectly competitive character of typical market situations is a departure from orthodox theory that was readily accommodated by neoclassical theorists simply by extending their conception of market types to include the "gray area" of markets that are neither purely competitive or purely monopolistic.

The insights about the functioning of the economy offered by John Maynard Keynes in *The General Theory of Employment, Money and Interest* (1936) sparked an intellectual crisis whose order of magnitude was considerably greater than that provoked by the theories of imperfect competition. Keynes's theory followed on the heels of renewed interest, during the 1920s, in the role of money and credit in generating business cycles. Skepticism about the effectiveness of policy measures to control the cycle prompted a number of English, Swedish, and Austrian writers to build on the investigations of Knut Wicksell. Chapter 16 examines their efforts to analyze the processes through which alternating periods of prosperity and depression are generated. Their analyses reflected a belief that the economy has an internal self-adjustment mechanism which is capable, after a period of depression, of restoring a full employment equilibrium.

The business-cycle theories of neoWicksellian thinkers notwithstanding, the experiences of the United States, England, and much of western Europe during the 1930s cast doubt on the ability of private enterprise economies to restore full employment through the operation of market forces. John Maynard Keynes perceived persistent unemployment as a problem which the prevailing paradigm could not explain. His *General Theory* challenges the validity of the neoclassical theory that an economy characterized by flexible wages and prices will have strong equilibrium tendencies. Chapter 17 examines his argument that money-wage cuts to stimulate employment would be self-defeating because they affect aggregate demand adversely.

He identified investment expenditures as a key component of aggregate demand and argued that, in a world of uncertainty even the encouragement of a policy of low interest rates cannot be relied on to restore a full employment equilibrium. His message was hailed as a major analytical breakthrough and was widely interpreted as an intellectual revolution.

Economic inquiry in the decades following *The General Theory* became predominantly macroeconomic in character; that is, it focused chiefly on the behavior of economic aggregates, among them consumption, investment, income, employment, and the price level. Keynes' original system was embellished, interpreted, and refined and became subjected to extensive empirical testing. Chapter 18 reviews the efforts of many of the professions' highly regarded members to fashion the body of macroeconomic principles which comprises Keynesian economics. The contributions which are particularly singled out for study, taken in alphabetical order, are those of Evsey Domar, James Duesenberry, Alvin Hansen, John R. Hicks, Milton Friedman, Don Patinkin, Arthur Pigou, Paul Samuelson, Robert Solow, and James Tobin. Their influence has been so pervasive that Keynes' terminology and his theory that employment and income are governed by aggregate demand commands almost universal acceptance. In this sense, at least, the Keynesian revolution has been successful, and the body of principles built on Keynes' system has become the paradigm on which most of the profession bases its research and teaching.

The monetarist interpretation of Keynesian principles has been particularly persuasive. Led by Nobel Prize winner Milton Friedman of the University of Chicago, monetarists have focused chiefly on explaining the difficulties of achieving the dual goals of full employment and price level stability. The perceived "trade-off" between unemployment and inflation, as implied by the Phillips curve apparatus, is a matter of special concern and is the basis for the monetary policy recommendations of Friedman and his associates.

The microeconomic aspects of the work of Chicago school economists have also been of major importance in shaping the research and teaching of the majority of the economics profession. Chapter 19 reviews the work of Gary Becker and his associates to extend the theory of individual choice in studying the behavior of households and related problems of maximizing behavior. They have also had a special interest in the effect which the assignment of property rights has on the allocation of society's resources. Ronald Coase, in particular, has pioneered in promoting law and economics as the chief interdisciplinary field of the social sciences.

Chicago school interests have been further extended toward the analysis of growth in underdeveloped economies via the agency of the market mechanism. Economists adhering to the libertarian philosophy of the efficiency of the market mechanism regard economic freedom as the most effective way of allocating resources in these economies as well as those which are already advanced. In microeconomic as in macroeconomic matters, mainstream economists have considerable faith in the positive role of the market mechanism and the limited need for intervention. Both on a micro- and on a macroeconomic level, this policy view is consistent with the underlying theoretical structure which has been developed.

The focus of Chapter 20, which concludes this book, is on the critics of mainstream economics, some of whom, like John Kenneth Galbraith, are extremely persuasive. The critics of orthodox economics also include contemporary followers of Keynes, among them Joan Robinson and Nicholas Kaldor in England, Sidney Weintraub in the United States, and writers associated with the New Left. Their criticisms are sounding a note of discord on the contemporary scene which cannot be neglected in assessing the present state of economics. Whether or not the magnitude of the discord is such that it can be judged as indicative of an intellectual crisis, it is a certainty that this dissent will leave its mark on future economic thought.

14

Dissenting Schools and Neoclassical Revival

INTRODUCTION

WHILE THE ISSUES of the dissent against tradition during the first three decades of the 20th Century were many and were differently emphasized and expressed by the various participants, they can be conveniently classified under major headings.

1. The continuing controversy about the use of the deductive method to establish general laws about the behavior of the economic system and those who participate in the economic process. This is an issue which members of the historical school continued to raise and in which they were joined by those who became associated with the American Institutionalist School.
2. The appropriateness of the concept of equilibrium, which the economist borrowed from quantum physics, to describe the behavior of the economic system.
3. The controversy about the assumptions from which deductive analysis proceeded. The validity of the assumption that sovereign consumers and producers behave rationally to maximize the outcome of their choices became a hotly debated issue. The relevance of marginal utility in guiding consumer choice was a related matter of controversy.
4. The reliability of the price system in allocating resources in a manner which is compatible with social welfare as well as private profit. Marshall had already given some attention to the problem of a divergence

between social and private costs and benefits in increasing and decreasing cost industries. But the conventional wisdom continued to view the role of the price mechanism as capable of producing optimal allocations of resources. Now the problem that he raised was about to be addressed again.

To anticipate the discussion which follows, it is appropriate to recognize that very few of these controversies have been definitively solved. Indeed, still other areas of controversy to be examined in the chapters which follow have since emerged. The period from Marshall to the present has been one of ongoing intellectual conflict. There has been a multifaceted revolt against the neoclassical tradition which has produced an equally multifaceted reaffirmation of its principles. The success of this counterrevolution is plainly in evidence in the predominantly neoclassical character of our more popular economics textbooks and college curricula. But the controversy continues; now a counter-counterrevolution is gathering force from several directions, which will be identified more fully in the concluding chapter of this book. Because developments that took place during the early decades of the 20th century were but a prelude to present-day discussions, understanding of what they involved is useful. Thus we turn our attention to the participants and the particular issues which each addressed.[1]

The Leading Participants

The critics of the neoclassical tradition protested against the philosophical and psychological premises from which economic laws are derived and the use of the deductive method for establishing them. From the point of view of the members of the German historical school and the Institutionalists these were related issues. Gustav Schmoller (1838–1917), the undisputed leader of the younger historical school left an impressive legacy of historical research which he hoped would provide the groundwork for the identification of economic laws that would be truly universal.

Schmoller's emphasis on the appropriateness of induction, via the study of history, was complemented, albeit from a different point of view, by Thorstein Veblen (1857–1929), who urged economists to study human behavior in its institutional setting. Human behavior is, in Veblen's view, dictated by the cultural setting of which economic activity is a part and within which it takes place. Behavior is dictated by institutions such as the family, the church, the school system, and the corporation, which are

---

[1] For a more detailed discussion of early 20th century challenges to the authority of the Cambridge School, see Ingrid H. Rima, "Neoclassicism and Dissent 1890–1930," in Sidney Weintraub, ed., *Modern Economic Thought* (Philadelphia: University of Pennsylvania Press), chap. 1.

relatively static in the short run but which are evolving over time. Impressed by his studies of anthropology and influenced by Darwin's theory of evolution in *Origin of Species,* Veblen decried the economists' reliance on the deductive method and on the concept of equilibrium which was borrowed from quantum physics. Biology and not physics is, in Veblen's view, the proper prototype for the study of economics.

The vigor and originality of Veblen's antiestablishment expressions, on a personal as well as a professional level, have left an unmatched legacy of anecdotes and stories.[2] His unorthodox behavior and views were already much in evidence during his undergraduate days at Carleton College, where he was introduced to economics by John Bates Clark. Clark was, at the time, engaged in developing the marginal productivity theory of factor prices, which earned him his reputation as America's foremost neoclassicist. Graduation from Carleton took Veblen briefly to Johns Hopkins where he was a classmate of John Dewey, studying philosophy under Charles Sanders Peirce, while also continuing his work in political economy. The intellectual influence of these two individuals, who subsequently founded that uniquely American school of philosophical thought known as pragmatism, made his sojourn at Johns Hopkins a significant interlude for the development of Veblen's later thinking and writing. But, transfer to Yale a year later, where he earned his Ph.D. degree, opened no academic doors for him, the recommendation of John Bates Clark notwithstanding. He spent the next seven years studying on his own before becoming a student once more, this time at Cornell University, where he studied anthropology, sociology, and economics under still another exponent of neoclassicism, J. L. Laughlin.

Laughlin later agreed to head the Economics Department of the University of Chicago with the proviso that Veblen be permitted to accompany him. It was in this environment that Veblen's long years of study in multiple disciplines came to fruition in his first published work, *The Theory of the Leisure Class* (1899). Though this was followed by many other works, among them *The Theory of Business Enterprise* (1904) and *The Engineers and the Price System* (1921), those Veblenesque expressions which are remembered best, such as "conspicuous consumption" and "captains of industry," were introduced in *The Theory of the Leisure Class.* His unique knack with descriptive phrases, his sharp antiestablishment wit, and unorthodox appearance and behavior is even better remembered than the ideas which his disciples perpetuated and elaborated into a school of thought generally called Institutionalism. A host of well-known followers in the Veblen tradition, among them Wesley Mitchell, John R. Commons, John Maurice Clark, C. E. Ayres, and John Kenneth Galbraith, are iden-

---

[2] Joseph Dorfman, *Thorstein Veblen and His America* (New York: The Viking Press, 1934).

tified by the label of Institutionalism which continues to be used, perhaps because no better one has come to mind.

Like Veblen, Arthur Cecil Pigou (1877–1959) was a man of broad intellectual concern. Indeed, the prizes he won for his essays "The Causes and Effects of Changes in the Relative Values of Agricultural Produce in the United Kingdom during the Last Fifty Years" and "Robert Browning as a Religious Teacher" (published as Pigou's first book in 1901) suggest that his interests were even more diverse than Veblen's. Like Veblen, he was also known for his somewhat eccentric behavior and unconventional dress.[3] But, unlike Veblen, Pigou presents one of the most paradoxical figures in the history of economics. He was, on the one hand, a pioneer in questioning the social efficacy of unregulated private capitalism and, on the other hand, the very epitome of the neoclassical tradition. He studied under Marshall and succeeded to his chair of political economy. It was his work which J. M. Keynes took, during the 1930s, as representative of "the classics," whose conclusions about the tendencies of the economy to fully employ its resources he refuted in *The General Theory of Employment, Interest, and Money*. Pigou's counterattack was to demonstrate that full employmnt is theoretically possible under the neoclassical assumptions of wage-price flexibility. But in his earlier works, particularly *The Economics of Welfare* (1920), he is among the critics of laissez-faire capitalism.

Pigou was, however, not a critic who maintained that the answer to society's problems is the replacement of the capitalistic system by an alternative one. Where others argued in favor of abolishing capitalism, whether by revolutionary or evolutionary means, Pigou explored the possibility of improving the existing system. The thrust of his theoretical arguments and policy recommendations commanded only limited interest at the time of their introduction. But it has recently been observed "now that the Keynesian Revolution has been digested and the political divisions of the thirties and forties have been reconciled in a system of welfare capitalism, economists are becoming increasingly occupied with policy problems of the kind with which Pigou was concerned, and in whose analysis he was a pioneer."[4]

INSTITUTIONAL DISSENT

The Veblenian Challenge

Although Veblen worked under two of the most respected neoclassical scholars of his day, his studies of man within the broader framework of anthropology and biology became the basis on which he rejected the assumption, fundamental to neoclassical economics, that human behavior in

---

[3] D. G. Champernowne, "Arthur Cecil Pigou, 1877–1959," *Royal Statistical Society Journal*, vol. 122, Pt. 11 (1959).

[4] Harry Johnson, "Arthur Cecil Pigou, 1877–1959," *Canadian Journal of Economics and Political Science*, vol. 26, no. 1 (February 1960), p. 155.

the economic sphere is rationally directed. He questioned the assumption that man has an inherent ability to calculate the economic gains and losses that result from his choices among the alternatives available to him. One of his most vitriolic criticisms is directed against the hedonistic conception that

> Mankind is, on the whole and normally (conceived to be), clear-sighted and far-sighted in its appreciation of future tenuous gains and losses, although there may be some inconsiderable difference between men in this respect.[5]

This conception of economic behavior does not, in Veblen's view, reflect the impact of the dymamic and "life process" aspects of the culture. These can be studied only within a framework derived from an evolutionary discipline. Thus Veblen regarded biology as being an inherently better prototype for studying economic behavior than physics, from which the economist derived his preoccupation with static equilibria.

Veblen sees the chief dynamic influences on human behavior as deriving from changes in technology, i.e., changes in "the methods of dealing with the material means of life." Man's technological activities are a reflection of his "instinct for workmanship," his "idle curiosity," and his "parental bent." The latter especially inclines him to direct his efforts toward improvement. These dynamic influences on human behavior conflict with those which are "ceremonial" and "taboo determined." The latter are essentially static and unchanging because they derive from social institutions, which change only slowly, if at all, from generation to generation. Thus, Veblen saw an essential dichotomy in all human behavior which reflected, on the one hand, the impact of a dynamic technology and, on the other, the static ceremonial influences derived from prevailing institutions. Ideally, therefore, economic science should be recast into a Darwinian framework. This would accommodate the essentially evolutionary character of consumer behavior.

Not only is the individual's conduct hedged about and directed by his habitual relations to his fellows in the group, but these relations, being of an institutional character, vary as the institutional scene varies. The wants and desires, the end and the aim, the ways and means, the amplitude and drift of the individual's conduct are functions of an institutional variable that is of a highly complex and wholly unstable character.[6]

It is clear that, in Veblen's view, consumption patterns are less the result of the rational calculation of marginal gains and losses than the result of habit, and the consumption patterns of others in the society who stimulate "emulative display" and "conspicuous consumption." This is the source of

---

[5] Thorstein Veblen, "The Limitations of Marginal Utility," *What Veblen Taught*, Wesley Mitchel, ed. (New York: Augustus Kelley, 1961), p. 155.

[6] Ibid., p. 165.

the fundamental dichotomy which characterizes consumer behavior. Society seeks to emulate the standards of consumer behavior set by a wealthy leisure class. But these standards do not satisfy man's need—derived from the "instinct of workmanship"—to engage in useful, welfare-serving activities. Man's technological bent is thus perverted by a culture which is oriented toward wasteful, ostentatious consumption. "The effect [of conspicuous waste] upon the serious activities of men is therefore to direct them with great singleness of purpose to the largest possible acquisition of wealth, and to discountenance work that brings no pecuniary gain."[7]

The chief implication of Veblen's observations is that a policy of laissez-faire does not automatically maximize consumer welfare. The functioning of the price system cannot be equated with human well-being when man's instinct for workmanship is perverted by patterns of consumption which emulate a wealthy leisure class. Thus, the state might do well to mitigate these undesirable influences by taxing items intended for conspicuous consumption to compensate those who experience psychological losses in consequence of their display.

Veblen's subsequent attack on the market system went even further. In *The Theory of Business Enterprise* he distinguished between making goods and making money as a basis for the observation that the monetary returns from investments are often directly proportionate to its negative affect on the life process of the society. The community is abused via the "advised idleness" of industrial plants and the "capitalization of inefficiency," which reduces output in order to maintain prices. Waste from this source is compounded by advertising directed at the sale of fashionable goods, which contribute to "the making of money" for business enterprise rather than "the making of goods" for consumer satisfaction.

The pervasiveness of these influences notwithstanding, Veblen saw the predominant role of business enterprise in the shaping of contemporary life as a temporary phenomenon which would eventually be destroyed by the machine process. His expectation was that individuals reared in the precise, orderly environment of a technocratic culture would eventually discard the ceremonies, taboos, and superstitions of yesteryear. The engineers and technolgists, who "make up the indispensable General Staff of the industrial system, will develop a "class consciousness" and take counter measures against the wastes and inefficiencies of the present system. Financial managers and absentee owners will then be rendered powerless through a "soviet of technicians." This group may comprise only a small fraction of the population, but a collapse of the old order will follow if the technological specialists engage in a general strike.[8]

---

[7] Thorstein Veblen, *The Theory of the Leisure Class* (New York: Modern Library, 1934), p. 112.

[8] Thorstein Veblen, *The Engineers and The Price System* (New York: The Viking Press, 1921).

J. M. Clark's Rejection of Marginal Utility Theory

Like Veblen, John Maurice Clark, the son of John Bates Clark, was concerned with emphasizing the shortcomings of the psychology on which neoclassical theory is founded. Nineteenth century psychologists conceived of the individual as engaging in rational calculation to satisfy given wants, whose origins required no explanation. Clark maintained that much human behavior reflects impulse and "monetary interests," rather than rational estimates of increments of marginal satisfaction.[9] The human mind is subject to myriad outside influences and is, in Clark's view, readily influenced, particularly by advertising which is largely geared to generating wants. Clark interprets this response as providing evidence that "what every man brings into the world of markets and trading is not wants but merely the raw material out of which economic wants for particular objects are manufactured."[10]

These observations lead him to the conclusion that marginal utility theory is premised on an oversimplified view of human nature. Human nature responds to external stimuli, many of which are an integral part of the industrial system. Thus Clark argues that it is necessary for economists to extend their inquiries beyond the satisfaction of existing wants. The theory of production ought to be developed to explain how businessmen create human wants and the reasons why individual and social utilities are not always maximized.

Clark further criticizes marginal utility theory for its implicit assumption that the choice process is psychologically costless. Following the psychologist William James, Clark maintained that the process of decision-making involves so much effort that people tend to limit the extent to which they exercise their freedom to choose. They tend to rely on habitual modes of behavior in order to avoid the psychological cost of choice. Behavior is thus less the result of continuous rational calculation, in the manner perceived by orthodox theorists, than it is circumscribed by habit and routine.

CONTROVERSY ABOUT THE PRICE MECHANISM AND RESOURCE ALLOCATION

Sidgwick and Pigou on "Externalities"

Another aspect of the challenge against the neoclassical tradition addressed itself to the circumstances under which governmental action should appropriately supersede private action in the economic sphere. From the time of Adam Smith it was recognized that there are certain undertakings

---

[9] J. M. Clark, "Economics and Modern Psychology," preface to *Social Economics* (New York: Farrar and Rinehart, Inc., 1936).

[10] Ibid., pp. 100–101.

so necessary to the commonweal but so unprofitable for the private businessman to undertake that their performance by government is essential. Certain other activities were also identified as requiring governmental regulation because they are of a unique public nature, or are performed under conditions of "natural monopoly." Common defense, industries regulated under common law as public institutions, and those few activities which individuals could not perform for themselves were viewed as appropriate activities for government. But, apart from recognizing these exceptional activities as appropriate for government to perform, the corollary of neoclassical analysis was that society's welfare is best served by a government which allows the market mechanism to function without restraint.

Although this sharply circumscribed role for government was generally accepted, the English economist, Henry Sidgwick (1838–1900), expressed his reservations even before Marshall published his *Principles*. Unlike his contemporaries, Sidgwick saw the possibility of a divergence between the private product and the social product.[11] He reasoned that an individual's claim to wealth is not, under all circumstances, the precise equivalent of his net contribution to society. There may be "externalities" associated with his activities which either impose costs on others for which he is not charged, or which yield benefits to others for which he is not paid. Sidgwick's now classic illustrative example hypothesized a lighthouse erected by an individual at his own expense for his own benefit which simultaneously yields benefits to others who are "free riders" in the sense that they bear no part of its cost. In other cases individuals have unreimbursed monetary or psychic costs imposed on them as a result of another's activities. In either case the private net product of an activity is not the equivalent of the social net product. Thus Sidgwick inferred there is a prima facie basis for government intervention on grounds other than those traditionally accepted.

Sidgwick's pioneering inquiry into the problem of the possibility and significance of divergences between the private and social product was raised anew by A. C. Pigou three decades later in his *Wealth and Welfare* (1920). Pigou considered it to be a major responsibility of the economist to identify the presence of externalities which caused divergences between marginal private and social products and to work out means to eliminate them.[12] For example, he argued that a railroad ought to be made to compensate farmers and other property owners whose crops and woodlands are damaged by the emission of sparks and smoke. Society's output is overestimated if this type of uncompensated damage is understated in the

---

[11] Henry Sidgwick, *The Principles of Political Economy* (1833), Book 3, especially chap. 4.

[12] A. C. Pigou, *Economics of Welfare,* 4th ed. (London: Macmillan and Company, 1932), pp. 129–30.

absence of a compensatory liability charge. The addition of such a charge to private costs makes it possible to identify the whole cost of an operation and thus provide a basis for eliminating the divergence between the private and social product. Regulation is therefore necessary in industries that do not operate under conditions of constant cost in order to prevent the misallocation of resources.

Pigou on Increasing and Decreasing Cost Industries

Pigou was also concerned to further explore Marshall's inquiry into the social significance of increasing and decreasing-cost industries and the possibility of using taxes and subsidies to regulate their outputs. Following Marshall, he argued that increasing-cost industries tend to attract excessive investment whereas constant- and decreasing-cost industries are predisposed toward underinvestment. His most provocative example of the limitations inherent in the market mechanism concerned the hypothetical case of highway traffic on alternative roads between two cities. One of the two roads is poorly surfaced and graded but, being sufficiently wide to accommodate whatever volume of traffic is likely to use it, it provides service under conditions of decreasing cost as the number of cars using it increases. The second road is significantly better with respect to surfacing and grading, but its narrowness limits its capacity. Service is, therefore, provided under increasing-cost conditions. The object of Pigou's example was to demonstrate that under pure competition traffic will tend to distribute itself so that the average cost of travel is the same on both roads. This balance occurs because the cost advantage of using the better but narrower road is offset as a result of the externalities associated with increasing congestion. It is then equally advantageous to use the wider, but otherwise inferior, road because the average cost per unit of travel would be no higher. This situation, however, will result in excessive traffic on the well-surfaced road and too little on the other because the route each user chooses is based on the marginal *private* cost of his choice.

The costs which users of the narrow road impose on others by the additional congestion their traffic causes does not concern them; they have no reason to include the *social costs* they generate in their private-cost calculations. Under competition the volume of traffic on each road will tend to be such that, in equilibrium, marginal and average private costs are equal for both alternatives. The marginal private cost which any particular car must pay as traffic increases on the narrow road, however, is less than the total social cost. This follows because the total social cost is the marginal private cost multiplied by the number of cars using this alternative. The larger the volume of traffic on the narrow road becomes, the larger the discrepancy between marginal private cost and total social cost becomes as a result of externalities. Given the volume of traffic, a user who is charged the amount at which the private average cost equals marginal cost is paying a price which is necessarily lower than the true marginal cost of adding an additional vehicle. Because of its failure to assess social costs, the market mechanism produces a tendency toward the misallocation of resources between increasing-cost and decreasing-cost industries.

The difference in the marginal social costs of using the narrow but otherwise superior road versus the wider but otherwise inferior road suggests that a pure gain could be achieved for all traffic by altering the use pattern which the market mechanism tends to establish. The transfer of one unit of traffic to the wider road would not impose a loss on the user who is shifted because the marginal private costs of service are the same on both routes in an equilibrium situation. The transfer would, however, decrease the marginal social cost of using the narrow road. Thus, rerouting traffic can produce a *net gain* to society. The question, therefore, arises how can a socially optimal distribution of traffic best be brought about? Pigou argued that this could be accomplished by imposing a tax equal to the difference between the marginal private and and marginal social cost on each vehicle using the narrow road. The route a user chooses to travel will then, as always, be guided by his estimate of the cost of traveling over alternative routes. The tax, however, will force him to include a monetary equivalent for the social costs he previously tended to exclude from his private cost estimates. The effect will be to reduce traffic on the narrow road until the true (i.e. inclusive of social costs) marginal cost of using it is equal to the marginal cost of using the wider but otherwise inferior road. Since the tax for the use of the narrow road is equal to the costs associated with excessive crowding, its imposition does not add to total travel costs. But, by increasing the money-cost of using the narrow road, it induces a redistribution of the total volume of traffic and thus contributes to the total welfare.

Clark's "Economics of Overhead Costs"

J. M. Clark pursued the question of the efficiency of the price mechanism in allocating resources from a different perspective. His inquiry into the economics of overhead cost is crucial to the development of a new type of economics he describes as "social." The concern of social economics is to examine the efficiency of the whole economic system in relation to achieving the economic aims of society rather than the efficiency of the individual entrepreneur in relation to maximizing business profits. Instead of proceeding in the traditional mode of neoclassical economics, which assumes that individual efficiency leads inevitably to collective efficiency, Clark maintains that "narrow commercial efficiency does not promote economic efficiency in the large."[13]

---

[13] J. M. Clark, "The Socializing of Theoretical Economics" in R. G. Tugwell, *The Trend of Economics,* p. 85.

A basic reason for the dichotomy between efficiency at the level of the firm and efficiency of the level of the economy in the aggregate derives from the unique and largely unrecognized role of overhead cost in a modern industrial economy. Clark maintained that the prevailing view of the nature of costs of production dates back to the domestic system and is not really appropriate to any later stage of industrial development. J. S. Mill, Robert Torrens, and William Nassau Senior gave some attention to the theory of fixed cost. But the general body of classical thought focused chiefly on the variable expenses of labor and raw material associated with specific units of output. These expenses are readily transferable from one operation to another, and even among industries, in response to changing conditions of demand. Overhead costs, which are chargeable to output as a whole, were not of great consequence to classical thinkers.

Later, the growth of the railroad and other public utility industries which experienced great variations in demand, focused attention on the importance of overhead expenses. The business-cycle investigations of Wesley Mitchell, Clark's close associate, who founded the National Bureau of Economic Research, provided detailed data concerning the ebb and flow of business activity from one phase of the business cycle to the next. These data supported Clark's contention that the 19th century view of the economy's productive capacity was totally outmoded. Productive capacity does not consist of a highly elastic capital fund which is easily reallocated from one economic activity to another. It is highly specific to particular industries and even the most efficient firms find themselves unable to use all their producing capacity during depression periods. Their problems are exacerbated because of the peculiar response of the durable goods industries to changes in consumer demand. Thus began Clark's concern with "magnified demand" or what present day economists term "the acceleration principle."[14]

The demand for capital goods is derived from increases in the demand for consumer goods. Sometimes production turns up without waiting for a change in consumer demand. "Guided by the rising prices rather than a statistical canvass of demand and supply, producers expand their production of capital equipment. When the rate of growth in the demand for consumer goods declines it is accompanied by a larger percentage decline in the demand for new capital equipment." Thus the principle of acceleration intensifies the expansion of investment in fixed capital during the upturn of the cycle. It similarly intensifies its contraction during the downturn, thus increasing the size of the capital stock which becomes idle overhead during the period of depression.

---

[14] Clark's earliest interest is expressed in his essay "Business Acceleration and The Law of Demand: a Technical Factor in Economic Cycles," *The Journal of Political Economy,* vol. 21 (March 1917), pp. 217–35. The problem is further investigated in *Studies in the Economics of Overhead Cost* (Chicago: University of Chicago Press, 1923), pp. 389–96.

The concept of overhead cost is, in Clark's view, as applicable to labor and raw material as it is to industrial equipment. Even though businessmen hire labor by the day or week when they adjust their labor supplies to the demands for output, it does not follow that labor is not an overhead cost to society. The true nature of labor as an overhead cost is obscured by contracts which make workers responsible for their own maintenance. The cost of maintaining labor during a depression is a social or collective overhead cost, which businessmen have passed on to the community. There is thus a conflict between private and social welfare which is reflected in the businessman's effort to preserve his profit margin by reducing output and employment at a time when the social interest requires that production and employment be preserved. Clark recognizes that "the search for standards of social value in the economic realm is a baffling task . . . [for we shall] presumably never discover a definite yardstick of social value comparable to the dollar yardstick of exchange values; but we may find standards by which those of the market may be revised or in some instances replaced."[15] Clark thus shares Veblen's doubts about the equilibrating tendencies of the economy while echoing Pigou's misgivings about the ability of the price mechanism to assure the well-being of society as a whole. This is the basis for his urging that economists devise ways to achieve the social control of business.[16]

THE COUNTERREVOLUTION: NEOCLASSICISM DEFENDED

Logical Positivism

The counterarguments to the criticisms examined above against neoclassical analysis and policy recommendations were as numerous and varied as the attacks that inspired them. But all were associated in one way or another with a philosophical movement known as Logical Positivism. Philosophically speaking, the 1920s and 1930s was an era of Logical Positivism, which held that the ideal of all science, including economics, is to be "value free." Senior's urging that the proper subject of economics is what *is,* and not what ought to be, was reechoed by John Neville Keynes in *The Scope and Method of Political Economy* (1891). It also became the uncompromising position of Lionel Robbins in his *Essay on the Nature and Significance of Economic Science* (1932). Robbins maintained that propositions which have ethical content are not appropriate to positive economics. The place of economics as a science requires that it limit itself

---

15 J. M. Clark, "Toward a Concept of Social Value," preface to *Social Economics,* p. 44.

16 For a sympathetic but well-balanced description of Clark's "social cost keeping" and "social-liberal planning," see Allan Gruchy, *Modern Economic Thought* (New York: Prentice Hall, 1947), chap. 5.

to two types of generalizations: tautologies which are generalizations derived by logical deduction from one or more premises and therefore acceptable a priori (i.e., without proof) and generalizations which are empirically verifiable.

Logical Positivism was inhospitable to the concept of utility as a cardinally measurable magnitude as well as to the kind of welfare analysis which emerged from it. Pigou's welfare analysis and Clark's social economics, both of which emphasized the possibility of divergences between social and private costs and benefits, were at least implicitly based on value judgments. As such they were inconsistent with the dictum of the Logical Positivists that economics must be value free. Logical Positivism is implicit in Frank Knight's rebuttal to Veblen and Pigou and in the neoclassical optimization theory that developed after the publication of John R. Hicks' *Value and Capital* (1939).

Frank Knight (1885–1946) was skeptical of positive action as a means of combating social and economic ills. Harkening back to the classical liberalism of Smith and Hume, he helped mold the economic views now associated with the economics faculty of the University of Chicago, which he joined in 1927. His mistrust of reformers never altered and was never more cogently expressed than in his 1950 presidential address to the American Economic Association in which he remarked, "when a man or group asks for power to do good, my impulse is to say, 'Oh, yeah, who ever wanted power for any other reason?' And what have they done when they got it? So, I instinctively want to cancel the last three words, leaving simply 'I want power,'—that is easy to believe."[17]

Sir John R. Hicks (1904–   ) of Oxford University became an especially important British participant in the reaffirmation of the neoclassical tradition. The refinement of modern utility, demand, and equilibrium analysis is, in large measure, attributable to the foundation he laid in *Value and Capital* (1939). It is largely due to Hicks that the Paretian technique of the indifference curve has become a standard tool of modern microeconomic analysis. He used this tool to demonstrate that it is possible to examine consumer behavior without resorting to the assumption that utility is a cardinally measurable magnitude.

His rationale for eliminating utility as a measurable magnitude (and the value judgments associated with such measurements) is that it makes it possible to eliminate latent elements of Utilitarianism in economics. As Hicks put it, "If one is a Utilitarian in philosophy, one has a perfect right to be Utilitarian in one's economics. But if one is not (and few people are Utilitarians nowadays) one also has the right to an economics free from Utilitarian assumptions."[18] Logical Positivism thus underlies Hicks' re-

---

[17] "The Role of Principles in Economics and Policies," *American Economic Review*, vol. XLI, March 1951, p. 29.

[18] J. R. Hicks, *Value and Capital*, 2d ed. (Oxford: Clarendon Press, 1946), p. 18.

construction of neoclassical demand theory and the new welfare economics quite as much as it underlies the thinking of Frank Knight and the Chicago tradition.

Knight on the Methodology of Economics and Consumer Sovereignty

It will be recalled that Veblen's rejection of the concept and *modus operandi* of "economic man" was basic to his disassociation from the neoclassical tradition. Frank Knight's effort to clarify the nature and role of economic man may thus be viewed as fundamental to his defense of neoclassicism. Knight agreed with Veblen that the determinants of man's behavior are multifaceted. But instead of insisting that all of these aspects be incorporated and reflected in the behavioral assumptions made by the economist, Knight maintains that it is not only proper but necessary to abstract from reality and focus on those aspects which are relevant to explaining economic behavior. Thus, the reasoning of the economist is predicated on the assumption that man, viewed in that dimension of his total existence which involves the material aspects of life, behaves in such a way as to maximize his gains both as a consumer of goods and services and as a producer. In making this abstraction the economist is following precisely the same procedure as the natural scientist who also excludes the influence of those variables whose operation is either irrelevant or prejudicial to the conclusion he is seeking to establish.

Economic man does not and, indeed, cannot approximate the man of the real world. But the abstraction is useful, in Knight's view, for helping us understand the purely economic dimension of human behavior. Pecuniary behavior is what the economist is seeking to explain. Knight therefore questions the distinctions Veblen makes between industrial and pecuniary employment and between conspicuous consumption and that which is not conspicuous. He reasons that economic activity is directed toward maximizing producer and consumer gains. Technological efficiency supports rather than thwarts pecuniary gain, and all consumption, beyond that essential to mere subsistence, is emulative in some degree. Knight therefore rejected Veblen's argument that consumer sovereignty is destroyed because people are conditioned to imitate the consumption patterns of the financially well-to-do and saw it simply as an expression of Veblen's personal disapproval of certain types of consumer behavior.

Not only is the consumer sovereign according to Knight, but the producer who, in an uncertain world, correctly anticipates what forms of production are most likely to find favor with consumers will be rewarded with profit; this is his return for bearing uncertainty. It comes to him as a residual, after all contractual obligations have been met, and only because there is no assurance that sovereign consumers will actually purchase what he has produced. Thus, Knight's contribution to the theory of profits is directly related to his rebuttal against Veblen's attack on consumer sovereignty.[19]

Knight's Response to Pigou

Pigou's argument in favor of using the device of taxes and subsidies to correct divergences between private and social marginal products was subjected to critical examination by Knight in "Fallacies in the Interpretation of Social Cost."[20] In this essay and subsequent writings, he reasserted the traditional neoclassical view that competition would tend to produce an efficient allocation of resources. Pigou's demonstration of the failure of the market mechanism, is, in fact, Knight urged, indicative of the failure of government to establish and protect private property rights.[21] The results Pigou anticipates with respect to highway use follow only if it is assumed that the owner of the narrow road fails to set a toll equivalent to the difference in value to the user between it and the wider, but otherwise inferior, road. As a profit-maximizing entrepreneur, the owner of the better road will charge a toll equivalent to the differential surplus or rent which is associated with the service of the good road. A toll that recaptures this differential surplus, which is rent in the Ricardian sense of the term, will be exactly equal to the tax prescribed by Pigou. Furthermore, it will cause traffic to adjust itself in such a way that social interests are not abused by private decisions to use alternative transportation routes. Thus, Knight maintains, Pigou's conclusion is not evidence of market failure calling for government interference, but rather evidence of the failure of government to identify and protect property rights.[22]

HICKS ON DEMAND THEORY

Indifference Curves and Optimum Allocation of Income

The reaffirmation of traditional theory by Hicks concerns utility and demand theory. The marginal utility theorists established the principle that a consumer maximizes his satisfaction from a given income when he spends it in such manner as to make

$$\frac{MU_x}{p_x} = \frac{MU_y}{p_y}$$

---

[19] Frank Knight, *Risk, Uncertainty and Profit* (Boston and New York: Houghton Mifflin Co., 1921).

[20] *Quarterly Journal of Economics,* vol. 38 (May 1924), pp. 582–606; reprinted in Kenneth B. Arrow and Tibor Scitovsky, eds., *Readings in Welfare Economics* (Homewood, Ill.: Richard D. Irwin, Inc., 1969), pp. 213–27.

[21] The best contemporary statement of this position is in Ronald Coase's "The Problem of Social Costs," *The Journal of Law and Economics,* vol. 3 (October 1960).

[22] Pigou eliminated this particular example from subsequent editions of *The Economics of Welfare* as a result of Knight's refutation.

Because this formulation is so closely associated with the presumption that consumers are rational and able to quantify utility, it became a source of embarrassment to mainstream thinkers. A logical escape, from the point of view of Professor Hicks, is to demonstrate that the economists' understanding of demand (and the allocation of income among alternative uses) is not predicated on either the assumption of rationality or the measurability of utility. To this end he revived the technique of the indifference curve from the work of Edgeworth and Pareto.

The indifference technique provides an alternative method for determining the optimum allocation of a consumer's income between two goods, say X and Y, given his income and the prices of the two goods. In Figure 14–1 the indifference curves labeled I, II, and III represent increasingly preferable combinations of two goods, X and Y, to a hypothetical consumer. Hicks has demonstrated that all indifference curves must slope downward and be convex to the origin of an indifference map such as shown in Figure 14–1. The reason is that the marginal rate of substitution of X for Y, which is the amount of Y the consumer is willing to give up for an extra unit of X, decreases as more of X is acquired.[23] The ratio between his income and the prices of the two goods determines the quantity of either or both which he could purchase. Thus a line of attainable combinations is drawn by joining the point on the vertical axis which represents the expenditure of all his income, I, on good Y at a price of p_{y_1} to the point on the horizontal axis which represents the expenditure of the entire income, I, on good X at a price of p_{x_1}. The second line on the diagram, drawn from point I/p_{y_1} on the vertical axis to point I/p_{x_2} on the horizontal axis, has no relevence to this discussion and will be explained presently.

The slope of the line of attainable combinations indicates the quantity of X the consumer would *have* to give up in order to obtain a unit of Y, given his income and price constraints. The slope of his indifference curve, however, expresses his *willingness* to give up X for Y. Thus, while the consumer can purchase any combination of X and Y permitted by his income, such as those represented by points *A, B,* or *C,* the optimum allocation of his income requires that he choose that combination which gives him the greatest total satisfaction. This is the combination at which the marginal

---

[23] John R. Hicks, *Value and Capital,* 2d ed. (Oxford: Clarendon Press, 1946), chap. 2. If an indifference curve were concave to the origin, the satisfaction of the marginal conditions would define a position of minimum satisfaction for a consumer rather than maximum satisfaction, for in such cases a consumer could improve his position by moving from the point of tangency between the price line and an indifference curve to either axis. The convexity of indifference curves is associated with the diminishing marginal rate of substitution between commodities. This condition is a second-order requirement, whereas the marginal conditions are of the first order. See Hicks, chap. 2; also J. Henderson and Richard Quandt, *Hicroeconomic Theory* (New York: McGraw-Hill Book Co., Inc., 1958), chap. 2, sec. 2–2.

FIGURE 14–1

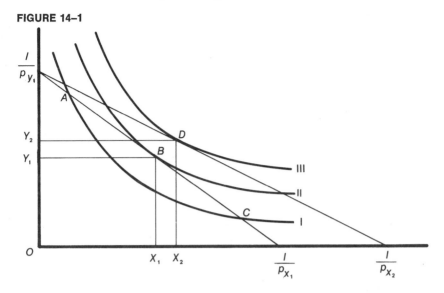

rate of substitution of X for Y is equal to the ratio of their prices. In Figure 14–1, it is the combination represented by *B,* the point of tangency between the price line and his highest indifference curve. Thus, given the prices of the two goods, and given his income, a consumer with an indifference map such as shown in Figure 14–1 maximizes his satisfaction when he takes quantities OX_1 and OY_1 of goods X and Y, because this combination places him on the highest possible indifference curve. However, unlike the older marginal utility analysis, satisfaction is not equated with specific measurable quantities of utility.

Derivation of a Demand Curve

Hicks showed that the concept of diminishing marginal utility is not essential to the construction of consumer demand curves. The typical downward slope of a demand curve may be derived with the aid of a family of indifference curves and various assumed budget constraints. For example, one point on an individual demand curve for commodity X may be derived from the indifference map in Figure 14–1. Given his income and the prices of goods X and Y, the quantity of commodity X which a hypothetical consumer would buy at price p_{x_1} is OX_1. This price-quantity relationship is therefore one point on the individual's demand curve for X, as shown in Figure 14–2.

In order to demonstrate that more X will be taken at a lower price, its price may be assumed to fall to p_{x_2}. Given his income, a consumer having

FIGURE 14–2

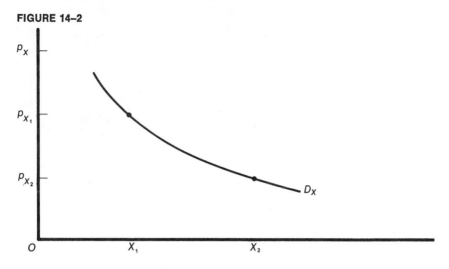

an indifference map such as that shown in Figure 14–1 can now purchase more of a good X at a lower price. Thus, there will be a new line of attainable combinations drawn from point I/p_{y_1}, which represents the ratio between the consumer's income and the price of good Y, to the point I/p_{x_2}, which represents the ratio between his income and a *new price* of good X. The new price line is tangent to the higher indifference curve III at D, and quantities OY_3 and OX_2 represent the optimum allocation of the consumer's income between goods X and Y. The relationship between the lower price, p_{x_2}, and the larger quantity, OX_2, is now a second point on the demand curve in Figure 14–2. This operation may be repeated using other assumed prices of X to establish other points of the demand curve. This demonstration, provided by Hicks, shows that downward sloping demand curves can be drawn independently of the assumption of diminishing marginal utility and the notion of utility measurable in cardinal terms.[24]

Although advocates of the indifference curve approach claim that the notion of measurable utility is avoided by using the concepts of the marginal rate of substitution, its critics maintain that the assumption of measurable utility and diminishing marginal utility is not less implicit in the

---

[24] Frank Knight objected to Hicks' technique of generating a demand curve by keeping the price of all other goods and money income constant, while changing the price of the good in question, which implies a change in real income. This procedure according to Knight separates consumption from production. The correct way of viewing their relation, according to Knight, is to follow Menger and recognize that production reflects the choices made by the consumer. See Frank Knight, "Realism and Relevance," *Journal of Political Economy,* vol. 52, pp. 289–318 (December 1944).

new formulation than it is in the older one.[25] They point out that a consumer cannot know which of several combinations are a matter of indifference to him unless he is able to estimate the amount of utility they represent and that there is a set of marginal utility curves underlying every set of indifference curves. Further, if the analysis is generalized so that the marginal rate of substitution expresses the relationship between one good and the best combination of other goods, this is the same thing as establishing the marginal rate of substitution between that good and money. The marginal rate of substitution then expresses the utility of that good in terms of the best combination of other goods or in dollars.

Separation of Income and Substitution Effects

Even if the indifference-curve approach does not really avoid the assumption of measurable utility, it has the advantage of making it possible to separate the income effect of a price change from the substitution effect. A conventional demand curve would show only that more will be taken at a lower price, but there is no way of knowing to what extent the increase is associated with the substitution of one good for other higher priced goods and to what extent it is due to the increase in real income which occurs when the price of a good is reduced.

Hicks demonstrated that the income effect of a price change can be separated from the substitution effect by introducing a compensating varia-

FIGURE 14–3

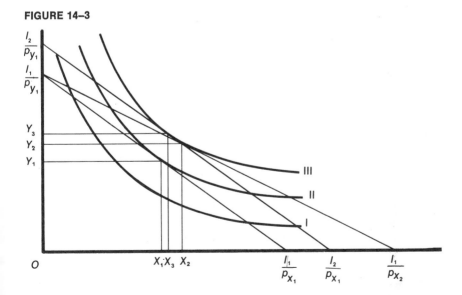

[25] See for example, Dennis Robertson, "Utility and All What?" *Economics Journal,* vol. 64 (December 1954).

tion in income which will enable a consumer to reach the same indifference curve made possible by an assumed change in the price of the good. Thus, in Figure 14–3 a new price line is drawn parallel to the original one drawn from I/p_{y_1} to I_1/p_{x_1}. It connects point I_2/p_{y_1} on the vertical axis, which represents the ratio between an assumed new income, I_2, and the price of good Y, to point I_2/p_{x_1} on the horizontal axis, which represents the ratio between the new income and the price of good X.

The assumed increase in income enables the consumer to reach indifference curve III and buy quantity OX_3 of X and OY_3 of Y. The initial move to indifference curve III was accomplished via the reduction in the price of X and the optimum purchase at the lower price was O_{x_2}. It is evident, therefore, that the increase in consumption from O_{x_2} to O_{x_3} is the result of the income effect, while the difference between O_{x_2} and O_{x_3} resulted from substitution effect. By way of contrast, the older marginal utility approach obscures the difference between these two effects because it does not lend itself to separating the income effect of a price change from the substitution effect.

THE NEW WELFARE ECONOMICS

Logical Positivism and the New Welfare Economics

As was seen in the preceding section, the persuasiveness of Logical Positivism was instrumental in recasting the problem of maximizing utility into a problem of *constrained choice* in which the rational agent selects the best outcome from among many possible outcomes. A further objective of Hicks' *Value and Capital* (1939) was to show how this logic could unify economic theory by treating the problem of producer behavior in terms of the same principles as consumer behavior. This completed the attack against latent elements of Utilitarianism in economics.[26] Thus, the new welfare economics (as distinct from the welfare economics of Marshall and Pigou) concerned itself only with the requirements for achieving an ethically neutral optimum with respect to production and consumption. It brought the era of welfare economics which began with Pigou's *Economic of Welfare* to a definitive close. The new welfare theorists searched for value-free propositions in the sense that they inquired only into the conditions under which the resources of a private ownership economy are best used to satisfy given wants within the framework of a given distribution of income. This is maximum welfare in the Paretian sense.

---

[26] It is relevant to note that while Hicks and Knight were both concerned with the reaffirmation of neoclassical economics that there was by no means agreement between them. Specifically, Knight was negative to Hicks' formalization of demand theory, precisely because it weakened the importance of analytical propositions regarding human behavior. See Frank H. Knight, "Realism and Relevance," *Journal of Political Economy*, vol. 52, December 1944.

Its task was (1) to identify the interdependence of consuming and producing sectors of a private ownership economic system with a given distribution of income and supply of resources, (2) to identify the function of the price system in reconciling the potentially conflicting choices of consumers and producers. The new welfare theorists of the 1930s thus continued the general equilibrium approach of Walras and Pareto. Their approach is value free and thus compatible with the aims of Logical Positivism in its conception of maximum welfare as a state in which there is no alternative distribution of commodities that can improve the position of anyone without making someone else worse off; nor is there an alternative allocation of factors that can yield a larger output *given the distribution of income and the supply of resources.* Papers published by A. Wald in 1936 and John von Neumann in 1938 provided mathematical proof that a competitive equilibrium is compatible with this conception of welfare.[27] Modern welfare theorists were thus returning to the central thesis of *The Wealth of Nations,* namely, that the divergent interests of consumers and producers as well as those who supply and those who hire factors of production are reconciled in a competitive market.

The choices that each participant makes, guided by the equimarginal principle, will insure that the following optimum conditions will be satisfied though each participant acts in his own self-interest.

1. *Optimum conditions of exchange.* Every household will purchase each pair of consumer goods it consumes until the marginal rate of substitution between them is equal for all households consuming both. Satisfaction of this condition implies that households cannot add to their satisfaction by further trade.

2. *Optimum conditions of production.* Given the technical conditions of production, each output will be produced with the optimal combination of factors. The marginal rate of substitution between each pair of productive factors being used to produce a particular product must be such that total output cannot be increased by factor substitution. Alternatively expressed, this condition means that factor substitution cannot reduce the factor cost of the product.

3. *Optimum composition of output.* The production of any product A implies the loss of an alternative product B. Thus the marginal rate of transformation between A and B must be such that it is not possible to increase the output of either without reducing that of the other. Together with the second condition, the satisfaction of this condition implies that the least cost has been achieved for every pair of outputs. That is, the marginal rate of transformation between pairs of

27 Wald's paper is translated as "On Some Systems of Equations in Mathematical Economics." *Econometrica* vol. 19 (October 1951), pp. 368–403. John von Neumann's paper is translated by Oskar Morgenstern as "A Model of General Equilibrium," *Review of Economic Studies,* vol. 13 (1945–46), pp. 1–9.

products is equal to the marginal rate of substitution between pairs of factors producing them. If the first condition is also satisfied, the marginal rate of substitution between pairs of products by each household will be equal to the marginal rate of substitution between them in production. Optimum in the producing sector will then be compatible with optimum in the consuming sector.[28]

The more important details of neoclassical optimization theory follow.

Optimum in the Consumer Sector

The Wald and von Neumann papers notwithstanding, rigorous mathematics are not necessary to demonstrate the simultaneous optima required for general equilibrium.[29] The attainment of optimum conditions of consumer exchange can be demonstrated with the aid of a box diagram such as is shown in Figure 14–4. This is drawn on the assumption that the quantity of two goods available for exchange between two consumers is Q_0

FIGURE 14–4

Quantity of good A

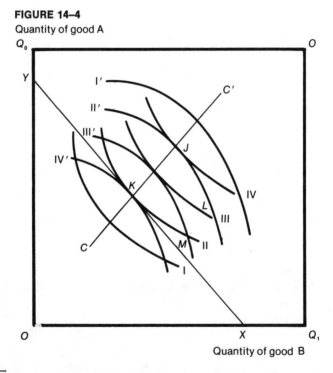

Quantity of good B

---

[28] Additional marginal conditions require optimal work-leisure combinations and between hours of work and the product produced and optimal allocations of factor inputs and product outputs through time.

[29] John R. Hicks, "Foundations of Welfare Economics," *Economic Journal,* vol. 49 (December 1939), pp. 696–712.

of good A and Q_1 of good B. Curves I, II, III, and IV represent successively better combinations of the two goods from the vantage point of one consumer, while curves I', II', III', and IV' show the same thing for a second consumer. The second set of indifference curves has simply been rotated to be convex to the origin O' (concave to O) and superimposed on the first set in order to visualize the trading opportunities between them. There are, of course, numerous other indifference curves which are not shown in the diagram.

Given their incomes and their indifference curves, a pair of consumers have various possible quantities of both goods which each could acquire by trade. Any point of intersection or tangency between two indifference curves represents a possible division of goods A and B between the two. It can be shown, however, that the consumers will tend to move toward some point on the line CC' through trade. For example, if point L represents the distribution of goods A and B between the two, the first consumer is on his indifference curve III, and the second is on his indifference curve II'. If point J is established by trade, the second consumer remains on indifference curve II', but the first moves up to his curve IV. In fact, every point on the line CC', which is drawn through the points of tangency between the two sets of indifference curves, represents a more preferred position for each of the two individuals than any point not on the curve. CC' is therefore known as a contract curve, and any exchange which results in a movement toward the contract curve may be construed as an increase in welfare.

In order to demonstrate which point on the contract curve becomes relevant as a result of trade, it is necessary to make some assumption concerning the rate of exchange between commodities A and B. If the rate of exchange is assumed to be OY of A or OX of B, a price line or line of attainable combinations can be drawn, shown by YX. As we have seen previously, each consumer will do best by seeking the point at which the price line is tangent to the highest indifference curve he can reach. In this case the preferred point for both will be K, at which the price line is tangent simultaneously to indifference curve II for the first consumer and to curve IV' for the second. K represents an optimum for the consuming sector in the sense that neither individual could move to a higher indifference surface by trading without pushing the other party to a lower one. Figure 14–4 therefore demonstrates that consumers will maximize their gains from exchange by moving to a point on the contract curve which equates the marginal rate of substitution between goods A and B for consumer 1 to that for consumer 2, and which equates both to the prevailing price ratio.[30]

---

[30] The reader should realize, if the case is one of bilateral trade, that is, trade between two monopolists, that individual maximizing behavior does not result in determinate equilibrium prices. Depending on their relative bargaining power, any

Pareto generalized this conclusion by defining optimum as a situation in which it is impossible to improve anyone's position by either exchange or production without diminishing that of someone else. The necessity for achieving optimum in the producing sector as well as the consuming sector is therefore implicit in Pareto's formulation, although complete exposition of the requirements of the general optimum did not appear until the 1930s, when they were spelled out by Lerner, Lange, Bergson, and Hicks.[31]

Optimum in the Producing Sector

The indifference curve technique for analyzing consumer behavior led Hicks to develop substitution curves and transformation curves to study the behavior of firms in the rational utilization of factor inputs and the production of outputs. Just as an indifference curve indicates the various combinations of two commodities which yield equal satisfaction to a consumer, so a *substitution curve,* or *isoquant,* shows various combinations of two factor imputs which yield the same total quantity of a given product.

Like an indifference curve, an isoquant curve will be convex to the origin. Because different resources are not perfect substitutes for one another, it will take increasing quantities of resource B to substitute for resource A in order to produce the same quantity of a product. This is the same thing as saying that the marginal rate of technical substitution of factor A for factor B is diminishing. The slope of an isoquant at any point measures the marginal rate of technical substitution of A for B at that point. In theory, the marginal rate of substitution of A for B to produce some output, X, may be either positive or negative. But rational producer behavior rules out a positive substitution ratio because it implies that the application of more of A *and* B results in the *same* output. Clearly, it would be unprofitable for a firm to use more than the minimum-factor input required to produce a particular volume of output. This is shown in

---

point along the contract curve is a possible equilibrium point. In the case of competitive exchange, such as that assumed in Figure 14–4, indeterminacy does not arise because relative prices are the same for all.

[31] Abba P. Lerner, "The Concept of Monopoly and the Measurement of Monopoly Power," *Review of Economic Studies,* vol. 1 (June 1934), pp. 57–75; "Economic Theory and Socialist Economy," ibid. vol. 2 (October 1934), pp. 51–61; "A Note on Socialist Economics," ibid. vol. 4 (October 1936), pp. 72–76; Hicks, "Foundations of Welfare Economics"; Abram Bergson, "A Reformulation of Certain Aspects of Welfare Economics," *Quarterly Journal of Economics,* vol. 52 (February 1938), pp. 310–34; also Oscar Lange, "Foundations of Welfare Economics," *Econometrica,* vol. 10 (July–October 1942), pp. 215–28.

The concept of the social optimum is introduced in chap. 6 of Pareto's *Manual,* and the marginal conditions are developed in the mathematical appendix, where they are used to demonstrate that perfect competition maximizes welfare.

FIGURE 14–5

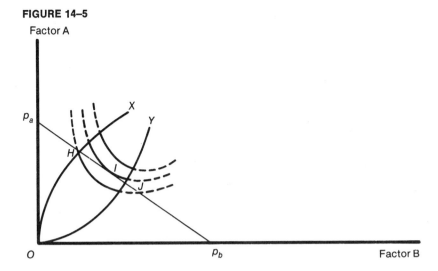

Figure 14–5, in which ridge lines X and Y are drawn to mark off the limits of rational-factor employment. Those portions of the isoquants which lie outside the ridge lines X and Y, as shown by the broken lines in Figure 14–5 are uneconomic factor combinations and are therefore not relevant to production decisions.

In order to determine the optimum output which can be produced with a given factor expenditure, it is necessary to know the prices at which the factors can be purchased. Assume that their prices are p_a and p_b, respectively. Thus the firm can purchase any combination of the two factors which lies on $p_a p_b$, which is the outlay or isocost curve. This curve connects that point on the vertical axis which represents the use of a given budget to purchase only factor A to that point on the vertical axis which represents the purchase of factor B only. It is therefore analogous to the price line in indifference curve analysis. The position of the budget or isocost line in Figure 14–5 indicates that the firm could purchase any factor combination lying on it, such as H, I, and J. But the best combination is I, for this combination enables the firm to achieve a bigger output, i.e., to produce on a higher isoquant, with a given factor input. This is the combination at which the ratio of the marginal rates of substitution between A and B is equal to the ratio of their prices. It is therefore the optimum factor combination. Generalizing this conclusion for all firms using A and B implies that the marginal rate of technical substitution must be the same for all firms using both factors. If this condition is not satisfied, it is possible to increase the total product by substituting one factor for another until a further shift will no longer add anything to the total product.

Maximum efficiency of resource use also requires that each firm produce an optimum amount of each product it turns out. The various combinations of two products, say A and B, which can be produced with a given input of factor X can be represented by a *transformation curve*. Unless the two products are jointly produced in fixed proportions, e.g., hides and meat, outputs of A must be sacrificed to obtain outputs of B, given the input of X. Thus a product transformation curve will be *concave* to the origin.[32] Its slope at any point measures the marginal rate of transformation between the two products or, what amounts to the same thing, the ratio of the marginal costs of the two products. The individual firm produces the optimum combination of two products, say A and B, with a given factor input when the marginal rate of transformation between them is equal to the ratio of their prices. If this condition is not satisfied, the firm could produce more of A and less of B (or vice versa) and add to its profits. Generalizing this conclusion to all firms producing A and B and paying the same price for their factor inputs implies that the ratio of their marginal rates of transformation to the marginal cost of producing the two goods must be equal. If this condition is not satisfied, a reallocation of production could increase the output of either or both products without any change in factor input or the output of other commodities.

The general equilibrium investigations of the new welfare theorists thus demonstrated that a competitive equilibrium can exist. This is essentially the problem posed by Adam Smith in 1776. Can the divergent interests of consumers seeking to maximize their satisfactions and producers seeking to maximize their profits be reconciled by the operation of the competitive price mechanism? Modern welfare analysis has answered this question affirmatively.[33] That is, it has shown that there exists a set of non-negative prices for each competitive market that would emerge and be compatible with consumer and producer optimization behavior.[34]

---

[32] If transformation curves were convex to their origins, satisfaction of the marginal conditions would define an economic minimum. Similarly, if isoquants were concave, satisfaction of the marginal conditions would define an economic minimum.

[33] Proof that rational pricing of the factors of production is even possible in a socialist economy was first offered by Oscar Lange and Fred M. Taylor, in *On the Theory of Socialism* (Minneapolis: University fo Minnesota Press, 1938). Their argument was a rebuttal to that of Ludwig von Mises that a socialist economy is necessarily chaotic because of the absence of a free price market. Von Mises' view is published in F. A. Hayck, ed., *Collectivist Economic Planning* (London: Routledge, 1935). See also the view of Enrico Barone. "The Ministry of Production in a Collectivist State," republished in the same volume.

[34] Paul Samuelson's *Foundation of Economic Analysis* (Cambridge: Harvard University Press, 1947) examines the relationship between stable states and equilibrium states. A parameter change in an unstable system will not necessarily produce a new equilibrium. See also "The Stability of Equilibrium, Comparative Statistics and Dynamics," *Econometrica* vol. 9 (April 1941), pp. 97–120.

CONCLUDING REMARKS

The objective of this chapter has been to investigate the continued development of post-Marshallian economics from the dissent associated with the American Institutionalists and Pigovian welfare economics to the reaffirmation by Knight, Hicks, and Samuelson that the price mechanism can reconcile diverging economic interests in a competitive private enterprise system. All of these writers have had a major impact on contemporary economics, some of which will be more fully explored in the chapters which follow. The heterodoxy of Veblen, Clark, and others who worked in the Institutionalist tradition are particularly evident in the writings of John Kenneth Galbraith, who is perhaps the foremost social critic of our day. Galbraith's observations about the power of the conventional wisdom over men's actions is not unlike the effect which Veblen attributed to institutions. Similarly, Galbraith's notion of the role of the dependence effect, which derives from the actions of producers who generate artificial or contrived wants to suit their own requirements as producers, casts as much doubt on the principle of consumer sovereignty as did Veblen's notion of conspicuous consumption.[35]

While Veblenian nuances are evident in the writings of such social critics as Galbraith, the specifics of Veblen's legacy to economics falls short of the avowed objective of reconstructing economic science. As a compromise, many modern Institutionalists have followed Wesley Mitchell in their reliance on quantitative empirical work.[36] They have also recognized the complementarity of their empirical work and pure theory. It is acknowledged that a successful empiricist needs to be able to formulate economic concepts and give precise expression to economic relationships. Thus, such quantitative workers as Mitchell looked toward the goal of being able to arrive at generalizations comparable to those neoclassicists arrived at by deductive analysis. This objective is not, of course, shared by all modern Institutionalists, some of whom continue to examine the economic process within its social and political framework while rejecting the Newtonian *Weltannschaung* they perceive in the still predominantly equilibrium analyses of neoclassical economics. A few even look toward a system of "economic sociology", such as was visualized by Veblen or Max Weber.[37]

While the results of Veblen's criticism of neoclassicism are less than positive, Pigou emerges, in retrospect, as a scholar who was considerably

---

[35] Galbraith's views are examined in more detail in Chapter 20 below.

[36] Wesley Mitchell, "Quantitative Analysis in Economic Theory," reprinted in *The Backward Art of Spending Money* (New York: Augustus Kelley 1937), pp. 22–36.

[37] Karl Mannheim has attempted to establish the sociology of knowledge as an integrated system of analysis in his *Ideology and Utopia* (New York: Harcourt, 1936).

ahead of his contemporaries in his concern about the discrepancies between the neoclassical theoretical model and the real world. Before the
publication of his *Wealth and Welfare* (1920), no one who commanded
the respect of the academic community, other than Henry Sidgwick, undertook to inquire about the social consequences which private actions for
profit might have. Pigou's distinction between private costs and social costs
constituted an analytical breakthrough which he himself helped to extend
by recommending that such problems of uncompensated damage as those
arising from air and water pollution in an urban-industrial environment,
might be dealt with through a system of fines and subsidies.

The legacy of Frank Knight's work is also much in evidence today.
Specifically his counterargument—that the misallocation of resources that
Pigou attributed to market failure is, in fact, related to the failure of government to clearly identify property rights—has laid the groundwork for
important contemporary work which inquires further into the relationship
between externalities of various sorts and property rights. Knight's influence is also apparent in both the analysis and policy recommendations of
the Chicago School. Chapter 19 below is devoted to examining the contributions of this very influential group of thinkers, whose most prominent
member, Milton Friedman, was honored with the Nobel Prize in Economics in 1976.

The influence of Hicks' work is also much in evidence in contemporary
theory. The inquiries that built on the foundations he laid, together with
Wald and von Neumann, clarified understanding of the conditions under
which a decentralized economic system, governed by the independent
choices of consumers and business firms in the market place, can achieve
efficient resource allocations. The general equilibrium analysis Hicks
revitalized in *Value and Capital* also became fundamental, as will be examined in Chapter 18, to the controversy between Keynes and the Keynesians who reaffirmed the traditions of neoclassical economics along different lines than those examined in this chapter.

While the work of Knight and Hicks during the 1930s left no doubt that
neoclassicism was alive and well, the dissent that preceded and accompanied it was merely a harbinger of the discontent with orthodox economics
that was to follow. An important aspect of this disenchantment, which has
not yet been examined, concerned the theory of value. The Marshallian
analysis of increasing returns and its relationship to the viability of the
competitive market soon became the central issue of another great debate.[38] This one climaxed during the early 1930s with the emergence of
the theories of nonperfect competition, which are the subject matter of the
following chapter. But this was not to be the end of the attack against the

---

[38] The opening salvo of this debate was J. H. Clapham's, "Of Empty Economic
Boxes," *Economic Journal,* vol. 32 (September 1922).

neoclassical model. The apparent tendency of capitalistic systems to experience cyclical disturbances produced conflicting hypotheses. These inquiries were climaxed by J. M. Keynes's attack against those aspects of the neoclassical analysis that relate to the macroeconomic question of the level of employment and output. Thus, the challenges to the neoclassical model which we have here examined were merely a prelude to the era of intellectual revolution which was to follow.

GLOSSARY OF TERMS AND CONCEPTS

Box diagram (sometimes called an Edgeworth box).   A closed diagram which encloses the total quantities of two goods available to be exchanged and the indifference curve families of a pair of potential trading partners.

Collective goods.   Goods which are consumed by the population as a whole, e.g., police protection, military hardware, etc.

Conspicuous consumption.   A term introduced by Veblen, which has become standard terminology, describing the kind of consumption behavior which is associated with a wealthy leisure class.

Consumer sovereignty.   A term describing individual ability and freedom to make rational choices among all alternative goods so that the marginal gain will tend to equal the marginal expenditure for each good.

Contract curve.   The curve formed by the locus of all the points of tangency between the indifference curves of potential trading partners.

Externalities.   Social costs (or benefits) that unintentionally accompany private production (or consumption) activities. Because these are not incorporated into market prices, it has been proposed that they be "corrected" via a system of taxes and bounties. Present concern focuses particularly on externalities which pollute the environment. The recipient of an unpaid benefit is sometimes referred to as a "free rider."

Income effect.   The change in the quantity of a good demanded as real income changes. The latter may be the result of a price change or a change in money income.

Indifference map.   A three dimensional representation of various combinations of a pair of goods, among which a consumer is indifferent. Indifference may equally well be represented by an indifference curve which will be convex to the origin and downward sloping because the rate at which one of the commodities will have to be substituted for the other will have to be increased in order for the individual to continue to be indifferent among the combinations.

Institutionalism.   A distinctively American school of economics, largely inspired by the work of Veblen, which emphasizes the necessity of studying economics as an evolutionary discipline.

Isoquant.   A curve illustrating the various combinations of two factors which can be traded off against one another to produce a specific quantity of a good. Each point on an isoquant curve represents the marginal rate of substitution between the two factors. Because the rate at which one factor will have to be substituted for another in order to keep output constant must increase, an isoquant, like an indifference curve, is convex to the origin.

Logical Positivism.   A philosophical movement identified with the view that all sciences, including economics, must be free of value judgments.

Magnified demand.   (The acceleration principle) Changes in the demand for consumer goods generate proportionately greater changes in the demand for capital goods (including inventories). A decline in the demand for a consumer good causes excess capacity and therefore may reduce the demand for new capital, even if consumer demand increases again.

Marginal cost pricing.   Government intervention to follow the rule that price should equal marginal cost for goods produced under decreasing cost conditions in order to facilitate the achievement of the competitive output.

Overhead cost.   The fixed costs of equipment and other capital that are associated with output as a whole.

NOTES FOR FURTHER READING

Veblen and Other Institutionalists

For a thoughtful account of the work of Veblen, J. M. Clark, Mitchell, Commons, and Tugwell by a leading modern Institutionalist, see Allan Gruchy, *Modern Economic Thought: The American Contribution,* (Englewood Cliffs, N.J.: Prentice-Hall, 1947). See also his *Contemporary Economic Thought* (New York: Augustus Kelley, 1972). Joseph Dorfman's *Thorstein Veblen and His America* (New York: Viking, 1934) remains a classic reference as does Wesley Mitchell's *What Veblen Taught* (New York: Viking Press, 1936) which includes among its essays, "The Preconceptions of Economic Science," a scathing attack on the philosophical foundations of economic orthodoxy. Veblen's article, "Why Economics Is Not an Evolutionary Science," *Quarterly Journal of Economics,* vol. 12 (July 1898), pp. 3–21, is outstanding as a methodological critique. For a more recent evaluation of Veblen's work see Douglas Dowd, ed., *Thorstein Veblen: A Critical Reappraisal* (Ithaca, N.Y.: Cornell University Press, 1958). William Breit and Roger L. Ransom present a lively review of writers of Institutionalist persuasion in *The Academic Scribblers* (New York: Holt Rinehart and Winston,

1971), especially chaps. 4, 5, 11, and 12. Veblen's own *Theory of the Leisure Class* (1899) which is readily available, is recommended as representative of Veblen's thought and style besides being the source of such familiar phrases as "conspicuous consumption." Kenneth Boulding's, "A New Look At Institutionalism," *Proceedings of the American Economic Association,* May 1957 and comments by discussants remains relevant.

Methodology

The classic inquiry is John Neville Keynes's *The Scope and Method of Political Economy* (1891; New York: Kelley & Millman Inc., 1955), which reviews the issues of the 19th century *Methodenstreit* and restates the neoclassical position. The modern conception of economics as a value-free science stems from Lionel Robbins, *An Essay on the Nature and Significance of Economic Science,* 2d ed. (New York: Macmillan, 1935). T. W. Hutchison examines the role of value judgments in economics in *Positive Economics and Policy Objectives* (Cambridge, Mass.: Harvard University Press, 1964). The essays by Jerome Rothenberg, C. W. Churchman, and R. B. Brandt in Part IV of the *Structure of Economic Science* (New York: Prentice-Hall, 1966). Sherman R. Krupp, ed., examine the role of value premises in economics. For Frank Knight's views on methodology, see Eva and Abraham Hirsch's "The Heterodox Methodology of Two Chicago Economists," *Journal of Economic Issues,* vol. 11, no. 4 (December 1975). Knight's article "Fallacies in the Interpretation of Social Costs," *Quarterly Journal of Economics,* vol. 38 (May 1924) is reprinted in K. Arrow and T. Scitovsky, eds., *Readings in Welfare Economics* (Homewood, Ill.: R. D. Irwin, Inc., 1969). John McKinney reviews the conservative political philosophy of Frank Knight and relates it to the modern Chicago tradition in "Frank H. Knight and the Chicago Libertarianism," *Journal of Economic Issues,* vol. 9, no. 4 (December 1975).

Demand Theory

The article by Ivor Pierce, "Demand Theory, Consumers' Surplus, and Sovereignty" in Sidney Weintraub, ed. *Modern Economic Thought 1945–1965* (Philadelphia: University of Pennsylvania Press, 1976), is especially recommended for its review of modern mathematical demand theory and for relating contemporary theorizing to the earlier work of the classicists and the marginal utility theorists.

Pigovian Welfare Economics

The brief discussion by T. W. Hutchison, *Review of Economic Doctrines;* chap. 18, is especially recommended. For a critical view see Hla Myint, *Theories of Welfare Economics* (New York: Augustus Kelley, 1965) chap. 10. The ethical problems of welfare economics are discussed in chap. 11 of the same volume.

General Equilibrium and Paretian Welfare Economics

E. J. Mishan reviews the field in "A Survey of Welfare Economics 1939–1959," *Economic Journal,* vol. 70 (1960).

E. Roy Weintraub reviews the place of general equilibrium analysis in contemporary economics in chap. 6, "General Equilibrium Theory," in Sidney Weintraub, ed., *Modern Economic Thought 1945–1965.*

15

Chamberlin, Robinson, and Other Price Theorists

INTRODUCTION

THE ASSUMPTION that the markets of the real world typically approximate the conditions which made them compatible with the economists' model of pure competition became a further matter of special concern during the 1930s. Marshall focused chiefly on the determination of commodity and factor prices in markets characterized by "freedom of industry and enterprise," because large numbers of buyers and sellers of homogeneous commodities and services were trading in them. He had a well developed model of monopoly, though he accorded the problem of pricing in this type of market much less attention than he lavished on the behavior of competitive markets. Further, the possibility that some markets might have characteristics that would enable individual sellers to exert some individual control over the prices they charged even though they were not monopolists was hardly perceived by him. Yet it is precisely this grey area of pricing in markets that are *neither* purely competitive nor purely monopolistic which became a major area of investigation during the 1930s.

Although the modern theory of price determination disregards Marshall's rigid compartmentalization of markets into the category of competition or monopoly, it is essentially Marshallian in inspiration. It is also Marshallian in its adherence to particular equilibrium methodology. Unlike the modern theory of optimal consumer and producer behavior and the new welfare economics examined in the preceding chapter, modern price theory does not rest on the marginal utility theory of value or the concept of general equilibrium.

One cannot help but speculate whether or not the more rigorous treatment of imperfectly competitive market structures by contemporary theorists was triggered by concern with the problem of "big business." It is certainly true that in the United States, at least, there was renewed public concern over the concentration of economic power during the 1920s and 1930s, and many institutional studies of the problem appeared at that time.[1] Still, no one could have been more concerned with the problem of monopoly than Marshall or John Bates Clark, though both conducted their theoretical analyses on the premise that most markets approximate free competition. While the problem of big business and its regulation may indeed have been more pressing in the 1930s than it had been 50 or so years earlier, there is no evidence that the new theoretical developments in the area of price theory were in any way a response to the challenge created by this aspect of the institutional environment.

If any environmental influences were at work in stimulating the development of price theory, they derived from the intellectual rather than the institutional environment. In particular, greater interest in mathematical economics focused attention on the work of Cournot, whose *Researches into the Mathematical Principles of the Theory of Wealth* (1838) was then nearing its 100th anniversary. Cournot's theory of monopoly and his conclusion that a monopolist will maximize profit when he equates the first derivative of total revenue (i.e., marginal revenue) to the first derivative of total cost (i.e., marginal cost) was the first major achievement of mathematical economics. It is understandable that a wider study of Cournot's work stimulated a more rigorous classification of market structures along the lines he suggested, along with greater terminological precision and development of new analytical concepts. The gaps in Marshall's analysis, particularly as they relate to pricing situations intermediate between competition and monopoly, also attracted able minds. More recently, it is the problem of oligopoly, or competition among a few sellers, which has been of greatest interest in the area of price theory. The paragraphs which follow will provide acquaintance with the names and brief biographical information about the main contributors to price theory since Marshall.

The Contributors to Modern Price Theory

With respect to the theory of monopoly, the improvement since Cournot has been mainly in terms of exposition. The main substantive contributions have been the theory of monopoly price discrimination and the development of the case of monopsony, or buyer monopoly, to parallel the tradi-

---

[1] Claire Wilcox, *Competition and Monopoly in American Industry,* Temporary National Economic Committee Monograph No. 21 (Washington, D.C.: U.S. Government Printing Office, 1941), A. A. Berle and G. C. Means, *The Corporation and Private Property* (New York: Commerce Clearing House, Inc., 1932); and Frank Fetter, *Masquerade of Monopoly* (New York: Harcourt Brace & Co., 1931).

tional case of seller monopoly. With respect to the theory of monopoly price discrimination, the most substantial contributions have come from Arthur C. Pigou (1877–1959) and Joan Robinson (1903–   ). Pigou's examination of the nature and results of monopoly pricing was conducted within the framework of the welfare analysis of his *Economics of Welfare,* which has already been discussed.

Other than Pigou's, the most substantive contribution to the theory of monopoly pricing is to be found in Robinson's *Economics of Imperfect Competition* (1933), which is also concerned with the analysis of pricing situations which lie in the gray area between pure monopoly and pure competition. Robinson, of Cambridge University, is perhaps the only woman to achieve recognition as an economic theorist. She rediscovered Cournot's first derivative of total revenue and christened it "marginal revenue," and her simple yet elegant geometry popularized the use of marginal cost and marginal revenue curves in price analysis. She also made the most substantial contribution of any contemporary writer since Pigou to the theory of monopoly price discrimination, besides developing the case of monopsony, or buyer monopoly, to parallel the traditional case of seller monopoly.

Her contributions are not, however, limited to the field of price theory. She is equally accomplished in the area of macroeconomic theory. Her *Introduction to the Theory of Employment* (1937) was the earliest effort to present the gist of Keynes's theory on an elementary level, and her *Essays on the Theory of Employment* (1936) examines the application of Keynesian theory to particular problems. Her latest work in this area, besides numerous articles and essays, is *The Accumulation of Capital* (1960), in which she has demonstrated the construction of a model of secular growth. Her essays on a wide variety of theoretical subjects are to be found in *Collected Essays of Joan Robinson* (1951), and she has also written *An Essay in Marxian Economics* (1942), besides her recent philosophical essay, *Economic Philosophies* (1962).

It is not, however, the theory of monopoly but the theory of monopolistic competition which constitutes the main refinement and extension of the work of Cournot and Marshall. Although both Cournot and Marshall examined monopoly behavior with respect to price, this case was regarded as one which is seldom encountered in the real world. Marshall lavished almost all of his concern on firms which produced their products under conditions of free competition, even though he noted, in his *Industry and Trade,* that competition and monopoly are "interlaced." Nowhere, however, did he examine the nature of this interlacing or its significance for price determination. Not until the 1920s and early 1930s did there emerge a growing concern with the gaps in Marshall's work, particularly with respect to pricing situations intermediate between competition and monopoly.

The most vulnerable part of Marshall's analysis proved to be the resort to "external economies" as a device for reconciling increasing returns with the assumption of pure competition. Their inherent incompatibility was clearly pointed out by Piero Sraffa (1898–   ) in his now classic article of 1926 on the laws of return.[2] Sraffa, an Italian who emigrated to England, where he studied under Marshall, eventually taught at Cambridge. His most distinguished works are his edition of Ricardo's collected works and personal correspondence and his monograph "The Production of Commodities by Means of Commodities."[3] But he is equally well known for his provocative article on the laws of return, which focused analytical attention on the main "dark spots" in the Marshallian theory of value and urged its reconstruction. Even though he did not participate further in bringing about this reconstruction, the keenness of his observations on the technical shortcomings of Marshall's long-run supply curve alone are sufficient to secure him a place among contemporary contributors to value theory.

Sraffa's 1926 article on the laws of return had already appeared when Edward Chamberlin (1899–1967), still a graduate student at Harvard in 1927, submitted a doctoral dissertation in which he undertook to examine the determination of prices in markets in which monopolistic and competitive elements are blended. This dissertation, *The Theory of Monopolistic Competition* (1933), appeared so nearly at the same time as Joan Robinson's *Economics of Imperfect Competition* in England that both writers are equally recognized as pioneers in the theory of pricing situations that are intermediate between pure competition and pure monopoly. Unlike Robinson, Chamberlin, who was a professor of economics at Harvard, devoted his professional efforts almost exclusively to exploring the various ramifications of his original thesis, including the implications of the theory of monopolistic competition for the theory of distribution.

While the leading contributions to contemporary literature on price theory are those of Chamberlin and Robinson, Heinrich von Stackelberg (1905–46) published his *Marktform und Gleichgewicht* (Market Structures and Equilibrium), which is especially concerned with duopoly and oligopoly, in 1934.[4] This work appeared in the period during which the National Socialist Party was achieving full power in the third Reich. It is interesting to note that von Stackelberg's conclusions with respect to the proper role of the state in oligopolistic markets is compatible with the policies of the Nazi Party, although von Stackelberg supported his conclusions by economic analysis.

Original contributions to the literature of price theory have been scant

---

[2] Piero Sraffa, "The Laws of Return under Competitive Conditions," *Economic Journal,* vol. 36 (December 1926),

[3] This analysis is based on Sraffa's interpretation of Ricardo's theory. Cambridge, Cambridge University Press, 1960.

[4] Translated as *Theory of the Market Economy* by Allen T. Peacock (New York: Oxford University Press, 1952).

since the three leading works of the 1930s. A notable contribution was made at the close of the decade by Robert Triffin (1911–   ), *Monopolistic Competition and General Equilibrium Theory* (1940), which provides an analytical comparison of the works of Chamberlin, Robinson, von Stackelberg, and others and suggests that the theory of monopolistic competition may provide the bridge needed to reconcile the particular equilibrium approach of Marshall with the general equilibrium approach of Walras.

SOME DARK SPOTS IN NEOCLASSICAL VALUE THEORY

Assumptions concerning the Firm's Demand Curve

While Marshall's theory of value is unquestionably superior to its predecessors, it nevertheless has certain shortcomings which made themselves increasingly apparent as time went on. One of these is the implicit assumption that most firms produce and sell their products under conditions of free competition, that is, in markets in which they must accept a price determined by the interaction of forces outside their individual control. The individual firm was conceived to have an infinitely elastic demand for its product at the going market price. Unless a firm was a monopolist, there was therefore no need to single it out for separate examination because its experience was essentially that of every other firm in its industry. Thus, Marshall solved the problem of determining the equilibrium price of a commodity in terms of the industry as a whole by setting an industry supply curve, which was conceived of as a simple summation of the supply curves of a large number of firms producing an essentially homogeneous commodity, against an industry demand curve, constructed by the summation of individual demand curves for a given product.

The shortcoming of this procedure is that it does not take into account the fact that buyers are not indifferent with respect to the seller from whom they buy a particular commodity. The causes for their preferences are, as Sraffa observed in his 1926 article, extremely diverse and "may range from long custom, personal acquaintance, confidence in the quality of the product, proximity, knowledge of particular requirements, and the possibility of obtaining credit to the reputation of a trademark, or sign or a name with high traditions, or to such special features of modeling or design in the product as, without constituting it a distinct commodity intended for the satisfaction of particular needs—have for their principal purpose that of distinguishing it from the products of other firms." Joan Robinson, in *The Economics of Imperfect Competition,* made essentially the same observations about the causes of buyer preferences and viewed their existence as the source of "imperfect" competition.[5] Edward Chamberlin likewise cites

---

[5] Joan Robinson, *The Economics of Imperfect Competition* (London: Macmillan & Co., 1933), pp. 89–90 (subsequently cited as *Imperfect Competition*).

essentially the same factors as creating what he terms "product differentiation," which significantly distinguishes the goods of one seller from those of his rivals and creates a market in which there is "monopolistic competition."[6]

Regardless of the particular method a seller uses to attract and hold customers, the effect of such techniques is always to make the demand (or sales) curve for his product less than perfectly elastic. This effect was succinctly expressed by Sraffa in his observation that "the peculiarity of the case of the firm which does not possess an actual monopoly but merely has a particular market is that, in the demand schedule for the goods produced by it, the possible buyers are entered in descending order according to the price which each of them is prepared to pay, not rather than go entirely without, but rather than not buy it from that particular producer instead of elsewhere."[7] That product differentiation will cause the demand (or sales) curves of an individual seller to diverge from the horizontal position it would have if no seller had any individual control over price was similarly pointed out by Chamberlin and Robinson.[8]

Product differentiation also has the effect of making a firm's demand curve and its cost curves interdependent, for the firm's demand curve then depends partly on the expenditure it makes to attract customers. Chamberlin, in particular, has distinguished between selling costs and production costs, and has pointed out that the existence of selling expenditures is *prima facie* evidence that the market is not one in which there is pure competition.[9] If a seller conducts a successful selling effort, "this means a shift of the demand curve for his product upward and to the right."[10] The position and slope of an individual seller's demand curve depend not only on his product but also on the extent to which he can, by his selling expense, build up preferences for his particular output as opposed to that of his rivals. It follows that when there is product differentiation, the sales and cost curves, and therefore the profits of rival firms, are interdependent in various degrees. Thus, there arises what Chamberlin has chosen to call the "group problem." His *Theory of Monopolistic Competition* lavishes great attention on defining the nature of group equilibrium and examining the mode of its establishment. Robinson's *Economics of Imperfect Competition,* though it parallels in many ways Chamberlin's work, is not concerned directly with the group problem at all, although it describes the

---

[6] Edward Chamberlin, *The Theory of Monopolistic Competition* (Cambridge, Mass.: Harvard University Press, 1933, revised 1948), p. 8 (subsequently cited as *Monopolistic Competition*).

[7] Sraffa, "The Laws of Return," p. 546.

[8] E. Chamberlin, *Monopolistic Competition,* p. 71; J. Robinson, *Imperfect Competition,* p. 21.

[9] E. Chamberlin, *Monopolistic Competition,* chap. 6.

[10] Ibid., chap. 7, p. 130.

phenomenon of product differentiation in almost the same language as Chamberlin.

Assumptions regarding the Laws of Return

An equally troublesome feature of the Marshallian analysis, along with his assumptions regarding the demand curve confronting the typical firm, is his treatment of the long-run laws of return and their effect on the industry supply curve. Marshall, it will be recalled, conceived of the possibility of long-run constant, decreasing, and increasing returns. He recognized that if it were possible for an individual firm, as distinct from an industry as a whole, to experience economies which would give it increasing returns to scale in the long run, free competition would be destroyed. He did not, however, believe that the economies from which increasing returns might derive are exclusively available to any one firm. He thought them to be the result of external economies equally available to all and therefore compatible with the continuation of competition. This conclusion was, in Sraffa's view, such a vulnerable part of Marshall's analysis of the long-run supply curve that he was led to make the following observation in his 1926 article:

> In the tranquil view which the modern theory of value presents us there is one dark spot which disturbs the harmony of the whole. This is represented by the supply curve, based upon the laws of increasing and diminishing returns. That its foundations are less solid than those of the other portions of the structure is generally recognized. That they are so weak as to be unable to support the weight imposed on them is a doubt which slumbers beneath the consciousness of many, but which most succeed in silently suppressing.[11]

The crucial question with respect to the long-run supply curve of a particular industry was, as Sraffa viewed the matter, the compatibility of Marshall's explanation of the tendency toward long-run increasing returns and decreasing supply price with his insistence on a particular equilibrium analysis. Particular equilibrium methodology requires that variations in output or demand in one industry have neither a direct nor an indirect effect on any other industry. Such long-run independence is unlikely, Sraffa contended, in industries subject to either diminishing or increasing returns because, in these cases, changes in the output of the commodity in question have an effect on the cost of using factors that also enter into the production of other commodities. The requirements of a particular equilibrium methodology are thus violated. He objected for the same reason to Marshall's reliance on external economies which result from the general progress of the industrial environment as a means of explaining why some

---

[11] Sraffa, "The Laws of Return," p. 536.

industries are able to enjoy long-run increasing returns. Such economies are compatible with the continuation of competitive conditions because they are equally available to all the firms in an industry. This is precisely the source of their appeal to Marshall; but, maintained Sraffa, a particular equilibrium analysis requires that the economies from which long-run decreasing costs derive be *internal* to the industry, even though they are external to the individual firms. "The only economies which could be taken into consideration would be such as occupy an intermediate position between these two extremes; but it is just in the middle that nothing, or almost nothing, is to be found. Those economies which are external from the point of view of the individual firm but internal as regards the industry in its aggregate, constitute precisely the class which is most seldom met with."[12] Sraffa therefore advised that we "abandon the path of free competition and turn in the opposite direction, namely, towards monopoly."

While few undertakings fit the case of pure monopoly, Sraffa believed that the theory of monopoly could provide a guide to the relationship between price and the quantity which can be sold when competition is absent for other reasons. The theory of monopoly is, therefore, useful to us in studying those cases in the real world (and they are in majority), which do not fit either the case of pure competition or pure monopoly but are "scattered along the intermediate zone." He also suggested that the task of reconstructing the theory of value could be immediately begun, for an analytical tool equal to the task was already at hand in Marshall's concept of monopoly net revenue.

The Monopoly Net Revenue Curve

Joan Robinson was among those who responded to Sraffa's urging that the time had come to reconstruct the theory of value. She regarded Marshall's tool of monopoly net revenue, however, as being unsatisfactory because "it introduces an artificial cleavage between monopoly and competition."[13] The firm under free competition maximizes profits or minimizes losses by equating its marginal cost to price. But since price (average revenue) is equal to marginal revenue in this case, the firm also equates marginal cost and marginal revenue. A monopolist will do precisely the same thing, although this is obscured when expressed in terms of monopoly net revenue. Actually, it matters not in the least whether we say, as did Marshall, that a monopolist maximizes profit by maximizing his net revenue or whether we say, as did Cournot, that a monopolist will maximize profit when he sets a price which will equate the first derivative of total revenue (marginal revenue) with the first derivative of total cost (marginal

---

12 Ibid., p. 540.

13 J. Robinson, *Imperfect Competition,* p. 54.

cost). The latter expression, however, has the advantage of being a principle which is equally applicable to competition and monopoly or any market structure combining elements of both.

Robinson sought to facilitate understanding of the problem of price determination by introducing the concept of marginal revenue and demonstrating the relationship between the average and marginal revenue curves of a monopoly firm as opposed to a purely competitive firm. Their difference derives, she explained, from the fact that under conditions of pure competition the individual firm does not depress market price by offering additional units for sale, with the result that its demand curve is infinitely elastic. Since there is no change in average revenue regardless of the volume of sales, marginal revenue does not change either. It is, therefore, graphically a horizontal line which is identical with that of average revenue. A monopolist, on the other hand, is supplying the total market, and his demand curve has the same characteristics as the industry demand curve for a purely competitive market. It is the summation of the demand curves of individual consumers and is therefore downward sloping. The price a monopolist can get for an additional unit of output is always less than can be gotten for a smaller volume. Average revenue declines as output increases, so that marginal revenue will be less than average revenue. Graphically, therefore, the marginal revenue curve will lie below the average revenue curve.[14]

Robinson's discovery of the marginal revenue curve has greatly facilitated both the verbal and the graphical exposition of the behavior of a firm as it maximizes profit or minimizes losses. It is much simpler to say that a firm equates marginal revenue and marginal cost than that it equates the first derivative of total revenue with the first derivative of total cost. In addition, the intersection of the marginal cost and marginal revenue curves as the determinant of a firm's output facilitates a much clearer graphic representation of the behavior of a firm than one which proceeds by means of average revenue and average cost. Chamberlin's diagrams in *The Theory of Monopolistic Competition* depict the behavior of firms with the help of average curves only. This diagrammatic technique is cumbersome in comparison with Robinson's, which employs marginal curves. Her terminology and her geometry have become standard for the profession.

Robinson herself demonstrated the versatility of her tool in her examination of monopoly price determination, particularly in the case of discriminating monopoly and buyer's monopoly. The equilibrium of the firm as distinct from the equilibrium of the group is her main concern and her main contribution to the extension of the neoclassical theory of value. It is therefore relevant to examine further what contemporary theorists have accomplished with respect to eliminating the "dark spots" in neoclassical

---

[14] Ibid., pp. 52–54.

value theory under two headings: The first is "Equilibrium of the Firm," which focuses on the individual seller of commodities in isolation from any rivals it may have. The second is "Equilibrium of the Group," which examines the impact rival sellers and buyers have on one another's behavior.

EQUILIBRIUM OF THE FIRM

The Conditions of Stable Equilibrium

Chamberlin and Robinson reflect the Marshallian origins of their work on price theory in their concern with establishment of equilibrium. Marshall's analysis was conducted almost wholly in terms of the industry, the notable exception being the case of monopoly, in which the firm is the industry. Contemporary theorists, on the other hand, having discarded the notion that the firms of an industry have infinitely elastic demand curves, are concerned with the individual firm as a separate entity. Robinson, following Sraffa's suggestion, proceeds by allowing the theory of monopoly to "swallow up" the analysis of competition. It is, however, not the behavior of the pure monopolist that Robinson is concerned with, but rather the behavior of a firm which is a monopolist of its own particular product. The equilibrium position of such a firm is necessarily affected by the nature of the reaction which its price-output decisions have on its competitors. Some method must therefore be devised to deal with the problem of interdependence.

In the latter respect there is a striking difference between Robinson's approach and Chamberlin's. Whereas Chamberlin is concerned with analyzing the nature of interdependence and the effect which the price-output decisions of one firm will have on those of its rivals, and therefore on the equilibrium of the group. Robinson makes the implicit assumption that every firm in the group but one is in equilibrium. It is thus possible for her to study in isolation the movement of that firm toward an equilibrium position, guided by the objective of maximizing its monetary profits. For this reason her analysis leaves the impression of being concerned with simple monopoly.

Since the individual firm is conceived to move toward its equilibrium position guided by the objective of maximizing its monetary profits, the first condition which must be satisfied is that its marginal revenue must equal marginal cost. Satisfaction of this condition will not, however, assure a stable equilibrium. Obviously, if the production of a larger output than the one at which $MC = MR$ adds more to total revenue than to total cost, it will pay a firm to expand. Robinson has therefore shown that equality between marginal cost and marginal revenue is only a first-order condition. The stability of monopoly equilibrium depends also on the relationship

FIGURE 15–1

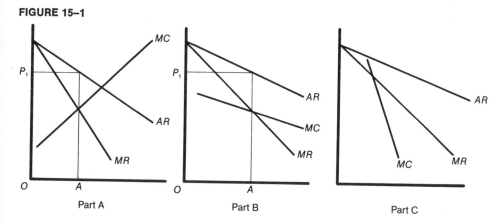

| Part A | Part B | Part C |

between the marginal revenue and marginal cost curves of a firm. A stable monopoly equilibrium requires as its second condition that the production of a larger output than that at which $MC = MR$ adds more to total cost than to total revenue, so that a further expansion of output is unprofitable. This is illustrated in Figure 15–1.

Since the marginal revenue curve of a firm will be downward sloping, unless it is a pure competitor, the second-order condition specified by Robinson for a stable equilibrium of a firm is satisfied if marginal cost is increasing or, at least, decreasing less rapidly than marginal revenue. In either case the MC curve cut the MR curve from below, as in Part A and Part B of Figure 15–1. If MC cuts MR from above, as in Part C of Figure 15–1, so that MC lies below MR for outputs larger than that at which $MC = MR,$ the second-order condition is not satisfied; i.e., the maximum profit is indeterminate, and there is no stable equilibrium price or output.[15]

Equilibrium When Monopoly Price Discrimination Is Possible

Monopoly price discrimination, or the practice of charging different prices to different buyers of a product or service, is the ultimate as a technique for profit maximization. It is possible only if a seller who is in a position to control his selling price has the additional power of distinguishing among his customers on the basis of differences in their demand elasticities. Customers having different demand elasticities for a particular product or service, as, for example, is the case with respect to most users of public utility service, enable a seller to group his buyers according to their demand elasticities and to charge a different price to each. The essential

---

[15] For a methematical approach to this and other aspects of pricing under nonperfect competition see James M. Henderson, and Richard E. Quandt, *Microeconomic Theory* (New York: McGraw-Hill Book Co., Inc., 1958), chap. 6.

requirement for discrimination is the effective segregation of the various parts of the total market. Pigou has shown that this depends on the nontransferability of various units of output and demand from one market to another.[16]

Pigou was, during the 1920s, greatly interested in the special price problems of railroads and showed that the factor of nontransferability is significant in explaining why a discriminatory price structure prevails in this field. A shipper who buys transportation service generally cannot resell a part of the service to some other shipper to whom the railroad has quoted a higher rate.[17] The same factor explains discriminatory rate patterns in the sale of public utility services generally. For example, gas or electric power is sold to industrial users at a lower rate than to residential users; but they cannot redistribute it, at least not without considerable expense, to residential users. Thus the ability of a utility to maintain a policy of price discrimination derives from the fact that ready transference of service from customer to customer is impossible. If units of a product or service were transferable from one market to another, a monopolist would, for all practical purposes, be forced to adhere to a single-price system.

A monopolist who can effectively segregate his markets and who is not subject to public regulation can maximize his returns by charging high prices to those customers whose demands are least elastic, while at the same time cultivating sales to other buyers, whose demands are more elastic, through the offer of low prices.[18] Robinson demonstrated that profits will be at a maximum when marginal revenue in each submarket is equal to the marginal cost of the whole product. That is, the total output of a discriminating monopolist is determined by the intersection of his marginal cost curve and the aggregate marginal revenue curve.

Profit maximization by a discriminating monopolist is shown in Fig. 15–2, in which MR_1 is the marginal revenue curve in the market having a less elastic demand and MR_2 is the marginal revenue curve in the market having a more elastic demand. They are derived from demand curves D_1 and D_2. The lateral summation of both demand curves results in the aggregate demand curve, AD. The aggregate marginal revenue curve, AMR, is obtained by summing MR_1 and MR_2. The total output is therefore OC,

---

[16] Arthur C. Pigou, *Wealth and Welfare* (London: Macmillan & Co., 1912) chap. 27. This work rejects the explanation of multiple railway rates offered by Frank W. Taussig. As early as 1891 Taussig argued that services being supplied by railroads are produced under conditions of joint cost. Following Marshall (see above p. 291), he reasoned that the services are not one homogeneous commodity but several commodities which are characterized by different elasticities of demand and consequently differing abilities to bear the joint cost of producing them. He thus concluded that multiple railway rates are compatible with pure competition and do not provide a basis for government ownership of railways.

[17] The freight forwarder does perform this function to a limited extent.

[18] J. Robinson, *Imperfect Competition*, chap. 15.

FIGURE 15–2

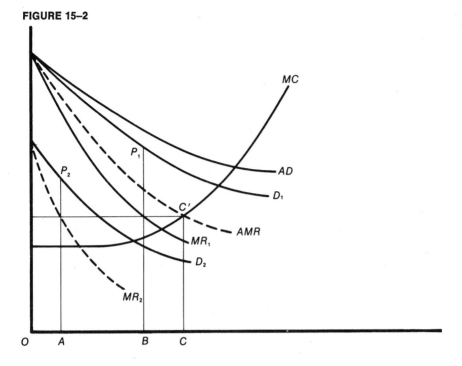

which is determined by the intersection of the aggregate marginal revenue curve with the marginal cost curve. It is comprised of output *OA,* sold at price P_2 to those whose demands are relatively more elastic, and *OB,* sold at P_1 to those whose demands are relatively less elastic. This is the output which maximizes profit for the discriminating monopolist, since marginal revenue in each market is equal to the marginal cost of the whole output. Monoply net revenue for output *OC* is the area under the aggregate marginal revenue curve (total revenue) minus the area under the marginal cost curve (total costs).[19]

The chief argument against monopoly is that it affects welfare adversely because it restricts output. Robinson, however, demonstrates that if production takes place under conditions of decreasing average cost, it contributes to the welfare of consumers instead of being detrimental to their interests because it may result in the offer of a larger output. If a monopolist is able to segregate his consumers into distinct market groups which he charges different prices, his output may be either equal to, greater than, or smaller than it would be if a single monopoly price were charged.

Output will be larger in consequence of price discrimination if the more

---

[19] Ibid., pp. 182–83, fig. 61.

elastic demand curve is concave while the less elastic curve is convex or linear. In this case the expansion in output sold in the first market at a price lower than the single monopoly price will be greater than the reduction in output sold in the second market at a price higher than the single monopoly price. This is so because discrimination results in an aggregate marginal revenue curve which is above the simple monopoly marginal revenue curve.[20] But if demand curves in both markets are linear, the aggregate marginal revenue curve will equal the simple monopoly marginal revenue curve, and output will be no larger than it would be under a single monopoly price. The only difference will be in the way in which output is allocated between the two markets and the price which is charged in each.

THE EQUILIBRIUM OF THE GROUP

Chamberlin's Concept of Small and Large Groups

The duopoly models of Augustin Cournot and Joseph Bertrand, which were discussed in Chapter 10 are a convenient beginning to an inquiry into what has become known as the group problem. It will be recalled that Cournot's and Bertrand's models were based on the highly artificial assumption of a conjectural variation of zero with respect to the behavior of competing duopolists. That is, each hypothesized a case in which the solution derives from the assumption that a duopolist behaves as though his rivals' behavior is independent of his own. Cournot hypothesized two sellers of a costless homogeneous commodity, each of whom tries to maximize his net revenue on the assumption that his competitor will not alter *the quantity* he offers for sale. Bertrand, ostensibly criticizing Cournot's solution to the duopoly problem, created a different model in which the competitors behaved on the assumption that, regardless of the rival's action; the other would keep his *price* unchanged.

The oligopoly case is an extension of the duopoly problem in which there are more than two sellers but the number is sufficiently small so that each seller realizes that his own behavior will influence not only the price at which he can sell but also his rivals' price policies. The solution to the small group or oligopoly problem depends on the assumptions the particular model makes with respect to the behavior of the various participants. The first among the several models we shall examine is that of Edward Chamberlin.

Chamberlin simplified the problem of analyzing the behavior of the group by assuming that all the firms have identical cost and demand functions. The group can then be described in terms of a single firm which is representative of all firms. The essential difference between the small group and the large group is to be found in the reaction pattern which any

---

[20] Ibid., pp. 190–93.

individual firm will stimulate among its competitors when it alters either its price, its product, or its selling expenses.[21] Chamberlin pictures this reaction pattern in terms of the elasticity and movement of the sales or demand curve confronting the individual firm. The demand curve confronting the representative firm depends on whether its sales are a function solely of its own price, or also of the prices charged by its competitors. The curve *dd* in Figure 15–3 shows how much the representative firm thinks it can sell at all possible prices, provided other firms keep their prices fixed instead of responding to price changes it might initiate. This kind of curve is associated only with a large group because in a case like this the impact of a price change by one firm on its competitors is likely to be negligible. The large group is, in this sense, akin to pure competition. But it is also akin to monopoly, in that each seller has a negatively sloped demand curve for his particular product. There are many sellers in the market, but their products are heterogeneous rather than homogeneous because of advertising and other techniques of product differentiation. The absence of homogeneous commodities enables each seller to determine his own profit-maximizing price, which may be quite different from that of other sellers with whom he is competing.[22] Chamberlin therefore introduced the term *monopolistic*

FIGURE 15–3

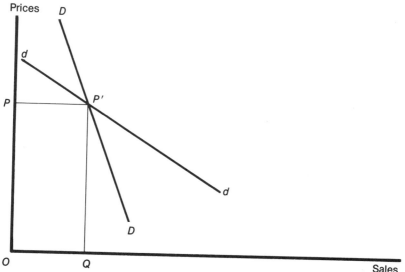

[21] E. Chamberlin, *Monopolistic Competition,* pp. 81–104.

[22] In "The Origin and Early Development of Monopolistic Competition," *Quarterly Journal of Economics,* vol. 75 (November 1961), pp. 515–43, Chamberlin relates that his investigation was influenced by Taussig's argument with Pigou about the effect of product heterogeneity on pricing. Taussig maintained multiple rates for railway service can be explained in terms of Marshall's joint supply thesis. Because the services bought by different groups of railroad customers are not homogenous commodities, they will not sell at uniform prices even under competition.

competition to describe it. He reasoned that if there is monopolistic competition, a price cut will significantly increase the sales of the firm that introduces it because the cut draws away customers from rivals. But the effect of the price cut is spread over so many competitors that the volume of sales it draws away from any one firm is too small to cause any one to alter its policy.

The *DD* curve in Figure 15–3, on the other hand, shows how much the representative firm thinks it can sell at all possible prices if its competitors always charge the same price it charges. This curve is drawn on the assumption that if a particular firm alters its price, say from *OP,* an identical change is made by every other firm in the group. The result is a sales curve which is less elastic than the *dd* curve the firm would face if it were able to alter its price and not call forth a similar price change by its competitors. If the market were comprised of only one firm, *DD,* and *dd* would be the same curve. But if there is more than one firm, the *DD* curve represents the actual market share the representative firm will enjoy at every possible price it might charge if competing firms charge exactly the same price it charges.[23] This will be the case only if the group is small.

Figure 15–3 also sheds some light on the tendency for oligopoly prices to remain rigid once they have been determined. Paul M. Sweezy suggested that in an oligopoly situation a seller is not confronted with the entire length of *DD* but with a "kinked" demand curve like *dP'D.*[24] If an oligopolist can raise his price above *OP* without his rivals following suit, but finds that the sales curve confronting him at prices above this level is a highly elastic curve like *dP',* a price increase cannot gain him a larger share of the market. If, on the other hand, he reduces his price below *OP,* only to find that his rivals do the same, a price cut will not increase his share of the market. Thus the demand curve confronting him at prices below *OP* is the relatively inelastic curve *P'D* in Figure 15–3. Sweezy therefore reasoned that because there is no incentive in a case like this either to raise or to lower price from *OP,* once an oligopolistic seller has fixed his price at this level, he will tend to keep it rigid, and so will his rivals.

Chamberlin's Equilibrium Analysis

Given its sales and cost curves, the representative firm of the group will maximize profits. While Chamberlin's diagrams demonstrate its behavior with the aid of average revenue and average cost curves, the same thing

---

23 Ibid., pp. 83–85.

24 Paul M. Sweezy, "Demand under Conditions of Oligopoly," *Journal of Political Economy,* vol. 47 (August 1939); also reprinted in Kenneth F. Boulding and George Stigler, *Readings in Price Theory,* vol. 6 (Homewood, Ill.: Richard D. Irwin, Inc., 1952). See also the empirical study by George Stigler on the basis of which the latter denies the existence of the kinked oligopoly demand curve ("The Kinky Oligopoly Demand Curve and Rigid Prices," *Journal of Political Economy,* vol. 55 [October 1947]).

can be more conveniently illustrated with diagrams which also show the now standard marginal cost and marginal revenue curves. Thus in Figure 15–4, if $DD = AR$ is the sales curve of the representative firm in a small group, and SMC and SAC are its short-run cost curves, output OQ will be offered for sale at a price of OP per unit assuming that rivals sell at an identical price.

At a price of OP, there will be a pure profit equivalent to the area $CC'P'P$. Whether pure profit will continue to be enjoyed depends on the entry of new firms into the market in response to higher than normal profits. If entry into the group is free, newcomers will encroach on the sales of existing sellers until pure profit has been eliminated. Thus, a long-run equilibrium with only normal profit is possible when the group is small. The very existence of a small group, however, usually implies that entry is restricted in some way. Chamberlin therefore conceives of small-group equilibrium as being compatible with any level of pure profit, even in the long run.

If, on the other hand, a group is large, new firms tend to be attracted by the presence of pure profits precisely as is the case when competition is pure. Thus, if there are pure profits, the group will move to a position of equilibrium in which pure profit is eliminated. Chamberlin pictured this move via the demand curve of the representative firm. Equilibrium is achieved when a sufficient number of new firms have entered to shift $DD = AR$ to a level at which it is tangent to the average cost curve, as in Figure 15–5, so that price equals long-run average cost. Total cost will then equal revenue, so that only a normal profit is made and net revenue is zero.

For the firm and the group both to be in equilibrium in the long run, it is

FIGURE 15–4

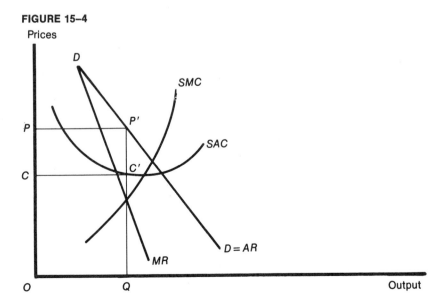

FIGURE 15–5

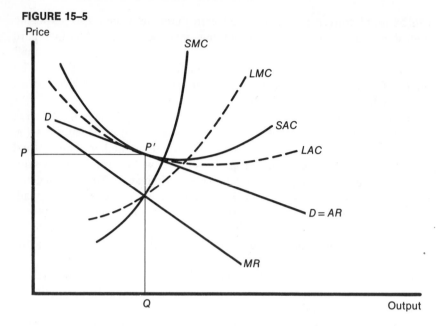

necessary that it be unprofitable to alter output from existing capacity; i.e., neither exit from nor entry into the group can occur. This condition requires that price equal short-run and long-run average cost, and that short-run and long-run marginal costs are increasing and equal to marginal revenue. This is shown in Figure 15–5, in which the curve $DD = AR$ is tangent to both the long-run and the short-run average cost curves. Short-run and long-run marginal costs are equal to marginal revenue at output OQ, and the price is equal to both long-run and short-run average cost at OP'. Thus, total revenue and total cost are both equal to $OQP'P$, and net revenue is zero. Chamberlin conceives of this result as being possible only if the group is large. If the group is small, which implies that entry is restricted, any level of positive profits can persist even in the long run.

In addition to the insight it provides into the difference between the behavior of oligopolistic firms and those which are monopolistically competitive, the preceding analysis also shows that the equilibrium output of firms producing under monopolistic competition cannot be optimal. This is because the demand curve will always be tangent to the average cost curve somewhere to the left of its lowest point, as in Figure 15–5. Price equals average cost but not marginal cost, as is the case under pure competition. Thus, in comparison with pure competition, the firm under monopolistic competition necessarily produces a smaller output at a higher average cost.[25] Does this mean that there is a waste of resources in monopolistically

---

[25] E. Chamberlin, *Monopolistic Competition*, pp. 113–16.

competitive markets? No definite answer can be given to this question. Product differentiation provides consumers with a variety of similar commodities among which to choose and the information advertising provides facilitates choice among them. Scarce resources that could be used in other alternatives are necessarily employed for these purposes, but the question as to whether consumers are, on balance, better off is a value judgment.

Robinson's "Full Equilibrium"

Robinson, unlike Chamberlin, draws no distinction between the large group and the small group. Yet, her concept of "full equilibrium," as expressed in the following quotation, coincides with Chamberlin's tangency solution for large-group equilibrium: "Full equilibrium . . . requires the double condition that marginal revenue is equal to marginal cost and that average revenue is equal to average cost. The double condition of full equilibrium can only be fulfilled when the individual demand curve of the firm is tangent to its average cost curve."[26] While she does not specifically limit the applicability of the tangency solution by distinguishing between the large group and the small one, she indirectly recognizes the effect which the absence of free entry has on profits. She observes that "in trades into which there is no possibility of entry, . . . there is no upper limit to profit, though there must be a lower limit at the level of profits which is just sufficient to maintain the existing number of firms in business."[27]

Robinson's definition of costs provides another possible way of reconciling her generalized tangency solution with pure profits. Her treatment of costs includes not only normal profits but also entrepreneurial and factor rents.[28] Chamberlin also includes factor rents and the wages of management as costs, but he has a less inclusive definition of normal profit than she does. Thus, the differences between Robinson's exposition and Chamberlin's of the requirements for equilibrium in the firm and industry appear to be mainly terminological in spite of the differences between them in the presentation of the oligopoly case.

The von Stackelberg Approach

Unlike Chamberlin and Robinson, Heinrich von Stackelberg was particularly concerned with the problem of few sellers. His *Marktform und Gleichgewicht* begins with the relatively simple case of duopoly and then proceeds to oligopoly, and finally to the additional complication of product differentiation.

In the case of two sellers, von Stackelberg conceived of each as being

---

[26] J. Robinson, *Imperfect Competition*, p. 94.

[27] Ibid.

[28] Ibid., p. 125.

confronted with the alternative of leadership or following the lead of his rival. The profit of each is a function of the output levels of both; but, unlike Cournot and Bertrand, who assumed conjectural variations of zero with respect to quantity and price, von Stackelberg assumes that both sellers are aware of their mutual interdependence. A follower will adjust his output to maximize his profit, given the decision of his rival, whom he assumes to be a leader with respect to output. The leader, on the other hand, maximizes his profit on the assumption that his rival acts the part of the follower.

An equilibrium solution is possible in the case of duopoly under von Stackelberg's assumption if one seller desires to assume a position of leadership while the other desires to be a follower, and both act accordingly. But if both wish to be followers and behave as though the rival is the leader, neither can realize his expectations. Similarly, if both decide that maximum profit is to be made by assuming the role of the leader, there will be disequilibrium. One of the two must change his behavior pattern and act as a follower before equilibrium can be reached.

Stackelberg believed that the usual market result in duopoly is one of disequilibrium rather than equilibrium. This belief implies that there is inherent conflict which can be resolved only by collusion or a fight to the finish in which one of the sellers is forced to yield to the leadership of the other. Disequilibrium and destructive competition are even more likely in the case of oligopoly. The interdependence among firms in this situation is such that the interplay of their actions cannot result in any economic equilibrium. This disequilibrium is the basis for von Stackelberg's view that direct action by the state or organizations like cartels is necessary to achieve equilibrium. However, his argument for the need for intervention by an authoritarian state is also compatible with the philosophy and techniques of the German National Socialist Party of the 1930s.

IMPERFECT COMPETITION AND FACTOR REWARDS

Factor Rewards under Competition

In general, a factor of production is said to be exploited if the payment it receives is less than its marginal physical product valued at its selling price.[29] In light of this definition, Robinson has investigated the relationship between factor rewards and their marginal productivities under conditions of buyer monopoly, or monopsony, in the factor market.[30] The

---

[29] Arthur C. Pigou, *Economics of Welfare,* 4th ed. (London: Macmillan & Co., 1952), p. 549.

[30] *Imperfect Competition,* chapter 18.

FIGURE 15–6

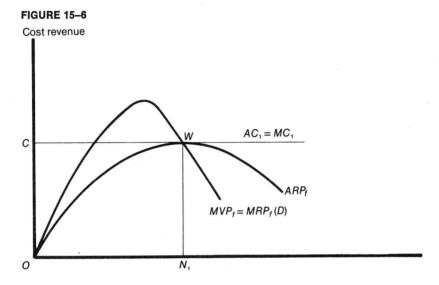

Cost revenue

$AC_1 = MC_1$

W

ARP_f

$MVP_f = MRP_f (D)$

C

O

N_1

impact of monopsony is most easily understood by examining the relationships which result in a competitive factor market first.

These relationships are illustrated in Figure 15–6 which assumes pure
competition in the selling market for a particular product and monopsony
in the market in which a factor, f, required for its production is purchased.
Curves ARP_f and $MVP_f = MRP_f$ show the average and marginal increments of value added by additional inputs of the variable factor when it is
used with other fixed inputs. $MVP_f = MRP_f$ (Marginal value product
equals marginal revenue product) because pure competition in the product
market is associated with $P = AR = MR$. The downward sloping portion of
the marginal productivity curve $MVP_f = MRP_f$ is the firm's demand curve
for the variable factor. Together with the factor supply curve, it determines
the quantity of the variable factor the firm will hire.

In a purely competitive factor market the supply curve of a factor is
represented as the perfectly elastic curve $AC_1 = MC_1$. In a long-run
equilibrium situation, $AC_1 = MC_1$ will be tangent to the average revenue
product curve at its maximum level. This tangency is represented by the
point "W" on the average revenue product curve in Figure 15–6. The
firm will maximize its gains from employing the variable factor when it
equates the marginal cost of its hire with the marginal revenue product
which can be gotten from the sale of its product. It will therefore hire
quantity ON_1, for which it will pay $OC = N_1W$ per unit. This payment is
equivalent to both the average revenue product and the marginal revenue
product of the factor. Thus, the factor receives the full value of its output.

Monopsony and Factor Exploitation

Robinson's analysis of the effect of monopsony begins with the observation that the factor supply-curves confronting a monopsonistic buyer cannot be infinitely elastic any more than the product demand curve confronting a seller who is not a pure competitor can be infinitely elastic. A firm who is a monopsonist in the purchase of a factor is confronted with upward sloping average and marginal cost curves.[31] The upward slope of these curves is significant because it alters both the quantity of that factor which will be hired in an equilibrium situation and the relationship between the marginal return to that factor and its marginal value product. When the marginal cost of hiring a factor lies above its average cost, as in the case when there is not pure competition in the factor market, the firm will employ a smaller quantity of the factor than it would under pure competition, and the price which it pays for its hire will be less than the value of its marginal product.[32]

These relationships are illustrated in Figure 15–7. In this diagram which represents the factor demand and supply curves of the monopsonistic buyer, the firm is confronted with upward sloping average and marginal cost curves like AC_2 and MC_2. Their shape reflects the inability of a monopsonist to purchase additional units of the same factor at an unchanged price as is the case in a purely competitive factor market. For purposes of comparison the perfectly elastic factor supply curve that characterizes a purely competitive factor market is reproduced from Figure 15–6.

Both a purely competitive buyer of a factor of production and a monopsonist will seek the most profitable level of a factor employment. This is the level at which its marginal cost of employment is equal to the factor's marginal revenue product. A monopsonistic employer following this principle would, as is illustrated in Figure 15–7, employ only quantity ON of the factor, as opposed to the larger quantity ON_1 which would be bought by a competitive buyer. It would pay the factor a reward equal to NR, its average product. The average revenue product of the factor, however, is less than NW, its marginal revenue product. Thus, there will be nonopsonistic exploitation in the amount of WR, which is the amount by which the value of the marginal revenue product of ON units of the factor exceeds NR, its price of employment.

Robinson suggests that these observations bear in an important way on the problem of factor exploitation. If the factor in question is labor, Robinson has shown that exploitation can be reduced or eliminated and employment increased by introducing a minimum wage at which the supply of

[31] Ibid., p. 220.
[32] Ibid., p. 250.

FIGURE 15–7

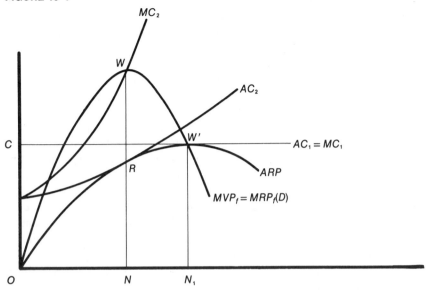

labor will be perfectly elastic.[33] In a situation such as that depicted in Figure 15–1 an enforced minimum wage rate of OC will eliminate exploitation and result in the employment of ON_1 labor units, which is the same as that which would obtain under pure competition.

CONCLUDING REMARKS

Modern price theory is, analytically speaking, largely a refinement of the work of Cournot and Marshall. These sources of inspiration are plainly evident in the static particular equilibrium framework within which optimal behavior is investigated in terms of the relationship between marginal cost and marginal revenue. This implies that whenever possible, a firm will continue to engage in a particular activity until the net gain at the margin is zero. If there are several activities, then ideally they should all be pursued until they yield the same marginal return.

The fundamental role of marginal analysis in modern price theory has raised the question as to whether businessmen actually employ marginal principles in their decision-making. Fritz Machlup has, for example, taken the position that businessmen employ marginal concepts without being aware of it.[34] Taken by itself, marginal analysis is, of course, only a tool

---

[33] Ibid., chap. 26, pp. 295–96.

[34] Fritz Machlup, "Marginal Analysis and Empirical Research," *American Economic Review,* vol. 36, no. 4 (September 1946).

for achieving optimal results. But what constitutes the best objective to seek is something else again. The basic premise of price theory continues to be that businessmen are concerned first and foremost with the maximization of profit.[35] Empirical studies of the pricing behavior of firms and the objectives they pursue, however, are still inclusive.

The price-output relationships which modern price theorists conceive to result as firms seek to maximize their profits depend very much on the structure of the market. Interest has centered primarily on those market situations which lie intermediate between pure competition and pure monopoly, i.e., monopolistic competition and oligopoly. Most modern theorists, following Chamberlin, conceive of a monopolistically competitive market as one in which each firm is in competition with so many rival producers of close substitutes that its long-run equilibrium position, like that of the pure competitor, is one in which there are no pure profits even though each is a monopolist of its own product. The oligopoly situation has, however, defied such neat packaging and it is in this area that modern price theory encounters its main difficulties.

The main feature of oligopoly is the interdependence of firms with respect to their decision-making. Every businessman in a market which is dominated by a few large firms knows that, in varying degrees, he will influence his rivals by his decision and, in turn, be influenced by them. Theorists from Cournot and Bertrand to Chamberlin, Robinson, and Stackelberg have constructed models based on different premises with respect to the behavior of rivals. Given their respective premises, each has provided a "solution" compatible with profit maximization. Each of these solutions is, however, only one of a wide variety of possible solutions each of which is perfectly tenable under the assumptions made.

Numerous writers have, in recent years, challenged the traditional assumption of profit maximization on various grounds. Herbert Simon has suggested that firms "satisfice" rather than maximize profit.[36] That is, the objective of a plant manager's activity is to achieve a satisfactory rate of profit, rather than a maximum figure. The interests of managers may well be different from those of stockholders, who frequently have limited knowledge about the firm's operations. Thus, managerial decisions in regard to salaries, size of staff, and other amenities do not necessarily coincide with the profit-maximizing objectives of stockholders.[37] The "satis-

---

[35] A. D. H. Caplan et al., *Pricing in Big Business: A Case Study Approach* (Washington, D.C.: Brookings Institution, 1958).

[36] Herbert Simon, *Models of Man* (New York: John Wiley and Sons, 1957).

[37] Robin Marris, *The Economic Theory of "Managerial" Capitalism* (New York: Free Press, 1965). E. Mansfield and H. Wein have observed that the behavior of middle management may similarly be at variance with the objectives of top management. See "A Study of Decision-Making within the Firm," *Quarterly Journal of Economics,* vol. 72 (November 1958).

ficing" aspirations of a firm may well change from year to year, depending on the economic and political climate. The outside pressures to which it is subjected, for example, declining demand or new competition, may also change. Thus, a firm may find it necessary to eliminate slack which it may be able to afford under other circumstances when it is less necessary to achieve economic efficiency. This is a market reality of which conventional theory, with its assumption that firms typically minimize costs, does not take cognizance.

Joan Robinson herself, 20 years after *The Theory of Imperfect Competition,* remarked that the "assumptions which were adequate are by no means [now] a suitable basis for an analysis of the problems of prices, production and distribution which present themselves in reality."[38] In particular, she notes that "the treatment of the entrepreneur and his profits in the *Economics of Imperfect Competition* is extremely primitive."[39] In order for the entrepreneur to survive and grow, "he must pursue profit, but he must avoid actions which, though profitable in the present, will change his future position. . . ." She remarks further that the profit available in a particular market is likely to be strongly influenced by the difficulty of entry. It is also noted that it is hard to generalize about profit rates and the "normal level of profits" and that the notion of "equilibrium size" with respect to a firm has little application to reality.

The theory of nonperfect competition has had another "spillover" of which notice should be taken. The wide variety of behavior patterns which are theoretically possible in oligopolistic markets has stimulated a new approach to the empirical investigation of industries and markets which has come to be called industrial organization. This approach has been working toward a synthesis of price theory and institutional market studies concerned with the concentration of economic power which predominated during the 1930s. Earlier studies lacked the theoretical orientation of contemporary studies,[40] which focus not only on market structures and interindustry differences in market structures, but attempt to associate these structural differences with significant differences in performance. Thus they are attempting to verify hypotheses which such theorists as Chamberlin, Robinson, and others have offered with respect to such matters as freedom

---

[38] Joan Robinson, "Imperfect Competition Revisited," *Economic Journal,* vol. 63 (September 1953), pp. 579–93.

[39] Robinson's footnote comment (p. 579) that she has never been able to grasp the distinction between monopolistic competition and imperfect competition is relevant. It appears to her that she and Chamberlin used the same assumptions where they dealt with the same questions and reached the same results.

[40] See Footnote 1 in this chapter for an identification of earlier studies. A seminal contemporary work in this area is J. S. Bain, *Industrial Organization* (New York: Wiley, 1959). A more recent treatment of the problem of market power is William G. Shephard, *Market Power and Economic Welfare* (New York: Random House, 1970).

of entry; selling costs and product quality; and selling costs and consumer choices, to mention only a few.

Thus far students of industrial organization have not derived much direction for their work from game theory. Nevertheless, game theory is not without promise as a method of studying the optimizing behavior of business firms. The principles of game theory demonstrate that rationality in an oligopoly situation does not necessarily require the maximization of net profits. Oligopoly is also compatible with achieving the maximum payoff, and the payoff may consist of a certain percentage of sales revenues, or a particular share of the market, or a particular return on invested capital and so forth. Thus, game theory may eventually help to resolve some of the seeming inconsistencies between the profit-maximizing assumptions of price theory and empirical observations about business behavior.

GLOSSARY OF TERMS AND CONCEPTS

Game theory.   This is concerned with alternative strategies and their related payoffs which are open to competitors. If a participant is pessimistic about his rival's probable counterstrategy, he is likely to choose a defensive strategy which will result in the maximum minimum gain (maximin). In a zero-sum (two person) game, if his opponent is similarly pessimistic, a defensive strategy will actually result in a large payoff for his competitor.

Kinked demand curve.   A demand curve associated with oligopolistic markets which is relatively elastic in the upper ranges and relatively inelastic in the lower ranges. It therefore displays a "kink" at which the selling price will tend to be rigid. This follows because it is not profitable to reduce price within that segment of the demand curve which is inelastic, and it is not possible to sell at higher prices within the segments in which demand is elastic.

Marginal revenue curve.   A curve showing the revenue which will be added from the sale of an additional unit of output. Under imperfect competition it will always be downward sloping (and will be below the average revenue curve) because additional output can only be sold at a reduced price. Mathematically it is the first derivative of the total revenue curve.

Monopolistic competition.   A market situation characterized by product differentiation.

Monopoly price discrimination.   A technique for maximizing profits which can be utilized by a monopolist who sells to different groups of buyers who can be identified on the basis of their demand elasticities. Buyers whose demands are relatively elastic will be offered a lower price than those whose demands are less elastic, provided it is impossible for the first group to resell to the second. The monopolist will divide output among his various markets in such manner as to equate marginal revenue in each market to the marginal cost of producing the output.

Monopsony. Buyer's monopoly.

Oligopoly. A market situation characterized by relatively few sellers each of whom produces a large enough share of the total output to be in a position to influence market price. Chamberlin called this the "small group" case as opposed to the large group in which individual firms can influence price. An oligopoly situation may also be characterized by product differentiation.

Product differentiation. Various techniques, among them packaging, trademarks, brand names, advertising for the purpose of creating buyer preference for a particular seller's product. If successful, it gives the seller some degree of freedom with respect to pricing.

NOTES FOR FURTHER READING

The logical starting point is Piero Sraffa's "The Laws of Return under Competitive Conditions," *Economic Journal,* vol. 36 (December 1926); reprinted in George Stigler and Kenneth E. Boulding, eds., *Readings in Price Theory,* vol. 6 (Homewood, Ill.: Richard D. Irwin, Inc., 1952). Chamberlin describes the origin of his approach in "Origin and Early Developments of Monopolistic Competition," *Quarterly Journal of Economics,* vol. 75 (November 1961), pp. 515–43. A. R. Burns' classic *Decline of Competition* (New York: McGraw-Hill Book Co., Inc., 1936) vividly describes the institutional conditions which accompanied Chamberlin's and Robinson's theoretical contributions.

Joe S. Bain and Robert L. Bishop provide reflective insight in "The Theory of Monopolistic Competition after Thirty Years: The Impact of Industrial Organization," *American Economic Review, Papers and Proceedings,* vol. 54, no. 3 (May 1964), and "The Theory of Monopolistic Competition after Thirty Years: The Impact on General Theory," *American Economic Review, Papers and Proceedings,* vol. 54, no. 3 (May 1964). The latter is reprinted in Ingrid H. Rima, ed., *Readings in the History of Economic Theory* (New York: Holt, Rinehart and Winston, 1970).

The welfare implications of monopolistic competition are examined by William J. Baumol, in "Monopolistic Competition and Welfare Economics," *American Economic Review, Papers and Proceedings,* vol. 54, no. 3 (May 1964).

The oligopoly problem is examined by William Fellner in *Competition among the Few* (New York: A. A. Knopf, Inc., 1949). Paul Sweezy's classic article demonstrating the "kinked demand curve" is "Demand under Conditions of Oligopoly," *Journal of Political Economy,* vol. 47 (August 1939); reprinted in K. E. Boulding and G. Stigler, eds., *Readings in Price Theory* (Homewood, Ill.: R. D. Irwin, Inc., 1952). Joan Robinson's "Imperfect Competition Revisited," *Economic Journal*, vol. 63 (September 1953) contains some pertinent observations about oligopoly, a problem which she omitted treating in *The Theory of Imperfect Competition*, not because she regarded it as unimportant, but because "I could not solve it" (p. 584). She notes, in particular, that the reaction of any entrepreneur must depend very much on how he expects others to behave. Rank and file firms "wait and see" until a recognized leader reacts to a new situation. On occasion "We find the apparently paradoxical phenomenon of the imperfection of competition keeping prices below the competitive level" (p. 589). This article is readily comprehensible to readers whose sophistication is not equal to reading her *Economics of Imperfect Competition* (London: Macmillan and Co., 1933) or Edward Chamberlin's *Theory of Monopolistic Competition* (Cambridge: Harvard University Press, 1933).

Chapter 8 added in the 1948 edition of Chamberlin's *Theory of Monopolistic Competition* extends the theory of monopolistic competition to examine its effect on factor employment and the relationship between factor rewards and the value of the marginal product they produce. Chamberlin concludes that, because of the downward slope of its demand curve, it may be impossible for a firm whose selling market is monopolistically competitive to pay any of its factors the value of their marginal products. This does not, however, imply to him that factors are being exploited in the usual sense of the term, for the tangency solution means that there are no pure profits. Chamberlin has, therefore, argued that to define exploitation as a payment which is less than a factor's marginal product is appropriate only under conditions of pure competition. If competition is not pure, the relationship between the total product and the marginal product is such that it is impossible to pay all factors the full value of their marginal products without exceeding the amount available for distribution.

16

Neo-Wicksellian Cycle Theorists

INTRODUCTION

WHILE THERE WAS MUCH CONFIDENCE during the 1920s that the study of business cycles was obsolete because a great deal had been learned about policy measures for controlling them, this optimism, which was not shared by all, was shattered by the Great Depression of the 1930s. As the industrial economies of the world experienced large scale unemployment, systematic analysis of business cycles began anew after some decades of relative neglect.

The chief feature of the new investigations was their concern with the central role of money and credit in bringing about or conditioning the business cycle. A number of Swedish followers of Knut Wicksell, as well as several English and Austrian writers, led the way in rejecting the quantity theory. Wicksell contended that monetary and real phenomena are interrelated and he offered the hypothesis that cumulative expansions and contractions in business are generated by a divergence between market and real rates of interest.

Wicksell's thesis was the starting point for all who identified monetary forces as playing a central role in generating, or at least facilitating, cyclical disturbances. Ralph G. Hawtrey of England was among the first to put money at the center of his scheme of causation with *Good Trade and Bad Trade* (1913), which anticipated his own later work. There was a general concern of the profession with the operation of monetary forces. Frederick von Hayek, Ludwig von Mises, and Fritz Machlup were among the Austrians who identified monetary forces, as they operated within the framework of modern banking systems, as essential to the disequilibrium between "lower and higher stages of production" that they identified as the chief feature of cyclical disturbance. Another group, among them Gustav Cassel, Arthur Spietoff, and Joseph Schumpeter, stress factors that operate in the sphere of production, such as inventions and discoveries which provide new investment opportunities, besides identifying monetary forces as indispensable accompanying factors in cyclical disturbance.

Wicksell's conception of a possible divergence between the market and natural rates of interest may also be thought of in terms of saving and investment magnitudes as they come into being as *ex ante* plans or expectations and as they are realized *ex post*. Some of Wicksell's Swedish followers, who are sometimes identified as members of the Stockholm School, emphasized the effect of divergences between saving (S) and investment (I) *ex ante* and *ex post* in bringing about cumulative expansions or contractions. Bertil Ohlin, Erick Lundberg, and Erick Lindahl are chief among those who adopted the *ex ante-ex post* construct. Their analyses are based on definitions of saving and investment which are compatible with the possibility that $S>I$ or $S<I$ at the planning stage. Divergences between saving and investment are conceived to generate a process through which, ultimately, $S=I$. This construct also had appeal for several English writers, among them Dennis Robertson and J. M. Keynes, who used it in his *Treatise on Money*. The work of all of these writers is neo-Wicksellian. Their common thread is emphasis on money as the active factor in producing changes in real magnitudes, and concern with analyzing the process of economc change in response to differences between expected and realized phenomena.

OVERINVESTMENT THEORIES

Hawtrey's Monetary Theory of the Business Cycle

Knut Wicksell's inquiry into the indirect mechanism of price change had already pioneered in the direction of effecting an integration of monetary analysis and real analysis. He identified the expansion of the capital goods sector, facilitated by bank credit during periods when the availability of bank reserves depressed market rates of interest below their natural level, as responsible for the prosperity phase of the business cycle. Conversely, a market rate that rises above the natural rate as reserve shortages emerge, was identified as the key force in a cumulative contraction. This analysis pointed in the direction of a monetary theory of the business cycle, besides demonstrating that the price level does not change directly as implied by the quantity theory of money, but indirectly as a result of changes in the interest rate.

Ralph Hawtrey pursued the theme of purely monetary causes of the cycle by emphasizing the critical role of variations in short term interest rates and cash lags on business behavior. "Variations in effective demand," says Hawtrey, "which are the real substance of the trade cycle, must be traced to changes in bank credit . . . which disturb equilibrium." According to his analysis the effective demand for commodities derives from the total money outlay of consumers. In equilibrium, consumers' outlay equals consumers' income. Further, consumption equals production; consumers and traders are neither increasing nor decreasing their cash balances; banks are not changing the volume of bank credit and there is no net export or import of gold. This equilibrium has extremely delicate balance, which is readily disturbed so that it will give way to cumulative disequilibrium.

The least likely source of disturbance in Hawtrey's view, anticipating Keynes's emphasis on the stability of the consumption function, is increased spending by consumers out of their balances. But release of cash by traders and increases of bank credit are another matter. Improvements in expectations cause traders to increase their working capital, and increases in reserves cause banks to lower their discount rates in order to stimulate loans. Hawtrey conceives traders to be extremely sensitive to changes in interest rates, which he thought to be a principal expense associated with working capital.

If banks release cash as a result of increasing loans to traders (or the latter move their idle deposits into circulation in larger volume on their own initiative), the aggregate money income of the community is increased. Given conventional attitudes toward cash balances, Hawtrey assumes the increased income will largely be spent, thus stimulating excess demand. This result sets up a cumulative process of expansion in which additional cash is released by traders and banks, which adds to consumer income and outlay. Trader's stocks are subsequently reduced, which encourages them to use idle balances and seek additional bank loans, which will be available as long as there are excess bank reserves; this process further increases consumer income and outlay.

There will be some sectors of the economy in which output cannot readily increase because of labor scarcities and/or capacity operations by plants. The price rise in this sector adds to the expansionary process because the relative short-run rigidity of wages and interest rates increases profits. Further borrowing is stimulated because consumers will want more cash. The cash drain, which may be exacerbated by an increase in imports and a flow of gold abroad, inevitably depletes bank reserves, which forces high interest rates and an end to the expansion. This discourages traders from investing in commodity stocks or inventory, and leads via lay-offs to a contraction in consumer income. Eventually consumer outlay and effective demand also contract; subsequently output and the volume of credit required for financing it declines. This sequence culminates in crisis and depression.

Hawtrey identifies the forces which will eventually halt the decline as getting underway during the contraction phase of the cycle. One such force is the easing of the reserve position of banks as depression continues to reduce cash needs and improve reserve ratios. Banks then assume more liberal attitudes about lending. Low interest coupled with falling stocks of goods facilitate revival. In short, variations in bank credit that result from changes in the state of reserves is, in Hawtrey's view, the sole cause of cyclical variations. "If the central bank waits for the flow [of credit] to affect its reserves . . . , we cannot escape from alternatives of feverish activity with depression and unemployment."[1] Most writers of the period would agree with Hawtrey that bank credit plays a critical role in the cycle; but, as is elaborated in the next several sections, they generally do not hypothesize a purely monetary theory of the cycle.

Hayek's Monetary Overinvestment Theory

Frederick Hayek is among those theorists who argued that monetary forces alone are not "sufficient" to explain the phenomenon of the business cycle. The instability of bank credit is the "ultimate" cause of cycles, but its impact is on the structure of production rather than on variations in the consumer's outlay.[2]

In Hayek's view the chief problem of business-cycle theory is to explain the extraordinary variations in the production of capital goods as compared with consumer goods. The structure of production reflects the allocation of resources between the consumer and capital goods industries of the economy and corresponds to the savings habits of the community. Increased savings reduce the interest rate and encourage increased roundaboutness or "lengthening" of the production process. Conversely, a decrease in saving raises interest rates and tends to shorten the process of production. Given the stability of spending habits, however, violent changes in the structure of production are unlikely, in Hayek's view, in the absence of an elastic money supply.

If the market rate of interest is below the natural rate, the volume of bank credit increases. Borrowers use their loans to expand the commitment of resources to the capital-goods industries. Thus, labor and other resources are bid away from the consumer-goods industries. The result is that shortages of consumer goods raise their prices and bring about "forced savings." The real capital required for more roundabout processes of production is thus "extorted" via rising prices, from consumers, who have not intentionally changed their consumption patterns.

---

[1] For a particularly precise statement of Hawtrey's view, see R. G. Hawtrey, "The Monetary Theory of the Trade Cycle," *Quarterly Journal of Economics,* vol. 41, 1926/27.

[2] Frederick Hayek, *Prices and Production,* 2d ed. (London: Macmillan, 1934).

Consumers can be kept from reverting to their original spending patterns as long as the market rate of interest is below the natural rate, viz. as long as banks have excess reserves. Thus, the process of transferring resources out of relatively shorter production processes (i.e., the consumer goods industries) into the capital-goods industries continues until banks are forced to halt the lending process by raising interest rates.

The structure of production cannot be restored to compatibility with the level of voluntary savings, in Hayek's view, without crisis and depression. The crisis that precedes depression reflects a shortage of real voluntary savings relative to the volume of investment that has taken place. There is overinvestment in the capital goods industries which, in effect, wipes out or, at a minimum, severely reduces the value of investments in capital-intensive industries. Thus workers and other resources are released from longer processes more rapidly than they can be reabsorbed into shorter processes. The result is large-scale unemployment and general deflation. Hayek thus agrees with Hawtrey that repeated episodes of prosperity and depression can be avoided only be exercising proper control over the size of the money supply. But whereas Hawtrey interprets cyclical disturbance as a strictly monetary phenomenon, Hayek interprets cyclical variations as reflecting changes in the structure of production that are incompatible with the voluntary savings choices of the community.

Both hypotheses are in the tradition of Wicksell in the sense that they represent a definitive break with the simplistic quantity theory view of the relationship between the quantity of money and the price level. Both maintain, on the contrary, that changes in the money supply affect the *real* magnitudes of the system. Money plays a decisive role in bringing about the cycle and periodically causing real maladjustments; but, in Hayek's theory, unlike Hawtrey's, the business cycle is not interpreted as a purely monetary phenomenon.

Other Considerations

While there are fundamental differences between Hawtrey's view that monetary movements are "sufficient conditions of the observed phenomena of the cycle" and Hayek's theory which stresses the role of forced saving brought about by monetary forces, a common feature of both theories is their presumption that businessmen are uniquely sensitive to small changes in the bank rate of interest. Their responsiveness to these changes is central to the mechanism which is purported to trigger cumulative upswings and downswings.

This hypothesis about the mechanism of change is at odds with contrary evidence that business is not much influenced by changes in the rate of interest, which are generally too small or too delayed to be very consequential. Long-term changes in capital production may be related to changes in interest rates, but short-term variations of the cyclical variety are more likely to be induced by spurts of invention and innovation and changes in the prospect for making profit.[3] There are a number of writers whose theories identify the unique role of *real* factors in producing cyclical disturbance, though they do not negate the contributory role of fluctuations in credit in exacerbating the influence of more fundamental real causes. Joseph Schumpeter's theory of innovation is among the more highly regarded real theories of the cycle.

THEORIES OF INNOVATION

Schumpeter's Theory of Innovation

Invention, innovation, and technological changes are among the most characteristic aspects of a competitive capitalistic economy. Joseph Schumpeter viewed their impact as being so pervasive that he interpreted the cyclical functuations and development experience of dynamic economies as having their origin in the changes they initiate.[4] According to his view of the process, innovational changes are spearheaded by the unique few who, by virtue of their vision and daring, assume a position of economic leadership. As their entreprenuerial expectations are enhanced, they generate a demand for new productive equipment to take advantage of the innovated opportunities. If these arise at a time when the economic system is in a state of equilibrium with all factors fully employed and entrepreneurs making zero profits (i.e., there is a static state), the equilibrium is disturbed. Innovation interrupts the circular flow because it is facilitated by bank credit, which enables innovators to bid resources away from other sectors of the economy.

As long as the banking system is able to provide credit, the system expands on a wave of innovation to a new level of prosperity because the profits of successful innovators are great and attract imitators whose investments carry the expansion into a full-blown prosperity. Innovation does more than alter the technical aspects of production and promote a prosperous business environment. Because of their inconsistency with existing economic relationships, innovations induce reorganizations in the sociological superstructure. The logic of Schumpeter's analysis of the far-reaching effects of innovation on the structure of society is quite reminiscent of

---

[3] In an alternative statement of his hypothesis, Hayek argued that variations in the structure of production will occur in response to changes in the level of profits; thus cyclical disturbances will occur even if interest rates are unchanged. See F. A. Hayek, *Profits, Interest and Investment,* (London: Routledge, 1939), essay I.

[4] Joseph A. Schumpeter, *The Theory of Economic Development,* translated by Redvers Opie (Cambridge, Mass.: Harvard University Press, 1954).

Marx's analysis of the impact of changes in the mode of production.[5] The imitators who follow on the heels of the captains of industry are less able than the original innovators, and they arrive at a less propitious time. Their miscalculations, coupled with the tightening of credit which accompanies the expansion of bank loans, tend to force marginal firms into bankruptcy. These failures are the harbingers of depression, for they reflect the necessity of correcting the errors which have been made in the process of expansion. Error correction is the painful process of weeding out inefficiencies. This process is, to Schumpeter, the essence of depression.

But, for all its destructiveness, depression is also creative in Schumpeter's view, for the gains of innovation are truly assimilated by the economy only during depression. Moreover, the struggle for survival which typifies depression also stimulates and encourages the next surge of innovation which will propel the economy to its next level of economic achievement. Thus, Schumpeter views the process of capitalist development as being inherently unstable because it is always accompanied by the turbulence of cyclical expansion and contraction. Depression is part of the growth process because it is during this phase of the cycle that the fruits of earlier innovation are assimilated. Depression also causes a more active search for methods to reduce costs, which is the chief impulse to innovation. The reduction of interest rates, which is characteristic of depression, makes inventions exploitable so that a new cycle of expansion is able to enter the scene.[6]

---

[5] It should not, of course, be inferred from this similarity that Schumpeter was intellectually sympathetic to Marx's analysis, for, on the contrary, he was opposed to Marx's thinking as he was, for quite different reasons, to Keynes's.

[6] There is still another aspect of Schumpeter's theory of capitalist development which is relevant, especially in relation to the views of Karl Marx and J. M. Keynes with whom he subsequently found himself locked in fundamental disagreement. In *Capitalism, Socialism, and Democracy* (New York: Harper & Bros., 1942) Schumpeter expressed the view that the process of capitalist development will not continue indefinitely. As long as the rugged individualism of early capitalism predominated, the system maintained its vitality. But with the growth of the corporation to a position of dominance, the control of industry has passed into the hands of hired managers. As a result, the position of the bourgeoisie has degenerated to that of a stockholder, so that instead of leading the capitalist process, it merely participates indirectly. Thus, Schumpeter, like Marx, believed that capitalism will eventually destroy itself, but for fundamentally different reasons. He thought capitalism was destined to lose its vitality not as a result of the increasing misery of the exploited proletariat, but rather because the bourgeoisie loses control of the entrepreneurial process. The productive system becomes not less efficient as capitalist development advances, but rather more so; but in spite of its technical superiority, the system will cease to command popular support because so few persons have the opportunity for individual action in a bureaucratic society. Capitalism, Schumpeter believed, will tend to become sociologically untenable. This is one reason why he rejected so violently Keynes's political economy with its prescriptions for reforming the capitalistic system. Quite apart from his belief that prescription has no place in scientific economics, Schumpeter was of the opinion that the measures proposed by Keynes would hasten capitalism's decline because they are inherently anticapitalistic.

Cassel's Theory of Innovation and Crisis Due to Undersaving

The Swedish economist Gustav Cassel was among those who, like Schumpeter, identified the force of progress as the chief cause of the cycle. But whereas Schumpeter traces the crisis which always follows expansion to price dislocations that occur when the gestation period is over and the results of innovation are ready for the market, Cassel attributes the end of the expansion to investment which is excessive relative to the supply of saving. According to Cassel, cycles, or "conjunctures," as he preferred to call them, are essentially the result of progress.[7] These forces include not only technical progress, which is the chief force, but also population growth and the opening of new countries and new resources. All innovations and discoveries generate large-scale opportunities to use fixed capital profitably on a large scale. A new "high conjuncture" develops when progress has lowered the cost of exploiting them relative to the existing rate of interest.

Rates of interest at the beginning of a period of high conjuncture are relatively low, which encourages investment plans. When profits are high, as they are in the beginning of a boom, saving and capital formation are at their highest. Much of this saving comes from profit makers, who tend to have high rates of savings.

Expansions commonly end abruptly, i.e., crises occur. These crises, in Cassel's view, are indicative of miscalculation. But what is miscalculated is not the needs of the community for fixed capital or the demands of consumers. What is miscalculated is the community's capacity to save. High conjuncture is dependent on the community's willingness to supply the savings which will facilitate the flow of resources into investment.[8] The process of expansion sharply limits the growth of savings; the scarcity of labor which characterizes prosperities raises wages at the expense of profits; and, as this occurs, the level of saving becomes inadequate relative to the needs of investors.

The capital shortage evidences itself in rising interest rates which make it difficult for businessmen to complete previously planned undertakings. The ability of the banking system to expand credit can offset these difficulties only temporarily for, as the prices of capital goods fall and enterprises are abandoned, the real scarcity of capital will become apparent. Thus, the essential cause of crises is, to Cassel, an undersupply of savings relative to the volume of fixed-capital production that has been undertaken on the basis of opportunities generated by innovation. Like Hayek, Cassel associates crisis with an insufficiency of saving. But, whereas Hayek blames the

---

[7] Gustav Cassel, *Theory of Social Economy,* vol. 2, rev. ed. (London: Ernest Benn Ltd, 1932), S. L. Barron, trans.

[8] *The Theory of Social Economy,* vol. 2, p. 649.

banking system for facilitating more round about production processes which force additional saving via higher consumer prices, Cassel associates cyclical instability with the forces of progress and innovation that characterize the capitalistic system. Whereas the monetary theorist like Hawtrey would control fluctuations by proper control of the money supply, Cassel (like Schumpeter) sees no way of overcoming cyclical instability except at the expense of curbing the progress and innovational activities of the capitalistic system.

THE SAVINGS-INVESTMENT CONTROVERSY

Anoher possible approach to explaining expansions and contractions in economic activity is to examine more specifically the savings-investment process. While the concepts of saving and investment and differences between them have arisen numerous times in the preceeding discussion, neither of these terms has been given precise definition. This is because the writers who used them thought that they could rely on their everyday meaning. Subsequent inquiry by the Stockholm School, as well as by Dennis Robertson and J. M. Keynes, made it apparent that this was not the case.

In the overinvestment theories reviewed above, equality of S and I is associated with an equilibrium state. If I exceeds S (i.e., $I>S$) within this framework, the result is inflation; an excess of S over I (i.e., $S<I$) produces deflation. These concepts lent themselves well to expressing what was generally inferred to be happening during periods of prosperity and depression. There remains, however, the matter of how saving and investment should be defined if one is to be consistent in speaking about differences between them.

Keynes's Treatise on Money

Keynes's *Treatise on Money* popularized the concept of an "excess of saving over investment" and an "excess of investment over saving" in English economic literature. Its novelty in the mid-1930s is attested to by the reference made to it as "the new-fangled view, sponsored by Mr. Keynes in his *Treatise,* that the volume of saving may be unequal to the volume of investment."[9]

In the *Treatise,* Keynes defined investment as the "value of unconsumed output"; savings was defined as "income minus consumption." Thus, an excess of saving over investment was defined to mean losses, while, by definition, an excess of investment over savings meant profits. Profits and

---

[9] Roy Harrod, "Mr. Keynes and Traditional Theory," *Econometrica,* vol. 5, 1937, p. 75.

losses were defined as the amount by which actual entrepreneurial income exceeds or falls short of the level which induces the entrepreneur to alter the rate of output and employment.

The short-run problem of changes in output, employment, and income is not the chief focus of the *Treatise*. Its main theme is the problem of price stability. According to its schematic, output is divided into what Keynes called "available" and "nonavailable" output. These categories correspond to consumption and capital goods output. The primary costs of production for both types of output are wage costs. In order for the price level to be stable over time, wage earners, together with profit receivers, must save enough of their income to equal the value of the "nonavailable output" (i.e., investment) produced. In other words, if the price level is to be stable, saving must equal investment. If this condition is not met, i.e., if $S<I$ or $S>I$, the price level will change. This will create windfall profits or losses which will cause the balance between saving and investment to be restored. For example, if there are windfalls, more resources will be utilized in the investment sector. The accompanying increase in the price level increases profits and at the same time reduces real wages, i.e., there is a transfer of income to capitalists. Their higher savings propensities generate an increase in total savings until their level is equal to the new level of investment.

The definitions of saving and investment which Keynes found useful in the *Treatise* for explaining price-level changes are discarded in his subsequent, and more famous, *General Theory of Employment, Money and Interest*. The following chapter will focus entirely on this work. What is important here is to recognize that he fashioned definitions of saving and investment in the *Treatise* that were compatible with his emphasis on the critical role of entrepreneurial decision-making with regard to investment as the chief determinant of the system. Further, he emphasized that investment decisions do not "automatically" match decisions to save out of the income. This point is as central to Keynes's later intellectual dispute with the "Classics" as his repudiation of the quantity theory of money.[10] Thus, there is a common thread running between the *Treatise* and *The General Theory*, in which his interest shifts from the problem of explaining price-level stability to the problem of explaining the phenomenon of less than full employment as the consumption sector finds it must accomodate itself to the decisions of the investment sector.

---

[10] It is worth noting that the *Treatise* also evidences Keynes's concern with the problem of income distribution, i.e., which of the two groups, wage earners or profit recipients, do the necessary saving and how does the change in the price level distribute the burden of nonconsumption (real saving) between them. There is implicit in the *Treatise* an alternate conception of income distribution that reflects institutional forces rather than factor productivities. These alternative explanations of income distribution are critical matters of current controversy.

The Ex Ante-Ex Post Construct of the Stockholm School

A group of Swedish writers, among them Erick Lundberg,[11] Bertil Ohlin,[12] and Gunnar Myrdahl[13] developed an alternative set of definitions to those proposed by Keynes in *The Treatise on Money*. Their scheme is to distinguish between plans or expectations and amounts that are actually realized for all magnitudes (i.e., income, savings, and investments). Magnitudes that are associated with plans are *ex ante* manifestations. Thus, households and businesses formulate plans to save based on the incomes they expect. Entrepreneurs expect certain demands, interest rates, costs of production, and prices, and they formulate their investment plans on the basis of these expectations. *Ex ante* magnitudes for the economy as a whole represent the summing up of these expectations.

There is no reason, according to this school, for planned saving and planned investment to be equal *ex ante*. But they will be equal *ex post,* How does this equality come about? An inequality between saving and investment *ex ante* sets into motion a process which causes realized income to be different from expected income, realized saving to be different from planned saving and new investment to differ from what was planned.[14] *Unexpected* income, *unexpected* new investment, and *unintentional* new saving materialize. An excess of investment *ex ante* over savings, has a stimulating effect and is characteristic of the prosperity phase of the cycle. Conversely, if savings exceed investment *ex ante,* retailers find themselves with greater stocks than they expected (unintentional investment) or lower receipts (unintentional dissavings). This generates a contraction (or alternatively, expansion, if *ex ante I>S*) which brings about equality between saving and investment *ex post*. No more can be saved than is compatible with realized income; the latter depends on entrepreneurial decisions about investment.

In general, then, and in spite of different definitions of saving and investment, Keynes and the Stockholm School are in agreement that saving and investment are made by different groups on the basis of different criteria and that entrepreneurial decisions about investment are the dominant factor in generating change. Both would agree that "forced saving" is not an appropriate term to apply to the increase in savings that accompanies an increase in income. Even though the increase is unexpected and unplanned, it is "unintentional" rather than "forced" in the Hayekian sense of the term. The terms *ex ante* and *ex post* seem more descriptive of the process

---

[11] *Studies in the Theory of Economic Expansion,* Nils G. Sahlin and Florianne Dahlberg, trans. (London: P. S. King & Staples, Ltd., 1937).

[12] *Studies in the Theory of Money and Capital* (London: G. Allen, 1939).

[13] *Monetary Equilibrium* (London: Hodge, 1939).

[14] Bertil Ohlin, "Some Notes on the Stockholm Theory of Saving and Investment," *Economic Journal,* vol. 47, 1937.

by which income changes are generated than is Keynes's own terminology. They are now quite standard terminology for referring to plans and the results that actually materialize.[15]

CONCLUDING REMARKS

Business-cycle theory progressed very rapidly during the 1920s and 1930s to the point where it was a major concern of writers who were, unlike Marx and other socialists, "respectably orthodox" politically and in their theories of value and distribution. Much of the inspiration came from the work of Knut Wicksell whose theory of the relationship between interest rates, the allocation of resources, the process of price change, and changes in the quantity of money was a fundamental departure from the simplistic quantity theory of money.

Not all theorizing about business cycles during this period was Wicksellian in origin. The most important alternative hypotheses are conveniently grouped under the heading of "underconsumption theories." These theories differ from one another in detail but share the common feature of attributing recurring crises and depressions to the inability of consumers to buy industry's products at prices that will cover their costs. In its popular form, this hypothesis is sometimes given expression in the statement that "workers cannot buy back their own product."

Major C. H. Douglas offered the "A+B Theorem" to explain the source of purchasing-power insufficiency.[16] According to his explanation the payments made by business consist of:

> A payments, which are made to individuals in the form of wages, salaries, and dividends.
> B payments, which are made into reserves for depreciation and payments to other businesses for raw material and equipment and interest on bank loans.

A payments provide a flow of purchasing power while B payments do not. Yet both A payments and B payments become part of price. Thus, there is a deficiency of purchasing power equal to B, which must be replaced in some way if production is not to be interrupted. This logic provides the basis for various schemes for "sharing the wealth."

---

[15] Another alternative construct developed during this period is that introduced by Dennis Robertson. Robertson thought in terms of periods he called "days." Income received during a given "day" is available for disposal only on the following "day." In his terminology saving is the difference between yesterday's income and today's expenditure. If income is increasing or decreasing, the income earned in any day is greater or less than the disposable income of that day. Thus, there is a disequilibrium of saving and investment which generates expansion or contraction. See D. H. Robertson, "Saving and Hoarding." *Economic Journal,* vol. 43 (September 1933).

[16] C. H. Douglas, *Credit-Power and Democracy* (London: Stanley Nott Ltd., 1935) and *Social Credit,* rev. ed. (New York: W. Norton & Co. Inc., 1933).

More sophisticated versions of the underconsumption hypothesis are associated with two Americans, W. T. Foster and W. Catchings, who jointly wrote numerous books and articles.[17] The essence of their argument is that the inadequacy of purchasing power is traceable to oversaving. Savings become the basis for bank credit which is advanced to producers. They make payments to workers and other income receivers which enables them to buy goods whose production has been financed with *previous* savings. Thus, unless banks advance even more credit, or the price level falls, purchasing power is insufficient to buy back the enlarged volume of production. This deficiency will increase at an increasing rate unless bank credit is expanded at an increasing rate. Banks cannot accomodate this need for credit, for sooner or later legal or customary reserve requirements limit their ability to create new credit. According to this hypothesis, it is impossible for society to save without causing crisis and depression.

A less extreme hypothesis is that savings are not, in and of themselves, the source of the trouble. Only savings which are in excess of some "optimum" amount are troublesome. Such an hypothesis was offered by J. A. Hobson, who was perhaps the most illustrious of all underconsumption theorists.[18] He argued that the amounts paid out in wages, rent, profit, and interest are, in general, sufficient to buy back the product of industry. In economies which are characterized by great inequalities in the distribution of income, however, many are so wealthy they are unable to spend their incomes. The lag of wages behind prices during prosperity limits the expenditures of a class that normally spends readily and transfers disproportionate amounts of income to nonwage earners. This adds to the flow of savings. Additional saving supports new investment, which eventually adds to the volume of output available for sale. Overproduction is thus inevitable in the sense that the increased stream of consumer goods, which is produced as increased saving supports new investment, cannot be absorbed at prices remunerative to producers. The "cure" in Hobson's view, is to be found in greater equality of income.

While underconsumption theories in various forms have been warmly received by the "man in the street," most professional economists sought the cause of the trade cycle in imbalances originating in the investment sector rather than in underconsumption. Following the lead of Wicksell, such writers as Hawtrey, Hayek, Cassel, Schumpeter and a host of others focused on the central role of elastic credit systems in generating the phases of the trade cycle. Though there are important differences among them, all are Wicksellian in implicating money, as generated by the credit system, as the active factor in determining the real magnitudes of the economy.

---

[17] See for example, W. T. Foster and W. Catchings, *Profits* (Boston: Houghton-Mifflin, 1925); also, "The Dilemma of Thrift," *Atlantic Monthly* (April 1926).

[18] See, for example, J. A. Hobson, *Economics of Unemployment* (London: Macmillan, 1922).

Hayek, Schumpeter, and Cassel conceive of the prosperity phase as being associated with the "lengthening" of the production process. They thus follow also in the tradition of the Austrians, such as Menger, Wieser, and Böhm-Bawerk. Hayek "blames" the phenomenon of the cycle on the elasticity of credit, while Schumpeter and Cassel, emphasizing the positive effect of innovation and their effect on entrepreneurial expectations, see the role of the banking system as being "accommodating" rather than initiating.

The notion of saving and investment as unrelated phenomena is evident in the writings of the overinvestment and innovation theorists. But an analytical construct designed to focus more precisely on differences between savings and investment magnitudes and the impact of such differences awaited the writing of J. M. Keynes, Robertson, and the Stockholm School. The critical feature of their analyses is their focus on the key role of entrepreneurial investment decisions in bringing about the changes in income levels at which savings and investment are equal *ex post*. These analyses pointed in the direction of future thinking, especially as it became crystalized in J. M. Keynes's *General Theory of Employment, Money, and Interest,* which is examined in the chapter that follows.

Although it includes "Notes on the Trade Cycle," *The General Theory* is not a theory of the business cycle. As such it signals an important shift of emphasis which distinguishes it from the analyses examined in this chapter. The hypothesis formulated by cycle theorists conceived of full employment as an equilibrium condition toward which the economy tended to return via the adjustment mechanism the theory purported to explain. The forces that generated revival from a depression were conceived to carry along the seeds of their own destruction. Ultimately crisis would cut short the prosperity phase and produce the cumulative decline from which it would eventually recover as forces of revival operated to restore a new equilibrium. This representation of alternating phases of prosperity and depression brought about by the economy's internal mechanism of self adjustment reflects an essentially different conception of its functioning than is presented by Keynes in *The General Theory*. His preconception, in this work, is not that of an economy which possesses strong equilibrium tendencies, but rather of a system in which disequilibrium can be a self-perpetuating state. Thus, we proceed to examine next the disequilibrium economics of J. M. Keynes.

GLOSSARY OF TERMS AND CONCEPTS

Business cycles.   Recurrent but nonperiodic fluctuations in general economic conditions. Each phase is believed to carry the seeds that bring about the succeeding phase. Thus *prosperity,* which is characterized by high employment, income, and prices, including interest rates, is interrupted by crisis which generates *recession* which degenerates into *depression* which continues until expansionary forces promote *revival* which eventually culminates in a new prosperity.

Ex ante and ex post phenomena.   The plans and expectations of households and business firms with respect to consumption, saving, income, and investment are *ex ante* phenomena. If the plans which households and business firms make with respect to saving and investment diverge from each other, it sets a process in motion which causes them to be equal as realized, or *ex post* magnitudes.

Innovation.   Schumpeter's term for changes in production and/or marketing processes which are introduced by uniquely talented entrepreneurs. They anticipate opportunities for making profit which are so fundamental that they induce reorganizations in the sociological superstructure while promoting the revival of the economy during the depression phase of the cycle.

Overinvestment theories and the cycle.   Theories which identify the "cause" of cyclical disturbance with excessive investment. Monetary theorists typically associate excessive investment with excessive credit expansion.

Underconsumption theories and the cycle.   Theories which identify the "cause" of cyclical disturbance with purchasing power insufficiencies. Some, like the A plus B theorem, attribute the deficiency to the presence of interbusiness payments which, unlike payments to individuals, do not finance the purchase of consumer goods. Others attribute purchasing power insufficiency to excessive saving by capitalists and high income groups. Depending on their special emphasis, underconsumption theories are akin to "oversaving" theories.

NOTES FOR FURTHER READING

The most useful general reference on the subject of business cycles is Gottfried Haberler's *Prosperity and Depression,* Harvard Economic Studies, no. 105 (Cambridge, Mass.: Harvard University Press, 1958; 4th ed. [New York: Atheneum, 1963] Business Machines Corporation). *Readings in Business Cycle Theory,* R. A. Gordon and Laurence R. Klein, eds. (Philadelphia: The Blakeston Company, 1944) contains numerous classic articles, including F. A. Lutz's "The Outcome of the Savings-Investment Discussion." Joseph Schumpeter's *History of Economic Analysis* (New York: Oxford University Press, 1954) part IV, chap. 8 contains a comprehensive discussion of theorizing about money, credit, and cycles. Clark Warburton's "The Misplaced Emphasis in Contemporary Business Fluctuation Theory," *Journal of Business of the University of Chicago,* vol. 19, reprinted in *Readings in Monetary Theory,* F. A. Lutz and L. W. Mints, eds. (New York: The Blakeston Company, 1951) laments the emphasis accorded to savings-investment relationships in explaining the depression of the 1930s to the neglect of "the erratic variation in the quantity of money." This article anticipates the current controversy between the Monetarists and the Keynesians, which will be examined in Chapter 18.

For those who have access to them, some of the older textbooks on business cycles which became obsolete with the popularity of contemporary macroeconomics may be useful. Among the more popular ones and still worth examining are Elmer C. Bratt, *Business Cycles and Forcasting* (Chicago: R. D. Irwin, Inc., 1948) and James A. Estey, *Business Cycles* (New York: Prentice-Hall, 1941).

17

The Disequilibrium Economics
of J. M. Keynes

INTRODUCTION

Life and Times (1883–1946)

THE IMPACT of *The General Theory of Employment, Interest and Money* in the profession and in the realm of public policy has exceeded that which could reasonably have been expected from even such a distinguished and influential thinker as John Maynard Keynes. The reason for its sweeping success, in the face of received doctrine and a generally negative reception in nonacademic circles at the time of its publication in 1936, is that it had something for everyone. One would have to go back to Adam Smith to find a comparable degree of persuasiveness with respect to public policy; to David Ricardo for the kind of rigorous analysis which inspires the deductive thinker; and to Karl Marx for someone who attracted sufficiently zealous and able followers to carry his message to the world.

Heredity appears to destined Keynes to make a distinguished contribution to the world.[1] His father was John Neville Keynes, Registrar of the University of Cambridge, whose *Scope and Method of Political Economy* (1891) is not only a classic in its field but remains an eminently useful

---

[1] Biographical details are readily available in the *London Times,* "Obituary," April 22, 1946; and in the biography by Roy F. Harrod, *The Life of John Maynard Keynes* (New York: Harcourt, Brace & Co., 1952). A bibliography of Keynes's extensive writings is appended to Seymour Harris, ed., *The New Economics* (New York: Alfred Knopf, 1947).

treatise on the subject of methodology to this day. His mother served as Mayor of Cambridge as recently as 1932. They educated their son at Eton and King's College, where he excelled in mathematics, besides studying the classics, philosophy, and economics, the latter under Henry Sidgwick and Alfred Marshall.

In 1906, having passed the civil service examination, he went into the India Office for two years before returning once more to King's College, where he specialized in teaching Marshall's *Principles of Economics*. The academic life, broadened to include cultural as well as business interests which provided a handsome additional income, suited him well.

But he was always involved in public affairs in one capacity or another, particularly with respect to matters of trade and finance. This aspect of his career was in perfect keeping with his predominantly pragmatic approach; economics as a pure science interested him far less than economics in the service of policy. Indeed, Keynes's contribution to the theory and practice of political economy must be seen in perspective against the war and interwar years in order to be fully understood and appreciated. These years were marked by the breakdown of trade relations and the gold standard during World War I, followed first by inflation, exchange rate instability, and balance-of-payments disequilibria and later by deflation and mass unemployment on an international scale. Theoretical examination of these catastrophic phenomena and, more important from Keynes's point of view, practical solutions to the problems they created were therefore the order of the day.

With the outbreak of World War II, Keynes devoted himself to questions concerning war finance and the ultimate reestablishment of international trade and stable currencies. His ideas on these matters were offered in a pamphlet, *How to Pay for the War* (1940) and in the Keynes plan for the establishment of an international monetary authority which he proposed in 1943. Although Keynes's plan was rejected, the proposal which was adopted at the 1944 Bretton Woods Conference, which Keynes attended as the leading British delegate, clearly reflected the influence of his thinking.

At the time of his death, early in 1946, shortly after working out the American loan agreement, he was the leading economist not only of England but of the world. He was a brilliant theorist but valued theory primarily as a guide to policy. Thus, Keynes, perhaps more than any other individual, is responsible for the return to what once was known as "political economy."

The Evolution of "The General Theory"

Though Keynes was schooled in traditional theory, his examination of the relationship between depression and monetary deflation after World War I led him to ponder the question of the ability of a free system to operate automatically at full-employment levels. The train of thought which ultimately developed out of this question later became the essence of Keynes's message.[2] Even his first publication, *Indian Currency and Finance* (1913), which is regarded as an outstanding examination of the functioning of the gold exchange standard, foreshadows his later view on the need for wise monetary policy in order to have economic stability. But this message first emerged clearly in *The Economic Consequences of the Peace* (1919), which won him international fame. In it, he presented, in addition to his vigorous polemic against reparations payments, a vivid examination of the breakdown of what he called "that extraordinary episode of laissez-faire capitalism." The picture he sketched was of a system made economically moribund by the passing of the conditions necessary to entrepreneurial success: a rapidly growing population and plentiful investment opportunities born of innovation and scientific progress. Thus, Keynes's *Weltanschauung* in the period after World War I was one of economic stagnation. Nothing was yet in sight of the theoretical schema of *The General Theory*, which was to be published more than a decade later during the worldwide depression of the 1930s. But there are few better examples in the history of economic thought of the relationship between the germination of an economic analysis and its crystallization into theoretical propositions than we find in *The Economic Consequences of the Peace* and *The General Theory of Employment, Interest and Money*.

His *Tract on Monetary Reform* (1923) was another stepping-stone to *The General Theory*. In it, he advocated that the volume of note issue be controlled by the central bank independently of the gold reserve as a means of achieving economic stabilization via price-level stabilization. Two aspects of this work are significant as regards the ultimate development of Keynes's thinking: The first is its unmistakably prescriptive nature; the second is its conception of money as an active agent in the economic process. Both are important signposts along the way to *The General Theory*.

The "economics as a guide for policy" character of Keynes's work is somewhat obscured in his *Treatise on Money* (1930). But that work contributed at least one other important principle which ultimately became embodied in *The General Theory*. This is the principle that decisions to save and decisions to invest are unrelated to one another. Their separateness was, however, glossed over—or better still, lost sight of—by those who conceived of the interest rate as a device to equilibrate savings and investment. It was in order to emphasize the separateness of these decisions and the idea that private thrift is not a virtue when investment opportunities are lacking, that Keynes adopted definitions of saving and investment

---

[2] Joseph A. Schumpeter has given a most lucid account of its gradual unfolding in "John Maynard Keynes, 1883–1946," *American Economic Review*, vol. 36, no. 4 (September 1946), reprinted in his *Ten Great Economists* (London: Oxford University Press, 1951).

in the *Treatise* which recognized the possibility of their diverging from each other. Gunnar Myrdahl, who followed Wicksell, had essentially the same distinction in mind when he identified savings and investment in terms of *ex ante* and *ex post* magnitudes.[3] Thus if $S>I$ (or in Myrdahl's terminology saving *ex ante* exceeds investment *ex ante*) there will be a cumulative contraction while $I>S$ will bring about a cumulative expansion. This formulation was intended not only as a tool for monetary theory, but also as a guide for monetary policy, the obvious goal of which is to keep $S=1$.[4] It proved to be one of the more successful of Keynes's many terminological innovations, though the *Treatise* as a whole was received with less applause than any previous work. While the definitions of savings and investment introduced in the *Treatise* were abandoned in *The General Theory*, the idea of savings and investment as separate phenomena and as magnitudes which are not equated by the interest rate is another of the foundation stones of *The General Theory*.

The completion of *The General Theory* only five years after the *Treatise* represents Keynes's crowning achievement. It is his magnum opus not only as a cumulation of his previous efforts, but also as his last major publication. It brought him so enthusiastic a following that there emerged a whole school which adopted and proliferated his ideas. Among those who carried Keynes's message to the world are a remarkable number who are notable and possibly even outstanding thinkers in their own right. Roy F. Harrod, Joan Robinson, and Richard F. Kahn are among the leading English economists whose thinking appeared to be progressing in the same general direction as Keynes's when *The General Theory* appeared. Alvin Hansen, Abba P. Lerner, and Paul A. Samuelson are among the leading Keynesians in the United States.[5] All have the distinction of having added in an original way to the body of theory which Keynes presented in *The General Theory of Employment, Interest and Money*.

The Revival of Macroeconomic Analysis

With the publication of *The General Theory*, macroeconomic analysis once more claimed the center of the stage. Not the allocation of resources

---

[3] Dennis Robertson's perception of the possibility of a divergence between saving and investment came as early as his *Banking Policy and the Price Level* (1926), rev. ed. (New York: Augustus Kelley, 1949).

[4] A still-useful examination of the nature and usefulness of the savings and investment terminology of the *Treatise on Money* is Frederick A. Lutz, "The Outcome of the Savings-Investment Discussion," *Quarterly Journal of Economics*, vol. 52 (August 1938), pp. 588–614; reprinted in American Economic Association, *Readings in Business Cycle Theory* (Philadelphia: The Blakiston Company, 1944).

[5] It is important to note, however, that there are major differences between the economics of Keynes and what is generally perceived of as "Keynesian economics." These differences are examined in depth in the chapter which follows.

among alternative uses, but rather whether resources would be employed at all became the primary question economic theory sought to answer. This is the question to which Keynes addressed himself and which he made the basis for his fight with the "classics." Keynes thoughtfully provides us with a footnote explaining his use of that term to include "the followers of Ricardo, those, that is to say, who adopted and perfected the theory of the Ricardian economics, including (for example) J. S. Mill, Marshall, Edgeworth and Prof. Pigou."[6]

Two things are worth noting before proceeding with the precise nature of Keynes's criticism of the classics. The first is that no single individual associated with the classical or neoclassical tradition ever held all the ideas that Keynes attributes collectively to all of them. What he did, in effect, was to create a convenient and more clearly defined target at which he could aim the shots he was about to fire. The second point is that the problem to which Keynes addressed himself, namely, the problem of the level of economic activity, is fundamentally different from that with which his classical and neoclassical predecessors concerned themselves.

Classical writers (i.e., the orthodox writers who preceded Marshall) were more concerned with the problem of long-run secular development than with the problem of cyclical disturbance. The latter problem was conceived of primarily as a problem of gluts and overproduction, and was considered to be self-correcting. Though the nature of the self-corrective mechanism was explored in only a cursory fashion, it was Say's law, with its dictum that supply creates its own demand, which provided the basis for their conclusion.

Neoclassical theorists, that is, those in the Marshallian tradition, were mainly concerned with the problem of optimizing and relating the price-determining process to the maximizing activities of individuals and firms. Thus, when Keynes focused his attention on the problem of disequilibrium, he was dealing with a problem his predecessors scarcely perceived. One would, for example, search Marshall's *Principles of Economics* in vain for any discussion of the problem of underemployment or its relationship to income determination. Yet, this is the essence of Keynes's problem and the basic difference between it and all that went before. It is the analysis of the problem of aggregate demand and the implications of this analysis for policy making which separates Keynes's theory from the traditional. Yet, Keynes was, by training, a strict neoclassicist. This is perhaps one reason why he was able to exert so much influence over his similarly trained contemporaries.

While Keynes's examination of the behavior of the macroeconomic vari-

---

[6] John Maynard Keynes, *The General Theory of Employment, Interest and Money* (New York: Harcourt, Brace & Co., 1936), p. 3. This work is cited hereafter in the footnotes as *The General Theory*.

ables that determine income and employment was static and short-run, he implicitly recognized the need to also examine long-run changes in these magnitudes and their effect on income and employment. It is necessary to go beyond the income-creating role of investment in order to inquire at what rate income and investment must grow to bring about the full employment of the incremental addition to the economy's productive capacity. Investigation of this problem is in the realm of growth theory, which Keynes himself did not study. But it became apparent as early as 1939 to Roy Harrod, who was eventually to become Keynes's biographer, that sustained growth is necessary if the growing capital stock resulting from new investment is to be fully utilized. Harrod's posing of the growth problem and the hypothesis he formulated about it are very much in the mode of Keynes's own disequilibrium economics. They are therefore examined briefly at the end of the present chapter as a refinement of the model Keynes developed as an alternative to the neoclassical model he criticized.

KEYNES'S CRITICISM OF NEOCLASSICAL POSTULATES

Wage Theory

The General Theory of Employment, Interest and Money is premised on Keynes's criticism of the neoclassical theory that an economy with flexible wages and prices tends automatically to generate full employment. This theory was implicit rather than explicit in a neoclassical thinking, which was concerned primarily with the problem of value and distribution and the allocation of resources among alternative uses. Its microeconomic bias is particularly evident in the postulates on which its wage theory is based.[7] These postulates are (1) that the marginal product of labor tends to fall as employment increases, (2) that the real wage of labor tends to equal its marginal product and to reflect the psychic disutility of employment at the margin, and (3) that the money-wage bargains made by workers and their employers also determine the level of real wages. Neoclassical thinkers concluded, on the basis of these postulates, that if there is unemployment, it must be due to workers' unwillingness to accept a reward which corresponds to their marginal productivity. It follows that an increase in employment can be brought about only by reducing money wages until they are equal, in real terms, to labor's marginal product.

Keynes, however, rejected this conclusion and maintained that unemployment resulted from what he termed "insufficient aggregate demand.[8] Given the state of the art, it is the level of employment and output which determines the marginal product of labor and, therefore, the real wage.

---

[7] Ibid., chap. 2.

[8] Ibid., p. 16.

Thus, he argued, the level of real wages is not determined independently of the level of employment. Moreover the level of real wages cannot be reduced simply by reducing the level of money wages. Money-wage cuts are not an effective way to reduce real-wage rates because the total demand for consumer goods is dependent mainly on labor income. The wage bargain determines only money-wage rates and not real-wage rates. "There may exist no expedient by which labor as a whole can reduce its real wage to a given figure by making revised money bargains with entrepreneurs."[9]

This brings to the foreground the postulate concerning the *reaction* of workers to wage cuts. Neoclassical theorists maintained that money wages tend to equal real wages and that the latter reflect the psychic disutility of employment at the margin. Workers reject offers of additional employment at lower money wages. Neoclassical thinkers regard their unemployment as *voluntary,* on the presumption that a reduction in money wages would increase job offers which workers reject.

The mechanism by which mainstream thinkers thought *real*-wage levels adjusted to make them compatible with full employment is important because employer incentive to expand employment requires a reduction in *real wages.* Competition among workers for jobs will tend to depress money-wage rates. In certain sectors of the economy in which production costs become lower along with wages, prices may also decline. The expectation, however, is that the *general* price level, which was thought to be determined by the relationship between the quantity of money and the volume of transactions, would *not* change. Therefore, reductions in money-wage rates in response to unemployment were regarded as a reliable (though admittedly painful) mechanism for reducing *real* wages and stimulating employment. Neoclassical economists thus interpreted persistent unemployment (as distinct from the frictional unemployment experienced by workers who are "between jobs") as being *voluntary.*

Keynes rejected the notion that workers who are unemployed and unwilling to accept reduced money wages are voluntarily unemployed. He agreed that workers generally *are* reluctant to accept cuts in their money wages. They will however *not* refuse to work at current money-wage rates if real wages are reduced as a result of an increase in the general price level. Keynes therefore maintained that workers are voluntarily unemployed only if they refuse to work in consequence of a rise in consumer prices, i.e., a cut in real wages. Worker unwillingness to accept a cut in money wages was not regarded as a major impediment to increasing employment because he thought it is generally not possible to decrease workers' real wages via money-wage reductions.

The difference between the classical analysis and Keynes's of the relationship between real wages and employment is demonstrated in Figure

---

[9] Ibid. p. 13.

FIGURE 17–1

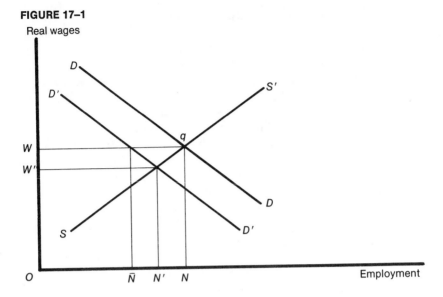

Real wages

17–1. Keynes accepted the classicist's principle that the demand for labor is a function of real wages. Thus *DD* represents the labor-demand curve for both the classical and Keynesian cases. The classical labor-supply curve is *SS′*, and the equilibrium amount of employment is *ON* at a wage rate of *OW*. In Keynes's view the supply of labor will be highly elastic at the going wage rate up to full employment; thus the Keynesian labor supply curve is *WqS′*. The significance of this labor-supply function, as opposed to one which is classically shaped, may be demonstrated by tracing the effects for both cases, assuming that depression causes the demand curve for labor to fall to *D′D′*.

In the classical view, a cut in money wages will also reduce real wages, say to *OW′*. All who wish to work at that real-wage level will be employed and *ON′* is the equilibrium volume of employment. Keynes disagrees with this analysis on the ground that a cut in money wages will be resisted; real wages therefore will not fall below *OW*. Given a labor supply curve of *WqS′*, employment will be no greater than *ON̄*. Keynes would identify this level of employment as an *underemployment* situation. It is indicative of disequilibrium in the sense that wage-price deflation is not a corrective force which can reasonably be counted upon to generate full employment. "Money illusion" by workers is a critical reason for disequilibrating forces.

Money illusion is said to exist whenever there is a reaction to a *monetary* magnitude, such as a money wage rather than its equivalent in real or purchasing power terms. Experience, Keynes observed, shows that workers reject money-wage reductions even in the face of unemployment, even though they do not respond adversely when rising commodity prices reduce real wages. Thus, they are reacting to money illusion.[10]

This observation is particularly crucial to Keynes's analysis because it reflects his view that exogenous forces such as labor unions, wage legislation, and customs establish money-wage rates. The mainstream view, from which he disassociated himself, is that economic forces which are internal or endogenous to the system and work through the price mechanism determine money-wage rates. Keynes's view that money-wage rates are exogenously determined (while the quantity of money is endogenous to the system) are basic to his rejection of the neoclassical tradition.[11]

The only circumstances under which Keynes agreed that falling money wages and prices might have favorable effects on employment would be if they exerted a monetary influence which revised interest rates downward. He thought the probable mechanism of this favorable effect, which has since become known as the Keynes effect, would be that the transactions demand for money would fall along with money wages and prices. If the total money stock is unchanged, the smaller cash requirement for transactions needs will free cash balances for the purchase of securities. This will raise security prices and reduce interest rates. Given the schedule of the marginal efficiency of capital, additional investments will then be profitable, so that the level of aggregate demand may increase until full employment is reached.

---

[10] A recent attempt by Axel Leijonhufvud to clarify Keynes's argument about worker unwillingness to accept money wage reductions in the face of unemployment interprets Keynes's perception of the functioning of the price mechanism in a new way and is relevant in this connection. In his *On Keynesian Economics and the Economics of Keynes* (London: Oxford University Press, 1966), Leijonhufvud argues that the automatic functioning of the system in classical theory requires that prices (1) disseminate the information necessary to coordinate the economic activities and plans of independent transaction units, and (2) provide the incentives for transaction units to adjust their activities in such a manner that they become consistent in the aggregate. He maintains that Keynes's perception of the functioning of the price system rejected the classical notion that this mechanism performs the function of transmitting price information in the short run. A worker's perception of what he is "worth" is unavoidably related to what he was worth only yesterday when he was laid off. It is also related to the experiences of workers in similar jobs who continue to work at much the same money wage as before. This sort of information causes the unemployed worker to resist significant wage cuts in order to regain employment. Interpreted in this way the problem of unemployment is an information problem. The defect in the information-feedback mechanism leads the system further away from equilibrium instead of restoring equilibrium. The imperfection of the information-feedback mechanism emerges in this interpretation as the basic reason why Keynes insisted that there "may exist no expedient by which labor as a whole can reduce its *real wage* to a given figure by making revised *money* bargains with entrepreneurs."

[11] These views also emerge prominently in the writing of contemporary followers of Keynes who see their work as continuing Keynes's rejection of neoclassicism. See Chapter 20. The basis for Keynes's view of money as endogenous is examined in connection with his analysis of investment and the money supply, p. 407.

While this is a theoretical possibility, Keynes hardly regarded it as a likely occurrence because, in a severe depression, the prices of long-term nonmoney assets are likely to be too low relative to money-wage rates to restore full employment. Keynes was inclined to interpret a downturn in activity as indicating that asset values are too low, rather than that wage rates are too high. This aspect of his diagnosis is clearly evidenced by his policy recommendation that, in the event of unemployment, the central bank should operate to force asset prices back up to a level at which the value of investment would be large enough to result in full employment at going wage rates. In other words, it is long-term interest rates rather than wage rates which should be brought down.

The Theory of the Interest Rate

The real impediment to stimulating employment during a depression is the difficulty of maintaining the aggregate demand for goods at a level associated with full employment. Classical and neoclassical thinkers recognized that an economy can experience gluts and lapses from full employment as a result of cyclical fluctuation. But, they argued, in the long run flexible commodity prices and wage rates prevent overproduction and unemployment, while interest rates can be relied on to channel all savings into investment. In terms of this logic, aggregate demand cannot be deficient in the long run because any income that is saved automatically becomes invested. Many of the business-cycle theorists who wrote between 1900 and 1936 were skeptical that the interest rate reliably performed this function. But it was Keynes's emphasis on the monetary aspects of interest-rate determination which brought to light the reasons why the interest rate cannot be relied on automatically to equilibrate savings and investment.

Neoclassical thinkers thought of the interest rate as being determined by the intersection of a positively sloped schedule of the supply of loanable funds and a negatively sloped schedule of the demand for funds, as shown in Figure 17–2. Elasticity may be deduced on the supply side of the market if a preference for spending versus saving is assumed and if the only motive for saving is the interest income it yields. The elasticity of the demand schedule may similarly be deduced from the schedule of the marginal productivity of capital. If, now, competition is assumed on both sides of the market so that the interest rate is free to fluctuate, it will settle at a level which equilibrates savings and investment.

Keynes, however, maintained that the interest rate does not automatically channel savings into investment in the manner conceived by neoclassical thinkers. The main reason for its inability to function in this way is that there is *an asset demand for money* as well as a transactions de-

FIGURE 17–2

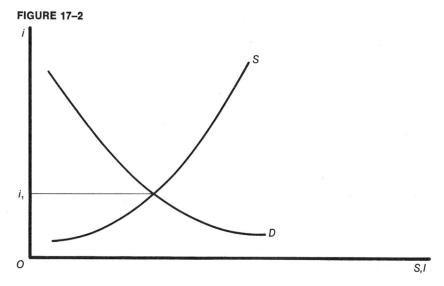

mand. Keynes regarded a demand for money per se as being perfectly rational because it satisfies a basic psychological need to hedge uncertainty. The hazard of predicting the future leads people to hold cash balances as a refuge. Thus, Keynes conceived of interest as a price for parting with *liquidity* (cash) rather than as a reward for abstinence. Interest can reward abstinence only in a full-employment economy, for this is the only circumstance in which additional investment necessarily curtails consumption. Thus, he regarded the neoclassical conception of interest as inappropriate to any but a full-employment economy.

Keynes further attacked the neoclassical theory of interest on the ground that the rate is indeterminate. According to this theory, the interest rate is determined by the intersection of a savings schedule and an investment-demand schedule, as in Figure 17–2. However, Keynes maintained, it is impossible to determine the position of the savings schedule until the level of income is known. There is a different level of savings for every level of income. Yet, we cannot know the income level without first knowing the volume of investment, and the latter depends not only on the productivity of new capital at the margin but also on the rate of interest. Changes in the investment-demand schedule and the savings-supply schedule are therefore interdependent and render the interest rate indeterminate within the neoclassical framework. What was needed, therefore, Keynes thought, was a new approach which would explain interest as a monetary phenomenon and integrate monetary theory into the general theory of income, output, and employment. His theory of aggregate effective demand was intended to provide such an approach.

KEYNES'S THEORY OF EMPLOYMENT, OUTPUT, AND INCOME

The Principle of Aggregate Effective Demand

In *The General Theory of Employment, Interest and Money,* Keynes introduced a radically new theoretical structure accompanied by an essentially new vocabulary to accomplish his "struggle of escape from habitual modes of thought and expression." His vocabulary has become incorporated even into introductory economics texts in spite of early difficulties. His theoretical structure, however, is significantly different from the income-expenditure models which are popularly thought of as Keynesian economics, particularly in America. These are not Keynes's models but are, rather, the product of several highly successful efforts at popularization.[12] This suggests, the usefulness of presenting Keynes's theory of employment, output and income in terms of *The General Theory* itself. There are important differences between Keynes's original work and the body of thought generally identified as "Keynesian".

Keynes notes that one of the main problems encountered in presenting an aggregate analysis is the choice of units. That is, aggregate analysis obviously requires some way of expressing both physical magnitudes (e.g., output and employment) and monetary magnitudes (e.g., income). Keynes simplified his analysis by restricting it to the short run in which organization, technique, and equipment can be assumed as given. Changes in output and employment will then closely parallel each other. Accordingly, Keynes chose to express the physical aspect of changes in the level of economic activity in terms of labor units of employment. He expressed the monetary aspects of changes in the level of economic activity in terms of a constant wage unit and conducted his analysis in money rather than in real terms.[13] His analytical reliance on a constant wage unit is consistent with his view that changes in the average rate of money wages alters the price level proportionately and in the same direction as money wages.[14]

Keynes taught that the economy's level of the economic activity is determined by the interaction of aggregate demand and supply schedules and that this level will not necessarily coincide with an employment level that provides jobs for all who are seeking them. He did not undertake to draw

---

[12] We particularly note among these Alvin H. Hansen, *A Guide to Keynes* (New York: McGraw-Hill Book Co., 1953); Dudley Dillard, *The Economics of John Maynard Keynes* (New York: Prentice-Hall, 1948); and Lawrence Klein, *The Keynesian Revolution* (New York: Macmillan Co., 1961). Paul Samuelson has perhaps been the leading disseminator of popular Keynesianism by virtue of his highly successful text, *Economics* (New York: McGraw-Hill, 1st ed., 1948; 10th ed., 1976).

[13] This approach is one of the features which distinguishes economics of Keynes himself from Keynesian economics. The income expenditure models in textbook presentations of aggregate economic activity are typically conducted in real terms.

[14] Cf. J. R. Hicks, *Crisis in Keynesian Economics* (New York: Basic Books, Inc., 1974).

aggregate demand and supply schedules, but his discussion indicates that, had he done so, his aggregate demand schedule would have related expected sales proceeds (converted into real terms by means of an index of wage rates) to the employment levels associated with the production of varying amounts of output.[15] The aggregate supply schedule, which Keynes called the *"Z"* function, is a schedule of the proceeds required to cover factor costs, including normal profit. It is a function of N, the level of employment, and is given in the short run. Thus $Z = \phi(N)$.

Aggregate demand is generated by the spending units of the economy (households, business firms, and government) and is not necessarily equal to aggregate supply. The sales proceeds which businessmen can expect to realize depends on the level of consumption and investment expenditures. The level of employment thus depends on the relationship between the aggregate demand function $D = f(N)$ and $Z = \phi(N)$ and is not necessarily full employment. Keynes therefore rejects the dictum of Say's Law that supply creates its own demand. Say's Law implies that every increase in output and employment which takes place as the economy expands along its aggregate supply curve is associated with corresponding increases in demand. Keynes is thus led to examine the determination of consumption and investment expenditures separately.

The Determination of Consumption Expenditures

Marshall recognized that saving is related to income, and J. M. Clark presented the idea of a "tendency toward saving a progressively larger proportion of our income as our income itself gets larger."[16] But it remained for Keynes to hypothesize that consumption is a stable function of real income.[17]

Keynes formulated his hypothesis concerning the relationship between consumption and income in terms of real income, i.e., money income "corrected" for price change in terms of a constant wage unit. His focus on real income in connection with consumption expenditures reflected his view that consumption behavior is not subject to "money illusion."[18] He makes reference to statistical evidence, but his hypothesis that "other things being equal" expenditures depend primarily on real income is an a priori rather than an empirical proposition.

---

[15] The well-known Keynesian Cross, which is presented in the following chapter, is due to the efforts of Keynesians, rather than Keynes. Chief among them is Paul Samuelson, who popularized the apparatus in his widely used text, *Economics*.

[16] J. M. Clark, *Economic Reconstruction* (New York: Columbia University Press, 1934), p. 109.

[17] *The General Theory,* chaps. 8–10.

[18] One of the curiosities of *The General Theory* is Keynes's belief that people see through the veil of money as consumers but are subject to money illusion as wage earners.

FIGURE 17–3

Consumption expenditures

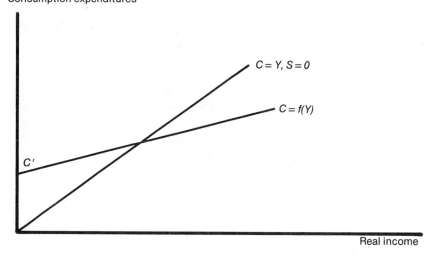

The consumption function, $C = f(Y)$, which is shown in Figure 17–3 as $C'C$, is premised on the assumption that changes in consumption expenditures are associated with changes in real income on the expectation that "other factors" which might affect consumption expenditures remain unchanged. These other factors are exogenous and, if they change, will produce *shifts* in the consumption function. Windfall gains or losses such as might occur in a stock-market boom or crash, major changes in expectations with respect to the availability of goods such as would be experienced in wartime, changes in fiscal policy, and major interest-rate changes are objective factors which Keynes mentioned as being capable of producing shifts in the propensity to consume out of given income if they occur. In the absence of unusual events, however, Keynes maintained that the propensity to consume out of a given income is a highly stable function of income because the subjective, or endogenous, factors which determine consumer behavior change only very slowly.[19]

These subjective factors are the psychological characteristics of human behavior and the social institutions and practices affecting the distribution of income and its disbursement. They are unlikely to change rapidly. People accustom themselves to certain living standards, and certain practices emerge with respect to the frequency of wage, dividend, and other payments and the size of retained earnings. These factors change so gradually that the slope and position of the consumption function are likely to be quite stable. This is the basis for Keynes's formulation of what he considered to be a "fundamental psychological law" with respect to deter-

---

[19] Ibid., p. 96.

mining the normal slope of the consumption function. This law is that "as a rule, and on the average, consumption will increase as income increases but not by as much as the increase in income."[20] Thus the value of the marginal propensity to consume, $\triangle C/\triangle Y$, which is the slope of the consumption curve, is less than unity. It will therefore cut through a curve such as the one drawn at a 45-degree angle in Figure 17–3 which shows how the consumption function would look if all income were spent. It follows that for a given dollar increase in real income the absolute increase in consumption will be less than the *absolute* increase in income. The implication is that, as the income level of an economy rises, consumption expenditures become a smaller component of aggregate demand.

This far-reaching hypothesis has, naturally enough, invited all manner of empirical testing.[21] When properly interpreted, Keynes's proposition has stood up remarkably well. U.S. Department of Commerce data show that for the economy as a whole, excluding abnormal periods such as the war and early postwar years, the marginal propensity to consume is less than one, just as Keynes maintained. But there eventually developed a considerable controversy about the nature of the long-run consumption function which will be discussed in the following chapter.

The Marginal Propensity to Consume and the Multiplier

Not Keynes, but R. F. Kahn has the distinction of having fathered the concept of the multiplier.[22] Kahn formulated the principle that an increase in investment has an expansionary effect which is greater than the increase in investment itself. Keynes subsequently recast the principle from its original form as a tool for analyzing the employment effects of public investment into a tool for analyzing the income effect of investment.

The importance of increments of new investment for increments of income had of course already been stressed by business-cycle theorists such as Wicksell, Hayek, Cassel, and Ohlin. But it was the formulation of the multiplier principle which revealed two fundamentals concerning the relationship between investment and income which were not clearly understood before. The first is that the expenditure of new money can have an expansionary effect on an economy with unemployed resources which is *larger* than the size of the expenditure itself. The second is that any expansionary process is necessarily limited and loses vitality because of leakages from the expenditure stream. Both of these insights raised intensely practical

---

[20] The consumption function has a positive intercept because $C > Y$ at low levels of income.

[21] For a particularly lucid account of these and related efforts at empirical testing, see Ronald Bodkin, chap. 4, "Keynesian Econometric Concepts" in Sydney Weintraub, ed., *Modern Economic Thought* (Philadelphia: University of Pennsylvania Press, 1976).

[22] R. F. Kahn, "The Relation of Home Investment to Unemployment," *Economic Journal,* vol. 41 (June 1931).

issues during the Great Depression of the 30s, when there was considerable interest in proposals to stimulate economic activity by the introduction of "scrip" money. Thus the theory of the multiplier made a very timely appearance.

Keynes reasoned that an increment of investment can initiate an expansionary process because it increases income and also consumption expenditures (unless the marginal propensity to consume is zero). This, in turn, eventually increases the demands for the factors of production and their incomes. Since a zero marginal propensity to consume is most unlikely, Keynes thought that an increment of investment would be certain to raise the income level by more than its own amount. Precisely how great the leverage will be depends on the marginal propensity to save. Any portion of an increment of new investment which leaks away from the current expenditure stream cannot generate additional new income.

For example, if one third of a new investment of $100,000 is saved rather than spent to finance new consumption, only $66,666.66 generates new income in the next period. If the propensity to save is such that one third of this amount is also drained into cash balances in the next period, national income will increase by an additional $44,444.44. Each successive round of expenditures will add an additional amount to national income. Given a marginal propensity to save of 0.33 (i.e., a marginal propensity to consume of two-thirds) a new investment of $100,000 will eventually, other things being equal, raise national income by three times the original amount, or $300,000. The multiplier, which is the reciprocal of the marginal propensity to save is equal to 3 when the marginal propensity to save is 0.33. Since the value of the marginal propensity to consume is somewhere in the range of zero to 100 percent, the value of the multiplier will be between 1 and infinity. The operational significance of the multiplier is that, other things being equal, it indicates the expansion in national income which may be expected from any income creating expenditure in consequence of its effect on consumption.[23]

---

[23] The multiplier may be derived as follows:

$$M = \frac{\Delta Y}{\Delta I} = \frac{\Delta Y}{\Delta S} = \frac{1}{\frac{\Delta S}{\Delta Y}} \tag{1}$$

$$\Delta Y = \Delta C + \Delta S \tag{2}$$

$$\frac{\Delta Y}{\Delta Y} = \frac{\Delta C}{\Delta Y} + \frac{\Delta S}{\Delta Y} - 1 \tag{3a}$$

$$\frac{\Delta S}{\Delta Y} = 1 - \frac{\Delta C}{\Delta Y} \tag{3b}$$

$$\therefore M = \frac{1}{1 - \frac{\Delta C}{\Delta Y}} \tag{4}$$

The increase in income associated with the operation of the multiplier principle can obviously only take place with a time lag. Yet Keynes chose not to emphasize the dynamic aspects of the multiplier and worked within a framework of a static conception of the multiplier. Thus the new equilibrium income level is conceived as occurring without time lag and is determined by the increment of new investment times a multiplier derived from some "normal" marginal propensity to consume.

Investment Expenditures: The Role of Expectations

Since increases in consumption expenditures are, in general, dependent on prior increases in income, Keynes emphasized the *volume of investment* as the crucial economic magnitude. In so doing he followed in the tradition of business-cycle theorists who pointed to investment as the key variable in the economy. Keynes's central question was: What determines the willingness of entrepreneurs to purchase new capital goods? The answer to this question depends on the relationship among three elements: the cost of the capital goods, the expected dollar yield, and the market rate of interest.

The inducement to invest in a capital asset will be strong if the prospective yield a purchaser expects it to produce compares favorably with its supply price. The prospective yield of a capital good is a series of annuities, $Q_1, Q_2, \ldots Q_n$, which are expected after deducting expenses, from the revenue the sale of its output is expected to yield. Its supply price is its replacement cost, "the price which would just induce a manufacturer newly to produce an additional unit of such assets." Thus the marginal efficiency of a particular type of capital is the relationship between the prospective net income from one more unit of that type of capital and the cost of producing it. More specifically, Keynes defines the marginal efficiency of capital as "the rate of discount which will make the present value of the series of annuities given by the returns expected from the capital asset during its life just equal to its supply price."[24] If C_r represents the replacement cost of a particular type of asset which is expected to yield returns over n years, the marginal efficiency of capital can be calculated by solving for r in the equation

$$C_r = \frac{Q_1}{(1 + r)} + \frac{Q_2}{(1 + r)^2} + \ldots \frac{Q_n}{(1 + r)^n}$$

Each successive return in the series will be received by the prospective purchaser only after the time between the beginning of the production process and the final sale of the product elapses. Returns must, therefore, be discounted over a period of time; the marginal efficiency of capital is

---

[24] *The General Theory*, p. 135.

the internal rate of return which equates the expected income stream and the supply price of the asset.[25]

It is important to note that while the marginal efficiency of capital is a rate, it is not the same thing as the rate of interest on money.[26] It is the relationship between r, the marginal efficiency of capital, and i, the rate of interest at which money can be borrowed, which determines whether a particular investment will be made or not. An investment will be made if $r>i$; the inducement to invest comes to an end when $r=i$, as it eventually will, because of the tendency for the marginal efficiency of capital to fall.

The value of a capital asset, once it has been produced (apart from its value as scrap), reflects its ability to yield capital income. Capital income is dependent on the *scarcity* rather than on the productivity of capital assets.[27] Thus Keynes lays much stress on the role of expectations in governing the investment-demand schedule. Expectations concerning the ability of a particular asset to continue yielding the same net return are revised downward as the physical quantity of a particular capital asset increases because the price at which output can be sold will diminish. Then, too, a capital good which has a long service life may eventually have to compete with equipment whose costs are less per unit of product, or which can be satisfied with a lower rate of return because the money rate of interest may then be lower. Thus, anticipations play a major role in determining the inducement to invest. It is not only the expected current yield of an asset which a prospective purchaser of new capital will take into account, but also the *future* yield, which is surrounded by an even greater degree of uncertainty and risk. The effect these factors have on the state of long-term expectations is vividly described in chapter 12 of *The General Theory*, which observes that the ability of entrepreneurs to estimate prospective yields is especially precarious because they are usually influenced by the expectations of those who deal in the stock market, no less than they are guided by the expectations of entrepreneurs themselves.[28]

A change in expectations will make itself fully felt on the level of employment only over a period of time. Thus Keynes speaks of "long period employment," which corresponds to a state of expectations which has prevailed for a sufficient length of time for its effect on employment to have worked itself out completely. The state of expectations is subject to con-

---

[25] Keynes himself pointed out that his marginal efficiency of capital is the same concept as Irving Fisher's "rate of return over cost" (ibid., p. 140).

[26] *The General Theory*, p. 165.

[27] Ibid., p. 213.

[28] Keynes regarded the relationship between the stock market and investment decisions as one of the least desirable features of laissez-faire capitalism. He remarks, "when the capital development of a country becomes the by-product of the activities of a casino, the job is likely to be ill-done." *The General Theory*, p. 159.

stant change; new expectations crystallize even before previous changes have fully worked themselves out. "The actually realized results of the production and sale of output will only be relevant to employment insofar as they cause a modification of subsequent expectations."[29] The latter "may change so frequently that the actual level of employment" will not coincide with the equilibrium level. This is, clearly, a *disequilibrium theory of employment and output*. Keynes is viewing changes in expectations and unrealized expectations as generating a response process in which employment and output become adjusted. These adjustments are not, however, perceived as necessarily producing equilibrium values of employment and output.

KEYNES'S MONETARY THEORY

The Money Supply: Its Origin in the Finance Process

Keynes's monetary theory—that is his conception of the origin of the money supply, the demand for it and the structure of interest rates—is the logical counterpart of his view of the relationship between the pricing of capital assets and the flow of investment output. Money "comes into existence along with debts, which are contracts for deferred payment. . . ."[30] The prospect of financial gain induces foreign and domestic business firms (and individuals) to enter into debt contracts. A considerable part of this financing takes place through the banking system, which interposes its guarantee between its depositors who lend it money and its borrowing customers to whom it loans money to finance the purchase of real assets.[31] Government may also initiate the demand process, which generates an endogenous increase in the money supply. Thus, Keynes's perception of a modern capitalistic economy characterized by a sophisticated banking system, which functions on the basis of fractional reserves, conceives of the money supply as originating in the finance process. The money supply will increase as long as investors perceive the marginal efficiency of capital (relative to the interest rate) as favoring the purchase of new capital goods and banks are willing to make debt contracts available to them. The effect of a change in the money supply is *on the level of interest rates rather than on the level of prices*. In contrast with Keynes the latter impact was envisioned by traditional theorists who held to the quantity theory of money.

---

[29] Ibid., p. 47.

[30] *Treatise on Money* (London: Macmillan, 1930), vol. 1, p. 3.

[31] J. M. Keynes, *"Essays in Persuasion,"* Collected *Writing of John Maynard Keynes* (London and New York: Macmillan and Co., St. Martin's Press for the Royal Economic Society, 1972), vol. 9, p. 151.

Liquidity Preference: The Demand for Money

Uncertainty regarding the future affects not only the marginal efficiency of capital and investment but also our willingness to part with our cash resources. To hold cash, says Keynes, "lulls our disquietude," and the rate of interest we demand for parting with liquid assets in exchange for earning assets measures the "degree of our disquietude." He therefore regarded interest as compensation for illiquidity and the determination of its rate as a monetary phenomenon arising out of the store-of-value function of money.[32]

Keynes's emphasis on the desire to hold money as a store of wealth represents a sharp break with his predecessors, who assumed that the only demand for money is for transactions purposes. Keynes maintains that money is demanded to satisfy three motives: the transactions motive, the precautionary motive, and the speculative motive. The amount of cash needed to carry on personal and business transactions and the additional amount desired to meet possible future contingencies varies directly with the economy's level of output. Since expenditures normally increase as business activity expands, the transactions-demand for money increases with national output and income. The precautionary demand for money also increases as the volume of business activity expands and is therefore functionally related to output. The amount of cash wanted for transactions and precautionary reasons is generally interest inelastic, though conceivably there may be some motivation for economizing the cash balances held for these purposes if interest rates become very high. The aggregate demand for money to satisfy the speculative motive, however, usually shows a continuous response to gradual changes in the rate of interest; i.e., there is a continuous curve relating changes in the demand for money to satisfy the speculative motive and changes in the rate of interest reflected in changes in the prices of bonds and debts of different maturities.[33]

Keynes's explanation of the demand for money as a store of value under uncertainty is easily understood in terms of the behavior of bond yields. Where there is an organized market, even though they are not exchange mediums, fixed-income bonds are not greatly inferior to money itself as highly liquid assets. Their disadvantage, however, is the risk of price change, which correspondingly alters their yield. If the market price of a bond rises, the ratio of its fixed dollar income to the bond price falls. Its yield, which is the income to be earned by illiquidity, is therefore falling. Low interest rates and bond yields may be less attractive to a wealth holder than cash itself, even though the latter earns no income at all. This is so

---

[32] *The General Theory*, pp. 166–72. See also John Maynard Keynes, "The General Theory," *Quarterly Journal of Economics*, vol. 51 (February 1937); also reprinted in Harris, *The New Economics*.

[33] *The General Theory*, p. 197.

FIGURE 17–4

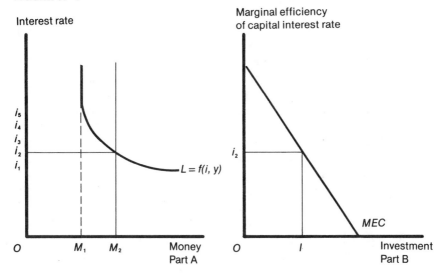

because when bonds are bought at a relatively high price (low yield), a subsequent small drop in price may be sufficient to wipe out the income earned from illiquidity. Cash is then a relatively more attractive asset than a bond. Thus the preference for liquidity for speculative purposes is virtually unlimited if the market is convinced that bond prices cannot rise further.

The relationship between interest rates and the demand for money is shown graphically by the L curve in Part A of Figure 17–4. Since some cash balances will be required at every income level irrespective of the interest rate, the segment of the curve representing the sum of the transactions and precautionary demands is shown as interest-inelastic at rates above i_4. The speculative demand for cash, however, is sensitive to small changes in the interest rate and approaches perfect elasticity when the rate is very low, e.g., at a level corresponding to i_1 in Part A of Figure 17–4. Thus the total demand for money, as represented by the L curve, is the sum of the transactions, precautionary, and speculative demands and is a function of the income level and the rate of interest. According to Keynes's liquidity preference theory, the interest rate is a monetary phenomenon which results from the interaction of the total demand for money and its supply. The supply of money depends primarily on the actions of the monetary authority and the commercial banks in response to the demand of individuals, businesses, and government. Thus, if the money supply is OM_2, as in Part A of Figure 17–4, the interest rate is i_2; OM_1 is the proportion of the money supply held for transactions and precautionary purposes, while M_1M_2 satisfies the speculative motive.

Part A of Figure 17–4 makes it apparent that in Keynes's analysis the interest rate equates the demand for and the supply of *money*. It does not, *as in the neoclassical analysis,* equate savings and investment.[34] Rather, it is the interest rate which, together with the marginal efficiency of capital, determines the level of investment, as shown in Part B of Figure 17–4.

The schedule of the marginal efficiency of capital is the schedule relating the demand for new capital goods to the expected rate of return. For simplicity, the curve has been assumed to be linear (although it is not possible, a priori, to know what its shape is). Its slope is necessarily negative because the net income stream which can be expected from additional units of a given capital good is certain to fall and its supply price is likely to increase. As long as the expected return from investment is higher than the rate of interest, it will be profitable to invest. Thus, when the interest rate is at i_2 and the investment-demand curve is as given in Part B of Figure 17–4, the volume of investment will be *OI*.

The central bank is generally capable of exerting pressure on interest rates because, under most circumstances, it is possible to buy or sell bonds by bidding their prices (and therefore interest rates) up or down, thereby inducing the public to hold either more or less cash. There is, however, a floor below which the interest rate is not likely to fall even when the monetary authority is seeking a policy of extreme monetary ease. Liquidity preference may become "virtually absolute in the sense that almost everybody prefers cash to holding a debt which yields so low a rate of interest" that the earnings from illiquidity do not offset the risk of loss on capital account.[35] It is evident from Part A of Figure 17–4 that an enlarged money supply could not reduce the rate of interest below i_1. The additional stock would be absorbed into hoards. This "liquidity trap" presents the main impediment to the effective use of monetary policy as an antidepression device. From an analytical point of view, it is the basis for Keynes's rejection of Say's identity.

It is evident that in Keynes's analysis, money is far from being the passive medium of exchange and unit of account that classical and neoclassical thinkers assumed it to be. It is, rather, an active determinant of

---

[34] Savings and investment are nevertheless equal in Keynes's system. There are two aspects to this equality. The first is definitional: Savings and investment are both defined as being equal to the unconsumed portion of current output. The second is an equilibrium relationship. Any change in investment causes a change in the income level and, given the propensity to consume, on the level of savings, so that when the adjustment process is complete, savings equal investment at the equilibrium-income level. Since the equality of savings and investment is an *ex post* phenomenon, many people prefer to define savings and investment in terms which recognize specifically *ex ante* (i.e., planned as opposed to realized) inequalities between them. The lengthy and not particularly fruitful controversy which developed concerning the relative merits of various savings-investment formulations is admirably reviewed by Lutz, *Readings.*

[35] *The General Theory,* p. 207.

the level of income, output, and employment because its relationship to the marginal efficiency of capital determines the worthwhileness of investment. Given the schedule of the marginal efficiency of capital, it is the rate of interest which determines the volume of real investment. Given the quantity of money as decided by the monetary authority, and given the level of output, wealth owners determine whether they will profit most from holding money or from holding other types of assets. The relative advantage of each alternative will be equal at the margin because wealth holders will shift from one alternative to another whenever one appears to offer a superior opportunity for gain. Thus the state of expectations, the preference for liquidity, the rate of interest, and the prospective yield on capital assets are all interrelated.[36]

The Relationship between Value Theory and Monetary Theory

Keynes lamented what he called the "false division" between the theory of value and distribution on the one hand and the theory of the general level of prices on the other. This dichotomy, already evident in the crudest statements of the quantity theory dating back to the preclassical economists, was perpetuated even in the refined presentations of Marshall and Fisher. Money was regarded as determining only the absolute level of prices, whereas relative prices were thought of as being determined by a set of equations which were independent of the absolute level of prices. One of Keynes's objectives was "to bring the theory of prices as a whole back to close contact with the theory of value."[37] He conceived of his theory of employment and output as providing the necessary link. In pursuit of his objective, Keynes makes some brief observations about the particular prices prevailing in single industries and then proceeds to "industry as a whole" and the general price level. He reminds us that particular prices reflect marginal costs, which depend partly on the industry's scale of operations and partly on the prices it has to pay for the factors it hires. He, therefore, reasons that as we pass to industry as a whole, it will be found that the general price level also depends partly on the factor prices which enter into marginal cost and partly on the scale of output as a whole, i.e., on the volume of aggregate affective demand and employment. Thus, the effect of a change in the quantity of money reflects the effect it has on these magnitudes.

Keynes thought a change in the quantity of money would affect the level of aggregate demand most readily through its influence on the interest rate and, through it, on investment.[38] He reasoned that as long as there is

---

[36] These interrelationships are examined by Keynes much more precisely in "The General Theory," *Quarterly Journal of Economics,* vol. 51 (February 1937) than in *The General Theory* itself.

[37] *The General Theory,* p. 29.

[38] Ibid., p. 298. See also above, p. 407.

unemployment, an increase in the quantity of money would spend itself partly in increasing the volume of employment and partly in raising the level of wages and prices. Keynes thus rejected the classical conclusion that relative prices and the rate of interest are independent of the quantity of money. Money, according to Keynes, is only "neutral," i.e., without impact on the real magnitudes of the economy in two special cases: one is full employment; the other is in the case of a "liquidity trap." In all other situations money is not neutral because, in the highly uncertain world in which we live, it provides the major link between the present and the future. Money is, as has already been noted in our discussion of the liquidity-preference theory of interest, an asset which may be held as an alternative to the income yielding assets. The demand for it is governed by changing expectations in an uncertain world. Changes in the quantity of money affect the rate of interest and, through it, the level of income, output, and employment. Thus, Keynes's focus on money and its relationship to the rate of interest is an integral part of his inquiry into the problem of disequilibrium in a dynamic, uncertain economy.

The Dynamic Aspects of Keynes's Analysis

It will be recalled that Keynes's model, relating as it did to the short run, assumed the stock of capital to be a constant magnitude. His concern with the investment process concentrated on its income (and employment) creating effect. It did not consider the capital-creating effect of investment. Will additions to the capital stock be utilized in production, or will they simply pose the problem of excess capacity?

Roy F. Harrod's "Essay in Dynamic Theory" emphasized that investment which results in a net addition to the stock of capital makes it necessary for the economy to grow or confront the problem of unemployed capital resources. Accordingly, he outlined a dynamic theory based on the marriage of the acceleration principle and the multiplier.[39] Whereas a static approach like Keynes's concerns itself with an instantaneous or timeless examination of economic variables, a dynamic analysis is concerned with their *rate of change*. The essential characteristic of a dynamic process (or system) is that it is self-generating over time, much like a servomechanism. Its motion through time is the result of its "built-in" response to an initial internal condition or its response to changing external conditions.[40]

The pattern which a particular process will generate over successive

---

[39] A multiplier-accelerator model envisions a sequence of the behavior of income over time which is constructed on the basis of the values of the multiplier ($1/\Delta S/\Delta Y$) and the acceleration coefficient $\Delta K/\Delta Y$.

[40] See Paul A. Samuelson, "Dynamic Process Analysis," in Howard Ellis, ed., *A Survey of Contemporary Economics*, vol. 1 (Philadelphia: Blakiston Co., 1949).

periods depends on the numerical value of its determining variables. If this value is a positive number greater than one, the process is one which increases at a geometric rate. The compound-interest problem is a classic economic illustration of the operation of this type of process. The value of a principal invested at a certain rate of interest increases at a geometric rate. Its value at the end of t period is determined according to the formula

$$X_{(t)} = (1 + r)^t X_0$$

where X_0 is the principal initially invested and r is the interest rate. This formula may be rewritten in a simpler form as

$$X_{(t)} = X_0 a^t$$

where $a = (1 + r)$. Any dynamic process which is characterized by growth, whether or not it is in the realm of economics, will behave according to the same principle as a sum of money invested at compound interest. That is, $X_{(t)}$ will increase exponentially as i increases and will, when shown graphically, result in a curve which is sloping upward at an increasing rate.

If the product of an initial magnitude, X_0, and the exponential value of the variables which determine its value in time, t, is a positive number greater than one, the process is one of growth. If, for example, $X_0 = 3$ and $a = 2$ the numerical values of the process are 3, 6, 12, 24, 48, . . . for $t = 0, 1, 2, 3, 4$, which produce the upward sloping curve associated with the growth process.[41]

It was not, however, until the post-World War II period that interest in the problem of growth really gained momentum. Harrod himself made an important contribution to its revitalization. But there is a related development which deserves mention, though it is not specifically related to Keynes's disequilibrium economics. This development, which is examined next, is Evsey Domar's formulation of an equation to express the rate of growth of national product which is required if excess capacity is not to develop.[42]

---

[41] If the value of a is equal to one, the process is self-sustaining without either growth or decay. If its value is a fraction less than one, e.g., ½, ⅓, ¼, the process is one of decay over time. That is, a magnitude whose value is determined by a fraction which is continuously raised to higher powers becomes progressively smaller and approaches zero.

A negative value will create still another pattern, namely, one of oscillation rather than steady exponential growth or decline. If, for example, $X_0 = 50$ and $a = -2$, an explosively oscillating pattern will be generated whose sequence is $+ 50 - 100 + 200 - 400 + 800$. . . . Or if a is a negative fraction which is less than one, the result is an oscillation which is dying out or becoming damped.

[42] Evsey Domar, "Capital Expansion, Rate of Growth and Employment," *Essays in the Theory of Economic Growth* (New York: Oxford University Press, 1957).

Domar's Growth Equation

Domar reasoned that the necessary growth rate of income required in order fully to employ a growing capital stock depends on the long-run savings function and the productivity of the additional increments of capital which result from net investment. The larger the volume of investment and the more each additional dollar of investment adds to productive capacity, the greater the rate at which income and investment will have to increase in order to give full employment to the growing capital stock. Specifically, the required rate of growth is the product of the marginal propensity to save, or the saving ratio, and the productivity ratio. Therefore, with a constant marginal propensity to save and a given productivity ratio, and full employment in year t, in order that full employment continue to obtain in year $t + 1$, investment and income will have to grow at an exponential or compound interest rate. That is, they will have to grow at a rate which is the product of the productivity ratio and the savings ratio. Domar's growth equation is, therefore,

$$\frac{\Delta I}{I} = os$$

where o is the productivity ratio and s is the savings ratio.[43]

To use Domar's own simple numerical example: If income per year is $150 billion and the marginal propensity to save, s, is 12 percent, in order that full employment be maintained, an amount of $150 (12/100) billion

---

[43] The productivity ratio is customarily designated by the symbol o. It is the reciprocal of the marginal value of the capital-output ratio $\Delta K/\Delta Y$, where K is the net increase in capital stock resulting from investment. Domar's formula can be derived in the following way:

$$o = \frac{\Delta Y}{\Delta K}$$

$$s = \frac{\Delta S}{\Delta Y}$$

$$M \text{ (the multiplier)} = \frac{1}{s}$$

Equate aggregate supply and aggregate demand by:

$$M \Delta I = I \cdot o$$

$$\frac{\Delta I}{s} = I \cdot o$$

Transposing:

$$\frac{\Delta I}{I} = s \cdot o$$

must be invested.[44] This will increase productive capacity by the amount invested multiplied by the productivity ratio, *o*. If *o* is 25 percent, the productive capacity of the economy will rise by the amount invested, *s*, times *o*, i.e., by

$$\$150 \left(\frac{12}{100}\right)\left(\frac{25}{100}\right) = \$4.5 \text{ billion.}$$

National income will therefore have to rise by the same annual amount. That is, its relative rise will have to equal the absolute increase in investment divided by the income itself, or

$$\frac{150\left(\frac{12}{100}\right)\left(\frac{25}{100}\right)}{150} = 3 \text{ percent,}$$

which is the value of *os*.

The significance of $\Delta I / I = os$ is that it is not sufficient, in Keynesian terms, for yesterday's savings to be invested today. Investment today must always exceed the savings of yesterday; the economy must continuously expand at a constant annual percentage (or compound interest) rate equal to the product of the marginal propensity to save and the average (to put it briefly) productivity of investment. If investment and income do not grow at the required rate, unused capacity will develop, and both capital and labor will be idle. It therefore becomes apparent that investment, by increasing productive capacity, can cause labor to be unemployed. The productivity effect of investment implies that investment, or the lack of it, presents a *twofold* problem: If investment is insufficient today relative to savings, there will be unemployment, but if enough is invested today, still more will have to be invested tomorrow in order to maintain full employment. This is the essence of the growth problem.

It should be obvious that the very existence of the growth problem derives from the stability of the savings function and the capital coefficient. If a reduction in investment tended automatically to be offset by an increase in consumption, the problem of maintaining the necessary rate of growth to give full employment to a growing capital stock would not exist. Similarly, if investment were accompanied by technological changes associated with the deepening of capital, productive capacity would grow less rapidly than if the capital coefficient remained constant or reflected technological changes of a capital-saving variety. Steady growth requires that the relationship between the savings and capital ratios be such that there will be continuous full employment of an accumulating stock of capital.

---

[44] Evsey Domar, "Expansion and Employment," *American Economic Review*, (March 1947), pp. 34–55. Republished in his *Essays in the Theory of Economic Growth*, pp. 83–108. Example appears on p. 92.

This condition is automatically assured when a constant proportion of income is added to capital every year and capital bears a constant ratio to income, for income will then expand continuously at a constant proportional rate.[45] Domar has the distinction of having formulated this principle in specific terms and of recognizing productive capacity as a key element in the growth problem, even though he was anticipated in its perception by Harrod.

While Domar's growth equation identifies the rate of growth of income and investment which is necessary fully to utilize the growing capital stock of an economy in which the marginal propensity to consume is less than one, his formulation is not, of course, a *theory* of economic growth. It does not offer a hypothesis which purports to explain—as did, for example, Schumpeter's theory of innovation—what forces propel the economy along an upward path. Nor was he concerned with the ability of an equilibrium growth rate to perpetuate itself or the related question of divergences from the growth rate and their consequences. His treatment of the growth problem is simply a straightforward application of the principle that any magnitude which is increasing over time must continue to increase exponentially, or it will either level off or decline. But it nevertheless constitutes a major step forward as far as dynamic economic theory is concerned, for the growth equation is an analytical tool which is fundamental to all contemporary theorizing on the problem of economic growth and fluctuation.

HARROD'S DYNAMIC ECONOMICS

Roy F. Harrod's "Essay in Dynamic Thory" reveals that as early as 1939, he fully appreciated the importance of making Keynes's employment theory dynamic. Accordingly, he outlined a dynamic theory based upon the marriage of the acceleration principle and the multiplier. The coefficients are assumed to operate without a time lag, thus producing a model in which income will grow geometrically. By proceeding in this manner, he specifically rejected the approach initiated by Tinbergen, which seeks to construct a dynamic theory by introducing time lags between certain adjustments. Harrod proceeded as he did on the ground that while the introduction of a lag will produce a model whose pattern is one of oscillation, "there is some doubt as to the nature of the trend on which the oscillation is superimposed."[46] Moreover, he thought it possible that the trend of

---

[45] Joan Robinson has spelled out the assumptions on which the models of continuously expanding economies are generally based. See "The Model of an Expanding Economy," *Economic Journal,* vol. 62 (March 1952); reprinted in Joan Robinson, *Collected Economic Papers,* vol. II (Oxford: Basil Blackwell, 1960), p. 74.

[46] Harrod, "An Essay in Dynamic Theory," *Economic Journal,* vol. 49 (March 1939), p. 14.

growth may *itself* generate forces making for oscillation. His objective was the formulation of a hypothesis to explain why this may be the case.

Quite apart from the merits of Harrod's approach, the case he presented in 1939 for a dynamic economics in the "Essay" was most eloquent. He observed that "once the mind is accustomed to thinking in terms of trends of increase, the old static formulation of problems seems stale, flat and unprofitable." As things turned out, however, it was not until the postwar period that interest in the problem of growth and fluctuation really gained momentum. Harrod himself revitalized matters by offering a volume of five readings entitled *Towards a Dynamic Economics* in 1948. Essentially, this volume fleshes out the theory presented in skeleton form ten years earlier. It attempts to explain not only the circumstances under which a steady rate of growth will be perpetuated, but also how an economy might fail to realize its potential and experience depression or be exploded into a too rapid expansion in which inflationary pressures are created. Harrod's theory is therefore a theory of short-run fluctuation quite as much as it is a theory of long-term growth.

Harrod's Warranted Rate of Growth and Its Perpetuation

The most important concept in Harrod's analysis is the "warranted rate of growth." It is defined as "that rate of growth which, if it occurs will leave all parties satisfied that they have produced neither more nor less than the right amount. Or, to state the matter otherwise, it will put them into a frame of mind which will cause them to give such orders as will maintain the same rate of growth."[47] The concept is also expressed symbolically as $G_w = s/v$, where G_w is the warranted growth rate, or $\Delta Y/Y$; s is the long-run constant average and marginal savings ratio; and $v = \Delta K/\Delta Y$ the *desired* ratio between an increment of induced investment and new output (income). This formulation reveals that Harrod's theory of growth is essentially a capital stock adjustment theory, i.e., the growth process is viewed as one which manifests itself in additions to capital stock which in turn increase income. Its Keynesian origins are plainly in evidence; paralleling the equilibrium requirement that desired savings must equal desired investment in the static Keynesian model, so in Harrod's growth form of the model the equilibrium requirement is that the desired ratio be maintained between the capital stock and the rate of output. If, now, the propensity to save is given, and the relationship between capital and output is a technological constant, it follows that the capacity to produce output will grow at a constant percentage rate determined by the productivity of additions to capital stock and the proportion of the increase

---

47 Ibid., p. 16.

in output devoted to the creation of new capital. It is plain, therefore, that Harrod's G_w, like Domar's *os,* is an exponential growth rate. Harrod has given us, in addition, however, a hypothesis concerning the origin of the forces which propel the economy along its steady upward path of growth and of the manner in which divergences may take place from the equilibrium path. This hypothesis is essentially a theory of entrepreneurial investment behavior in which the key role is played by the effect of expectations and hence desires on induced investment.

Harrod, like many other business-cycle theorists, reasons that the psychology of human behavior is such that in the absence of evidence to the contrary the business community expects that economic conditions in the foreseeable future will generally be similar to those of the immediate past. The behavior of businessmen is predicated on the assumption that they can safely project current economic events into the future. Thus, Harrod's conception of the warranted rate of growth implies that the rate of growth of income in period t will be followed by an equal rate of growth in period $t + 1$, i.e., $G_t = G_{t+1}$. This is the case because the anticipations of period G_t were in fact realized, so that business firms, projecting satisfactory output and investment decisions into the following period, expect a similar rate of growth in the following period which, in turn, tends to perpetuate itself precisely because businessmen behave in such a way that expectations are realized.

It is worth noting that Harrod's theory envisions businessmen as repeating in period $t + 1$ not the *amount* of output and capital outlays of period t, but their rate of growth. This is essential to the whole concept of the warranted rate of growth, for the latter is the growth rate which insures the full utilization of the productive capacity represented by the new capital stock of the period.

In addition to the warranted growth rate, there is another growth rate which Harrod identifies as "the natural growth rate," or G_n. When the economy is growing at its natural rate, the ratio of an increment of induced investment to output is the maximum consistent with the full employment of is resources and the rate of technological progress. Contrary to what one might expect, there is no inherent tendency for this rate to obtain. The warranted growth rate *may* coincide with the natural growth rate; the desired ratio of induced investment to new output. $\Delta K/\Delta Y$ is then equal to the actual ratio $\Delta K^*/\Delta Y^*$, and the warranted growth rate coincides with the natural growth rate. However, the warranted growth rate may diverge from the natural growth rate; these divergences are, according to Harrod's theory, the source of cyclical fluctuations.

If G_w exceeds G_n, the *desired* ratio of induced investment to new output, $\Delta K/\Delta Y$, will exceed $\Delta K^*/\Delta Y^*$, the actual ratio. The economy will experience a tendency toward stagnation because the growth rate of savings and investment, and thus the capital stock, is greater than that associated with the full employment of labor resources. Excess capacity will therefore appear and dampen business expectations. Investment will decline further, so that the actual growth rate will be still further below the warranted growth rate. Only more investment could have avoided this decline. Thus we are confronted with a seemingly paradoxical situation in which the only way the capacity resulting from some previous level of investment can be fully utilized is by investing even more. If $G_n > G_w$, the *actual* ratio, $\Delta K^*/\Delta Y^*$, will exceed $\Delta K/\Delta Y$, the desired ratio, and the economy will experience a state of secular exhilaration; actual investment is less than acceleration-induced planned investment. Existing capital stocks will be utilized intensively and provide high rates of return, so that there is a continuous stimulus to new investment. Harrod's warranted rate of growth is thus seen as being inherently unstable. Divergences from G_w are not associated with the development of corrective counterbalancing forces. On the contrary, any divergence from G_w leads to an even greater divergence.

The unstable character of Harrod's warranted rate of growth derives from the assumption that there is no lag between the receipt and the spending of income. The absence of an investment lag is evident in its formulation as $G_w = s/v$. With respect to the volume of induced investment, this means that changes in income are instanteously followed by investment outlays. Because the model does not assume an investment lag, induced investment is treated as a function of the current income of which it is itself a component. Thus, if income increases between period t and t_1 acceleration-induced investment will take place which increases income and induces still more investment, and thus income. The change thus perpetuates itself in the same period. Conversely, a reduction in income is instantaneously reflected in a self-perpetuating reduction of the income level. Harrod's system is, therefore, one which will either "explode" and produce an astronomically large income or else break down. It is thus a disequilibrium model which is entirely consistent with Keynes's own work which intended, first and foremost, to examine economic disequilibrium.

CONCLUDING COMMENTS

John Maynard Keynes wrote to George Bernard Shaw in 1935 that the book he was writing on economic theory would revolutionize the way the world thinks about economic problems. His prophecy has been amply fulfilled, for *The General Theory* has changed our conception of the essential nature of the economic problem. From the time of the classics, the economic problem had been thought of in terms of the unending struggle between scarcity and unlimited human wants. In the era of Malthus and Ricardo, this struggle was given expression in the controversy over the Corn Laws. When John Stuart Mill wrote, the Corn Laws were no longer at issue, but his vision of the stationary state was nevertheless premised on the solution of the scarcity problem via the intercession of human wisdom, especially as it relates to population growth. Marshall and the marginalists changed the focus of the problem to the level of the individual economic entity, e.g., the consumer, the employer, and the industry; but they did not change the conception of the problem as being inherently one of scarcity. Their concern was with the allocation of resources among alternative uses, and they therefore continued the classical conception of the economic problem as having itst origin in the scarcity of resources.

The awareness that the economic problem had another aspect, namely, "poverty in the midst of plenty," came to Keynes after World War I. But the general view that the economic problem is one of scarcity persisted into the depression. Only prolonged unemployment on a mass scale eventually made it apparent that scarcity is not the only dimension of the economic problem. The rational allocation of resources is the sole problem only when all resources seeking employment can be absorbed into the production process. Keynes argued that the level of employment depends on the level of aggregate demand and showed that even an economy with flexible wages, prices, and interest rates may not be restored automatically to full employment. A full-employment equilibrium is only one of many possible equilibria and the classical and neoclassical analysis is therefore a special rather than the general case.

Keynes's emphasis on the inability of the system to make automatic adjustments because of imbalances between consumption and production reminds us immediately of the Marxian analysis. Marx, too, emphasized the inherent instability of the capitalistic system and, like Keynes, found investment to be the crucial factor. Marx attributed the declining rate of profit to the inability of capitalists to realize surplus value from investment. This, in turn, meant that the ability to accumulate capital inhibited investment and therefore delayed revival. Keynes, on the other hand, saw the problem as being rooted not in impediments to accumulation, but in impediments to investment, which caused an insufficiency of aggregate demand.

But while both Marx and Keynes stressed factors affecting investment as the cause of breakdown, there are important differences between the two systems. One of these is that Marx's system is inseparable from his conception of the social relationships underlying commodity exchange and, consequently, the labor theory of value. The increasing exploitation of labor, coupled with the decreasing rate of profit and of surplus value, leads to increasingly severe breakdowns, which are the prelude to the destruction of the capitalistic system. For Keynes, the main factors causing breakdowns are derived from basic human propensities. He thus saw a basis for government intervention when aggregate demand is inadequate to create full employment. But he regarded the destruction of capitalism as being neither desirable nor inevitable. On the contrary, he felt that the essentials of the capitalistic system could be preserved without sacrificing full employment if government exercises the proper controls. Precisely what the nature of this intervention should be Keynes did not examine in detail. But the social philosophy which underlies the concluding chapter of *The General Theory* is that there are certain areas which should not be left to individual initiative. Keynes suggests that:

> The state will have to exercise a guiding influence on the propensity to consume, partly through its scheme of taxation, partly by fixing the rate of interest, and partly, perhaps, in other ways. Furthermore, it seems unlikely that the influence of banking policy on the rate of interest will be sufficient by itself to determine the optimum rate of investment. . . . [But it] is not the ownership of the instruments of production which it is important for the state to assume. If the state is able to determine the aggregate amount of resources devoted to augmenting the instruments and the basic rate of reward to those who own them, it will have accomplished all that is necessary.[48]

Thus, what Keynes proposed is essentially a mixed economy in which investment is socialized but in which private self-interest will continue to function in all areas in which it is compatible with full employment. He regarded this as "the only practicable means of avoiding the destruction of existing economic forms in their entirety and as the condition of the successful functioning of individual initiative."

It is apparent that to Keynes himself, the theory of aggregate effective demand was presented as an anchor for his policy recommendations to England during the 1930s. There is no question that *The General Theory* contributed in a significant way to the acceptance by government of the responsibility for maintaining the level of employment at satisfactory levels. Fiscal policy has come into its own since the time of *The General Theory*.[49] There is also no doubt that the popularity of *The General Theory* in the pre-World War II period derived in no small measure from the fact that it took a positive approach to the problems of its day.

This is not to say, however, that *The General Theory* cannot be divorced from the specific problems of the 1930s. The principle of aggregate effective demand, which is the core of Keynes's theory, is independent of this particular institutional setting and is neutral as far as policy is concerned. The introduction of the principle of aggregate effective demand in *The General Theory* marks a milestone in the history of economic analysis because it is the culmination of a number of earlier efforts to

---

[48] *The General Theory,* p. 378.

[49] What does seem strange, however, is that *The General Theory* has so frequently been interpreted as being a polemic against monetary policy. To anyone familiar with Keynes as a monetary theorist, the importance of monetary policy is implicit in *The General Theory.*

develop an alternative to the quantity-theory approach to aggregate demand. The difference between the quantity-theory approach and Keynes's approach is that the latter conceives of aggregate demand as the sum of consumption and investment expenditures rather than as the money stock times its velocity of circulation. The expenditure stream is separated in order to take account of the factors affecting these two independently determined magnitudes. The quantity-theory approach, by way of contrast, makes no analytical distinction between consumer demand and investment demand but simply assumes that income which is not used for consumer goods purchases will, because of a flexible interest rate, be used for capital goods purchases. The proportions in which consumer goods and capital goods are bought may become altered as their relative prices and utilities change, but all will find a market at some price. In short, the theory of aggregate demand implicit in the quantity theory is precisely the same as that which is implicit in Say's law. Thus, Keynes avoids the neoclassical conclusion that sales proceeds will necessarily cover the cost of producing the full-employment output because the money value of that output is associated with the creation of an equivalent money income.

The notion that money is demanded as an asset to offset the uncertainty of the future and the view that the supply of money is an exogenous variable that responds, via the lending activities of financial institutions to the "animal spirits" that determine investor behavior, are companion notions to the principle of aggregate demand. The investment expenditures of businessmen and the consumption expenditures of households are the chief components of aggregate demand in a closed economy. Finally, there is the view that aggregate demand and employment cannot be raised by a reduction in money wages. Money wages are, according to Keynes, chiefly the result of institutional forces. Workers cannot achieve downward revisions in their real wages by the simple expedient of accepting reduced money wages. If unemployment is accompanied by an asset demand for money, which is likely at very low rates of interest, there may be no mechanism by which an economy with unemployed resources can recover from an unemployment disequilibrium.

The years that followed the publication of *The General Theory* witnessed the emergence of a counterrevolution. Many of the ideas and analytical tools which Keynes initiated were challenged or reinterpreted in such a fundamental way that they lost much of their original intent. These developments are so crucial to understanding contemporary macroeconomics, that they deserve a separate chapter which follows.

GLOSSARY OF TERMS AND CONCEPTS

Aggregate effective demand.   The total demand for output based on consumption and investment expenditures.

Aggregate demand function. Relation of the proceeds employers expect from the sale of the output to different levels of employment on the basis of consumption and investment expenditures. Keynes represented this function as $D = f(N)$ where N is employment.

Aggregate supply schedule. Relation of the proceeds employers consider necessary to earn from the sale of the outputs produced at different levels of employment in order to make it profitable to provide each level (i.e., $Z = \phi(N)$).

Capital stock adjustment growth models. Dynamic models inspired by *The General Theory* (but not created by Keynes himself) in which the growth process is visualized as consisting of additions to capital stock, which in turn increase income and employment levels. Domar's growth equation, which specifies that $\dfrac{\Delta I}{I} = os,$ implies that the stock of capital (I) must increase at a rate which is the product of the savings ratio (s) and the productivity ratio (o) if excess capacity and unemployment are to be avoided.

Consumption function. Relates consumption expenditures to *real* income. This implies that consumers, unlike wage earners, are not subject to money illusion.

Keynes effect. The stimulative effect of a wage-price reduction on employment which operates if interest rates fall relative to the marginal efficiency of capital, in response to a reduced transactions demand for money at a lower income level.

Keynes's fundamental psychological law. Keynes suggested that "as a rule, and on the average, consumption will increase as income increases but not by as much as the increase in income." From this it follows that the marginal propensity to consume, that is, the rate at which consumption increases, given an increase in income, is less than proportionate. (i.e., $\dfrac{\Delta C}{\Delta Y} < 1$)

Liquidity trap. An accumulation of idle balances at very low rates of interest.

Marginal efficiency of capital. The rate of discount at which an expected series of earnings from a capital good is equal to its supply price.

Multiplier effect. The expansion in national income which may be expected from any income-creating expenditure in consequence of its effect on consumption. Mathematically it is equal to the reciprocal of the marginal propensity to save or

$$M = \frac{1}{1 - \dfrac{\Delta C}{\Delta Y}}.$$

Static versus dynamic analysis. A static approach concerns itself with an instantaneous or timeless examination of economic variables. A dynamic analysis is concerned with the rate of change in economic variables. The motion through time of a dynamic process results from its "built-in" response to an initial internal condition.

Steady state growth. The rate of growth at which the total output of the economy and its stock of capital grow together at a constant proportionate rate which reflects the rate of increase of the population and the rate of increase in output per man.

Warranted rate of growth. That rate of growth which maintains the same rate of growth as was previously achieved. This rate is to be distinguished from the *natural rate,* which is the maximum rate of growth consistent with the full employment of all resources and the rate of technological progress.

NOTES FOR FURTHER READING

There is no substitute for Keynes's *The General Theory of Employment, Interest and Money* (New York: Harcourt, Brace, 1936). It is difficult reading, as Keynes himself warns in the Preface, in which he addresses "my fellow economists," adding the hope "that it will be intelligible to others." For the most part, the hope appears to have been in vain. Nevertheless, moderately advanced readers can profitably read Book I, which comprises the first 34 pages and chapter 4 in Book II. Chapter 5, "Expectation as Determining Output and Employment" is nontechnical but deceptive in its simplicity. Keynes's article "The General Theory of Employment," *Quarterly Journal of Economics,* vol. 51 (February 1937), and Jacob Viner's "Mr. Keynes on the Causes of Unemployment," *Quarterly Journal of Economics,* vol. 51 (November 1936), provide some insight into the immediate controversy Keynes's *General Theory* stirred up. Viner's review of the *General Theory* identified Keynes's liquidity-preference functions as being, in essence, the same as the Cambridge k, which made velocity a function of the interest rate. Keynes's rebuttal to Viner emphatically rejected this interpretation.

Keynes's "Alternative Theories of the Rate of Interest," *Economic Journal,* vol. 47 (June 1937), pp. 241–52 and "The Theory of the Rate of Interest," *Readings in the Theory of Income Distribution,* vol. 3 (Philadelphia: Blakiston, 1946), pp. 418–24 virtually complete the bibliography of Keynes's writings about his theory of employment, before his untimely death.

Inquiry into the dynamic aspects of Keynes's theory properly begins with Roy F. Harrod's "An Essay in Dynamic Theory," *Economic Journal,* vol. 49 (March 1939). Evsey Domar completed *Essays in the Theory of Economic Growth* (London: Oxford University Press, 1957) shortly before the publication of Harrod's "Second Essay in Dynamic Theory," *Economic Journal,* vol. 70 (June 1960).

18

Keynesians, Monetarists, and the Reaffirmation of the Neoclassical Tradition

THE BODY OF IDEAS developed by Keynes himself, the "economics of Keynes," as distinct from "Keynesian Economics," which is the work of those who embellished, interpreted, and refined the original system, has passed into history.[1] The *Treatise on Money* and *The General Theory* have become classics and share the common fate of being known largely through secondary sources. The 40 years that have elapsed since the publication of *The General Theory* have witnessed a phenomenal amount of empirical and theoretical work built on Keynesian foundations. The main thrust of the empirical work has been to try to verify Keynes's theoretical constructs.[2] The most important of these early empirical findings concerned the consumption function. Subsequent important empirical findings resulted from the research of James S. Dusenberry, James Tobin, Milton Friedman, Arthur Smithies, and the well-known trio Franco Modigliani, Albert Ando, and Richard Brumberg who did much of their work together.[3]

Important work has also estimated the numerical value of the multiplier

---

[1] The distinction between "Keynesian Economics" and the "Economics of Keynes" was made by Axel Leijonhufvud in *On Economics and The Economics of Keynes* (New York: Oxford University Press, 1966).

[2] Keynes himself attempted some evaluation of his work against that done by Colen Clark for the United Kingdom and Simon Kuznets for the United States. See *The General Theory*, pp. 102–4.

[3] A particularly useful summary of this empirical work is in Ronald Bodkin, "Keynesian Econometric Concepts: Consumption Functions, Investment Functions, and "The Multiplier" in Sidney Weintraub, ed., *Modern Economic Thought* (Philadelphia; University of Pennsylvania Press, 1976), chap. 4.

and the responsiveness of investment demand to interest rates. Empirical research also attempted to establish the demand for money to test Keynes's concept of liquidity preference and its related "liquidity trap" hypothesis. More recently, macroeconomic models of the economy as a whole have been developed, the best known among them being the St. Louis Model of the Federal Reserve Bank of St. Louis and the larger Wharton Model of the University of Pennsylvania's Wharton School under the direction of Lawrence Klein.

While these efforts at empirical research have yielded important results, our interests are more specifically focused on developments in theoretical economics that came after *The General Theory*. Several are of particular interest because they reflect a counterrevolution against Keynes's economics, and a reaffirmation of the tradition that separates the economics of Keynes from many of the macroeconomic developments which followed. The "Keynesian Cross" and the ISLM (investment, savings, liquidity-preference, money) apparatus, which have become mainstays of contemporary macroeconomics even at the textbook level are products of the counterrevolution. In conjunction with the "real balance effect," the ISLM apparatus has been used to demonstrate the possibility of a general equilibrium among commodity, money, and labor markets. A major concern of this chapter is to explain these developments as reflecting a return to the neoclassical tradition Keynes rejected, despite the frequent observation that "we are all Keynesians now."

A second concern of this chapter is to examine the body of doctrine and policy prescriptions that have come to be known as Monetarism. The third is to examine the hypothesis that there is a trade-off between inflation and unemployment which is associated with an apparatus known as the Phillips curve. A final concern is the neoclassical view of the phenomenon of economic growth. The principal question in this connection is whether, as in the Harrod model examined at the end of the last chapter, the "animal spirits" of entrepreneurs cause the secular behavior of the economy to be inherently explosive and unstable. Neoclassical writers have developed alternative models in which this is not the case. They have developed models in which a mechanism is postulated which keeps the economy on a steady-state growth path. These neoclassical growth models, together with Keynesianism and Monetarism, represent the schools of thought associated with the counterrevolution against Keynes.

KEYNESIAN ECONOMICS

The "Keynesian Cross"

"Keynesian Economics," as distinct from the "Economics of Keynes," began its development almost before the ink of *The General Theory* was dry! In 1937, Professor John R. Hicks, Keynes's compatriot, undertook to reinterpret Keynes's message in terms of the neoclassical tradition, in his article, *"Mr. Keynes and the Classics, A Suggested Reinterpretation."*[4] Its impact was temporarily delayed by an interpretation of Keynes that became associated with the "Keynesian cross."

The essentials of the model from which the Keynesian cross is derived are usually represented in terms of five equations. The first two represent the "real," or commodity sectors of the economy. In the consumption function:

$$C = C(Y,r) \qquad (18\text{--}1)$$

C represents consumption expenditures, Y is real income and r represents the interest-rate structure. The investment relationship in which I is real investment is represented as:

$$I = I(r) \qquad (18\text{--}2)$$

The next two equations represent the money, or bond, market. The liquidity preference function in which L is the money demand function is written:

$$L = L(Y,r) \qquad (18\text{--}3)$$

The fourth equation

$$M = M^* \qquad (18\text{--}4)$$

represents the money supply created by the monetary authority and is assumed to be an exogenous constant.

The final equation

$$C + I = Y \qquad (18\text{--}5)$$

completes the system.

This system may be simplified by substituting equations (1) and (2) into (5) to derive a single equation with two unknowns

$$C(Y,r) + I(r) = Y$$

which can be equated with $M = L(Y,r)$, which expresses equality between the money supply and the demand for it. The model is thus determinate.

The system may also be represented geometrically as in Figure 18–1A, which shows real expenditures on the vertical axis and output on the horizontal axis. The aggregate-supply curve is given expression as a 45-degree line. This line represents the $C + I = Y$ output combinations compatible with the condition $C = Y$, $S = 0$. The consumption function is

---

[4] *Econometrica,* vol. 5 (1937), pp. 147–59. For a more extensive review of Keynesianism than is given here, see the various contributions to Sidney Weintraub's *Modern Economic Thought, part 1,* especially his own chap. 3, "Hicksian Keynesianism: Dominance and Decline."

FIGURE 18–1

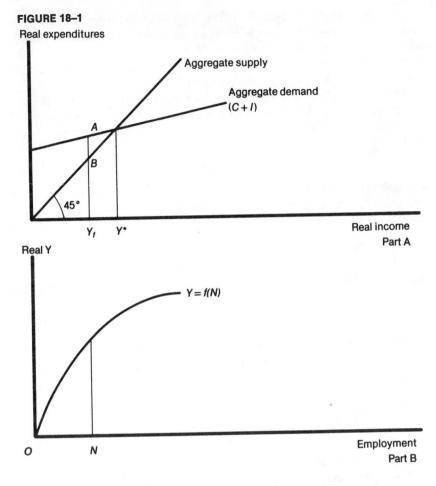

Part A

Part B

represented with a positive intercept, for at low-income levels saving is negative. The addition of (real) investment outlays results in the curve $C + I$, which represents expenditures on consumption and investment. Its intersection with the aggregate-supply curve determines the equilibrium level of output. Given the production function relating output to employment as in Part B of Figure 18–1, the level of employment N is determinate.

Paul Samuelson viewed the intersection of the aggregate demand and supply curves which comprise the "Keynesian cross" as having a significance on a par with the Marshallian cross of intersecting demand and supply curves because it provides a guide for fiscal policy.[5] If, as in Figure

---

[5] "The Simple Mathematics of Income Determination," *Income, Employment and Policy: Essays in Honor of Alvin H. Hansen* (New York: Norton and Co., 1948), p. 135.

18–1A, the full employment volume of output is represented as Y_f and the economy equilibrates at Y^*, there is an "inflationary gap" which is equivalent to AB. This excess of purchasing power has been interpreted as providing a rationale for higher tax collections and/or reduced government expenditures to lower the $C + I$ curve so that it intersects aggregate supply at Y_f.

Conversely, if $C + I$ were to intersect aggregate demand so that equilibrium output is to the *left* of Y_f and therefore smaller than that associated with full employment, a *deflationary* gap is deemed to exist. This situation came to be interpreted as being amenable to expansionary fiscal policy instruments such as reduced tax collections and greater government expenditures which would generate a multiplier and perhaps even an acceleration effect.[6]

The Hicks-Hansen ISLM Apparatus

Despite the attractive simplicity of the Keynesian cross model, it had a shortcoming that led to its eventual displacement by a new apparatus comprised of two composite curves, *IS* and *LM*. The logic of the *ISLM* apparatus will be most easily perceived in relation to Keynes's views of the neoclassical theory of the interest rate. As noted in the preceding chapter, Keynes maintained that neoclassical theory did not provide a determinate solution of the interest rate because the savings-supply schedule, which, together with the investment-demand schedule, is supposed to determine the rate, is itself dependent on the income level.[7] Yet the income level is not known until the volume of investment is known, and the latter itself depends on the interest rate. In other words, the interest rate is indeterminate because the savings-supply schedule and the investment-demand schedule are interdependent.

Hicks countered that Keynes's criticism of indeterminacy is equally applicable to his own theory of the interest rate. The liquidity-preference schedule and the supply schedule of money also do not yield a determinate rate of interest because there is a different liquidity-preference schedule for every level of income. Even though the schedule of liquidity preference for speculative purposes is independent of the level of income, it is necessary to know the income level in order to know what the transactions and precautionary demands for money will be. Thus, the criticism of indeterminancy of interest rate determination which Keynes leveled against the neoclassical theory was held to be equally applicable to his own.

---

[6] Paul A. Samuelson, "Interactions between the Multiplier Analysis and the Principle of Acceleration," *Review of Economics and Statistics*, vol. 21, no. 2 (May 1939). In *Crisis in Keynesian Economics*, J. R. Hicks observed that "Keynesianism became fiscalism because interest-rate reductions came to be viewed as unreliable for expanding investment expenditures," p. 33.

[7] See above, pp. 398–99.

FIGURE 18–2

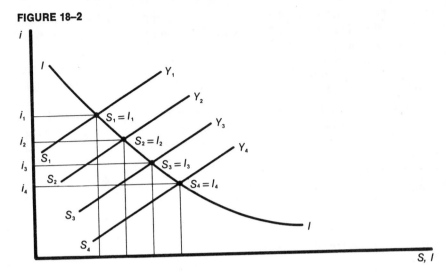

Hicks' "Suggested Reinterpretation" demonstrated that Keynes's theory and the neoclassical theory can together provide a determinate solution because they include all of the variables of the interest-rate problem.[8] These variables are (1) the savings function, (2) the investment-demand function, (3) the liquidity-preference function, and (4) the quantity of money. They have been combined to construct two new curves, the *IS* curve and *LM* curve.

The *IS* curve is derived from the relationship between the investment-demand schedule and a family of curves showing savings as a function of both income and the interest rate. Figure 18–2 shows a different savings schedule for every possible combination of interest rate and income level. Thus, when income is Y_1, the savings schedule is S_1Y_1, and, given the investment demand curve, savings will equal investment at interest rate i_1. Similarly, when income is Y_2, savings will equal investment at i_2. The locus of all the points at which saving and investment are equal yields what Hansen and Hicks have called the *IS* schedule. As shown in Figure 18–3, the *IS* function expresses interest as a function of three variables: savings, investment, and the income level. It is the *IS* function which, together with a curve which has become known as the *LM* function, determines the rate of interest.

The *LM* curve is derived from the relationship between a family of liquidity-preference curves and the schedule of the money supply. There is a different liquidity-preference schedule at every income level; hence the family of curves L_1Y_1, L_2Y_2, L_3Y_3, L_4Y_4, as shown in Figure 18–4. These

---

[8] Alvin Hansen also provides a demonstration in *A Guide to Keynes*, chap. 7.

FIGURE 18–3

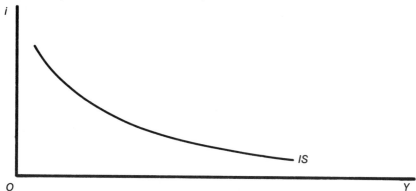

curves, together with *M,* the money supply made available by the monetary authority, show the various combinations of income levels and interest rates which are consistent with the willingness of the public to hold the money supply in its balances. Thus, if the income level is Y_1, the demand for money will be equal to the supply at interest rate i_1. But the same money supply will be held at a higher rate of interest if the income level is higher. Therefore, it is impossible to determine what the interest rate will be solely from the relationship between the family of liquidity-preference curves and the schedule of the money supply. It is possible to establish that at each level of income the given quantity of money will be held at a different rate of interest. That is, there is a different rate of interest which is compatible with the condition $L = M$ at every income level. Thus, in Figure 18–4, $L = M$ at an interest rate of i_1 when income is Y_1; $L = M$ at an interest rate of i_2, when income is Y_2; and so forth. Together with the

FIGURE 18–4

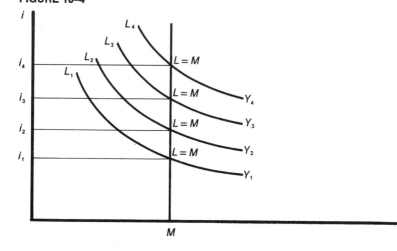

FIGURE 18–5

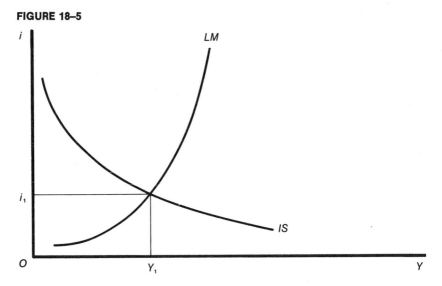

money supply, these combinations provide the data for the *LM* curve in Figure 18–5.

The upward slope and increasing inelasticity of the *LM* curve shows that with a given quantity of money, a greater preference for liquidity will result in a higher interest rate rather than a greater volume of hoards. It should also be observed that higher income-levels will be associated with higher interest-rates because at higher income-levels the transactions and precautionary demands for money increase, so that there is less left out of a given money stock to satisfy the speculative motive. This puts an upward pressure on the interest rate and accounts for the increasing inelasticity of the *LM* curve.

Figure 18–5 also shows the *IS* curve from Figure 18–3, which relates interest rates, income levels, and various possible savings and investment equilibria. Since two of these variables are also required for the construction of the *LM* curve, the two curves can be shown on the same graph. The interest rate may then be conceived of as being determined by the intersection of the *LM* and *IS* curves, which bring together the supply of money as the four variables of the problem. The intersection point of the two curves represents a stable monetary equilibrium if realized savings and investment are equal to planned savings and investment, and if the amount of money people wish to hold is equal to the actual money stock.

The Real Balance Effect and General Equilibrium

The full Keynesian model conceives of the economy as consisting of four aggregate markets. The money and bond markets in which interest rates are determined involve stocks, and the commodity and labor markets in which goods prices and wage rates are determined involve flows. Unlike the Keynesians, Keynes maintained that there is no mechanism which can achieve a general equilibrium among the commodity, labor, and money markets.[9]

The rebuttal to Keynes's view that there is no tendency toward general equilibrium is central to the counterrevolution. Under the leadership of Pigou and Don Patinkin, it has been argued that Keynes did not adequately recognize the impact and significance of price changes on the real value of money balances and wealth as a mechanism for restoring equilibrium. The *real-balance effect* reflects the effect of the real value of money balances (i.e., of M/P where M represents stock of money and P is the price level) on expenditures for consumption and investment. Patinkin argued that, in principle, flexible prices and wage rates can restore commodity, money, and labor markets to equilibria which are consistent with full employment.

The relationships he perceived may be illustrated in terms of the diagrams in Figure 18–6. In Part A aggregate demand is represented by the *IS* curve, which is assumed to be at IS_1. Given the stock of money, *LM* represents the demand for cash balances at different interest rates and

FIGURE 18–6

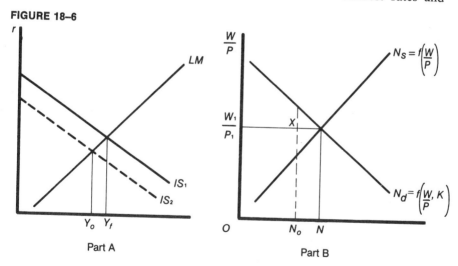

Part A

Part B

[9] Keynes himself, however, appears to have appreciated the possibility of constructing the *IS* curve on the basis of the neoclassical formulation. He even said specifically that the level of income and the interest rate must be "uniquely correlated." See *The General Theory*, pp. 178–81. From this, later writers formulated general equilibrium models in which, given the consumption (savings) schedule, the investment-demand schedule, the liquidity-preference schedule, and the quantity of money, the interest rate and the level of income are mutually determined. The contention of many modern followers of Keynes, among them Sidney Weintraub, is that the economics of Keynes is incompatible with a general equilibrium model. Their disagreement is fundamental to the counter-counterrevolution now underway to refute the analyses of the Keynesians and the Monetarists. See Chapter 20 below.

income levels. *LM* and *IS₁* establish that the commodity market is willing to absorb the full employment output Y_f which firms desire to produce at the real wage rate W_1P_1. As shown in Figure 18–6B, W_1P_1 is consistent with employment for *ON* workers, when N_s is the supply curve of labor at various possible real-wage rates and N_d the demand-curve for labor at various real-wage rates, given the stock of capital K.

What is the nature of the forces which operate if aggregate demand falls to *IS₂*? Recall Keynes's argument that a deficiency of aggregate demand results in involuntary unemployment which is not automatically corrected even if the wage-price structure is flexible downward. He would not expect the aggregate demand-curve to be restored to the *IS₁* level. But Patinkin argues, Keynes's view "overlooks the direct influence of the real balance effect on this demand. Similarly it overlooks the supply side of the commodity market which, by its excess demand, generates this effect."[10] He reasons that a decrease in commodity-demand will create an excess commodity supply; that is, a supply which is excessive in the sense that it exceeds what the market is willing to absorb at a given price. Thus, commodity prices will be bid down. Further, excess commodity supply will have repercussions in the labor market; i.e., the demand for labor will decrease to, say, ON_0. If wages and prices are both flexible downward and fall proportionately, the real wage remains at W_1P_1 which is consistent with the employment of *ON* workers rather than the smaller volume ON_0. Patinkin, thus, describes employment ON_0, which is represented by point x in Figure 18–6B, as reflecting the "involuntary departure of firms from their labor demand curves." He sees it as the counterpart, from the employers' point of view, of involuntary unemployment from labor's point of view.

It does not follow, however, in Patinkin's view, that the economy need languish indefinitely in a disequilibrium state. The decrease in commodity demand results in a price decline which sets into motion a dynamic process. It increases the value of net liquid assets which affects consumption expenditures in the same way as an increase in income.[11] The rise in consumption expenditures restores the *IS* curve from *IS₂* back to *IS₁*. The commodity market is then again willing to purchase output Y_f.

The demand for labor is pulled up concurrently to a level which is appropriate to the unchanged real-wage rate. When firms are again able to sell Y_f units of output, they will be able to return to their labor-demand curves and hire *ON* workers as before. This equilibrium-position differs from the original one only in having lower levels (in money terms) of wages, prices,

---

[10] Don Patinkin, *Money, Interest and Prices*, 2d ed. (New York: Harper and Row, 1965), p. 325.

[11] The net liquid assets of the private sector are the sum of "outside" money, i.e., money for which there is no corresponding private liability (which excludes most commercial bank deposits) and the interest-bearing government debt.

and interest rates. Patinkin contends that the equilibrating process is not changed if wages and prices do not initially fall in the same proportion, but it does have the effect of a "prolongation of the dynamic process into which the economy is thrown by an initial decrease in demand."

In what way does this analysis narrow the analytical distance between Keynes and classical economics? Patinkin agrees with Keynes that worker unwillingness to accept money-wage cuts cannot be identified as the source of involuntary unemployment nor the cause of its persistence. His reasoning reinforces Keynes's contention that involuntary unemployment is the result of inadequate aggregate demand in the commodity market and need not, as the classicists contended, have its origin in wage rigidities. Patinkin identifies the "offending rigidities" as "the rigidities of sovereign consumers and investors unwilling to modify their expenditure habits on short notice." The wealth effect may not be immediately operative in the equilibrating process.[12] Thus, Patinkin's essential conclusion is that involuntary unemployment is a phenomenon of economic dynamics, . . . "granted full flexibility of prices, it is still highly possible that a deflationary process will not work, due to the dynamic factors involved."[13]

Adverse microeconomic distributional effects are among the impediments to a restoration of equilibrium. For example, a price decline may encourage consumption by those who are in debt less than consumption by creditors is discouraged. Alternatively, it may be that there is no price decline which will have an encouraging effect on either consumption or investment expenditures. Looked at in terms of the impact of successively decreasing price levels on savings (which are a function of the real value of cash balances, as well as the interest rate and the income level), it may be that most of the additional real funds resulting from price declines will be added to cash balances. That is, the marginal utility of additional consumption may decrease more rapidly than the marginal utility of cash balances. Thus Patinkin concludes that even if prices are fully flexible downward, falling prices might not be effective in restoring full employment because of the dynamic factors at work. In the absence of a reliable automatic adjustment-process the burden for restoring employment to acceptable levels then falls on appropriate policy measures. As interpreted by Patinkin, "the Keynesian position [as distinct from Keynes's] . . . states that even with uncertainty full employment would eventually

[12] Patinkin, *Money, Interest and Prices,* p. 343; also note pp. 651–64 in "Empirical Investigations of the Real-Balance Effect," which suggests that the evidence on the real-balance effect is inconclusive. Patinkin's model assumes outside money which is an asset without a corresponding debt. But if there is also inside money, the price level has no effect on real wealth. A price reduction makes an asset holder richer in real terms and a debtor poorer; i.e., the net effect of a price change is zero if there is inside money.

[13] Don Patinkin, "Price Flexibility and Full Employment," *Readings in Monetary Theory* (New York: The Blakeston Company, 1951).

be generated by a policy of price flexibility; but the length of time that might be necessary for the adjustment makes the policy impractical."[14]

Keynesianism and the Phillips Curve

One of the limitations of the ISLM apparatus is that it does not link real magnitudes of output and employment to the monetary magnitudes of price and wage levels. The necessity for establishing this link became evident as the difficulties of achieving the dual goals of full-employment and price-level stability without wage and price controls became apparent.[15] It is in this connection that Keynesian economists pressed into service the results of a study (1958) by A. W. Phillips which employed British data to relate the rate of wage increases to the percent of unemployment of the civilian labor-force.

The convex, downward sloping curve plotted by Phillips for Great Britain for the period 1861–1913 is reproduced in Figure 18–7 from the original study.[16] This study shows a fairly close relationship between the percent change in wage-rates and the percent of the civilian labor-force unemployed, for each of three periods, 1861–1913, 1913–48, and 1948–57, studied. Omitting the years, largely associated with wars, during which import-prices rose rapidly enough to generate a wage-price spiral, and assuming a productivity increase of 2 percent per year, Phillips's conclusion for the United Kingdom was that the money-wage level could become stabilized with 5.5 percent rate of unemployment. An alternative interpretation is that the rate of increase of money wages could be held down to the 2 to 3 percent increase in productivity with about 2.5 percent of the labor force unemployed.

The relationships exhibited by the Phillips curve between money-wage rate changes and unemployment do not, in and of themselves, support any hypothesis about the cause of inflation. The Phillips curve tells us only that the tighter the labor market, the greater the upward pressure on wage rates. However, the correlation between wage changes $\Delta w/w$ and U, the rate of unemployment, has been interpreted as providing a basis for *inferences* about increases in the general price level by linking it to changes in money wage rates.[17] That is, money wage rate-changes are taken as a proxy for

---

[14] Ibid.

[15] Both Keynes and Joan Robinson anticipated this problem. See J. M. Keynes, *The General Theory,* pp. 298–302, and Joan Robinson, *Essays in the Theory of Employment* (New York: The Macmillan Co., 1937), chapter 1.

[16] A. W. Phillips, "The Relation between Unemployment and the Rate of Change of Money Wage Rates in the United Kingdom 1862–1957," *Economica,* vol. 25, (1958), pp. 283–99.

[17] Paul Samuelson and Robert Solow made the first empirical estimate of the Phillips curve for the United States in "Analytical Aspects of Anti-Inflation Policy," *American Economic Review, Papers and Proceedings,* vol. 1 (1960). They conclude

price-level changes on the premise that market prices reflect a fairly stable markup over wage-costs.

A convenient way of representing this relationship is in terms of a price equation which has been found useful in econometric research:

$$P = kw/A$$

in which P is the price level, w is average wages and salaries in money terms, k is the average price markup over unit labor costs, and A is the average productivity of labor. The markup equation of price-change implies that wage-increases that exceed productivity-increases are associated with inflationary price increases and higher unemployment.[18] If the relationship between unit labor costs, the markup, and average prices is reliable, then, according to the unemployment and wage rate relationship of the Phillips' curve, the rate of inflation is necessarily associated with the level of unemployment. The tighter the labor market, the greater the upward pressure on wage rates and prices. The "trade-off" between rates of unemployment and rates of inflation is reflected in the convex shape of the Phillips curve. This is the basis for the belief, which has persisted up to the recent past, that policy makers can choose among alternative rates of unemployment and rates of inflation. This belief has currently been shaken by the "puzzle" of simultaneous increases in unemployment and rates of inflation.

Some writers have argued that a wage-price spiral cannot occur without the acquiesence of the monetary authority.[19] In their view, money is an *exogenous* magnitude. This interpretation is the basis for much of the hiatus between Keynesians, who are chiefly concerned with constructing general equilibrium models of the economy, and "positive economists" (among them Milton Friedman), who are chiefly concerned with identifying the relationship between money income and the quantity of money for the purpose of developing a guide to policy. The absence of a price level in both the Keynesian cross model and the ISLM model (both are presented in *real* terms) made them suspect as analytical tools for analyzing the

---

that if wage increases do exceed productivity increases, an unemployment rate of 5 to 6 percent of the labor force would persist. Alternatively to maintain unemployment at the 3 percent level, the price index would have to rise by as much as 48.5 percent each year. Studies by Bhatia and France indicate even more pessimistic curves, the latter indication approximately 10 percent unemployment existing when the annual wage inflation-rate is 2.4 percent. See R. J. Bhatia, "Unemployment and Rate of Change in Money Earnings in the United States, 1900–1959," *Economica*, vol. 28 (August 1961), pp. 285–96.

[18] It is relevant to note that this conception of the relationship among money, wages, labor productivity and inflation is consistent with Keynes' own view. See R. F. Harrod *Reforming the World's Money* (London: MacMillan and Co., 1965). See also Sidney Weintraub, *Keynes and the Monetarists* (New Brunswick: Rutgers University Press, 1973) pp. 24–25.

[19] See, for example, Susan and Michael Wachter, "Money Wage Inflation," in Sidney Weintraub, ed., *Modern Economic Thought,* chap. 16.

FIGURE 18–7

Rate of change of money wage rates, percent per year

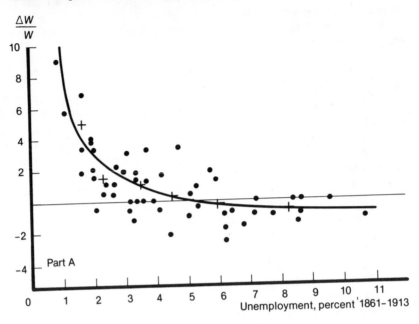

Part A

Unemployment, percent 1861–1913

Rate of change of money wage rates, percent per year

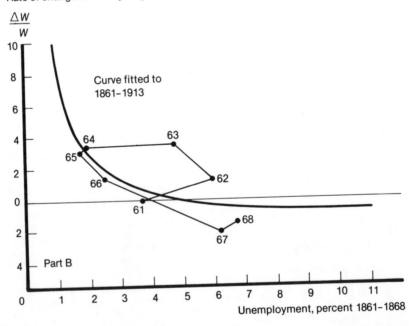

Curve fitted to 1861–1913

Part B

Unemployment, percent 1861–1868

Source: A. W. Phillips: "The Relation between Unemployment and the Rate of Change in Money Wage Rates in the United Kingdom 1862–1957," *Economica*, vol. 25 (1958), p. 285.

problem of inflation. This lack gave impetus to the modern quantity theory of the Monetarists as an alternative analytical and policy tool.

MONETARISM

Reaffirmation of the Importance of Money

The place of the quantity-theory in the thinking of classical and neo-classical writers has been noted several times. The essence of their views is that changes in the price-level are attributable to changes in the quantity of money. Autonomous changes in *v*, the velocity of circulation, were not expected, except during transition periods, because of the unchanging nature of spending habits and the institutional factors governing them.

The concern of modern economists with the role of money and the potential of monetary policy to achieve employment and price-level goals has changed over time. It was accorded little interest during the 1930s and 1940s. Thus, the publication of Milton Friedman's *Studies in the Quantity Theory of Money* in 1956 reflects a reassessment which has been in progress in more recent decades about the role of money and the place of monetary policy.[20] The essence of its message, and of the research it stimulated, is that "money matters." Unlike the Keynesians whose ISLM apparatus reduces money to a *numeraire* (common denominator) in a general equilibrium-model, the Monetarists, led by Milton Friedman, focused on the importance of specifically analyzing the demand for money and formulating a "positive theory" for the guidance of policy.[21]

The "Modern" Quantity Theory

The fundamental question that the theory of the demand for money seeks to answer is why do people hold money which is not an income-earning asset rather than productive goods or interest-bearing securities? In Friedman's view the demand for money by the wealth-owning units of the society can be examined within the framework of the theory of consumer choice.[22] Thus the demand for money depends on (*a*) the total wealth to be held in various forms (which is analogous to the budget constraint); (*b*) the price of and the return on this (and alternative) forms of wealth; and (*c*) the tastes and preferences of wealth-owning units.

Total wealth includes all sources of what Friedman terms "permanent"

---

[20] *Studies in the Quantity Theory of Money* (Chicago: The University of Chicago Press, 1956.) Friedman has been honored with the Nobel Prize (1976) for his contribution to economics.

[21] For a more detailed summary of the monetarist position see Richard T. Selden, "Monetarism," Sidney Weintraub, ed., *Modern Economic Thought*.

[22] Milton Friedman, *Studies in the Quantity Theory of Money*, p. 4.

income.[23] It includes (a) "money," which is identified as "claims" that are acceptable for making payments at a fixed nominal value; (b) bonds; (c) equities; (d) physical goods; and (e) human capital. A wealth-owning unit is conceived to allocate total wealth among these alternatives to maximize "utility," taking into consideration the possibility of converting one form of wealth into another. There is utility to be derived from holding part of one's wealth in the form of money; thus the holder of money alters his money holdings "until the value to him of the addition to the total flow of services produced by adding a dollar to his money stock is equal the reduction in the flow of services produced by subtracting a dollar from each of the other forms in which he holds assets."[24] As in all demand-analyses predicated on maximizing a utility-function, the demand for money is independent of the nominal unit used to measure money variables. Thus, the demand for money is a demand for *real* balances as a function of *real* variables.

Quantity theorists maintain that the demand for money (in real terms) is highly stable and are satisfied that there is empirical evidence to verify this hypothesis. Philip Cagen's study, in particular, identified the stability of the *real* demand for money with his finding that changes in the rate of change of prices affects the *nominal* quantity of money demanded.[25] The higher the rate of change of prices, the less the nominal quantity of money held will be because it makes alternative forms of holding wealth more attractive. Friedman regards the stability of the money-demand function (in terms of real balances) to be one of the few "constants" that economists have been able to identify.

Friedman's Permanent Income Hypothesis

Keynes thought it a reasonable proposition that consumption will, as a general rule, increase less than in proportion to an increase in income. This view became much debated after his work was published. Three sets of facts have been utilized by various investigators to test this proposition empirically. There are data on aggregate savings and income for the period 1869–1958 collected by the 1971 Nobel Prize winner in economics, Professor Simon Kuznets; budget studies for 1935–36 and 1941–42, by the National Resources Committee and the U.S. Bureau of Labor Statistics; and, finally, Department of Commerce data on aggregate saving and income published yearly since 1929. The Kuznets data show that, decade by decade, there has been a long-run constant ratio between consumption and income of about 88 percent. Thus they do not show any tendency for the

---

23 Friedman's permanent income concept is examined in the section which follows.

24 Friedman, *Studies,* p. 14.

25 Philip Cagen, "The Monetary Dynamics of Hyperinflation," in M. Friedman, ed., *Studies in the Quantity Theory of Money,* pp. 25–117.

proportion of income saved to rise with income. But available budget studies suggest that the savings ratio increases with income. Department of Commerce data support the thesis that the ratio of savings to income varies over the trade cycle. Of course, such evidence does not necessarily mean that the *long-run relationship* between consumption and income may not be a proportional one. Friedman is among those advancing the hypothesis that the true long-run relationship between consumption and income is a proportional one.[26]

Friedman's view that consumption behavior depends on "permanent income," i.e., on the resources an individual expects to have at his disposal over a lifetime, is closely related to his finding that the demand for real-money balances is stable. His theory seeks to extend Keynes's initial inquiry into consumption-behavior.

His approach is to distinguish between the permanent and transitory components of income and consumption. Thus, income includes a permanent component, Y_p, and a transitory component, Y_t. Similarly, there is a permanent consumption-component, C_p, and a component which is transitory, C_t. Permanent income, in the Friedman sense, is determined by two factors: the wealth of the consumer unit expressed as the present value of a stream of expected future receipts and the rate at which they are discounted.

The ratio (k) between permanent income (Y_p) and permanent consumption (C_p) depends on the rate of interest (r), the ratio of "non-human" wealth to income (w), and a composite variable (u) whose value reflects the propensity to consume of consuming units which are different with respect to age and taste. The ratio k is, however, independent of permanent income, and Friedman asserts that transitory consumption (C_t) is unrelated to transitory income (Y_t). The "measured" consumption established from cross-section data as the sum of permanent and transitory consumption depends on permanent income rather than measured income. That is, consuming units are envisioned as determining their consumption on the basis of the returns expected from resources received over a lifetime. Expenditures represent a constant proportion (k) of the permanent-income level. The various transitory factors, such as unexpected bills or income losses which produce deviations between observed income and expenditures and their permanent levels are random factors. Symbolically:

$$Y = Y_p + Y_t$$
$$C = C_p + C_t$$
$$C_p = kY_p$$
$$k = f(r, w, u)$$

---

[26] This is also the view of Franco Modigliani and Richard Brumberg. See their "Utility Analysis and the Consumption Function: An Interpretation of Cross-Section Data," reprinted in H. R. Williams and J. D. Hufnagle, eds., *Macroeconomic Theory: Selected Readings* (New York: Appleton-Century-Crofts, 1969), p. 102.

While the difficulty of measuring permanent income and consumption makes the permanent-income hypothesis difficult to test, Friedman has established some empirical support for it. Using time-series aggregates he has established that (1) after allowances are made for transitory components of consumption and income, the ratio k of permanent consumption to permanent income seems to have been constant since 1897; and (2) the income-elasticity of consumption rises as the period of observation to which a consumption-function is fitted increases, which suggests that transitory components become less important over a longer time period. Thus, the theory predicts a long-run consumption-function in which consumer expenditures are a constant proportion of income.[27]

The Perverse Effect of Monetary Expansion on Interest Rates

In Friedman's view the stability, in real terms, of the demand for cash balances is responsible for the perverse effect which monetarists believe changes in the quantity of money have on long-term rates of interest. The

---

[27] Many nonmonetarists have also advanced hypotheses to explain why the long-run relationship between consumption expenditures and income is proportional. James Duesenberry (in *Income, Savings, and the Theory of Consumer Behavior,* Harvard Economic Study, no. 87, 1959) has advanced the view that consumption depends not only on the absolute level of current income, but more particularly on the level of current income relative to the income-peak previously achieved. This hypothesis reflects his disagreement with two of Keynes's fundamental assumptions. These are (1) that every individual's consumption-behavior is independent of that of every other individual, and (2) that consumption-relations are reversible in time. Given the distribution of income, there are strong psychological and sociological reasons which cause an individual's desire to increase his consumption-expenditures to be functionally related to his percentile-position in the income-distribution pattern. It follows that the proportion of income saved is a function of the same variable. Duesenberry is, therefore, led to the following conclusions:

1. At any one moment, the proportion of income saved will be higher for the higher income groups than for low income groups.
2. If income increases, while the proportional distribution remains constant, the ratio of savings to income will be constant.

Arthur Smithies also supports the view that the long-run relationship between consumption and income is a proportional one. His explanation emphasizes the tendency toward upward drift of the consumption-function. He has suggested several reasons why such an upward secular shift of the consumption-function—that is, an increase in consumption relative to income and essentially independent of its growth —has taken place in the United States. One is that population has become increasingly urbanized. Since a rural population typically saves more and spends less than an urban one, the shift of population to cities is probably a factor which has contributed to the upward drift of the consumption-function. The constant stream of new consumer-goods which have become available, along with the emergence of various financial institutions catering to satisfying demands for consumer-credit, is probably another factor. The change in the age-composition of the population is still another factor which has probably served to increase consumption-expenditures independently of the income-level. The retired population has also increased, so that a larger percentage of people are consumers without being current income earners. See Arthur Smithies, "Forecasting Postwar Demand," *Econometrica,* vol. 13, (January 1945).

growth of the money supply will stimulate spending and raise income. This will raise the liquidity-preference schedule and the demand for loans.[28] It may also raise prices, which will reduce the *real* quantity of money. These effects, Friedman maintains, tend to reverse the initial downward pressure that money expansion has on interest rates and return them to their previous level. "The *initial* impact of increasing the quantity of money at a faster rate is to make interest rates lower for a time than they would otherwise have been. But this is only the beginning of the process, not the end."[29] Indeed, monetarists argue that a higher rate of monetary expansion will ultimately correspond to a *higher,* not lower level of interest rates than would otherwise have prevailed because it will generate the *expectation* of further increases in the price level. Since the demand for real balances is stable, the nominal demand for money increases, which increases rather than decreases the rate of interest. Thus, Friedman argues, interest rates cannot be "pegged."[30]

Nor is it possible for the monetary authority to adopt a "target" for unemployment. Monetarists maintain that the immediate effect on unemployment of changes in the rate of expansion of the money supply is similarly different from the delayed effect. There is, in their view, a level of unemployment at any moment of time which is consistent with the structure of *real* wage rates. Real wage rates are tending, on the average, to increase at a "normal" secular rate that is compatible with the rate of capital formation and technological improvements, and there is a "natural rate of unemployment" consistent with them. It is the relationship between real-wage and money-wage changes that explains why the trade-off postulated by the Phillips curve between money-wage changes and the unemployment rate is a short-run trade-off.[31] Thus Friedman argues that the Phillips curve is vertical in the long run. The trade-off between inflation and unemployment is the temporary result of unanticipated (i.e., a rising rate of) inflation.

Friedman's Recommendations for Monetary Policy

Friedman's recommendations for controlling the money supply are predicated on his identification of what monetary policy can and cannot accomplish. The monetary authority can control the *nominal* quantity of

---

[28] Milton Friedman, "The Role of Monetary Policy," *American Economic Review,* vol. 58 (March 1961), pp. 1–17.

[29] It is relevant to point out that much of the ongoing controversy between the monetarists and writers who profess to be working in the tradition of Keynes (as distinct from the Keynesians) turns on their analysis of the demand for money. See Chapter 20 below.

[30] Friedman, "The Role of Monetary Policy," p. 7.

[31] Ibid., p. 8.

money (i.e., its own liabilities) and thereby control *nominal* magnitudes, such as the price level, exchange rates, and the nominal level of national income. But it cannot use control over nominal quantities to peg real quantities such as the rate of unemployment, the real rate of interest, the real quantity of money, or the level of real national income.[32]

The chief objective of monetary policy should, in Friedman's view, be to prevent money itself from becoming a source of major disturbance. What is required is to provide a "stable environment" within which consumers, producers, employees, and employers are reasonably assured "that the average level of prices will behave in a known [preferably stable] way in the future."

This is a function which, in an earlier era, was performed by the gold standard. There are persuasive reasons for the demise of the gold standard but, according to Friedman, "the monetary authority could operate as a surrogate for the gold standard." He recommends to this end that the monetary authority adopt a policy of increasing the money supply (however defined) at some specified and unchanging rate. If the money supply is defined as consisting of currency and commercial bank deposits, the rate of increase which he has estimated would be suitable is between 3 to 5 percent per year.[33] A publicly stated policy of a steady rate of monetary growth is, he believes, the most important contribution the monetary authority can provide to facilitate economic stability.

Keynes versus the Monetarists

What separates modern Monetarists from the Keynes of *The General Theory* (and contemporary followers of Keynes)? Clearly, it cannot be said that the view that "money matters" is attributable to the Monetarists and not to Keynes. Keynes's particular concern with the nature and role of money has been emphasized at several junctures. It is incorrect, in view of this emphasis, to construe his limited faith in monetary policy during severe depression to mean that he thought money did not matter.

What separates Keynes from the Monetarists thus turns, in simplest terms, on the question of whether money-wage rates or the quantity of money is the key endogenous variable of the system. In viewing money as an asset which is demanded to circumvent uncertainty and which comes into existence as a result of the debt-creating activities of commercial banks, Keynes identified money as being *endogenously* generated within the system (and explainable in terms of the economist's tools). Money-wages, on the other hand, are the outcome of institutional arrangements and therefore *exogenous* to the system. According to Keynes's view, the

---

[32] Ibid., pp. 10–11.

[33] Friedman, "The Role of Monetary Policy," pp. 1–17.

collective bargaining activities of unions, legal wage minima, and customs of various kinds impinge on demand and supply forces to a degree which makes it impossible to explain wage-behavior in terms of the market-mechanism. Monetarists and Keynesians conceive of the quantity of money as being generated by policy and as exogenous to the system while real wages are established endogenously via the operation of the price-mechanism. These differences, as will be seen in Chapter 20, are also fundamental to the *counter-counter* revolution which modern followers of Keynes are now conducting against the Monetarists and Keynesians whose work has been reviewed in this chapter.

NEOCLASSICAL GROWTH MODELS

The reaffirmation of the neoclassical tradition in the period of counter-revolution that followed the publication of *The General Theory* manifested itself in a variety of ways. The development of the ISLM apparatus examined above and the general-equilibrium approach it implies together with the restatement of the quantity-theory and its related view of monetary policy and positive economics, are chief among them. A further aspect of the ongoing influence of neoclassical conceptions is concern with the problem of economic growth.

The resurgence of interest in the theory of economic growth during the early post-World War II days was noted at the end of the last chapter. Roy Harrod's contribution not only revitalized concern with the problem of growth, but served to focus attention on the question of stability.[34] A model in which growth is conceived to proceed at a constant rate is one which has a steady-state growth. Steady-state growth is, analytically speaking, the counterpart of long-period equilibrium in static theory.

An economy may be identified as exhibiting stable growth if a divergence from the equilibrium or steady-state path causes reactions which tend to bring the system back to equilibrium. In Harrod's model, as has been seen, movement along the steady-state path is possible only if warranted growth G_w is equal to G_n, the natural rate of growth, the highest rate of growth that can be achieved, given the parameters of the system. Harrod concluded that equality between G_w and G_n is possible only in the special case in which all business expectations are fulfilled. Any divergence between G_w and G_n, instead of resulting in self-correction, only serves to accentuate the departure from the steady-state path. Harrod concluded therefore that full-employment steady-state growth is, in general, not possible. Harrod's model is thus in the tradition of Keynes' disequilibrium economics.

---

[34] See above, p. 419. This interest was partly the result of intense economic competition between the Iron Curtain countries and the free world and partly the result of concern about the (different, but not unrelated) problems of underdeveloped countries.

Writers who construct growth-models that depict an economy in which steady-state growth is possible reject the assumptions on which the Harrod-Domar models are based. The critical assumptions of these models, as was set forth in the preceding chapter, is that production-functions are characterized by fixed coefficients, so that substitution between labor and capital is not possible, and that the propensity to save is constant. Writers of neoclassical persuasion have developed models in which these assumptions have been relaxed.[35] For example, the Harrod-Domar assumption of fixed coefficients may be relaxed by allowing for substitutability between labor and capital in the production-function. Another way is to construct a model in which the savings-income ratio is assumed to be flexible. A third way is to introduce economically induced changes in the rate of population-growth instead of assuming that population and the labor force are determined by the operation of noneconomic demographic forces. Making one or the other of these changes in the original Harrod-Domar model affects either the warranted-rate growth or the natural rate of growth and serves to bring them into equality with each other. These approaches are neoclassical in the sense that divergences of the system from equilibrium cause factor-price changes that bring the system back to the steady-state path.

Neoclassical Models: The Variable Capital-Output Case

Models in which the capital-output ratio is variable rather than fixed in response to changes in factor-prices occupy an important place in the most recent literature on growth-theory. Robert Solow of Harvard and Paul T. Samuelson of Massachusetts Institute of Technology are among the U.S. economists who are closely associated with the construction of such neoclassical models as are the Englishmen, T. W. Swan and James E. Meade. Solow has characterized the Harrod-Domar models as "balanced on the knife-edge of equilibrium-growth." This balance depends on the assumption that production takes place under conditions of fixed proportions. "If this assumption is abandoned, the knife-edge notion of unstable balance seems to go with it."[36]

The model developed by Robert Solow is designed to demonstrate this proposition. It is predicated on the assumption that output consists of a single composite commodity produced by labor and capital. It assumes that the labor force increases as a result of population growth, which reflects the

---

[35] J. R. Hicks has shown that one way of constructing a model that will not "explode" in the Harrodian manner is to introduce lags in consumption and investment. See John R. Hicks, "Mr. Harrod's Dynamic Theory," *Economica*, vol. 16, no. 62 (May 1949) pp. 106–21.

[36] Robert M. Solow, "A Contribution to the Theory of Economic Growth," *Quarterly Journal of Economics*, vol. 70 (February 1956).

operation of noneconomic exogenous factors. It assumes technological change to be absent, so that the rate of increase in the labor force is, in effect, equivalent to Harrod's natural rate of growth. The problem, then, is to determine whether there is a rate of increase in the stock of capital which is consistent with the rate of growth of the labor force. If there is, the warranted rate is equal to the natural rate; i.e., the knife-edge conditions of the Harrod model are satisfied. But if these two rates are not initially equal, Solow demonstrates that the inherent instability of the Harrod model is not inevitable.

Models of the Solow variety are noclassical in that the rate of growth is determined by decisions on the supply side, made in response to price adjustments. Their crucial difference from the Harrod-Domar model is that they are characterized by a production-function which has alternative capital-labor and, therefore, capital-output ratios. The Harrod problem of divergence between the natural rate and the warranted rate is avoided by the choice of a production method with a capital-intensity which checks any tendency for capital stock to grow at a rate different from the rate of population growth.

For example, if the savings associated with full employment are in excess of what is required to enable the capital stock to grow at the same rate as the labor force, the warranted rate of growth will be above the natural rate. The real rate of interest will tend to fall in this situation. As a result, a deepening of capital, which increases the capital-labor ratio and therefore the capital-output ratio, tends to take place. This serves to reduce the warranted rate of growth as well as the savings ratio. The deepening process continues as long as the warranted rate is above the natural rate. When the warranted rate has fallen to the level of the natural rate, growth takes place along the steady-state path. Saving will then have been reduced to a level at which the capital stock grows at the same rate as the labor force.

Conversely, if the size of the initial capital stock is such that the warranted rate is below the natural rate, capital and output will grow at a faster rate than the labor force until the warranted rate of growth is equal to the natural rate. In short, the model shows that the natural rate of growth and the warranted rate of growth are not inherently divergent from each other if a method of production is chosen in which the capital intensity is appropriate to the size of the capital stock. If the interest rate is flexible, the neoclassical model envisions growth occurring at the long-run natural rate, by virtue of the variability of the equilibrium or warranted rate of growth. An important implication of this model, in contrast with the Harrod-Domar models, is that it downgrades the significance of savings and capital accumulation as the "engine" of economic growth.

Critics of neoclassical growth-models are similarly concerned with the essential question of assumptions. Thus they doubt the relevance of a model in which substitution between labor and capital is assumed. Substitutability, it is contended, is unlikely in economies characterized by rigid factor prices. Even more important, it may not be possible to alter methods of production quickly enough to be compatible with changed K/L and K/Y ratios. Changes in the relative quantities of capital and labor employed in production involves changes in the types of labor performed and the forms in which capital is used. Even if factor prices are flexible in substantial conformity with the assumption of the neoclassical model, the time required to plan and alter production methods may impede the achievement of the K/L and K/Y ratios that are necessary for steady state growth.[37]

Adjustment via Induced Changes in the Natural Rate

The adjustment needed to bring about equality between the natural and warranted rates of growth may, theoretically, take place via a change in the natural rate instead of through a change in the warranted rate. It will be recalled that the natural rate is the maximum growth-rate consistent with the full employment of resources and the rate of technological progress. Given the labor requirements per unit of output, the natural rate of growth cannot be greater than the rate of growth of the labor supply.

A model in which the warranted growth-rate and the natural growth-rate are brought to equality via a change in the natural rate can be constructed by dropping the assumption that the rate of population growth is determined by noneconomic forces. Growth-models typically assume the rate of growth of the labor supply is an exogenous constant. In principle, however, economically induced changes in the rate of growth of population can be incorporated into growth-models.

There are various ways of doing this. But all are Malthusian in inspiration in the sense that they conceive of birth and death rates as resulting from the operation of economic forces. The Malthusian hypothesis has it that the supply of labor is perfectly elastic at a real wage corresponding to subsistence. Given a fixed supply of land and no technical progress, the growth of population and hence total output is presumed to depend on the capitalists' propensity to save out of profits. That is, a relationship between income (output) and population and between population and the real wage is postulated. A high real wage is presumed to induce a high rate of population growth and output. Increases in population, in turn, reduce the capital-to-labor ratio which adversely affects income and real wages. If the rate of growth of population responds to real wages, the natural growth rate may be envisioned as being reduced until it coincides with the warranted rate.

---

[37] See D. Hamburg, *Economic Growth and Instability* (New York: W. W. Norton, 1956) and chap. 17 in *Modern Economic Thought*, Sidney Weintraub, ed.

While there are growth models of Malthusian inspiration, there is only limited interest in models incorporating changes in the rate of growth of the labor supply. Demography, which is the study of population behavior, remains a specialized area of inquiry in spite of pioneering efforts to examine population behavior in response to economic stimuli.[38] There has been relatively greater interest among economists in those aspects of growth that are associated with changes in technique and technological progress.[39] Neoclassical models have been constructed in which investment is associated with capital of different "vintages" that are associated with technologies that prevailed at various points of time. The nature and role of "human capital" as distinct from physical capital has also challenged the interest of neoclassical economists. Part of this interest was originally sparked by the growth problem and evidenced by an effort to estimate the proportion of growth associated with the quality of the labor force as distinct from its size.[40] On a more theoretical level, Kenneth Arrow has worked out a growth model in which "experience," i.e., improvements in human capital that are the product of learning, is the engine of progress.[41] Experience is seen as facilitating improvements in the design of new machines which serves to reduce the labor requirements per unit of output. Investment does not increase the productivity of labor employed on existing machines, but it does increase the productivity of labor working on machines subsequently designed and built.[42]

While the growth phenomenon is closely related to the quality of the labor force, the economists' interest in investment in human capital is only peripherally related to problems of growth. The most important theoretical and empirical work has taken place within the context of decision-making by the household. As such, human capital analysis is of limited importance in connection with the macroeconomic topics explored in this chapter.[43]

---

[38] Simon Kuznets, "Long Swings in the Growth of Population and Related Economic Variables," *Proceedings of the American Philosophical Society,* vol. 102, no. 1 (February 1958). Also Richard Easterlin, *Population, Labor Force and Long Savings in Economic Growth* (New York: Natural Bureau of Economic Research, 1968).

[39] Edwin Mansfield, *The Economics of Technological Change* (New York: W. W. Norton Co., Inc., 1968).

[40] Theodore W. Schultz, "Rise in the Capital Stock Represented by Education in the United States 1900–1957" in S. Mushkin, ed., *Economics of Higher Education* (Washington, Department of Health, Education and Welfare, 1962).

[41] Kenneth Arrow, "The Economic Implications of Learning by Doing," *Review of Economic Studies,* vol. 29 (June, 1962).

[42] N. Kaldor and J. Mirrlee in "A New Model of Economic Growth," *Review of Economic Studies,* vol. 29 (June 1962) have presented a more complex model of growth which incorporates both the learning process and rates of increase in gross investment. That is, learning is viewed as a function of the rate of increase of gross investment. In the Kaldor-Mirrlee model, investment enhances productivity because it generates opportunity of learning new methods.

[43] Its place in Friedman's permanent income hypothesis, however, merits emphasis.

But it is a major topic of the "new microeconomics" which is examined in the chapter that follows.

CONCLUDING COMMENTS

The concern of this chapter has been to underscore the continuing vitality of the neoclassical tradition. The Keynesian revolution was hardly underway before it was countered by Professor Hicks' suggested "reinterpretation." The ISLM apparatus reflects a perception of reality or "world view" besides being an analytical tool. It conceives of an economic system in which commodity, factor, and money markets tend toward general equilibrium via the functioning of the price-mechanism. The possibility that the mechanism may not be effective in the presence of dynamic forces and prices that are not fully flexible is recognized. This is the basis for the Keynesian argument that monetary and fiscal policy are needed to supplement the price mechanism.

The ISLM apparatus is at a particular disadvantage when focus shifts to examining the behavior of money magnitudes. The price level is abstracted from the ISLM model; the role of money in this general equilibrium model is to serve as a *numeraire*—one commodity among many that serves as an exchange medium. Thus, the Phillips curve which relates changes in unemployment rates and wage rates, the latter serving as a proxy for changes in the general price level, has been pressed into service in order to explain the relationship between unemployment and prices.

To confront the problem of explaining *simultaneous* increases in the price level and unemployment-rates, which is inconsistent with the Phillips curve hypothesis, monetarists have focused on the relationship between changes in the money supply, the nominal-income level and the price-level. The monetarist position is that inflation cannot take place without the acquiesence of the monetary authority. They interpret the demand for money by households as a highly stable demand for *real* balances. Changes in the quantity of money therefore affect interest rates perversely; *initially* increases in the quantity of money reduce interest rates and stimulate the economy. But as rising prices reduce the *real* quantity of money, interest rates become higher because of the expectation of further price increases.

Neoclassicists conceive of real-wage rates as tending, on the average, to be increasing at a secular rate which is compatible with the rate of increase in capital formation and technological improvements. Thus, according to the neoclassical view, the forces determining wage rates are endogenous to the system while those determining the quantity of money are exogenous. Keynes believed matters to be quite the other way around! In his system the money supply is determined endogenously as financial institutions respond to investment decisions by creating "debt" money, and wage rates are established by exogenous social and political factors.

The dichotomy between contemporary interpreters of Keynes is also evidenced in the growth models they have constructed and the policy implications that have been deduced from them. The models that have emanated from Cambridge, Massachusetts, reflect the influence of the neoclassical tradition in their reliance on changing capital-labor and capital-output ratios in response to relative changes in wage and interest rates. The disagreement between those who are of neoclassical persuasion on the question of growth and those who, like Roy Harrod, and his associates at Cambridge, England, believe they have developed growth models which reflect a closer fidelity to the spirit of Keynes' own work has produced the ongoing "Cambridge controversy." Not all who are associated with the neoclassical position are at Cambridge, Massachusetts; John R. Hicks and James Meade are leading English proponents of the neoclassical position. Opposition to the neoclassical view is being led chiefly by writers associated with Cambridge, England—the late Michael Kalecki, Joan Robinson, Luigi Passinetti, and Nicholas Kaldor. Like Keynes, their emphasis is on the independence of investment decisions from savings propensities. Investment-decisions are conceived to be governed by the expectations and "animal spirits" of entrepreneurs. The implication of these models, which will be examined briefly in our concluding chapter, is that steady economic growth is unlikely. This conception of the behavior of the economic system over time presents a sharp contrast with the neoclassical view that the forces that predominate in modern capitalistic economies are those which are compatible with steady-state growth.

GLOSSARY OF TERMS AND CONCEPTS

Real-balance effect. An increase in the real value of cash balances which might operate to increase the volume of real spending and shift the consumption function upward.

Vertical Phillips curve. A graphic representation of the "natural" rate of unemployment consistent with a zero expectation of price change. It has been hypothesized (by Friedman and his followers) that the trade-off between employment and wage increases is observable only in the short run. Policy measures to reduce unemployment below the natural rate raise wage rates and generate inflationary expectations. Short-run Phillips curves therefore shift upward and restore unemployment to its natural level. This logic is associated with the accelerationist view of unemployment and inflation.

"Modern" quantity theory. Modern quantity theorists (e.g., Friedman) maintain that the demand for cash balances is stable in real terms. The process of increasing the nominal quantity of money at a faster

rate reduces interest rates only temporarily. The expectation of further increases in the price-level reduces the real value of the balances held. Since the demand for real balances is stable, the nominal demand for money increases, which increases rather than decreases the rate of interest. Because this adversely affects the level of income and employment, the monetarist position is to advocate a policy of increasing the money supply at a steady unchanging rate.

NOTES FOR FURTHER READING

On Keynesian Economics:

Dudley Dillard's *The Economics of John Maynard Keynes* (New York: Prentice Hall, Inc., 1948) did much to popularize the income-expenditure model that has come to be associated with Keynesianism in America. For a more sophisticated interpretation, see Alvin H. Hansen's *A Guide to Keynes* (New York: McGraw-Hill Book Co., 1953). Chap. 7 presents Hansen's effort to reconcile the neoclassical theory of the interest rate with Keynes' liquidity-preference theory via the ISLM apparatus. Hicks' somewhat earlier reconciliation is "Mr. Keynes and the Classics: A Suggested Reinterpretation," *Econometrica,* vol. 5 (1937) pp. 147–59. Don Patinkin integrates labor market equilibrium in "A Patinkin-Revised Version of Price Flexibility and Full Employment," in J. Lindauer, ed., *Macroeconomic Readings* (New York: Free Press 1968). This is a very succinct restatement of the analysis presented in *Money, Interest and Prices,* 2d ed. (New York: Harper and Row, 1965).

The Phillips curve originated in A. W. Phillips' "The Relationship Between Unemployment and the Rate of Change of Money Wage Rate in the United Kingdom 1862–1957," *Economica,* vol. 25 (1958). For the Samuelson-Solow empirical estimate of the Phillips curve relationship in the United States see "Analytical Aspects of Anti-Inflation Policy," *American Economic Review, Papers and Proceedings,* vol. 1, 1960. See also Milton Friedman, "The Role of Monetary Policy," *American Economic Review,* vol. 52 (March 1972). Sidney Weintraub criticizes these and related aspects of Keynesianism in chap. 3 of his *Modern Economic Thought* (Philadelphia: University of Pennsylvania Press, 1977), pp. 45–66. See also Paul Davidson's "Post Keynes Monetary Theory and Inflation" in the same volume, especially pp. 275–78.

On Monetarism

The classic reference is Milton Friedman, "The Quantity Theory of Money —A Restatement" in Milton Friedman, ed., *Studies in the Quantity Theory of Money* (Chicago: University of Chicago Press, 1956). The same volume contains Philip Cagen's "The Monetary Dynamics of Hyperinflation," in which the stability of real demand for money is established empirically. The development of monetarism is reviewed by Richard Selden's "Monetarism" in Sidney Weintraub's *Modern Economic Thought,* pp. 309–26.

Martin Bronfenbrenner and F. D. Holzman present a comprehensive survey of alternative approaches to the problem of inflation in "Inflation Theory," *American Economic Review*, vol. 53 (1963), which is usefully supplemented by Susan and Michael Wachter, "Money Wage Inflation," in Weintraub's *Modern Economic Thought*, pp. 309–26. Friedman gives a succinct statement of his policy views in "The Role of Monetary Policy" *American Economic Review*, vol. 48 (March 1961), pp. 1–17.

Long-Run Consumption Functions

Milton Friedman's "The Permanent Income Hypothesis" is reprinted in H. R. Williams and J. D. Hufnagle, eds., *Macroeconomic Theory: Selected Readings* (New York: Appleton-Century-Crofts, 1969). A summary of Duesenberry's hypothesis is in Duesenberry, James S. "Income-Consumption Relations and Their Implications," in *Income, Employment and Public Policy*, Essays in Honor of Alvin H. Hansen (New York: W. W. Norton, 1948, pp. 54–81).

Neoclassical Growth Theory

The classic article is Robert Solow's "A Contribution to the Theory of Economic Growth," *Quarterly Journal of Economics*, vol. 70 (February 1956). A companion piece to this seminal article is T. W. Swann's, "Economic Growth and Capital Accumulation," *Economic Record*, vol. 32 (November 1956), pp. 334–36. Joseph Stiglitz and Hirofumi Uzawa have collected the most relevant articles in *Readings in the Modern Theory of Economic Growth* (Cambridge, Mass.: Massachusetts Institue of Technology, 1969). Neoclassical growth theory is elsewhere reviewed by P. A. Neher in *Economic Growth and Development* (New York: John Wiley and Sons, 1971). For a concise summary, see Karl Shell, whose chapter on "Neoclassical Growth Models" is among the contributions to Sidney Weintraub's *Modern Economic Thought* already cited.

19

The Chicago School of
Political Economy

INTRODUCTION

"Yes, virginia, there is a Chicago School." In response to the question as to whether "the Chicago School of economics" is a recognizable and meaningful designation Professor Martin Bronfenbrenner responded emphatically in the affirmative.[1] There *is* a group of professional economists who have taught or studied at the University of Chicago or other institutions (among them The University of California at Berkeley, Stanford, and MIT) where they have come under the energizing influence of the Chicago view and share an identifiable intellectual bond. Although their professional association is very loose, and they disagree about many specifics, they are nevertheless relatively homogeneous with respect to their methodology, philosophy, and policy preferences.

What are the distinctive attributes of the members of the Chicago school? A useful starting point for cataloguing these attributes in a meaningful way is to take note of a recent reference to them as "The Chicago

---

[1] Martin Bronfenbrenner, "Observations on the Chicago School(s)," *Journal of Political Economy,* 1962. This article responded to the question raised concerning the possibility of identifying a Chicago School by H. Lawrence Miller, Jr. in "On the Chicago School of Economics," *Journal of Political Economy,* vol. 70 (1962), pp. 72–75. Contrary to Bronfenbrenner's affirmative response, George Stigler's "Comment" in the same issue (pp. 70–71) maintains there "is no simple harmony in the methodological views of the economists Miller names as 'Chicagoan.'" Stigler interprets Miller's statement as a "less than complete sketch of the views of Milton Friedman" whom he prefers to identify as "the leader of the Berkeley-Cambridge axis."

school of libertarian economics."[2] Whatever the differences among them (and they are numerous), Chicago economists are, first and foremost, advocates of an individualistic market economy. It is the *degree* of his advocacy which sets the Chicagoan apart from the other economists, who may also prefer a predominantly market-oriented economy but who do not necessarily believe that individual liberty (political as well as economic) cannot exist outside of a free enterprise system, or that a free enterprise system is more productive than any other system. A further, and related, difference between Chicagoans and other economists is the Chicagoans' belief that the market economy is characterized by commodity prices and wage rates which are by and large flexible. This view is, as was seen in the preceding chapter, an integral part of the Chicagoans' analysis of the functioning of the macroeconomy. Chicago economists tend to be less concerned with and give less weight than other economists to the implications of oligopoly and labor unions, largely because they maintain that these do not significantly alter the essentially competitive nature of the economy. Their concern with questions relating to the distribution of income and wealth is similarly limited.

On the positive side, Chicagoans are committed to the usefulness and relevance of a theory of individual choice predicated on the assumption that sovereign consumers are capable of maximizing behavior. With the aid of empirical tests, they have brought within the purview of the economist an impressive range of problems which have been traditionally viewed as lying outside of economics.

There is, as is to be expected, considerable difference among individual Chicagoans.[3] Thus, Friedman and those associates who share his concern about the price level and monetary economics should be identified separately from Gary Becker, Jacob Mincer, Ronald Coase, and others who are chiefly concerned with problems of allocative efficiency. The latter are chiefly responsible for the development of the "new" microeconomics. This chapter will focus chiefly on their concerns since the monetarist concerns of Friedman and others were discussed in the preceding chapter. These concerns are (1) the problem of allocative efficiency with respect to the time and income resources of the individual household, (2) allocative efficiency in market activities which involve common property, and (3) the role of the market mechanism in promoting economic growth in less

---

[2] See Duncan J. Folley, "Problem vs. Conflicts? Economic Theory and Ideology," *American Economic Review, Papers and Proceedings,* vol. 65 (May 1975).

[3] It is also important to recognize the nonmonolithic character of those associated with Chicago. Paul Douglas and Harry Millis, both outstanding labor economists, and the Socialist Oscar Lange were among the Chicagoans who held dissenting views during the 1930s. More currently, Tjallings Koopmans and Jacob Marshak, who were at the University of Chicago until 1954 cannot be identified as committed to the propositions that have come to be associated with the Chicago School. This observation also applies to Lloyd Meltzer.

developed countries. The nature and role of property rights is an integral part of this inquiry. The interests of Chicagoans are thus very diverse. But there is a *leitmotif* that will become apparent as the highlights of their concerns are examined. Their common intellectual debt to Frank Knight and the Austrians is a useful starting point.

THE ALLOCATIVE EFFICIENCY OF THE HOUSEHOLD

The Menger-Knight Heritage

The microeconomic propositions formulated and subjected to empirical testing by modern Chicagoans builds chiefly on the work of Carl Menger as interpreted and transmitted by Frank Knight. Their analyses proceed from the premise that choice is governed by individual perceptions of the utility associated with alternative courses of action. Following Menger, Knight maintained that the relevant cost of any economic decision is the utility of the alternatives which are sacrificed. No resource has any value other than that imputed to it by the consumer, whose objective it is to maximize the returns his given supply of resources yields. Knight credits Menger for establishing that this principle is valid.

> It is to the everlasting credit and renown of Menger . . . that he not only grasped the utility principle but extended and applied it in two directions: in the field of complementary goods and in that of indirect goods. He reiterated . . . the principle that costs are simply the values of cost goods, which values are *derived from* or reflect the value of some final consumption good, and that this value, in turn, is that of the "need satisfaction" dependent upon a small portion or increment (*Teilquatität*) of the final good in question. This is perhaps as accurate a statement as can be put into words . . . of the general principle that explains, as far as it goes, all valuation.[4]

Modern writers in the Chicago tradition have built on this Menger-Knight perspective of the relationship between utility and cost (i.e., the "cost" of any choice is the utility lost in choosing one alternative rather than another) to explore the behavior of the household in managing its time and income resources. An impressive range of topics which are traditionally examined by sociologists or psychologists has come within their scope of analysis. Using the framework provided by economic theory, the new microeconomics has examined such topics as the allocation of time to education and training as investment in "human" capital, the rearing of children, criminal behavior as an alternative to market behavior, and

---

[4] Frank Knight, *Introduction to Carl Menger's Principles of Economics,* by James Dingwall and Bert Hoselitz, trans. and ed. (Glencoe, Ill.: The Free Press, 1950), p. 15.

choice among sex partners.[5] These inquiries represent contemporary efforts to explore Knight's classic observation: "To live, in the human plane, is to choose."[6] The modern microeconomists' emphasis on time as a scarce allocable input reflects, it should be noted, a different conception of time than the Marshallian one which relates to processes maturing through time.

Courtship and Marriage

Study of the family and relationships among its members is generally considered to lie in the intellectual domain of sociologists and social psychologists. Chicagoans have chosen to ignore this traditional division of intellectual labor and made the family unit the focal point of analysis. Viewed in this light, the family is a producing unit. It is, in effect, a "firm" which utilizes time and other resources at its disposal to produce the utilities desired by family members.[7] Within this analytical framework, marriage is identified as a contract in which the parties have made commitments with respect to the time each will allocate to market and nonmarket activity, including housework, further schooling and training, leisure, and the bearing and rearing of children. Thus, Becker conceives of dating and engagement as providing opportunities for couples to work out "the rules of the game" and arrive at the contractual arrangement under which they will live their life together.[8] According to this line of reasoning, the search for a marriage partner is extended until the expected marginal benefit is equal to the marginal cost. Courtship is, in this sense, an investment process which is expected to eventuate into the flow of returns associated with marriage. It "produces" a flow of returns or benefits in the form of goods and services that the family desires and which "matures out" over the expected life of the marriage contract. Children are included among

---

[5] A further extension of these principles by Becker into the realm of social interactions is to be found in "A Theory of Social Interactions," *Journal of Political Economy,* vol. 82 (November–December 1974). Special attention is directed to the effects of different kinds of income change on charitable contributions and expenditure to allocate envy. For a popular exposition of application of the theory of choice to problems generally not treated by economists, see Richard B. McKenzie and Gordon Tullock, *The New World of Economics* (Homewood: Richard D. Irwin Inc., 1975).

[6] Frank Knight, "Economic Psychology and the Value Problem" (1925) reprinted in *The Ethics of Competition and other Essays* (New York: Augustus Kelley, 1951), p. 88.

[7] Gary Becker, "A Theory of the Allocation of Time," *The Economic Journal,* September 1965.

[8] Gary Becker, "A Theory of Marriage: part I," *Journal of Political Economy,* vol. 81 (July–August 1973), pp. 813–46 and "A Theory of Marriage: part II," *Journal of Political Economy,* vol. 82, supp. (March–April 1974), pp. 511–526.

these "goods," as is the sex relationship, companionship, and social life usually associated with marriage.

The "net benefit" of the marriage relationship reflects the difference between the flow of the benefits it yields and the costs it imposes. Improved efficiency in the production of wanted goods and services as a result of specialization and division of labor in the household and trade among family members is a major benefit. A chief cost, which is among several which must be evaluated in order to assess the net return from a family relationship, is that associated with joint decision-making. In general, it is more costly to make a decision when the preferences of both parties need to be taken into account. From this, Chicagoans infer that agreements between the partners regarding the domain in which each has autonomy (e.g., wives typically assume the responsibility for meal planning) minimize the costs of decision-making. These costs tend to increase directly with the number of family members (i.e., older children) and the extent of their participation in the process of decision-making and production. Family arrangements requiring members to assume a share of responsibility for the performance of household tasks is, in effect, akin to a tax which is imposed to pay for a collective good which is not necessarily shared equally.

The analytical framework of the family unit has also been used for examining the allocation of time by family members between work in the home and work in the market. One of its implications is that the traditional female role of homemaking and caring for children is not wholly dictated by socially determined values. These do play a role, but the chief determinant is the relative value of the labor time of men and women in the market place.[9] The "cost" of a woman's time in the performance of household and child-care duties is the wage she loses by remaining outside the market. Since men typically command higher wages than their partner (either because they are more productive or experience less discrimination), having men engage in market activity while women work in the home typically minimizes the household's cost of producing the goods it wants.

Child Production

Essentially the same analytical apparatus which was used to study female labor force participation has been extended to examine the decision-making process with respect to the production of children. These inquiries

---

[9] Jacob Mincer has undertaken to test the hypothesis that female labor-force participation reflects the net benefit from market activity as compared with work in the home. See "Labor Force Participation of Married Women, a Study of Labor Supply," in R. Marshall and R. Perlman, eds., *An Anthology of Labor Economics* (New York: John Wiley and Sons, 1972).

reflect a renewed interest of economists in population problems which were very much in the purview of classical economists but were subsequently neglected by their modern counterparts. Extensive work by Gary Becker, and others at the National Bureau of Economic Research, has contributed significantly toward reaffirming the economists' interest in demographic questions.[10] Becker has undertaken to examine questions relating to population behavior using conventional tools of microeconomic analysis. Thus he has suggested that from the standpoint of economics, children might be considered as consumer goods which, in common with other commodities, yield satisfactions but can be acquired only at a price. The "price" of children consists of the time and goods sacrificed in bearing and rearing them. There are direct costs congealed in the prices of goods and services associated with their birth and nurture, and the additional indirect cost of the time parents spend with their children.

Assuming that the care of children falls largely on the mother, the price of the mother's time is a major component of the overall "price" of children. From this it may be inferred that an increase in female wage rates or fringe benefits raises the "price" of children and thus potentially reduces the demand for them. By the same reasoning, and assuming that children are not inferior goods, the demand for them is, presumably, positively related to income.[11] This logic has provided a basis for the hypothesis that each level of "satisfaction" a household can achieve, given its income, is compatible with various combinations of children and other goods among which the household is "indifferent."[12]

Attitudes about having children are so traditional that the very suggestion of a "trade-off" between children and goods is unfamiliar and perhaps even repugnant. But it is precisely the objective of the new microeconomics to demonstrate that the usual assumption of rationality with respect to household decision-making applies to all aspects of household behavior, including family planning. It is their view that the rationality assumption implies nothing more than that children may be viewed as sources of satisfaction (or psychic income) and that the household responds to economic variables, i.e., prices and incomes, in making its choices.

R. A. Easterlin of the University of Pennsylvania has extended this logic in an attempt to explain the reversal of the long-run trend of delining fertility rates that occurred after 1940.[13] He offered the hypothesis that

[10] Gary Becker, "An Economic Analysis of Fertility," *Demographic and Economic Change in Developed Countries* (Princeton: Princeton University Press, 1960), pp. 209–31.

[11] If a good is inferior, the demand for it declines as income rises.

[12] Richard A. Easterlin, *Population, Labor Force and Long Swings in Economic Growth* (New York: National Bureau of Economic Research, 1968), chap. 5.

[13] R. A. Easterlin, "Population" in N. Chamberlin, ed., *Contemporary Economic Issues* (Homewood, Ill.: Richard D. Irwin, Inc., 1973).

after 1940, couples planning their families were typically earning average real incomes that exceeded those of their parents at a comparable stage in their lives. The increase in their incomes, relative to that of their parents, encouraged them to enjoy higher standards of consumption—including more children.

The decline in fertility rates which began in 1957, in spite of continued high income levels can, according to Easterlin, be explained by much the same logic. Couples planning their families in the 1960s had grown up as dependent members of households in which the average income was above that which they were presently achieving for themselves. Thus, their actual income was low relative to their desired income based on their parents' earnings. The decline in the ratio of actual to desired income during the 1940s is interpreted by Easterlin as anticipating the decline in fertility rates that became apparent in 1957. His hypothesis is consistent with the work of those associated with the Chicago School and is of particular interest to us because it exemplifies the effort to extend the economists' conventional range.[14]

LAW AND ECONOMICS: THE PROPERTY RIGHTS APPROACH TO PRICING

The Chicago School's concern with allocational efficiency has still another dimension. It is among its concerns to analyze how the assignment of property rights affects the choices of decision-makers and, through them, the allocation of society's resources. Property rights are the legally sanctioned relations among persons (and businesses) that arise from the existence and utilization of scarce resources. A leading proponent of the property rights approach conceives of economics as "the study of property rights over scarce resources. The question of economics, or of how prices should be determined, is the question of how property rights should be defined and exchanged, and on what terms."[15] Chicagoans thus promote law and economics as the leading interdisciplinary field of the social sciences. R. H. Coase's now classic article, "The Problem of Social Costs," has given this interdisciplinary effort direction, and *The Journal of Law and Economics,* which is published at the University of Chicago, provides a forum for research emanating from Coase's article.[16]

---

[14] Easterlin's hypothesis has provoked considerable controversy among demographers. Some of this literature is reviewed in Harvey Leibenstein, "An Interpretation of the Economic Theory of Fertility: Promising Path or Blind Alley," *Journal of Economic Literature,* vol. 12 (June 1974), pp. 457–70.

[15] A. A. Alchian, *Pricing and Society,* Occasional Paper, no. 17 (Westminster: The Institute of Economic Affairs, 1967), pp. 2–3.

[16] Ronald Coase, "The Problem of Social Costs," *The Journal of Law and Economics,* vol. 3 (October 1960), reprinted in Robert and Nancy Dorfman, eds., *Economics of the Environment* (New York: W. W. Norton, 1972).

The Coase Theorem

The problem of "externalities," which was addressed by the Pigou-Knight controversy, has been a matter of continuing concern to economists. It will be recalled that externalities arise in production or consumption when the activities of one party generate costs (or benefits) for a second party for which he is not compensated (or for which he does not pay). The problem involved is readily apparent if the impact of "externalities," or unpriced costs and benefits, is explored in terms of production and/or consumption functions. Consider, for example, a production function such as $q = q (x_1 \ldots x_n; y_1 \ldots y_n)$ in which q represents output (or consumption if the function is an individual welfare function), the x's represent the priced inputs and the y's the unpriced inputs. Because the latter have a zero price, their allocation among alternative uses is not price directed. Virtually every firm which produces goods utilizes not only the inputs which it purchases or leases at a market price but also some inputs for which it pays nothing at all. A major category of unpriced inputs is the service provided by the assimilative capacity of the environment; in a free market producers use the waste receptor capabilities of water, air, and land resources *without charge.* Pigou would have argued that in the absence of regulation (e.g., waste emission standards, or pollution charges) there will be no incentive for either producers or consumers to limit their utilization of what appears to them to be a "free" good or service, though it is obviously not free when viewed from the standpoint of society as a whole.

Coase examined the possibility that individual action, as opposed to authority, might suffice as an instrument for dealing with externalities in a context that differs from the Pigou-Knight inquiry. He notes that the courts have been called on many times to determine what is an appropriate action in particular cases in which damages have been inflicted as a result of what the economist calls "externalities." Their findings have, in Coase's view, an implication for the economists' concept of "factors of production."

Productive factors are generally thought of as physical entities. Coase suggested that the concept might usefully be given a legal definition; that is, factors of production may be thought of as rights to engage in certain physical acts.[17] Thus, the concept of land as a factor of production implies that the owner of land has the "right to carry out a circumscribed list of actions. The rights of the landowner are not unlimited. . . . For example, some people may have the right to cross his land. Furthermore, it may or may not be possible to erect certain types of buildings or to grow certain crops or to use particular drainage systems on the land."[18] If factors of

---

[17] R. H. Coase, "The Problem of Social Cost," *The Journal of Law and Economics,* vol. 3 (October 1960), pp. 43–44.

[18] Ibid.

production are thought of as *rights,* then the "cost of excercising a right (to use a factor of production) is always the loss which is suffered elsewhere in consequence of that right—the inability to cross land, to park a car, to build a house, to enjoy a view, to have peace and quiet, or to breathe clean aid."[19] In short, when property rights are assigned, there is necessarily a reciprocal denial.

The reciprocal relationship which is inherent in the assignment of property rights is interpreted by Coase as providing insight into the way in which parties engaged in conflicting activities can resolve their differences without outside intervention. There are several arrangements by which externalities can be "internalized." For example, the parties might make an agreement according to which the damaged party (A) pays the party inflicting the damage (B) to modify its activities. Or, if B has a legal right against A, A might pay B for putting up with an optimal amount of the loss it is causing B to experience. Thus, the Coase theorem proceeds from the rational two-party bargain, which is shown as capable of capturing economic efficiency without social interference.[20]

Coase recognizes that the market has its limits because the transactions costs of setting matters right may be prohibitively high. If this is the case, the problem is given to the legal system to decide the proper allocation of resources.[21] If the costs of allowing the market to function are in excess of the costs of the allocating resources by means of a legal decision, it is the function of the court to apply the test of "which party's interest has the greatest market value."[22] That is, in cases in which the functioning of the market is precluded because of transactions' costs, Chicagoans identify the function of the courts to make the "correct" decision based on the principle of opportunity cost. The premise is that resources tend always to gravitate toward their highest valued uses in a free market. Legal decisions which

---

[19] Ibid., p. 44.

[20] Coase notes the case of Sturgis vs. Bridgeman (1879). Sturgis, a physician, bought a property next door to a candy factory, which had been in operation for several decades. The doctor had been practicing at his location without complaint for eight years when he constructed a new consulting room on that part of property located near the confectioner's machinery. When he experienced difficulty in examining his patients, he brought suit to enjoin the candy factory from making noise and vibrations. In ruling in favor of the physician, the court observed that "any other decision would have had a prejudicial effect upon the development of land for residential purposes." The court believed it was determining how the land was used. In Coase's interpretation, the court was, in fact, assigning a right to the physician and imposing a loss on the confectioner by forcing him to relocate his factory. He concludes that resort to the courts was unnecessary in this type of situation and that the parties could have struck a bargain which would have "internalized" the externality.

[21] R. A. Posner, *Economic Analyses of Law* (Boston: Little, Brown and Co., 1972), p. 320.

[22] Ibid.

affect the use of resources will thus be consistent with economic principle if the courts invoke the principle of opportunity price in their decisions.[23]

The Chicago View of Public Utility Regulation

In light of their interest in the relationship between law and economics, it is not surprising that members of the Chicago School have taken a special interest in the institution of public regulation and its effects. Early members of the Chicago School, among them Henry Simons and Frank Knight, were opposed to social control of monopoly through regulation and recommended public ownership of such natural monopolies as railroads and power industries. This was the dominant Chicago view throughout the 1930s and 1940s, which was a period during which public regulation was greatly extended in the United States.

The stance of the Chicago School on public regulation underwent a drastic change in the late 50s and early 60s, when Stigler, Friedman, Coase, and others re-examined the economic effects of regulation and proposed a new solution to the natural monopoly problem. The essence of this solution was that private monopoly can result in a competitive level of profits without regulation. Friedman expressed the view that "the conditions making for technical monopoly frequently change and I suspect that both public regulation and public monopoly are likely to be less responsive to such changes in conditions, to be less readily capable of elimination than private monopoly."[24] The present Chicago view that private monopoly is superior to government regulation and public ownership is attributable in some measure at least to the support it has gotten from Friedman, though the theoretical bases for this position is more specifically associated with Harold Demsetz's competitive bidding principle.

How can private monopoly be reconciled with a competitive level of profits in the absence of direct price-earning regulation? Demsetz has argued that a competitive level of profits can be achieved indirectly via an auctioning process.[25] Government can award a franchise or operating license to the highest bidder who offers to serve consumers at the lowest price. Competition among bidders for the award would force earnings down to the level a competitive market would generate. The competitive

---

[23] Critics of this view maintain that it serves chiefly to make law the instrument of existing social order. See, for example, H. H. Liebhafsky, "Price Theory as Jurisprudence," *Journal of Economic Issues,* vol. 10 (March 1976). Liebhafsky argues that price theory as jurisprudence is an exercise in logical positivism suspended in mystical natural law philosophy.

[24] Milton Friedman, *Capitalism and Freedom* (Chicago: University of Chicago Press, 1962), p. 28.

[25] Harold Demsetz, "Why Regulate Public Utilities?" *Journal of Law and Economics,* vol. 11 (April 1968), pp. 55–66.

auctioning process has been particularly urged in connection with the development of off-shore gas and oil development as an alternative to the existing system of discretionary licenses.[26] The aim of competitive bidding for royalties would be to reconcile natural monopoly with competitive profit levels without resort to government regulation.

In recent years the Chicago School has extended its arguments against direct governmental control to support its view that the free market offers solution to the energy crisis. The essence of their position is that demand and supply forces are capable of establishing a proper balance between lower and higher valued uses of energy. Alchian recommends the use of the bidding process to bring down prices if the cartel of producers restricts supply.[27] He argues that this technique for promoting a market solution under oligopoly will promote access to the U.S. market and thereby limit the economic rents which the cartel can enjoy. This recommendation reflects the Chicago School's present preference for market solutions even in the case of natural monopoly which, historically, they would have subjected to public ownership.

THE CHICAGO VIEW OF DEVELOPING ECONOMIES

The Perspective

Chicago economists have also had a particular interest in the economics of underdeveloped countries. A major influence in shaping their perspective was the recognition that economic growth cannot be wholly explained in terms of additions to an economy's stock of physical capital and number of workers.[28] The residual, which is the name given to that portion of growth not accounted for by increases in the stock of physical capital and increases in the labor force, has been attributed in part to technical progress and in part to improvements in human capital.

Chicagoans, as already noted, have had a particular interest in the process and significance of investment in human capital which they have examined in many different connections, one of which is the matter of economic development. A major study undertaken by Theodore W. Schultz focused on identifying the portion of investment in human capital which is represented by education.[29] Numerous studies examine the requisites for

[26] Kenneth Dam, "The Evolution of North Sea Licensing Policy in Britain and Norway," *Journal of Law and Economics,* vol. 17 (October 1974).

[27] A. A. Alchian, "No Time to Confuse," *Institute of Contemporary Studies,* vol. 9 (1972), p. 15.

[28] Kuznets, Simon, *Modern Economic Growth* (New Haven: Yale University Press, 1966).

[29] T. W. Schultz, "Rise in the Capital Stock Represented by Education in U.S. 1900–1957" in S. Muskin, ed., *Economics of Education,* Washington, 1962.

manpower development in particluar countries with a view also to identifying alternative strategies for developing human resources.[30]

Complementing their concern with the role of human capital in the development process is the Chicago School's view of human nature as being universally responsive to market incentives.[31] Many economists take the position that market-oriented behavior is limited to capitalistic economies in which work habits and entrepreneurial activity have traditionally experienced the spur of monetary rewards. Chicagoans, however, maintain that while people in underdeveloped countries are often viewed as strangers to the idea of maximizing gains, there is evidence that the supply of effort is responsive to the incentive of improved rates of remuneration and that wants are elastic through time in large parts of the underdeveloped world.[32]

Their belief that this behavior pattern prevails is the basis for the Chicago view that the market mechanism can stimulate efficiency and growth in an underdeveloped economy more effectively than the alternative policy of governmental planning as an instrument of economic development.[33] "What is required in underdeveloped countries is the release of the energies of millions of able, active, and vigorous people . . . an atmospere of freedom, of maximum opportunity for people to experiment, and of incentive for them to do so in an environment in which there are objective tests of success and failure—in short in a vigorous, free capitalistic market."[34]

The necessity for encouraging the emergence of "entrepreneurial personalities" in underdeveloped countries is a matter of special concern to Chicagoans. Assuming the distribution of entrepreneurially talented people is approximately the same in developed and in underdeveloped countries, they emphasize the need for underdeveloped countries to provide a social

---

[30] See, for example, F. H. Harbison and C. A. Myers, *Education, Manpower and Economic Growth: Strategies of Human Resource Development* (New York: McGraw-Hill Book Company, 1964).

[31] For this point of view, see Harry G. Johnson, *Money, Trade and Economic Growth* (London: George Allen and Unwin, 1962). This view also underlies the approach to economic development of some prominent textbooks. See, for example, Henry J. Bruton, *Principles of Economic Development* (Prentice-Hall, 1965).

[32] Writers who have studied the economies of South East Asia and Africa have especially noted the readiness with which these populations accept consumer and capital goods brought to their notice and within their means. Bauer and Yancey maintain there are also many examples that "the inhabitants of poor countries (e.g., Cyprus and Uganda) generally are well informed as producers and consumers, and that they are responsive to changes in the alternatives open to them." Cf. P. T. Bauer and Basil S. Yancey, *The Economics of Underdeveloped Countries* (Chicago: The University of Chicago Press, 1957), p. 88.

[33] Harry G. Johnson, *Money, Trade, and Economic Growth,* especially, pp. 152–53, 156–59, 160–63.

[34] Milton Friedman, "Foreign Economic Aid: Means and Objectives," *Yale Review* (Summer 1958), p. 509.

environment that does not militate against development and which contributes in a positive way to its realization. Thus, they urge government to facilitate private investment by supplying information and data not generally available to individual entrepreneurs. Education, free elections, and nationwide radio are regarded as especially useful for opening up an otherwise closed society.[35] These measures are expected to contribute to a social environment of economic opportunity which encourages the mobility and adaptability of economic agents. This is the kind of environment in which economic development will require a minimal administrative apparatus and very little policing other than the provision of a legal system for the enforcement of contracts.[36]

It is recognized that there are objections to relying on the market mechanism as an instrument of growth.[37] Harry Johnson specifically notes that the pattern of income distribution produced by the market may be unjust and socially undesirable. But in his view it is "unwise for a country anxious to enjoy rapid growth to invest too strongly on policies aimed at ensuring economic equality and a just income distribution."

A second objection to relying on the market mechanism as the instrument of growth is that it may not produce as high a rate growth as is desirable because it may not sufficiently stimulate saving and investment. The counterargument offered by the Chicago School is that it is preferable to stimulate saving by offering high market rates of interest and to stimulate investment by tax concessions, subsidies, and cheap credit. As they see matters, it is dangerous to have government underwrite investment because it contributes to "the creation of vested industrial interests inimical to further development and resistant to technical change."[38]

Trade versus Inflation as an Instrument of Development

Most underdeveloped countries have a strong orientation to foreign trade. Typically they are characterized by a high ratio of export production to total output in the cash sector of the economy, a strong propensity to import, a high proportion of foreign-owned enterprises and an inflow of long term capital. In the early stages of development the foreign trade sector tends to grow faster than the rest of the economy.[39] Economists concerned with studying developing countries have, therefore, examined their problems within the context of their external environment.

Trade doctrine as developed by Ricardo and Mill asserted that compara-

---

[35] Bruton, *Principles,* pp. 258–59.

[36] Johnson, *Money, Trade, and Economic Growth,* especially chap. VII.

[37] Ibid.

[38] Ibid.

[39] W. A. Lewis, *The Theory of Economic Growth* (London: Allen and Unwin, 1955), p. 342.

tive differences in labor costs determine in what products nations will specialize and, consequently, what they will export and import. Since factors of production are typically not mobile internationally, trade itself becomes the alternative to factor movements as a mechanism for adapting productive activity to natural and population resources. The expectation is that factor prices and incomes will tend toward equality as a result of international trade.

Contrary to what the equilibrium theory of international trade predicts, however, the interplay of market forces has not produced these equalizing tendencies among countries. In underdeveloped countries international trade has stimulated the production of primary products which employ mostly unskilled labor. The demand for these products is often inelastic with the result that technological improvement in their production tends to transfer the advantages of cheapening production to the importing countries. The question of what is appropriate policy in face of the worsening of the terms of trade experienced by underdeveloped countries is a matter of considerable controversy. Chicago economists continue to put their faith in the positive contribution which free trade will make to growth and urge the necessity of working towards the elimination of trade impediments. The counterargument is that it is necessary for the underdeveloped countries to cut themselves off from those that are more developed and mobilize the capital resources they require for industrialization via the route of the "forced saving" that accompanies inflation and other policy measures.[40]

Inflation is expected to promote development in two ways: First it redistributes income from workers and peasants, who typically have a low propensity to save, to capitalist entrepreneurs who have a high propensity to save and invest. Second, it is expected to promote investment by raising the nominal rate of return from investment relative to the rate of interest. Both arguments are rejected by members of the Chicago School.

Harry Johnson has extended the concept of "inflationary expectation" to the problems of underdeveloped economies. His argument is that all income groups become adjusted to the expectation of inflation during a sustained inflationary process. As a result the effect of inflation is not to redistribute income from workers and savers to capitalist entrepreneurs, but rather to redistribute it from holders of money balances to the monetary authority who issues money of steadily depreciating real value. There is an inflationary tax on money balances which the public attempts to evade by reducing their holdings. The reallocation of resources to consumption impedes development and may outweigh the positive contribution which inflation makes to growth.[41] In short, Chicagoans argue that infla-

---

[40] See Gunnar Myrdal, "Development and Underdevelopment," National Bank of Egypt 15th Anniversary Commensuration Lectures, Cairo, 1956.

[41] Harry G. Johnson, "Is Inflation the Inevitable Price of Rapid Development?" *Economic Policies toward Less Developed Countries* (Washington, D.C.: The Brookings Institution, 1967).

tion will discourage rather than encourage saving. In their view, inflation has a further adverse effect because it encourages the allocation of resources into forecasting and searching for alternatives which hedge against uncertainty. This distorts the allocation of resources and encourages the waste of inflation-gathered resources on consumption because it encourages policies of protectionism and exchange control. The Chicago position is, thus, to urge against economic nationalism and in favor of free international trade. They consider it the responsibility of the more advanced nations to facilitate the development process by reducing barriers to trade that handicap their less developed neighbors.[42]

CONCLUDING COMMENTS

Considering the extraordinarily wide range of the intellectual concerns of Chicago economists, it seems useful to return to the question posed at the beginning of this chapter. To wit: Is there a group of economists associated with the University of Chicago who are relatively homogenous with respect to their methodology, philosophy, and policy preferences, and who are in a position to reach and persuade a sufficiently sizeable segment of the economics profession to insure the extension and further proliferation of their ideas? The very diversity of their interests would appear to militate at the very outset against identifying a unifying theme. Besides the monetarism (and the various macroeconomic concerns it implies) of Friedman and his associates, various aspects of family life have become the focus of a number of writers among whom Becker and Mincer are the most prolific, both in terms of their own writing and research and the number of doctoral students they have trained. Their work has helped to close the gap between economics, sociology, and psychology. Another identifiable group has undertaken to explore the relationship between economics and the law, with Coase as a leading figure. Harry Johnson was (until his untimely death in 1977), and Peter T. Bauer is among those at Chicago who devoted their attentions to development economics and various aspects of international trade.

The common thread which links these diverse inquiries together is that they have built on the work of Frank Knight as an economic theorist, as a methodologist, and as a social philosopher. These "three hats" of Frank Knight are scarcely separable from each other and they are similarly blended in the work of most of his followers. From the standpoint of economic principle, the starting point of Knight's analysis, which is clearly reflected in the present Chicago tradition, is his commitment to the principle that sovereign consumers are capable of maximizing behavior. Given freedom, each individual uses his available means to achieve his own ends and each transaction reflects a choice among alternatives. Expressed in the

---

[42] Ibid.

language of the economist, the choices of the autonomous individual are conceived to be governed by the universal principle of opportunity cost. Thus, the objective of the economist is to arrive at a body of scientific (i.e., value free) truths predicated on individual freedom to choose among alternatives.

Most of Knight's teaching as a theorist and as a methodologist reflects his commitment as a philosopher to the dictum that "to live on the human plane is to choose." The essence of freedom is *possibility,* as distinct from coercion which implies "denial of possibility." Thus economic freedom became for Knight the essential freedom because he saw it as underlying all other forms of freedom—religious, political, and intellectual.[43] The perfect market which is the "embodiment of complete freedom" is identified as ideal in the sense that man's capability for maximizing behavior is most completely realized under these conditions. Efficient resource allocation thus became inextricably interwoven with the perfect market in Knight's thinking and teaching.

The 30 years that Knight spent at Chicago, to which he returned in 1927, after a brief association with the State University of Iowa, were dedicated to articulating the utility principle and extolling economic laissez-faire, though he was not blind to the necessity for "extensive legislation to prevent intolerable divergences from free market conditions."[44] His commitment is very much in evidence in the *Journal of Political Economy* during the years when he shared its editorship with Jacob Viner. Approximately three quarters of the articles published by that journal from 1930 to 1946 were the product of Chicago faculty or former students.[45] In more recent years this journal, together with *The Journal of Law and Economics,* continued the tradition which crystalized during the tenure of Knight, Viner, and Henry Simons.[46] Their work reflects an ongoing search to identify the operation of the market system of rewards and penalties.[47]

---

[43] Frank Knight, "Ethics and Economic Interpretation" in *The Ethics of Competition* (New York, Harper and Brothers, 1935), pp. 19–43.

[44] Frank Knight "Abstract Economics as Absolute Ethics," *Ethics,* vol. 76 (April 1966), pp. 163–77.

[45] The status of the *Journal of Political Economy* as a house organ is not unique. *The Economic Journal* published at Cambridge University (England) and the *Quarterly Journal* published at Harvard University (Cambridge, Mass.) have exhibited a similar preference for publishing articles written by its faculty and former students.

[46] Martin Bronfenbrenner in "Observations on the Chicago School(s)" suggests that there are *two* Chicago Schools; "the departure of Jacob Viner and the passing of Henry Simons are the dividing lines between. The pre-war school which included Knight, Viner, and Simons exhibits more concern with price level and less with money supply than the post-war school. It also had more concern with economic freedom and allocative efficiency."

[47] See, for example, R. Kessel, "Price Discrimination in Medicine," *Journal of Law and Economics,* vol. 1 (October 1958), pp. 20–53 and S. Rottenberg, "The Baseball Players Labor Market," *Journal of Political Economy,* vol. 64 (June 1956), pp. 242–58.

Their concerns are reflected in the doctoral dissertations of their graduate students, which are largely empirical and heavily concentrated in the fields of land economics, labor economics (a classification which includes the economics of the household), and monetary economics.[48] Within these areas the Chicago approach is characterized by efforts to reaffirm (typically with the aid of empirical work) the efficacy of the individualistic market economy. This is accompanied by a fear of power aggregates, whether these are concentrated in the hands of "big business" or "big government" and a preference for a competitive market structure.

It is at precisely this juncture that the Chicago School invites the most rousing criticism. Critics argue that Chicagoans (especially the present generation) are prone to blur the distinction between the actual market and the ideal market represented by perfect competition. This presents a strong contrast with Chicagoans as Simons who strongly favored laissez-faire but did not hesitate to advocate the socialization of industries in which the market performed poorly.[49] Modern Chicagoans, as already noted, fear government interference as the greater evil and look to the market to restrain monopoly. Many others in the profession are skeptical of this policy stance. Unlike members of the Chicago School, large segments of the profession identify the discrepancy between actual market conditions and perfect competition as being significantly greater than Chicagoans believe it to be. Nor do they have the faith most Chicagoans seem to have in the ability of competitive capitalism to separate economic and political power to a degree which will enable them to offset one another. They emphasize that the market system has, in fact, produced large inequities in the distribution of income. Chicagoans are wont to interpret these inequalities as reflecting the free choices of rich and poor alike.

Against this view many nonChicagoans interpret income inequalities as reflecting the failure of competition which they charge Chicagoans with failing to identify because they neglect the specifics of the institutional environment of modern capitalism. This critique is an essential part of the ongoing controversy between traditional economists and those who have rejected mainstream views. Just as Marx, Veblen, Roscher, and their followers dissented from the traditional economics of their day, so modern writers, among them Galbraith and other Neo-Institutionalists, The "New Radicals," and the "Post-Keynesians" associated with Cambridge (England) University are addressing themselves to re-examining the tenets of contemporary macro- and microeconomics that were developed in this

---

[48] This is in significant contrast with the greater concern at Harvard and Columbia Universities with economic history and development, public finance and fiscal policy, international economics, and industrial organization. See the report for the year 1959–60 in *American Economic Review*, vol. 50 (September 1960), pp. 864–91.

[49] See Henry Simons, "A Positive Program for Laissez-Faire: Some Proposals for a Liberal Economic Policy," reprinted in *Economic Policy*, pp. 40–77.

chapter and the one which preceded it. The problems of contemporary society—especially the conundrum of inflation and unemployment, but also the unhappy results of numerous programs of social reform—have become so pressing that the critics of mainstream economics are being heard even in the academic circles of professional societies. It, therefore, seems increasingly appropriate to bring our inquiry into the development of economic analysis to a close in our concluding chapter with a brief survey of the main thrust of contemporary criticism.

GLOSSARY OF TERMS AND CONCEPTS

Coase theorem. Economic efficiency can be achieved without resorting to legal action by various arrangements which "internalize" externalities; e.g., there is an optimal amount a damaged party may pay the party inflicting damage to modify its activities. Legal intervention is available unless transactions' costs are so high that the costs of allocating resources via the market mechanism exceed those of legal determination.

Human capital investment. The allocation for resources for education, training, moving, etc., for the purpose of increasing the expected future income stream. Chicagoans explain these allocations in terms of the principle of rational household behavior.

Property rights. Relations established by law among persons (and businesses) that involve the use of scare resources.

NOTES FOR FURTHER READING

General

A trio of selections, H. Lawrence Miller, "On the Chicago School of Economics," *Journal of Political Economy,* vol. 70 (1962), pp. 72–75; Martin Bronfenbrenner, "Observations on the Chicago School(s)," and George Stigler's "Comment" all in the same journal, are an excellent starting point for perspective concerning the school as a whole. For greater detail and insights into areas of controversy, there is no better source than the symposium on the Chicago School sponsored by The Association For Evolutionary Economics and published in their *Journal of Economic Issues.* The first group appears as vol. 9 (December 1975), and the concluding group appears as vol. 10, no. 1 (March 1976). The following articles from this volume are of particular interest: Eva and Abraham Hirsh, "The Heterodox Methodology of Two Chicago Economists"; Ezra Mishan's "The Folklore of the Market"; John P. Henderson's "The History of Thought in the Development of the Chicago Paradigm"; C. Wilber's and Jon D. Wisman's "The Chicago School: Positivism or Ideal Type"; and H. H. Liebhafsky's "Price Theory as Jurisprudence."

The New Microeconomics

See especially the seminal articles by Gary Becker, "A Theory of the Allocation of Time," and "A Theory of Marriage part I," *Journal of Political Economy,* vol. 51 (July–August 1973), pp. 813–46, and "A Theory of Marriage, part II," *Journal of Political Economy,* vol. 82 supp. (March–April 1974), pp. 511–26, and "An Economic Analysis of Fertility," *Demographic and Economic Change in Developed Countries* (Princeton: Princeton University Press, 1960), pp. 209–31.

Law and Economics: The classic reference is Ronald Coase, "The Problem of Social Costs," *The Journal of Law and Economics,* vol. 3 (October 1960). Erik Furubotn and Svetozar Pejovich have surveyed the property rights literature in "Property Rights and Economic Theory: A Survey of Recent Literature," *Journal of Economic Literature,* vol. 8, no. 4 (December 1972). For a particularly pointed critique of the property-rights approach, see H. H. Liebhafsky, "Price Theory as Jurisprudence," *Journal of Economic Issues,* vol. 10 (March 1976).

International Trade and Economic Development: Harry G. Johnson's *Money, Trade and Economic Growth* (London: George Allen and Unwin, 1962) is representative of the Chicago perspective. For a more recent policy statement, see his monograph, *Economic Policies toward Less Developed Countries* (The Brookings Institution, 1967). Jere R. Behrman's chapter "Development Economics" in Sidney Weintraub's *Modern Economic Thought* complements the discussion of the text though it is much broader in scope and does not specifically identify analyses or points of view associated with Chicagoans. Its brief survey of pre-1950 thought on development economics and modern trends is particularly useful.

20

Some Modern Iconoclasts and Contemporary Controversy in Economics

The Participants and Issues of Current Controversy

EVERY SCIENCE has its dissenters; there are always some who are disenchanted with the methods and/or conclusions of the normal science activities of those working within the prevailing tradition or paradigm. These are the persons who engage in what Thomas Kuhn described as "extraordinary research" directed against traditional tenets and beliefs.

Except for Marx, Veblen, and Keynes, the iconoclasts of economics are accorded little space in the textbooks on the history of economics. This is undoubtedly because the crises of economics, including that provoked by the great depression of the 1930s, did not result in revolutions which destroyed the prevailing paradigm.[1] Even the so-called Keynesian revolution failed, in the minds of some of his contemporary followers, to capture his theoretical system.[2] His great impact was on the shaping of policy, fiscal

---

[1] Economics is thus quite different from the natural sciences in which unresolved crises produced revolutions and new paradigms, e.g., the Ptolemaic system was wholly supplanted by the Copernican and Newtonian paradigms. Subsequently, the inability of 19th century scientists to verify any motion of the earth through space was resolved by Albert Einstein's theories of relativity, which hypothesized that time and space are both relative rather than absolute as implied by Newton. The scientific community as a whole embraced Einstein's theory, i.e., it became the new paradigm just as the Copernican system replaced the Ptolemaic system. In economics, old theories do not fade away.

[2] Alfred S. Eichner and J. A. Kregel, "An Essay in Post-Keynesian Theory: A New Paradigm in Economics," *Journal of Economic Literature,* vol. 13 (December 1975), pp. 1293–1314.

as well as monetary—to control the vicissitudes of the modern industrial economy.

While there has been a reaffirmation of the neoclassical tradition which is reflected in the works of Hicks, Patinkin, et al., and the Chicago tradition, controversy in economics is by no means stilled. On the contrary, there are a number of economists whose "extraordinary research" seeks to destroy the neoclassical economics paradigm and replace it by an alternative one. John Kenneth Galbraith, Professor Emeritus of Harvard University is, in all likelihood, the most widely read among contemporary dissenters. Besides being very much in the public eye as an advisor of presidents, he is a recent past president of The American Economic Association (1971) and has a Veblenesque wit reminiscent of the intellectual forbear whose tradition he is helping to perpetuate. In his 1972 address to the American Economic Association he observed that contemporary theory has no "useful handle for grasping the economic problems that now beset . . . modern society" which leaves a "whole galaxy of . . . urgent economic issues largely untouched."[3]

Modern radical economists are considerably to the left of Galbraith in terms of their politics and their economics. The rapidity with which their ideas have gained currency since 1969, when a group of young rebels demanded to be heard at the convention of the American Economic Association, is due, at least in part, to the intellectual sympathy displayed by Galbraith and other well established economists, among them Kenneth Boulding, Martin Bronfennbrenner, Robert Heilbroner, and Daniel Fusfeld. During 1971, when Galbraith was president of the American Economic Association, the radical contingent from Harvard University was well represented at the annual convention. Their organization originated when a group of Harvard graduate students and faculty tried (unsuccessfully at first) to add a course to the economics curriculum which aimed at examining and resolving a host of controversial issues, among them poverty, discrimination, pollution, the Vietnam War, inflation, and unemployment.

The Post-Keynesians are a third group of dissenters. These one-time associates of Keynes have been joined by a younger generation; together they are seeking to develop an alternative to the prevailing neoclassical paradigm which incorporates a microeconomic foundation into Keynes' macroeconomic model. Cambridge (England) economists, among them Joan Robinson, Nicholas Kaldor, James Mirrlees, and Luigi Passinetti, are thus far the main contributors to the post-Keynesian literature that has emerged as a counter-counterrevolution against the neoclassical reinterpretation of Keynes' work that was examined in Chapter 18. This group of

---

[3] Kenneth Galbraith, "Power and the Useful Economist," *American Economic Review,* 63 (March 1973), pp. 2–3.

dissidents still commands only a small group of adherents in this country; most of these reflect the intellectual influence of Sidney Weintraub of the University of Pennsylvania.[4]

THE GALBRAITHIAN CHALLENGE

The "New Industrial State" and the "Technostructure"

John Kenneth Galbraith views the present American economy as the product of its advanced technology.[5] The economy is a "technostructure" comprised of giant corporations which require minimum levels of earnings to assure their survival, growth, and technical virtuosity. Their needs have rendered obsolete the assumption that firms seek to maximize profits; power in the present industrial state is no longer associated with capitalists and entrepreneurs, but with a technostructure which includes salaried managers who "must eschew personal profit making." The assumption that they will do for the stockholders what they are forbidden to do for themselves weakens, in Galbraith's view, the tenability of the profit-maximizing assumption on which neoclassical analysis is predicated.

Galbraith's observations about the magnitude of the product differentiation that characterizes most markets has also raised anew the Veblenian question of consumer sovereignty. Firms that are able to manipulate consumer demand via advertising have an impact on the ability of the consumer to make rational choices among alternatives.

Galbraith, therefore, regards the traditional view that the consumer is sovereign as being untenable in the affluent society which modern technology makes possible. The creation of new wants is essential to the survival and growth of the modern corporation because the productive capacity of today's technostructure is so vast. Thus there has emerged what Galbraith calls the "dependence effect"; a higher level of want creation, generated by advertising and other techniques designed to manipulate consumer demands, is made necessary because of the greater ability of the technostructure to satisfy wants.[6] The implications of these observations about consumption go considerably beyond those of the theories of imperfect competition. They are also different from Veblen's view of "pecuniary emulation" as a cultural phenomenon. Galbraith would, however, agree with Veblen that the relationship between consumption and production cannot be explained in neoclassical terms. Orthodox economics cannot

---

[4] See for example his *Keynes and The Monetarists* (New Brunswick, N.J.: Rutgers University Press, 1970).

[5] Kenneth Galbraith, *The New Industrial State,* New American Library ed. (Boston: Houghton Mifflin Company, 1967), p. 128.

[6] Kenneth Galbraith, *The Affluent Society* (Boston: Houghton Mifflin Company, 1958), p. 158.

explain either the emergence of the technostructure or how consumer sovereignty became supplanted, via the dependence effect, by *producer* sovereignty.

In his *Economics and the Public Purpose* (1973), Galbraith's argument concerning the dependence effect and the creation of "contrived" wants is modified somewhat to make selling efforts compatible with some level of actual want satisfaction at the consumer level. But his more important insight is that producer efforts at want creation is a "safe" form of competition among ostensibly rival producers. Instead of competing for larger shares of each other's markets, they are concerned with promoting the growth of the entire industry. The survival requirements of giant corporate enterprises thus present a different perspective on the phenomena of growth than is inherent in the mainstream view of neoclassical economics.

The Planning System

Galbraith interprets the development of giant corporations as organizational entities as the outcome of extensive planning at the level of the firm. His inquiry also explores the relationship between their planning system and the state. Government, especially via the Department of Defense, is now a major customer of business enterprise. Congress and governmental and public regulatory agencies typically have a symbiotic relationship with big business; their interests are mutually compatible. Witness the classic phrase, "What's good for General Motors is good for the country."

The goals of organized labor are also interpreted by Galbraith as being compatible with those of the corporate structure. In his view, the historical enmity between labor and industry is reconciled within the framework of the technostructure. Because giant corporations can pass on wage increases in the form of higher prices, their interests are not really incompatible with those of "big labor." Here is a perception of the functioning of the economy in which only the consumer appears to be lacking a powerful advocate. Thus, Galbraith's *Weltanschauung* is probably closer to that of "the man in the street" than the perception of the economy's functioning inherent in mainstream economics. Although his social criticism has invited no small measure of adverse comment, many highly respected economists agree that the questions Galbraith raises concerning the "quality of life," as it is shaped by the modern technostructure, are relevant.

THE CHALLENGE OF RADICAL ECONOMICS

The Radical Paradigm

The modern radical school—sometimes referred to as the new left—emerged during the 1960s. It has a considerable intellectual debt to the economics of Karl Marx, though it is by no means wholly Marxian. Its Marxist aspect is evident chiefly in its historical perspective and its view that society is an integrated system whose economic, political, and social aspects are interrelated and inseparable. These interrelationships are interpreted as reflecting the "mode of production," which modern radical economists construe in the Marxian sense to refer not simply to the technology embodied in production processes, but also to the ownership of the means of production and, therefore, the social relationships among classes.[7]

"The most important and most distinctive feature of the mode of production in capitalist societies is its organization of labor by means of the wage contract."[8] The governance of labor's economic status by the wage contract reflects its "property-less" state. Workers have no alternative but to work for wages and have their surplus products appropriated by those owning the means of production.

Modern radicals have added a number of new insights of a sociological nature to their Marxian interpretation of the economic relationships among classes. Particular interest attaches to the problem of worker alienation and the role of various institutions, specifically the school and the family unit, in supporting and perpetuating of the capitalistic system. Those who own capital and control the work process nurture the development and maintenance of institutions that are compatible with the kinds of work habits and attitudes (e.g., punctuality and regular attendance) which are supportive of capitalism.

In the system's present phase of monopoly capitalism, a major change has been identified with respect to the characteristics of the working class. Radicals note that when the factory system first emerged, the handicraft workers of the preceding age became obsolete; the worker thus became alienated from his job as his separate skills and crafts gradually became obliterated by the requirements of the factory system for "labor pure and simple." Raw labor power required only the most general skills that are quickly learned on the job.

With the continued technological advance that characterizes the present phase of capitalism, the requirement for more specific work skills emerged again for many workers. These are typically learned via on-the-job training. Since the training process is expensive, today's capitalists, unlike those of past decades, have an interest in retaining the workers they have trained as "quasi-fixed" factors, and tend to encourage uninterrupted job tenure. Their requirements promote what radical economists refer to as "stratified" labor markets.

---

[7] David M. Gordon, *Theories of Poverty and Underemployment* (Lexington, Mass.: D. C. Heath and Company, Lexington Books, 1972), pp. 56 ff.

[8] David M. Gordon, *Theories of Poverty,* p. 3.

Depending on their race, sex, and class, certain workers are identified as likely to exhibit the kind of stable work habits essential to capitalist production. Minorities, including women who traditionally have had unstable work patterns, are thus shunted into lower strata of the labor market. Here they are confronted with entry jobs that are not only low paying, but do not provide job training or benefits. These workers are alienated by their work experiences and tend to have high turnover rates. Because employees have little or nothing invested in their training, they typically bear the brunt of the unemployment that accompanies a decline in aggregate demand. Their unstable employment experiences, in turn, is likely to be associated with poverty levels of living, typically in urban slums.[9] Poverty, sexism, and racism is thus inherent, in the view of the radical economists, in the functioning of capitalism.

Even the state functions to serve the interests of the capitalist class. The primary function of the state is to protect private property. In a mature system like ours, the degree of state action required to preserve the interests of the capitalists is minimal; capitalists "do not need the state to enhance their position, only to assure it."[10]

A further feature of the radical paradigm, which also reflects its Marxian heritage, is its interpretation of the competitive forces of capitalism as functioning "inevitably [to] spur owners of capital to protect themselves against their competitors by producing more goods and accumulating more and more profit."[11] The drive toward capital accumulation and productive capacity underlies the great internal contradictions which characterize capitalism. On the one hand, the necessity for division of labor creates an interdependence among men as producers; at the same time capitalist production requires ruthless competition to insure individual survival. A further contradiction of capitalism is that conflict about the sharing of the surplus product persists in spite of the fact that the system has the productive capability to provide adequately for all members of society.

Can Capitalism Survive?

Unlike some of the more moderate critics of the neoclassical paradigm and the capitalist system, modern radical economists do not envision the possibility of "correcting" capitalism's faults. No amount of "social engineering" in the form of equal opportunity legislation, desegregated schools, "head start" and government sponsored worker-training and retraining programs can remedy the basic fault of the capitalistic system. The rela-

---

[9] Ibid., pp. 66–81.

[10] Edwards and MacEwan, "Radical Approach to Economics," *American Economic Review, Papers and Proceedings*, vol. 60 (1970), p. 350.

[11] Gordon, *Theories of Poverty*, p. 60.

tionship between the state and the capitalist class is such that measures threatening the relative share of the capitalist class preclude any really meaningful program to redistribute income. The only effective cure for the ills of capitalism is the destruction of the system itself.

THE CHALLENGE OF POST-KEYNESIAN THEORY

The criticisms which some of Keynes's contemporary followers are levelling at mainstream thinkers are chiefly directed at the neoclassical interpretation of *The General Theory* that followed J. R. Hicks' article "Mr. Keynes and the Classics: A Suggested Reinterpretation." In response to this reaffirmation of neoclassicism, some of Keynes's former associates, together with a small number of younger generation economists at Cambridge (England) and an even smaller number of American economists, have mounted a "counter-counterrevolution" against Keynesianism and Monetarism. They are working to develop "a generalization of *The General Theory*."[12] The theoretical nature of the post-Keynesian critique, especially in comparison with Galbraith's challenge and that offered by modern radicals, has made it virtually inaccessible to the lay reader. In spite of their lack of popular appeal, however, post-Keynesians appear to be having an intellectual impact that is formidable in relation to the smallness of their numbers.

The starting point of their challenge is their argument that current orthodox theory is incompatible with Keynes's analysis. Neoclassical theory is also found wanting because it neglects institutional aspects of the economy which they maintain, in common with Galbraith, Heilbroner, and the modern radicals, must be incorporated to provide a tenable basis for analysis. Among these institutional aspects, they particularly emphasize the predominant role of monopolistic elements in the production and sale of output and the historical determination of the distribution of income between wage earners and shareholders. Whereas neoclassical thinkers believe that the distribution of income is explainable in terms of the marginal productivity of variable factor inputs, post-Keynesians maintain that wages and other income shares are determined by social and political institutions.

On a theoretical level their work harkens back to Keynes's objective "to bring the theory of prices as a whole back to close contact with the theory of value" through the link provided by his theory of employment and output. Examination of the microeconomic foundations of Keynes's macroeconomic analysis was, therefore, given early identification as an important task. The development of inflationary pressures at the end of the 1950s, which many believed were not satisfactorily explained by monetarist

---

[12] See Joan Robinson, *The Rate of Interest and Other Essays* (London: Macmillan, 1952).

theories, led to an alternative theory to explain inflation which focused on the relationship between money wage rates and labor productivity.

Other aspects of the post-Keynesian analysis derive from Keynes's perception of the economy's inherent tendency toward disequilibrium rather than equilibrium. Robert Clower is among those who have urged that much of contemporary macro-theory is irrelevant in consequence of Hicks's "transmogrification" of Keynes's analysis; "Keynesian wine simply did not go well in Walrasian bottles."[13] Contemporary followers have particular interest in the impact of uncertainty in generating investment environments which render capitalistic economics inherently unstable and therefore incapable of progressing along a steady state growth path. These efforts to develop what has been termed a "post-Keynesian paradigm" are examined in greater detail in the sections which follow.[14]

Weintraub's "Classical" Keynesianism[15]

An early effort to counter the influence of Hicks' "suggested reinterpretation" of Keynes's work was initiated by Sidney Weintraub who undertook to link the theory of employment and output with the theory of value and distribution via the aggregate-supply function. It will be recalled that the aggregate-supply schedule (the Z function) was not explicitly stated in the Keynesian system and came to be represented as a 45 degree line. Because this simplification obscures the cost and productivity conditions of the economy, Weintraub has undertaken to show that the aggregate-supply function can be derived from the supply curve of the firm.[16] The latter curve, it will be recalled, is that portion of the firm's marginal cost curve which lies above average variable cost, and it indicates the output the firm is willing to sell at each price. It is upward sloping because, for a given stock of capital, additional inputs of labor eventually yield diminishing returns. The industry short-run supply function, which is the lateral summation of the marginal cost curves of the firms, relates industry output with expected market prices. Since employment is correlated with output, an aggregate-supply function (i.e., a function relating employment with re-

[13] Robert S. Clower, "Reflections on the Keynesian Perplex," *Zeitschift für National-Ökonomie*, 35 (1975), p. 6.

[14] See Alfred S. Eichner and Jan A. Kregel, "An Essay on Post-Keynesian Theory: A New Paradigm in Economics," *Journal of Economic Literature*, vol. 13 (December 1975).

[15] Weintraub conceives of his version of Keynesian economics as being "classical" in the sense that it reflects Keynes' own view of the role of money; specifically money in the real world is not merely one commodity among many that serves as *numeraire* as in the general equilibrium model; it is an active factor in determining income and employment that is generated in the finance process.

[16] Sidney Weintraub, "A Macroeconomic Approach to the Theory of Wages," *The American Economic Review*, vol. 46, no. 5 (December 1956).

quired sales revenues) can be derived for each industry. Then the aggregate money-supply schedule for the economy as a whole can be built up by the process of aggregating the required revenue-employment functions for all industries. An alternative way of expressing this is to say that the aggregate money-supply function relates each level of employment to the GNP level required to support it.

The aggregate-supply function thus derived is in money, not real terms, and may normally be expected to rise to the right at an increasing rate as does OZ in Figure 20–1. This shape reflects the increasing significance of diminishing returns in individual production functions as employment increases while capital stock remains unchanged. Its upward slope implies that prices rise with employment because diminishing returns increase marginal costs and, therefore, the revenues required to make increased employment profitable. Every point on the aggregate-supply function reflects the relationship between employment and money outlays, and has an implicit price level.[17]

The aggregate (money)-demand function in Figure 20–1 shows the expenditures *expected* from consumption and investment as the level of employment increases. Every point on the DD function, therefore, also has a price level implicit in it which corresponds to a point on the aggregate supply curve. For example, in Figure 20–2 the price level implicit in Z_2 is also implicit in D_2 while the (lower) price level implicit in Z_1 is also implicit in D_1. The intersection of the aggregate-demand and supply functions determines the equilibrium level of employment ON.

FIGURE 20–1

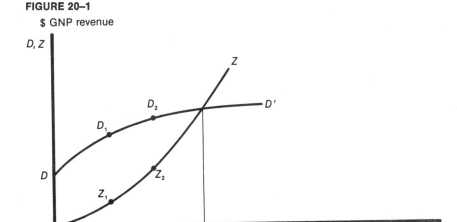

$ GNP revenue

D, Z

Z

D_2

D'

D_1

D

Z_2

Z_1

O N Employment

---

[17] It is important to recall that the aggregate demand and supply schedules depicted in the Keynesian cross are represented in real rather than money terms. (See Chapter 18, p. 428). Modern writers working in the tradition of Keynes view their emphasis on monetary magnitudes as a hallmark of their approach.

By presenting aggregate-supply and aggregate-demand functions in money terms, Weintraub's apparatus is also specifically designed to treat the problem of inflation. He rejects the theory of inflation inherent in the Phillips curve linkage of wage-rate and price-level increases and also its implied trade-off between inflation and unemployment. His alternate theory focuses on the relationship between money wage rate changes and productivity changes to explain inflation. His reasoning is that a change in the money wage will produce a shift in both the aggregate-demand curve, via its influence on consumer spending, and the aggregate-supply function via its effect on industry supply curves. The aggregate-supply function Z_1 in Figures 20–1 and 20–2 reflects a given rate of money wages w, and a constant markup, k, over the wage bill. If the average wage rate in the economy increases to w_2, there will be an upward shift of both the aggregate-demand and aggregate-supply functions to D_2 and Z_2. Aggregate demand shifts upward via the effect of the higher wage on income and consumption; aggregate supply shifts upward via the effect of the higher wage on cost of production.

The position of the Z function reflects the relationship between wage rates and labor productivity and is critical, according to Weintraub, for understanding inflation. If average money wages rise while labor productivity remains constant or rises proportionately less than wages, the leftward shift of the Z function from Z_1 to Z_2 will be greater than the upward shift of aggregate demand from D_1 to D_2. The result is that the higher average money wage is associated with a *smaller* volume of employment N_2 and a *higher* price level. It is thus hypothesized that, depending on their relationship to labor productivity, higher money wages can be associated not only with *less employment* but also with a *higher price level*. Thus, micro-theory and macro-theory are joined in a manner which, in Wein-

FIGURE 20–2

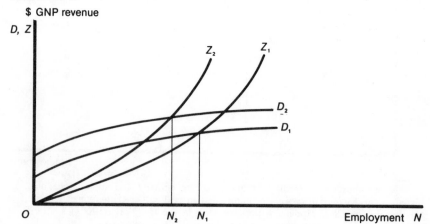

traub's view, satisfies more closely Keynes's own objective of bringing the theory of prices as a whole into close contact with the theory of value.[18]

Instability, Uncertainty, and Finance

The arguments of the (neoclassical) Keynesians, as we have seen, imply that in the absence of strong exogenous shocks, the economy tends toward equilibrium. Keynes himself was, however, more inclined to emphasize the possibility of endogenous *instability* which is related to the relationship between the pricing of capital assets and the flow in investment. This perspective of systematic instability as opposed to macroeconomic equilibrium tendencies is being emphasized by contemporary post-Keynesians who are challenging the orthodox interpretation.

A key aspect of systematic instability is inherent in the uncertainty which characterizes the real world. Several contemporary economists who are writing in the tradition of J. M. Keynes emphasize the impossibility of transforming uncertainty into certainty via the calculus of probability.[19] Firms are confronted with the need to make decisions concerning asset investment and finance as well as production, and the decision rules which orthodox economics presumes them to follow are, in the view of the critics, not relevant in a world of uncertainty.[20]

The effect of uncertainty surrounding the financing decisions of individual firms is compounded in a sophisticated capital-using economy because there are multiple capital assets and financial instruments. More important, the prevailing practice is to finance long-term capital assets via "speculative financing," that is, via the issuance of new debt.[21] Since the future is unknowable, such financing takes place amidst environments of alternating (and unpredictable) euphoria or despair. A fundamentally un-

---

[18] For a recent exposition see his chap. 3, "Hicksian Keynesianism," in *Modern Economic Thought* (Philadelphia: University of Pennsylvania Press, 1977). Earlier expositions include *An Approach to the Theory of Income Distribution* (Philadelphia: Chilton Press, 1958) and *A Keynesian Theory of Employment Growth and Income Distribution* (Philadelphia: Chilton Press, 1965). Weintraub's wage-cost markup hypothesis of inflation may also be represented in terms of the equation $P = kw/A$ in which w = the average money wage, A the average productivity of labor, and k the average markup of unit prices over unit-labor costs. In his view of the economic process, the price level is resolved once the money-wage rate is given. See *Classical Keynesianism, Monetary Theory and the Price Level* (1961), p. 41–64.

[19] See in particular, Paul Davidson, *Money and the Real World* (London: Macmillan and Co., 1972), pp 10–11, G. L. S. Shackle, *The Years of High Theory* (Cambridge: Cambridge University Press) and Douglas Vickers, *Financial Markets in the Capitalist Process* (Philadelphia: University of Pennsylvania Press, 1978).

[20] Douglas Vickers, "Financial Theory of the Firm," in Sidney Weintraub, ed., *Modern Economic Thought* (Philadelphia: University of Pennsylvania Press).

[21] Hyman Minsky, *John Maynard Keynes* (New York: Columbia University Press, 1975).

stable environment is thus generated. Instability with respect to asset values, income, prices, and employment are inherent characteristics of capitalistic economies. Employment and income disequilibria are the consequence of the unstable investment environment that is generated by uncertainty.

Growth and Dynamics

Other writers pursue the theme of uncertainty to examine the problem of economic change over time. The dynamic aspects of post-Keynesian theory can be traced to the influence of Roy Harrod's growth formula $G = \frac{s}{v}$ in which G is the rate of national income, s is the average propensity to save, and v is the capital/output ratio.[22] Neoclassical growth theorists, as we have seen, focus on changes in the aggregate capital and labor components of the production function in response to their relative scarcities and prices in order to explain the economy's tendency to expand along what they perceive as the steady-state growth path.[23] By contrast, the post-Keynesian approach modifies the assumption that s, the average propensity to save, is constant by assuming that changes in the distribution of income and differences in the propensity to save out of different incomes affects aggregate savings ratios.

Numerous growth hypotheses have been formulated, chiefly by Cambridge University economists, which incorporate a variable savings-income ratio, which causes the warranted rate of growth s/v to converge with the natural rate. (It will be recalled that in the neoclassical models the variable-capital output ratio caused the warranted and natural rates of growth to converge.) Models predicated on a variable savings-income ratio are Keynesian in the sense that they conceive of investment decisions as being independent of savings propensities instead of being governed by savings, as in the classical models.

Nicholas Kaldor's model is one of several which builds on this assumption.[24] His model hypothesizes a savings-income ratio which depends on the distribution of income. The savings of wage earners and profit receivers are postulated as being functionally related to their incomes and the propensity to save out of profit, s_π, is assumed to be greater than s_w, the propensity to save out of wages. In the special classical case, in which the propensity to save out of wages is zero, the propensity to save for the economy as a whole is the propensity to have out of profit, s_π, multiplied by π/y, the ratio of profit to income. Since the capital-output ratio is assumed given, which implies that the coefficients of production are fixed,

---

[22] See Chapter 17 above.

[23] See Chapter 18 above.

[24] Nicholas Kaldor, "Alternative Theories of Distribution," *Review of Economics Studies,* vol. 23 (1956).

relative factor rewards are *independent* of factor productivities.[25] Thus the distribution of income is variable and savings can change to be compatible with whatever adjustments of investment and the warranted growth rate are necessary to maintain the economy on an equilibrium path of growth. The distinguishing feature of these models, as compared with the static Keynesian model which preceded them, is that the equality of saving and investment is brought about through changes in the *distribution* of income rather than changes in its *level*.

While the post-Keynesians begin with an examination of the conditions required for steady-state growth, their chief objective is to explain why, in fact, the expansion path of a free enterprise economy is so erratic.[26] Their analysis conceives the rate of expansion to be related to the distribution of income. Recalling the world of the classical economists, national income is conceived as being divided into wage income and profits. Income from wages is presumed to be wholly spent on consumption. That is, savings out of wages is zero, while the marginal propensity to save of capitalists (i.e., nonwage earners) who receive profits through their ownership of the means of production, is 100 percent. Profit is thus the only source for financing investment, and the expenditures of capitalists controls the rate of investment.

Another important proposition put forward by post-Keynesians, is that instead of being confronted with increasing costs firms are, in fact, facing constant costs over the relevant range of their outputs; i.e., the conventional U-shaped cost curves of neoclassical analysis are not experienced.[27] It follows that profits—a residual income—are thus an increasing function of the rate at which capacity is utilized, which depends on the level of demand.

Given the production technique and the money-wage rate, the higher the growth rate, the higher the ratio of profit (i.e., nonwage income) to wages. This will result in a higher level of investment and a greater share of national income going to capitalists in the form of profit relative to the lower share going to workers in the form of wages. Post-Keynesians thus focus particularly on the distribution of income; ". . . one of the insights that can be derived from the post-Keynesian theory is that it is possible for the level of income to workers to be increasing at the same time that their share of the national income is declining."[28]

Unlike neoclassical theorists, post-Keynesians do not assume that in-

---

[25] This is a key difference from the neoclassical model.

[26] Alfred S. Eichner and Jan Kregel, "An Essay on Post-Keynesian Theory: A New Paradigm in Economics," *Journal of Economic Literature,* vol. 13 (December 1975).

[27] Joan Robinson and J. Eatwell, *Introduction to Economics* (London: McGraw-Hill, 1974), p. 168. This view of cost behavior is not, however, exclusive to Robinson and her colleagues.

[28] Eichner and Kregel, "An Essay on Post-Keynesian Theory," p. 1298.

dividual firms are chiefly price takers equating marginal cost and marginal revenue. Nor do they accept the neoclassical conclusion that wages reflect the marginal productivity of labor. They view the nominal (money) wage as being exogenously determined and as reflecting, in particular, the bargaining strength of unions.

The *real* wage is established by the rate of discretionary expenditures which is consistent with the relative distribution of income between residual and nonresidual income recipients. What especially matters is not the distinction between social classes as much as the distinction between quasi-contractual and residual forms of income.[29] In an economic system dominated by large corporations, the economy's savings propensity is that of the corporate sector. The savings behavior of large corporations is thus a key determinant of the distribution of income, and the level of income.[30] These savings are a prime source of "discretionary" expenditures (investment) which are the primary factor determining the level of economic activity. The analysis of the post-Keynesian suggests that, if the rate of growth of discretionary expenditures is not equal to the warranted rate of growth, the economy will tend to move off its growth path and experience a cyclical pattern around that trend line. Their chief interest is thus in shorter period cyclical movements quite as much as the analysis of long-run steady-state expansion.

Eichner and Kregel have summarized what they consider to be the relevant differences between the prevailing neoclassical position and the challenge that is being leveled against it by post-Keynesian thinkers under headings reproduced in Table 20–1. It recapitulates in an easily read format the differences which post-Keynesians maintain sets their work apart from orthodox economics. Its emphasis on the key role of the megacorp is consistent with many of Galbraith's observations in *The New Industrial State;* its emphasis on the institutional aspects of the income distribution process is consistent with the perception held by modern radicals.

Speculation about the future fate of these attacks on mainstream economics is necessarily beyond the scope of this book. But there seems to be a consensus that, while neoclassical economics is alive, it is no longer considered to be wholly well. It is, however, premature to speculate whether the crisis will produce a genuine intellectual revolution, or whether mainstream economics will, as in the past, be capable of sufficient reconstruction and reinterpretation to accommodate the criticisms and alternative interpretations reviewed in this chapter.

---

[29] J. Kregel, *The Reconstruction of Political Economy: An Introduction to Post-Keynesian Economics* (New York: Wiley, 1973), chap. 11.

[30] In this connection, Eichner focuses on the pricing policy of the megacorp as a determinant of its rate of saving. A. S. Eichner, "A Theory of the Determination of the Mark-up under Oligopoly," *Economic Journal,* vol. 83 (December 1973), pp. 1184–1200.

TABLE 20–1

A Comparison of Neoclassical and Post-Keynesian Theories

Aspect	Post-Keynesian Theory	Neoclassical Theory
Dynamic properties	Assumes pronounced cyclical pattern on top of a clearly discernible secular growth rate	Either no growth, or steady-state expansion with market mechanisms assumed to preclude any but a temporary deviation from that growth path
Explanation of how income is distributed	Institutional factors determine a historical division of income between residual shareholders, with changes in this distribution depending on changes in the growth rate	The distribution of income explained solely by variable factor inputs and the marginal productivity of those variable factor inputs
Amount of information assumed to be available	Only the past is known, the future is uncertain	Complete foresight exists as to all possible events
Conditions that must be met before the analysis is considered complete	Discretionary income must be equal to discretionary expenditures	All markets cleared with supply equal to demand in each of those markets
Microeconomic base	Imperfect markets with significant monopolistic elements	Perfect markets with all micro units operating as price takers
Purpose of the theory	To explain the real world as observed empirically	To demonstrate the social optimality if the real world were to resemble the model

Source: W. S. Eichner and J. A. Kregel, "An Essay on Post-Keynesian Theory: A New Paradigm in Economics," *Journal of Economic Literature,* vol. 13 (December 1975), p. 1309.

NOTES FOR FURTHER READING

Galbraith's leading works are *The Affluent Society* (Boston: Houghton Mifflin, 1964); *The New Industrial State* (Boston: Houghton Mifflin, 1967); and *Economics and the Public Purpose* (Boston: Houghton Mifflin, 1973). Two particularly readable evaluations of Galbraith's work by Myron E. Sharpe are "The Galbraithian Revolution," *Challenge: The Magazine of Economic Affairs* (September–October 1973), and *John Kenneth Galbraith and Lower Economics,* rev. ed. (New York: International Arts and Sciences Press, 1974).

Donald M. Gordon is among the several writers associated with the "new" radical economics. See his *Theories of Poverty and Underemployment* (Lexington, Mass.: D. C. Heath and Co., Lexington Books, 1972) and, as editor, *Problems in Political Economy: An Urban Perspective* (Lexington, Mass.: D. C. Heath and Co., 1971). He is also a co-author with Michael Reid and Richard C. Edwards of "A Theory of Labor Market Segmentation," *American Economic Review,* vol. 63 (1973), pp. 359–65. Richard C. Edwards and

Arthur MacEwen are co-authors of "A Radical Approach to Economics," *American Economic Review, Papers and Proceedings,* vol. 60 (1970), pp. 352–63. Howard M. Wachtel's "Class Consciousness and Stratification in the Labor Process" is in *Review of Radical Political Economics,* vol. 6 (1974), pp. 1–31. Raymond S. Franklin and William P. Tabb, discuss the common commitments of radical economists in "The Challenge of Radical Political Economics," *Journal of Economic Issues,* vol. 8 (1974), pp. 124–50. Daniel P. Fusfeld's "Types of Radicalism in American Economics," *Papers and Proceedings of the American Economics Association* (May 1973), pp. 145–51 examines the place the radical economics in the history of economic thought with special concern to identify the ethical and moral preconceptions of the radical position.

"An Essay on Post-Keynesian Theory: A New Paradigm in Economics," *Journal of Economic Literature,* vol. 12 (December 1975), co-authored by Alfred S. Eichner and Jan A. Kregel, is especially recommended for a readable overall account of the post-Keynesian critique and the alternative paradigm they propose. The dean of the American post-Keynesian movement is Sidney Weintraub, whose many works include, *A General Theory of the Price Level, Output, Income Distribution and Economic Growth* (New York: Chilton, 1959) and *A Keynesian Theory of Employment, Growth and Income Distribution* (New York: Chilton, 1966). His influence is particularly evident in the work of such younger scholars as Paul Davidson and Hyman Minsky. See their respective works: *Money and the Real World* (London: Macmillan, 1972), and *John Maynard Keynes* (New York: Columbia University Press, 1975). Also interesting in connection with present rethinking about the place of general equilibrium analysis in contemporary macroeconomics is an article by Robert Clower (who some years ago was also "captured" by the notion of general equilibrium) entitled 'Reflections on the Keynesian Perplex," *Zeitschrift für National-Ökonomie,* 35 (1975).

E. Ray Canterberry's *The Making of Economics* (Belmont: Wadsworth Press, 1976) is particularly recommended as a readable and perceptive attempt to interpret the future direction of economics.

INDEXES

INDEX

Index to Glossary of Terms and Concepts

Index of Names

Index of Subjects

This book has been set in 10 and 9 point Times Roman, leaded 2 points. Part numbers are set in 24 point (large) Helvetica Medium and part titles in 24 point (small) Helvetica. Chapter numbers are 48 point Helvetica Medium and chapters titles in 18 point Helvetica. The size of the type page is 27 by 45½ picas.